FROM THE WADSWORTH SERIES IN SPEECH COMMUNICATION

Babbie	*The Basics of Social Research*
Babbie	*The Practice of Social Research*, Ninth Edition
Barranger	*Theatre: A Way of Seeing*, Fourth Edition
Braithwaite/Wood	*Case Studies in Interpersonal Communication: Processes and Problems*
Campbell	*The Rhetorical Act*, Second Edition
Campbell/Burkholder	*Critiques of Contemporary Rhetoric*, Second Edition
Cragan/Wright	*Communication in Small Groups: Theory, Process, Skills*, Fifth Edition
Crannell	*Voice and Articulation*, Third Edition
Freeley/Steinberg	*Argumentation and Debate: Critical Thinking for Reasoned Decision Making*, Tenth Edition
Govier	*A Practical Study of Argument*, Fourth Edition
Hamilton	*Essentials of Public Speaking*
Hamilton/Parker	*Communicating for Results: A Guide for Business and the Professions*, Sixth Edition
Jaffe	*Public Speaking: Concepts and Skills for a Diverse Society*, Third Edition
Kahane/Cavender	*Logic and Contemporary Rhetoric: The Use of Reason in Everyday Life*, Eighth Edition
Larson	*Persuasion: Reception and Responsibility*, Ninth Edition
Littlejohn	*Theories of Human Communication*, Sixth Edition
Lumsden/Lumsden	*Communicating with Credibility and Confidence*
Lumsden/Lumsden	*Communicating in Groups and Teams: Sharing Leadership*, Third Edition
Miller	*Organizational Communication: Approaches and Processes*, Second Edition
Morreale/Spitzberg/Barge	*Human Communication: Motivation, Knowledge, and Skills*
Orbe/Harris	*Interracial Communication: Theory Into Practice*
Peterson/Stephan/White	*The Complete Speaker: An Introduction to Public Speaking*, Third Edition
Rubin/Rubin/Piele	*Communication Research: Strategies and Sources*, Fifth Edition
Rybacki/Rybacki	*Communication Criticism: Approaches and Genres*
Samovar/Porter	*Intercultural Communication: A Reader*, Ninth Edition
Samovar/Porter	*Communication Between Cultures*, Fourth Edition
Trenholm/Jensen	*Interpersonal Communication*, Fourth Edition
Ulloth/Alderfer	*Public Speaking: An Experiential Approach*
Verderber	*The Challenge of Effective Speaking*, Eleventh Edition
Verderber	*Communicate!*, Ninth Edition
Verderber/Verderber	*Inter-Act: Interpersonal Communication Concepts, Skills, and Contexts*, Ninth Edition
Wood	*Communication Mosaics: An Introduction to the Field of Communication*, Second Edition
Wood	*Communication in Our Lives*, Second Edition
Wood	*Communication Theories in Action: An Introduction*, Second Edition
Wood	*Gendered Lives: Communication, Gender, and Culture*, Fourth Edition
Wood	*Interpersonal Communication: Everyday Encounters*, Second Edition
Wood	*Relational Communication: Continuity and Change in Personal Relationships*, Second Edition

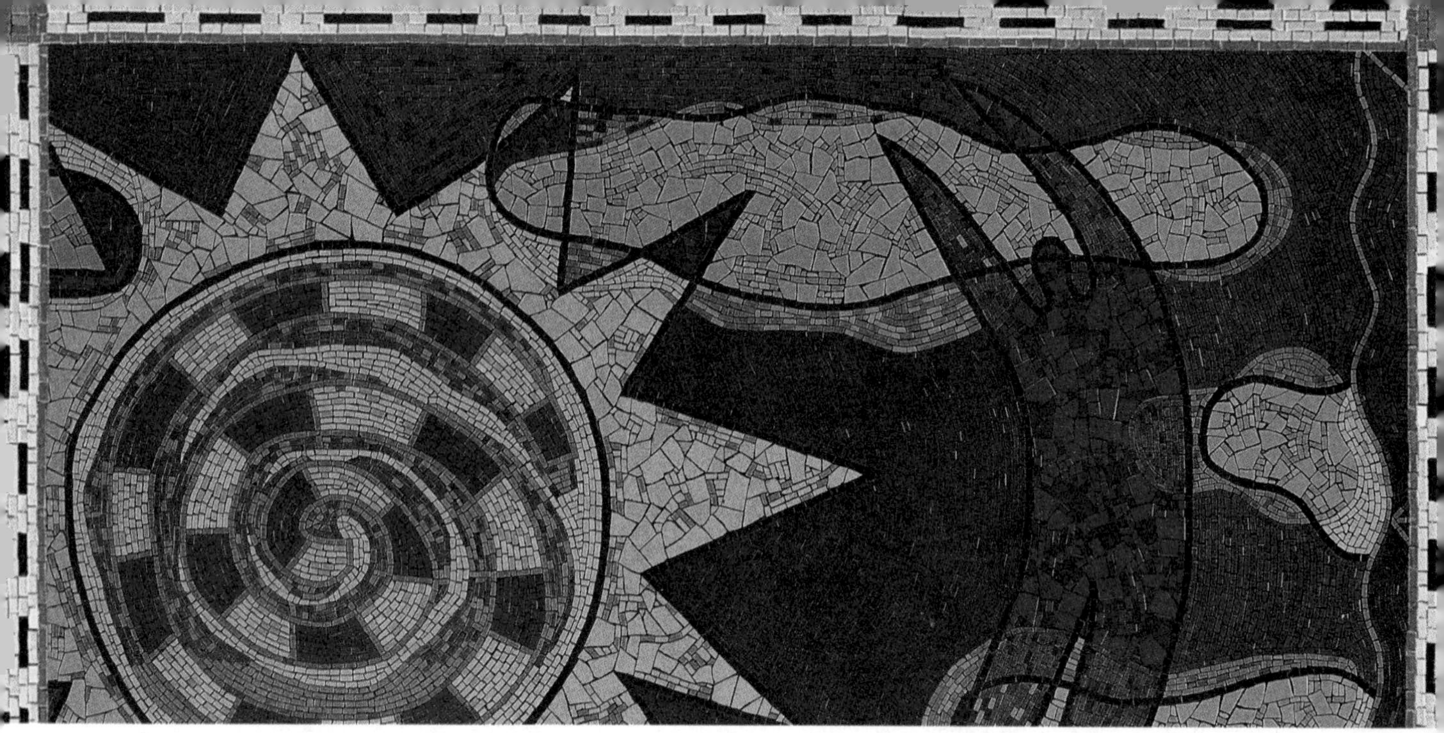

Communication Mosaics

An Introduction to the Field of Communication

Second Edition

Julia T. Wood

The University of North Carolina at Chapel Hill

Australia • Canada • Mexico • Singapore • United Kingdom • United States

Executive Editor: Deirdre Cavanaugh
Publisher: Clark Baxter
Marketing Manager: Stacey Purviance
Marketing Assistant: Kenneth Baird
Project Editor: Cathy Linberg
Print Buyer: Barbara Britton
Permissions Editor: Robert Kauser
Production: Electronic Publishing Services Inc., NYC
Text and Cover Designer: Lisa Delgado, Delgado Design, Inc.
Photo Researcher: Sarah Evertson, ImageQuest

Copy Editor: Electronic Publishing Services Inc., NYC
Chapter Opening Images: Lisa Delgado, Delgado Design, Inc.
Cover Image: Jose Ortega, *Una raza, Un Mundo, Universo (One Race, One World, One Universe)* owned by MTA New York City Transit and commissioned by Metropolitan Transportation Authority. Photography by © David Lubarsky
Cover Printer: Phoenix Color
Compositor: Electronic Publishing Services Inc., NYC
Printer/Binder: Courier Kendallville, Inc.

Printed in the United States of America
2 3 4 5 6 7 04 03 02 01

For permission to use material from this text, contact us by
Web: http://www.thomsonrights.com
Fax: 1-800-730-2215
Phone: 1-800-730-2214

Library of Congress Cataloging-in-Publication Data
Wood, Julia T.
Communication mosaics: An introduction to the field of communication/Julia T. Wood.—2nd ed.

p. cm.

Includes bibliographical references and index.
ISBN 0-534-57249-9
1. Communication. 1. Title.
P90.W6185 2000
302.2—dc21 99-462110

For more information, contact

Wadsworth/Thomson Learning
10 Davis Drive
Belmont, CA 94002-3098
USA
http://www.wadsworth.com

International Headquarters
Thomson Learning
International Division
290 Harbor Drive, 2nd Floor
Stamford, CT 06902-7477
USA

UK/Europe/Middle East/South Africa
Thomson Learning
Berkshire House
168-173 High Holborn
London WC1V 7AA
United Kingdom

Asia
Thomson Learning
60 Albert Street, #15-01
Albert Complex
Singapore 189969

Canada
Nelson Thomson Learning
1120 Birchmount Road
Toronto, Ontario M1K 5G4

Brief Contents

For Daniel
and
the fantastic foolybear:
And what could she say?

Contents

PART II

Preface

I wrote *Communication Mosaics* to support introductory courses that survey the broad and exciting field of communication. Unlike other forms of the introductory course, the survey approach doesn't emphasize in-class student performances, such as giving speeches and engaging in task discussion. Instead, the survey course aims to provide a more comprehensive view of the communication field, giving attention to topics and contexts that cannot be covered in performance-oriented courses. The focus on conceptual understanding of the breadth and importance of communication in many spheres of life allows the survey course to serve a greater number of students than typically can be accommodated in introductory courses that include performance.

Response to the first edition of this book indicates that many faculty want a textbook that is specifically designed to support a survey approach to the introductory course. Student feedback to the first edition indicates that students, too, find it useful to take a course that gives them an expansive introduction to the communication discipline. In addition to welcoming the approach of this book, faculty and students have been generous in offering feedback that I have used to improve the second edition.

In the pages that follow I explain my vision of this book and the features I weave into it. As I discuss the book, I'll note changes I made in preparing the current edition.

COMMUNICATION AS A MOSAIC

As the title of the book suggests, communication is an intricate mosaic that is made up of many parts. The parts are distinct, yet they are also interrelated—all of them work together to create the whole of communication. This book increases students' awareness of the importance of basic communication skills and processes and shows students how those common elements surface in specific settings where people communicate. Part I of *Communication Mosaics* introduces students to the discipline of communication and then explains basic processes and skills that are common to a range of communication situations and goals. In response to faculty feedback on the first edition of this book, I moved the chapter on climate from its former location as Chapter 6 to its new location as Chapter 3. The basic communication skills and processes are:

- perceiving and understanding
- creating communication climates

- engaging in verbal communication
- engaging in nonverbal communication
- listening and responding
- adapting communication to people and contexts

These basic skills and processes shape the character and effectiveness of communication in a wide range of settings, although how each one functions differs from context to context. For example, we may use different listening skills when talking with a close friend and when interviewing for a job. Part II of the book shows how these basic processes and skills function in eight specific types of communication:

- communication with ourselves
- communication in personal relationships
- communication in groups and teams
- communication in organizations
- communication in interviews
- public speaking
- mass communication
- technologies of communication

FEATURES OF *COMMUNICATION MOSAICS*

Accenting this book are five features that enhance students' learning and ensure the scholarly integrity of content.

Accessible, Conversational Style

Students are most likely to read and learn from a book that engages them personally. To prepare myself to revise *Communication Mosaics*, I read reviews by faculty and over 1,000 student reviews of the first edition. Nearly all students who wrote a review said that the personal writing style motivated them to read chapters and made the book more accessible and applicable to their lives. For this reason, in the current edition, I retain the conversational style that invites students to think with me and that lets them know a real person is behind the words they are reading. I refer to myself as "I," rather than "the author," and I address students as "you," rather than "the student." I also use informal language, such as contractions, just as people do in everyday conversations. In the opening chapter of the book, I introduce myself to students so that they know something about my view of communication and my motivations for writing this book. Another way in which I've personalized my writing style is including examples and reflections from my own life.

Foundation in Research and Theory

A textbook is only as good as the research and theory on which it is built. *Communication Mosaics* draws on the impressive research and theory developed by scholars of communication. Although I include important work from scholars in other fields, I draw most heavily on the published research of communication scholars because it is most directly relevant. Instructors who are familiar with the first edition of this book will notice that the current edition includes more than 100 new references to studies that were published since the first edition went to press.

Integrated Attention to Social Diversity

Social diversity is one of the most basic facts of life in the 21st century. The United States and the world include people of different ages, sexual orientations, races and ethnicities, sexes, abilities, and economic circumstances. These differences among people directly affect their communication. Thus, the idea of universal communication goals and principles must be replaced with understandings of how goals and principles are used differently by diverse people and how communication is adapted to contexts.

Communication Mosaics emphasizes social diversity in three specific ways. First, Chapter 7 offers in-depth coverage of the relationships between communication and culture: How cultural factors influence communication style, how communication shapes culture, and how we adapt our ways of communicating to particular people and contexts. Second, I weave research on social diversity into all chapters of the book. For example, Chapter 4 notes general differences in traditional African American communication and European American communication. Chapter 9 explains differences in how women and men typically communicate in personal relationships. Chapter 12 includes research on how ethnicity affects interviewees' communication. Third, examples in the chapters, as well as photographs, feature a wide range of people.

Integrated Attention to Technologies of Communication

Technology increasingly infuses our lives, and this is reflected in *Communication Mosaics*. Every chapter includes examples and research related to technologies of communication. Chapters also include special features that inform students about web sites where they may learn more about particular forms and contexts of communication. The questions that follow each chapter also direct students to web sites  that extend the chapter's coverage by highlighting technology resources. Another way in which I emphasize communication technologies is with a full chapter on the topic. Chapter 15 deals exclusively with various technologies of communication that have changed, or will soon change, how we live and work. This chapter has been revised substantially, because technologies of communication have changed greatly in  just the few years since the first edition appeared. Students who use this book automatically receive a four-month free subscription to **InfoTrac College Edition**—a world-class, online library that gives students access to articles from hundreds of academic journals and magazines and to texts of speeches.

Student Commentaries

Woven into each chapter are commentaries from students' journals and papers. Although students at my university wrote most of the commentaries, there are also ones sent to me by students at other universities. I include student commentaries because in my 25 years of teaching I've learned that students have much to teach each other and me. The student commentaries show how different people relate communication principles and research to their own lives.

Pedagogical Features

In this book I include five features to maximize student learning.

For Your Information. Featured in each chapter are "For Your Information" boxes that highlight communication research and the role of communication in everyday life. I use these to call students' attention to particularly interesting and important aspects of communication in a variety of settings.

Sharpen Your Skill. Each chapter also includes "Sharpen Your Skill" exercises that invite students to apply skills and principles discussed in the text. Some of these exercises encourage students to practice a particular skill. Others invite students to observe how communication concepts and principles discussed in the text show up in everyday interactions. Still others ask students to reflect on the ways in which particular skills, theories, or concepts have shaped who they are and how they communicate.

End of Chapter Questions. Following each chapter are questions that encourage students to reflect on what they have read and to extend and apply the material presented in the chapter. Questions at the end of each chapter include one or more that guide students to web sites that can enlarge their understanding.

Learning Objectives. Opening each chapter are key learning objectives. These orient students to the chapter that follows and help them organize how they read and study the material.

Highlighting of Key Terms. Within each chapter I boldface key concepts and terms that students should learn. All boldfaced terms are repeated in a list at the end of each chapter to encourage students to check their retention after they have read the chapter. Boldface terms are also defined in the glossary at the end of the book.

Resources for Students and Instructors

Accompanying this book is an integrated suite of resources that support both students and instructors.

Instructor Resources. Instructors who adopt this book may request a number of resources to support their teaching.

- The **Instructor's Resource Manual** offers guidelines for setting up your course, sample syllabi, chapter-by-chapter outlines of content, suggested topics for lectures and discussion, and a wealth of class-tested exercises and assignments. It also includes a test bank.
- **ExamView** for Windows and Macintosh is a fully integrated resource for creating and using test items. This resource includes all of the test items found in the *Instructor's Resource Manual.*
- **CommLink: Multimedia Presentation Tool for Human Communication** is a searchable database of art, media, CNN videos, and PowerPoint slides to support teaching. CommLink also offers the ability to import information from

previously created lectures or classroom activities. A set of full-color transparencies for overhead projection and a set of PowerPoint slides are also available to instructors.

- Also available to instructors adopting this book are video resources. **CNN Videos** provide film clips that feature communication in groups and teams, personal relationships, public speaking, mass media, and other contexts. **Student Speeches for Critique and Analysis Video** includes a speech of introduction, two impromptu speeches, and three persuasive speeches. Among the featured speeches are ones that include visual aids and ones by students for whom English is a second language. Accompanying this resource is the **Instructor's Guide to the Student Speeches for Critique and Analysis Video**, which assesses each speech on the video and suggests questions for class discussion.

- **The Teaching Assistant's Guide to the Basic Course** is available to instructors who adopt this textbook. Katherin Hendrix, who is on the faculty at the University of Memphis, prepared this resource specifically for new instructors. Based on leading communication teacher training programs, this guide discusses some of the general issues that accompany a teaching role and offers specific strategies for managing the first week of classes, leading productive discussions, managing sensitive topics in the classroom, and grading students' written and oral work.

Both Students and Instructors. Thomson Learning Web Tutor™ on WebCT and BlackBoard is available when you adopt this textbook. This content-rich, Web-based teaching and learning tool is filled with pre-loaded content tied directly to the text and is ready to use as soon as you and your students log on. At the same time, you can customize the content in any way you choose. For students, **Web Tutor** offers real-time access to a full array of study tools, including flashcards (with audio), practice quizzes, online tutorials, and Web links. Use **Web Tutor** to provide virtual office hours, post your syllabi, set up threaded discussions, track student progress with the quizzing material, and more.

Student Resources. Students who purchase *Communication Mosaics* will find a rich array of resources to enhance and extend their learning.

- The **Student Companion** to this edition provides students with interactive summaries of chapter content, vocabulary lists, self-tests, and practical activities that guide them to develop skills in communicating and apply those skills in their everyday interactions. The *Companion* also integrates web and InfoTrac activities into its coverage.

- With this text, students automatically receive a free four-month subscription to **InfoTrac College Edition**, which is an online library with extensive holdings in communication.

- Nancy Goulden of Kansas State University is the author of **InfoTrac College Edition Student Activities Workbook for Communication**, which can be ordered for a minimum cost. This workbook extends the text by providing extensive individual and group activities related to public speaking.

- **Speech Interactive: Student Speeches for Critique and Analysis** is a multimedia CDROM that helps students prepare for speech performances and reinforces the textbook's discussion of the importance of listening critically to public communication.

- **Service Learning in Communication Studies: A Handbook** was prepared by Rick Isaacson, who directs service learning at San Francisco State University. The handbook describes ways to integrate service learning into the basic communication course and prepares students to work effectively with agencies and organizations.
- **WebTutor on WebCT** is a web-based dynamic study guide that helps students check their understanding and retention of communication concepts and principles.
- **A Guide to the Basic Course for ESL Students** may be purchased for a small fee. It features FAQs, helpful URLs, and strategies for managing communication anxiety.

ACKNOWLEDGMENTS

Although only my name appears as the author of this book, I could not have written it without the help of many people. I want to take a moment to acknowledge the support and assistance of a number of people who have influenced how I think and write.

I am deeply indebted to the Wadsworth team. Everyone on that team has been extraordinarily professional and helpful throughout the evolution of this book. Leading that team is Deirdre Cavanaugh, Executive Editor of Communication. I consider myself blessed to have Deirdre as my editor. She routinely exceeds the formal requirements of her position by offering substantive suggestions and creative insights that enhance the quality of books we publish. She is also a friend whose warmth and generous spirit add much to my life and work. In addition to Deirdre, I am grateful to other members of the team at Wadsworth: Cathy Linberg, extraordinary project editor; Dory Schaeffer, former editorial assistant who had the uncanny ability to juggle an overwhelming set of responsibilities and let nothing slip through the cracks; Patty O'Connell of Electronic Publishing Services Inc., production editor who coordinated the team for this book; Carol Peschke, copy editor; and Lisa Delgado of Delgado Design, Inc., who designed the text and cover. This book is truly a collaborative effort that involved and reflects the contributions of everyone on the team.

I am also grateful to scholars and teachers of communication who reviewed the first edition and my proposal for revision and who offered valuable feedback that shaped this edition of *Communication Mosaics*. Reviewers were: Rebecca Parker, Western Illinois University; Joy L. Hart, University of Louisville; Belle A. Edson, Arizona State University, Joseph B. Zubrick, University of Maine-Presque Isle; Mark A. Schlesinger, University of Massachusetts-Boston; Matt McAllister, Virginia Tech; Stephanie J. Coopman, San Jose State University; David W. Worley, Indiana State University; Marjukka Ollilainen, Virginia Tech; Jess K. Alberts, Arizona State University; Guy Warner, Augusta State University; Jodee Hobbs, Northeast Louisiana University; Marcia Dixson, Indiana-Purdue at Fort Wayne; Carol Dostal, Indiana-Purdue at Fort Wayne; Patrick Herbert, Northeast Louisiana University; Susan Cain Giusto, Augusta State University; Scott Vitz, Indiana-Purdue at Fort Wayne; Mary Allen, Valencia Community College; Diane O. Casagrande, West

Chester University; Bobbie R. Klopp, Kirkwood Community College; Sandra Metts, Illinois State University; Kim P. Niemczyk, Palm Beach Community College; Nan Peck, Northern Virginia County College; Helen M. Sterk, Marquette University; and Sue L. Wenzlaff, Austin Peay State University.

The ideas in this book were also influenced by students in my classes, as well as students around the country who generously gave me feedback on the first edition of this book. In class discussions, conferences, email notes, and written comments students push me to do more and tell me what communication issues are prominent in their lives. Invariably, students teach me at least as much as I teach them. Because students are so thoughtful, I include many of their thoughts as *Student Voices* in this book.

Finally, I thank those who are my intimates. For more than 25 years Robert Cox has been my partner in love, life, and work. He is my greatest fan and my most rigorous critic, and both his support and his criticism shape all that I write. Robbie is unfailingly generous in listening to my ideas and providing perceptive feedback that enriches what I write. Special friends, LindaBecker and Nancy, sharpen my thinking and writing by testing my ideas against their experiences communicating with others. My sister Carolyn remains one of the most positive, perceptive, and delightful presences in my life, as do my youngest friends, Cam who is 17, Michelle who is nine, Daniel who is six, and Harrison who just turned one. These children continuously remind me of the magic and wonder in human relationships. And of course I must express my appreciation to the four-legged members of my family: Madhi the wonder dog, Sadie Ladie, and Ms. Wicca. When Robbie and my two-footed friends are asleep and I am writing, it's Madhi, Sadie, and Wicca who keep me company and who occasionally offer their feedback on my work.

Julia T. Wood
Spring 2000

Communication Mosaics

An Introduction to the Field of Communication

Introduction to *Communication Mosaics*

LEARNING OBJECTIVES

To understand

1. The roles of communication in your life
2. Which skills and processes are common to communication in diverse situations
3. How personal identity shapes communication and social life
4. The themes and features of this book

- Your romantic partner claims that you avoid dealing with conflict in your relationship. You know it's true, but you don't know how to communicate about conflict.
- While browsing on the World Wide Web you find a message that contains racist and sexist slurs. You think you should respond but aren't sure what to say.
- You sense that your friend feels on guard during a conversation, and you want to say something to reduce the defensiveness between you, but you don't know what to say.
- You've been invited to interview for your dream job, and getting it depends on communicating effectively in the interview. You wonder how to do that.
- A group to which you belong is working on recycling programs for the community, but the group is so disorganized that it's getting nowhere. You wonder how you could participate to make discussion more efficient and orderly.
- You've noticed a new employee at your part-time job and would like to ask for a date, but you're not sure how communication on the job might be affected if the two of you were romantically involved.
- At the end of this term your romantic partner will graduate and take a job in a city that's a thousand miles away. You're concerned about sustaining intimacy when you have to communicate across the distance.

- At work you're assigned to a team that includes people from Korea and Mexico. You aren't sure how to interpret their styles of communicating or how to interact effectively with them.
- A major political personality speaks at your campus, and you attend. You try to listen carefully, but you aren't sure how to evaluate what the speaker says.

From the moment we rise until we go to bed our days are filled with communication challenges and opportunities. Unlike some subjects you study, communication is relevant to virtually every aspect of your life. We communicate with ourselves when we work through ideas, psych ourselves up for big moments, and talk ourselves into or out of various courses of action. We communicate with others to build and sustain personal relationships, perform our jobs and advance in our careers, and participate in social and civic activities. Even when we're not physically around other people, we are involved in communication as we interact with mass media and communication technologies. All facets of our lives involve communication. Although we communicate continuously, we aren't always effective. People who have inadequate communication knowledge and skills are limited in their efforts to achieve personal, professional, and social goals. On the other hand, people who communicate well have a strong advantage in personal, social, professional, and civic life. Thus, learning about communication and developing your skills as a communicator are foundations for a successful life.

Communication Mosaics is designed to introduce you to basic communication processes and skills that influence your effectiveness in a range of communication situations. It's useful to think of communication as a mosaic made up of basic processes and skills. In various contexts we arrange the elements differently, and the result is variations in the appearance of the mosaic. In Part I we focus on six fundamental communication processes. Part II traces how those basic communication processes operate in situations ranging from communication with yourself to communication on the World Wide Web. Reading this book will sharpen your understanding of fundamental processes and skills pertinent to the myriad forms and settings of human communication. First, I introduce myself and describe the special features of this book.

Tom Levy/Photo 20-20

■ *Informal communication is constant on most campuses. What can you infer about these people from their nonverbal behavior?*

INTRODUCTION TO THE AUTHOR

As an undergraduate I enrolled in a course much like the one you're taking now. It was an introductory class in which we studied a variety of communication forms and contexts. In that course I became fascinated by the field of communication, and my interest has endured for more than 20 years. Today I am still captivated by the field—more than ever, in fact. I see communication both as a science that involves skills and knowledge of research and as an art that reflects human imagination and wisdom in adapting basic processes and skills to diverse situations. Because communication is central to personal identity and cultural life, it is one of the most dynamic and growing areas of study in higher education. It is a field that offers insights, skills, and knowledge relevant to our personal and collective well-being.

When I was a student, I always wondered about the authors of my textbooks. Who were they? Why did they write a book? Unfortunately, the authors never introduced themselves in their books. I want to start our relationship differently by telling you something about myself. I am a 48-year-old middle-income European American woman who has strong spiritual beliefs. For more than 25 years I have been married to Robert Cox, a professor of communication at my university and a national leader of the Sierra Club. As is true for all of us, who I am affects what I know and how I think, act, feel, and communicate. Thus many of the ideas and examples in the chapters that follow reflect what I have learned during my 27 years as a researcher and teacher of communication. I have taught and conducted research on group communication, leadership, interaction in personal relationships, communication theory, social influences on communication, and gender, communication, and culture. My experiences communicating with others are another source of examples that I use to illustrate the communication processes, concepts, and skills we will discuss in this book. Research by other scholars also informs my perspective. The hundreds of references cited in this book have shaped how I understand human communication and how I introduce you to the field.

Other facets of my identity also influence what I know and how I write. My race, gender, socioeconomic level, and sexual orientation have given me certain kinds of insight and have limited other insights. As a woman, I understand discrimination based on sex because I've experienced it. However, I do not have personal knowledge of racial discrimination because Western culture confers privilege on me as a European American. Being middle income has shielded me from personal experience with hunger, poverty, and biases against the poor, and being heterosexual has spared me from being the direct target of homophobia. Who I am also reflects

© Dan Sears/UNC Press Bureau

■ *Julia T. Wood*

my roles as a daughter, wife, friend, aunt, professional, and member of spiritual and civic groups. Likewise, your identity influences what you know and how you communicate. Think about how your identity and experiences shape what you know and how you interpret others and their styles of communicating. If you reflect on this issue, I suspect you will discover how profoundly your identity shapes your personal choices and your views of social life.

Although our identity limits what we personally know and experience, it doesn't completely prevent insight into people and situations different from our own. From conversations with others and from reading, I have gained some understanding of communication styles that differ from my own as well as kinds of discrimination and privilege that I haven't personally experienced. I've also learned from others who communicate in situations that are unfamiliar to me. In our increasingly diverse world, we need to learn about a variety of people, lifestyles, personal and social milieus, and cultures. We need to understand and communicate effectively with people who differ from us. What we learn by studying and interacting with people of different cultural heritages expands our appreciation of the richness and complexity of humanity. In addition, learning about and forming relationships with different people enlarges our repertoires of communication skills. Throughout *Communication Mosaics* we discuss ways in which membership in different cultural and social groups affects communication goals and styles.

INTRODUCTION TO *COMMUNICATION MOSAICS*

To provide a context for your reading, let me share my vision of this book. *Communication Mosaics* introduces you to basic communication processes, concepts, and skills that are relevant to a range of goals and settings of interaction. The title reflects the idea that communication is an intricate mosaic of skills that are distinct yet interrelated. The six basic communication skills and processes emphasized in this book are these:

- Perceiving and understanding others
- Creating and sustaining communication climates
- Engaging in verbal communication
- Engaging in nonverbal communication
- Listening and responding to others
- Adapting communication to people and contexts

These skills are not isolated from one another; in fact, each is related to all others. For example, how we perceive others is related to the ways we create and interpret verbal and nonverbal communication. How we interact with co-workers affects and is affected by our verbal and nonverbal styles of communication. The interaction climates we establish in personal and professional relationships are shaped by questions we ask, statements we make, and nonverbal behaviors. Our skill in communicating with doctors depends on our ability to listen critically, ask questions, and adapt our communication to the context of a medical conference. The basic communication processes you'll study in this book are present in all forms and contexts of communication.

Coverage

Because communication is a continuous part of life, we need to understand processes and skills that are relevant to a range of forms and functions of communication. Part I of this book introduces you to key processes and principles of communication that shape what happens when people interact in various situations. Part II extends Part I by applying the basic processes and skills to a broad spectrum of communication encounters: communication with yourself, interaction with friends and romantic partners, teamwork, communication in organizations, interviewing, public speaking, mass communication, and communication technologies. These topics can be adapted to the interests, needs, and preferences of individual classes and instructors.

Students

Communication Mosaics is written for anyone who is interested in human communication. It is equally appropriate for majors and nonmajors. If you are a prospective communication major, this book and the course it accompanies will give you a firm foundation for more advanced study. If you are majoring in another discipline, they will give you a sound basic understanding of communication and opportunities to strengthen your skills as a communicator.

Learning about communication should be enjoyable. I don't think textbooks have to be dry or burdened with unnecessary jargon. When it's necessary to use specialized terms, I define them so that you and I share an understanding of what they mean. I've written this book in an informal, personal style to make it more interesting to read. Throughout the chapters that follow I refer to myself as *I* rather than *the author*, and I use contractions (*can't* and *you're* instead of the more formal *cannot* and *you are*), as we do in normal conversation. To enlarge our conversation beyond just you and me, all chapters include reflective comments from students at my university and other campuses around the country. To protect privacy I've changed the names of students who wrote the commentaries.

Theory and Practice

Communication Mosaics reflects my conviction that theory and practice go together. Years ago renowned scholar Kurt Lewin said, "There is nothing so practical as a good theory." His words remain true today. In this book I've blended theory and practice so that each draws on and enriches the other. Effective practice is theoretically informed: It is based on knowledge of how and why the communication process works and what is likely to result from different kinds of communication. At the same time, effective theories have pragmatic value: They help us understand experiences and events in our everyday lives. Each chapter in this book is informed by the impressive theories and research generated by scholars of communication, as well as scholars in other fields. The perspectives and skills recommended reflect current knowledge of effective communication practices.

FEATURES

To prepare this book, I read many reviews of the first edition. Some reviews were prepared by faculty who teach communication. In addition, I read more than 1,000 reviews from students who had used the first edition as a textbook. The students' comments were especially helpful in guiding my work on this edition of the book. I believe it retains the strengths that faculty and students found in the first edition and addresses some of their requests for increased coverage of some topics. In response to faculty feedback, Chapter 1 now includes a brief history of the communication field and a discussion of methods of conducting research in communication. Also in response to faculty requests, this edition includes discussion of how basic communication processes apply to a range of communication situations. Faculty also wanted the chapter on creating climates of communication to come earlier in the book. Thus, I have moved it from its former position as Chapter 6 to Chapter 3 in this edition. Both students and faculty urged me to provide greater attention to technology. In response, this edition integrates technology thoroughly into all chapters. In every chapter you will find examples of how communication technologies affect how we live and work. The questions for discussion at the end of each chapter include one or more questions focused specifically on technology. Also, Chapter 14 reflects changes in communication technologies since the first edition went to press.

The changes in this edition, along with the vision that motivated the first edition, result in six features that I want to call to your attention. Understanding each feature's contribution to the mosaic of communication will allow you to use the book effectively.

Technology Emphasis

Technology increasingly pervades our personal, public, and professional lives. Among the many technologies that affect how we live and work are communication technologies, which connect us with people and services around the world. More than 90% of U.S. college students in 1999 used the Internet to conduct research for their classes (McCollum, 1999). In addition, two thirds of today's college students regularly use email and more than half join online discussions in chat rooms ("Connecting with the Future," 1999; Weiss, 1999). To reflect the increasingly technological nature of our society, this edition of *Communication Mosaics* emphasizes technology in three ways. First, discussion of technology is woven into every chapter. Current research and examples of communication using technologies appear in all chapters. You'll also find lots of Web sites that you might want to visit to learn more about specific facets of communication.

Second, Chapter 15 is devoted exclusively to technologies of communication so that you can learn how they affect patterns and meanings of interaction and how they affect the social fabric. Third, technology is emphasized through the *InfoTrac College Edition* that accompanies this textbook. This fully searchable online library allows you to search for information on specific communication topics and to read and print out complete speeches and research articles in academic journals and popular magazines. Because *InfoTrac College Edition* is updated regularly, you'll find it a very valuable source of current information.

Integrated Attention to Cultural Diversity

Social diversity is woven into this book. The United States and the world have always been culturally diverse. However, much popular and academic writing has inadequately recognized and represented the diversity of human beings and the lives we lead. In recent years a number of textbooks have dealt with diversity by adding comments about various groups into general discussions. For instance, a chapter on leadership might examine how Western middle-income Caucasian men lead and then add a few paragraphs about female leadership. A chapter on communication in personal relationships might focus on interaction between heterosexuals and only briefly mention communication in gay and lesbian commitments. This approach to diversity was an important first step in the effort to broaden understandings of the social world.

In this book I extend early efforts by making diversity an important and continuous element in the communication mosaic. I integrate cultural diversity in the text in two ways. First, Chapter 7, "Adapting Communication to People and Contexts," focuses on the ways in which our member-

© Dan Bosler/Tony Stone Images

© Frank Siteman/Index Stock

■ *What differences in interaction style can you identify in these two photos? How are the people adapting their communication to suit diverse settings?*

fyi

LEARNING ABOUT MULTICULTURALISM

The Multicultural Pavilion is a rich resource designed for educators, students, and activists. This online resource center offers full texts of speeches such as Abraham Lincoln's "Gettysburg Address" and Martin Luther King Jr.'s "I Have a Dream." In addition, it provides scholarly papers and an impressive bibliography for those who want to learn more. To access this site, go to http://curry.edschool.virginia.edu/curry/centers/multicultural.

ship in cultures and social groups influences our communication and our interpretations of others' communication. Second, discussion of cultural diversity is blended into all chapters in Part II of the book. For example, Chapter 9, on personal relationships, identifies differences in how women and men generally communicate and provides clues about how the sexes can translate each other's language. Chapter 11, on communication in organizations, highlights the implications for communication of our increasingly diverse work force. This book's integrated attention to cultural diversity will extend your insight into the complex relationships among culture, identity, and communication in all settings. In addition, it will enhance your ability to participate effectively in a culturally diverse world.

David

As an African American male I sometimes feel as though I am a dash of pepper atop a mountain of salt. I have attended many classes where I was the only African American out of 50 or even 100 students. In these classes the feeling of judgment is cast down upon me for being different. Usually what I learn about is not "people," like the course says, but white people. Until I took a communication course the only classes that included research and information on African Americans were in the African American curriculum. This bothered me because white Americans are not the entire world.

Student Commentaries

The comment above is from David, who wrote to me after using my book in a course he took at a college in the western United States. David's comment illustrates both the importance of integrated attention to cultural diversity and the value of student commentaries. In my classes students teach me and each other through their insights, experiences, and questions. Because I believe students have much to teach all of us, I've included reflections written by students at my university and other campuses. As you read the student commentaries, you'll probably identify with some, disagree with others, and be puzzled by still others. Whether you agree, disagree, or are perplexed, I think you'll agree that the student voices expand the text and spark thought and discussion in your class and elsewhere.

For Your Information

Communication Mosaics also includes inserts that highlight information about communication. These are set off from the rest of the text in *FYI* (For Your

U.S. DEMOGRAPHICS IN THE TWENTY-FIRST CENTURY

The United States is home to a wide range of people with diverse ethnic, racial, cultural, and geographic backgrounds. And the proportions of different groups are changing.

The U.S. Census Bureau (1998; Larmer, 1999), predicts the following shifts in the ethnic makeup of the United States through the middle of the twenty-first century.

	2005	2050
African Americans	12%	14%
Asians	4%	8%
Caucasians	71%	53%
Hispanics	13%	25%

Information) *boxes.* I use these to introduce ideas that merit special attention and to highlight particularly interesting findings from communication research. Material in the FYI features may serve as a springboard for class discussions. You'll notice that some FYI boxes have a special icon in the corner. This alerts you to the fact that the box will suggest one or more Web sites you can visit to learn more about the topic.

Sharpen Your Skill

A fifth feature is *Sharpen Your Skill,* which brings to life the concepts we discuss by showing you how to apply basic skills in your own life. I suggest ways you might develop your communication skills and ways to be more sensitive to communication processes and principles in everyday situations. You're invited to apply communication principles and skills as you interact with and observe others. Some *Sharpen Your Skill* activities suggest ways to develop a particular communication skill through practice. Others encourage you to discover how a specific communication principle or theory shows up in interactions you observe or in which you participate.

Aids to Learning

I've included four aids to retention and learning. First, I open each chapter with key Learning Objectives to highlight important topics that will be covered. Reading the objectives as you begin a chapter will help you focus your attention as you study the chapter. Rereading the objectives after completing the chapter allows you to check your understanding of ideas and issues that have been discussed. Second, each chapter concludes with a summary that condenses the main topics in each chapter into a few paragraphs. Third, at the end of each chapter you'll find a list of key terms introduced in bold type and discussed in the chapter. You can test your comprehension of conceptual material by asking yourself whether you understand each concept in the list. Finally, each chapter includes several questions for further reflection on your part and discussion with others. These questions invite you to extend and apply material covered in chapters and to use Web resources to learn more.

Writing this book is a way for me to share my enthusiasm for communication with you. I hope you'll enjoy reading *Communication Mosaics* as much as I enjoyed writing it. If so, both of us will have spent our time well.

FOR FURTHER REFLECTION AND DISCUSSION

1. How does your identity shape how you think, act, feel, and communicate? How has it influenced what you know? Recall my discussion in this Introduction of how my identity affects my knowledge and behavior. Using my discussion as a guide, reflect on how your identity shapes your beliefs and practices.
2. Learn more about the field of communication by visiting the Web site of the National Communication Association at http://www.natcom.org.
3. Think about the various forms and contexts of communication: intrapersonal (communication with yourself), personal relationships, groups, and public speaking. In which contexts is your communication most effective? In which contexts do you want to become more skillful? At the outset of the course you might make a contract with yourself to focus on improving in one or two areas.
4. Do you agree that theory and practice are natural allies? As a class, discuss the importance of theories in everyday life. How do they affect your behavior and your interpretation of people, situations, and events?
5. Media often refer to the emergence of multiculturalism. Yet in this Introduction I claim that the United States and the world have always been multicultural, but that only recently has this been recognized. Do you agree that multiculturalism is not new but awareness of it is? Do you think awareness of multiculturalism is appropriate and valuable?
6. Use your *InfoTrac College Edition* to find out about relationships between culture and communication. Enter the site, select EasyTrac, and type in the key words *culture and communication*. Review resources that appear.

The Field of Communication

LEARNING OBJECTIVES

To understand

1. The value of studying communication
2. The history of the field of communication
3. How communication scholars conduct research
4. The breadth of the contemporary communication discipline
5. How communication is defined
6. The processes and skills that unify the many forms and contexts of communication
7. The levels of meaning in communication
8. What careers are open to people with strong backgrounds in communication

Mike exits from his email program and reflects on how amazing it is to "talk" with Jack, who is thousands of miles away. He wonders how it would be to communicate with Jack in person—would they like each other and find it easy to interact? Shrugging, he walks across his room and gets a notebook out of his backpack. It's a draft agenda for meeting with his student government team. At first Mike, who is an undergraduate, found it difficult to work on teams. In high school the emphasis was on individual initiative, achievement, and leadership. Now teams are the big thing. To be effective in the team environment, Mike has had to learn new ways of interacting, presenting ideas, and evaluating effectiveness. Somewhat to his own surprise, Mike's involvement with a number of teams has convinced him that teamwork often is superior to individual efforts.

After spending 30 minutes making notes on the draft agenda, Mike sees Pat walking toward his room. She is a first-year resident assistant whom he has been mentoring. He gets up, welcomes her, and spends the first 10 minutes creating a climate in which she feels comfortable and supported. Then he praises her strengths: efficiency, commitment to students in her dorm, and insights. Once Pat is aware that he values her skills, Mike introduces the idea that she doesn't seem very team oriented, which is important for resident assistants. As he broaches the topic, he notices that she tenses, which he interprets as a sign that she is uncomfortable. She tells him she doesn't like to rely on others. Perceiving Pat as having a high need to control outcomes, Mike talks with her about his difficulties in letting go of personal control when working with teams. Pat responds well to his self-disclosure by opening up about her reservations. When Pat leaves 20 minutes later, Mike feels the conversation went well. He jots down a few notes about what he learned as he listened to her.

Mike then dashes off to meet Marylyn and Walt for lunch. They talk about companies that are interviewing on campus. Informally comparing perceptions with one another is a primary way that he, Walt, and Marylyn stay informed about job opportunities.

As he walks back to his dorm after lunch, Mike thinks about his date with Coreen later that evening. He wonders whether she'll want to talk about the relationship again. He doesn't understand why she wants to talk about the relationship unless they need to resolve some issue. He's also noticed that some women in student government perceive interpersonal issues in the group but that he doesn't see these issues. Back in his room Mike focuses on his speech to a group of thirty new members of student government. So that he can adapt his comments to the goals and concerns of the people with whom he'll be speaking, Mike thinks back to his experiences as a newcomer to student government.

Like Mike, most of us communicate continuously in our everyday lives. There's not a moment in his day when he's not communicating: chatting with friends on email, researching topics on the Internet, mentoring Pat, relying on the informal network during lunch, watching television and listening to radio programs, pondering his relationship with Coreen, and preparing a presentation to give to thirty people.

Even if you don't pursue a career such as sales, teaching, or law, all of which require strong speaking skills, communication will be essential in your work. You may want to persuade your boss you deserve a raise, represent your neighborhood in a zoning hearing, be a spokesperson for environmental issues, or participate in work teams. You will have conflicts with co-workers, romantic partners, and friends. To advance in your career you'll need to know how to build good climates in work teams. You may need to deal with co-workers who tell racist jokes or harass you sexually. You should reflect on whether others might perceive your communication as sexist or racist. Communication skills are vital to personal and professional well-being and to the health of our society.

In this book you'll gain insight into communication and enhance your ability to communicate effectively in a variety of situations. Part I of *Communication Mosaics* introduces you to six basic communication processes that apply to all settings:

- Perceiving and understanding (Chapter 2)
- Creating healthy communication climates (Chapter 3)
- Engaging in verbal communication (Chapter 4)
- Engaging in nonverbal communication (Chapter 5)
- Listening and responding to others (Chapter 6)
- Adapting communication to people and contexts (Chapter 7)

In Part II of *Communication Mosaics* we'll see how these six basic processes pertain to diverse forms and settings of communication. You can become a more effective communicator in multiple situations if you understand common processes and learn the skills associated with them.

WHY STUDY COMMUNICATION?

Because you've been communicating all your life, you might wonder why you need to study communication. One answer is that formal study can improve skill. Some people have a natural talent for singing or basketball. Yet they could be even more effective if they took voice lessons or studied theories of offensive and defensive play. Likewise, even if you communicate well now, learning about communication can make you more effective.

Theories and principles of communication also help us make sense of what happens in our everyday lives, and they help us to have influence. For instance, learning about gender-based differences would help Mike understand why Coreen and other women enjoy talking about relationships more than men in general do. Mike's skill in mentoring Pat reflects his understanding of the importance of a good communication climate and his ability to use verbal and nonverbal communication to reduce her defensiveness. Because Mike perceives and listens to others, he sensed that Pat felt uneasy, and he communicated in a way that reduced her discomfort. His listening skill also served him well at the lunch with Marylyn and Walt. Mike understands that effective communicators adapt to particular contexts and people, and this insight guides him as he prepares his speech. Knowledge of basic communication processes helps Mike maximize his effectiveness in all spheres of his life.

This chapter establishes foundations for studying communication. We'll first discuss the importance of communication in our lives. Second, we'll discuss the field of communication so that you can appreciate its rich history and primary methods of conducting research. Next we'll survey areas in the communication field and highlight themes that unify the different areas. Finally, we will identify careers for communication specialists.

IMPORTANCE OF COMMUNICATION

You spend more time communicating than doing anything else. We talk, listen, think, share confidences with intimates, ask and answer questions, participate on teams, attend public presentations, exchange information with co-workers, watch television programs, and so forth. From birth to death communication is central to our personal, professional, and civic lives.

Personal Life

George Herbert Mead (1934) said that humans are talked into humanity.* He meant that we gain personal identity by communicating with others. In our earliest years our parents told us who we were: "You're smart," "You're so strong," "You're such a funny one." We first see ourselves through the eyes of others, so their messages form important foundations of our self-concepts. Later we interact

*I use the American Psychological Association (APA) style of citation. "Mead (1934)" refers to a work by Mead that was written in 1934. "Mead (1934, p. 10)" or "(Mead, 1934, p. 10)" refers to page 10 of Mead's 1934 work. Complete citations appear in the references, beginning on page 361.

YOUR COMMUNICATION ACTIVITIES

To find out how important communication is in your life, monitor your activities for the next 24 hours. (The activities may overlap, so your total may exceed 100%):

1. What percentage of time do you spend listening to others?
2. What percentage of time do you spend talking with yourself about ideas, plans, and options?
3. What percentage of your time do you spend communicating with friends and romantic partners?
4. How much time do you devote to group and public communication?
5. How much time do you spend talking with co-workers?
6. How often do you interact with people from other cultures?
7. How much time do you spend communicating on email and the Web?

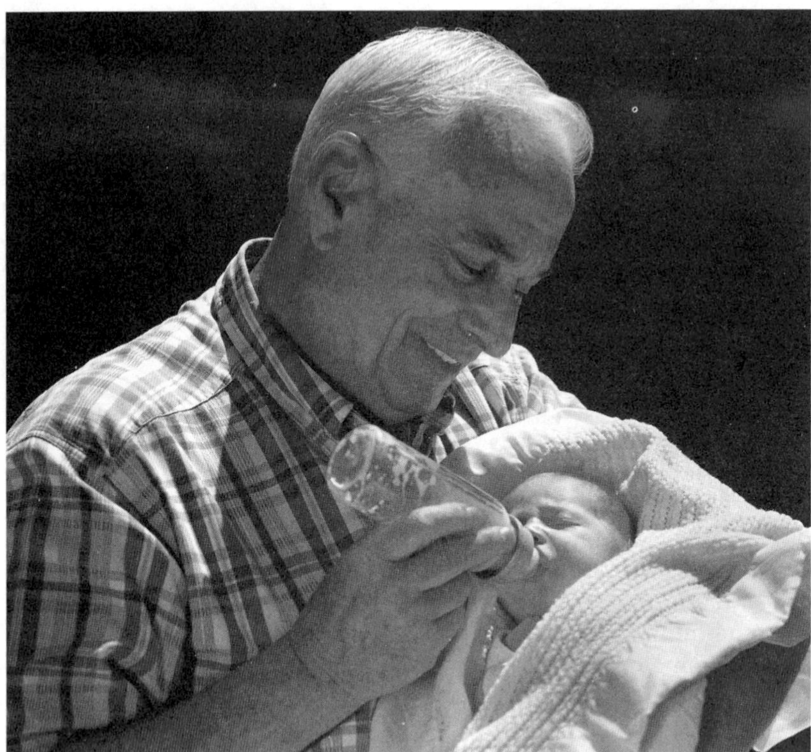

■ *What message is this grandfather conveying about how he views his grandchild? How might his communication affect this child's self-concept?*

© CORBIS

with teachers, friends, romantic partners, and co-workers who communicate their views of us. Thus, how we see ourselves reflects the views of us that others communicate.

The profound connection between communication and identity is dramatically evident in children who are deprived of human contact. Case studies of children who were isolated from others show that they have no concept of themselves as humans, and their mental and psychological development is severely hindered by lack of language.

Communication also directly influences our physical well-being. Research consistently shows that communicating with others promotes health, whereas social isolation is linked to stress, disease, and early death (Crowley, 1995). People who lack close friends have greater levels of anxiety and depression than people who are close to others (Hojat, 1982; Jones & Moore, 1989). Heart disease is also more common among people who lack strong interpersonal relationships (Ruberman, 1992). Women with metastatic breast cancer double their average survival time when they belong to support groups in which they talk with others (Crowley, 1995). Some women with widespread breast cancer who belonged to support groups survived 15 years or longer after the study of the connection between interpersonal contact and health was done (McClure, 1997). Steve Duck (1992), a scholar of interpersonal communication, reports that people in disturbed relationships tend to suffer from low self-esteem, headaches, alcoholism, cancer, sleep disorders, and other physical problems. Clearly, healthy interaction with others is important to our physical and mental well-being.

Personal Relationships

Communication is a key foundation of personal relationships. We build connections with others by revealing our private identities, asking questions and listening to the answers, working out problems, remembering shared history, and planning a future. Marriage counselors have long emphasized the importance of communication for healthy, enduring relationships (Beck, 1988; Gottman & Carrère, 1994; Scarf, 1987). A primary distinction between relationships that endure and those that collapse is

fyi

GHADYA KA BACHA

Ghadya Ka Bacha, or the wolf boy, was found in 1954 outside a hospital in Balrampur, India. He had calloused knees and hands as if he moved on all fours, and he had scars on his neck, suggesting he had been dragged about by animals. Ramu, which was the name the hospital staff gave the child, showed no interest in others but became very excited once when he saw wolves on a visit to the zoo. Ramu lapped his milk from a glass instead of drinking as we do, and he tore apart his food. Most doctors who examined Ramu concluded he was a wolf boy who had grown up with wolves and who acted like a wolf, not a person.

Source: Shattuck, 1980

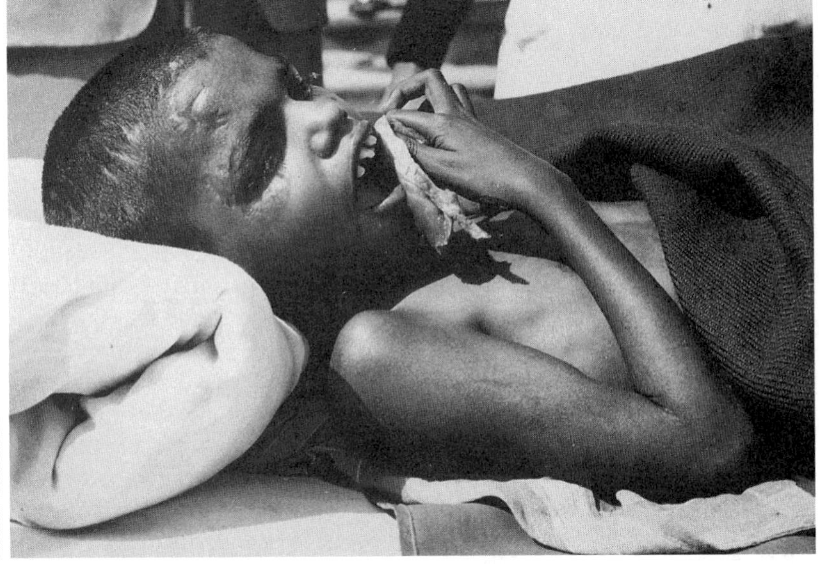

Archive Photos/APA

In this photo Ramu is eating raw meat. What do Ramu's behaviors suggest about how we develop self-concepts?

effective communication. Couples who learn how to discuss their thoughts and feelings, adapt to each other, and manage conflict constructively tend to sustain intimacy over time.

Communication is important for more than solving problems or making disclosures. For most of us, everyday talk and nonverbal interaction are the essence of relationships (Barnes & Duck, 1994; Duck, 1994a, 1994b; Spencer, 1994). Although dramatic moments affect relationships, it is unremarkable, everyday interaction that sustains the daily rhythms of our intimate connections (Berger & Kellner, 1964). Partners weave their lives together through small talk about mutual friends, daily events, and other mundane topics. Couples involved in long-distance romances say their biggest loss is not being able to share small talk (Gerstel & Gross, 1985).

Sandy

When my boyfriend moved away, the hardest part wasn't missing the big moments. It was not talking about little stuff or just being together. It was like we weren't part of each other's life when we didn't talk about all the little things that happened or we felt or whatever.

fyi

COMMUNICATION AND MARRIAGE

How important is communication to marriage? How much does poor communication contribute to divorce? A national poll conducted in 1998 found answers to these questions. Regardless of age, race, sex, or economic standing, Americans say communication problems are the number one cause of divorce. Fifty-three percent of those polled said lack of effective communication was the principal cause of divorce. Other causes lagged far behind. When asked what the primary reason for divorce was, 29% said money problems, 7% said interference from relatives, and 5% said sexual problems.

To learn more about this poll, view the complete results at http://www.natcom.org/research/Roper/how_americans_communicate.htm.

Professional Life

Communication skills are critical for success in professional life. The importance of communication is obvious in professions such as teaching, law, sales, and counseling, where talking and listening are central to effectiveness. Many attorneys, counselors, and businesspeople major in communication before pursuing specialized training (Morreal & Vogl, 1998).

In other fields the importance of communication is less obvious but nonetheless present. One survey found that 79% of New York City corporate executives ranked the ability to express ideas verbally as the most important qualification in hiring and evaluating employees (Silverstone, Greenbaum, & MacGregor, 1987). Health care professionals rely on communication skills to talk with patients about medical problems and courses of treatment and to gain cooperation from colleagues, patients, and families for continued care (Berko, Wolvin, & Wolvin, 1992). According to a 1998 poll, people who feel they are effective communicators are more successful in a variety of careers (http://www.natcom.org/research/Roper/how_americans_communicate.htm).

Even highly technical jobs such as computer programming, accounting, and film editing require communication skills. Specialists have to be able to listen carefully to the needs of their clients and customers. They also need to be skilled in explaining technical ideas to people who lack their expertise. When the National Association of Colleges and Employers asked 480 companies to identify the applicant qualities that were most important in their hiring decisions, communication skills were at the very top of the list (Schneider, 1999). Developing good communication skills is important no matter what your career goals are.

Civic Life

Communication skills are also important for the health of our society. From painting on the walls of caves to telling stories in village squares to interacting on the Internet, people have found ways to communicate with each other to build a common social world. To be effective, citizens in a democracy must be able to express ideas and evaluate the ethical and logical strength of claims other people advance. To make informed judgments, voters need to listen critically to candidates' arguments and responses to questions. We also need to listen critically to speakers who make proposals about goals for the institutions at which we work, as well as those on which we depend for services.

Communication skills are especially important for effective, healthy interaction in a socially diverse world. In pluralistic cultures such as ours, we need to understand and work with people who differ from us. Healthy civic and social engagements depend on our ability to listen thoughtfully to a range of perspectives and to adapt our communication to diverse people and contexts.

Luanne

I feel so awkward trying to talk with people who weren't raised in the United States like I was.

Sometimes it seems that they have a totally different way of talking than I do, and we don't understand each other naturally. But I've been trying to learn to understand people from other places, and it really is making me realize how many different ways of communicating people have. With so many cultures now part of this country, nobody can get by without learning how to relate to people from other cultures.

When Luanne was a student in one of my courses, she and I talked several times about the concern she expresses in her commentary. Luanne realized she needed to learn to interact with people whose backgrounds are different from hers if she is to be effective. Like Luanne, you can develop skill in communicating effectively with the variety of people who make up Western society on the brink of the twenty-first century.

Communication, then, is important for personal, relationship, professional, and civic and cultural well-being. Because communication is a cornerstone of human life, your decision to study it will serve you well.

HISTORY OF THE COMMUNICATION FIELD

In your introductory course in communication, you will find that communication has a rich and distinguished intellectual history. As the title of this book suggests, communication is like a mosaic that has many parts, each of which contributes to the overall character of the field. One theme in the mosaic of communication dates back more than 2,000 years. In ancient Greece, philosophers such as Aristotle and Isocrates viewed rhetoric as central to civic life. Aristotle taught citizens how to analyze listeners, discover ideas for communication, organize messages effectively, develop proof to support claims, and deliver speeches that could move listeners. For centuries after Plato and Aristotle taught in the Athenian forums, rhetoric held a premier spot in liberal education in Europe and the United States. Following Aristotle's view that rhetoric is a practical art, teachers of rhetoric provided pragmatic advice to students who wanted to be effective speakers in public contexts. During the nineteenth century many of the most prestigious universities in the United States had chairs of rhetoric, held by distinguished scholars and civic leaders. Among these was future president John Quincy Adams, who held the first Boylston Professor of Rhetoric Chair at Harvard University (Foss, Foss, & Trapp, 1991). During the 1800s and early 1900s, rhetoric was taught as a practical art that prepared people for responsible participation in civic life. The emphasis on teaching that marked this period explains why the first national professional organization, founded in 1914, was named the National Association of Teachers of Public Speaking.

A second prominent theme in the communication mosaic emerged in the middle part of the twentieth century. Following the two world wars, communication professionals became interested in social issues that went far beyond public speaking. Members of the discipline felt an urgent need to understand the connections between communication and Hitler's rise to power, the development of prejudice against social groups, willingness to follow an authoritarian leader, the effects of propaganda, and changes in attitudes and beliefs. This broadening of the field's interest explains why the national organization changed its name to the Speech Association of America. In 1969 the name was changed again to the Speech Communication Association, and in the mid-1990s it became the National Communication Association, which is its name today. The name changes reflect the field's evolving interests in diverse contexts and forms of communication.

During the mid–twentieth century another part of the mosaic of communication emerged: scientific, empirical research, which affected virtually all of the social sciences and humanities. Marking the advent of scientific research in the communication field was the formation of the International Communication Association (ICA) in 1950. Whereas the National Communication Association (then called Speech Association of America) was steeped in the humanities, ICA allied itself with the scientific tradition. This tradition led many communication scholars to favor quantitative forms of research as they sought to learn more about such issues as the factors that influence a speaker's credibility, the effects of following rational models of decision making, the responses of group members to different leadership styles, and the impact of various kinds of evidence on persuasion.

The 1960s and 1970s saw a new motif in the communication mosaic. In the United States, this was a time of unprecedented social and political upheaval. The civil rights movement and the second wave of the women's movement shook up long-standing patterns of personal and social relations. At the same time, the counterculture surged and brought with it new ideas about how people should interact and what was really important in life. Responding to these currents in social life, the communication discipline expanded its interests to encompass interpersonal communication. Historically the introductory course in communication had been public speaking, but it became interpersonal communication at many colleges and universities in the 1960s and 1970s. Additional courses such as nonverbal behavior, family communication, and interaction in intimate relationships emerged and were welcomed by students. The interpersonal emphasis also affected group communication courses, adding sensitivity training and human relations to the traditional coverage of rational decision making. Both humanistic and scientific perspectives on communication continued to shape research and teaching during this time.

Beginning in the late 1970s and continuing through the 1990s, another theme ascended in the communication field. An interest in social issues reshaped all areas of the field, including rhetoric, which broadened its scope beyond the study of individual speakers. Rhetorical scholars began to study social movements, such as the black power movement and the anti-Vietnam War movement, and they studied more than the public speeches that were part of those movements. They also analyzed how coercive tactics were used, how symbolic strategies for defining issues worked, and how social movements challenged and changed broadly held cultural practices and values. Scholars in other areas shared an interest in critical perspectives that focus on ways in which communication shapes and is shaped by the historical, social, and political contexts in which it occurs. Thus, faculty in interpersonal communication conducted research and taught about how new technologies affect personal relationships through online dating, how events such as the Million Man March and movements such as third-wave feminism influence the communication of individual women and men, and how national trends such as downsizing and outsourcing affect workers on the job and in their personal lives.

As this brief historical overview shows, the field of communication has always been sensitive to the ever-changing needs of individuals and society. Perhaps this is why the field has expanded, even during periods of downsizing in many colleges and universities. Just as the citizens of Athens found that Aristotle's teachings helped them prepare for effective participation in their society, today's students realize that the modern field of communication offers them remarkably effective skills for participating in the world in which they live.

CONDUCTING RESEARCH IN COMMUNICATION

Like other scholarly disciplines, communication is based on knowledge gained from rigorous research. Much of the research described in this book explores how and why communication works as it does and why it sometimes doesn't work as we intend. So that you can understand how scholars acquire knowledge, we'll discuss three primary approaches to communication research. These three approaches are not incompatible. Many scholars rely on multiple approaches to study how communication works.

Quantitative Research

Scholars use **quantitative research methods** to gather information in numerical form. There are many specific methods of quantitative research; we'll discuss three that are widely used by communication researchers. Descriptive statistics describe human behavior in terms of quantity, frequency, or amount. For example, in the 1998 survey mentioned earlier in this chapter, we saw that 53% of Americans think ineffective communication is the principal cause of divorce. Kelly McCollum reports that in 1999, 93% of college students use the net for educational purposes.

A second method of quantitative research is surveys, which are instruments, questionnaires, or interviews that measure how people feel, think, act, and so forth. Surveys are very valuable when a researcher wants to discover general trends for a particular group of people, which could be members of one institution or Americans as a whole, for example. Surveys are often used in organizations to gain information about employee morale, response to company policies, and relationships between job satisfaction and factors such as leadership style, participation on teams, and quality of communication among coworkers. Once survey data are gathered, they may be analyzed using a variety of statistical methods that help researchers detect patterns in communication and assess their strength and importance.

A third method of quantitative research is experiments, which are studies in which researchers control the context and what happens in it to measure how one variable that may be manipulated (called independent variable) affects other variables (called dependent variables). Linda Acitelli (1988) conducted an experiment to learn whether women and men differ in their desire to engage in relationship talk. She had half of the participants in her study read scenarios in which a husband and wife discussed a conflict or problem in their relationship. The other half of the respondents read scenarios in which a husband and wife engaged in general talk about their relationship when there was no specific problem or issue. Acitelli found that both women and men thought the relationship talk was satisfying when there was a problem, but when there was no specific tension to be resolved, women thought relationship talk was significantly more satisfying than men did.

Qualitative Research

A second approach used by many scholars of communication is **qualitative research methods,** which provide nonnumerical knowledge about the character of communication. Qualitative methods are especially valuable when researchers want to study aspects of communication that cannot easily be quantified, such as meanings of experience, the function of rituals in organizational life, and how we feel about and engage in online communication. Three methods of qualitative research are most prominent in the communication discipline.

Textual analysis is an interpretation of symbolic activities. Text is not restricted to formal written texts or orally presented speeches. Scholars who engage in textual analysis might interpret the meaning of the AIDS quilt, community-building rituals among refugees, self-disclosures in chat rooms on the Web, and stories told in families.

Another qualitative method is ethnography, in which researchers try to discover what symbolic activities mean by immersing themselves in those activities and their contexts and gaining insight into the perspectives of those who are native to the context. At the center of ethnographic research is a commitment to understanding what communication means from the perspective of those involved in it, rather than that of an outside, objective researcher. Dwight Conquergood, a distinguished ethnographic scholar, has provided insight into the meaning of communicative practices among Laotian refugees (1986) and Chicago street gangs (Conquergood, Friesema, Hunter, & Mansbridge, 1990). To achieve this, Conquergood lived in those communities and participated in their daily activities so that he could learn how his subjects perceive what they are doing and what it means.

A third important method of qualitative scholarship is historical research, which provides knowledge about significant past events, people, and activities. Historical research is favored by many rhetorical theorists and critics, perhaps because it allows them to uncover important insight into key thinkers who shaped the field, such as Socrates, Plato, and St. Augustine (Conley, 1990), and pivotal rhetorical works, such as Elizabeth Cady Stanton's speech "The Declaration of Sentiments," which was the keynote address at the first women's rights convention in 1848 (Campbell, 1989), and Martin Luther King Jr.'s "I Have a Dream" speech in 1963 (Cox, 1989). The data for historical scholarship include original documents, such as drafts of speeches and notes for revision, records that describe events and public reaction to them, and biographical studies of key figures.

Critical Research

The third main approach to communication scholarship is **critical research methods,** in which scholars identify and challenge communication practices that oppress, marginalize, or otherwise harm individuals and social groups. Critical scholars think that the traditional research goals of understanding, explanation, and prediction are insufficient if academics want the knowledge they generate to have practical consequences. Thus, critical scholars are passionately committed to using their research to advance social awareness and progress. For this group, specific communication practices are seen as means of reflecting, upholding, and sometimes challenging cultural ideology. For example, the practice in many organizations of punching a time clock upholds the notion that workers are responsible to those who have the means to own and run businesses. The meaning of the practice of punching a time clock is tied to an overall ideology that stipulates who does and does not have power in society.

Some critical scholars (Grossberg, 1997) contribute through original theorizing that helps us understand how certain groups and practices become dominant and how dominant ideologies are sometimes challenged and changed in a society. Other critical scholars engage in empirical work to reveal how particular practices work and whom they benefit and harm. For example, Lana Rakow's (1992) critical analysis of television advertisements shows that they harm many women by advancing unrealistic and unachievable ideals of beauty. Mary Strine (1992) and Brian Taylor and Charles Conrad (1992) engaged in critical analysis to illuminate the ways in which practices in some organizations condone sexual harassment and define it as "how things work."

Each approach to research is valuable, and each has contributed to the overall knowledge that makes up communication as a scholarly discipline. In this book you'll encounter research reflecting all three of the primary approaches we've discussed. Some research is highlighted in FYI boxes so that you can appreciate how scholars generate knowledge about human communication.

DEFINING COMMUNICATION

So far we've been using the word *communication* as if we agreed on what it means. Yet the word has many definitions. In 1970, communication theorist Frank Dance counted more than 100 distinct definitions of communication proposed by experts in the field. In the years since that survey, even more definitions have surfaced. By drawing from these multiple definitions, we can define **communication** as a systemic process in which people interact with and through symbols to create and interpret meanings.

Features of Communication

The definition of communication has three important facets. We'll discuss each of them.

Process Communication is a **process,** which means that it is ongoing and always in motion. It's hard to tell when communication starts and stops because what happened before we talk with someone may influence our interaction, and what occurs in a particular encounter may affect the future. That communication is a process means it is always in motion, moving forward and changing continuously. We cannot freeze communication at any one moment.

Systemic Communication takes place within **systems.** A system consists of interrelated parts that affect one another. In family communication, for instance, each family member is part of the system. In addition, the physical environment and the time of day are elements of the system that affect interaction. People interact differently in a living room than they do on a beach, and we may be more alert at certain times of day than others. The history of a system also affects communication. If a family has a history of listening sensitively and working out problems constructively, when someone says, "There's something we need to talk about," the others are unlikely to become defensive. On the other hand, if the family has a record of nasty conflicts and bickering, the same comment might arouse strong defensiveness. A lingering kiss might be an appropriate way to show affection in a private setting, but the same action would raise eyebrows in an office.

Communication is also affected by the larger systems within which it takes place. For example, different cultures have distinct understandings of appropriate verbal and nonverbal behaviors. Many Asian cultures place a high value on saving face, so Asians try not to cause personal embarrassment to others by disagreeing overtly. It would be inappropriate to perceive people from Asian cultures as passive simply because they don't assert themselves in the same ways that many Westerners do. Arab cultures consider it normal to be nearer to one another when talking than most Westerners find comfortable. And in Bulgaria, head nods mean no rather than yes (Munter, 1993). Thus, to interpret communication we have to consider the systems in which it takes place. In Chapter 7 we'll discuss different communication practices in diverse cultural contexts.

Symbolic Communication is symbolic. It relies on **symbols,** which are abstract, arbitrary, and ambiguous representations of other things. We might symbolize love by giving a ring, saying "I love you," or closely embracing the other person. A promotion might be symbolized by a new title and a larger office. Later in this chapter and also in Chapter 4 we'll have more to say about symbols. For now, just remember that human communication involves interaction with and through symbols.

Meanings Finally, our definition focuses on **meanings,** which are at the heart of communication. Reflecting on the evolution of the communication discipline, distinguished scholar Bruce Gronbeck (1999) notes that the field has moved increasingly toward a meaning-centered view of human communication. Meanings are the significance we bestow on phenomena, or what they signify to us. We do not find meanings in experience itself. Instead, we use symbols to create meanings. We ask others to be sounding boards so we can clarify our thinking, figure out what things mean, enlarge our perspectives, check our perceptions, and label feelings to give them reality. In all these ways we actively construct meaning by interacting with symbols.

Communication has two levels of meaning (Watzlawick, Beavin, & Jackson, 1967). The **content level of meaning** is the literal message. If someone says, "You're crazy," the content level of meaning is that you are insane. The **relationship level of meaning** expresses the relationship between communicators. In our example, if a friend says, "You're crazy" and smiles, you would probably conclude that the person likes you and is kidding around. On the other hand, if the person who says you're crazy is a supervisor who is responding to your request for a raise, you might interpret the relationship level of meaning as a signal that your supervisor is not impressed with your work. And if the person saying you're crazy is your therapist, you might interpret yet another meaning.

Models of Communication

Theorists create models to describe how things work. Over the years scholars in communication have developed a number of models that reflect increasingly sophisticated understandings of the communication process.

Linear Models Harold Laswell (1948) advanced an early model that described communication as a linear, or one-way, process in which one person acts on another person. His was a verbal model consisting of five questions that described early views of how communication works:

Who?
Says what?
In what channel?
To whom?
With what effect?

Claude Shannon and Warren Weaver (1949) refined Laswell's model by adding the feature of **noise.** Noise is anything that interferes with the intended meaning of communication. Noises may distort understanding. Figure 1.1 shows Shannon

Figure 1.1 Linear Model of Communication

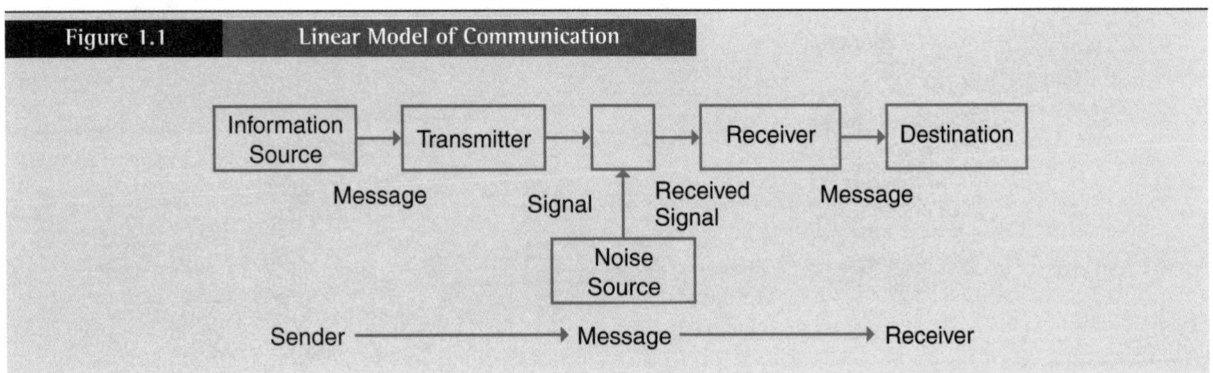

Source: Adapted from Shannon & Weaver, 1949.

and Weaver's model. Although early models, such as those by Laswell and Shannon and Weaver, were useful starting points, they are too simplistic to capture the complexity of human communication.

Interactive Models The major shortcoming of linear models was that they portrayed communication as flowing in only one direction, from a sender to a receiver. Commenting on this limitation, Bruce Gronbeck (1999) noted that linear views are inaccurate because communication processes "are bi-directional, not unidirectional; are dialogic, not monologic; and hence are processes best described not by bullets or arrows hitting their targets, but rather by congregations of voices together building the frameworks of shared meanings" (p. 13). The linear model suggests that a person is only a sender or a receiver. Furthermore, it suggests that listeners passively absorb senders' messages and do not respond. Clearly, this isn't how communication occurs. In the example that opened this chapter, Mike listened to Pat while he was talking with her. She was sending him nonverbal messages while she listened to him. Similarly, as you talk to friends, you notice whether they seem interested. If they nod, you're likely to continue talking; if they yawn, you might stop. In communication, people affect each other.

When communication theorists realized that listeners respond to senders, they added a new feature to models. **Feedback** is a response to a message. Feedback may be verbal or nonverbal, and it may be intentional or unintentional. Wilbur Schramm (1955) depicted feedback as a second kind of message. In addition, Schramm pointed out that communicators create and interpret messages within personal fields of experience. The more communicators' fields of experience overlap, the better they can understand each other. Remember how Mike's initial resistance to teamwork gave him some common ground with Pat?

Lori Ann

I was born in Alabama, and all my life I've spoken to people whether I know them or not. I say hello or something to a person I pass on the street just to be friendly. When I went to a junior college in Pennsylvania, I got in trouble for being so friendly. When I spoke to guys I didn't know, they thought I was coming on to them or something. And other women would just look at me like I was odd. I'd never realized that friendliness could be misinterpreted.

Adding fields of experience to models clarifies why misunderstandings sometimes occur. You jokingly put a friend down, and he takes it seriously and is hurt. You offer to help someone, and she feels patronized. Adding fields of experience and feedback allowed Schramm and other communication scholars to develop models that portray communication as an interactive process in which both senders and receivers participate actively (Figure 1.2).

Figure 1.2 Interactive Model of Communication

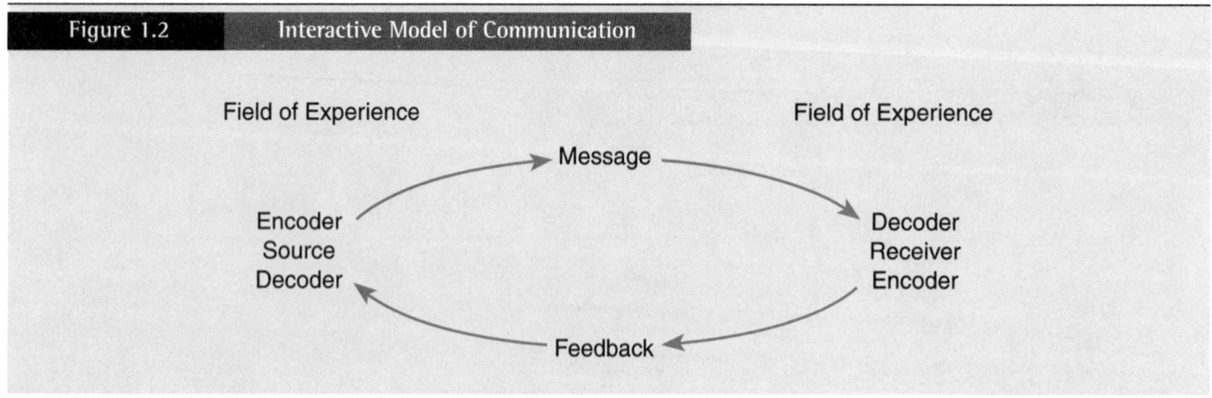

Source: Adapted from Schramm, 1955.

Transactional Models Although an interactive model was an improvement over the linear one, it still didn't capture the dynamism of human communication. The interactive model portrays communication as a sequential linear process in which one person communicates to another, who then sends feedback to the first person. Yet people may communicate simultaneously instead of taking turns. Also, the interactive model designates one person as a sender and another person as a receiver. In reality, communicators both send and receive messages. While handing out a press release, a public relations representative watches reporters to see whether they express interest; both the speaker and the reporters are "listening" and both are "speaking."

A final shortcoming of the interactional model is that it doesn't portray communication as changing over time as a result of what happens between people. For example, Mike and Coreen communicated in more reserved ways on their first date than they do after months of seeing each other. What they talk about and how they interact have changed over time. To be accurate, a model should include the feature of time and should depict communication as varying rather than as constant. Figure 1.3 is a transactional model that highlights the features we have discussed.

Consistent with what we've covered in this chapter, our model includes noise that can distort communication. Noise includes sounds such as a lawn mower or background chatter, as well as interferences inside communicators, such as mental biases and preoccupation, that hinder effective listening. In addition, our model emphasizes that communication is a process that is continuously changing. How people communicate varies over time and in response to their history of relating. The support Mike gave to Pat becomes part of all their interactions in the future.

The outer lines on our model emphasize that communication occurs within systems that affect what and how people communicate and what meanings they create. Those systems, or contexts, include shared systems of the communicators (campus, town, and culture) and the personal systems of each communicator (family, religious associations, friends). Also note that our model, unlike previous ones, portrays each person's field of experience and his or her shared fields of experience as changing over time. As we encounter new people and grow personally, we alter how we interact with others.

Finally, our model doesn't label one person a sender and the other a receiver. Instead, both are defined as communicators who participate equally, and often simultaneously, in the communication process. This means that at a given moment in communication, you may be sending a message (speaking or wrinkling your brow), listening to a

Figure 1.3 Transactional Model of Communication

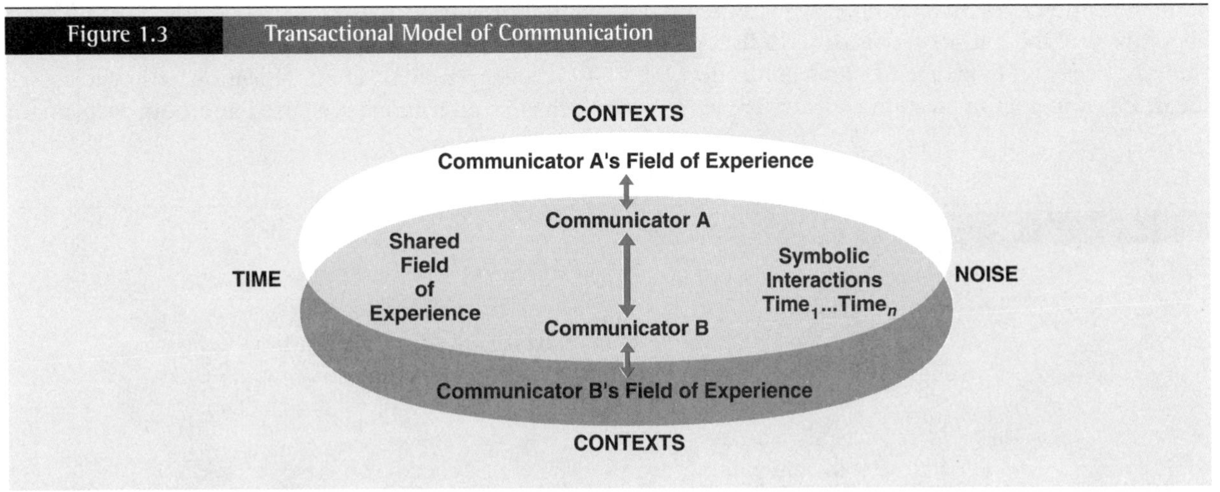

Source: Adapted from Wood, 1997, p. 21.

message, or doing both at the same time (interpreting what someone says while nodding to show you are interested). Now that we understand what communication is, let's explore the many facets that make up this field.

BREADTH OF THE COMMUNICATION FIELD

The study and teaching of communication began more than 2,000 years ago. Originally, the field focused almost exclusively on public communication. Aristotle, the famous Greek philosopher mentioned earlier in this chapter, believed that effective public speaking was essential to citizens' participation in civic affairs. He taught his students how to develop and present persuasive speeches to influence public life. Although public speaking remains a vital skill, it is no longer the only focus of the communication field. The modern discipline can be classified into ten areas.

Intrapersonal Communication

Intrapersonal communication is communication with ourselves, or self-talk. You might be wondering whether *intrapersonal communication* is another term for *thinking*. In one sense, yes. Intrapersonal communication does involve thinking because it is a cognitive process that occurs inside us. Yet, because thinking relies on language to name and reflect on ideas, it is also communication (Vocate, 1994).

Chiquella

I figure out a lot of things by thinking them through in my head. It's like having a trial run without risk. Usually, after I think through different ideas or ways of approaching someone, I can see which one would be best.

One school of counseling focuses on enhancing self-esteem by changing how we talk to ourselves (Ellis & Harper, 1977; Rusk & Rusk, 1988; Seligman, 1990). For instance, you might say to yourself, "I blew that test, so I'm really stupid. I'll never graduate and, if I do, nobody will hire me." This kind of talk lowers self-esteem by convincing you that a single event (blowing one test) proves you are totally worthless. Therapists who realize that what we say to ourselves affects our feelings urge us to challenge negative self-talk by saying, "Hey, wait a minute. One test is hardly a measure of my intelligence. I did well on the other test in this course, and I have a decent overall college record. I shouldn't be so hard on myself." What we say to ourselves can enhance or diminish self-esteem.

We engage in self-talk to plan our lives, rehearse different ways of acting, and prompt ourselves to do or not do particular things. Intrapersonal communication is how we remind ourselves to eat in healthy ways ("No saturated fats"), show respect to others ("I need to listen to Grandmother's story"), and check impulses that might be destructive ("I'll wait until I'm calmer to say anything").

Intrapersonal communication also helps us rehearse alternative scenarios and how each might

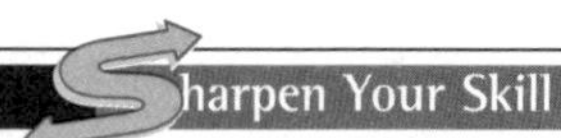

ANALYZING YOUR SELF-TALK

Pay attention to the way you talk to yourself for the next day. When something goes wrong, what do you say to yourself? Do you put yourself down with negative messages? Do you generalize beyond the specific event to describe yourself as a loser or as inadequate?

The first step in changing negative self-talk is to become aware of it. We'll have more to say about how to change negative self-talk in Chapter 8.

turn out. To control a disruptive group member named Nelson, Cass might consider telling him to shut up, suggesting that the group adopt a rule that everyone should participate equally, and taking Nelson out for coffee and privately asking him to be less domineering. She'll think through the three options, weigh the likely consequences of each, and then choose one to put into practice. We engage in internal dialogues continuously as we reflect on experiences, sort through ideas, and test alternative ways of acting.

Figure 1.4 The Communication Continuum

Interpersonal Communication

A second major emphasis in the field of communication is **interpersonal communication,** which deals with communication between people. Interpersonal communication is not a single thing but rather a continuum that ranges from quite impersonal to highly interpersonal (see Figure 1.4; Wood, 1999, 2000b). The more we interact with a person as a distinct individual, the more interpersonal the communication is. Using this criterion, a deep conversation with a friend is more interpersonal than a casual exchange with a clerk.

Scholars of interpersonal communication study how communication creates and sustains relationships and how partners communicate to deal with the normal and extraordinary challenges of maintaining intimacy over time (Canary & Stafford, 1994; Duck & Wood, 1995; Spencer, 1994). Research shows that intimates who listen sensitively and talk openly have the greatest chance of sustaining a close relationship over time.

Some interpersonal communication researchers study how gender, ethnicity, and sexual preference influence communication. In later chapters we'll discuss research on the different communication goals and styles that different social groups tend to use.

Group and Team Communication

A third branch of the field is small group communication, including communication in therapy groups, social groups, decision-making committees, and work teams. Small group research focuses on leadership, member roles, group features, agendas for achieving group goals, and managing conflict. In Chapter 10 we'll consider how we adapt basic communication processes to be effective in groups and teams.

Dennis Gouran (1982), a scholar of group communication, emphasizes the importance of critical thought in rational group decision making. He has identified forms of communication that advance and interfere with rational decision making, and he has developed strategies that help group members avoid impediments to effective group work. Other scholars of small group communication have concentrated on communication processes that transform a collection of individuals into a cohesive group. In this area, the work of Ernest Bormann and his associates is particularly important (Bormann, 1975; Bormann, Putnam, & Pratt, 1978). Bormann claims that group cohesion and identity often crystallize through **fantasy themes,** which are symbolic chains of ideas that spin out in a group and capture its social and task themes. The talk of politicians often suggests that they view their parties as warring opponents. When politicians speak of "attacking the other side's plan," "defending" their agenda, and "refusing to give ground," they create a fantasy chain that defines the parties as warring factions. Fantasy themes frame how group members think and talk about what they are doing.

Public Communication

Public speaking remains an important branch of the communication field. Even though many people will not pursue careers that call for extensive formal speaking, most of us will have opportunities to speak to others. In addition, we all will be in situations where speaking up is a responsibility. My editor makes presentations to her sales representatives to explain what her books are about and how to spotlight important features to professors who may wish to use them in their courses. I recently coached my doctor, who was asked to address her colleagues on a development in treatment of renal disease. My plumber presents workshops to his staff to inform them of new developments in plumbing products and to teach them how to communicate effectively with customers. My sister relies on public speaking skills to try cases in court and to raise money to support a center for abused children. A friend of mine recently took a leading role in organizing a union in her company. My editor, doctor, plumber, sister, and friend don't consider themselves public speakers, but public speaking is a part of their lives, and doing it well is important to their success.

Rhetorical critics study important communication events such as Martin Luther King Jr.'s "I Have a Dream" speech and debates on public policies. Critics often take a role in civic life by evaluating how well public figures support their positions and respond to challenges from opponents. Scholars of public communication are also interested in discovering and teaching principles of effective public speaking. As we will see in Chapter 13, we know a great deal about what makes speakers seem credible to listeners and how credibility affects persuasion. Research has also enlightened us about the kinds of argument, methods of organizing ideas, and forms of proof that listeners find ethical and effective. If Mike studied this body of research, he could glean useful guidelines for his speech.

Organizational Communication

Communication in organizations is another growing area of interest. Work by communication scholars has identified communication skills that enhance professional success, and they have traced the effects of various kinds of communication on morale, productivity, and commitment to organizations. Scholars of organizational communication study interviewing, listening, leadership, new technologies of communication, and decision making.

In addition, scholars have begun to focus substantial attention on organizational culture and personal relationships in professional settings. **Organizational culture** is made up of understandings about identity and codes of thought and action that members of an organization share. Some organizations think of themselves as families. From this understanding emerge rules for how employees should interact and how fully they should commit to work. Studies of organizational culture also shed light on the continuing problem of sexual harassment. Some institutions have developed cultures that treat sexual harassment as the normal way "we do things around here" (Strine, 1992). A number of communication scholars have analyzed how some institutions trivialize complaints about sexual harassment and sustain an organizational culture that implies that sexual harassment is acceptable (Bingham, 1994; Clair, 1993; Conrad, 1995; Taylor & Conrad, 1992).

Another area of increasing interest is personal relationships among co-workers. As we expand the hours we spend on the job, it is natural for the number of personal relationships among co-workers to increase. Furthermore, because the majority of women work full or part time today, opportunities for romantic and sexual relationships in the workplace have increased. Obviously, this adds both interest and complications to life in organizations. Co-workers may also be close friends, a relationship that is complicated if one person has more status than the other. Communication scholar Ted Zorn (1995) analyzed "bosses and buddies," relationships in which one friend is the boss of the other. Zorn discovered a number of ways people cope with the often contradictory rules for communication between friends and between superiors and subordinates. He identified potential values and hazards of friendships on the job.

Melbourne

It was a real hassle when my supervisor and I started going out. Before, he gave me orders like he did all the other servers, and none of us thought anything about it. But after we started dating, he would sort of ask me, instead of tell me, what to do, like saying, "Mel, would you help out in section seven?" Another thing was that if he gave me a good station where tips run high, the other servers would give me trouble

A CAN-DO CULTURE

In July 1994 a Colorado wildfire became a raging inferno in which fourteen firefighters lost their lives. An investigation revealed that a primary contributor to the loss of lives was a "can-do" culture among firefighters. Trained to believe that they can do what others cannot and that they can perform heroic feats, the firefighters didn't observe critical safety regulations. Ironically, the can-do culture essential for success in a dangerous job led to disregard for important cautions and the loss of fourteen lives.

because they thought he was favoring me because we go out. And when he gave me a bad station, I'd feel he was being nasty for personal reasons. It was a mess being his employee and his girlfriend at the same time.

Personal relations on the job also require that women and men learn to understand each other's language. In a number of ways, women and men communicate differently, and they often misunderstand one another (Wood, 1998, 2001c). For example, women tend to make more "listening noises" such as "um," "uh-huh," and "go on" than men. If men don't make listening noises when listening to women colleagues, the women may mistakenly think the men aren't listening. Conversely, men are likely to misinterpret the listening noises women make as signaling agreement rather than simply interest. Such misunderstandings can strain professional relations. Some scholars of organizational communication study and conduct workshops on effective communication between the sexes (Murphy & Zorn, 1996).

Interviewing Communication

Interviews serve many functions, including hiring, reprimand, job review, research, and problem solving. Although each type of interview has distinct goals, it has features in common with the other types. For example, most interviews rely heavily on a question-and-answer format. In Chapter 12 we will consider how basic communication processes pertain to interviewing, and we'll focus extensively on the hiring interview so that you can understand how it works and prepare to communicate effectively when you are searching for a job.

Mass Communication

One of the most exciting areas of the modern field of communication is mass communication. From a substantial body of research, we have learned a great deal about how media represent and influence cultural values. For instance, using young models in ads and hiring young and beautiful women as television news reporters and anchors perpetuates the cultural feminine ideal, which centers on youth and beauty. Films that portray men as daring, brave, and violent perpetuate strength and boldness as masculine ideals.

Media sometimes reinforce cultural stereotypes about race and ethnicity. For example, television shows and movies most often cast African Americans in supporting roles, not principal roles. In addition, entertainment programming often portrays black men as lazy and unlawful or casts them as athletes or entertainers (Evans, 1993; "Sights, Sounds," 1992). Robert Entman (1994), a communication professor at Northwestern University, points out that major network news programs are likely to show black defendants in mug shots without names but offer multiple pictures and names of white defendants. This difference may contribute to perceptions of African Americans as an undifferentiated group. Thus, we should ask ethical questions about the ways that media portray events and social groups.

Although the Asian American population has tripled since 1970 and now numbers eight million, Asian Americans seldom appear on prime-time television shows (Wong, 1994). Hispanic Americans and Asian Americans are often cast in the roles of villains or criminals (Lichter. Lichter, Rothman, & Amundson, 1987). Communication scholars heighten awareness of how media shape—and sometimes distort—our perceptions of ourselves and society.

Franklin

I hate the way television shows African Americans. Most of the time they are criminals or welfare cases or drunks or Uncle Toms. When I watch TV, I understand why so many people think blacks are dumb, uneducated, and criminal. We're not, but you'd never know it from watching television.

Technologies of Communication

We are in the midst of a technological revolution that provides us with the means to communicate in more ways at faster speeds with greater numbers of people throughout the world than has ever before been possible. How do new technologies and the accompanying acceleration of the pace of interaction influence how we think, work, and form relationships? Some scholars caution that new technologies may undermine human community (Hyde, 1995), whereas others celebrate the social networks and productivity technology allows (Lea & Spears, 1995). Still others claim that new communication technologies will fundamentally transform how we think and process information (Chesebro, 1995).

Winston

I live through my modem. That's how I stay in touch with friends at other schools, and I even "talk" daily with my mom, who has an email system in her office. I think if I couldn't communicate with these people, the relationships would deteriorate or completely die. I think that's what happened to a lot of relationships before we had email.

Clearly, the verdict on the effects of new technologies will not be in for some time. Meanwhile all of us struggle to keep up with our increasingly technological world. When I was an undergraduate student, I typed my papers on a typewriter. Today any student without access to a computer is at an academic disadvantage. Ten years ago we relied on letters and phone calls to communicate across distance. Today overnight mailing services, faxes, and email make it possible for us to communicate almost immediately with people on the other side of the world. During college and for the first decade of my career,

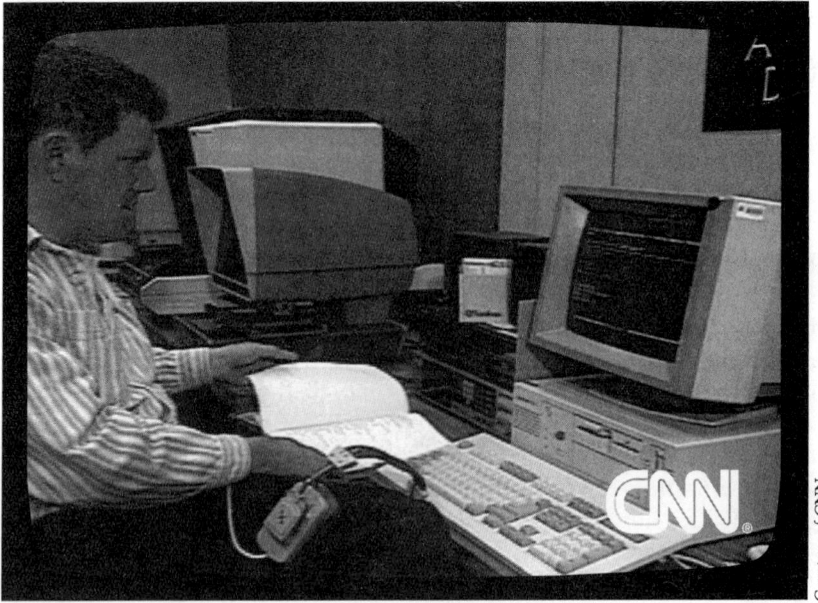

■ *In our era, technologies of communication are standard in both work and personal contexts.*

Courtesy of CNN

Sharpen Your Skill

YOUR MEDIATED WORLD

How do new technologies of communication affect your interactions? If you use the Internet, how are your electronic exchanges different from face-to-face interactions? Have you made any acquaintances or friends through electronic communication? Did those relationships develop differently from ones formed through personal contact? Do you feel differently about people whom you haven't ever seen and those whom you see face to face?

I had to go to libraries to find books and articles for my research. Today students conduct much of their research on the World Wide Web or specialized information services on the Internet. Communication scholars will continue to study whether emerging technologies merely alter how we communicate or actually change the kinds of relationships we build.

Intercultural Communication

Although intercultural communication is not a new area of study, its importance has grown in recent years. The United States has always been made up of many peoples, and demographic shifts in the last decade have increased the pluralism of this country. Increasing numbers of Asians, Latinos and Latinas, Eastern Europeans, and people with other ethnic backgrounds immigrate to the United States and make their homes here. They bring with them cultural values and styles of communicating that differ from those of citizens whose ancestors were born in the United States.

Meikko

What I find most odd about Americans is their focus on themselves. Here everyone wants to be an individual who is so strong and stands out from everyone else. In Japan it is not like that. We see ourselves as parts of families and communities, not as individuals. Here I and my are the most common words, but they are not often said in Japan.

Studying intercultural communication increases our insight into different cultures' communication styles and meanings. For example, a Taiwanese woman in one of my graduate classes seldom spoke up and wouldn't enter the heated debates that are typical of graduate classes. One day after class I encouraged Mei-Ling to argue for her ideas when others challenged them. She replied that doing so would be impolite. Her culture considers it disrespectful to contradict others. In the context of her culture, Mei-Ling's deference did not mean that she lacked confidence.

A particularly important recent trend in the area of intercultural communication is research on different cultures within a single society. Cultural differences are obvious in communication between a

THE FAMILY CIRCUS. By Bil Keane
11-30
©1998 Bil Keane, Inc.
Dist. by Cowles Synd., Inc.
"...lead us not into temptation, but deliver us from e-mail..."

LEARNING ABOUT INTERCULTURAL COMMUNICATION

The Web provides abundant resources for learning about communication between people from different cultures. One of the best sites offers many links to multicultural and intercultural sites of interest. Check out the Society for Cross Cultural Research's Web site at http://www.fit.edu/CampusLife/clubs-org/sscr/resources.html.

Nepali and a Canadian. Less obvious are cultural differences in communication between people who speak the same language. Within the United States are distinct cultures based on race, gender, sexual preference, and other factors. Larry Samovar and Richard Porter (1994) have identified distinctive styles of communication used by women, men, African Americans, whites, Native Americans, gay men and lesbians, people with disabilities, and other groups in our country. African Americans belong to a communication culture that encourages dramatic talk, verbal duels, and other communication routines that have no equivalents in European American speech communities (Houston, 1994; Houston & Wood, 1996). Recognizing and respecting different communication cultures increases personal effectiveness in a pluralistic society.

Ethics and Communication

A final area of study and teaching in the field focuses on the relationship between ethics and communication. Because all forms of communication involve ethical issues, this area of interest is both a focus of scholarship in its own right and an integral part of all other areas in the discipline. For instance, ethical dimensions of intrapersonal communication include the influence of stereotypes on how we judge others.

In the realm of interpersonal communication, honesty, compassion, and fairness in relationships are ethical concerns. Conformity pressures that sometimes operate in groups are an ethical issue. The area of organizational communication includes ethical questions about the right of institutions to regulate employees' personal lives. Do companies have a right to refuse insurance to employees who smoke, sky dive, or race cars on their own time? Ethical issues also surface in public communication. For example, does speaking for oppressed groups misrepresent their experiences or even reinforce oppression by keeping others silent (Alcoff, 1991)?

From interpersonal to public situations, people confront such ethical issues as concealing evidence, misusing statistics, or misrepresenting information. Attitudes and actions that encourage or hinder freedom of speech are relevant to a range of communication contexts. Are all members of organizations equally empowered to speak? Is it right for audiences to shout down a speaker with unpopular views? How does the balance of power between partners affect each person's freedom to express himself or herself in a relationship? Because ethical issues infuse all forms of communication, I will weave ethical themes into each chapter of this book.

UNIFYING THEMES AND PROCESSES IN THE COMMUNICATION FIELD

After reading about the many different areas in communication, you might think that the field is a collection of unrelated interests. That isn't accurate. Although there are distinct elements in the communication mosaic, there are also common themes that unify the diverse areas that make up the discipline.

Unifying Themes

Enduring concerns with symbolic activities, meaning, and ethics unify the diverse areas in communication.

Symbolic Activities Symbols are the basis of language, thinking, and nonverbal communication. Symbols are arbitrary, ambiguous, and abstract representations of other phenomena. For instance, a wedding band is a symbol of marriage in Western culture, *Julia* is a symbol for me (my name), and a smile is a symbol of friendliness. Symbols allow us to reflect on our experiences and ourselves. Symbols also allow us to share experiences with others, even if they have not had those experiences themselves. We will discuss symbols in greater depth in Chapters 4 and 5, which deal with verbal and nonverbal communication, respectively.

Meaning Closely related to interest in symbols is the communication field's concern with meaning. The human world is a world of meaning. We don't simply exist, eat, drink, sleep, and behave. Instead, we imbue every aspect of our lives with significance, or meaning. When I feed my dog, Madhi, she eats her food and then returns to her canine adventures. However, we humans layer food and eating with meanings beyond merely satisfying hunger. Food often symbolizes special events or commitments. For example, kosher products reflect commitment to Jewish heritage, turkey is commonly associated with commemorating the first Thanksgiving in the United States (although vegetarians symbolize their commitment by *not* eating turkey). Eggnog is a Christmas tradition, and dreidels and potato pancakes are Hanukkah staples. Birthday cakes celebrate an individual, and we may fix special meals to express love to others.

Some families consider meals an occasion to come together and share lives, whereas in other families meals are battlefields where family tensions are played out. A meal can symbolize status (power lunches), romance (candles, wine), a personal struggle to stick to a diet, or an excuse to spend two hours talking with a friend. Humans imbue eating and other activities with meaning beyond their functional qualities. Our experiences gain significance as a result of the values and meanings we attach to them.

Because we are symbol users, we actively interpret events, situations, experiences, and relationships. We use symbols to name, evaluate, reflect, and share experiences, ideas, and feelings. Through the process of communicating with others we define our relationships. Do we have a friendship or something else? How serious are we? Do we feel the same way about each other? Is this conflict irresolvable or can we work it out and stay together?

■ *What do you infer about this person based on the context and what she is doing?*

Benita

It's funny how important a word can be. Nick and I had been going out for a long time and we really liked each other, but I didn't know if this was going to be long term. Then we said we loved each other, and that changed how we saw each other and the relationship. Just using the word love transformed who we are.

To study communication, then, is to study how we use symbols to create meaning in our lives. As we interact with others, we build the meaning of friendship, team spirit, and organizational culture (Andersen, 1993; Wood, 1992a, 2000b). Leslie Baxter says that "relationships can be regarded as webs of significance" spun as partners communicate (1987, p. 262). By extension, all human activities are webs of significance spun with symbols and meaning.

Ethics A third theme that unifies the field of communication is concern with ethical dimensions of human interaction. **Ethics** is a branch of philosophy that focuses on moral principles and codes of conduct. What is right? What is wrong? What makes something right or wrong? Communication inevitably involves ethical matters because people affect each other when they interact. Thus, it's important to think seriously about what sort of moral guidelines we should follow in our communication and in our judgments of others' communication.

One ethical principle that is applicable to a broad range of situations is allowing others to make informed and willing choices. Adopting this principle discourages us from deceiving others by distorting evidence, withholding information, or coercing consent. Another important principle for ethical communication is respecting differences among people. Embracing this guideline deters us from imposing our ways and our values on others, whose experiences and views of appropriate communication may differ from our own. In later chapters we'll elaborate on these and other ethical guidelines for communication.

Basic Processes of Communication

Communication scholars have identified six basic communication processes. They are basic because they are foundations for effective communication in all kinds of interactions. Yet the key processes take different forms in various situations. This chapter introduces the six communication processes, and remaining chapters in Part I of the book will elaborate on each one in turn.

Perceiving and Understanding Central to communication is perceiving ourselves, others, situations, and experiences. Our **perceptions** influence how we communicate and how we interpret others' communication in any setting. In Chapter 2 we will explore how perception influences and is influenced by communication.

Creating Interaction Climates A second basic communication process is creating climates for interaction. **Communication climate** is the psychological mood or emotional feeling surrounding communication. In intimate relationships, desirable climates might be warm and supportive, whereas in televised news broadcasts the ideal climate might be professional and energized.

Engaging in Verbal Communication A third basic communication process is using and interpreting verbal symbols. Symbols allow us to make sense of our world and to create our identities and our relationships with others.

Engaging in Nonverbal Communication Paralleling verbal communication is the intricate system of nonverbal behavior, which affects how others perceive us and our communication and how we interpret others.

Listening and Responding Communication is more than talking. Equally important to effective interaction is **listening,** which is an active process that involves more than hearing; it also means being mindful, selecting and organizing information, interpreting communication, responding, and remembering. We can improve our listening by recognizing and controlling factors that hinder good listening and by adapting how we listen to diverse situations and goals.

Adapting to Contexts Finally, adapting to contexts is a basic communication process. Communication has no single all-purpose formula. What is effective depends on the context in which interaction transpires and the people with whom we are interacting. For example, if you are explaining an idea to a close friend, you probably use informal language and small gestures, and you link your ideas to your friend's interests. If you want to explain the same idea to an audience of 500 people, you would probably use more formal language, larger gestures, and perhaps visual aids, and you would discuss a greater range of issues to interest the diverse listeners.

Enduring concerns with symbols, meaning, and ethics and consistent attention to six basic processes of communication unify the many different areas in the field.

CAREERS IN COMMUNICATION

Studying communication prepares you for a wide array of careers. As we've seen, communication skills are essential to success in most fields. In addition, people who major in communication pursue a number of careers.

Research

Communication research is a vital and growing field of work. Academics who combine teaching and research in faculty careers conduct many studies. In this book you'll encounter a good deal of academic research, and you'll be able to evaluate what we learn from doing it.

In addition to academic research, communication specialists do media research on everything from message production to marketing (Morreal & Vogl, 1998). Companies want to know how people respond to different kinds of advertisements, logos, and labels for products. Before naming a new cereal or beer, companies test market various names. Retailers' bottom line depends on understanding how customers will respond to different communication strategies. In addition, businesses research the audiences reached by different media such as newspapers, magazines, radio, and television. People who understand communication and who have research skills are qualified for careers in communication research.

Education

Teaching others about communication is another exciting career path for people with extensive backgrounds in the field. Clearly, I am biased toward this profession because I've had a 27-year love affair with teaching communication. I find nothing more exciting than opening students' eyes to the power of communication and working with them to improve their skills. Across the nation, communication teachers at all levels are finding growing opportunities. Secondary schools, junior colleges, colleges, universities, technical schools, and community colleges offer communication classes and often whole curricula.

The level at which people are qualified to teach depends on how extensively they have pursued the study of communication. Generally a bachelor's degree in communication education and a teaching certificate are required to teach in elementary and secondary schools. A master's degree in communication qualifies a person to teach at community colleges, technical schools, and some junior colleges and colleges. The doctoral degree in communication generally is required for a career in university education, although some universities offer short-term positions to people with master's degrees (Morreal & Vogl, 1998).

Although generalists are preferred for many teaching jobs, at the college level people can focus on areas of communication that particularly interest them. For instance, my research and teaching focus on interpersonal communication and gender and communication. My partner, who is also on the faculty in my department, specializes in environmental advocacy and social movements. Other college faculty concentrate in such areas as oral traditions, intercultural communication, family communication, organizational dynamics, and performance of literature.

Communication educators are not restricted to communication departments. In recent years more and more people with advanced degrees in communication have taken positions in medical and business schools. Good doctors have not only specialized medical knowledge but also good communication skills. They know how to listen sensitively to patients, how to explain complex problems and procedures, and how to provide comfort, reassurance, and motivation. Similarly, good businesspeople know not only their business but also how to explain it to others, how to present themselves and their company or product favorably, and so on. Because communication is essential for doctors and businesspeople, increasing numbers of medical and business schools are creating permanent positions for communication specialists.

Mass Communication

Careers in mass communication are attractive to many people with backgrounds in communication. Strong communication skills are necessary for many facets of mass communication, ranging from conducting interviews as background research to reporting stories on radio or television or in newspapers. Script writing and directing are additional careers in mass communication that require solid understandings of communication and skill in basic communication processes.

Training and Consulting

Consulting is another field that welcomes people with backgrounds in communication. Businesses want to train employees in effective group communication skills, interview techniques, and interpersonal interaction. Some large corporations, such as IBM, have entire departments devoted to training and development. People with communication backgrounds often join these departments and work with the corporation to design and teach courses or workshops that enhance employees' communication skills.

In addition, communication specialists may join or form consulting firms that provide particular kinds of communication training to government and businesses. One of my colleagues consults with corporations to teach men and women how to understand each other's language and work together. Another of my colleagues consults with organizations to help them develop work teams that interact effectively. I sometimes prepare workshops for educators who want to learn how to use communication to stimulate students' interest and learning. Other communication specialists work with politicians to improve their presentational style and sometimes to write their speeches. I consult with attorneys on cases involving charges of sexual harassment and sex discrimination. I help them understand how particular communication patterns create hostile, harassing environments, and I collaborate with them to develop trial strategy. In addition, I sometimes testify as an expert witness on whether sexual harassment or sex discrimination occurred. Other communication consultants work with attorneys on jury selections and advise lawyers about how dress and nonverbal behaviors might affect jurors' perceptions of clients.

Human Relations and Management

Because communication is the foundation of human relations, it's no surprise that many communication specialists build careers in human development or human relations departments of corporations. People with solid understandings of communication and good personal communication skills are effective in careers such as public relations, personnel, grievance management, negotiations, customer relations, and development and fund raising (Morreal & Vogl, 1998). In each of these areas, communication skills are the primary requirements.

Communication degrees may also open the door to careers in management. The most important qualifications for management are not technical skills but abilities to interact with others and to communicate effectively. Good managers are skilled in listening, expressing ideas, building consensus, creating supportive climates, and balancing task and interpersonal concerns in dealing with others. Developing skills such as these gives communication majors a firm foundation for effective management.

fyi

CAREERS IN COMMUNICATION

Learn more about the careers open to people who have strong training in communication. In 1998 the National Communication Association published the fifth edition of *Pathways to Careers in Communication.* In addition to discussing careers, this booklet provides very useful information on the National Communication Association and its many programs. To read this publication online, go to http://www.natcom.org/publications/pathways/5thEd.htm.

Summary

In this chapter we've taken a first look at human communication. We noted its importance in our lives, discussed how the field evolved historically and how scholars conduct research, and learned that a transactional model most accurately represents the dynamism of communication.

Like most fields of study, communication includes many areas, which have evolved over its long and distinguished intellectual history. We described ten areas that make up the modern field of communication, and we noted that these areas are unified by abiding interests in symbolic activities, meanings, and ethics and by a common interest in basic processes that form foundations of personal, interpersonal, professional, and mediated communication.

In the final section of this chapter we considered career opportunities open to people who specialize in communication. The field of communication offers an array of exciting career paths for people who enjoy interacting with others and who want the opportunity to be part of a dynamic discipline that evolves continuously to meet changing needs and issues in our world.

FOR FURTHER REFLECTION AND DISCUSSION

1. Using each of the models discussed in this chapter, describe interaction and transaction in your class. What does each model highlight and obscure? Which model better describes and explains communication in your class?
2. Interview a professional in your field of choice. Identify communication skills she or he thinks are most important for success. Which of those skills do you already have? Which skills do you need to develop or improve? How can you use this book and the course it accompanies to develop the skills you need to be effective in your career?
3. As a class, discuss particular topics and skills that interest you. How might you highlight these during the course of the term? You might agree to have project groups that study and make presentations to the class on communication topics that you consider especially important.
4. Visit the Web site for the National Communication Organization at http://www.natcom.org. Access one or more pages on the site that are particularly relevant to your interests in communication.
5. Go to the placement office on your campus and examine descriptions for available positions. Record the number of job notices that call for communication skills.
6. This is a good time to start using your *InfoTrac College Edition* so that you will be comfortable relying on it as you read the chapters to come. Go to http://www.infotrac-college.com/wadsworth. Enter your password and spend 30 minutes perusing some of the resources available in this online library.

KEY TERMS

Quantitative research methods
Qualitative research methods
Critical research methods
Communication
Process
System
Symbol
Meaning
Content level of meaning
Relationship level of meaning
Noise
Feedback
Intrapersonal communication
Interpersonal communication
Fantasy theme
Organizational culture
Ethics
Perceptions
Communication climate
Listening

Perceiving and Understanding

LEARNING OBJECTIVES

To understand

1. Why perceptions differ among people
2. How social roles affect perception
3. What the self-serving bias is
4. How perceptions shape our views of others
5. Whether it is useful to try to read others' minds
6. How we can sharpen our perceptions

Last year my sister, Carolyn, visited me with her 9-year-old daughter Michelle, 6-year-old son, Daniel, and 13-month-old son, Harrison. Robbie and I had cleaned our home and put a vase of fresh flowers in their room. As Carolyn walked through the house, she picked up a glass paperweight, two small sculptures, a set of darts Robbie and I throw for recreation, and a souvenir saber from Nepal. "Got to kid-proof the house," Carolyn explained. She moved the flowers to the top of a tall bureau, saying, "Your rugs don't need all this water spilled on them." Carolyn perceived our home in terms of dangers to her children (the saber and darts) and objects that youngsters might accidentally damage (crystal, sculptures). Because we don't have young children, Robbie and I hadn't perceived these objects as potential hazards. Our perceptions reflected our individual interests and experiences. Perceptions—and differences between people's perceptions—are major influences on human communication.

This chapter focuses on a basic communication process: **perception,** which is critical to our efforts to create meaning. Perception is the process by which we notice and make sense of experience and stimuli around us. To explore the relationships between perception and communication, this chapter discusses three interrelated facets of perceiving and considers primary influences on how people perceive and why they sometimes differ in their perceptions. We'll conclude the chapter by identifying ways in which skillful perception can improve our effectiveness as communicators.

THE PERCEPTION PROCESS

Perception is an active process of selecting, organizing, and interpreting people, objects, events, situations, and activities. The first thing to notice is that perception is an active process. We are not passive receivers of what is "out there" in the external world. Instead, we select only certain things to notice, and then we organize and interpret what we have selectively noticed. What anything means to us depends on which aspects of it we attend to and how we organize and interpret what we notice. Perception and communication influence each other. Perception shapes how we understand others' communication and the choices we make in our own communication. For example, if you perceive someone as hostile, you are likely to communicate defensively or to minimize interaction. Communication also influences our perceptions of people and situations. The language and nonverbal behaviors other people use affect our perceptions of whether they are intelligent, friendly, and so forth.

Perception consists of three interrelated processes: selecting, organizing, and interpreting. These processes blend into one another. We organize perceptions even as we select what to perceive, and we interpret in an ongoing manner. Each process affects the other two. What we notice about people influences how we interpret them; our interpretation of a situation directs us to selectively notice certain, and not other, aspects of the setting.

Selection

Stop for a moment and notice what is going on around you right now. Is music playing in the background? Or do you perhaps hear several different kinds of music from different places? Is the room warm or cold, messy or clean, large or small, light or dark? Is laundry piled in the corner waiting to be washed? Can you smell anything—food cooking, the odor of cigarette smoke, traces of cologne? Who else is in the room and nearby? Do you hear other conversations? Is the window open? Can you hear muted sounds of activities outside? Is it raining? Now think about what's happening inside you. Are you tired or hungry? Do you have a headache or an itch anywhere? On what kind of paper is your book printed? Is the type large, small, easy to read?

Chances are that you weren't conscious of most of these phenomena when you began reading the chapter. Instead, you focused on reading and understanding the material in the book. You selectively attended to what you defined as important in this moment, and you were unaware of many other things going on around you. This is typical of how we live our lives. We can't attend to everything in our environment because far too much is there and most of it isn't relevant to us at a particular time.

A number of factors influence which stimuli we notice. First, some qualities of external phenomena draw our attention. For instance, we notice things that **STAND OUT** because they are larger, more intense, or more unusual than other phenomena. So we're more likely to hear a loud voice than a soft one and to notice a bright shirt more than a drab one. We also notice what matters to us, so out of a long list of messages that appears when you open your email, you're likely to notice one from a friend. Change also compels attention, which is why we become more attentive if a speaker shows a slide to enliven a speech or a new person joins a dialogue on the Internet.

Sometimes we deliberately influence what we notice by talking to ourselves (Mead, 1934). We tell ourselves to be alert if we have to drive when we're tired. We remind ourselves to speak loudly if we are addressing a large group without a microphone. We remind ourselves not to interrupt during team discussions. These are examples of intrapersonal communication based on selective perception.

Education is a process of learning to tell ourselves things we haven't previously noticed. Right now you're learning to be more conscious of the selectiveness of your perceptions, so in the future you will notice your selectivity more. In English courses you learn to recognize how authors craft characters and use words to create images. In on-the-job training you learn what you are expected to notice and do. Eli illustrates how selective perception operates in one sphere of his life.

Eli

A couple of years ago I went on a week-long hike in the Cranberry Back Country. Fortunately, the guys I went with knew a lot more about wilderness than I did. They taught me how to tell poisonous plants from ones that are safe to eat,

© James Holland/Stock, Boston

■ *What draws your eye in this photo? Why*

and they showed me how to read signs to figure out what wildlife inhabited an area. Before that trip I never noticed when branches were bent and I'd certainly never been able to tell how large an animal had bent them.

Our needs, interests, and motives influence what we choose to notice. If you're bored in your job, you're likely to notice ads for other jobs. If you are interested in politics, you're likely to pay attention to political stories in the news. If you've just broken up with a partner, you're more likely to notice attractive people than if you are in a relationship. Motives also explain the oasis phenomenon, in which thirsty people in a desert see an oasis although none is present. If we want something badly, we may perceive it when it doesn't exist.

Organization

We don't perceive randomly; instead, we organize our perceptions in meaningful ways. **Constructivism** is a theory that states that we organize and interpret experience by applying cognitive structures called **cognitive schemata,** or just **schemata.** We rely on four schemata to make sense of phenomena: prototypes, personal constructs, stereotypes, and scripts.

Prototypes

Prototypes are knowledge structures that define the clearest or most representative examples of some category (Fehr, 1993, p. 89). For example, you probably have a prototype of a great teacher, a true friend, and a superb team leader. You may also have prototypes of other cultures based on what you have witnessed in mass media. A prototype is an ideal for the category. We use prototypes to define the exemplar of a category: Jane represents confidence, Burt exemplifies a comfortable, casual friend, Ned is an ideal co-worker. The person who exemplifies the whole group is the prototype for each category. We classify people in categories by asking which of our prototypes they most closely resemble. We then consider how they measure up to the prototype, or ideal, of the category.

Damion

My ideal of a friend is my buddy Jackson. He stood by me when I got into a lot of trouble a couple of years ago. I got mixed up with some guys who used drugs, and I started using them too. Pretty soon the coach caught onto me and he suspended me from the team. That made me feel like a total loser, and I got deeper into drugs. But Jackson didn't give up on me, and he wouldn't let me give up either. He took me to a drug center and went there with me every day for 3 weeks. He never turned away when I was sick or even when I cried most of one night when I was getting off the drugs. He just stood by me. Once I was straight, Jackson went with me to ask the coach about getting back on the team.

Personal Constructs **Personal constructs** are mental yardsticks that allow us to measure people and situations along bipolar dimensions of judgment (Kelly, 1955). Examples of personal constructs are *intelligent–unintelligent, kind–unkind*, and *trustworthy–untrustworthy*. How intelligent, kind, and trustworthy is a speaker, group member, or co-worker? Whereas prototypes help us decide into which broad category a person or event fits, personal constructs allow us to make more detailed assessments of particular qualities of phenomena we perceive.

Nai Lee

One of the ways I look at people is by whether they are individual or related to others. In Korea we think of ourselves as members of families and communities. The emphasis on individuals was the first thing I noticed when I came to this country, and it is still an important way I look at people.

Winowa

People have a stereotype of Native Americans. People who are not Native Americans think we are all alike—how we look, how we act, what we believe, what our traditions are. But that isn't true. The Crow and Cherokee are as different as people from Kenya and New York. Some tribes have a history of aggression and violence; others have traditions of peace and harmony. We worship different spirits and have different tribal customs. All these differences are lost when people stereotype us all as Native Americans.

THE CENSUS BUREAU'S DILEMMA

Systems of organizing or classifying are arbitrary constructions invented by humans. Yet we sometimes act as if the ways we have classified things are intrinsically right. Consider the dilemma of the U.S. Census Bureau, which found that its method of classifying races no longer works.

The mushrooming diversity of our country has created problems for the Census Bureau and other demographic trackers. The racial categories they use were created in 1978, and they are no longer adequate to classify people with diverse languages, cultures, and ethnic heritages. Lumping diverse groups into single categories such as Asian (Japanese, Chinese, Taiwanese, Nepalese, etc.) or Native American (Crow, Lumbee, Paiute, etc.) is inappropriate. The prevailing classifications count Middle Easterners as white, and Alaskans as Alaskan Natives rather than people born in the United States. Another deficiency of existing categories is their inability to acknowledge people who have multiracial identities—and this may be most of us.

Social critic Eric Bates asks, "Counting and grouping people by racial categories helps us fight discrimination—but does it also perpetuate racism by institutionalizing false racial distinctions? Can we preserve 'race' as a useful statistical device and yet find ways to acknowledge that such measurements can never truly reflect our rich diversity as a people?" (Bates, 1994, p. 15).

In any context we rely on a limited set of personal constructs. If you are thinking about a person as a date, you're likely to rely on constructs such as *fun–not fun, intelligent–not intelligent,* and *attractive–unattractive.* When perceiving a co-worker, you're more likely to rely on constructs such as *reliable–unreliable, cooperative–uncooperative, experienced–inexperienced,* and *motivated–unmotivated.* Constructs such as *fair–unfair, knowledgeable–not knowledgeable,* and *interesting–not interesting* may guide your perceptions of teachers. We assess people in terms of how they measure up on the constructs we use, not on all the constructs that could be used. Thus, we may not perceive qualities that are not highlighted by the constructs we apply.

Stereotypes **Stereotypes** are predictive generalizations about people and situations. Based on the category in which we place someone or something, and how it measures up against personal constructs we apply, we predict what it will do. For instance, if you define someone as a liberal, you might stereotype the person as likely to vote Democratic, support social legislation, recycle, and so forth. You may have stereotypes of fraternity and sorority members, professors, athletes, and people from other cultures. Stereotypes don't necessarily reflect actual similarities among phenomena that you group into a single category. Our stereotypes may keep us from seeing differences between people we have grouped into a category.

Stereotypes may be accurate or inaccurate. In some cases we have incorrect understandings of a group, and in other cases some members of a group don't conform to the behaviors we think are typical of a group as a whole. Although we need stereotypes in order to predict what will happen, we should remember that they are selective and subjective.

Phyllis

I'll tell you what stereotype really gets to me: the older student. I'm 38 and working on a B.A., and I'm tired of being treated like a housewife who's dabbling in courses. Some students treat me like their mother, not a peer. And some faculty are even worse. One professor told me that I shouldn't worry about grades because I didn't have to plan a career like the younger students. Well, I am planning a career, I am a student, and I am serious about my work.

Scripts The final cognitive schemata we use to organize perceptions are **scripts,** which are guides to action. A script is a sequence of activities that define what we and others are expected to do in specific situations. Although we're often unaware of them, scripts guide many of our daily activities. You have a script for greeting casual acquaintances as you walk around campus ("Hey, how ya doing?"; "Fine"; "See ya."). You also have scripts for first dates, talking with professors, and relaxing with friends. Scripts organize perceptions into lines of action.

Prototypes, personal constructs, stereotypes, and scripts are cognitive schemata that organize our thinking about people and situations. We use them to make sense of experience and to predict how we and others will act.

SIZING UP OTHERS

Pay attention to the cognitive schemata you use the next time you meet a new person. First notice how you classify the person. Do you categorize her or him as a potential friend, date, colleague, and so on? Next, identify the constructs you use to assess the person. Do you focus on physical constructs (*attractive–unattractive*), mental constructs (*intelligent–unintelligent*), psychological constructs (*secure–insecure*), or interpersonal constructs (*eligible–committed*)? Would different constructs be prominent if you used a different prototype to classify the person? Now, note how you stereotype the person. What do you expect him or her to do based on the prototype and constructs you've applied? Finally, identify your script, or how you expect interaction to unfold between you based on your perceptions.

Interpretation

To create meaning, we interpret what we have noticed and organized. **Interpretation** is the subjective process of creating explanations for what we observe and experience.

Attributions

To interpret experiences, we ask why something happens or why someone says or does or doesn't do a particular thing. **Attributions** are explanations of why things happen and why people act as they do (Heider, 1958; Kelley, 1967).

Attributions have three dimensions. The first is the internal–external locus, which attributes what a person does to internal factors ("he's angry") or external factors ("the traffic jam frustrated him"). The second dimension is stability, which explains actions as the result of stable factors that won't change ("she's a nervous person"; "this job is always stressful") or temporary (unstable) occurrences ("she's nervous right now because of a big deal she's closing"; "this is a stressful period at work"). Finally, the dimension of control attributes responsibility for actions either to people ("she doesn't try to control her temper") or to factors beyond their personal control ("she has a chemical imbalance"). Figure 2.1 illustrates the three dimensions of attribution.

Chandra

I wait tables to make money for school. It used to be that when I didn't make good tips, I would say that the customers were cheap or in bad moods or my manager assigned me to a slow station. When I made good tips, I always thought that it was because I am such a considerate server. Then we got a new manager who told me that I made better tips when I was feeling good. He pointed out that I was really friendly and attentive to customers when I was in a good mood but that I could be careless when I felt down.

Self-Serving Bias

Research shows that we tend to construct attributions that serve our personal interests (Hamachek, 1992; Sypher, 1984). Thus, we are inclined to make internal and stable attributions for our positive actions and our successes.

ATTRIBUTION PATTERNS AND RELATIONSHIP SATISFACTION

Investigations have shown that happy and unhappy couples have distinct attribution styles (Bradbury & Fincham, 1990; Fletcher & Fincham, 1991). Happy couples make relationship-enhancing attributions. Such people attribute nice things a partner does to internal, stable, and global reasons. "She got the film for us because she is a good person who always does sweet things for us." They attribute unpleasant actions by a partner to external, unstable, and specific factors. "He yelled at me because all the stress of the past few days made him short with everyone."

Unhappy couples use reverse attribution patterns. They explain nice actions as resulting from external, unstable, and specific factors. "She got the tape because she had some extra time today." They see negative actions as stemming from internal, stable, and global factors. "He yelled at me because he is a nasty person who never shows any consideration to anybody else."

Negative attributions encourage pessimistic views and sap motivation to improve a relationship. Whether positive or negative, attributions may be self-fulfilling prophesies.

Figure 2.1 Dimensions of Attributions

Dimension		
Locus	Internal	External
Stability	Stable	Unstable
Controllability	Within personal control	Beyond personal control

We're also likely to claim that good results come about because of the personal control we exerted. For example, you might say that you did well on a test because you are a smart person (internal) who is always responsible (stable) and studies hard (personal control). On the other hand, we tend to avoid taking responsibility for negative actions and failures by attributing them to external and unstable events that are beyond personal control. To explain a failing grade on a test you might say that you did poorly because the professor (external) put a lot of tricky questions on that test (unstable) so that regardless of how hard you studied, you couldn't do well (outside of personal control). This phenomenon is known as **self-serving bias,** and it can distort our perceptions, leading us to take excessive credit for what we do well and to deny responsibility for our failings.

We've seen that perception involves three interrelated processes. The first of these, selection, involves noticing certain things and ignoring others within the totality of what is going on. The second process is organization, wherein we use prototypes, personal constructs, stereotypes, and scripts to order what we have selectively perceived. Finally, we engage in interpretation to make sense of the perceptions we have gathered and organized. Attributions are a primary way we explain what we and others do. Although we discussed each process separately, in reality they may occur in different orders and they interact continuously. Thus, our interpretations shape the knowledge schemata we use to organize experiences, and how we organize perceptions affects what we notice and interpret. We're now ready to consider some factors that influence what and how we perceive.

INFLUENCES ON PERCEPTION

Last year I went to a neighborhood picnic at which a neighbor who did not attend was the subject of discussion. The absent person had been behaving oddly ever since he moved into our neighborhood. He had thrown a rock at one person's dog, been seen going into one neighbor's house when nobody was home, been verbally abusive to several members of the community, and begun shooting squirrels and birds. At the picnic neighbors were comparing stories of what he had done and what it meant. A woman who is a psychologist ventured the opinion that he was suffering from depression and perhaps guilt, which had overcome his judgment. The legal aspects of his behavior were the focus of an attorney's comments—he suggested that the man could be arrested for breaking and entering and verbal harassment. A third person who had recently left her abusive partner was clearly terrified that our neighbor posed a threat to all of us. Those of us who have dogs and cats in our families were concerned for the safety of our pets. As this example illustrates, people don't always perceive in the same ways. How each of us perceived our neighbor was shaped by many factors in our background and training. What we perceive and how we interpret our perceptions depends on many factors.

Physiological Factors

The most obvious reason that perceptions vary among people is that we differ in our sensory abilities and physiologies. The five senses are not the same for all of us. Music that one person finds deafening

fyi

IT'S NEVER OUR FAULT!

Have you ever had an argument with your boyfriend or girlfriend and thought later that your partner's behavior was inappropriate, inconsiderate, or mean? Have you also thought that your own behavior was justified and appropriate? If so, you're in good company. In 1999 Astrid Schutz reported her study of married couples in southwest Germany. Relying on qualitative methods, Schutz independently interviewed each spouse about a particular marital conflict. Schutz then coded the interviews to learn how spouses perceived the conflict process. Schutz interpreted the data to discover who was labeled as the person who did or said something that was objectionable or failed to do or say something that should have been done or said. Schutz also coded interviews to reveal who each partner labeled as the person who objected to the behavior or lack of behavior. Finally, Schutz coded each person's account of the conflict using twenty-seven dimensions that described attributions, needs, and feelings. She then used chi-square tests, a statistical method that measures the significance of differences, to measure the differences between how partners described conflicts.

Schutz found that each person tended to describe the conflict in a manner that faulted his or her partner. Most accounts labeled the partner's behavior or lack of behavior as the problem responsible for conflict. She also found that most people described their own behaviors as reasonable, appropriate, well-intentioned, and justified in light of the other's behavior. On the other hand, most people described their partners' behaviors as unfair, irrational, inconsiderate, ill-intentioned, and unjustified. This study adds support to the well-documented tendency of people to engage in self-serving biases when they interpret their own and others' actions.

is barely audible to another. Salsa that is painfully hot to one diner may seem mild to someone else. On a given day on my campus students wear everything from shorts and sandals to jackets, a sign that they have different sensitivities to cold. Some people have better vision than others and some are color-blind. These differences in sensory abilities affect our perceptions.

Our physiological states also influence perception. If you are tired, stressed, or sick, you're likely to perceive things more negatively than when you are well and rested. For instance, a playful insult from a friend might anger you if you're feeling down, but it wouldn't bother you if you felt good. Each of us has a biorhythm, which influences how alert we are at different times of day. I'm a morning person, so that's when I prefer to teach classes and write. I am less alert and creative late in the afternoon.

Age is another factor that influences our perceptions. The older we get, the richer is our perspective for perceiving situations and people. Thus, compared to a person of 20, someone who is 60 has a more complex fund of experiences to draw on in perceiving. Throughout my twenties I was easily upset when my classes didn't go well or when I experienced writing blocks. Often I became disheartened because of problems I perceived as significant. In my mid-thirties my father died after a long illness that drained him and those who cared for him: my mother, my sister, my partner, my brother-in-law, and me. After his death, a less than perfect class or a bad day's writing didn't seriously distress me because I had a very different perspective on problems and bad times.

The extent of discrimination still experienced by women and minorities understandably discourages

many college students. I am more hopeful than some because I have seen significant changes in my lifetime. When I attended college, women and minorities were not admitted on an equal basis with Caucasian men. When I entered the job market, few laws protected women and minorities against discrimination in hiring, pay, and advancement. The substantial progress made during my life leads me to perceive that society can change inequities that still exist.

■ *One gift of growing older is enriched perspective. What might these people be able to share that two 20-year-olds could not?*

Expectations

Imagine that a friend tells you she wants you to meet a person whom she describes as "one of the greatest people I've ever met—he's funny, and considerate, and so interested in other people. You'll find him really easy to talk to and lots of fun." Chances are you would expect to like the new person and would in fact perceive the good qualities your friend led you to expect. If your friend had instead said, "This guy is a real drag. He's always cracking bad jokes and he's self-centered," you might expect not to like the man and you might see only his shortcomings.

Based on a series of studies, John Bargh (1997, 1999) reports that how we act may be affected by subliminal priming of perceptions. In one study participants were told that they would be taking two tests. The researcher told each participant to go in a room and take a test and then come out of the room and find the researcher to progress to the second test. One half of the participants then took a test that presented them with a group of terms related to politeness. The other half of participants took a test that presented them with a group of terms related to rudeness. When participants finished the test and went to look for the researcher, they found the person talking with another person. Sixty-three percent of the participants who had worked with the terms related to rudeness interrupted the researcher's conversation, but only 17% of the participants who had worked with politeness terms interrupted the conversation. Apparently their perceptions of what is appropriate behavior were affected by exposure to words that made rudeness or politeness salient to them.

Expectations affect our perceptions in a variety of communication situations. If we are told in advance that a new person on the job is a real team player, we're likely to notice the new employee's cooperative behaviors and not to see competitive or self-serving behaviors that the new person may also present. If we're forewarned that a speaker tends to distort facts, we're likely to perceive unethical representations of information in the speech. On the other hand, if we're told that the speaker is trustworthy, we may listen less critically and not perceive misrepresentations. Our sense of time has been radically reshaped by communication technologies that lead us to expect extremely quick exchanges. Just a decade ago, most people expected replies to business correspondence within a week to 10 days. Now, many people expect nearly instant responses and they grumble if an email message isn't answered for several hours.

The influence of expectations on communication is the basis of **positive visualization,** which is a technique used to reduce speaking anxiety by guiding apprehensive speakers through imagined positive speaking experiences. This technique allows people to form a mental picture of themselves as effective speakers and to then enact that mental picture in actual speaking situations (Hamilton, 1996).

Researchers report that positive visualization is especially effective in reducing chronic communication apprehension (Ayres & Hopf, 1990; Bourhis & Allen, 1992). The goal of positive visualization is to create detailed positive images of yourself in communication situations. Such visualizations encourage positive expectations for your actual communication.

Cognitive Abilities

In addition to physiological, cultural, and social influences, perception is shaped by our cognitive abilities. How elaborately we think about situations and people and the extent of our knowledge of others affect how we select, organize, and interpret experiences.

Cognitive Complexity

People differ in the number and type of knowledge schemata they use to organize and interpret people and situations. **Cognitive complexity** is the number of constructs (remember, these are bipolar dimensions of judgment) used, how abstract they are, and how elaborately they interact to shape perceptions. Most children have fairly simple cognitive systems. They rely on few schemata, focus more on concrete constructs (*tall–not tall*) than abstract psychological ones (*secure–insecure*), and often don't perceive relationships among different perceptions (how is security related to extroversion?). For instance, toddlers may

---

fyi EXPECTATIONS AND PERCEPTION

A class experiment (Secord, Bevan, & Katz, 1956) asked racially prejudiced and unprejudiced Caucasians to describe African Americans pictured in photographs. The prejudiced viewers "saw" stereotypical racial characteristics such as broadness of noses and fullness of lips, even when those features were not objectively present. The unprejudiced viewers did not "see" stereotypical racial qualities. This study demonstrates that expectations powerfully mold what we see.

IN YOUR MIND'S EYE

Positive visualization can enhance success in a variety of situations. Businesses coach managers to visualize successful negotiations and meetings. Athletes learn to imagine playing well, and those who engage in positive visualization improve as much as athletes who physically practice their sport. According to psychologists, we act like the person we see ourselves as being. Applying this to athletics, business, or speaking, it seems that successful people are those who see themselves as successful.

Sources: Lau, 1989; Porter & Foster, 1986.

call every adult male *Daddy* because they don't make cognitive distinctions among men.

Adults also differ in cognitive complexity, and this affects the accuracy of our perceptions. If you can think of people only as good or bad, you have limited ways of perceiving others. Similarly, people who focus on concrete data tend to have less sophisticated understandings than people who also perceive psychological data. For example, you might notice that a person is attractive, tells jokes, and

Sharpen Your Skill

VISUALIZING POSITIVE COMMUNICATION

First, imagine yourself speaking to three of your friends about a topic that matters to you. Now visualize your friends as nodding and asking questions that tell you they are interested in what you say. Notice that they are looking intently at you and their postures are attentive.

Now imagine that someone you don't know joins your friends and you continue speaking. It's okay if you feel a little anxious, but visualize the stranger as becoming attentive to your communication. Notice how the new person looks at you with admiration.

Next, imagine that you are asked to speak on the same topic to a student group and you agree. Visualize the room in which you speak: It is a small conference room in the campus student union. The room seems warm and comfortable. When you enter, twenty people are there to hear you. Notice that they smile when you walk to the front of the room. See how they look at you expectantly because they are interested in your topic.

Visualize yourself starting your talk. You begin by telling the listeners that, like them, you are a student. Notice that they nod and acknowledge the connection. Feel yourself relaxing and feeling confident. Then you tell them what you will cover in your talk. Notice how your words flow easily and smoothly. See the nods and smiles of your listeners. As you speak, they act interested and seem impressed by your knowledge. When you are through, the listeners break into spontaneous applause.

talks a lot. At a more abstract psychological level you might infer that the behaviors you observe reflect a secure, self-confident personality. This is a more sophisticated explanation because it includes perceptions of why the person acts as she or he does.

What if you later find out that the person is quiet in classes? Someone with low cognitive complexity would have difficulty integrating the new information with earlier observations, either dismissing the new information because it doesn't fit or replacing the former perception with the more recent data and redefining the person as shy. A more cognitively complex person would integrate all the information into a coherent account. Perhaps a cognitively complex person would interpret the person as more confident in social situations than academic ones.

Research shows that cognitively complex people are flexible in interpreting complicated phenomena and are able to integrate new information into how they think about people and situations. People who are less cognitively complex tend to ignore information that doesn't fit their impressions or to throw out old ideas and replace them with new impressions (Crockett, 1965; Delia, Clark, & Switzer, 1974). Either way, they screen out some of the nuances and inconsistencies that are part of human nature.

Person-Centeredness **Person-centeredness** is the ability to perceive another as a unique individual. When we perceive distinctions between people, we can adapt our communication to particular individuals. Effective public speakers perceive differences between audiences and adapt their presentations to the specific expectations, knowledge, and interests of each distinct audience. Thus, an effective campaigner may adopt a different speaking style and emphasize different topics when talking with elderly citizens, elementary school children, members of unions, and business executives.

To adapt communication to others, we must understand something about them. In relationships that aren't highly personal, communicators sometimes tailor messages to the general characteristics of groups. For example, more educated people tend to be more critical and informed, so effective speakers include strong evidence and show respect for listeners' knowledge when addressing people with high levels of education. Because uncertainty and change foster anxiety, effective managers communicate reassurance and provide maximum information to subordinates during times of organizational change. To be effective in a job interview, an interviewee should do research to learn about the history and image of the company and to find out what the company looks for in new employees.

We have different degrees of insight into people with whom we interact. You need to know your intimates well to create satisfying relationships; you need to know professors and co-workers less well but well enough to work with them; you need to know clerks only well enough to transact business. As we get to know someone better, we gain insight into how he or she differs from others in their group ("Rob's not like other political activists"; "Ellen's more interested in people than most computer science majors"). The more we interact with someone and the greater variety of experiences we have together, the more knowledge we gain about their motives, feelings, and behaviors. As we come to understand others as individuals, we fine-tune our perceptions of them. Consequently, we rely less on stereotypes to perceive them.

Person-centeredness is not the same as empathy. **Empathy** is the ability to feel with another person—to feel what he or she feels in a situation. Feeling with another is an emotional response that some scholars believe is not really possible. Our feelings tend to be guided by our emotional tendencies and experiences, so it may be impossible to feel precisely what another person feels. A more realistic goal is to learn to adopt dual perspective so that you adapt your communication to other people's frames of reference (Phillips & Wood, 1983; Wood, 1982, 2000b).

Steve

You really have to know somebody on an individual basis to know what they like and want. When I first started dating Sherry, I sent her red roses to let her know I thought she was special. That's the "lovers' flower," right? It turns out there were zillions of red roses at her father's funeral. Now they make Sherry sad because they remind her he's dead. I also took her chocolates once before I found out that she's allergic to chocolate. By now I know what she likes, but my experience shows that the general rules don't always apply to individuals.

When we take the perspective of others, we try to grasp what their perceptions and meanings are. To do this we have to suspend our own perspective and perceptions long enough to enter the world of another person. This allows us to gain some insight into their point of view, so we can communicate more effectively with them. At a later point in interaction we may choose to express our perspective or to disagree with another's views. This is appropriate and important in honest communication, but voicing our views is not a substitute for the equally important skill of attempting to understand another's perspective.

Social Roles

Our social roles also shape our perceptions. Both the training we receive to fulfill a role and the actual demands of the role affect what we notice and how we interpret and evaluate it. Because I'm a teacher, my perceptions of classes focus on how interested students seem, whether they appear to have read assigned material, and whether what they're learning is useful in their lives. Students have told me that they think about classes in terms of number and difficulty of tests, whether papers are required, and whether the professor is interesting. We have different perspectives on what classes are. When I am consulting with attorneys, I am more careful to state evidence for the ideas and suggestions I offer than I am in casual conversations with friends.

The professions people enter influence what they notice and how they think and act. In the earlier example, members of my community perceived our odd neighbor differently because of our distinct professional roles, as well as other factors. The attorney in the group focused on the legal—or illegal—nature of the neighbor's behavior and the psychologist's training led her to perceive his behaviors as evidence of emotional problems.

■ *How do you check perceptions when communicating on the Internet or through email?*

Cultural Factors

Membership in a culture influences perceptions. A **culture** consists of beliefs, values, understandings, practices, and ways of interpreting experience that a number of people share (Klopf, 1991). Western culture emphasizes technology and its offspring, speed. We expect things to happen fast—almost instantly. Whether it's instant photos, 5-minute copying, instant messages to people on our buddy lists when we're online, or 1-hour Martinizing, we

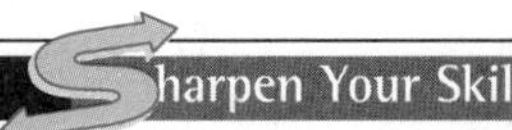

Sharpen Your Skill

NOTICING INDIVIDUALISM

How do the individualistic values of our culture influence our perceptions and activities? Check it out by observing the following:

- How is seating arranged in restaurants? Are there large communal eating areas or private tables and booths for individuals or small groups?
- How are living spaces arranged? How many people live in the average house? Do families share homes?
- How many people share a car in your family? How many cars are there in the United States?

The United States is a fiercely individualistic country that expects and rewards personal initiative. Other cultures, including Hispanic and Asian ones, are more collectivist and define identity in terms of membership in family and community rather than individuality. Because families are more valued in collectivist cultures, elders are given great respect and care. Rather than perceiving themselves as autonomous, as is typical in cultures that value individualism, people in communal cultures tend to think of themselves as members of and accountable to groups.

© Dave Bratruff/Artistry International

■ *Notice the number of generations that make up this Japanese family. Would a typical American family look like this?*

The difference between collectivist and individualistic cultures is also evident in child care policies. Countries that are more communal have policies that reflect the value they place on families. In every developed country except the United States, new parents, including adoptive parents, receive a period of paid parental leave, and some countries provide nearly a year's paid leave (Wood, 2001b).

live at an accelerated pace (Wood, 2000b). We express mail letters, fax memos, email notes, jet across the country, and microwave meals. Some writers suggest that emphasis on speed may diminish patience and our willingness to invest in long-term projects, such as relationships (Toffler, 1970, 1980). In countries such as Nepal and Mexico, life proceeds at a more leisurely pace, and people spend more time talking, relaxing, and engaging in low-key activity.

Differences based on physiology, expectations, cognitive abilities, social roles, and cultural membership affect how we perceive and interpret others and experiences. By extension, all these influences on perception affect how we communicate with ourselves and others.

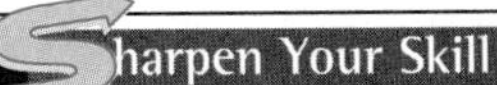

Sharpen Your Skill

DETECTING CULTURAL INFLUENCES ON PERCEPTION

How do values in Western culture affect your everyday perceptions and activities? See whether you can trace the concrete implications of several cultural values:

1. Productivity
2. Individualism
3. Speed
4. Youth
5. Wealth

Example: **Competitiveness.** This value is evident in concrete practices such as competitive sports, grading policies, vying for power in businesses, and attempts to get the last word in casual conversations.

Reflect on the influence of cultural values on your perceptions and activities.

GUIDELINES FOR DEVELOPING SKILL IN PERCEIVING

Perceiving and understanding are skills you can develop. In the pages that follow we'll identify four guidelines for enhancing skills in perceiving people and situations in ways that facilitate effective communication.

Avoid Mind Reading

Because perception is subjective, people differ in what they notice and in the meaning they attribute to it. One of the most common problems in communication is **mind reading,** which is assuming we understand what another person thinks or feels. When we mind read, we act as if we know what's on someone else's mind, and this can get us into considerable trouble. We can misinterpret co-workers' absence from meetings if we assume that it signals disinterest instead of competing commitments. Mind reading is also a common cause of tension between spouses (Gottman, 1993; Gottman, Markman, & Notarius, 1977).

Consider a few examples of the problems mind reading can cause. One person might assume a friend was late because he or she was angry about what happened yesterday. This guess could well be wrong. Mind reading also occurs when we say or think, "I know he's upset" (has he said he is upset?) or "She doesn't care about me anymore" (maybe she is too preoccupied or worried to be attentive). We also mind read when we tell ourselves we know how somebody else will feel or react or what they'll do ("I can't reprimand Pete in the annual performance review because he'll take it personally"). The truth is that we don't really know what others think or perceive—we're only guessing. When we mind read, we impose our perspectives on others instead of allowing them to say what they think. This can cause misunderstandings and resentment because most of us prefer to speak for ourselves.

Check Perceptions with Others

The second guideline follows directly from our insight that mind reading is seldom advisable. Because perceptions are subjective, checking our perceptions with others is a good idea. In the earlier example, it would be wise to ask, "Why are you late?" If the friend is angry, it might be valuable to ask, "Why are you angry?" It's especially important to check perceptions when communicating online because we don't have access to many of the nonverbal cues that help us interpret face-to-face communication. Sarcasm, irony, and other forms of communication may not be obvious online. Checking perceptions enhances clarity between people and invites productive dialogue, not blame and defensiveness.

Perception checking is an important communication skill because it helps people arrive at mutual understandings of each other and their interaction. To check perceptions, you should first state what you have noticed. For example, a person might say, "Lately you've seemed less pleased with my work." Then the person should check whether the other perceives the same thing: "Do you feel you've been dissatisfied with my work?" Finally, it's appropriate to invite the other person to help you understand her or his behavior. So in the example, if the other person agrees to being less pleased with our work, we could say, "Can you give me some insight into what specifically is unsatisfactory?" (If the other person doesn't agree that she or he is less pleased with your work, a useful question might be, "Is there some reason why you've given me less feedback and not offered me additional assignments?").

When checking perceptions, it's important to use a tentative tone rather than a dogmatic or accusatory one. This minimizes defensiveness and encourages good discussion. Just let the other person know you've noticed something and would like that person to clarify his or her perceptions of what is happening and what it means.

Distinguish Facts from Inferences

Effective communicators distinguish between facts and inferences. A fact is based on observation or proof. An **inference** is an interpretation that goes beyond what you know to be fact. For example, a student consistently comes to class late, sits at the back of the room, and often dozes during discussions. The teacher might infer that the student is rude and unmotivated. Defining the student as rude and unmotivated goes beyond the facts. The facts might be that the student has a job that ends right before the class, so the student is late and tired from working.

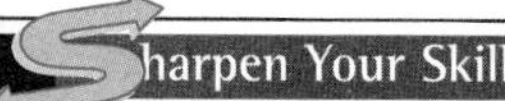

Sharpen Your Skill

PERCEPTION CHECKING

To gain skill in perception checking (and all communication behaviors), you need to practice. Try this:

1. Monitor your tendencies to mind read, especially in established relationships in which you feel you know your partners well.
2. The next time you catch yourself mind reading, stop. Instead, tell the other person what you are noticing and invite her or him to explain how she or he perceives what's happening. First, find out whether your partner agrees with you about what you noticed. Second, if you agree, find out how your partner interprets and evaluates what is happening.
3. Engage in perception checking for 2 or 3 days so that you have lots of chances to see what happens. When you've done that, reflect on the number of times your mind reading was inaccurate.
4. Think about how your perception checking affected interaction with your friends and romantic partners. Did you find out things you wouldn't have known if you'd engaged in mind reading?

Sharpen Your Skill

DISTINGUISHING FACTS FROM INFERENCES

Identify each of the following statements as a fact or an inference:

1. There are fifty states in the United States.
2. HIV/AIDS is caused by immoral sexual activity.
3. Women have a maternal instinct.
4. German shepherds have a tendency to suffer hip dysplasia.
5. Students who come to class late are disrespectful.
6. Acid rain can destroy trees.
7. College students earn money for dating and clothes.
8. Older students aren't career oriented.
9. Evelyn made a total score of 690 on her SAT.
10. Evelyn would not do well in college.

Statements 1, 4, 6 and 9 are facts; statements 2, 3, 5, 7, 8, and 10 are inferences.

It's easy to confuse facts and inferences because we sometimes treat the latter as the former. When we say, "The student is rude," we've made a statement that sounds factual, and we may then regard it that way ourselves. To avoid this tendency, substitute more tentative words for *is*. For instance, "The student seems rude" and "This student may be being rude" are more tentative statements that keep the speaker from treating an inference as a fact.

Monitor the Self-Serving Bias

We discussed self-serving bias earlier in this chapter. You'll recall that it involves attributing our successes and nice behaviors to internal and stable qualities that we control and attributing our failures and bad behaviors to external, unstable factors beyond our control. Because this bias can distort perceptions, we need to monitor it carefully. **Monitoring** is the process of calling behaviors or

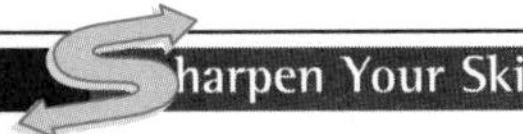

Sharpen Your Skill

USING TENTATIVE LANGUAGE

To become more sensitive to the tendency to confuse facts and inferences, pay attention to the language you use for the next 24 hours when you describe people and interactions. Listen for words such as *is* and *are*, which imply factual information. Do you find instances in which more tentative language would be more accurate?

Now extend your observations to other people and the language they use. When you hear others say "She is," "They are," or "He is," are they really making factual statements, or are they making inferences?

THE TRUTH, THE WHOLE TRUTH, AND NOTHING BUT THE TRUTH

Research (Trotter, 1975) shows that eyewitness testimony may not be as accurate as we often assume. Studies show that witnesses' perceptions are shaped by the language attorneys use. In one experiment, viewers were shown a film of a traffic accident and then asked, "How fast were the cars going when they *smashed* into each other?" Other viewers were asked how fast the cars were going when they *bumped* or *collided*. Viewers testified to significantly different speeds, depending on which word was used in the question.

In a separate experiment, viewers were shown a film of a traffic accident and then filled out a questionnaire that included questions about things that had not actually been on the film. Viewers who were asked, "Did you see *the* broken headlight?" more often testified that they saw it than did viewers who were asked, "Did you see *a* broken headlight?" The accidents that viewers "saw" were shaped by the words used to describe them.

other phenomena to our attention so that we can observe and regulate them. Try to catch yourself in the act of explaining away your failures or adverse behaviors as not your fault and taking personal credit for accomplishments that were helped along by luck or situational factors.

Monitoring self-serving bias also has implications for how we perceive others. Just as we tend to judge ourselves generously, we may judge others harshly. Monitor your perceptions to see whether you attribute others' successes and admirable actions to external factors beyond their control and their shortcomings and blunders to internal factors they can (should) control. If you do this, substitute more generous explanations for others' behaviors and notice how that affects your perceptions of them.

Words crystallize perceptions. Until we label an experience, it remains nebulous and less than fully formed in our thinking. Only when we name our feelings and thoughts do we have a clear way to describe and think about them. But just as words crystallize experiences, they can freeze thought. Once we label our perceptions, we may respond to our labels rather than the actual phenomena.

Summary

In this chapter we've discussed perception, which is a second basic communication process. As we have learned, perceiving involves selecting, organizing, and interpreting experiences. These three facets of the perception process are not separate in practice; instead, they interact so that each one affects the others. What we selectively notice affects how we organize and interpret the phenomenon. At the same time, our interpretations influence what we notice in the world around us. Selection, organization, and interpretation interact continuously in the process of perception. Our sensory capacities and physiological conditions affect what we perceive. In addition, expectations, cognitive abilities, social roles, and cultural context influence how we perceive experiences and how we communicate with ourselves and others.

Skillful perceiving enhances communication. We discussed four guidelines for enhancing your skills in perceiving. First, because people perceive differently, we should avoid mind reading. Extending this, we discussed the importance of checking perceptions, which involves stating how you perceive something and asking how another person perceives it. A third guideline is to distinguish facts from inferences in our perceptions and the symbols we use to label them. Finally, monitoring self-serving bias helps us perceive ourselves more accurately. We need to know when we are making factual descriptions and when we are making inferences that require checking.

FOR FURTHER REFLECTION AND DISCUSSION

1. Pay attention to how you communicate with people with whom you have both online and face-to-face contact. What differences can you identify in how you communicate in each medium? What differences can you identify in how others communicate when they are talking with you online and in person?
2. How do physiological factors affect your perceptions? Are you more alert at a particular time of day? How do your biorhythms affect your daily schedules?
3. Read a local paper and pay attention to how the language in stories shapes your perceptions of events and people. Identify examples of selective reporting.
4. For 24 hours, keep a list of instances in which you hear others state inferences in factual language. How widespread is this pattern? Learn more about fact–inference confusion and other ways in which language and perception affect our thinking by visiting the Web site of the Institute of General Semantics at: http://www.general-semantics.org/institute/.
5. Think of someone you know who is person-centered. Describe the specific skills this person uses and how they affect his or her communication.
6. Go to a grocery store and notice how products are placed on shelves (eye level versus lower) and the colors and designs on product packaging. Identify factors discussed in this chapter that are used to make products stand out and gain shoppers' attention.

KEY TERMS

Perception
Constructivism
Cognitive schemata
Schemata
Prototypes
Personal constructs
Stereotypes
Scripts
Interpretation
Attribution
Self-serving bias
Positive visualization
Cognitive complexity
Person-centeredness
Empathy
Culture
Individualism
Mind reading
Inference
Monitoring

Creating Communication Climates

LEARNING OBJECTIVES

To understand

1. How communication creates interpersonal climates
2. Whether conflict is healthy in relationships
3. How we can assert ourselves and also respect others
4. The values and risks of self-disclosing

- You have scheduled a performance review with Simon, who began working for you six months ago. You need to call his attention to some problems in his work while also showing that you value him and believe he can improve his performance.
- You know your friend Steve is worried about not having gotten any offers after interviewing with sixteen companies. You want to let him know it's okay for him to talk with you about his concerns.
- You have agreed to talk to a group of parents who are concerned about drugs at your school. You know the parents are worried and may regard you as just a spokesperson for the school. To be effective you'll have to show that you share their concerns and that they can trust you.

In each of these scenarios, achieving your goals depends on your ability to create an effective **communication climate,** which is the overall tone of interaction. Openness and trust are necessary in order to convey support while giving criticism, helping a friend feel comfortable disclosing fears, and opening lines of communication with parents. Communication climate influences collaboration on project teams, communication with intimates, reporting stories in media, online interaction, and speaking to large audiences. Creating and sustaining healthy communication climates is a basic communication process that affects what happens in any context where interaction occurs.

This chapter focuses on climate as a cornerstone of effective communication. We'll begin by defining *climate.* Next we'll discuss self-disclosure, a form of communication that can promote an open climate of communication if used appropriately. Third, we'll identify specific kinds of communication that foster distinct communication climates. In the fourth section of the chapter we'll consider the role of conflict in relationships, and we'll see that creating healthy communication climates helps us manage conflict constructively in personal and professional relationships. Finally, we'll discuss guidelines for creating and sustaining healthy communication climates.

COMMUNICATION CLIMATE

Communication climate is the emotional tone of a relationship between people who are interacting. Perhaps you feel foggy-headed when the sky is overcast and feel upbeat when it's sunny. Do you respond differently to the various seasons? In much the same way that physical climates influence moods, communication climates affect how people feel and interact with one another. We feel on guard when a supervisor blames us, a co-worker acts superior, someone flames us on the Internet, or a friend judges us. In each case, the communication climate is overcast.

Creating constructive climates is a basic skill that influences the effectiveness of communication in all contexts. On the job, we need to create supportive productive climates that foster good work relationships and outcomes. In social relationships, healthy climates allow us and others to feel at ease. In personal relationships, we want climates that let us disclose private feelings and thoughts without fear of criticism or ridicule. Effective climates for public speaking situations foster trust and respect between speakers and listeners. Thus, communication climates are basic to all settings and forms of interaction.

SELF-DISCLOSURE

Self-disclosure is the revelation of personal information about ourselves that others are unlikely to learn in other ways. We self-disclose when we express private hopes and fears, intimate feelings, and personal experiences, perceptions, and goals. Self-disclosures vary in how personal they are. To a co-worker who is upset about not receiving a promotion, you might disclose your experience in not getting a promotion some years ago. To your best friend, you might disclose more intimate feelings and experiences. The key characteristic of self-disclosure is that it communicates information about us that others are unlikely to learn if we don't tell them. Although we don't reveal our private selves to everyone and don't do it a great deal of the time even with intimates, self-disclosure is an important kind of communication.

Self-disclosure has notable values. First, sharing personal feelings, thoughts, and experiences often enhances closeness between people. By extension, when others understand our private selves, they can communicate more sensitively with us. Self-disclosing also tends to encourage others to self-disclose to us, so we may gain insight into them. Finally, self-disclosure can affect what we know about ourselves and how we feel about who we are. For example, if we reveal a shortcoming to a colleague or tell a friend about an incident of which we're ashamed and the other person doesn't judge us negatively, we may find it easier to accept ourselves and feel comfortable with that person.

Self-Disclosure and Personal Growth

A number of years ago, Joseph Luft and Harry Ingham created a model that describes different kinds of knowledge related to individual growth and awareness (Luft, 1969). They called the model the *Johari Window*, which is a combination of their first names, Joe and Harry (Figure 3.1).

Four types of information are relevant to the self. Open, or free, information is known to both us and others. Your name, major, work experience, and tastes in music are probably information that you share easily with others. Our co-workers and casual acquaintances often know information about us that is in our open area.

The blind area contains information that others know about us but we don't know about ourselves. For example, others may perceive us as leaders, even though we don't see ourselves that way. Co-workers and supervisors may recognize strengths, weaknesses, and potentials of which we are unaware.

The third area in the Johari Window includes hidden information, which we know about ourselves but choose not to reveal to most others. You might not tell many people about your vulnerabilities or about traumas you've experienced. You might conceal self-doubts when interviewing for a job. Even

Figure 3.1 The Johari Window

	Known to self	*Unknown to self*
Known to others	OPEN AREA	BLIND AREA
Unknown to others	HIDDEN AREA	UNKNOWN AREA

with our closest intimates we may choose to preserve some areas of privacy.

The unknown area is made up of information about ourselves that neither we nor others know. This consists of your untapped resources, untried talents, and unknown reactions to experiences you've never had. You don't know how you will manage a crisis in your professional life until you've been in one, you can't tell what kind of parent you will be unless you've had a child, and you can't tell how you would respond to serious disability unless you experience it.

Consuela

I had worked at my job for four years and never considered trying to advance. One day my supervisor called me in, and I thought, "Oh no, what have I done wrong?" He told me he had recommended me for a management training program because he thought I had managerial potential. Now I am a manager and I get good evaluations of my work, but I didn't see this possibility until my supervisor did first.

Because a healthy self-concept requires knowledge of yourself, it's important to gain access to information in our blind and unknown areas. To reduce your unknown area, you might enter unfamiliar situations, including chat rooms and Web sites that lie outside your normal interests. You might also try novel activities, interact with people whose cultural background differs from yours, and experiment with new ways of communicating. To decrease your blind area, you could ask others how they perceive you. To diminish your hidden area, in carefully chosen relationships in which trust has been established, you might reveal information that you do not share with most people.

Self-Disclosure and Closeness

According to researchers, self-disclosure is both a gauge of intimacy and a means of enhancing closeness, especially among Westerners (Derlega & Berg, 1987; Hansen & Schuldt, 1984). Yet people vary in their perceptions of the link between disclosure and intimacy. For some people talk is a primary way to develop intimacy, whereas other people regard sharing experiences and being together as more conducive to closeness than talking intimately.

Self-disclosure should take place gradually and with appropriate caution. It's unwise to tell anyone too much about ourselves too quickly, especially if revelations could be used against us. We begin by disclosing superficial information ("I haven't had experience in this kind of assignment," "I'm afraid of heights"). If a person responds to early disclosures with acceptance, we're likely to reveal progressively more intimate information ("My father served time in prison," "I'm not very skillful at reprimanding people for poor work"). If the person accepts these disclosures, communication may continue to deepen.

In the early stages of relationship development, reciprocity of disclosure seems important. If you mention a personal weakness to a new acquaintance, you'll be more comfortable if the other person shares a weakness, too. Most of us are willing to keep disclosing to a person we don't know well only as long as the other person is also revealing personal information (Cunningham, Strassberg, & Hann, 1986).

© M. Antman/The Image Works

© IPA/The Image Works

■ *Many men communicate closeness with few or no words, whereas women tend to talk to build intimacy.*

This principle also applies to contexts other than personal relationships: For example, when we self-disclose to a co-worker we are likely to feel a bit nervous if no reciprocal disclosure is forthcoming. The need to reciprocate disclosures immediately recedes in importance once a stable relationship is established.

Although self-disclosing is important early in relationships, it is not a primary communication dynamic in most enduring relationships. When we're first getting to know colleagues, friends, or intimate partners, we have to reveal parts of ourselves and learn about them, so disclosures are necessary and desirable. However, in relationships that endure over time, disclosures make up little of the total communication. Once co-workers have established a friendly working relationship, the bulk of their communication will focus on task issues, not further personal disclosures. In intimate relationships, frequency of disclosure tends to decline over time, yet partners continue to reap the benefits of the trust and depth of personal knowledge created by early disclosures. Also, partners do continue to disclose new experiences and insights to one another; it's just that mature relationships usually see less disclosure than embryonic ones. When a friendship, romance, or close working relationship wanes, typically the

fy*i*

DIFFERENT MODES OF CLOSENESS

Recent research suggests that the sexes may not differ much in the importance they place on closeness, but they may differ in how they create and experience intimacy.

Many women disclose personal thoughts and feelings as a primary way of enhancing intimacy. This is called *closeness in dialogue*. For many men, however, intimate talk and self-disclosure are not the primary paths to closeness. Instead, they often bond with others through doing things together. This is called *closeness in the doing*. The two modes of closeness are different yet equally valid.

Source: Wood & Inman, 1993.

depth of disclosure decreases (Baxter, 1987). We are reluctant to entrust others with our secrets and personal emotions when we no longer want closeness or when we sense the other is pulling away.

Janet

Josh and I have been married for 15 years. At first we shared a lot of personal information and private thoughts with each other, but we don't do that much now. Yet just knowing he knows me in ways no one else does makes me feel close to him. All the experiences and feelings we shared earlier help us understand things that happen now. We don't even have to discuss some things. We know how the other feels because we have shared so much over the years.

Sid

For three years Tom and I worked together, and we were really close. We knew everything about each other, and it was real easy to talk about anything, even problems or failures. But last year he stopped talking about himself. At first I just kept telling him what was going on with me, but then I got to feeling awkward—like I was more exposed than he was. Then I found out he had teamed up with another guy to open a franchise. When he stopped disclosing to me, it was a signal that our relationship was over.

Appropriate self-disclosure is important because it can foster trust and closeness, insight into ourselves, and knowledge of others. Self-disclosure is one form of communication that affects communication climates. To understand more fully how we shape interaction climates, we turn now to a discussion of confirming and disconfirming communication.

LEVELS OF CONFIRMATION AND DISCONFIRMATION

Philosopher Martin Buber (1957, 1970) believed that each of us needs confirmation to be healthy and to grow. The essence of confirmation is valuing. We all want to feel we are valued by co-workers on the job, audiences in public speaking settings, and intimates in personal relationships. When others confirm us, we feel appreciated and respected. When they disconfirm us, we feel discounted and devalued.

Few climates or relationships are purely confirming or disconfirming. In most, some communication is confirming whereas other messages are

THE RISKS OF SELF-DISCLOSURE

Along with potential values, self-disclosure also entails risks. The risks of self-disclosure found by communication researchers include that

- Others might reject you.
- Others might think less of you and you would lose face.
- Sharing needs and private feelings can expose incompatibilities in relationships.
- Others can use private information against you.
- You may have less power in a relationship once the other person knows your weaknesses.
- Revealing some private thoughts could hurt others.

Source: Derlega, Metts, Petronio, & Margulis, 1993.

disconfirming, or communication cycles between being confirming and disconfirming (Figure 3.2).

Communication scholars have extended insight into confirming and disconfirming climates (Cissna & Sieburg, 1986). They have identified three levels of confirmation that affect communication climates.

Recognition

The most basic form of confirmation is **recognition** that another person exists. We do this with nonverbal behaviors (a smile, hug, handshake, maintaining eye contact, looking up when someone enters your office) and verbal communication ("Hello," "Good to meet you," "I see you're home"). We disconfirm others at a fundamental level when we don't recognize their existence. For example, you might not speak to or look at a person when you enter a room or might not look at a teammate who comes late to a meeting. Not responding to another's comments is also a failure to give recognition. In Chapter 5 we will discuss how silence is sometimes used to disconfirm another's existence.

Acknowledgment

A second and more positive level of confirmation is **acknowledgment** of what another feels, thinks, or says. Nonverbally, we acknowledge others by nodding our heads or by making strong eye contact to show we are listening. Verbal acknowledgments are direct responses to others' communication. If a friend says, "I'm really worried that I blew the LSAT exam," you could acknowledge that by responding, "So you're scared that you didn't test well on it, huh?" This paraphrasing response acknowledges both the thoughts and feelings of the other person. If a co-worker tells you, "I'm not sure I have the experience to handle this assignment," you could acknowledge that disclosure by saying, "Sounds as if you feel this is a real challenge."

We disconfirm others when we don't acknowledge their feelings or thoughts. For instance, if you responded to your friend's statement about the LSAT by saying, "Want to go out and throw some darts tonight?" your response would be an irrelevancy that ignores what your friend said. We also fail to acknowledge others if we deny the feelings they communicate: "You did fine on the LSAT."

Lisa

I'm amazed by how often people won't acknowledge what I tell them. A hundred times I've been walking across campus, and someone's come up and offered to guide me. I tell them I don't need help, but they put an arm under my elbow to guide me. I am blind, but I can think just fine. I know if I need help. Why can't they acknowledge that?

Lisa makes an important point. To disregard another's statements is to disconfirm the person.

Endorsement

The final level of confirmation is **endorsement.** Endorsement involves accepting another person's feelings or thoughts as valid. You could endorse the friend who is worried about the LSAT by saying, "It's natural to be worried about the LSAT when you have so much riding on it." You could endorse your colleague at work by saying, "I'd be worried too if I were taking on a new responsibility." We don't endorse others when we reject their thoughts and feelings. For example, it would be disconfirming to say, "How can you complain about a new responsibility when so many people are being laid off? You

Figure 3.2 Continuum of Communication Climates

Confirming climate	Mixed climate Cycling climate	Disconfirming climate

should be glad to have a job." This response rejects the validity of the other person's expressed feelings and is likely to close the lines of communication between the two of you.

When we confirm someone, we say, "You matter to me, I care what you feel or think, and I accept your feelings and thoughts." When we disconfirm another, we say, "You don't exist, your ideas don't matter, I deny what you think and feel." Disconfirmation is not mere disagreement. Disagreements, after all, can be productive and healthy. What is disconfirming is to be told that we or our ideas are crazy, wrong, stupid, or deviant.

If you think about what we've discussed, you'll probably find that the relationships in which you feel most valued and comfortable are those with high degrees of recognition, acknowledgment, and endorsement.

Confirming and disconfirming messages are a primary means by which we create communication climates (Figure 3.3 on p. 67). We'll now consider other forms of communication that affect climates.

DEFENSIVE AND SUPPORTIVE CLIMATES

Communication researcher Jack Gibb studied the relationship between communication and climate (1961, 1964, 1970). He began by noting that in some climates we feel defensive, whereas in others we feel supported. Gibb identified six types of communication that promote defensive climates and six contrasting types of communication that foster supportive climates.

Wayne

I've gotten a lot of disconfirmation since I came out. When I told my parents I was gay, Mom said, "No, you're not." She and Dad both said I was just confused. They refuse to acknowledge I'm gay, which means they reject me. My older brother told me being gay is a sin against God. Now what could be more disconfirming than that?

Evaluation Versus Description

We tend to feel defensive when others evaluate us. Few of us are comfortable when we are the targets of judgments (Eadie, 1982; Stephenson & D'Angelo, 1973). It's not surprising that Wayne felt defensive when his parents and brother made evaluations—very negative ones—of his gayness. Even positive evaluations may provoke defensiveness because they imply that another person feels entitled to judge us. Examples of evaluative statements are "You have no discipline," "It's dumb to feel that way," "I approve," "You shouldn't have done that," and "That's a stupid idea."

Descriptive communication doesn't evaluate others or what they think and feel. Instead, it describes behaviors without passing judgment. In

CONFIRMATION AND DISCONFIRMATION IN ONLINE COMMUNICATION

Confirming and disconfirming communication is not restricted to face-to-face interactions. It also establishes climates in online communication. To gain insight into the particular forms of communication that create confirming and disconfirming climates, visit a chat room of your choosing. Take notes on communication that expresses or denies recognition, acknowledgment, and endorsement of others. What differences do you sense in the climates in chat rooms dominated by confirming versus disconfirming communication?

GUIDELINES FOR COMMUNICATING WITH PEOPLE WITH DISABILITIES

Effective communication can help create supportive climates when we interact with people who have disabilities. The following guidelines for a healthy climate are provided by AXIS, an organization dedicated to the dignity and rights of people with disabilities.

- When talking with someone who has a disability, speak directly to the person, not a companion or interpreter.
- When introduced to a person with a disability, offer to shake hands. People who have limited hand use or who have artificial limbs can usually shake hands.
- When meeting a person with a visual impairment, identify yourself and anyone who is with you. If a person with a visual impairment is part of a group, preface comments to him or her with a name.
- You may offer assistance, but don't provide it unless your offer is accepted. Then ask the person how you can best assist (ask for instructions).
- Treat adults as adults. Don't patronize people in wheelchairs by patting them on the shoulder or head; don't use childish language when speaking to people who have no mental disability.
- Respect the personal space of people with disabilities. It is rude to lean on a wheelchair; that is part of a person's personal territory.
- Listen mindfully when talking with someone who has difficulty speaking. Don't interrupt or supply words. Just be patient and let the person finish. Don't pretend to understand if you don't. Instead, explain what you understood and ask the person to correct you or otherwise clarify the communication.
- When you talk with people who use wheelchairs or crutches, try to position yourself at their eye level and in front of them to allow good eye contact.
- It is appropriate to wave your hand or tap the shoulder of people with hearing impairments as a way to get their attention. Look directly at the person and speak slowly, clearly, and expressively. Face those who lip read, face a good light source, and keep your hands, cigarettes, and gum away from your mouth.
- Relax. Don't be afraid to use common expressions such as "see you later" to someone with a visual impairment or "did you hear the news?" to someone with hearing difficulty. They're unlikely to be offended and may turn the irony into a joke.

Source: Adapted from AXIS Center.

Figure 3.3 Levels of Confirmation and Disconfirmation

	Confirming Messages	*Disconfirming Messages*
Recognition	**You exist.**	**You don't exist.**
	"Hello."	**Silence**
Acknowledgment	**You matter to me.**	**You don't matter.**
	I hear what you say.	**I am not listening.**
	I'm sorry you're hurt.	**You'll get over it.**
	I know you're worried.	**Let's drop the subject.**
Endorsement	**What you think is true.**	**You are wrong.**
	What you feel is okay.	**You shouldn't feel what you do.**
	I feel the same way.	**Your feeling doesn't make sense.**
	What you feel is normal.	**It's stupid to feel that way.**

Chapter 4 we'll discuss *I* language, in which the speaker takes responsibility for what she or he feels and avoids judging others. For example, saying "I feel upset when you scream" describes what the person speaking feels or thinks, but it doesn't evaluate another. On the other hand, if you say, "You upset me," you evaluate the other person and hold her or him responsible for what you feel or do. "I felt hurt when you said that" describes your feelings, whereas "You hurt me" blames another for your feelings.

Descriptive language may refer to others, but it does so by describing, not evaluating their behavior (for example, "You seem to be less involved in team meetings lately" versus "You're not involved enough in our team"; "You've shouted three times today" versus "Quit flying off the handle"). Nonverbal communication can turn descriptive words into an evaluative message. Thus it's important to keep facial cues and other nonverbal messages as nonevaluative as the words themselves.

Certainty Versus Provisionalism

Certainty language is absolute and often dogmatic. It suggests there is only one valid answer, point of view, or course of action. Because certainty proclaims an absolutely correct position, it slams the door on further discussion. Leaders can stifle creativity and team cohesion if they dogmatically state what the team should produce. There's no point in talking with people who demean any point of view but theirs. Certainty is also communicated when we repeat our positions in response to others' ideas.

Monika

My father is totally closed-minded. He has his ideas and everything else is crazy. I told him I was majoring in communication studies, and he said I'd never get a job as a speech writer. He never asked what communication studies is, or I would have told him it's a lot more than speech writing. He always assumes that he knows everything about whatever is being discussed. He has no interest in information or other points of view. I've learned to keep my ideas to myself around him—there's no communication.

One form of certainty communication is **ethnocentrism.** Ethnocentrism is a perspective based on

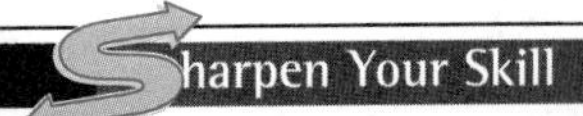

Sharpen Your Skill

USING DESCRIPTIVE LANGUAGE

To develop skill in supportive communication, translate the following evaluative statements into descriptive ones:

Evaluative	**Descriptive**
This report is poorly done.	This report doesn't include background information.
You're lazy.	______________________
I hate the way you dominate conversations with me.	______________________
Stop obsessing about the problem.	______________________
You're too involved.	______________________
You're excluding me from the team.	______________________

the assumption that our culture and its norms are the only right ones. For instance, someone who says, "It's disrespectful to be late" reveals insensitivity to societies that are less time conscious than the United States. Certainty is also evident when we say, "My mind can't be changed," "Only a fool would think that," or "There's no point in further discussion."

An alternative to certainty is provisionalism, which expresses openness to other points of view. Provisional communication signals that we are willing to consider alternative positions, and this encourages others to voice their ideas. Provisional language does not encourage others to perceive they have lost face in the interaction. Provisional communication includes statements such as "The way I tend to see the issue is . . .," "One way to look at this is . . .," and "It's possible that. . . ." Note that each comment shows that the speaker realizes that other positions also could be reasonable. Tentative communication reflects an open mind, which is why it invites continued conversation.

Strategy Versus Spontaneity

Most of us feel on guard when we think others are being devious or trying to manipulate us. Defensiveness is a natural response when we think others are using strategies in an effort to control us. Effective communication requires thought, planning, and efforts to adapt to others so that we can share meaning, but that doesn't necessarily mean communication must be manipulative. Strategic communication, in contrast, does not have the goal of sharing meaning. Quite the contrary: It aims to manipulate one person by keeping motives or intentions hidden (Eadie, 1982). An example of strategic communication is this: "Would you do something for me if I told you it really matters?" If the speaker doesn't tell us what we're expected to do, it feels like a set-up.

We may also feel someone is trying to manipulate us with a comment such as "Remember how I helped you with that project you were behind on last month?" After a preamble like that, we suspect a trap of some sort. Nonverbal behaviors may also convey strategy, as when a speaker pauses a long time before answering a question or refuses to look at listeners. A sense of deception pollutes the communication climate.

Spontaneity stands in contrast to strategy. Spontaneous communication may well be thought out, yet it is also open, honest, and not manipulative. "I really need your help with my computer" is more spontaneous than "Would you do something for me if I told you it really matters?" Likewise, it is more spontaneous to ask for a favor in a straightforward way ("Would you help me?") than to preface a request by reciting everything you've done for someone else. Many people say that they enjoy online communication because it can be so spontaneous, especially in fast-moving chat rooms. Whereas strategic communication cultivates distrust, spontaneous interaction fosters supportive communication climates.

Control Versus Problem Orientation

Similar to using strategies, controlling communication attempts to dominate others. For instance, it is controlling for someone to insist that his or her preference should prevail over others' preferences. Whether the issue is trivial (which movie to see) or serious (which policy a group will recommend), controllers try to impose their point of view on others. Winning an argument or having the last word is more important than finding the best solution.

Controlling communication prompts defensiveness because the relationship-level meaning is that the people exerting control think they have greater power, rights, or intelligence than others. It's disconfirming to be told our opinions are wrong, our preferences don't matter, or our ideas are faulty. Controlling communication is particularly objectionable when it is combined with strategies. For example, a wife who earns a salary higher than her husband's might say to him, "Well, I like the Honda more than the Ford you want, and it's my money that's going to pay for it." The speaker not only pushes her preference but also implies that her salary gives her greater power.

Rather than imposing a preference, problem-oriented communication focuses on resolving tensions and problems. The goal is to come up with something that everyone finds acceptable. Here's an example of problem-oriented communication: "It seems that we have really different ideas about how to get started on this task. Let's talk through what each of us wants and see whether there's a way for all of us to achieve what we need." Note how this statement invites collaboration and confirms the other people and the team's relationship by expressing a desire to meet all members' needs. Problem-oriented communication tends to reduce conflict and foster an open interaction climate (Alexander, 1979; Civickly, Pace, & Krause, 1977). One strength of focusing on problems is that the relationship level of meaning emphasizes that the communicators care about each other. In contrast, controlling behaviors aim for one person to triumph over the other, an outcome that undercuts harmony.

Neutrality Versus Empathy

We tend to become defensive when others act in a neutral manner, especially if we are talking about personal matters. Research on interview climates finds that defensiveness arises when an interviewer appears withdrawn and distant (Civickly et al., 1977). Neutral communication implies indifference to others and what they say. Consequently, it may be interpreted as disconfirming.

In contrast to neutrality, expressed empathy confirms the worth of others and concern for their

■ *How is the woman on the left communicating support and empathy to her friend?*

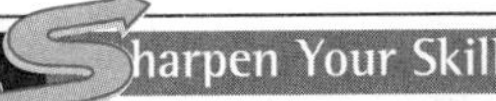

Sharpen Your Skill

ASSESSING COMMUNICATION CLIMATE

Use the behaviors we've discussed as a checklist for assessing communication climates. The next time you feel defensive, ask whether others are communicating superiority, control, strategy, certainty, neutrality, or evaluation.

In a communication climate that you find supportive and open, ask whether the following behaviors are present: spontaneity, equality, provisionalism, problem orientation, empathy, and description.

To improve defensive climates, be a model of supportive communication. Resist the tendency to respond defensively. Instead, be empathic, descriptive, and spontaneous, show equality and tentativeness, and be problem oriented.

thoughts and feelings. We communicate empathy when we say, "I can understand why you feel that way," "It sounds like you really feel uncomfortable with your job," or "I don't blame you for being worried about the situation." Gibb stressed that empathy doesn't necessarily mean agreement; instead, it conveys respect for others and what they think and feel. Especially when we don't agree with others, it's important to show that we respect them as people. Doing so fosters a supportive climate and keeps lines of communication open, even if differences continue to exist.

Superiority Versus Equality

Most of us feel on guard with people who act as if they are better than we are. Consider several messages that convey superiority: "I know a lot more about this than you"; "You don't have my experience"; "Is this the best you could do?"; "You really should go to my hairdresser." Each of these messages says loud and clear, "You aren't as good (smart/competent/attractive) as I am." Predictably, the frequent result is that we try to save face by shutting out people and messages that belittle us.

Carl

I am really uncomfortable with one of the guys on my team at work. He always acts like he knows best and that nobody else is as smart or experienced. The other day I suggested a way we might improve our team's productivity, and he said, "I remember when I used to think that." What a putdown! You can bet I won't go to him with another idea.

We feel more relaxed and comfortable when communicating with people who treat us as equals. At the relationship level of meaning, expressed equality communicates respect and equivalent status between people. This promotes an open, unguarded climate in which interaction flows freely. We may have special expertise in certain areas and still show regard for others and what they think, feel, and say. Creating a climate of equality allows everyone to be involved without fear of being judged inadequate.

We've seen that confirmation, which may include recognizing, acknowledging, and endorsing others, is the basis of healthy communication climates. Our discussion of defensive and supportive communication enlightens us about specific kinds of communication that express confirmation or disconfirmation. With this foundation, we're ready to consider the role of conflict in human relationships and how communication allows us to manage it productively.

CONFLICT AND COMMUNICATION

Conflict exists when people who depend on each other have different views, interests, values, responsibilities, or objectives and perceive their differences as incompatible. You want to set up a time each day when you and a friend will both be online for instant messages, but your friend doesn't want to do that. You believe money should be enjoyed, and your partner believes in saving for a rainy day. You favor one way of organizing a work team and your colleague prefers another. When we find ourselves at odds with people, we need to resolve conflict, preferably in a way that doesn't harm the relationship.

The presence of conflict doesn't mean a relationship is in trouble, although how people manage conflict does affect relationship health. Conflict is a sign that people are involved with each other. If they weren't, differences wouldn't matter and wouldn't need to be resolved. Co-workers argue because they care about issues that affect all of them; doctors and patients often work through conflicts about health practices in order to arrive at solutions that work for both; romantic partners can engage in conflict when they feel that the relationship is in jeopardy. For the most part, we have conflict only with people who matter to us. This is a good point to keep in mind when tensions arise because it reminds us that a strong connection underlies the conflict.

Conflict May Be Overt or Covert

Conflict may be overt or covert. **Overt conflict** exists when people express differences in a straightforward manner. They might discuss a disagreement, honestly express different points of view, or argue heatedly about ideas. In each case, differences are out in the open.

Carlotta

My roommate doesn't tell me when she's mad or hurt or whatever. Instead, she plays these games that drive me crazy. Sometimes she refuses to talk to me and denies that anything is wrong. Other times she "forgets" some of my stuff when she gets our groceries. I have to guess what is wrong because she won't tell me. It strains our friendship.

Yet much conflict isn't overt. **Covert conflict** exists when people camouflage disagreement and express it indirectly. When angry, a person may deliberately do something to hurt or upset another person but deny any motive to hurt. For instance, if you're annoyed that your roommate left the kitchen a mess, you might play the stereo when she or he is sleeping. Passive aggression is a form of covert conflict that sidesteps the real problems and issues. It's virtually impossible to resolve conflicts when we can't communicate openly about our differences.

Conflict May Be Managed Well or Poorly

How we handle conflict determines whether it benefits us and our relationships or creates lasting wounds.

fyi

CRISIS AS OPPORTUNITY

The Chinese word for *crisis* is made up of two characters: One means danger, and the other means opportunity.

The character on the left means "danger." The character on the right means "opportunity." Together they make up the Chinese word for *crisis.*

Views of Conflict How we perceive conflict affects how we deal with it. One of the greatest influences on our views of conflict is our cultural background. Societies such as the United States accept conflict and assertive competition. Other societies teach people to avoid conflict and to seek harmony with others. How people respond to conflict reflects one of three distinct orientations: **lose–lose, win–lose,** and **win–win.** Each of these is appropriate in some situations; the challenge is to know when each view is constructive.

The lose–lose approach to conflict assumes that conflict results in losses for everyone. One of my colleagues avoids conflict whenever possible because he feels everyone loses when there is disagreement. The lose–lose view presumes that conflict cannot produce positive outcomes. Although the lose–lose perspective usually is not beneficial, it has merit in specific circumstances. Some issues aren't worth engaging. For instance, my partner, Robbie, and I have very different ideas about the appropriate timetable for airline travel. He prefers to get to the airport at least 90 minutes before a flight, whereas I prefer to arrive just a few minutes in advance. For the first years of our marriage this was a source of discord that made travel unpleasant for us. Finally, I decided that the schedule was a dumb thing to argue about, and I simply planned to leave when Robbie preferred. We also disagree on cars, but Robbie defers to my preference because cars matter more to me than him. It's sometimes appropriate to defer on work teams when only trivial issues are at stake or when we aren't strongly committed to our point of view.

The win–lose orientation to conflict assumes that one person wins at the expense of the other. A person who sees conflict as a win–lose matter thinks disagreements are battles that can have only one victor. What one person gains is at the other's expense, and what one person loses benefits the other. Partners who disagree about whether to move to a new location might lock into a yes–no mode in which they can see only two alternatives: Move or don't move. They make no effort to find a mutually acceptable solution, such as moving to a third place that meets both partners' needs adequately or temporarily having a long-distance relationship so each person can maximize professional opportunities. The more person A argues for moving, the more B argues for not moving. Eventually, one of them "wins," but at the cost of the other and the relationship. A win–lose orientation toward conflict tends to undermine relationships because someone has to lose. There is no possibility that both can win, much less that the relationship can. For this reason, win–lose orientations should really be called *win–lose–lose* because when one person wins, both the other person and the relationship can lose.

Before you dismiss win–lose as a totally unconstructive view of conflict, let's consider when it might be effective. Win–lose can be appropriate when we have low commitment to a relationship and little desire to take care of the person with whom we disagree. When you're buying a car, for instance, you want the best deal you can get, and you have little concern for the dealer's profit. I adopted a win–lose approach to conflict with doctors when my father

fyi

WIN–WIN ATHLETICS

Americans view sports as competitions in which one person or team wins and the other loses. This perspective is in dramatic contrast to the Japanese attitude toward athletics. In baseball, for instance, the goal is not for one team to win but for the teams to tie. The Japanese play for ties because that way nobody loses face. When everyone plays hard and competitively, yet nobody loses, that's a perfect game!

The Japanese aim to win championships by only slim margins. One team may be many games ahead at a point in the season, but by the end of the season that team will trim its lead to one or two games. This preserves the face of the other teams because they don't lose by an embarrassing margin.

Source: Public Broadcasting Service, 1988.

was dying. The doctors weren't doing all they could to help him because they saw little value in investing time in a dying patient, but I wanted everything possible done to comfort my father. We had opposing views, and I cared less about whether the doctors were happy and liked me than about "winning" the best medical care for my father.

The win–win view of conflict assumes that there are usually ways to resolve differences so that everyone gains. For people who view conflict as win–win, the goal is to come up with a resolution that all parties can accept. A person is willing to make some accommodations in order to build a solution that lets others win, too. When partners adopt win–win views of conflict, they often find solutions that neither had thought of previously. This happens because they are committed to their own and the other's satisfaction. Sometimes win–win attitudes result in compromises that satisfy enough of each person's needs to provide confirmation and to protect the health of the relationship.

What we learned about perception in Chapter 2 reminds us that how we perceive and label conflict powerfully affects what it means to us and how we craft resolutions. We're unlikely to find a win–win solution when we conceive conflict as win–lose or lose–lose.

Bizarro

Tess

One of the roughest issues for Jerry and me was when he started working most nights. The time after dinner had always been "our time." When Jerry took the new job, he had to stay in constant contact with the California office. Because of the time difference, at 6 P.M. when Jerry and I used to do something together, it's only 3 P.M. on the West Coast and the business day is still going. I was hurt that he no longer had time for us, and he was angry that I wanted time he needed for business. We kept talking and came up with the idea of spending a day together each weekend, which we'd never done. Although my ideal would still be to share evenings, this solution keeps us in touch with each other.

Responses to Conflict A second influence on how we communicate during conflict is our accustomed style of responding to tension. A series of studies identified four responses to conflict (Rusbult, 1987; Rusbult, Johnson, & Morrow, 1986; Rusbult & Zembrodt, 1983; Rusbult, Zembrodt, & Iwaniszek, 1986). Figure 3.4 summarizes these responses to conflict, which are active or passive, depending on whether they address problems. Responses are also constructive or destructive in their effect on relationships.

The exit response involves leaving a relationship, either by walking out or by psychologically withdrawing. "I don't want to talk about it" is a vocal exit response. Because exit is forceful, it is active; because it fails to resolve tension, it can be destructive. The neglect response occurs when a person denies or minimizes problems. "You're making a mountain out of a molehill" is a neglect response that denies that a serious issue exists. The neglect response is also disconfirming because it fails to acknowledge and respect how another feels. Neglect can be destructive because it evades difficulties, but it does so passively by avoiding discussion. The loyalty

YOUR VIEW OF CONFLICT

Could you identify your perception of conflict from this discussion? To check, answer these questions:

1. When conflict seems about to occur, do you
   a. Marshal arguments for your solution?
   b. Feel everyone is going to get hurt?
   c. Feel there's probably a way to satisfy everyone?
2. When involved in conflict, do you
   a. Feel competitive urges?
   b. Feel resigned that everyone will lose?
   c. Feel committed to finding a mutual solution?
3. When you disagree with another person, do you
   a. Assume the other person is wrong?
   b. Assume neither of you is right?
   c. Assume each of you has good reasons for what you think and feel?

A answers indicate a win–lose view of conflict; B answers suggest a lose–lose view; C answers reflect a win–win view.

response is staying committed to a relationship despite differences. Loyalty involves hoping that things will get better on their own. Loyalty is silent allegiance, so it is passive. Because loyalty doesn't end a relationship and preserves the option of addressing tension later, loyalty can be constructive. Finally, voice is an active constructive strategy that responds to conflict by talking about problems and trying to resolve differences. A person who says to a co-worker, "I want to talk about the tension between us" exemplifies the voice response to conflict.

Although most people have one or two habitual responses, we can develop skill in other styles of responding. Constructive strategies (voice and loyalty) are advisable for relationships that you want to maintain. Of those two, voice is stronger because it actively intervenes to address conflict. Loyalty may be useful as an interim strategy when people need time to reflect or cool off before dealing with tension. Once you understand your current ways of responding to conflict, you can consider whether you want to develop skill in alternative styles.

Figure 3.4 Responses to Relationship Distress

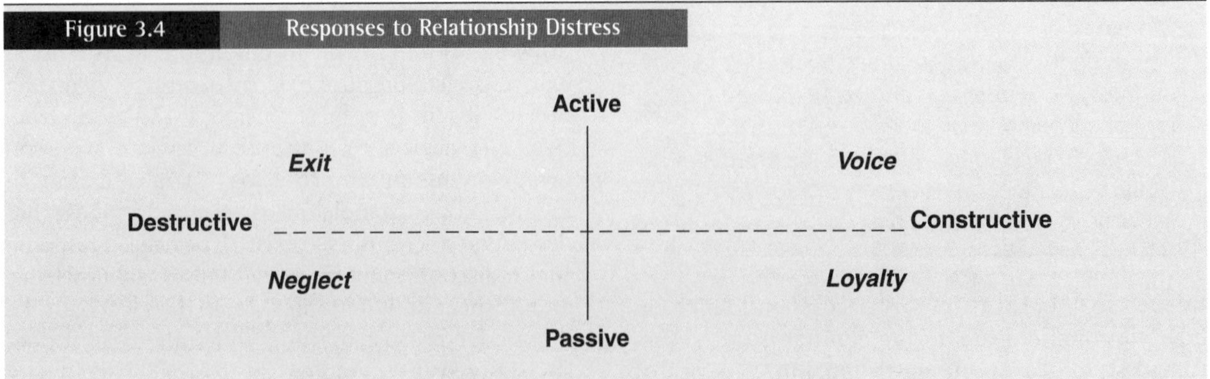

fy*i*

FAIR FIGHTING

Like cholesterol, conflict has good and bad forms. In their 1973 book *The Intimate Enemy: How to Fight Fair in Love and Marriage,* George Bach and Peter Wyden state that conflict can benefit relationships if it is managed well. One value of conflict is that it lets partners air problems, worries, or resentments before they fester. Conflict also has the potential to expand partners' understandings of each other. An argument about a specific issue often provides broader information about why partners feel as they do and what meanings they attach to the issue. These values can be realized if partners practice good communication skills.

Conflict Can Be Good for Individuals and Relationships

Although we tend to think of conflict negatively, it can benefit us and our relationships in several ways. When managed constructively, conflict can help us grow personally and professionally, and it can strengthen our connections with others. Conflict is an opportunity for us to deepen our insight into our ideas and feelings and to learn from the differing perspectives of others. Conflict prompts us to consider different points of view. Based on what we learn, we may change our opinions, behaviors, or goals. Conflict can also increase our insight into ourselves, relationships, and situations.

GUIDELINES FOR CREATING AND SUSTAINING HEALTHY COMMUNICATION CLIMATES

So far we've discussed relationships between communication, climate, and conflict. To translate what we've covered into pragmatic information, we'll discuss five guidelines for building and sustaining healthy climates.

Accept and Confirm Others

Throughout this chapter we've seen that confirmation is a cornerstone of healthy communication climates. Although we can understand how important confirmation is, it isn't always easy to give it. Sometimes we disagree with others or don't like certain things they do. Communication research tells us that people expect real friends to give honest feedback, even if it isn't always pleasant to hear (Rawlins, 1994). This implies that we have an ethical responsibility to be honest in our communication. It is false friends who tell us only what we want to hear. We can offer honest feedback within a context that assures others we value and respect them, as Dan's commentary illustrates.

Dan

When I first came to school here, I got in with a crowd that drank a lot. At first I drank only on weekends, but pretty soon I was drinking every night and drinking more and more. My grades were suffering, but I didn't stop. Then my friend Betsy told me she wanted to help me stop drinking. The way she talked to me, I knew that she was being honest because she cared. She was a better friend than all my drinking buddies, because she cared enough not to let me hurt myself. All my buddies just stood by and said nothing.

Affirm and Assert Yourself

It is just as important to affirm and accept yourself as to do that for others. You are no less valuable than others, your needs are no less important, and your preferences are no less valid. It is a misunderstanding to think that the interpersonal communication principles we've discussed concern only how we behave toward others. They pertain equally to how we should treat ourselves. Thus, the principle of confirming people's worth applies equally to others and ourselves. This implies that you need to communicate your thoughts and feelings to give others a chance to confirm you. A sound ethic is to assert our feelings, ideas, and preferences while honoring those that others have. If you don't assert yourself in the workplace, you give up the possibility of influencing the quality of work produced. If you don't assert yourself in personal relationships, you undercut your own and your partner's respect for your ideas, feelings, and needs.

Maria

Ever since I was a kid, I have muffled my own needs and tried to please others. I thought I was taking care of relationships, but actually I was hurting them, because I felt neglected. My resentment poisoned relationships in subtle but potent ways. Now I'm learning to tell others what I want and need, and that's improving my relationships.

Unlike aggression, assertion doesn't involve putting your needs above those of others. But unlike deference, assertion doesn't subordinate your needs to those of others. Assertion also differs from passive aggression, in which a person blocks or resists while denying she or he is doing that. Assertion is a matter of clearly and nonjudgmentally stating what you feel, need, or want. This should be done without disparaging others and what they want. You should simply state your feelings in an open descriptive manner. Figure 3.5 illustrates how aggression, assertion, and deference are different.

Even when people disagree or have conflicting needs, each person can state her or his feelings and confirm the other's perspective. Usually, there are ways to acknowledge both viewpoints, as Dean's comments illustrate.

Dean

My supervisor did an excellent job of letting me know I was valued when I got passed over for a promotion last year. He came to my office to talk to me before the promotion was announced. He told me both I and the other guy were qualified but that he had seniority and also field experience I didn't have. Then he assigned me to a field position for 6 months so I could get the experience I needed to get promoted. His talk made all the difference in how I felt about staying with the company.

Figure 3.5 Aggression, Assertion, and Deference

Aggressive	*Assertive*	*Deferential*
I demand that we spend time together.	I'd like to create more time for us.	If you don't want to spend time with each other, that's okay with me.
Get this report done today. I need it.	I need to have this report today. Can you manage that?	I need this report today, but if you can't get it done, that's all right.
Tell me what you're feeling, I insist.	I would like to understand more of how you feel.	If you don't want to talk about how you feel, okay.
I don't care what you want; I'm not going to a movie.	I'm really not up for a movie tonight.	It's fine with me to go to a movie if you want to.

Respect Diversity Among People

Just as individuals differ, so do relationships in personal and professional life. There is tremendous variety in what people find comfortable, affirming, and satisfying in interpersonal interaction. It's counterproductive to try to force all people and relationships to fit into a single mode. For example, you might have one co-worker who enjoys a lot of verbal banter and another who is offended by it. There's no need to try to persuade the second co-worker to engage in verbal teasing or the first one to stop doing so. You may like disclosing in online communication, but some of the people you meet online don't share that preference. The differences between people create a rich variety of ways we can build and sustain relationships.

Because people and relationships are diverse, we should strive to respect a range of communication choices and relationship patterns. In addition, we should be cautious about imposing our meaning on others' communication. People from different social groups, including distinct groups in the United States, have learned different communication styles. What Westerners consider to be openness and healthy self-disclosure may feel offensively intrusive to people from some Asian societies. European Americans can misinterpret as abrasive the dramatic, assertive speaking style of many African Americans. Especially in the workplace, it's important to understand that people vary widely in communication styles. To communicate effectively, we need to respect diversity among people.

It's appropriate to ask others (nonjudgmentally) to explain behaviors that are not familiar to you. This lets them know that they matter to you, and it allows you to gain insight into different perspectives on interaction.

Valaya

One of the most hard adjustments for me has been how Americans assert themselves. I was very surprised that students argue with their teachers. We would never do that in Taiwan. It would be extremely disrespectful. I also see friends argue, sometimes very much. I understand this is a cultural difference, but I have trouble accepting it. I learned that disagreements very much hurt relationships.

Time Conflict Effectively

A fourth guideline for creating effective communication climates is to use timing to foster constructive conflict. There are three ways to use timing so that conflicts are most likely to be civil and productive. First, try to engage in conflict when both people are able to be fully present and mindful. Most of us are irritable when we are sick, tired, or stressed, so conflict is unlikely to be constructive. It's also generally more productive to discuss problems in private rather than in public settings. If time is limited or we are rushing, we're less likely to take the time to deal constructively with differences. It's impossible to express ourselves clearly, listen well, be confirming, and respond sensitively when a stopwatch is ticking in our minds.

A second guideline for timing is to be flexible about when you deal with differences. Constructive conflict is most likely when everyone's needs are accommodated. Some people prefer to tackle problems as soon as they arise, whereas other people need time to reflect before interacting. If one person feels ready to talk about a problem, but the other doesn't, it's wise to delay discussion if possible. Of course, this works only if the person who is ready agrees to talk about the issue at a later time.

A third way to use timing to promote positive conflict is **bracketing**, which marks off peripheral issues for later discussion. In the course of conflict a variety of issues often surface. If we try to deal with all of them, we are sidetracked from the immediate problem. Bracketing other concerns for later discussion lets us keep conflict focused productively. Keep in mind, however, that bracketing, like the parliamentary procedure of tabling motions, works only if people actually do return to the issues they set aside.

Show Grace When Appropriate

Finally, an important principle to keep in mind during conflict is that **grace** is sometimes appropriate.

Although the idea of grace has not traditionally been discussed in communication texts, it is an important part of spiritual and philosophical thinking about ethical dimensions of human communication. You don't have to be religious or know philosophy to show grace. All that's required is a willingness to sometimes excuse someone who has no right to expect your compassion or forgiveness. Showing grace when appropriate is equally important in personal and professional relationships.

Grace is granting forgiveness or putting aside our needs or helping another save face when no standard says we should or must do so (Wood, 1999). Rather than being prompted by rules or expectations, grace springs from a generosity of spirit. Grace is not forgiving when we *should* be gracious (for instance, excusing people who aren't responsible for their actions). Also, grace isn't allowing others to have their way when we have no choice (deferring when our supervisor insists, for example). Instead, grace is unearned and unnecessary kindness. For instance, two roommates agree to split chores, and one doesn't do her share because she's got three tests that week. Her roommate might do all the chores even though there is no expectation for this generosity. It's also an act of grace to defer to another person's preference when you could impose yours. Similarly, when someone hurts us and has no right to expect forgiveness, we may choose to forgive anyway. We do so not because we have to, but because we want to. Grace is a matter of choice.

Grace is given without strings. We show kindness, defer our needs, or forgive a wrong *without any expectation of reward or reciprocity*. Grace isn't doing something nice to make a co-worker feel grateful or indebted to us. Nor is it grace when we do something with the expectation of a payback. For an act to be one of grace it must be done without conditions or expectations of return.

Grace is not always appropriate, and it can be exploited by people who take advantage of kindness. Some people repeatedly abuse and hurt others, confident that pardons will be granted. When grace is extended and then exploited, extending it again may be unwise. However, if you show grace in good faith and another takes advantage, you should not fault yourself. Kindness and a willingness to forgive are worthy moral precepts. Those who abuse grace, not those who offer it, are blameworthy.

Because Western culture emphasizes assertion and protection of self-interests, grace is not widely practiced or esteemed. We are told to stand up for ourselves, not let others walk on us, and not tolerate transgressions. It is important to honor and assert ourselves, as we've emphasized throughout this book. Yet self-assertion can work in tandem with being generous toward others.

None of us is perfect. We all make mistakes, hurt others with thoughtless acts, fail to meet responsibilities, and occasionally do things we know are wrong. Sometimes there is no reason others should forgive us when we wrong them; we have no right to expect exoneration. Yet human relations must have some room for redemption, for the extension of grace when it is not required or earned.

The guidelines we've discussed combine respect for self, others, relationships, and communication. Using these guidelines should enhance your ability to foster healthy affirming climates in your relationships with others.

Summary

In this chapter we've explored self-disclosure and communication climates as foundations of interaction with others. Self-disclosure allows us to share ourselves with others, gain insight into ourselves, and build closeness in relationships. Self-disclosure doesn't occur in a vacuum. Instead, it is most likely when the communication climate is affirming, accepting, and supportive.

A basic requirement for healthy communication climates is confirmation. Each of us wants to feel valued, especially by those for whom we care most deeply. When partners recognize, acknowledge, and endorse each other, they give the important gift of confirmation. They say, "You matter to me." We discussed particular kinds of communication that foster supportive and defensive climates in relationships.

Communication that fosters supportive climates also helps us manage conflict constructively. We discussed lose–lose, win–lose, and win–win approaches to conflict and explored how each affects interaction. In addition, conflict patterns are influenced by whether people respond by exiting, neglecting, being loyal, or giving voice to tensions. In most cases voice is the preferred response because it is the only response that allows people to actively and constructively deal with conflict.

To close the chapter, we considered five guidelines for building healthy communication climates. The first one is to accept and affirm others, communicating that we respect them, even though we may not always agree with them or feel the same as they do. A companion guideline is to accept and assert ourselves. Each of us is entitled to voice our thoughts, feelings, and needs. Doing so allows us to honor ourselves and to help others understand us. A third guideline is to respect diversity among people. Humans vary widely, as do their preferred styles of communicating. When we respect differences among people, we gain insight into the fascinating array of ways that humans interact.

The fourth and fifth guidelines concern communicating when conflicts arise. We learned that we can make choices about timing that increase the likelihood of constructive climate. In addition, we discussed the value of showing grace—unearned and unrequired compassion—when that is appropriate.

FOR FURTHER REFLECTION AND DISCUSSION

1. Think about the most effective work climate you've ever experienced. Describe the communication in that climate. How does the communication in that situation reflect skills and principles discussed in this chapter?
2. Visit a chat room or discussion forum that interests you. Identify instances of self-disclosure made by participants in the conversation and how others respond to those disclosures. Are the patterns you observe in online communication consistent with information presented in this chapter?
3. Consider the ethical principles reflected in the communication behaviors discussed in this chapter. What kinds of ethical principles underlie confirming communication and disconfirming communication?
4. Interview a professional in the field of work you plan to enter or return to after completing college. Ask your interviewee to describe the kind of climate that is most effective in his or her work situation. Ask what specific kinds of communication foster and impede a good working climate. How do your interviewee's perceptions relate to material covered in this chapter?
5. Use your *InfoTrac College Edition* to read recent reports on assertion. After entering the site, select *EasyTrac* and type in the key word *assertion.* Read two articles that are provided.
6. How often do you use exit, voice, loyalty, and neglect responses to conflict? What are the effects?
7. When do you find it most difficult to confirm others? Is it hard for you to be confirming when you disagree with another person? After reading this chapter, can you distinguish agreeing with, approving of, and confirming another person?

KEY TERMS

Communication climate
Self-disclosure
Recognition
Acknowledgment
Endorsement
Ethnocentrism
Conflict
Overt conflict
Covert conflict
Lose–lose
Win–lose
Win–win
Bracketing
Grace

Engaging in Verbal Communication

LEARNING OBJECTIVES

To understand

1. That language can affect us profoundly
2. How labels affect meaning
3. That language is a process, so meanings and symbols change over time
4. That communication is rule guided
5. How punctuation influences the meaning of communication

Many children in the United States hear the nursery rhyme "Sticks and stones can break my bones, but words can never hurt me." By now most of us have figured out that it isn't true. Words can hurt us, sometimes deeply. Words can also enchant, comfort, teach, amuse, and inspire us. We use language to plan, dream, remember, evaluate, and reflect on ourselves and the world around us. We also use language to define who we are and to represent ourselves to others. Words are powerful aspects of everyday life.

The human world is made up of symbols and meanings. We use symbols to express ourselves and to imbue our lives and activities with significance. The symbols used by others, including figures in mass media, shape how we perceive and regard people, events, and issues. In this chapter we take a close look at verbal communication, and we explore how words allow us to create meaning for ourselves, others, relationships, and situations. We begin by defining symbols and discussing principles of verbal communication. Next we'll examine how symbolic abilities enable us to create meanings for ourselves, others, and our experiences. Finally, we'll identify guidelines for using verbal communication effectively. In Chapter 5 we'll explore the companion system, nonverbal communication.

SYMBOLS AND MEANING

We experience life through symbols, which are the ways we represent people, events, and all that goes on around us and in us. In any moment we notice only certain things, and it is those that we symbolize. Once we symbolize something, we tend to perceive and respond to it in terms of the label we have used. For example, if you meet a new person and notice that he talks a lot about himself, you might label him arrogant or self-centered. The label you impose then leads you to perceive behaviors that are consistent with your label and not to perceive behaviors that are inconsistent with your label: his sense of humor, kindness, and so forth. What this person means to you is shaped by the symbols you use to define him. To appreciate the profound ways in which symbols affect our lives, we'll discuss what they are and how they affect us.

Features of Symbols

Verbal communication refers to the spoken or written word. **Nonverbal communication,** which we will discuss in Chapter 5, includes all aspects of communication other than words, such as facial expressions, dress, and tone of voice. Verbal communication consists of symbols, which represent feelings, ideas, objects, and people. For instance, your name is a symbol that represents you. *Dormitory* is a symbol for a particular kind of building. *Democracy* is a symbol for a particular political system. Symbols have three qualities: They are arbitrary, ambiguous, and abstract.

Arbitrary Symbols are **arbitrary,** which means they are not intrinsically connected to what they represent. For instance, the word *modem* has no natural relationship to the instrument that allows us to connect to the Internet and Web. Certain words seem right because as a society we agree to use them in particular ways, but they have no natural correspondence with their referents. Because meanings are arbitrary instead of necessary, they change over time. In the 1950s most people understood the word *gay* to mean lighthearted and merry; today it is generally understood to refer to homosexuals. The word *apple* used to refer exclusively to a fruit and *mouse* used to refer to a rodent, whereas today both words are at least as likely to refer to computers.

Language also changes as we invent new words. Through mass communication commentators have enlarged the political vocabulary with such terms as *Watergate* (which was followed by *Irangate* and *Monicagate*), *gender gap,* and *political correctness. Cyberspace, hyperlink, information superhighway, hypertext,* and *World Wide Web,* or *WWW,* are terms we've invented to refer to communication technologies. To express feelings in online communication, people have invented emoticons such as :) for smile, :(for frown, <g> for grin, and LOL for laughing out loud.

fyi

HOW WORDS HURT US

To understand how powerfully words can affect us, consider how you feel about the following words and phrases:

Drunk	Alcoholic	Person with a problem	
Feminazi	Bra-burner	Radical feminist	
Nigger	Negro	Black	African American
Kike	Hebrew	Jew	Jewish person
Queer	Fag/dyke	Homosexual	Gay/lesbian
Chick	Bimbo	Girl	Woman
God squader	Jesus freak	Bible thumper	Christian
Honkey	Whitey	White	Caucasian

© Michael Grecco/Stock, Boston

■ *In this photo of a computer convention, what words can you see that didn't exist or were used very differently 10 years ago?*

Ambiguous Symbols are also **ambiguous,** which means they don't have clear-cut, precise meanings. Degrees of uncertainty exist about what any symbol means. "A good friend" means someone to hang out with to one person and someone to confide in to another. Christmas and Hanukkah have distinct connotations for people with different religious commitments, and Thanksgiving means different things to many Native Americans and European Americans. "Affirmative action" summons distinct meanings for people who have experienced discrimination and those who have not. The meaning of these words varies as a result of cultural contexts and individuals' experiences.

Although verbal symbols don't mean exactly the same thing to everyone, within a culture many symbols have an agreed-upon range of meanings (Mead, 1934). In learning to communicate, we learn not only words but also the meanings and values of our society. Thus, all of us know that dogs are four-footed creatures, but each of us also has personal meanings based on dogs we have known and how our families and culture regard dogs. In some countries dogs are often used as food—not a meaning for dogs in the United States! Conversely, many Westerners eat beef, whereas Hindu cultures regard cows as sacred.

The ambiguity of symbols can lead to the misunderstandings that sometimes plague communication. We tend to assume that others have the same meanings for words that we do. A friend recently told me of misunderstandings that arose when he tried to negotiate a contract with a Japanese firm. My friend, Erik, said that when he made his initial proposal, O-Young, who represented the Japanese company, had nodded his head and said, "This is very good." Encouraged, Erik made additional suggestions, and O-Young smiled and responded, "This is a fine idea" and "I admire your work on the project." Yet O-Young consistently refused to sign the contract that contained Erik's proposals. Finally, another U.S. businessperson explained to Erik that Japanese culture regards it as rude to refuse another person directly. To someone socialized in Japanese society, outright disagreement or rejection causes another person to lose face, and that is to be avoided at all costs. Once Erik understood that apparently favorable responses did not mean O-Young agreed with him, their negotiations became much more constructive. The United States developed a training program in cultural sensitivity to prepare delegates to participate in the 1995 United Nations Conference on Women. The

fyi

OUR MULTICULTURAL LANGUAGE

Although the term *multicultural* has only recently come into popular usage, our society and our language have always been multicultural. See whether you recognize the cultural origins of the following everyday words (Carnes, 1994):

1. Brocade
2. Chocolate
3. Cotton
4. Klutz
5. Khaki
6. Silk
7. Skunk
8. Gingham
9. Noodle
10. Zombie

Answers: 1, Spanish; 2, Nahuatl Native American tribe; 3, Arabic; 4, Yiddish; 5, Hindi; 6, Greek; 7, Algonquian Native American tribe; 8, Malay; 9, German; 10, Kongo.

delegates were told that many Asian women would not sign agreements and contracts even if they seemed to give verbal and nonverbal indications of agreement. Like O-Young, they tend to avoid voicing disagreement overtly.

Problems arising from the ambiguity of language often surface. A supervisor criticizes a new employee for "inadequate quality of work." The employee assumes the supervisor wants more productivity; the supervisor means that the employee should be more careful in proofing material to catch errors. Americans who go to war and those who conscientiously object and refuse to go claim to be patriots. Similarly, spouses often have different meanings for "doing their share" of home chores. To many women it means doing half the work, but to men it tends to mean doing more than their fathers did, which is still less than their wives do (Hochschild & Machung, 1989; Wood, 1998).

According to counselor Aaron Beck (1988), a common problem in relationships is language that creates ambiguity. For instance, Anya might ask her husband, Bryan, to be more loving, but she and he have different understandings of what being more loving means. Consequently, Bryan may do more housework to express his love, whereas Anya wanted them to spend more time together. Suggesting that a co-worker should be more responsive doesn't specify what you want. To minimize ambiguity, we should be as clear as possible when communicating. Thus, it's more effective to say, "I would like for you to look at me when I'm talking" than to say, "I wish you'd be more attentive."

Abstract Finally, symbols are **abstract,** which means they are not concrete or tangible. They stand for ideas, people, events, objects, feelings, and so forth, but they are not the things they represent. In using symbols we engage in a process of abstraction whereby we move further and further away from external or objective phenomena. The symbols we use vary in abstractness. *Reading matter* is an abstract term that includes everything from philosophy books to the list of ingredients on a cereal package. *Book* is a less abstract word. *Textbook* is even less abstract. And *Communication Mosaics* is the most concrete term because it refers to a specific textbook.

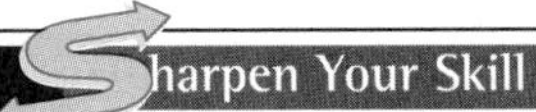

COMMUNICATING CLEARLY

To express yourself clearly, it's important to translate ambiguous words into concrete language. Practice translating with these examples:

Ambiguous language	Clear language
You are rude.	I don't like it when you interrupt me.
We need more team spirit.	____________________
I want more freedom.	____________________
Let's watch a good program.	____________________
Your work is sloppy.	____________________
That speaker is unprofessional.	____________________

Ron

A while ago I told my girlfriend I needed more independence. She got all upset because she thought I didn't love her anymore and was pulling away. All I meant was that I need some time with the guys and some for just myself. She said that the last time a guy said he wanted more independence, she found out he was dating out on her.

Our perceptions are one step away from the phenomena because perceptions are selective and subjective. We move a second step from phenomena when we label a perception. We abstract even further when we respond not to behaviors or our perceptions of them but to the label we impose. This process can be illustrated as a ladder of abstraction (Figure 4.1), a concept developed by two early scholars of communication, Alfred Korzybski (1948) and S. I. Hayakawa (1962, 1964).

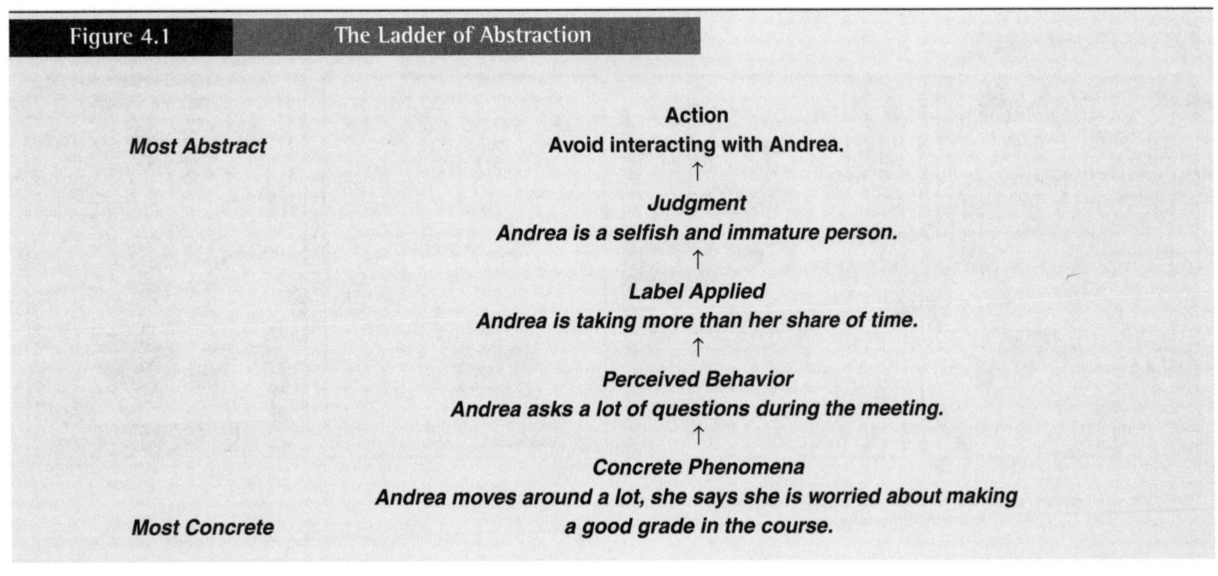

Figure 4.1 The Ladder of Abstraction
Most Abstract
Action
Avoid interacting with Andrea.
↑
Judgment
Andrea is a selfish and immature person.
↑
Label Applied
Andrea is taking more than her share of time.
↑
Perceived Behavior
Andrea asks a lot of questions during the meeting.
↑
Concrete Phenomena
Andrea moves around a lot, she says she is worried about making a good grade in the course.
Most Concrete

As our symbols become increasingly abstract, the potential for confusion mushrooms. One way this happens is overgeneralization. Mass communication often relies on highly general language to describe groups of people. Terms such as *welfare class, immigrants,* and *tax-and-spend Democrats* encourage us not to notice distinctions between people who receive welfare, people who immigrate to the United States, and people who are Democrats.

Overly general language can distort how partners think about a relationship (Beck, 1988). They may make broad negative statements such as "You never go along with my preferences" or "You always interrupt me." In most cases highly abstract communication involves overgeneralizations that are inaccurate. Yet by symbolizing experience this way, partners frame how they think about each other. Researchers have shown that we are more likely to recall behaviors that are consistent with how we've labeled people than ones that are inconsistent (Fincham & Bradbury, 1987). When we say a friend is insensitive, we're likely to notice instances in which he is insensitive and to overlook times when he is sensitive. Similarly, if we label a co-worker lazy, we predispose ourselves to perceive laziness and not to perceive her conscientiousness. We can minimize misunderstandings by using specific language instead of abstract terms (Patton & Ritter, 1976). Saying, "You interrupted me a moment ago" is clearer than "You're so dominating."

Principles of Using Symbols to Create Meaning

Now that we understand that symbols are arbitrary, ambiguous, and abstract representations of other phenomena, we're ready to consider three principles of communication.

Interpretation Creates Meaning Because symbols are abstract, ambiguous, and arbitrary, we have to interpret symbols to determine what they mean (Duck, 1994a, 1994b; Shotter, 1993). Interpretation is an active, creative process we use to make sense of experiences. Although we're usually not conscious of the effort we invest in interpreting words, we continuously engage in the process of constructing meanings.

When somebody says "Get lost," you have to think about the comment and the person who made it to decide whether it's an insult, a friendly needling, or a colloquial way to say you are out of line. People for whom English is a second language find idioms such as "get lost" even more difficult to interpret than native speakers do. What the words mean depends on the relationship between communicators, as well as the self-esteem and previous experiences of the person who is told to get lost. Similarly, if you say "hello" to someone who makes no response, you have to decide how to interpret the silence. Is the person ignoring you, angry with you, or preoccupied?

Doonesbury BY GARRY TRUDEAU

Communication Is Guided by Rules Rules that we learn in the process of being socialized into a particular culture set the pattern for our communication (Argyle & Henderson, 1985; Shimanoff, 1980). **Communication rules** are shared understandings among members of a particular culture or social group about what communication means and what behaviors are appropriate in various situations. Children are often taught that *please* and *thank you* are magic words that they should use. We learn that *sir* and *ma'am* are polite words to use when addressing our elders or people who have authority over us. In the course of interacting with our families and others, we unconsciously absorb rules that guide how we communicate and how we interpret others' communication. Research shows that children begin to understand and follow communication rules by the time they are 1 or 2 years old (Miller, 1993).

Two kinds of rules govern communication (Cronen, Pearce, & Snavely, 1979; Pearce, Cronen, & Conklin, 1979). **Regulative rules** regulate interaction by specifying when, how, where, and with whom to communicate about certain things. For instance, European Americans generally don't interrupt when someone is making a formal presentation, but in more informal settings interruptions may be appropriate. Some African Americans follow a different rule; it specifies that audience members should participate in public speeches by calling out responses. Thus, for some African American audiences at speaking events, the call–response pattern is an appropriate form of communication. The rules of other cultures say that interrupting in any context is impolite.

Sherita

I play with a rock group. It took me and the others in my group a while to figure out that white audiences liked our music. You know right away if black audiences like what you're doing because they shout out during songs or even join in. But white people wait until the end of a number to respond, and then they may just clap but not call out any praise. For the longest time I thought they didn't like our music because they didn't speak out during numbers.

Some families have a rule that people cannot argue at the dinner table, whereas other families regard arguments as a normal accompaniment to meals. Families also teach us rules about how to communicate in conflict situations (Honeycutt, Woods, & Fontenot, 1993; Jones & Gallois, 1989; Yerby, Buerkel-Rothfuss, & Bochner, 1990). Did you learn that it's appropriate or inappropriate to yell at others during conflict? Regulative rules also define when, where, and with whom it's appropriate to show affection and disclose private information. Regulative rules vary across cultures so that what is considered appropriate in one society may be regarded as impolite or offensive elsewhere.

Constitutive rules define what a particular communication means or stands for. We learn which behaviors communicate interest (listening, asking questions), professionalism (punctuality, high-quality work), and rudeness (ignoring). We also learn what communication is expected if we want to be perceived as a good friend (sharing confidences, defending our friends if others criticize them), a responsible employee (making good contributions in group meetings, creating supportive climates), and a desirable romantic partner (offering support, expressing affection). We learn constitutive and regulative rules in the process of interacting with others in our society. Like regulative rules, constitutive rules are shaped by cultures.

Rules that tell us when to communicate, what to communicate, and how to interpret others' verbal and nonverbal communication guide our everyday interaction. Casual social interactions tend to adhere to rules that are widely shared in a society. Interaction between intimates also follows rules, but these are private rules that reflect special meanings partners have created (Beck, 1988; Fitzpatrick, 1988; Wood, 1982, 2000b). Television networks follow rules for what can and cannot be said and shown during specific times and rules for how often they insert commercials. Chat rooms develop specific and often unique rules for how people express themselves and respond to one another. Every organization develops a distinctive culture, which includes rules about how members interact with one another.

Few rules are hard and fast. Like communication itself, most rules are subject to change. When we decide a rule is not functional, we negotiate

COMMUNICATION RULES

Think about the regulative and constitutive rules you follow in your verbal communication. For each item listed here, identify two rules that guide your verbal behavior:

Regulative Rules

List rules that regulate your verbal communication when

1. Talking with elders
2. Interacting at dinner time
3. Having first exchanges in morning
4. Greeting casual friends on campus
5. Talking with professors

Constitutive Rules

How do you use verbal communication to show

1. Trustworthiness
2. Ambition
3. Disrespect
4. Support
5. Anger

After you've identified your rules, talk with others in your class about the rules they follow. Are there commonalities among your rules that reflect broad cultural norms? What explains differences in individuals' rules?

changes in it. A company may find that its rule for making decisions by consensus no longer works once the company has tripled in size, so voting becomes a constitutive rule to define what counts as decision making. When we don't have a rule for a particular kind of interaction, we invent one and often negotiate and refine it until it provides the assistance we want in structuring communication. When couples have a child, they often find they don't have any guidelines for new communication situations, so they develop rules: "It is appropriate to tend to the baby while talking with each other," "We take turns eating so one of us is free to hold the baby," or "Interrupting our activities if the baby cries does not count as rudeness."

It's important to understand that we don't have to be aware of communication rules in order to follow them. For the most part we're really not conscious of the rules that guide how, when, where, and with whom we communicate about various things. We may not realize we have rules until one is broken and we become aware that we had an expectation. A study by DeFrancisco (1991) revealed that spouses have a clear pattern in which husbands interrupt wives and are unresponsive to topics wives initiate. The couples were unaware of the rules, but their communication nonetheless sustained the pattern. Becoming aware of communication rules empowers you to change those that do not promote good interaction, as Emily's commentary illustrates.

Emily

My boyfriend and I had this really frustrating pattern about planning what to do. He'd say, "What do you want to do this weekend?" And I'd say, "I don't know. What do you want to do?" Then he'd suggest two or three things and ask me which of them sounded good. I would say they were all fine with me, even if they weren't. And this would keep on forever. Both of us had a rule not to impose on the other, and it kept us from stating our preferences, so we just went in circles about any decision. Well, two weekends ago I talked to him about rules, and he agreed we had one that was frustrating. So we invented a new rule that says each of us has to state what we want to do, but the other has to say if that is not okay. It's a lot less frustrating to figure out what we want to do since we agreed on this rule.

Punctuation Affects Meaning We punctuate communication to interpret meaning. Like the punctuation you studied in grammar classes, **punctuation** of verbal communication is a way to mark a flow of activity into meaningful units. Punctuation is our view of when interaction begins and ends (Watzlawick, Beavin, & Jackson, 1967).

To decide what communication means, we establish its boundaries. Usually this involves deciding who initiated communication and when the interaction began. If a co-worker suggests going out to lunch together, you might regard the invitation as marking the start of the interaction. If you return another person's phone call, you might perceive the original call as the beginning of the episode.

When we don't agree on punctuation, problems may arise. If you've ever heard children arguing about who started a fight, you understand the importance of punctuation. Communication on the Internet and World Wide Web is often punctuated differently by different participants who join the dialogue at different times. I once read a message that was a defense of flaming (dramatically disparaging others on the Internet). Because I view flaming as discouraging freedom of speech, I wrote a critical response to the message. The person to whom I wrote replied that the message that disturbed me was a sarcastic reply to an earlier message that I had not seen. Because people enter electronic dialogues at different times, it's difficult to know who launched a particular topic or which messages initiate ideas and which are responses to earlier messages. New members of organizations may not understand relationships (allies and enemies) or when and why particular words came into use.

In personal relationships a common instance of conflicting punctuation is the demand–withdraw pattern (Figure 4.2; Bergner & Bergner, 1990; Christensen & Heavey, 1990; James, 1989). In this pattern, one person tries to create closeness with personal talk, and the other strives to maintain autonomy by avoiding intimate discussion. The more the first person demands personal talk ("Tell me what's going on in your life"; "Let's talk about our future"), the more the second person withdraws ("There's nothing to tell"; "I don't know about the future"; silence). Each partner punctuates interaction as starting with the other: The demander thinks, "I pursue because you withdraw," and the withdrawer thinks "I withdraw because you pursue."

Figure 4.2 The Demand–Withdraw Pattern

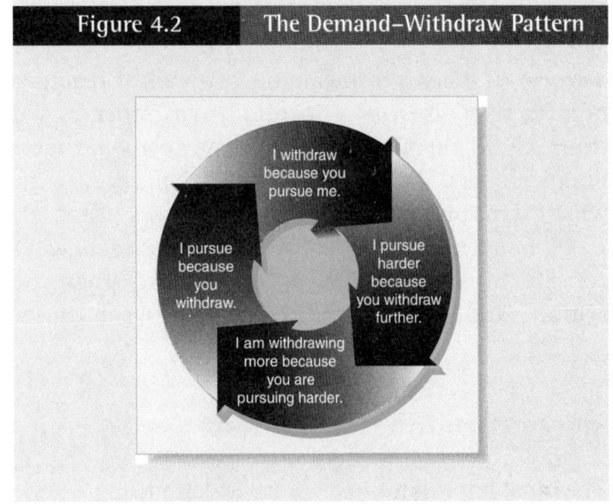

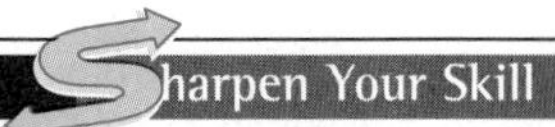

PUNCTUATING INTERACTION

The next time you and another person enter an unproductive cycle, stop the conversation and discuss how each of you punctuates interaction.

1. What do you define as the start of interaction?
2. What does the other person define as the beginning?
3. What happens when you learn about each other's punctuation? How does this affect understanding between you?

There is no objectively correct punctuation because it depends on subjective perceptions. When people don't agree on punctuation, they don't share meanings for what is happening between them. To break out of unconstructive cycles, such as demand–withdraw, people need to realize that they may punctuate differently and to discuss how each of them experiences the pattern.

Interpretation, communication rules, and punctuation influence the meaning we assign to communication. These three principles highlight the creativity involved in constructing meaning. We're now ready to probe how we use symbolic abilities in our everyday lives.

SYMBOLIC ABILITIES

The ability to use symbols allows humans to live in a world of ideas and meanings. Instead of reacting unreflectively to our concrete environments, we think about them and sometimes transform them. Philosophers of language have identified six ways in which symbolic capacities affect our lives (Cassirer, 1944; Langer, 1953, 1979). As we discuss each, we'll consider how to recognize the constructive power of symbols and minimize the problems they can cause.

Symbols Define Phenomena

The most basic symbolic ability is definition (Wood, 1992a, 1994a). We use words to define ourselves, others, experiences, relationships, feelings, and thoughts. A friend of mine separates his savings into accounts designated for travel, retirement, and emergencies. Last spring he told me he couldn't afford a summer vacation because he'd used up his travel fund. I pointed out that he had extra money in his emergency fund that he could use for a vacation. "No," he replied, "that account isn't for vacations." He had defined the accounts in specific ways that shaped his view of what money was available for various expenses. The symbols we use define what things mean to us.

The labels we use to define others affect how we see them. When we label someone, we focus attention on particular aspects of that person and her or his activities. At the same time, we necessarily obscure other aspects of that person's identity. A person might be a father, a conservative, a concerned citizen, and a demanding supervisor. Each label directs our attention to certain aspects of the person and away from others. We might talk with the conservative about editorials on government policies, discuss community issues with the concerned citizen, seek advice on child rearing from the father, and try to clarify the expectations of the supervisor. If we define someone as an Asian American or a Latina, that may be all we notice about the person, although there are many other aspects of her. This suggests that the words we use to define others have ethical implications. **Totalizing** occurs when we respond to a person as if one label totally represented who that person is. We fix on one symbol to define someone and fail to recognize many other aspects of who the person is. Some people totalize gay men and lesbians by noticing only their sexual orientation. Interestingly, we don't totalize heterosexuals on the basis of their sexual orientation. Totalizing also occurs when we dismiss people by saying "She's old," "He's a yuppie," or "She's just a jock." Totalizing is not the same as stereotyping. When we stereotype someone, we define the person in terms of characteristics of a group. When we totalize others, we negate most of who they are by spotlighting a single aspect of their identity (Wood, 1998).

Orest

A lot of people relate to me as Asian, like that's all I am. Sometimes in classes teachers ask me to explain the "Asian point of view," but they do not ask me to explain my perspective as a pre-med major or a working student. I am an Asian, but that is not all that I am.

The symbols we use affect how we think and feel. If we describe our work in terms of frustrations, problems, and disappointments, we're likely to feel negative about our job. On the other hand, if we describe rewards, challenges, and successes, we're likely to feel more positive about our work. The way we define experiences in relationships also affects how we feel about them. Several years ago my colleagues and I asked romantic couples how they defined differences between them (Wood, Dendy, Dordek, Germany, & Varallo, 1994). We found that some people defined differences as positive forces that energize a relationship and keep it ... Others defined differences as problems or ba... closeness. We noted a direct connection be... how partners defined differences and how th... acted. Partners who viewed differences as constructive approached their disagreements with curiosity, interest, and an expectation of growth through discussion. In contrast, partners who labeled differences as problems dreaded disagreements and tried to avoid talking about them.

People who consistently use negative labels to describe their relationships heighten their awareness of what they don't like and diminish their perceptions of what they do like (Cloven & Roloff, 1991). In contrast, partners who focus on good facets of relationships are more conscious of virtues in partners and relationships and less bothered by flaws (Bradbury & Fincham, 1990; Fletcher & Fincham, 1991).

Mass communication also defines people and events, sometimes in ways that are biased. Conservative commentator Rush Limbaugh uses terms such as *feminazis* and *fembots,* which reflect and foster negative perceptions of feminists. On the other end of the political spectrum, liberal Democratic commentators often refer to Republicans as "captives of special interests." We should be mindful of how the language we hear affects our perceptions and actions.

Symbols Evaluate Phenomena

Language is not neutral; it is laden with values. In fact, it's impossible to find language that is completely neutral or objective. We describe people we

fyi THE WHORF–SAPIR VIEW OF LANGUAGE

Studies by anthropologists reveal that language guides our perceptions. The language of the Hopi Indians makes no distinction between objects and actions, whereas English uses nouns and verbs, respectively. The English word *snow* is the only word we need to define frozen white precipitation that falls in winter. Arctic cultures, where snow is a major aspect of life, have a rich snow vocabulary, with words for powdery snow, icy snow, dry snow, wet snow, and so forth. The distinctions are important to designate snows that affect wildlife, travel conditions, and so forth (Whorf, 1956).

like with language that accents their good qualities and downplays their flaws ("my friend is self-confident"). Just the reverse is true of our language for people we don't like ("my enemy is arrogant"). Restaurants choose language that enhances the attractiveness of menu entries. A dish described as tender milk-fed veal sautèed in natural juices and topped with succulent chunks of lobster sounds more appetizing than one described as meat from a baby calf that was kept anemic to make it tender, slaughtered, cooked in blood, and topped with a crustacean that has been boiled to death.

Communication contains degrees of evaluation. We might describe people who speak their minds as *assertive, outspoken, courageous,* or *authoritarian.* Each word has a distinct connotation. The language we use also has ethical implications in terms of how it affects others. Most people with disabilities prefer not to be called *disabled* because that totalizes them in terms of a disability. The term *African American* emphasizes cultural heritage, whereas *Black* focuses on skin color. Designations for homosexuals are in transition. The term *homosexual* has negative connotations, and words such as *dyke* and *faggot* are even more negative. Some gay men and lesbians use the term *sexual orientation* to make the point that they didn't choose their sexual inclination. Others use the term *sexual preference* to show that their sexuality is a matter of choice, not genetics. Still others speak of *affectional preference* to signal that their commitment includes the entire realm of affection, not just sexual activity.

Loaded language is words that strongly slant perceptions and thus meanings. Loaded language encourages negative views of older citizens. Terms such as *geezer* and *old fogy* incline us to regard older people with contempt or pity. Alternatives such as *senior citizen* and *mature person* reflect more respectful attitudes.

Maynard

I'm as sensitive as the next guy, but I just can't keep up with what language offends what people anymore. When I was young, Negro *was an accepted term, then it was* black*, and now it's* African American. *Sometimes I forget and say* black *or even* Negro, *and I get accused of being racist. It used to be polite to say* girls, *but now that offends a lot of the women I work with. Just this year I heard that we aren't supposed to say* blind *anymore, and we're supposed to say* visually impaired. *I just can't keep up.*

Probably many of us sympathize with Maynard, who was 54 when he took a course with me. Keeping up with changes in language is difficult, and occa-

REAPPROPRIATING LANGUAGE

An interesting communication phenomenon is the reappropriation of language. This happens when a group reclaims terms others use to degrade it and treats those terms as positive self-descriptions. Reappropriation aims to remove the stigma from terms that others use pejoratively.

Some feminists and women musicians have reappropriated the term *girl* to define themselves and to resist the general connotations of childishness. One collective of punk rock female bands calls itself Riot Grrrls. Some gay men and lesbians have reappropriated the term *queer* and are using it as a positive statement about their identity.

Southern writer Reynolds Price developed cancer of the spine that left him paraplegic. He scoffs at terms such as *differently abled* and *physically challenged;* he refers to himself as a *cripple* and others who do not have disabilities as *temporarily able-bodied.*

fyi

NONDISCRIMINATION IN HOUSING

Whoops! Real estate ads may lead to lawsuits if they contain language that excludes certain groups. "Great view" excludes people with visual impairments, "walking distance to shops" offends people in wheelchairs, "master bedroom" suggests sexism, "family room" discriminates against childless couples and singles, and "newlyweds" excludes gay and lesbian couples who cannot be legally married.

In 1994 Pennsylvania's Association of Realtors, Newspaper Association, and Human Relations Commission issued a list of about seventy-five unacceptable words and phrases for real estate ads, including the following:

Bachelor pad	Couples	Mature
Children	Traditional	Senior citizens
Private	Newlyweds	Exclusive

sionally we will offend someone unintentionally. Nonetheless, we should try to learn what terms hurt or insult others and avoid using them. We also should tell others when they've referred to us in ways we dislike. As long as you speak assertively but not confrontationally, others are likely to respect your ideas.

Symbols Organize Experiences

Words organize our perceptions of events and experiences in our lives. As we learned in Chapter 2, the categories into which we place people influence how we interpret them and their communication. A criticism may be viewed as constructive if made by a friend but insulting if made by someone we classify as an enemy. The words don't change, but their meaning varies depending on the category into which we place the person speaking them. The organizational quality of symbols also allows us to think about abstract concepts such as justice, integrity, and good family life. We use broad concepts to transcend specific concrete activities and enter the world of conceptual thought and ideals. Because we think abstractly, we don't have to consider each object and experience individually. Instead, we can think in general terms.

Our capacity to abstract can also distort thinking. A primary way this occurs is stereotyping, which is thinking in broad generalizations about a whole class of people or experiences. Examples of stereotypes are "Management doesn't care about labor," "Teachers are smart," "Jocks are dumb," "Feminists hate men," "Religious people are good," and "Conflict is bad." Notice that stereotypes can be positive or negative generalizations.

Common to all stereotypes is classifying an experience or person into a category based on general knowledge of that category. When we use terms such as *Native Americans, lesbians, white males,* and *working class,* we may see only what members of each group have in common and not perceive differences among individuals in the group. What's lost is awareness of the uniqueness of the individual person. Clearly, we have to generalize. We simply cannot think about each and every thing in our lives as a specific instance. However, stereotypes can blind us to important differences among phenomena we lump together. Thus, we have an ethical responsibility to monitor stereotypes and to stay alert to differences among things we place in any category.

Symbols Allow Hypothetical Thought

Where do you hope to be 5 years from now? What is your fondest childhood memory? What would you do if you won the lottery next week? What would it be like to live in Africa? To answer these questions you must engage in **hypothetical thought,** which is thinking about experiences and ideas that are not part of your concrete daily reality. Because we can think hypothetically, we can plan, dream, remember, set goals, consider alternative courses of action, and imagine possibilities.

Hypothetical thought is possible because we are symbol users. Words give form to ideas so that we can hold them in our minds and reflect on them. We can contemplate things that have no real existence, and we can remember ourselves in the past and project ourselves into the future. Our ability to inhabit past, present, and future explains why we can set goals and work toward them, even though we do not realize the goal immediately (Dixson & Duck, 1993). For example, you've invested many hours in attending classes, studying, and writing papers because you have the idea of yourself as someone with a college degree. The degree is not real now, nor is the self that you will become once you have the degree. Yet the idea is sufficiently real to motivate you to work hard for many years. You can imagine yourself wearing academic regalia at your graduation, think of yourself as having a degree, and visualize yourself working in the career you plan to enter.

Hypothetical thought can enrich personal relationships by allowing intimates to remember shared moments. One of the strongest glues for intimacy is the ability to remember a history of shared experiences (Bellah, Madsen, Sullivan, Swindler, & Tipton, 1985; Wood, 1995). Because they can remember rough times they have weathered, intimates can often get through trials in the present. Language that symbolizes a shared future ("When we're rocking on the porch at 80") also fuels intimacy. We interact differently with people we don't expect to see again than with those who are continuing parts of our lives. Talking about future plans and dreams, another use of hypothetical thought, knits intimates together because it makes real the idea that more is yet to come (Acitelli, 1993; Duck, 1990).

Hypothetical thought also allows us to imagine being in places we have never visited. Television programs show us faraway countries and expose us to people with different values, traditions, and ways of living. When we listen to or see programs and films about other cultures, we can think about these cultures and imagine visiting them.

Duk-Kyong

Sometimes I get very discouraged that I do not yet know English perfectly and that there is much I still do not understand about customs in this country. It helps me to remember that

Julia T. Wood

■ *Couples communicate about past experiences and family events. How does this affect intimacy?*

THINKING HYPOTHETICALLY

Think about some aspect of yourself with which you aren't fully satisfied. Describe yourself in terms of that facet of your identity. Then describe that aspect of yourself as it was 5 years ago and how you want it to be 5 years from now.

Example

Today:	I interrupt people too often.
Five years ago:	I interrupted others continuously, and I didn't even realize I did it.
Five years from now:	I want to interrupt only occasionally and when appropriate.
Today:	I ______________________.
Five years ago:	I ______________________.
Five years from now:	I ______________________.

when I came here two years ago I did not speak English at all, and I knew nothing about how people act here. Seeing how much progress I have made helps me to not be discouraged with what I do not yet know.

Thinking hypothetically helps us improve who we are. We notice progress we have made when we can remember earlier versions of ourselves, and we motivate further self-growth when we envision additional improvements in ourselves. Using your ability to think hypothetically can enable you to chart a path of continuous growth.

■ *My niece Michelle just told me she was learning to read, a big development in her life. How might this self-reflection affect how Michelle thinks about herself?*

Symbols Allow Self-Reflection

Just as we use verbal symbols to think about times in the past and future, we use them to reflect on ourselves. We think about our existence and reflect on our actions. Mead (1934) considered self-reflection to be a foundation of human identity. He believed that our capacity to use symbols to think about ourselves was responsible for civilized society. According to Mead, the self has two aspects: the **I** and the **me.** The *I* is the spontaneous, creative self. The *I* acts impulsively in response to inner needs and desires, regardless of social norms. The *I* is the part of you that wants to send a really nasty email message to a chat room visitor whom you find offensive. The *me* is the socially conscious part of self that monitors and moderates the *I*'s impulses. The *me* reflects on the *I* from the social perspectives of others. The *me* is the part of you that says, "Hey, don't send that message or you'll get flamed." The *I* is impervious to social conventions, but the *me* is keenly aware of them. If your supervisor criticizes your work, your *I* may want to tell that boss off, but your *me* censors that impulse and reminds you that subordinates are not supposed to criticize their bosses.

Because we have both spontaneous and reflective parts of ourselves, we can think about who we want to be and set goals for becoming the self we desire. We can feel shame, pride, and regret for our actions—emotions that are possible because we self-reflect. We can control what we do now by casting ourselves forward to consider how we might feel about our actions later.

Tiffany

My mother-in-law thinks it's wrong that I go to school instead of being a full-time homemaker and mother. She constantly criticizes me for neglecting my children and home. So many times I have wanted to give her an earful and tell her to butt out of my family, but I stop myself by reminding myself that in the long-term it's important to me and my husband and the kids to maintain decent relations.

Self-reflection also empowers us to monitor ourselves. When we monitor ourselves, we (the *me*) notice and evaluate our (the *I*'s) impulses and may modify them based on our judgments (Phillips & Wood, 1983; Wood, 1992a). For instance, during a discussion with a co-worker you might say to yourself, "Gee, I haven't heard half of what this person said because I've been preoccupied with my own thoughts. I need to focus on what she's saying." Based on your monitoring, you might listen more carefully, give feedback, and ask questions to show interest. Effective public speakers monitor audiences. If members of the audience start looking restless or bored, speakers adapt by changing speaking pace or volume or by introducing a visual aid to add interest. When interacting with people from different cultures, we monitor by reminding ourselves they may not operate by the same values and communication rules that we do. Self-reflection allows us to monitor our communication and adjust it to be effective and ethical.

Self-reflection also allows us to manage the image we present to others. When talking with teachers and supervisors, you may consciously use language that represents you as respectful, attentive, and responsible. When interacting with parents, you may repress some language that surfaces in discussions with your friends. When communicating with someone you'd like to date, you may use language that is personal and conveys friendli-

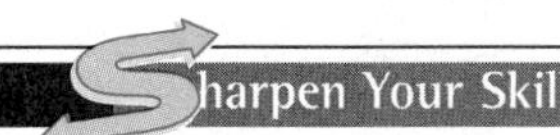

I–ME DIALOGUES

To see how your *I* and *me* work together, monitor your internal dialogues. These are conversations in your head as you consider different things you might say and do.

Monitor your *I–me* dialogues as you talk with a professor, a friend, and a romantic partner. What creative ideas and desires does your *I* initiate? What social controls does your *me* impose? What urges and whims occur to your *I*? What social norms does your *me* remind you of?

How do the *I* and *me* work together? Does one sometimes muffle the other? What would be lost if your *I* became silent? What would be missing if your *me* disappeared?

ness. We continuously use language to manage the images we project in particular situations and with specific people.

Symbols Define Relationships and Interaction

A sixth way in which symbols create meaning in our lives is by defining relationships and interaction. Our verbal communication conveys messages about how we perceive ourselves and others. "Mr. Buster" symbolizes a more formal relationship than "Phil." We also use verbal communication to regulate interaction. We signal we want to speak by saying, "Excuse me" or "Let me jump in here." We invite others to speak by saying, "Do you have an opinion about this?" or "I'd like to hear what you think about the issue."

You'll recall that in Chapter 1 we discussed two levels of meaning: content and relationship. Verbal communication, as well as nonverbal communication, conveys three dimensions of relationship-level meanings (Mehrabian, 1981).

Responsiveness One facet of relationship-level meaning is responsiveness. Through questions and statements of agreement or disagreement we show our interest in others' communication. When we give thoughtful feedback to a colleague, we show responsiveness. When we ask an interviewee to elaborate ideas, we demonstrate interest in him or her. Different social and cultural groups learn distinct rules for showing responsiveness. For instance, women generally display greater verbal responsiveness than men (Montgomery, 1988; Ueland, 1992), and Koreans tend to limit verbal responses.

Liking A second dimension of relationship-level meaning is liking. We communicate liking through verbal symbols when we say, "We missed you while you were away from work," "I care about you," "It's good to see you," and so forth. Conversely, we verbally communicate dislike by saying, "Bug off," "I don't have time right now," or "I don't want to see you anymore." In addition to these general rules shared in Western society, particular social groups instill more specific rules. Masculine socialization emphasizes emotional control and independence, so men are less likely than women to verbalize their feelings. Feminine socialization encourages many women to verbalize inner feelings.

Power The third aspect of relationship-level meaning is power. We use verbal communication to define

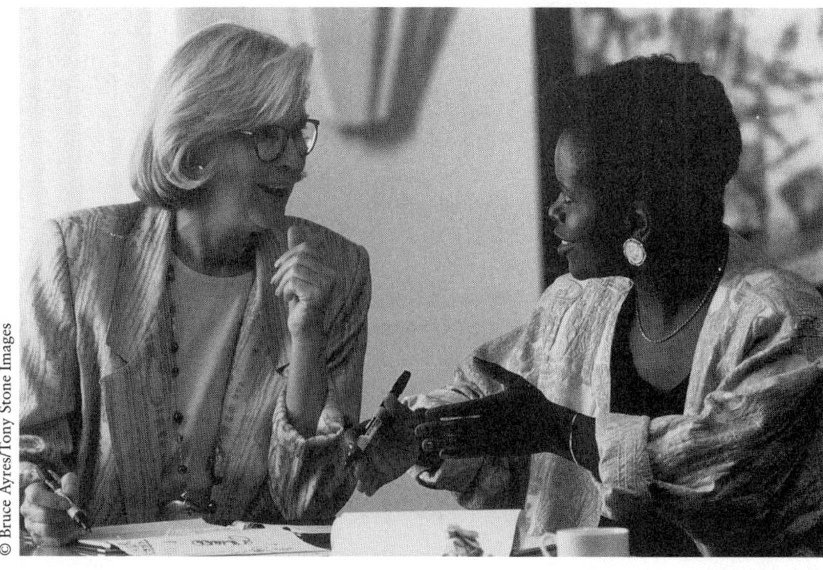

■ *What relationship-level communication are these two co-workers expressing?*

JAPANESE AND AMERICAN STYLES OF NEGOTIATION

Japanese Style	American Style
Understate initial position or state it vaguely.	Overstate initial position to seem strong.
Leak bottom line informally to move toward agreement.	Keep bottom line secret to preserve power.
Stress areas of agreement.	Attempt to win arguments.
Avoid contention.	Be adversarial.
Negotiate to avoid failure for either side.	Negotiate to win for their side.

Source: Weiss, 1987.

dominance and to negotiate for status and influence. Men typically exceed women in efforts to establish control over others. Research has shown that men are more likely than women to exert control verbally by dominating conversations, having the last word, interrupting, and correcting others (DeFrancisco, 1991). People in positions of power in organizations often express control with authoritative statements such as "That's how it's going to be" and "I've heard all I want to hear."

Summing up, we use language to define and evaluate phenomena, organize experiences, think hypothetically, self-reflect, and define relationships and interaction (Figure 4.3). Each ability helps us create meaning in our personal, professional, and social relationships.

Figure 4.3 Symbolic Abilities

1. **Symbols define phenomena.**
2. **Symbols evaluate phenomena.**
3. **Symbols allow us to organize experiences.**
4. **Symbols allow us to think hypothetically.**
5. **Symbols allow self-reflection.**
6. **Symbols define relationships and interactions.**

GUIDELINES FOR EFFECTIVE VERBAL COMMUNICATION

The five guidelines that follow will help you use verbal communication effectively.

Strive for Accuracy and Clarity

Because symbols are arbitrary, abstract, and ambiguous, the potential for misunderstanding always exists. In addition, individual and cultural differences foster varying interpretations of symbols. Although we can't completely eliminate misunderstandings, we can minimize them.

Be Conscious of Levels of Abstraction

We can reduce the likelihood of misunderstandings by being conscious of levels of abstraction. Much confusion results from language that is excessively abstract. For instance, a professor says, "Your papers should demonstrate a sophisticated conceptual grasp of material and its pragmatic implications." Would you know how to write a paper to satisfy the professor? Probably not, because the lan-

fyi

GENERAL SEMANTICS

General semantics is a theoretical approach to communication that was prominent in the early part of the twentieth century (Wood, 2001a). Alfred Korzybski was a Polish scientist, linguist, and philosopher who believed that many human difficulties arise from careless, imprecise language habits. In 1929 he founded the General Semantics Institute, which was incorporated in 1938.

Korzybski's training as a physical scientist taught him to appreciate precision in thought and language and to believe that careful, empirical observation is essential to clear thinking and informed beliefs and attitudes. Applying these basic principles to language, Korzybski (1933) developed general semantics, which provides guidelines for using language precisely and being careful and reflective in making observations and inferences. General semanticists formulated guidelines for communication that you are reading about in this book, including indexing language and recognizing levels of abstraction.

To learn more about general semantics and the communication principles it offers, visit the Web site at http://www.general-semantics.org/institute/.

guage is abstract and unclear. Here's a more concrete description: "Your papers should include definitions of the concepts and specific examples that show how they apply to your personal life." This second statement offers a clearer explanation of what the professor expects.

Abstract language is not always inadvisable. The goal is to use a level of abstraction that suits particular communication objectives and situations. Abstract words are appropriate when speakers and listeners have similar concrete knowledge about what is being discussed. For example, long-term friends can say, "Let's just hang out" and understand the activities implied by the abstract term *hang out*. More concrete language is useful when communicators don't have shared experiences and interpretations. For example, early in a friendship the suggestion to hang out would be more effective if it included specifics: "Let's hang out today—maybe watch the game and go out for pizza." Abstract language may also be useful when a communicator wants to create strategic ambiguity, so that meaning is *not* crystal clear. Politicians routinely use abstract language because it allows them to claim later that what they are saying is consistent with the strategically ambiguous statements made earlier.

Yet abstract language often contributes to misunderstandings. For example, online communication is easily misunderstood because it lacks many of the nonverbal cues that clarify meaning and it is often condensed to phrases and incomplete thoughts. Abstract language may also promote misunderstandings when people talk about changes they want in one another. For example, "I want you to show more initiative in your work" could mean that the person who is speaking wants the other person to work more hours, take on new projects, or seek less direction from supervisors. Vague abstractions promote misunderstanding if people don't share concrete referents for the abstract terms.

Qualify Language

Another strategy for increasing the clarity of communication is to qualify language. Two types of language require qualification. First, we should qualify generalizations so that we don't mislead ourselves or others into mistaking a general statement for an absolute one. "Politicians are crooked" is a false statement because it overgeneralizes. A more accurate statement would be, "A number of politicians have been shown to be dishonest." Qualifying reminds us of limitations on what we say.

We should also qualify language when describing and evaluating people. A **static evaluation** is an assessment that suggests that something is unchanging. Static evaluations are particularly troublesome when applied to people: "Ann is selfish," "Don is irresponsible," "Vy is rude." Whenever we use the word *is,* we suggest that something is fixed. In reality we aren't static but continuously changing. A person who is selfish at one time may be generous at other times. A person who is irresponsible on one occasion may be responsible in different situations.

Ken

Parents are the worst for static evaluations. When I first got my license 7 years ago, I had a fender bender and then got a speeding ticket. Since then I've had a perfect record, but you'd never know it from what they say. Dad's always calling me "hot rodder," and Mom goes through this safety spiel every time I get ready to drive somewhere. You'd think I was the same now as when I was 16.

Index Verbal Symbols

Indexing is a technique developed by early communication scholars to remind us that our evaluations apply only to specific times and circumstances (Korzybski, 1948). To index, we would say "Ann$_{\text{June 6, 1997}}$ acted

Sharpen Your Skill

QUALIFYING LANGUAGE

Study the qualified and unqualified statements listed here. In the three examples, the first statement is unqualified; the second is qualified.

Foreign cars are better than American ones.	Hondas and Mazdas generally require less maintenance than Fords and Chevys.
Science courses are harder than humanities courses.	Many humanities majors find natural science courses harder than humanities courses.
Television is violent.	Many commercial programs include a lot of violence.

Practice your skill in qualifying language by providing appropriate restrictions for the following unqualified assertions:

Teaching assistants aren't as good as professors.

Affirmative action gives jobs to unqualified people.

Men are more competitive than women.

Textbooks are boring.

selfishly," "$\text{Don}_{\text{on the task committee}}$ was irresponsible," and "$\text{Vy}_{\text{in college}}$ was rude." See how indexing ties description to a specific time and circumstance? Mental indexing reminds us that we and others are able to change in remarkable ways.

Own Your Feelings and Thoughts

We often use verbal language in ways that obscure our responsibility for how we feel and what we think. For instance, people say, "You made me mad" or "You hurt me," as if what they feel is caused by someone else. The language we use can attribute our responses to others' actions. "You're so demanding" really means that you feel pressured by what someone else wants or expects. Feeling pressured is your response. Even though others' behaviors can influence us, they seldom actually determine how we feel. Our feelings and thoughts result from how we interpret others' communication. Although how we interpret what others say may lead us to feel certain ways, it is *our* interpretations, not others' communication, that guide our responses. In certain contexts, such as abusive relationships, others may powerfully shape how we think and feel. Yet even in these extreme situations we need to remember that we, not others, are responsible for our feelings. We can disapprove of what others do without surrendering control of our thoughts, feelings, and actions. Telling others they make you feel some way is also likely to arouse defensiveness, which doesn't facilitate healthy personal or professional relationships.

Effective communicators take responsibility for themselves by using language that owns their thoughts and feelings. They claim their feelings and do not blame others for what happens in themselves. To take responsibility for your feelings, rely on *I* language rather than *you* language. Figure 4.4 gives examples of *I* and *you* language.

There are two differences between *I* and *you* language. First, *I* statements own responsibility, whereas *you* statements project it onto another person. Second, *I* statements offer considerably more description than *you* statements. *You* statements tend to be accusations that are abstract and that don't identify specific behaviors or feelings. This is one reason that *you* language is ineffective in promoting change. *I* statements, on the other hand, provide concrete descriptions of behaviors without holding the other person responsible for how we feel.

Some people feel awkward when they first start using *I* language. This is natural because most of us have learned to rely on *you* language. With commitment and practice, however, you can learn to communicate with *I* language. Once you feel comfortable using it, you will find *I* language has many advantages. It is less likely than *you* language to make others defensive, so *I* language opens the doors for dialogue. *I* language

Figure 4.4 ***I* and *You* Language**

***You* Language**	***I* Language**
You hurt me	I feel hurt when you ignore what I say.
You make me feel small	I feel small when you tell me that I'm selfish
You're really domineering	When you shout I feel dominated
You humiliated me	I felt humiliated when you mentioned my problems in front of your friends.

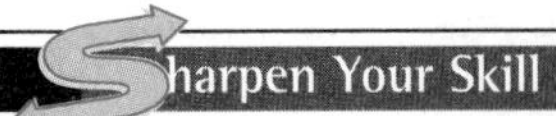

USING *I* LANGUAGE

For the next three days, whenever you use *you* language, try to rephrase what you said or thought in *I* language. How does this change how you think and feel about what's happening? How does using *I* language affect interaction with others? Are others less defensive when you own your feelings and describe—but don't evaluate—their behaviors or motives? Does *I* language facilitate constructive changes?

Now that you're tuned into *I* and *you* language, monitor how you feel when others use *you* language about you. When a friend or romantic partner says, "You make me feel . . .," do you feel defensive or guilty? Try teaching others to use *I* language so your relationships can be more honest and open.

is also more honest. We deceive ourselves when we say, "You make me feel . . ." because others don't control how we feel. Finally, *I* language is more empowering than *you* language. When we say, "You did this" or "You made me feel that," we give control of our emotions to others. This reduces our personal power and by extension our motivation to change what is happening. Using *I* language allows you to own your feelings while also explaining to others how you interpret their behaviors.

Summary

In this chapter we've explored the basic skill of engaging in verbal communication. Verbal symbols shape who we are, what we do, and what our experiences mean. Because they are arbitrary, ambiguous, and abstract, symbols do not have objective concrete meanings. Instead, their significance reflects our life experiences, as well as the views of our culture and social groups to which we belong.

To create meaning with language and to interact with others, we follow rules of communication and we punctuate interaction. Regulative rules, as we have seen, specify when, where, with whom, and how we communicate verbally. In addition, we follow constitutive rules that define the meaning of specific forms of verbal communication within particular social groups. A final aspect of creating the meaning of communication is punctuating beginnings and endings of interactions.

The ability to use verbal language allows humans to create meaning in their lives. By defining, evaluating, and classifying phenomena, language allows us to order our experiences and feelings. In addition, we use verbal symbols to think hypothetically, self-reflect, and define relationships and interactions. Our ability to use symbols is a key foundation of communication and human life. We increase the effectiveness of our verbal communication when we strive for accuracy and clarity in language, own our thoughts and feelings, and qualify language appropriately. In Chapter 5 we'll see how nonverbal communication complements and extends verbal communication by allowing us to create meaning.

FOR FURTHER REFLECTION AND DISCUSSION

1. Visit the Institute of General Semantics Web site at http://www.general-semantics.org/institute.
2. To appreciate the importance of symbolic capacities, imagine the following: living only in the present without memories or hopes and plans; thinking only in terms of literal reality, not what might be; and having no broad classifications to organize experience. With others in the class, discuss how your life would be different without the symbolic abilities discussed in this chapter.
3. In the chapter we learned that language names experiences and that language is continuously evolving. For instance, terms such as *date rape* and *cyberspace* are recent additions to our language. Can you think of experiences, feelings, or other phenomena for which we don't yet have names? What might we call a lesbian or gay couple with children: Are both parents mommies in lesbian couples and daddies in gay ones? What is a good term for describing someone with whom you have a serious romance? *Boyfriend* and *girlfriend* no longer work for many people. Do you prefer *significant other, romantic partner, special friend,* or *lover?*
4. Visit chat rooms and online discussion forums and notice the screen names that people use. How do the names people create for themselves shape perceptions of their identities? What screen names do you use? Why did you choose these?
5. Pay attention to *I* and *you* language in your communication and that of others. What happens when you change a *you* statement to an *I* statement? Does it change how you feel about what is happening?

KEY TERMS

Verbal communication
Nonverbal communication
Arbitrary
Ambiguous
Abstract
Communication rules
Regulative rules
Constitutive rules
Punctuation
Totalizing
Loaded language
Hypothetical thought
I
Me
Static evaluation
Indexing

Engaging in Nonverbal Communication

LEARNING OBJECTIVES

To understand

1. What nonverbal communication is
2. Whether nonverbal communication is learned or instinctual
3. To what extent we can read others' nonverbal behavior
4. How nonverbal communication regulates interaction
5. How nonverbal communication expresses the balance of power between people
6. How nonverbal communication expresses cultural values
7. What silence means

Ben Thompson had traveled to Japan to negotiate a joint business venture with Haru Watanabe. They seemed to see the mutual benefit of the project, yet Thompson felt something was wrong in their negotiations. Every time they talked, Watanabe seemed uneasy and refused to hold eye contact. Thompson wondered whether Watanabe was trying to hide something. Meanwhile, Watanabe wondered why Thompson was so rude if he wanted them to work together.

Maria noticed a nice-looking guy who was studying two tables away in the library. When he looked up at her, she lowered her eyes. After a moment she looked back at him just for a second. A few minutes later he came over, sat down beside her, and introduced himself.

Liz Fitzgerald gave a final glance to be sure the dining room table was just right for dinner: the placemats and blue linen napkins were out, and the silver and glasses sparkled; the bowl of flowers in the middle of the table added color; and the serving dishes were warmed and ready to be filled with roast beef, buttered new potatoes, and rice pilaf. Liz whisked balsamic vinegar and olive oil together, added a trace of basil, and sprinkled it on the spinach salad just before calling the family to dinner.

Across town, Benita Bradsher was also preparing dinner for her family. She put a big spoon in the pot of mashed potatoes and transferred it from the stove to the kitchen table. Next she piled paper napkins, knives, spoons, and forks in the middle of the table. She took the ground beef casserole from the oven, put it on a potholder on the table, and called her family to dinner.

Many of us grew up hearing that actions speak louder than words. The wisdom of this axiom is that nonverbal communication can be as powerful as or more powerful than words. Facial expressions can express love, suspicion, interest, anger, and hatred. Body postures can convey relaxation, nervousness, boredom, and power. Physical objects can symbolize professional identity (stethoscope, briefcase), personal commitments (wedding band, school sweatshirt), and lifestyle (comfortable furniture casually arranged versus stiff furniture in formal rooms). In this chapter we explore the fascinating realm of nonverbal interaction. We will identify principles of nonverbal communication and then discuss types of nonverbal behavior and guidelines for nonverbal effectiveness.

The examples that opened this chapter illustrate the power of nonverbal communication. In the first case, Thompson and Watanabe have difficulty because of different nonverbal communication norms in Japan and the United States. Ben Thompson has learned that eye contact is a sign of honesty and respect, so he looks directly at Haru Watanabe when they talk. In Watanabe's culture, however, direct eye contact is considered rude and intrusive, so he doesn't meet Thompson's gaze and feels uncomfortable when Thompson looks directly at him.

In the library we see a clear example of gendered patterns of nonverbal communication. Maria follows feminine communication norms by indirectly signaling her interest and by waiting for the man to initiate contact. He in turn enacts the rules of masculine communication culture by gazing directly at her and moving to her table.

In the final example, nonverbal communication reflects differences in socioeconomic level. Whereas Liz Fitzgerald sets her table with cloth napkins, placemats, silver, crystal, and a vase of flowers, Benita Bradsher sets her table with pans off the stove and a casual pile of utensils and paper napkins that people can take. What each woman serves and how she sets her table reflect the teachings of social groups to which she belongs and the time she has to prepare a meal.

Gender, ethnicity, sexual orientation, socioeconomic level (or status), and membership in social groups are aspects of our identities that we communicate day in and out. Recognizing this, Candice West and Don Zimmerman (1987) note that we "do gender" all the time by behaving in ways that symbolize femininity or masculinity according to our culture's views. We also "do" race, class, and sexual orientation by nonverbally symbolizing those facets of identity. Nonverbal communication, like its verbal cousin, allows us to establish identity, express thoughts and feelings, reflect on ourselves, define relationships, and create climates. Like words, nonverbal communication powerfully shapes meaning in our lives.

■ *How do these men's nonverbal behaviors reflect their distinct cultural backgrounds?*

PRINCIPLES OF NONVERBAL COMMUNICATION

Nonverbal behavior is a major dimension of human communication. It includes all aspects of communication other than words. In addition to gestures and body language, nonverbal communication includes *how* we utter words (inflection, volume), features of environments that affect meaning (temperature, lighting), and objects that affect personal images and interaction patterns (dress, jewelry, furniture). The nonverbal system accounts for 65 to 93 percent of the total meaning of communication (Birdwhistell, 1970; Mehrabian, 1981). This suggests that nonverbal behaviors make up more of our overall communication than verbal ones. We'll consider five principles of nonverbal communication.

Nonverbal Communication Can Be Ambiguous

Like verbal communication, nonverbal behavior can be ambiguous. We can never be sure that others understand the meanings we intend to express with our nonverbal behavior. Conversely, we can't know whether they read meanings into our behaviors that we do not intend. The ambiguity of nonverbal communication also arises because meanings vary over time. Spreading apart the first two fingers meant victory during the world wars and came to stand for peace during the 1960s. Both victory and peace are arbitrary meanings for a particular nonverbal behavior.

Nonverbal behaviors also reflect and perpetuate distinct organizational identities: bankers, attorneys, and many other professionals are expected to wear business suits or dresses, whereas companies such as Apple encourage employees to wear jeans and other informal attire. Each way of dressing reflects a particular organizational ethos. In formal organizations employees often work behind closed doors in private offices and do not enter another's office unless they have business to conduct. In more informal organizations, employees may work in common space or in offices with open doors, and casual visiting is a normal part of daily interaction.

Like verbal communication, nonverbal communication is learned and guided by rules. For example, we understand that people take turns speaking and that we should whisper in libraries. We know that we are supposed to raise our hands if we want to ask a question during a lecture but don't need to raise our hands to speak when interacting with friends. We dress differently for religious services, classes, dates, and job interviews. Insignia that nonverbally communicate rank define people in the military, and salutes are the standard way to acknowledge other military people.

Nonverbal Behavior Can Interact with Verbal Communication

Communication researchers have identified five ways in which nonverbal behaviors interact with verbal communication (Malandro & Barker, 1983). First, nonverbal behaviors may repeat verbal messages. For example, you might say "yes" while nodding your head. In making a public presentation, a speaker might hold up one, two, and three fingers to

■ *To what extent does Jesse Jackson's effectiveness as a speaker depend on his strong gestures and facial expressions?*

signal to listeners movement from the first to the second to the third point of a speech. Second, nonverbal behaviors may highlight verbal communication, as when you use inflection to emphasize certain words: "This is the *most serious* consequence of the policy I'm arguing against."

Third, we use nonverbal behavior to complement, or add to, words. When you see a friend, you might say, "I'm glad to see you" and underline the verbal message with a smile. When joking in an email message, you might add the emoticon :). Speakers often emphasize verbal statements with forceful gestures and increases in volume and inflection, and capital or boldfaced letters are used to symbolize the same emphasis in online communication. Fourth, nonverbal behaviors may contradict verbal messages, as when a group member says, "Nothing's wrong" in a hostile tone of voice. Finally, we sometimes substitute nonverbal behaviors for verbal ones. For instance, you might roll your eyes to show that you disapprove of something. In all these ways nonverbal behaviors augment or replace verbal communication.

Nonverbal Communication Can Regulate Interaction

You generally know when someone else is finished speaking, when a professor welcomes discussion from students, and when someone expects you to speak. Nonverbal cues, more than verbal ones, tell us when to speak and keep silent (Malandro & Barker, 1983). We signal that we don't want to be interrupted by averting our eyes or by increasing our speaking volume and rate. When we're finished talking, we look at others to signal, "Okay, now someone else can speak." Most Westerners invite specific people to speak by looking directly at them (Wiemann & Harrison, 1983), yet eye contact is used less to regulate interaction in many Asian cultures. Speakers step back from a podium to signal that they are finished. Although we're usually unaware of how nonverbal actions regulate interaction, we rely on them to know when to speak and when to remain silent.

Nonverbal Communication Can Establish Relationship-Level Meanings

You'll recall that the relationship level of meaning defines individuals' identities and relationships between people. Nonverbal communication can be powerful in expressing relationship-level meanings (Keeley & Hart, 1994). In fact, some communication scholars call nonverbal communication the relationship language because it so often expresses how people feel about one another (Burgoon, Buller, Hale, & de Turck, 1984; Sallinen-Kuparinen, 1992).

We use nonverbal communication to convey three dimensions of relationship-level meanings that we discussed in Chapter 4: responsiveness, liking, and power. Yet how people communicate responsiveness, liking and disliking, and power depends on the rules of their cultures.

Responsiveness We use eye contact, inflections, facial expressions, and body posture to show interest in others, as Maria did in one of the examples that opened this chapter. In formal presentations and

Hagar reprinted with special permission of King Features Syndicate

casual conversations, we signal interest by holding eye contact and assuming an attentive posture. As the example with Haru Watanabe and Ben Thompson reveals, however, all cultures do not interpret eye contact in the same way. To express disinterest, Westerners tend to avoid or decrease visual contact and adopt a passive body position or turn away from another person. Members of Asian cultures are less likely to overtly express disinterest. Also, harmony in people's postures and facial expressions may reflect how comfortable they are with each other (Berg, 1987; Capella, 1991). In a cohesive team, many nonverbal behaviors typically signal that members are responsive to one another. In less cohesive groups, nonverbal behavior shows less responsiveness. Happy couples sit closer to one another and engage in more eye contact than unhappy couples (Miller & Parks, 1982; Noller, 1986, 1987). Similarly, in work settings people who like one another often sit together and exchange eye contact.

Maryam

Americans do more than one thing at a time. In Nepal, when we talk with someone, we are with that person. We do not also write on paper or have television on. We talk with the person. It is hard for me to accept the custom of giving only some attention to each other in conversation.

Liking Nonverbal behaviors are keen indicators of whether we feel positive or negative about others. Smiles and friendly touching among Westerners usually are signs of positive feelings, whereas frowns and belligerent postures express antagonism (Keeley & Hart, 1994). Political candidates shake hands, slap backs, and otherwise touch people whose votes they want. These are general rules of Western society; particular social groups instill more specific rules. For example, women generally sit closer together and engage in more eye contact and more friendly touching than men (Montgomery, 1988; Reis, Senchak, & Solomon, 1985).

Ellen

Secretaries are the best decoders. They can read their bosses' moods in a heartbeat. I am a secretary, part time now that I'm taking courses, and I can tell exactly what my boss is thinking. Sometimes I know what he feels or will do before he does. I have to know when he can be interrupted, when he feels generous, and when not to cross his path.

Power We use nonverbal behaviors to assert dominance and to negotiate status (Henley, 1977). Compared to women, men assume more space and use greater volume and more forceful gestures to assert their ideas (Hall, 1987; Major, Schmidlin, & Williams, 1990). Men are also more likely to move into others' space, as the man in the library moved to Maria's table in one of the examples that opened this chapter. In addition, men tend to use gestures and touch to exert control (Henley, 1977; Leathers, 1986). Powerful people such as bosses touch those with less power such as secretaries more often than vice versa (Spain, 1992).

Ramona

In my home my father sits at the head of the table, and he has his chair in the family and his workroom. My mother does not have her chair, and she has no room of her own, either. This accurately reflects the power dynamics between them.

As Ramona observes, space also expresses power relations. The amount of space people have often directly reflects their power. The connection between power and space is evident in the fact that CEOs usually have large, spacious offices, entry-level and midlevel professionals have smaller offices, and secretaries often have minuscule workstations, even though secretaries often store and manage more material than executives. A widely understood regulative communication rule specifies that people with status or power have the right to enter the space of people with less power, but the converse is not true. Space may reflect power differences among family members. Adults usually have more space than children, and men, like Ramona's father, are more likely than women to have their own rooms and sit at heads of tables.

Silence, a powerful form of nonverbal communication, can also be a means to exert control. We sometimes use silence to stifle others' conversation in meetings. Silence accompanied by a glare is doubly powerful in conveying disapproval. Interviewers sometimes use silence to let interviewees know that they are not satisfied with answers given and to prompt interviewees to elaborate. In a number of Native American cultures and some Asian cultures, silence signals mindful attentiveness.

Nonverbal Communication Reflects Cultural Values

Like verbal communication, nonverbal patterns reflect rules of specific cultures. This implies that most nonverbal communication isn't instinctual but is learned in the process of socialization. For instance, dress considered appropriate for women varies across cultures, with some women in some countries wearing miniskirts, whereas some women in other countries wear veils. Cultures vary in the interpretations attached to many nonverbal behaviors, including eye contact, comfortable distance between people, touching, silence, and use of time.

Have you ever seen the bumper sticker that says "If you can read this, you're too close"? That slogan proclaims North Americans' fierce territoriality. We want our private spaces and we resent, and sometimes fight, anyone who trespasses on what we consider our turf. We want to have private homes, and many people want large lots to increase the distance between them and others. In more collectivist cultures people tend to be less territorial. For instance, Brazilians routinely stand close to one another in shops, buses, and elevators, and when they bump into each other, they don't apologize or draw back, as U.S. citizens do.

Western culture prizes time, and that is evident in the presence of clocks in homes and public spaces and in the nearly universal watches, which are not worn by people in many other cultures. Westerners' time-consciousness is also reflected in the many technological devices that are now part of many people's daily attire. We carry pagers, have cell phones in our cars, and have laptop computers or palm computers that allow us to maintain nearly instant contact with others. Orientations toward time are less rigid in many cultures, including Haiti, Jamaica, and Mexico.

Norms for touching also reflect cultural values. In one study Americans, who are somewhat reserved, were observed engaging in an average of only two touches an hour. The emotionally restrained British averaged no touches per hour. Parisians, long known for emotional expressiveness, touched 110 times per hour. Puerto Ricans touched most, averaging 180 touches an hour (Knapp, 1972).

Yumiko

I try to teach my daughter to follow the customs of my native Japan, but she is learning to be American. I scold her for talking loud and speaking when she has not been addressed, but she tells me

■ *These Pakistani women wear the veils that are traditional for women in their culture. Do veils express modesty or repression of women? Do they reflect individual or cultural values, or both?*

all the other kids talk loud and talk when they wish. I tell her it is not polite to look directly at others, but she say everyone looks at others here. She communicates as an American, not a Japanese.

Patterns of eye contact also reflect cultural values. U.S. society values frankness and assertion, so meeting another's eyes is considered appropriate and a demonstration of personal honesty. Yet in many Asian and northern European countries, direct eye contact is considered abrasive and disrespectful (Hall, 1969). In Brazil, eye contact is often so intense that people from the United States consider it staring, which they find rude.

The five principles of nonverbal communication we have discussed provide a foundation for exploring specific kinds of nonverbal communication.

Sucheng

In United States each person has so much room. Every individual has separate room to sleep and sometimes another separate room to work. Also, I see that each family here lives in a separate house. People have much less space in China. Families live together, with sons bringing their families into parents' home and all sharing the same space. At first when I came here, it felt strange to have so much space, but now I sometimes feel very crowded when I go home.

TYPES OF NONVERBAL BEHAVIORS

Because so much of our interaction is nonverbal, this symbol system includes many kinds of communication. In this section we will consider nine forms of nonverbal behavior, noticing how we use each to create and interpret meanings:

- Kinesics (face and body motion)
- Haptics (touch)
- Physical appearance
- Artifacts (personal objects)
- Proxemics (personal space)
- Environmental factors
- Chronemics (perception and use of time)
- Paralanguage (vocal qualities)
- Silence

Kinesics

Kinesics is a technical term that refers to body position and body motions, including those of the face. Our bodies communicate a great deal about how we see ourselves. A speaker who stands erectly and appears confident announces self-assurance, whereas someone who slouches and shuffles may seem to say, "I'm not very sure of myself." We also communicate moods with body posture and motion. For example, someone who is walking quickly with a resolute facial

FREEDOM OF (NONVERBAL) SPEECH

Nonverbal communication has been costly for some sports stars. When German midfielder Stefan Effenberg made an obscene gesture to fans during a world cup match in the summer of 1994, his coach promptly kicked him off the squad. When Miami Dolphins linebacker Bryan Cox flipped an obscene gesture in Buffalo, the National Football League slapped him with a $10,000 fine that was later reduced to $3,000.

Private athletic teams can make their own rules, but the First Amendment protects most nonverbal behavior by everyone else. Thus, attorney Louis Sirkin successfully defended a motorist who insulted a traffic officer with an obscene hand gesture.

Source: "Be Civil," 1994, p. A1.

expression appears more determined than someone who saunters along with an unfocused gaze. We sit rigidly when we are nervous and adopt a relaxed posture when we feel at ease. Audiences show interest by alert body posture.

Body postures and gestures may signal whether we are open to interaction. Speakers who stay behind podiums and read notes are often perceived as less open than speakers who interact more actively with audiences. Someone who sits with arms crossed and looks downward seems to say, "Don't bother me." That's also a nonverbal strategy students sometimes use to dissuade teachers from calling on them in class. To signal that we'd like to interact, we look at others and sometimes smile. We also use gestures to express how we feel about others. We use one hand gesture to say "okay" and a different one to communicate contempt. During the 1968 Olympics in Mexico City, two U.S. track medalists, Tommie Smith and John Carlos, raised black gloved fists on the victory stand, a gesture of black unity at the height of the civil rights movement. Their action, which was highly controversial, enraged the head of the International Olympic Committee, which threatened to expel the whole U.S. team if Smith and Carlos were not punished. They were suspended from the U.S. team and given 48 hours to leave the Olympic grounds.

Our faces are intricate messengers. The face alone is capable of more than a thousand distinct expressions that result from variations in tilt of head and movements of eyebrows, eyes, and mouth (Eckman, Friesen, & Ellsworth, 1971). Our eyes can shoot daggers of anger, issue challenges, express skepticism, or radiate love. The face is particularly powerful in conveying liking and responsiveness (Keeley & Hart, 1994; Patterson, 1992). Many speakers smile to suggest that they are open and friendly.

How we position ourselves relative to others may express our feelings toward them. On work teams, friends and allies often sit together and competitors typically maintain distance. Dissatisfied

fyi

CLEVER HANS

In the early 1900s, Herr von Osten trained his horse Hans to count by tapping his front foot. Hans learned quickly and was soon able to multiply, add, divide, subtract, and solve complex math problems. He could count the number of people in a room or the number of people wearing eyeglasses. Herr von Osten took Hans on a promotional tour. At shows he would ask Hans to add 5 and 8, divide 100 by 10, and do other computations. In every case Hans performed flawlessly, leading others to call him "Clever Hans." But skeptics wanted to test Hans's mathematical abilities.

The first test involved computing numbers that were stated on stage by people other than von Osten. Using his foot, Hans pounded out the correct answers. However, he didn't fare so well on the second test, in which one person whispered a number into Hans's left ear and a different person whispered a number into his right ear. Hans was told to add the two numbers and pound out the sum, an answer not known by anyone present. Hans couldn't solve the problem. On further investigation it was deduced that Hans could solve problems only if someone he could see knew the answer. When Hans was given numbers and asked to compute them, viewers leaned forward and tensed their bodies as Hans began tapping his hoof. When Hans tapped the correct number, onlookers relaxed their body postures and nodded their heads, which was Hans's signal to stop tapping. Hans was clever not because he could calculate but because he could read nonverbal communication (Sebeok & Rosenthal, 1981).

couples keep their distance and exchange few smiles and eye gazes (Miller & Parks, 1982). Smiles and warm gazes signal that we like others and are happy being around them (Walker & Trimboli, 1989).

Poets call the eyes the mirrors of the soul for good reason. Our eyes communicate important and complex messages about how we feel. If you watch infants, you'll notice that they focus on others' eyes. Babies often become terrified if they can't see their mothers' eyes, but they aren't bothered when other parts of their mothers' faces are hidden (Spitz, 1965). As adults we often look at eyes to judge emotions, honesty, interest, and self-confidence. This explains why strong eye contact tends to heighten the credibility of public speakers in Western societies. Yet eye contact is not universally regarded as positive. Among traditional Hasidic Jews, for example, boys are taught not to look into women's eyes.

Haptics

Haptics is nonverbal communication involving physical touch. Touch is the first of our five senses to develop (Leathers, 1986), and many communication scholars believe that touching and being touched are essential to healthy life. Research reveals that babies in dysfunctional families are touched less often and less affectionately than babies in healthy families. In disturbed families parents sometimes push children away and handle them harshly, nonverbally signaling rejection (Birdwhistell, 1970).

Touching also communicates power and status. People with high status touch others and invade others' spaces more than people with less status (Henley, 1977). Gendered patterns of touch reflect cultural views of women as more touchable than men. Parents touch sons less often and more roughly than they touch daughters (Condry, Condry, & Pogatshnik, 1983). These patterns early in life teach the sexes different rules for using touch and responding to the touches of others. As adults women tend to engage in touch to show liking and intimacy (Montgomery, 1988), and they may feel uneasy objecting to unwanted touch (Le Poire, Burgoon, & Parrott, 1992).

Emily

One of the other servers at the restaurant where I work bothers me. He doesn't really do anything wrong, I guess, but he touches my hand or brushes against me when he doesn't have to. I wish he would stop, but I don't want to say anything that might make him uncomfortable.

Physical Appearance

Western culture places an extremely high value on **physical appearance** and on specific aspects of appearance. We first notice obvious physical qualities such as sex, skin color, and size. Based on physical qualities, we may make inferences about others' personalities. In one study, researchers found that people associated plump bodies with laziness and weakness. The researchers found that subjects thought thin, angular physiques reflect youthful, hard-driven, stubborn personalities and that athletic body types reflect strong, adventurous, self-reliant personalities (Wells & Siegel, 1961). Although these associations may have no factual basis, they can affect decisions about hiring, placement, and promotion.

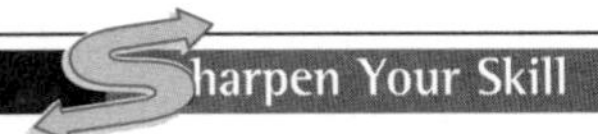

COMMUNICATING CLOSENESS

What do your nonverbal behaviors say about how you feel toward others? To find out, interact with someone you like and feel comfortable with, a stranger, and someone you dislike. How close do you sit or stand to each of the three people? How does your posture differ? What facial expressions and eye contact do you use with each person?

Cultures prescribe ideals for physical form. Western cultural ideals today emphasize thinness in women and muscularity and height in men (Wolf, 1991). This general cultural standard is qualified by ethnic identity. Traditional African societies perceive full-figured bodies as symbols of health, prosperity, and wealth, all of which are desirable (Villarosa, 1994). African Americans who embrace this value accept or prefer women who weigh more than the ideal for European American women (Thomas, 1989; Root, 1990).

Class membership modifies ethnic views about weight. According to a recent survey, African American women who are affluent or poor tend to have strong cultural identities that allow them to resist Caucasian preoccupations with thinness. On the other hand, middle-income African American women who are upwardly mobile may deemphasize their ethnic identities, and they are more susceptible to anxiety about weight and to eating disorders (Villarosa, 1994).

Cass

I've been dieting since I was in grammar school. I'm 5'5" and weigh 102 pounds, but I want to weigh less. I look at the models in magazines and the women in films, and they are so much slimmer than I am. I have to watch everything I eat and exercise all the time, and I'm still too fat.

Physical appearance includes both physiological characteristics, such as eye color and height, and ways that we manage our physical appearance, such as dieting, dyeing hair, having plastic surgery, wearing colored contact lenses, selecting clothes to covey particular images, and applying make-up. We can manage many facets of the physical impression we create, and Westerners seem increasingly interested in doing so.

Artifacts

Artifacts are personal objects we use to announce our identities and personalize our environments. Clothing is one of the most common forms of artifactual communication. Although clothing has become more unisex in recent years, once you venture beyond the campus context, gendered styles are evident. Many women wear makeup, dresses that may have lace or other softening touches, high-heeled shoes, jewelry, and hose. Typically, men wear less jewelry, and their clothes and shoes are functional. Men's clothing is looser and less binding, and it includes pockets for wallets, change, keys, and so forth. In contrast, women's clothing tends to be tailored and often doesn't include pockets, so women need purses to hold personal items. In recent years many stores have begun to carry a greater range of styles in clothing and jewelry, so people can acquire artifacts that express their cultural heritage. Indians may wear

fyi A FIGURE THAT DOESN'T ADD UP

Barbie, the so-called dream girl, has a figure that no human could have. Translating her to real-life size, Barbie measures 40"–18"–32" (Quindlen, 1994). G.I. Joe is no more realistic. Since he was introduced in 1964, each new model has been more muscular, so that he now has biceps and abs that no normal man could develop (Angier, 1999).

Although real people may not be able to match Barbie or G.I. Joe, they certainly are tinkering a good bit with their genetic endowments. More than 825,000 facial surgeries are performed every year, mostly on people with annual incomes of less than $50,000 (Sharlet, 1999). Both women and men have surgery to remake noses, lift faces, remove lines, and enlarge and reduce various parts of the body (Bordo, 1999; Gilman, 1999a, 1999b; Haiken, 1997; Mirzoeff, 1998; Peiss, 1998).

saris, Native Americans may wear jewelry with tribal symbols, and African Americans may wear clothes and jewelry of traditional African design.

Artifacts also express gender prescriptions. Many hospitals still use blue and pink blankets for boys and girls. In families, sons may get toys that encourage rough play (trains) and competitiveness (baseballs, toy weapons), whereas daughters get toys that cultivate nurturing (dolls) and attention to appearance (makeup kits, frilly clothes) (Caldera, Huston, & O'Brien, 1989; Lytton & Romney, 1991).

Artifacts announce professional identity. Nurses and doctors wear white and often drape stethoscopes around their necks; executives carry briefcases, whereas students more often tote backpacks. White-collar professionals tend to wear tailored outfits and dress shoes, whereas blue-collar workers often dress in jeans or uniforms and boots. The military requires uniforms that define individuals as members of the group. In addition, stripes, medals, and insignia signify rank and accomplishments.

We also use artifacts to define settings and personal territories. When the president speaks, the setting usually is decked with symbols of national identity and pride such as the flag. At annual meetings of companies, the chair usually speaks from a podium that bears the company logo. In much the same manner, we claim our private spaces by filling them with objects that matter to us and that reflect our experiences and values. Lovers of art adorn their homes and offices with paintings and sculptures that reflect their interests. Religious families often express their commitments by displaying pictures of holy scenes and the Bible, Koran, or another sacred text. Professionals may decorate their offices with expensive furniture and framed awards to announce their status or with pictures of family to remind them of people they cherish. Web sites, too, are defined by artifacts such as photos, animations, and colors that express the creators' personalities and interests.

Jagat Man Lama

To make my home here I had to put out my statue of Buddha and make the small shrine that each of us keeps in our home in my country. Seeing it is important for me to feel in comfort. I think that when I really felt like where I now live is home is when the smell of incense became part of the apartment so that I smell it faintly when I open the door each day. That makes me feel at home.

© Stephen Huyler

■ *These women in India repaint the entries to their homes each day. These "painted prayers" ask Lakshmi, goddess of abundance and fertility, to bless their homes.*

CULTURAL RULES OF GIFT GIVING

Giving gifts can lead to misunderstandings when the giver and recipient are from different cultures. A Chinese person might not appreciate a gift of a clock because clocks symbolize death in China. Giving a gift to an Arab person on first meeting would be interpreted as a bribe. Bringing flowers to a dinner hosted by a person from Kenya would cause confusion because in Kenya flowers express sympathy for a loss. In Switzerland, giving red roses is interpreted as a signal of romantic interest. Also, the Swiss consider even numbers of flowers bad luck, so never give a dozen.

Sources: Axtell, 1990a, 1990b.

In her 1990 book *Composing a Life,* Mary Catherine Bateson comments that we turn houses into homes by filling them with objects that matter to us. We use mugs given to us by special people, nurture plants to enliven indoor spaces, wear t-shirts from places we've visited, and hang posters and pictures that announce our artistic preferences.

Proxemics and Personal Space

Proxemics refers to space and how we use it (Hall, 1968). Every culture has norms for using space and for how close people should be to one another. In the United States we interact with social acquaintances from a distance of 4 to 12 feet but are comfortable with 18 inches or less between us and friends or romantic partners (Hall, 1968).

Space also announces status, with greater space being assumed by those with higher status. Substantial research shows that women and minorities generally have less space than European American men in the United States (Spain, 1992). The prerogative to invade someone else's personal space is also linked to power, with those having greater power being most likely to trespass into others' territory (Henley, 1977). Reflecting gendered socialization, many men respond aggressively when their space is invaded, whereas women typically yield their space (Fisher & Byrne, 1975).

How people arrange space reflects how close they are and whether they want interaction. Rigidly organized businesses may have private offices with closed doors and little common space. Couples who are highly interdependent tend to have more common space and less individual space in their homes than do couples who are more independent (Fitzpatrick, 1988; Fitzpatrick & Best, 1979; Werner, Altman, & Oxley, 1985). Similarly, families that enjoy interaction arrange furniture to invite conversation and eye contact. In families that seek less interaction, chairs may be far apart and may face televisions instead of each other (Burgoon, Buller, & Woodhall, 1989; Keeley & Hart, 1994).

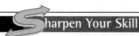

ARTIFACTUAL IDENTITY MESSAGES

What do your artifacts say about you? Are your clothes casual or formal? Are they traditional, the latest fad, or something uniquely your style? If you wear jewelry, does it suggest you are playful (novelty jewelry), rich (real gold and precious stones), or a member of an ethnic group?

What do the objects in your home convey about your values, interests, and the important people in your life?

ENVIRONMENTAL RACISM

According to Robert Cox, former national president of the Sierra Club, "The term 'environmental racism' describes a pattern whereby toxic waste dumps and hazardous industrial plants are located in low income neighborhoods and communities of color. It's no coincidence that industries expose our most vulnerable communities to pollutants and carcinogens that they seldom foist on middle and upper class people. The pattern is very clear: The space of minorities and poor people is often invaded and contaminated, but the territory of more affluent citizens is respected" (R. Cox, personal communication).

People invite or discourage interaction by how they arrange office spaces. Some professors and executives have desks that face the door and a chair beside the desk to promote open communication with people who come to their offices; other professionals turn their desks away from the door and place chairs opposite their desks to preserve status.

Environmental Factors

Environmental factors are elements of settings that affect how we feel, think, and act. For instance, we feel more relaxed in rooms with comfortable chairs than ones with stiff furniture. Candle-lit rooms invite romantic feelings, and churches, synagogues, and temples use candles to foster respectfulness.

Restaurants use environmental features to control how long people spend eating. For example, low lights, comfortable chairs or booths, and soft music are often part of the environment in upscale restaurants. On the other hand, fast-food eateries have hard plastic booths and bright lights, which encourage diners to eat and move on. To maximize profit, restaurants want to get people in and out as quickly as possible. Studies show that fast music in restaurants speeds up the pace of eating; on average, people eat 3.2 mouthfuls a minute when the background music is slow and 5.1 mouthfuls a minute when rock music is played (Bozzi, 1986; "Did You Know?" 1998).

Chronemics

Chronemics refers to how we perceive and use time to define identities and interaction. Nonverbal communication scholar Nancy Henley (1977) reports that we use time to negotiate and convey status. She has

Sharpen Your Skill

ENVIRONMENTAL AWARENESS

Think of two places where you feel rushed and two where you linger. Describe the following about each place:

1. How is furniture arranged?
2. What kind of lighting is used?
3. What sort of music and sound are in the place?
4. How comfortable is the furniture?
5. What colors and art do you see?

Can you draw any generalizations about environmental features that promote relaxation and those that do not?

fyi

FENG SHUI

Does your home encourage a free flow of energy? Does it foster prosperity, health, and happiness? If not, the problem could be bad feng shui (pronounced "fung shway").

Feng shui is a 3,000-year-old Asian art that focuses on relationships between external environments and the inner self (Kaufman, 1996; Spear, 1996; Wydra, 1998).

Feng shui is still widely practiced in much of Asia and has recently found its way westward. For $200 to $500 an hour, a feng shui consultant will come to your home or office and help you arrange the space to promote blessings, fortune, and the life force (chi). He or she will advise you to get plants with rounded leaves to promote upward and outward energy, to get the red out of your bedroom if you suffer from lack of sleep or put more red in the bedroom if your problem is lack of passion, and to use mirrors and lights to enhance, diminish, or redirect energy. Feng shui is based on a complex grid called a *bagua* that charts nine specific elements that affect the flow of energy. Many principles of feng shui are consistent with findings from research on nonverbal communication.

Several Asian cultures place special emphasis on environmental features thought to influence patterns of interaction, feelings, and moods. The ancient Asian art of feng shui aims to arrange furniture and walls to be in harmony with the earth. When an environment is in harmony with the earth, it is assumed that those in that environment will be similarly in harmony with the natural world and their positive energies (Wydra, 1998).

The Feng Shui Institute was founded by Nancilee Wydra, who has degrees in psychiatric social work and interior design. Her goal is to translate the ancient art of feng shui into a practice that is viable in contemporary Western societies. In addition to writing books on feng shui, Wydra writes a national column and appears on national television. To learn more about her and the Feng Shui Institute, visit the Web site at http://www.windwater.com/wydra/html.

identified a cultural rule that stipulates that important people with high status can keep others waiting. Conversely, people with low status are expected to be punctual in Western society. It is standard practice to have to wait, sometimes a good while, to see a doctor even if you have an appointment. This carries the message that the doctor's time is more valuable than yours. Professors can be late to class and students are expected to wait, but students are sometimes reprimanded if they appear after a class begins. Subordinates are expected to report punctually to meetings, but bosses are allowed to be tardy. Chronemics expresses cultural attitudes toward time. Western societies value time, so they value speed (Keyes, 1992; Schwartz, 1989). Thus we want computers, not typewriters, and we replace software programs and modems as soon as faster versions hit the market. We often try to do several things at once to get more done, rely on the microwave to cook faster, and take for granted speed systems such as instant copying and photos (McGee-Cooper, Trammel, & Lau, 1992). Many other cultures have far more relaxed attitudes toward time and punctuality. In many South American countries it's normal to come late to meetings or classes, and it's not assumed that people will leave when the scheduled time for ending arrives. Whether time is savored and treated casually or compulsively counted and hoarded reflects larger cultural attitudes toward living.

The length of time we spend with different people reflects our priorities. A manager spends more time with a new employee who seems to have executive

fy*i*

ALL IN A DAY'S WORK

North Americans and Germans differ in the time they invest in work. The typical job in Germany requires 37 hours a week, and the law guarantees a minimum of five weeks' paid leave each year. Stores close on weekends and four of five weeknights so that workers can have leisure time. In the United States, jobs typically require 44 to 80 hours a week, and many workers can't take more than a week's leave at a time. Furthermore, many U.S. workers take second jobs even when their first jobs allow a comfortable standard of living. Germans can't understand this, because "free time can't be paid for." Personal time is considered so precious in Germany that it's illegal to work more than one job during holidays, which are meant to let people restore themselves (Benjamin & Horwitz, 1994, p. B1).

potential than one who seems less impressive. A speaker gives a fuller answer to a question from a high-status member of the audience than a person with less status. We spend more time with people we like than those we don't like or who bore us. Researchers report that increased contact among college students is a clear sign that a relationship is intensifying, and reduced time together signals decreasing interest (Baxter, 1985; Dindia, 1994; Tolhuizen, 1989).

Chronemics also involves expectations of time, which are influenced by social norms. For example, you expect a class to last 50 or 75 minutes. Several minutes before the end of a class period, students often close their notebooks and start gathering their belongings, signaling the teacher that time is up. A similar pattern is often evident in business meetings. We expect religious services to last approximately an hour, and we might be upset if a rabbi or minister talked for two hours. These expectations reflect our culture's general orientation toward time, which is that it is a precious commodity to be hoarded and saved (Lakoff & Johnson, 1980). Many everyday expressions reflect the cultural view that time is like money, a valuable and limited resource to be used wisely: "You're *wasting* my time," "This new software program will *save* some time," "That mistake *cost* me three hours," "I've *invested* a lot of time in this class," and "I'm *running out* of time."

Paralanguage

Paralanguage is communication that is vocal but is not actual words. Paralanguage includes sounds, such as murmurs and gasps, and vocal qualities such as volume, rhythm, pitch, and inflection. Our voices are versatile instruments that tell others how to interpret us and what we say. Vocal cues signal others to interpret what we say as a joke, threat, statement of fact, question, and so forth. Effective public speakers know how to modulate inflection, volume, and rhythm to enhance their verbal messages.

We use vocal cues to communicate feelings to friends and romantic partners. Whispering, for instance, signals confidentiality or intimacy, whereas shouting conveys anger or excitement. Depending on the context, sighing may communicate empathy, boredom, or contentment. Research shows that tone of voice is a powerful clue to feelings between marital partners. Negative vocal tones often reveal marital dissatisfaction (Gottman, Markman, & Notarius, 1977; Noller, 1987). Negative intonation may also signal dissatisfaction or disapproval in work settings. A derisive or sarcastic tone can communicate scorn clearly. On the other hand, a warm voice conveys liking, and a playful lilt suggests friendliness.

Our voices affect how others perceive us. To some extent we control vocal cues that influence image. For instance, we can deliberately sound confident in job interviews or when asking for a raise. The president adopts a solemn voice when announcing military actions. Most of us know how to make ourselves sound apologetic, seductive, or angry when those images suit our purposes. In addition to the ways we intentionally use our voices, natural and habitual vocal qualities affect how others perceive us. For instance, someone with a pronounced Bronx accent may be perceived as brash, and someone with a southern drawl may be stereotyped as lazy.

PRACTICING PARALANGUAGE

Say *really* so that it means

1. I don't believe you.
2. Wow! That's amazing.
3. That doesn't square with what I've heard.
4. I totally agree.

Say *get lost* so that it means

1. I want you out of here.
2. That's a dumb idea.
3. I'm crazy about you.

Rayna

When I first moved to United States, I didn't understand many words and idioms. I did not understand "a bird in the hand is worth two in the bush" meant it is smart to hold on to what is sure. I did not understand "hang a right" meant to turn right. So when I did not understand, I would ask people to explain. Most times they would say the very same thing over, just louder and more slowly, like I was deaf or stupid. I felt like saying to them in a very loud slow voice, "I am Indian, not stupid. You are stupid."

Our ethnic heritage influences how we use our voices. In general, African American speech has more vocal range, inflection, and tonal quality than European American speech (Garner, 1994; Kochman, 1981). Paralanguage also reflects gender. Men's voices tend to have strong volume, low pitch, and limited inflection, features that conform to cultural views of men as assertive and emotionally controlled. Women's voices typically have higher pitch, softer volume, and more inflection, features consistent with cultural views of women as emotional and deferential. Socioeconomic level influences pronunciation, rate of speech, and accent.

Silence

A final type of nonverbal behavior is **silence,** which is a lack of communicated sound. Although silence is quiet, it can communicate powerful messages. "I'm not speaking to you" speaks volumes. Silence can convey different meanings. For instance, it can symbolize contentment when intimates are so comfortable they don't need to talk. Silence can also communicate awkwardness, as you know if you've ever had trouble keeping conversation going on a first date.

Jin Lee

In the United States, people feel it is necessary to talk all of the time, to fill in any silence with words and more words. I was not brought up that way. In my country it is good to be silent some of the time. It shows you are listening to another, you are thinking about what the other says, you are respectful and do not need to put in your words.

Some parents discipline children by ignoring them. No matter what the child says or does, parents refuse to acknowledge the child's existence. The silencing strategy may also surface later in life. We sometimes deliberately freeze out others when we're angry with them. In some military academies, such as West Point, silencing is a method of stripping a cadet of personhood if the cadet is perceived as having broken the academy's honor code. On the job, silence may signal disapproval—peers often ostracize whistle-blowers and union busters. People who violate the rules of chat rooms may be silenced by getting no responses to their messages. Audiences sometimes shout down speakers they dislike; when angry, romantic partners may refuse

OBSERVING NONVERBAL COMMUNICATION

To determine whether research findings about nonverbal communication apply in real life, go to three of the places listed here and observe. Describe environmental features and artifacts in the settings. Also notice proxemics, kinesics, chronemics, haptics, and paralanguage. Are your observations consistent with research we've discussed?

1. Expensive retail stores and discount stores
2. Executive and secretarial offices
3. Faculty club and student cafeterias
4. Library and student union
5. College administrative buildings and classroom buildings on campus

Describe how nonverbal factors reflect the different identities of these contexts and the kinds of activities and interactions each invites and discourages.

to speak; and the Catholic Church excommunicates people who violate its canons.

We've seen that nonverbal communication includes kinesics, haptics, physical appearance, artifacts, proxemics, environmental features, chronemics, paralanguage, and silence. The final section of this chapter identifies guidelines for improving nonverbal communication.

GUIDELINES FOR EFFECTIVE NONVERBAL COMMUNICATION

Nonverbal communication, like verbal communication, can be misinterpreted. The following two guidelines should reduce nonverbal misunderstandings in your interactions.

Monitor Your Nonverbal Communication

Think about the preceding discussion of ways we use nonverbal behaviors to announce our identities. Are you projecting the image you desire? Do others interpret your facial and body movements in ways consistent with the image you want to project? Do friends ever tell you that you seem uninterested when you're really interested? If so, you can monitor your nonverbal actions so that you more clearly communicate your involvement and interest in conversations. To reduce the chance that work associates will think you're uninterested in meetings, use nonverbal behaviors that others associate with responsiveness and attention.

Have you set up your spaces so that they invite the kind of interaction you prefer, or are they arranged to interfere with good communication? Paying attention to nonverbal dimensions of your world can empower you to use them more effectively to achieve your interpersonal goals.

Be Tentative When Interpreting Others' Nonverbal Communication

Although popular advice books promise to show you how to read nonverbal communications, no sure-fire formula exists. It's naive to think we can decode something as complex and ambiguous as nonverbal communication. People who believe that may misjudge others.

In this chapter we've discussed findings about the meanings people attach to nonverbal behaviors. We can never be sure what a particular behavior means to specific people in a given context. For instance, we've said that satisfied couples tend to sit closer together than unhappy couples. As a general rule this is true. However, sometimes contented couples prefer autonomy and like to have distance. Partners may also avoid physical closeness when one has a cold or flu. People socialized in non-Western cultures learned distinct rules for proxemics. Because nonverbal communication is ambiguous and personal, we should not assume we can interpret it with precision. An ethical principle of communication is to qualify interpretations of nonverbal behavior with awareness of personal and contextual considerations.

Personal Qualifications Generalizations about nonverbal behavior state what is generally the case. They don't tell us about the exceptions to the rule. Although eye contact generally is a sign of responsiveness, some people close their eyes to concentrate when listening. Often people who cross their arms and condense into a tight posture are expressing hostility or lack of interest in interaction. However, the same behaviors might mean that a person is cold and trying to conserve body heat. Most people use less inflection and adopt a slack posture when they're not really interested in what they're talking about. However, the same behaviors may mean only that we're tired.

Derrick

I'd like to tell off those jerks who write the popular books on reading nonverbal communications. One of the things they say is that crossing your legs a certain way means you're closed. Well, I have a bum knee from football, and there's only one way I can cross my legs. It doesn't mean anything about whether I'm open or closed. It means my knee doesn't work.

Because nonverbal behaviors are ambiguous and vary among people, we need to be cautious about how we interpret these behaviors. A key principle to keep in mind is that we construct the meanings we attach to nonverbal communication. A good way to keep this in mind is to rely on *I* language, not *you* language, which we discussed earlier. *You* language might lead us to inaccurately say of someone who doesn't look at us, "You're communicating lack of interest." A more responsible statement would use *I* language to say, "When you don't look at me, I feel you're not interested in what I'm saying." Using *I* language reminds us to take responsibility for our judgments and feelings. In addition, we become less likely to make others defensive by inaccurately interpreting their nonverbal behavior.

Contextual Qualification Like the meaning of verbal communication, the significance of nonverbal behaviors depends on the contexts in which they occur. Our nonverbal communication reflects the various settings we inhabit. We are more or less formal, relaxed, and open depending on context. Most people are more at ease on their own turf than someone else's, so we tend to be more relaxed in our homes and offices than in other people's homes and business places. We also dress according to context. When I am on campus or in business meetings, I dress in good clothes, but at home I usually wear jeans or running clothes.

Immediate physical settings are not the only factor that affects nonverbal communication. As we have seen, all communication reflects the values and understandings of particular cultures. We are likely to misinterpret people from other cultures when we impose the norms and rules of our culture on them. A Tibetan woman who makes little eye contact is showing respect by the norms in her country, although a North American might view her as evasive. This suggests that we have an ethical responsibility not to assume that our interpretations apply to the behaviors of others.

Eleni

I have been misinterpreted very much in this country. My first semester here a professor told me he wanted me to be more assertive and to speak up in class. I could not do that, I tell him. He said I should put myself forward, but I have been brought up not to do that. In Taiwan that is very rude and ugly, and we are taught not to speak up to teachers. Now that I have been here for 3 years I sometimes speak in classes, but I am still more quiet than Americans. I know my professors think I am not so smart because I am quiet, but that is the teaching of my country.

Even within the United States we have diverse communication cultures, and each has its rules for nonverbal behavior. Ethical communicators try to adopt dual perspective when interpreting others, especially when they and we belong to different cultures. To enhance your awareness of cultural influences on communication, Chapter 7 deals with that topic in detail.

Summary

In this chapter we've explored the fascinating world of nonverbal communication. We learned that nonverbal communication is symbolic and functions to supplement or replace verbal messages, regulate interaction, reflect and establish relationship-level meanings, and express cultural membership. These five principles of nonverbal behavior help us understand the complex ways in which nonverbal communication operates and what it may mean.

We discussed nine types of nonverbal communication, each of which reflects cultural rules and expresses our personal identities and feelings toward others. We use nonverbal behaviors to announce and perform our identities, relying on actions, artifacts, and contextual features to embody what our culture has taught us is appropriate for our gender, race, class, sexuality, and ethnicity. Because nonverbal communication is ambiguous, we construct its meaning as we notice, organize, and interpret nonverbal behaviors that we and others enact. Effectiveness requires that we learn to monitor our nonverbal communication and to exercise caution in interpreting that of others.

FOR FURTHER REFLECTION AND DISCUSSION

1. Attend a gathering of people from a culture different from yours. It might be a meeting at a Jewish temple if you're Christian, an African American church if you are white, or a meeting of Asian students if you are Western. Observe nonverbal behaviors of the people there: How do they greet one another, how much eye contact accompanies interaction, and how close to one another do people sit?
2. Use your *InfoTrac College Edition* to review recent articles in *Environmental Action Magazine* and *Journal of Environmental Health*. Do you find evidence that the toxic waste dumps and other environmental hazards are disproportionately located in the space of some groups of Americans?
3. Describe the spatial arrangements in the home of your family of origin. Was there a room in which family members interacted a good deal? How was furniture arranged in that room? Who had separate space and personal chairs in your family? What do the nonverbal patterns reflect about your family's communication style?
4. Think about current gender prescriptions in the United States. How are men and women "supposed" to look? How are these cultural expectations communicated? How might you resist and alter unhealthy cultural gender prescriptions?
5. Is it ethical to interpret the nonverbal communication of people from other cultures from the perspective of your culture?
6. Is it ethical to use nonverbal behaviors to suggest that you think or feel differently than you actually do?
7. Use your *InfoTrac College Edition* to compare advertisements in magazines targeted primarily to white readers (for example, *Better Homes and Gardens*) and black readers (*Ebony*). Identify differences in the physical shapes of models and in the number of ads for weight loss.

KEY TERMS

Kinesics
Haptics
Physical appearance
Artifacts
Proxemics
Environmental factors
Chronemics
Paralanguage
Silence

Listening and Responding to Others

LEARNING OBJECTIVES

To understand

1. How listening and hearing differ
2. How effective listening adapts to different goals and situations
3. How we can improve our listening skills
4. Whether it is a good idea to express positive judgments of others when we listen to them
5. How to listen effectively

"Got a minute?" Stan asks as he enters Suzanne's office.

"Sure," Suzanne agrees, without looking up from the report she is reading for a meeting later today. Lately, her supervisor has criticized her for being unprepared for meetings, and she wants to be on top of information today.

"I'm concerned about Frank. He's missed several days lately, and he's late half the time when he gets in to work," Stan begins. "He hasn't given me any explanation for his absences and tardiness, and I can't keep overlooking it."

"Yeah, I know that routine," Suzanne says with irritation. "Last month Barton missed two days in a row and left early several other days."

"That's exactly what I'm talking about," Stan agrees. "I can't let Frank disregard rules that everyone else follows, but I don't want to come down too hard on him, especially when I don't know why he's missing so much time."

"I told Barton that I'd had it and from now on he could either be at work when he should be or give me a darned good reason for why he wasn't," Suzanne says forcefully. Her mind wanders back to relive the confrontation with Barton.

"I wonder if the two situations are really similar," Stan says.

Suzanne realizes she was lost in her own thoughts. "Sorry, I didn't catch what you said," she says.

"I was wondering if you're saying that I should handle Frank like you handled Barton," Stan says.

"You have to enforce the rules, or he'll walk all over you." Suzanne's eyes drift back to the report she was reading when Stan dropped by.

"I hate to be so hard on Frank," Stan says.

"Remember last year when Cheryl kept missing work? Well, I tried to be subtle and hint that she couldn't skip work. In one ear and out the other. You have to be firm."

"But Frank's not like Barton or Cheryl," Stan says. "He's never tried to run over me or shirk his work. I have a hunch something is going on that is interfering with his work. Cheryl and Barton both had patterns of irresponsibility."

"I don't think my staff is any less responsible than yours. I'm a good supervisor, you know," Suzanne snaps.

"That's not what I meant. I just meant that I don't think I need to hit Frank over the head with a two by four," Stan says.

"And I suppose you think that's what I did?"

"I don't know. I wasn't there. I'm just thinking that maybe our situations are different," Stan says.

How would you describe the conversation between Stan and Suzanne? Is Suzanne a good communicator? Is she sensitive to Stan's concerns? Does she respond helpfully to him?

When we think about communication, we usually focus on talking. Yet **listening** is at least as important as talking in the communication process. As obvious as this is, few of us devote as much energy to listening as we do to talking.

In the conversation between Stan and Suzanne, poor listening is evident in several ways. First, Suzanne is preoccupied with a report she is reading. Reading it diverts her attention from Frank and limits her ability to maintain eye contact and give Frank nonverbal responses to his comments. If she really wants to listen to Stan, she should put the report aside. A second problem is Suzanne's tendency to monopolize the conversation, turning it into an occasion to discuss *her* supervisory problems instead of Stan's concerns about Frank's behavior. Third, Suzanne listens defensively, interpreting Stan as criticizing her when he suggests that he might act differently. Like Suzanne, most of us listen less well than we could much of the time. When we listen poorly, we are not communicating well.

Studies of people ranging from college students to professionals show that the average person spends 45% to 53% of waking time listening to others (Barker, Edwards, Gaines, Gladney, & Holley, 1981; Weaver, 1972). We listen in classes, at public lectures, to television and radio, in conversations, during interviews, on the job, and when participating in teamwork. If we add the time we listen while doing other things, the total listening time is even greater.

Ineffective listening can be costly. When people don't listen well on the job, they may miss information that can affect their professional effectiveness and advancement. Ineffective listening in the classroom diminishes what students learn and how they perform on tests. In personal relationships poor listening can hinder our understanding of others, and we may respond less sensitively than we might. Not listening well to public communication leaves us unfamiliar with important issues and uninformed when we cast our votes. Learning to listen well enhances personal, academic, social, and professional effectiveness.

This chapter explores listening, which is the fifth basic communication process. First, we'll consider what's involved in listening and discuss obstacles to effective listening. Next we'll examine common forms of ineffective listening. The third section of the chapter explains skills required for good listening in various situations. Finally, we'll identify ways to improve listening effectiveness.

fy*i*

WHO LISTENS?

We might do well to heed wisdom offered by Mother Teresa in an interview with Dan Rather (Bailey, 1998).

> RATHER: "What do you say to God when you pray?"
>
> MOTHER TERESA: "I listen."
>
> RATHER: "Well, what does God say?"
>
> MOTHER TERESA: "He listens."

WE LISTEN TO A BOOK A DAY

The average student listens to the equivalent of a book a day, talks approximately a book a week, reads about a book a month, and writes the equivalent of a book a year.

Source: Buckley, 1992.

THE LISTENING PROCESS

Although we often use the words *listening* and *hearing* as if they were synonyms, actually they're not. **Hearing** is a physiological activity that occurs when sound waves hit functional ear drums. Hearing is not the only way we receive messages. We also receive them through sight, as when we notice nonverbal behaviors, read lips, or use American Sign Language (ASL). In addition to physically receiving messages, listening involves being mindful, selecting and organizing information, interpreting communication, responding, and remembering (Figure 6.1).

Being Mindful

Mindfulness occurs when we decide to focus on what is happening in the moment (Wood, 1997). When you are mindful, you don't think about what you did yesterday or the report you're reading or a problem in your relationship. Instead, mindful listeners focus on the people with whom they are interacting. Some people like email because they can choose when to go online and can do so only when they are prepared to attend mindfully to others. We demonstrate mindfulness with verbal and nonverbal signals that we are paying attention and interested in what others say (Bolton, 1986).

Figure 6.1 The Listening Process

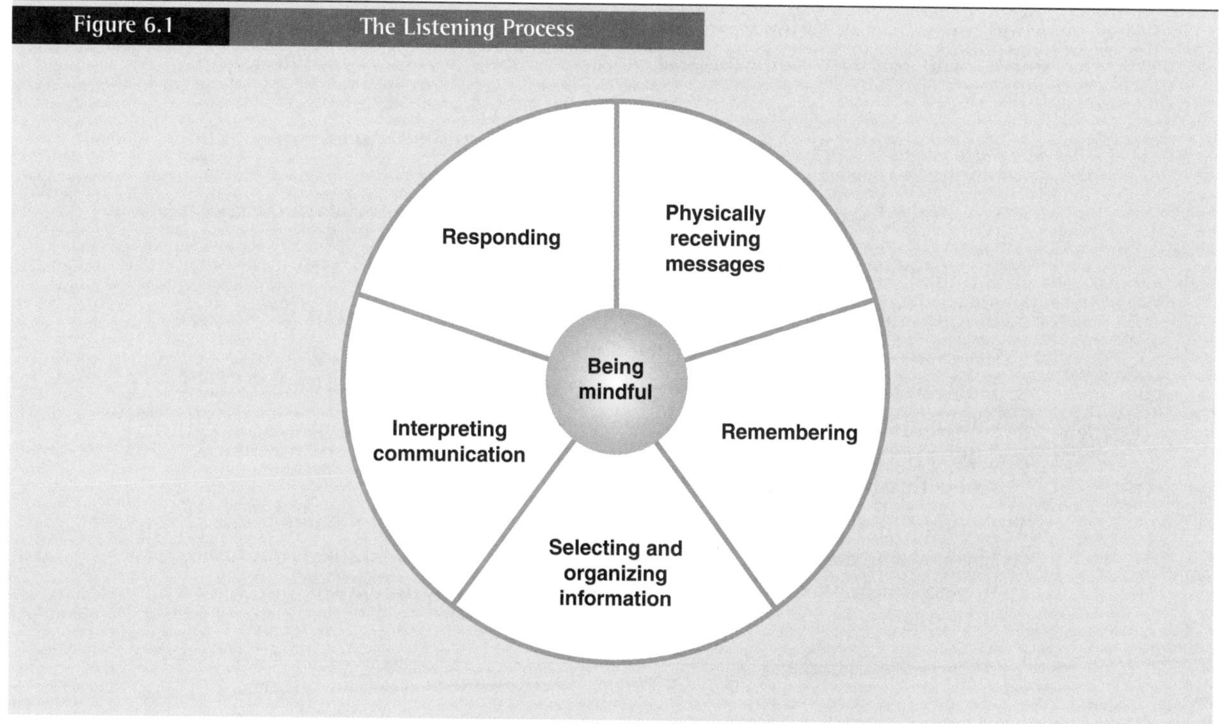

Simone

The best listener I've ever met was Nate, a guy I worked with on the campus newspaper. He wrote the best stories on special speakers who came to campus. At first I thought he just got more interesting personalities to interview than I did. But then he and I had a couple of joint interviews, and I saw how he listened. When an interviewee was talking, Nate gave the person his undivided attention—like there was nobody else and nothing else around. People really open up when you treat them like the most interesting person in the world.

Being mindful isn't a talent that some people have and others don't. Instead, it's an ethical commitment to attend fully to another person. No amount of technique will make you a good listener if you don't choose to be mindful. Thus, your choice of whether to be mindful is the foundation of how you listen—or fail to. The importance of choosing to listen mindfully is recognized by successful executives. Pamela Kruger (1999) talked with business leaders and concluded that "Leaders must know how to listen. . . . But first, and just as important, leaders must *want* to listen" (p. 134).

Mindfulness enhances communication in two ways. First, attending mindfully to others increases our understanding of how they feel and what they think about what they are saying. When we concentrate on another's communication, we gain insight into their thoughts and feelings. Second, mindfulness promotes more complete communication by others. When we really listen to others, they tend to elaborate on their ideas and express their feelings in greater depth. Mindfulness is a continuous part of effective listening; as such, it affects all other aspects of the listening process.

Sharpen Your Skill

BEING MINDFUL

Mindfulness is a skill that develops with commitment and practice. Zen Buddhists, who emphasize mindfulness, offer these guidelines for becoming more mindful:

1. Empty your mind of thoughts, ideas, and plans so that you are open to listening to another.
2. Concentrate on the person with whom you are communicating. Say to yourself, "I want to focus on this person and what she or he is saying and feeling."
3. If your mind does wander, don't criticize yourself. Instead, just refocus on the person you are with and what she or he is saying.
4. Don't be surprised if distracting thoughts come up or if you find yourself thinking about your responses instead of what the other person is saying. This is natural. Just push away diverting thoughts and refocus on the person with whom you are talking.
5. Evaluate how well you listened when you were focusing on being mindful. If you aren't as fully engaged as you want to be, remind yourself that mindfulness is a habit of mind and a way of living. Developing it requires considerable practice.

Physically Receiving Communication

In addition to being mindful, listening involves physically receiving communication. We might receive it by hearing sounds, interpreting nonverbal behaviors, or reading lips or using ASL. Sometimes we physically receive a message, and this causes us to become mindful; in other instances choosing to be mindful allows us to receive communication we might otherwise miss.

Most of us take hearing for granted. However, people who do not hear well may have difficulty receiving oral messages. When we speak with someone who has a hearing impairment, we should face the person and verify that we are coming across clearly. Our ability to receive messages also declines if we are tired or stressed. You may have noticed that it's hard to sustain attention in long classes. Physical reception of messages is also hampered by others talking around us, TVs and radios, or competing visual cues.

Other physiological factors influence how and how well we listen. Women and men seem to differ in how they listen. As a rule, women are more attuned than men to what is going on around them. Men tend to focus, shape, and direct their hearing in specific ways, whereas women are more likely to notice contexts, details, and tangents, as well as major themes in interaction (Weaver, 1972). The discrepancy between rates of speaking and hearing also influences listening. The average person can understand approximately 300 words a minute, yet the average person speaks at a rate of approximately 100 words per minute. This leaves a lot of free time for listeners to sort and interpret speech.

Selecting and Organizing Communication

The third element of listening is selecting and organizing material. As we noted in Chapter 2, we don't perceive everything around us. Instead, we selectively attend to some aspects of communication and disregard others. What we attend to depends on many factors, including physiological influences, expectations, cognitive structures, social roles, and cultural membership. Our preoccupations can hamper listening, as Suzanne's involvement with her report impeded her ability to listen to Stan. If you want to communicate effectively, you should take responsibility for controlling thoughts and concerns that can interfere with listening. Once again, mindfulness comes into play. Choosing to be mindful doesn't guarantee that our minds won't stray, but it does mean that we will bring ourselves back to the moment.

We can monitor our tendencies to attend selectively by remembering that we are more likely to notice stimuli that are intense, loud, or unusual. Thus, we may overlook communicators who don't call attention to themselves with volume and bold gestures. If we're aware of this tendency, we can guard against it so that we don't miss out on people and messages that may be important. Some researchers claim that teachers unintentionally give more attention and encouragement to male than female students because men communicate more assertively (Gabriel & Smithson, 1990; Sadker & Sadker, 1986; Spender, 1989). The same listening bias can occur in work settings because many women tend to be less outspoken than their male colleagues.

Once we've selected what to notice, we organize the stimuli to which we attend. As you'll recall from Chapter 2, we use cognitive schemata to organize our perceptions. As you listen to other people, you decide how to categorize them by deciding which of your prototypes they most closely resemble: friend with a problem, professional rival, supervisor, and so forth. You then apply personal constructs to assess whether they are smart or not smart, honest or deceitful, reasonable or unreasonable, open to advice or closed, and so on. Next, you apply stereotypes to predict what they will do. Finally, you choose a script that seems appropriate to follow in interacting.

When a friend is distraught, you can reasonably predict that he needs to ventilate and may not want advice until he has first had a chance to express his feelings. On the other hand, when a co-worker comes to you with a problem that must be solved quickly, you assume she might welcome concrete advice or collaboration. Your script for responding to the distraught friend might be to say, "Tell me more about what you're feeling" or "You sound really upset—let's talk." With a colleague who is facing a deadline, you might adopt a more directive script and say, "Here's what I suggest to fix the problem and stay on schedule."

Carlos

What I do when someone else is talking makes a difference in what they say. If I look interested and nod my head a lot, they keep talking and get more animated. But if I look away, they wind down and stop talking.

Carlos has recognized that listeners actively construct meaning. When we define someone as emotionally upset, we're likely to rely on a script that tells us to back off and let her air her feelings. On the other hand, if we perceive someone as confused, we might follow a script that tells us to help him clarify his feelings. It's important to realize that *we construct others and their communication* by the schemata we use to organize our perceptions of them. Because our perceptions can be wrong, we should be ready to revise them in the course of interacting.

Interpreting Communication

The fourth aspect of listening is **interpretation.** When we interpret, we put together all that we have selected and organized to make sense of communication. Effective interpretation depends on your ability to understand others on their terms. Certainly, you won't always agree with other people's feelings and thoughts. Recognizing others' viewpoints doesn't mean you agree with them; it does mean you make an earnest effort to grasp what they think and feel. This is an ethical responsibility of listening.

Maggie

Don and I didn't understand each other's perspective, and we didn't even understand that we didn't understand. Once I told him I was really upset about a friend of mine who needed money for an emergency. Don told me she had no right to expect me to bail her out, but that had nothing to do with what I was feeling. He would have seen the situation in terms of rights, but I didn't and he didn't grasp my take. Only after we got counseling did we learn to listen to each other instead of listening through ourselves.

To respect another person's perspective is to give a special gift. What we give is regard for another person and a willingness to open ourselves to that person's way of looking at the world. Too often we impose our meanings on others, we try to correct or argue with them about what they feel, or we crowd out their words with ours. As listening expert Robert Bolton has observed, good listeners "stay out of the other's way" so they can learn how the speaker views the situation (1986, p. 167).

THE POWER OF LISTENING

To test the effect of responsive listening, researchers taught students in a college psychology course to give different responses to their professor. The professor in the class was a boring lecturer who read his notes in a monotone, seldom gestured, and did little to engage students. After the first few minutes of class the students changed their postures, kept greater eye contact, nodded, and so forth. Shortly after the students began responding, the lecturer started using gestures, increased his speaking rate and inflection, and began interacting with students visually and verbally. Then, at a prearranged signal, the students stopped showing interest. Within a few minutes the lecturer returned to his old lecture style. The students' responses affected the professor's communication.

Source: Bolton, 1986.

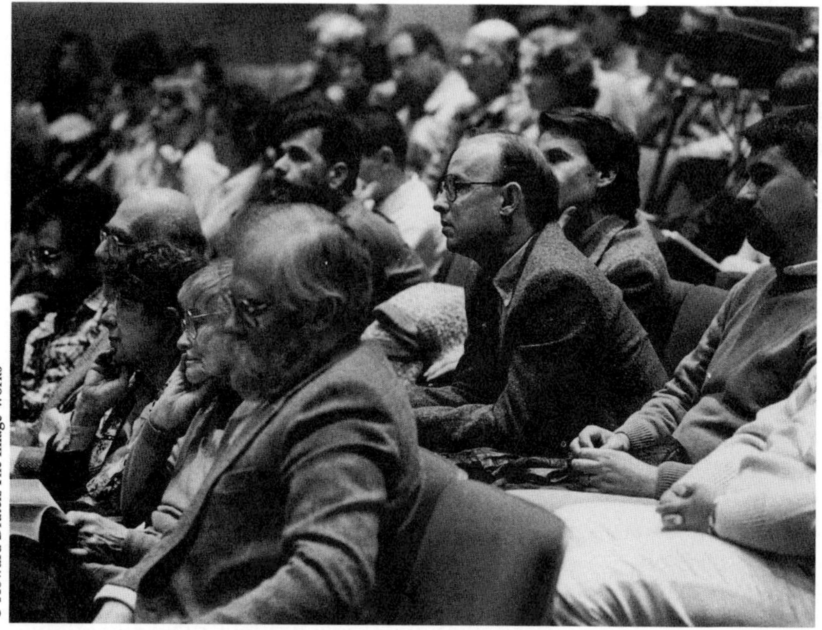

© Howard Dratch/The Image Works

■ *Listeners communicate with public speakers. If you were the speaker, how would you interpret the messages from these listeners?*

Responding

Effective listening involves **responding,** which is expressing interest, asking questions, and otherwise showing that we are attentive. As we noted in Chapter 1, communication is a transactional process in which we simultaneously receive and send messages. Skillful listeners give signs that they are involved in interaction, even though they are not speaking at the moment.

We don't respond only when others finish speaking but throughout interaction. At public presentations audience members show interest by looking at speakers, nodding their heads, and adopting attentive postures. Nonverbal behaviors, such as looking out a window, making notes to yourself, and slouching, signal that you aren't involved. We also show lack of involvement or interest by, for instance, yawning or staring blankly (Ernst, 1973).

Good listeners show that they're engaged. The only way that others know we are listening is through our feedback. Indicators of engagement include an attentive posture, head nods, eye contact, and vocal responses such as "Mm-hmm" and "Go on." When we demonstrate involvement, we communicate that we care about the other person and what she or he says.

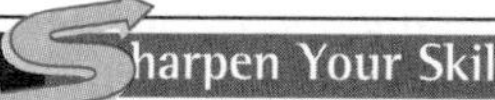

RESPONSIVE LISTENING

Test the effect of responsive listening. The next time a friend talks to you, signal interest by removing distractions, keeping eye contact, nodding your head, and so forth. How does your friend react? How is her or his communication affected by your responsiveness?

Repeat this exercise in a team situation. When other members of the team speak, express your interest and attention through nonverbal communication that signals involvement. How do various members of the group respond?

Remembering

Many listening experts regard **remembering** as the final aspect of the listening process. Remembering is not simply recalling literal messages. Instead, it is being able to recall your interpretation of messages. As we have noted, we continuously interpret others' communication to form meanings. Early scholars of listening found that we remember less than half of a message immediately after we hear it (Nichols & Stevens, 1957). After about 8 hours we recall only about 35% of our interpretations of most messages. Because we forget about two-thirds of the meanings we construct from others' communication, it's important to make sure we hang on to the most important third (Fisher, 1987). Selectively focusing our attention is particularly important when we listen to presentations that contain a great deal of information. Later in this chapter we'll discuss strategies for improving memory.

Listening is a complex process that involves being mindful, physically receiving messages, organizing, interpreting, responding, and remembering. Let's now consider hindrances to the listening process.

OBSTACLES TO EFFECTIVE LISTENING

Obstacles to good listening arise in communication situations and within us.

Situational Obstacles

Learning about situational hindrances to listening can help us guard against them or compensate for the interference they create.

Message Overload The sheer amount of communication in our lives makes it difficult to listen fully to all of it. **Message overload** occurs when we receive more messages than we can effectively process. For good reason our era has been dubbed the information age. Each day we are inundated by messages from media (newspapers, magazines, television, radio), electronic systems (email, telephone, Internet, bulletin boards, faxes), and other people (parents, friends, children, teachers, supervisors, subordinates). We simply can't be mindful and totally involved in all the messages that come our way. Instead, we have to make choices about which communication gets our attention.

Message overload often occurs in academic settings; readings and class discussions are laden with detailed information. Message overload may also occur when communication occurs simultaneously in multiple channels. For instance, you might suffer information overload if a speaker is presenting information orally while showing a slide with complex statistical data. In such a situation it's difficult to decide whether to focus your listening energy on the visual or the oral message.

Message Complexity Listening may also be impeded by **message complexity,** which exists when a message we are trying to understand is highly complex, is packed with detailed information, or involves intricate reasoning. The more detailed and complicated ideas are, the more difficult they are to follow and retain. Many jobs today are so specialized that communication among co-workers involves highly complex messages. We're tempted to tune out people who use technical vocabularies, focus on specifics, and use complex sentences. Effective communicators make an effort to reduce the complexity of their messages and to avoid unnecessary jargon. When speakers don't translate complex ideas into understandable language, effective listeners have to invest more effort. When listening to messages that are dense with information, taking notes can improve retention.

Environmental Distractions A third impediment to effective listening is **environmental distractions,** which are occurrences that interfere with effective listening. Sounds around us can divert our attention or even make it difficult to hear clearly. At a rally or a ball game you have to shout to the person next to you. Although most sounds aren't as overwhelming as the roar of a crowd, noise exists in all communication situations. It might be a television in the background, side comments during a conference, or muffled traffic sounds from outside.

Jimmy

It's impossible to listen well in my apartment. Four of us live there, and at least two different stereos are on all the time. Usually, there's also a TV going, and there may be conversations or phone calls too. We're always asking each other to repeat something or skipping over whatever we don't hear. If we go out to a bar or something, the noise is just as bad. Sometimes I think we don't really want to listen and all the distractions protect us from having to.

To listen effectively, we should reduce environmental distractions. It's considerate to turn off a television or turn down music if someone wants to talk with you. Closing a door eliminates hallway noises. Private conversations can be deferred until after a group meeting so that they don't interfere with listening. Professionals often have their phone calls held when they are talking with clients or business associates. Even when we can't eliminate distractions, we can usually reduce them or change our location to one that is more conducive to good listening.

Internal Obstacles to Listening

In addition to situational impediments, factors within us can hinder listening.

Auturro

Last week I got a letter from my family in which my mother said the monsoons had hurt their crops and so they would not make much money at the market. I was very worried because my family does not have savings—we live year to year and crop to crop. After a couple of days I realized that I did not know what had happened in any of my classes. I read my notebooks and I had notes that were good, but I didn't remember ever hearing what the notes were about.

Preoccupation One of the most common hindrances to listening is preoccupation. When we are absorbed in our thoughts and concerns, we can't focus on what someone else is saying. Perhaps you've attended a class right before taking a test in another class and later realized you got virtually nothing out of the first class. That's because you were preoccupied with the upcoming test. If you open your email box and find twenty messages, you may be preoccupied by feeling obligated to read and respond to all of them, so you are not fully, mindfully focused on reading and responding to each one as you open it. In the example that opened this chapter, Suzanne's preoccupation with a report impeded her ability to listen to her colleague. When we are preoccupied with our thoughts, we aren't mindful.

Prejudgments A second internal obstacle to good listening is the tendency to prejudge others or their ideas. Sometimes we think we already know what someone will say, so we don't listen carefully. In other cases we decide in advance that others have nothing to offer us, so we tune them out. If a co-worker has not had ideas that impressed you in the past, you might assume that nothing of value will surface in today's conversation. The risk is that you might miss a good idea. Keeping an open mind when listening to topics or speakers with which you disagree is also advisable. You can miss out on important information and perspectives if you prejudge speakers or topics.

Keith

My parents are so quick to tell me what I think and feel or should think and feel that they never listen to what I do feel or think. Last year I told them I was thinking about taking a year off from school. Before I could explain why I wanted to do this, Dad was all over me about the need to get ahead in a career. Mom said I was looking for an easy out from my studies. What I wanted to do was work as an intern to get some hands-on experience in media production, which is my major. I wasn't after an easy out and I do want to get ahead, but they couldn't even hear me through their own ideas about what I felt.

We also make prejudgments when we mind read. We assume we know what another feels, thinks, and is going to say, and we then fit their message into our preconceptions. This can lead us to misunderstand what they mean because we haven't really listened to them on their terms. Prejudgments disconfirm other people by denying them their voices. Instead of listening openly to them, we force their words into our preconceived mind-sets. When we impose our prejudgments on others' words, at the relationship level of meaning we express a disregard for them and what they say. Prejudgments also affect the content level of meaning because we may not grasp important content when we decide in advance that someone has nothing of value to say. This can be costly on the job, where we are expected to pay attention and understand information even if we don't like it or the person expressing it.

Lack of Effort Listening is hard work: We have to be mindful, focus on what others say, interpret and organize messages, remember, and respond. We also have to control distractions inside ourselves and in situations. Sometimes we aren't willing to invest the effort to listen well. In other instances, we want to listen, but we're tired, ill, or distracted by other matters. When this happens, it's effective to postpone interaction until you have the energy to listen mindfully. If you explain that you want to listen well, the other person is likely to appreciate your honesty and your commitment to listening.

Not Recognizing Diverse Listening Styles A final hindrance to effective listening is not recognizing and adjusting to different listening styles that reflect diverse cultures and social groups. For example, Nepalese give little vocal feedback during conversation because they consider it disrespectful to make sounds while someone else is talking. Other cultures exhibit differences in listening rules based on age, ethnicity, gender, and other aspects of identity.

There are also differences between social groups in the United States. Some African Americans engage in a more participative listening style than European Americans. Thus, some African Americans call out responses to a speaker as a way to show interest. A speaker who doesn't understand this pattern is likely to misinterpret the responses as rude interruptions. Conversely, some African Americans may perceive European American listeners as disinterested because they don't call out during a speech. If you realize that people differ in how they listen and express interest, you are unlikely to misinterpret others.

Nancy

I was amazed the first time I went to a black church. Members of the congregation kept speaking back to the minister and exclaiming over what they liked. At first I was alienated, but after a while I got into the spirit, and I felt a whole lot more involved in the service than I ever had in my own church.

Forms of Ineffective Listening

Now that we've discussed obstacles to effective listening, let's identify common forms of ineffective listening. Some may seem familiar because you and others probably engage in these at times.

Pseudolistening **Pseudolistening** is pretending to listen. When we pseudolisten, we appear attentive, but our minds are really elsewhere. Sometimes we pseudolisten because we don't want to hurt a friend who is sharing experiences, even though we are preoccupied with other things. We also pseudolisten when communication bores us but we have to appear interested. Superficial social interaction and boring lectures are communication situations in which we may consciously choose to pseudolisten so that we seem polite even though we really aren't involved. On the job we may need to appear interested in what others say because of their positions. Pseudolistening is inadvisable, however, when we need to understand another's communication.

Monopolizing **Monopolizing** is hogging the stage by continuously focusing communication on ourselves instead of the person who is talking. Two tactics are typical of monopolizing. One is conversational rerouting, in which a person shifts the topic of talk to himself or herself. For example, if Ellen tells her friend Marla that she's having trouble with her roommate, Marla might reroute the conversation by saying, "I know what you mean. My roommate is a real slob." And then Marla launches into an extended description of her roommate problems. In the workplace, people with higher status may shift conversations to themselves and their accomplishments. As a result, they don't listen to others. In both personal and work relationships, rerouting takes the conversation away from the person who is talking and focuses it on the self.

Interrupting can occur in combination with rerouting, so that a person interrupts and then introduces a new topic. In other cases, diversionary interrupting involves questions and challenges that are

Peanuts reprinted by permission of United Feature Syndicate, Inc.

not intended to support the person who is speaking. Monopolizers may fire questions that express doubt about what a speaker says ("What makes you think that?" "How can you be sure?" "Did anyone else see what you did?") or prematurely offer advice to establish their command of the situation and perhaps to put down the other person ("What you should do is . . ." "You really blew that." What I would have done is . . ."). Both rerouting and diversionary interrupting monopolize conversations. They are the antithesis of good listening.

It's important to realize that not all interruptions are attempts to monopolize communication. We also interrupt the flow of others' talk to show interest, voice support, and ask for elaboration. Interrupting for these reasons doesn't divert attention from the person speaking; instead, it affirms that person and keeps the focus on her or him.

Selective Listening A third form of ineffective listening is **selective listening,** which involves focusing only on particular parts of communication. We listen selectively when we screen out parts of a message that we dislike or find boring. We also listen selectively when we attend only to communication that interests us or with which we agree.

One form of selective listening is focusing only on aspects of communication that interest us or correspond with our opinions and feelings. We screen out message content that doesn't interest us or square with our ideas. If you are worried about a storm, you may listen selectively to weather reports and disregard news, talk, and music on the radio. Students often become highly attentive in classes when teachers say, "This is important for the test." In the workplace we may become more attentive when communication addresses topics such as raises, layoffs, and other matters that may affect us directly.

Gretchen

I know I screen out communication about problems in nursing homes. Last year we had to put my mother in one; with two kids under 6 years old, we just couldn't give Mom the medical care and the attention she needs. But I can't let myself read articles on abuses in nursing homes or listen to radio and television coverage of problems.

Selective listening also occurs when we reject communication that bores us or makes us uncomfortable. Because we don't like what someone says, we may not listen when we or our work is criticized. We may also screen out communication that makes us uncomfortable. A smoker may choose not to listen to messages about the dangers of smoking. We all have subjects that bore or bother us, and we may be tempted not to listen to communication about them.

Defensive Listening **Defensive listening** involves perceiving personal attacks, criticisms, or hostile undertones in communication where none is intended. When we listen defensively, we assume others don't like, trust, or respect us, and we read these motives into whatever they say, no matter how innocent their communication actually is. Some people are generally defensive, expecting insults and criticism from all quarters (a stable attribution about others). They hear threats and negative judgments in almost anything said to them. Thus, an innocent remark such as "Have you finished your report yet?" may be perceived as criticism or as suspicion that the work isn't being done.

In other instances defensive listening is confined to areas where we judge ourselves inadequate or times that we feel negative about ourselves. A woman who fears she is not valued in her job may interpret committee assignments as signs that she is not well regarded, a person who feels unattractive may perceive genuine compliments as false, and someone who has been laid off may perceive work-related comments as personal criticism.

Ambushing **Ambushing** is listening carefully for the purpose of gathering ammunition to use in attacking a speaker. Political candidates routinely listen carefully to their opponents in order to undercut them. Ambushing may also plague work life, especially in organizations that encourage employees to compete with one another in order to stand out. These employees display no openness, make no effort to understand the other's meaning, take no interest in recognizing value in what another says, and do not want genuine dialogue.

Eric

One brother at my [fraternity] house is a real ambusher. He's a pre-law major, and he loves to debate and win arguments. No matter what somebody talks about, this guy just listens long enough to mount a counterattack. He doesn't care about understanding anybody else, just about beating them. I've quit talking when he's around.

Literal Listening **Literal listening** involves listening only to the content level of meaning and ignoring the relationship level of meaning. When we listen literally, we do not listen to what's being communicated about the other person or our relationship with that person. Literal listening neglects others' feelings and our connections with them.

GUIDELINES FOR EFFECTIVE LISTENING

The key guideline for effective listening is to adapt to specific communication goals and situations. Two major kinds of listening, **informational and critical listening** and **relationship listening,** require different skills and attitudes. We'll discuss how to be effective in these two kinds of listening and identify other types of listening.

Informational and Critical Listening

Much of our listening has the purpose of gaining and evaluating information. We listen for information in classes and professional meetings, when we are

Sharpen Your Skill

IDENTIFY YOUR INEFFECTIVE LISTENING HABITS

Identify times when you have listened ineffectively:

1. Describe a situation in which you pseudolistened.
2. Describe a time when you monopolized communication.
3. Report on a time when you listened defensively.
4. Discuss an example of ambushing someone.
5. Describe an instance when you listened selectively.
6. Identify a time when you listened literally.

Repeat the exercise by identifying times when others engaged in each type of ineffective listening.

learning the ropes of a new job, during reports of important news stories, and when we need guidance on everything from medical treatment to directions to a new place. In all these cases the primary purpose of listening is to gain and understand information.

Closely related to informational listening is critical listening: We listen to make judgments of people and ideas. Like informational listening, critical listening requires attending closely to the content of communication. Yet critical listening goes beyond just gaining information for the purposes of analysis and evaluation and for analyzing and evaluating the people who express the information. We decide whether a speaker is credible and ethical by judging the thoroughness of a presentation, accuracy of evidence, carefulness of reasoning, and personal confidence and trustworthiness. Informational and critical listening call for similar skills in organizing and retaining information. Critical listening also calls for skill in evaluating information.

Be Mindful The first step in listening to information critically is to make a decision to attend carefully, even if material is complex and difficult. This may mean that you time conversations, whether by phone, online, or face-to-face, so that you have the mental energy to be mindful. Don't let your mind wander if information gets complicated or confusing. Avoid daydreaming and stay focused on learning as much as you can. Later, you may want to ask questions if material isn't clear or if you have reservations about evidence or logic.

Control Obstacles You can also minimize distractions. You might shut a window to block out traffic noises or adjust a thermostat so that room temperature is comfortable. In addition, you should minimize psychological distractions by emptying your mind of the many concerns, ideas, and prejudgments that can interfere with attending to the communication at hand.

Ask Questions Asking speakers to clarify their messages or to elaborate allows you to understand information you didn't grasp at first and to deepen your insight into content you did comprehend. Recently, I listened to a talk on national economic issues. After a fairly technical speech, audience members asked these questions: "Could you explain what you meant by the M2 money supply?" "How does inflation affect wages?" and "Can you clarify the distinction between the national debt and the deficit?" These questions showed that the listeners had paid attention and were interested in further information. Questions compliment a speaker because they show that you are interested and want to know more.

© James Wilson/Woodfin Camp & Associates

■ *This park official is teaching visitors how to protect themselves from Lyme disease. Are the visitors using good listening skills?*

Critical listening often calls for more probing questions of speakers and their content. "What is the source of your statistics on the rate of unemployment?" "Is a 7-year-old statistic on welfare current enough to tell us anything about welfare issues today?" "Have you met with any policy-makers who hold a point of view contrary to yours? What is their response to your proposals?" "I noticed that all the sources you quoted were fiscal conservatives. Does this mean your presentation and your conclusions are biased?" "Do you stand to benefit personally if we vote for what you are advocating?"

It's especially important and appropriate for nonnative speakers to ask questions if they don't understand language. People who have learned English as a second language may not understand idioms such as "in a heartbeat" (fast), "not on your life" (very unlikely), or "off the wall" (wacky). Sensitive communicators avoid or explain idioms if nonnative speakers are present. If speakers don't define colloquial language, listeners should request elaboration.

Use Aids to Recall To remember important information, we can apply principles of perception we discussed in Chapter 2. For instance, we learned that we tend to notice and recall stimuli that are repeated. To use this principle to increase your retention, repeat important ideas to yourself immediately after hearing them. This moves new information from short-term to long-term memory (Estes, 1989). Repeating the names of people when you meet them can save you the embarrassment of having to ask them to repeat their names.

Another way to increase retention is to use mnemonic (pronounced "ni-monic") devices, which are memory aids that create patterns that help you remember what you've heard. For instance, the mnemonic device MPSIRR is made up of one letter representing each of the six parts of listening (Mindfulness, Physical reception, Selecting and organizing, Interpreting, Responding, Remembering). You can also invent mnemonics to help you recall personal information. For example, ROB is a mnemonic for remembering that Robert from Ohio is studying Business.

Organize Information A third technique to increase your retention is to organize what you hear. When communicating informally, most people don't order their ideas carefully. The result is a flow of information that isn't coherently organized and so is hard to retain. We can impose order by regrouping what we hear. For example, suppose a friend tells you that he's confused about long-range goals, doesn't know what he can do with a math major, wants to locate in the Midwest, wonders whether graduate school is necessary, likes small towns, needs some internships to try out different options, and wants a family eventually. You could regroup this stream of concerns into two categories: academic information (careers for math majors, graduate school, internship opportunities) and lifestyle preferences (Midwest, small town, family). Remembering those two categories allows you to retain the essence of your friend's concerns, even if you forget many of the specifics. Repetition, mnemonics, and regrouping enhance retention.

Relationship Listening

Listening for information focuses on the content level of meaning in communication. Yet often we're as concerned or even more concerned with the relationship level of meaning, which has to do with feelings and

---

fyi

MISSING THE BOAT IN COMMUNICATION

Many people for whom English is a second language don't understand slang used by native speakers. Nonnative speakers may miss the boat if speakers use idioms such as "kick the bucket," "chew the fat," "far out," "hit the road," "this car's a real lemon," "hangdog expression," "cooked goose," "hang a right," or "bail out." Informality is inappropriate if it creates barriers to understanding.

Source: Lee, 1994.

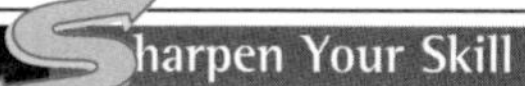
Sharpen Your Skill

IMPROVING RECALL

Apply the principles we've discussed to enhance memory.

1. The next time you meet someone, repeat his or her name to yourself three times after you are introduced. Do you find that the name sticks better?
2. After your next communication class, take 15 minutes to review your notes in a quiet place. Read them aloud so that you hear as well as see the main ideas. Does this increase your retention of material?
3. Invent mnemonics that help you remember basic information in communication.
4. Organize complex ideas by grouping them into categories. To remember the main ideas of this chapter, you might use major subheadings to form categories: listening process, obstacles to listening, and listening goals. Then the mnemonic LOG (Listening, Obstacles, Goals) could help you remember those topics.

relationships between communicators. We engage in relationship listening when we listen to a friend's worries, let a romantic partner tell us about problems, counsel a co-worker, or talk with a parent about health concerns. Specific listening attitudes and skills enhance our ability to listen supportively (Nichols, 1996).

Be Mindful The first requirement for effective relationship listening is mindfulness, which is also the first step in informational listening. When we're listening in order to support, however, we should focus on understanding feelings that may not be communicated explicitly. Thus, mindful relationship listening involves looking for what is between the words, the subtle clues to feelings and perceptions. As listening scholar Gerald Egan notes, "Total listening is more than attending to another person's words. It is also listening to the meanings that are buried in the words and between the words and in the silences in communication" (1973, p. 228).

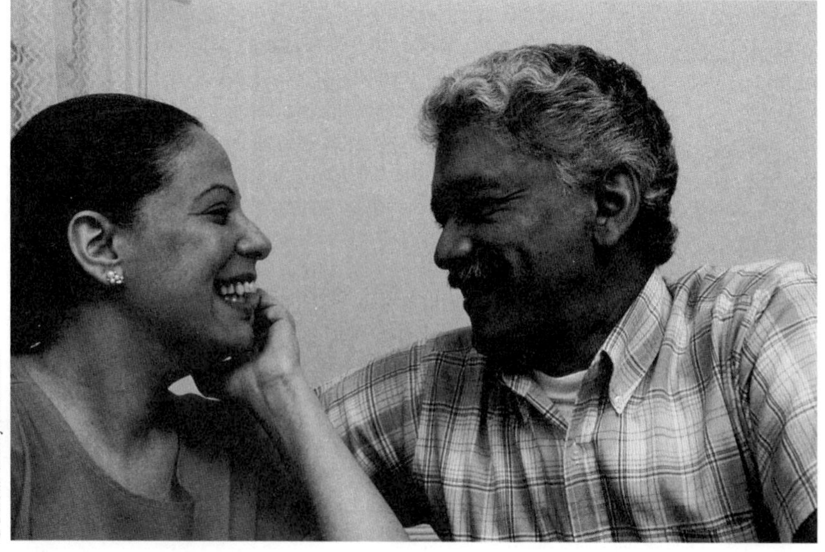
© Rhoda Sidney/PhotoEdit

■ *What might this woman do differently if she were engaging in critical listening instead of relationship listening?*

Jose

My best friend makes it so easy for me to tell whatever is on my mind. She never puts me down or makes me feel stupid or weird. Sometimes I ask her what she thinks, and she has this way of telling me without making me feel wrong if I think differently. What it boils down to is respect. She respects me and herself and so she doesn't have to prove anything by acting better than me.

Suspend Judgment When listening for the purpose of providing support, it's important to avoid judgmental responses. When we judge, we add our evaluations to other people's experiences, and this moves us away from them and their feelings. Our judgments may also lead others to become defensive and unwilling to talk further with us. To curb judgment, we can ask whether we really need to evaluate right now. Even positive evaluations ("That's a good way to approach the problem") can make others uneasy and less willing to communicate openly with us. The other person may reason that if we make positive judgments, we could also make negative ones. Only if someone asks for our evaluation should we offer it when we are listening to offer support. Even if our opinion is sought, we should express it in a way that doesn't devalue others. Sometimes people excuse strongly judgmental comments by saying, "You asked me to be honest" or "I mean this as constructive criticism." Too often, however, the judgments are not constructive and are more harsh than candor requires. Good relationship listening includes responses that communicate respect and support.

Strive to Understand the Other's Perspective One of the most important principles for effective relationship listening is to concentrate on grasping the other person's perspective (Nichols, 1996). This means we have to step outside of our point of view at least long enough to understand another's perceptions. We can't respond sensitively to others until we understand their perspective and meanings. To do this we must put aside our preconceptions about issues and how the other person feels and try to focus on their words and nonverbal behaviors for clues about how they feel and think.

One communication skill that helps us gain insight into others is the use of **minimal encouragers.** These are responses that gently invite another person to elaborate. Examples of minimal encouragers are "Tell me more," "Really?," "Go on," "I'm with you," "Then what happened?," "Yeah?," and "I see." We can also use nonverbal minimal encouragers such as a raised eyebrow to show that we're involved, a nod to signal that we understand, or widened eyes to demonstrate that we're fascinated. Minimal encouragers say we are listening and interested. They encourage others to keep talking so we can grasp what they mean. Keep in mind that these are *minimal* encouragers. They shouldn't take the focus away from the other person. Effective minimal encouragers are brief interjections that prompt, rather than interfere with, the flow of another's talk.

Paraphrasing is a second way to learn what others mean. To paraphrase, we reflect our interpretations of others' communication back to them. For example, a friend might confide, "I'm really scared my kid brother is messing around with drugs." We could paraphrase this way: "It sounds as if you think your brother may be taking drugs." This paraphrase allows us to clarify whether the friend has any evidence of the brother's drug involvement. The response might be, "No, I don't have any reason to suspect him, but I just worry because drugs are so pervasive in high schools now." This tells us that the friend's worry is about general trends, not evidence that her brother is using drugs.

Paraphrasing also helps us figure out what others feel. If someone screams, "I can't believe he did that to me!" it's not clear whether the person is angry, hurt, or upset. We could find out what the person is feeling by saying, "You seem really angry." If anger is the emotion, the speaker could agree; if not, he or she could clarify feelings by explaining further. Paraphrasing also allows us to check whether we understand another person's meaning: "Let me see if I followed you. What you're saying is that. . . ."

A third way to enhance understanding of others is to ask questions. For instance, we might ask, "How do you feel about that?" or "What do you plan to do?" Another reason we ask questions is to find out what a person wants from us. Sometimes it isn't clear whether someone wants advice, a shoulder to cry on, or a safe place to vent feelings. If we can't figure out what's wanted, it's appropriate to

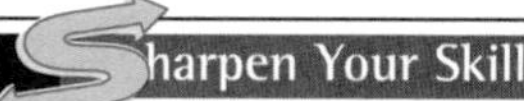

PRACTICING PARAPHRASING

Developing skill in paraphrasing others' messages enhances communication. Practice your paraphrasing skill by creating paraphrases of the following comments:

1. "I don't know how they expect me to get my work done when they don't give me any training on how to use this new software program."
2. "I've got three midterms and a paper due next week and I'm behind in my reading."
3. "Can you believe it? This is the fifth rejection letter I've received. I thought all the time I spent interviewing would produce better results."
4. "My parents don't understand why I need to go to summer school, and they won't pay my expenses."
5. "My son wants to go to summer school and expects us to come up with the money. Doesn't he understand what we're already paying for the regular school year?"

ask. "Are you looking for advice or a sounding board?" "Do you want to talk about how to handle the situation or just air the issues?" Asking directly signals that we really want to help and allows others to tell us how we can best do that.

Express Support Once you have understood another's meanings and perspective, relationship listening should focus on communicating support. This doesn't necessarily require us to agree with another's perspective or ideas. It does call upon us to communicate support for the person. To illustrate how we can support people even if we don't agree with their position, consider the following exchange between a son and his father.

SON: Dad, I'm changing my major to acting.

FATHER: Oh.

SON: Yeah, I've wanted to do it for some time but I hesitated because acting isn't as safe as accounting.

FATHER: That's certainly true.

SON: Yeah, but I've decided to do it anyway. I'd like to know what you think about the idea.

FATHER: The idea worries me. Starving actors are a dime a dozen. It just won't provide you with any economic future or security.

SON: I understand acting isn't as secure as business, but it is what I really want to do.

FATHER: Tell me what you feel about acting—why it matters so much to you.

SON: It's the most creative, totally fulfilling thing I do. I've tried to get interested in business, but I just don't love that like I do acting. I feel like I have to give this a try, or I'll always wonder if I could have made it. If I don't get somewhere in 5 or 6 years, I'll rethink career options.

FATHER: Couldn't you finish your business degree and get a job and act on the side?

SON: No. I've got to give acting a full shot—give it everything I have to see if I can make it.

FATHER: Well, I still have reservations, but I guess I can understand having to try something that matters this much to you. I'm just concerned that you'll lose years of your life to something that doesn't work out.

SON: Well, I'm kinda concerned about that too, but I'm more worried about wasting years of my life in a career that doesn't turn me on than about trying to make a go of the one that does.

FATHER: That makes sense. I wouldn't make the choice you're making, but I respect your decision and your guts for taking a big gamble.

This dialogue illustrates several principles of effective relationship listening. First, note that the father's first two comments are minimal encouragers that invite his son to elaborate on his thoughts and feelings. The father also encourages his son to explain how he feels. Later, the father suggests a compromise solution, but his son rejects that and the father respects the son's position. It is important that the father makes his position clear, but he separates his personal stance from his respect for his son's right to make his own choices. Sometimes it's difficult to listen nonjudgmentally, particularly if we don't agree with the person speaking, as in this example. However, if your goal is to support someone, sensitive, responsive involvement without evaluation is the ideal listening style.

OTHER PURPOSES OF LISTENING

In addition to listening for information, to make critical evaluations, and to provide support, we listen for pleasure and to discriminate.

Listening for Pleasure

Sometimes we listen for pleasure, as when we attend concerts or play CDs. Listening for enjoyment is also a primary purpose when we go to comedy shows or when an acquaintance tells a joke. When listening for pleasure, we don't need to concentrate on organizing and remembering as much as when we listen for information, although retention is important if you want to tell the joke to someone else later. Yet listening for pleasure does require mindfulness, hearing, and interpretation.

Listening to Discriminate

In some situations we listen to make fine discriminations in sounds in order to draw sound conclusions and act appropriately in response. For example, doctors listen to discriminate when they use stethoscopes to assess heart functioning or chest congestion. Parents listen to discriminate a baby's cries for attention, food, reassurance, or a diaper change. Skilled mechanics can distinguish engine sounds far more keenly than most other people. Mindfulness and keen hearing abilities are skills that assist listening to discriminate.

Mindfulness is a prerequisite for effective listening of all types. With the exception of mindfulness, each listening purpose tends to emphasize particular aspects of the listening process and to put less weight on others. Whereas evaluating content is especially important in listening critically, it is less crucial when listening for pleasure. Hearing acoustic nuances is important when listening to discriminate but not vital to listening for information. Selecting, organizing, and retaining information matter more when we are listening for information than when we are listening for pleasure. Deciding on your purpose for listening allows you to use the particular communication skills that are most pertinent.

Summary

According to the ancient philosopher Zeno of Citium, "We have been given two ears and but a single mouth, in order that we may hear more and talk less." Thousands of years later his comment remains wise. Listening is a major and vital part of communication, yet too often we don't consider it as important as talking. In this chapter we've explored the complex and demanding process of listening.

We began by distinguishing between hearing and listening. The former is a straightforward physiological process that doesn't require effort on our part. Listening, in contrast, is a complicated process involving being mindful, hearing, selecting and organizing, interpreting, responding, and remembering. Listening well requires commitment and skill.

Both obstacles in ourselves and hindrances in situations and messages jeopardize effective listening. Message overload, complexity of material, and external noise are external obstacles to listening. In addition, our preoccupations and prejudgments, lack of effort, and not recognizing differences in listening styles can hamper listening. The obstacles to listening often lead to various forms of ineffective listening, including pseudolistening, monopolizing, selective listening, defensive listening, ambushing, and literal listening. Each form of ineffective listening prevents us from being fully engaged in communication.

We also discussed different purposes for listening and identified the skills and attitudes that advance each purpose. Informational and critical listening require us to adopt a mindful attitude and to think critically, organize and evaluate information, clarify understanding by asking questions, and develop aids to retention of complex material. Relationship listening also requires mindfulness, but it calls for other distinct listening skills. Suspending judgment, paraphrasing, giving minimal encouragers, and expressing support enhance the effectiveness of relationship listening.

FOR FURTHER REFLECTION AND DISCUSSION

1. Review the types of ineffective listening discussed in this chapter. Do any describe ways in which you attend (or don't attend) to others? Select one type of ineffective listening in which you engage and work to minimize it in your interactions.
2. Use your *InfoTrac College Edition* to learn about the importance of listening in the workplace. Select *PowerTrac* and then select the *Journal of Human Resources*. Review the last four issues and notice how often principles discussed in this chapter are mentioned.
3. What do you see as ethical principles that guide different listening purposes? What different moral goals and responsibilities accompany informational and critical listening and relationship listening?
4. As a class, discuss the idea of mindfulness. As we saw in the chapter, mindfulness isn't a technique or specific skill but a commitment to attentiveness. Is it possible to learn mindfulness? Is it something we can improve with practice?
5. Keep a record of your listening for 2 days. How much of your listening is informational, critical, relational, for pleasure, and to discriminate? Describe differences in how you listen to meet each goal.
6. Use your *InfoTrac College Edition* to read speeches that emphasize listening. Select *Vital Speeches,* then type in the key word *listening*.

KEY TERMS

Listening
Hearing
Mindfulness
Interpretation
Responding
Remembering
Message overload
Message complexity
Environmental distractions
Pseudolistening
Monopolizing
Selective listening
Defensive listening
Ambushing
Literal listening
Informational and critical listening
Relationship listening
Minimal encouragers
Paraphrasing

Adapting Communication to People and Contexts

LEARNING OBJECTIVES

To understand

1. That effective communication adapts to people and contexts
2. How cultural membership affects communication
3. How culture and social groups shape individuals' communication
4. How gender affects communication
5. The different ways in which people respond to differences in communication styles

Myra is a good doctor. She has a firm technical understanding of physiology, and she is well trained in diagnostic methods and the values and risks of various treatments and medications. She deals with all her patients in the same way, using a consistent style.

Aaron is also a good doctor. Like Myra, he has good technical knowledge and diagnostic skills, and he is well read on the advantages and dangers of treatments and medications. Myra does not devote much time to talking with her patients, and she treats all of them similarly. Aaron spends a lot of time talking with each patient before doing examinations or considering treatment. Based on conversations with patients, he adapts his communication style to suit individual patients' needs and expectations. When he sees Pat, who is fearful, Aaron is reassuring and comforting but tells Pat little about technical aspects of his medical condition. When treating Lee, however, Aaron discusses clinical issues, often providing Lee with complicated technical information. Sometimes Lee and Aaron even collaborate to make diagnoses and decide on methods of treatment. Pat has little education and expects doctors to take charge, whereas Lee is an accomplished chemist who has substantial scientific knowledge and an interest in knowing technical details of medical conditions.

Both Myra and Aaron are technically skilled. Yet Myra treats each patient the same way, whereas Aaron adapts his style of practicing medicine to individual patients. He can be directive ("Take this medicine three times a day and eliminate alcohol") or collaborative ("Let's figure out together how to treat your stress"). He knows when to encourage patients ("You've done a great job of cutting back on cigarettes. Pretty soon I'll bet you quit entirely") and when to challenge patients ("I don't think you have the determination to give up cigarettes"). At times he listens and responds empathically ("I understand what a rough time this is for you"), and at other times Aaron responds more critically ("Not making time for regular physical exercise is just adding to your stress level").

The major difference between how Myra and Aaron practice medicine is that Myra follows a standard formula, whereas Aaron adapts to particular patients and situations. Most people would consider Aaron a more effective doctor because he not only has technical knowledge and skills but also knows how to modify them to fit a range of people and situations.

In this chapter we consider the sixth basic communication process: adapting to people and contexts. This process modifies the other processes we've discussed by accenting the importance of adapting how we use verbal and nonverbal symbols and how we perceive, listen, and create climates to respond to diverse goals, situational demands, and people with whom we interact. We'll open the chapter by surveying the importance of adaptation as a basic communication process. Next, we will elaborate an idea introduced in Chapter 1: All communication occurs within contexts. The third section of the chapter explores culture as a major context that influences how people communicate. We then consider ways in which distinct social groups, or standpoints, within cultures shape styles of communication. Finally, we will identify guidelines for adapting communication effectively.

ADAPTATION AS A BASIC COMMUNICATION PROCESS

Like medicine, communication may be practiced in formulaic or creative ways that are sensitive to contexts and people. You could learn a number of basic communication skills, yet you would not communicate effectively unless you also understood how to adapt to different situations, people, and communicative goals. Effective communicators understand that the basic processes we've discussed in preceding chapters must be tailored to fit the communicative norms, rules, and expectations of particular contexts.

No standard, one-size-fits-all formula for effective communication exists. The kind of language that is effective in talking with a five-year-old may not be effective in speaking with adults. The climate that sustains a close friendship is not the same as the climate that invigorates a project team. When we are listening to a co-worker, our goal may be to gain information. When we are attending a public presentation on a new policy proposal, critical listening is appropriate, whereas in a conversation with a troubled friend, our listening should be sensitive to relationship-level meanings. These examples highlight the importance of adapting communication to various contexts and people. The examples also reiterate a theme of *Communication Mosaics:* Basic processes of communication pertain to all forms and contexts of interaction. The key point, and the focus of this chapter, is that effective communicators tailor their interaction to specific people and contexts. In addition to developing competence in the five skills we discussed in previous chapters, effective communicators are able to adapt to the opportunities and constraints of diverse settings and people.

COMMUNICATION IS SYSTEMIC

Communication theorists and researchers recognize that communication occurs in contexts that affect how it operates and what it means. Consequently, we can't understand the communication of group leaders, public speakers, or dysfunctional people unless we examine them in the systems in which they occur.

A system is a group of interrelated and interacting parts that function as a whole. Four principles explain the implications of viewing communication as a system.

All Parts of Communication Are Interrelated

Communication systems consist of interdependent parts that interact continuously and affect one another. Consequently, if you change any part of a system, you change the entire system. When a new person joins a team, changes reverberate throughout the entire team. In response to the new part of the system, the team develops new patterns of interacting, subgroups realign, and team performance changes.

SPONGES, NEWTS, AND COMMUNICATION

A Viennese biology professor named Ludwig von Bertalanffy pioneered research on systems. He puzzled over such questions as why a live sponge that is forced through a sieve spontaneously reorganizes itself. Why do cells transplanted from the leg of a newt to its tail result in growth of a second tail instead of a leg? When an organ is injured, why do other organs take over the functions of the damaged organ (Hampden-Turner, 1982, p. 158)?

Von Bertalanffy concluded that life forms are organized wholes that seek to sustain themselves (von Bertalanffy, 1951, 1967). This explains why newts grow tails, not legs, in the tail area of their bodies, why sponges reconstitute themselves, and why organisms compensate for injured organs. Von Bertalanffy believed that all life forms—social as well as biological—are complex organized wholes that he called *systems*. His insights into life were considered so valuable that he was nominated for a Nobel Prize just before his death in 1971 (Hampden-Turner, 1982).

Communication Systems Are Organized Wholes

This second principle emphasizes the idea that we can't understand any part of a system in isolation from other interrelated parts. Because systems are organized wholes, they must be seen and studied as a totality of interacting elements (Hall & Fagen, 1956). Before systems theory was developed, therapists often worked with disturbed members of families and tried to "fix" the person who supposedly was causing problems for the family life. Thus, alcoholics might be separated from their families and given therapy to reduce the motivation to drink or

■ *This Iraqi family communicates differently than Westerners. What can you infer about Iraqi culture from the dress, artifacts, and proxemics?*

increase the desire not to drink. Often, however, the alcoholic who was "cured" resumed drinking shortly after rejoining the family. The reason is obvious if we think systemically. In many dysfunctional families the "problem person" is assisted by other family members. Perhaps the spouse denies the person has a problem, and children try to cover for the alcoholic parent's lapses to minimize friction in the family. The problem is the whole system, in which a person's alcoholic tendencies interact with codependent patterns of other family members.

In a similar manner, organizations sometimes send managers to leadership training programs but do not provide training to the manager's subordinates. When the manager returns to the office and uses the new leadership techniques, subordinates are distrustful and resistant. They were accustomed to the manager's former style, and they haven't been taught how to deal with a new style of leadership.

Kelly

My wife wanted us to get counseling. I wasn't interested, so she went to see a therapist on her own. But the therapist told her there was no point in working with one person in a troubled marriage. I finally agreed to go, and now I know the therapist was right. Aimee and I couldn't fix our marriage by changing what either one of us did. We had to change how we interacted—what we were together—and that required both of us to be involved.

A Whole System Is More Than the Sum of Its Parts

This third principle reminds us that communication systems are more than the aggregate of their parts. Communication systems such as families, groups, organizations, and societies evolve, change, discard old parts and patterns, and generate new forms of interacting. Over time, interaction among parts of a system creates new elements. Groups and teams develop norms that regulate communication and histories of success and failure that influence members' confidence and team spirit. When new topics are introduced on electronic bulletin boards, new subscribers join, old ones leave, and lines of communication between people are reconfigured. Personal relationships grow beyond the two original parts (partners) to include trust or lack of trust, shared experiences, and private vocabularies. As people alter patterns of self-talk (perhaps by censoring negative thoughts), their self-concepts and ways of interacting also change. Systems include not only their original parts but also what is created as a result of interaction.

Living systems vary in how open they are. **Openness** is the extent to which a system affects and is affected by outside factors and processes. Some tribal communities, such as those in the imperiled rain forests, are virtually closed systems that have little interaction with outside people and events. Yet most human systems are fairly open to interaction with larger systems that surround them. Each of us affects and is affected by families, work associates, and friends, as well as television, radio, magazines, and communication technologies. The more open a system is, the more factors influence what happens in it. Mass media and communication technologies are expanding the openness of most societies and, thus, the influences on them and their ways of life.

Communication Systems Strive for but Cannot Sustain Equilibrium

This is a paradoxical but important premise about communication systems. On one hand, they seek to achieve a state of equilibrium, or **homeostasis.** That's why families create routines, organizations devise rituals, individuals develop habits, groups generate norms, online communities develop conventions and abbreviations, and societies maintain traditions.

Yet living systems cannot sustain absolute balance or equilibrium. Change is inevitable and continuous. Sometimes it's abrupt (a member quits the team), at other times it's gradual (a team member's participation progressively declines); sometimes influences outside a system prompt change (the legislature demands that faculty teach more classes), in other cases the system generates change internally (faculty volunteer to teach more classes). To function and survive, members of the system, like the sponge, must continuously adjust and change.

Communication systems attempt to maintain a steady state by resisting change, *and* they are dynamic entities that cannot avoid changing. This helps us understand why we sometimes deny or try

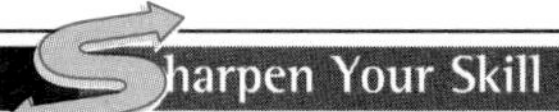

Sharpen Your Skill

TRACKING SYSTEMIC CHANGE

How do you deal with changes in your life? Think about one specific relationship, perhaps a long-standing friendship or a well-established work relationship. Recall a time when something major happened—you and your friend had to separate because of jobs or school, your parents divorced or remarried, your company restructured.

The following questions will prompt you to trace how the change reverberated throughout the entire relationship and how you responded to the change:

1. How did the change affect interaction routines in the relationship?
2. How did changes in interaction routines affect trust, closeness, and understanding between people?
3. How did the change affect your relationships with other people? (Did you form or strengthen other friendships when a friend moved away? Did you become less close to one of your parents after they divorced?)
4. How did you try to maintain equilibrium in the face of the change? (Some couples try to call daily when they are forced to have a long-distance relationship. Younger children often deny that their parents have separated for good. Older children sometimes regress in an effort to retain their share of attention in the wake of a new baby's arrival.)

Don't stop with these questions. Go on to identify the ripple effects of the change in your relationship system and the ways in which you both resisted and adapted to the change.

to avoid changes that disrupt our habitual ways of acting. At the same time, it explains why we seek novelty and appreciate changes in our lives and the new perspectives they bring.

Because communication is systemic, effectiveness requires adapting to particular contexts. In Part II of this book we will discuss specific contexts such as organizations, mass media, and interviewing. Before focusing on specific contexts, however, we should consider the single largest system that influences communication: **culture.**

COMMUNICATING IN A CULTURALLY DIVERSE WORLD

Communication is closely linked to culture because communication expresses, sustains, and alters culture. Your culture directly shapes how you communicate, teaching you whether interrupting is appropriate, how much eye contact is polite, and whether conflict is desirable. We are not born knowing how, when, and to whom to speak, just as we are not born with attitudes about different sexual orientations, religions, genders, and races. We acquire attitudes as we interact with others, and we then reflect cultural teachings in how we communicate.

Although the word *culture* is part of our everyday vocabulary, it's difficult to define. Culture is part of everything we think, do, feel, and believe, yet we can't point to a thing that is culture. Most simply defined, culture is a way of life. It is a system of ideas, values, beliefs, customs, and language that is passed from one generation to the next and that sustains a particular way of life (Spencer, 1982, p. 562).

Anthropologist Edward T. Hall noted, "You touch a culture in one place and everything else is affected" (1977, p. 14). In a culture, the interacting, interrelated parts affect one another and the whole. For example, the technological revolution that began in the 1970s has had multiple and far-reaching repercussions. Communication technologies allow us to interact with people who are not geographically near us. Today many people sustain and even form friendships and romantic relationships over the Internet (Lea & Spears, 1995). Telecommuting allows people who previously worked in offices to do their jobs in their homes. The speed at which organizations expect work to be done has accelerated with each newer, faster form of technological communication. Technologies change how, where, and with whom we communicate, just as they alter the boundaries of work and personal life. Because cultures are holistic, no change is isolated from the overall system. Four premises clarify how cultures affect and are affected by communication.

Bob

It's almost impossible to bring up children in a nonsexist way. My wife and I gave dolls and trucks to our son and daughter, we encouraged both of them at sports and cooking. We never emphasized being thin to our daughter or developing muscles to our son, but they learned that anyway. Our 12-year-old came home from school the other day saying she was going on a diet—and she's not fat. Every female movie star and singer is skinny, so she gets the culture's message despite what we try to teach her at home.

We Learn Culture in the Process of Communicating

We learn a culture's views and rules in the process of communicating (Klopf, 1991). By observing others and being exposed to mass communication we learn language (the word *dog*) and what it means (a pet to love or a food to eat). This allows members of a society to share meanings. Children aren't born knowing how to eat with forks and knives, chopsticks, or fingers; they aren't born thinking that dresses and suits or saris are appropriate dress; at birth they don't know whether to decorate parts of their bodies with tattoos or jewelry; they don't enter the world thinking of themselves as individuals or members of groups. We learn our culture's rules about these and countless other matters in the process of communication.

We learn culture in a variety of communication contexts. You learn to respect your elders or to devalue them by how you see others communicate with older people, what you hear others say about them, and how they are portrayed in media. We learn what body form is valued by what we see in media and how we hear others talk about people of various physical proportions. From the moment of birth we begin to learn the beliefs, values, norms, and language of our society. Both conscious and unconscious learning are continuous processes through which we internalize the particular ways of life in our culture. By the time we are old enough to realize that culture is learned, we've internalized many of our culture's perspectives and practices.

Multiple Cultures and Social Groups May Coexist in a Single Geographic Location

When we speak of different cultures, we often think of societies that are geographically distinct. For instance, India, South America, Africa, and Korea have separate

fyi LEARNING TOGETHERNESS

Traditional Korean schools teach children to identify with a group. Bathroom breaks are a collective enterprise: All children in a class go to a large room and use the bathroom together (Ferrante, 1995). In the United States that would be considered at least immodest and perhaps vulgar. The Asian view of personal identity as rooted in larger groups explains why Asians who lose face feel they have humiliated their entire families and communities.

cultures. Yet geographic separation isn't what defines a culture. Instead, a culture exists when a distinct way of life shapes what a group of people believes, values, and does. Groups with distinct ways of life can coexist in a single society or physical territory.

Most societies have a dominant, or mainstream, way of life. Although many groups may exist within a single society, not all identify equally and exclusively with the dominant culture. European, heterosexual, land-owning, able-bodied men who were Christian at least in heritage, if not in actual practice, created mainstream Western culture. Yet Western society includes many groups outside the cultural mainstream (Wood & Duck, 1995a, 1995b). Gay men, lesbians, and bisexuals experience difficulty in a society that communicates that they are not normal and refuses to grant them social recognition or legal rights. Mainstream customs often ignore the traditions of people who follow religions such as Judaism, Hinduism, and Buddhism.

We are affected not only by the culture as a whole but also by our particular location within the culture (Haraway, 1988; Harding, 1991). **Standpoint** is the social, symbolic, and material circumstances of particular social groups that shape members' perspectives on themselves, others, communication, and social life. **Standpoint theory** claims that a culture includes a number of social groups that distinctively shape perceptions, identities, and opportunities of members. Race, gender, class, and sexual preference are primary ways in which Western culture groups people. Although we may all realize that our society attaches differential value to different social groups, each of us is only one race, class, and sex, and each of us has a particular sexual orientation. Our experiences as members of particular social groups shape the way we perceive the world and ourselves and the ways we communicate.

In an early discussion of standpoint, philosopher Georg Wilhelm Friedrich Hegel (1807) pointed out that standpoints reflect power positions in society. To illustrate, he noted that masters and slaves perceive slavery very differently. Extending Hegel's point, we can see that those in positions of power have a vested interest in preserving the system that gives them privileges. Thus, they are unlikely to perceive its flaws and inequities. On the other hand, those who are disadvantaged by a system are able to see inequities and discrimination (Harding, 1991; Wood, 1993a).

Nonverbal communication reflects the perspective of dominant groups in a culture. For example, the dominance of people without disabilities is reflected in the number of buildings that do not have ramps and bathroom facilities for the disabled and public presentations that do not include signers for people with hearing limitations. Many campus and business buildings feature portraits of white men but few of women or people of color.

■ *Passing tradition from one generation to the next is how cultures sustain themselves. In this photo a Jewish elder is instructing a young boy in Jewish traditions.*

COMMUNICATING CULTURE

Locate a standard calendar and the academic calendar for your campus. Which of the following holidays of different cultural groups are recognized and treated as holidays by suspension of normal operations in communities and campuses?

Christmas	Passover
Yom Kippur	Kwanzaa
Elderly Day	Martin Luther King Day
Hanukkah	Easter

What do calendars communicate in recognizing or not recognizing important events of various cultures?

Mostafa

I went to a black college for two years before transferring here, and it's like two different worlds. There I saw a lot of brothers and sisters all the time, and I had black teachers. There were portraits of black leaders in buildings and black magazines in the bookstore. Here I've had only one black teacher, and I see fifty whites for every one black on campus. I've yet to see a black person's portrait hung in any campus building, and I have to go to specialty stores to buy black magazines. The whole atmosphere on this campus communicates "White is right."

Verbal communication also reflects the distinctive values of different cultures. For example, many Asian languages include numerous words to describe particular relationships: my grandmother's brother, my father's uncle, my youngest son, my oldest daughter. This linguistic focus reflects the cultural emphasis on family relationships (Ferrante, 1995; Triandis, 1990). English has fewer words to describe specific kinship bonds, which suggests that Western culture places less emphasis on ties outside the nuclear family.

Many Asian cultures also revere the elderly, and this too is reflected in language. "I will be 60 tomorrow" is a Korean saying that means "I have enough years to deserve respect." In contrast, Western cultures tend to prize youth, and English has more pos-

PROVERBS EXPRESS CULTURAL VALUES

"A zebra does not despise its stripes." Among the Masai of Africa, this saying encourages acceptance of things and oneself as they are.

"No need to know the person, only the family." This Chinese axiom reflects the belief that individuals are less important than families.

"The child has no owner." "It takes a whole village to raise a child." These African adages express the idea that children belong to whole communities, not just biological parents.

To learn about proverbs in other cultures, including Turkey and Palestine, consult these Web sites: http://www.columbia.edu/~sss31/Turkiye/proverbs.html and http://www.barghouti.com/folklore/proverbs/.

Source: Adapted from Samovar & Porter, 1991, p. 113.

itive words associated with youthfulness and negative words with seniority. The Western preoccupation with time and efficiency is evident in the abundance of words that refer to time (*hours, minutes, seconds, days, weeks*) and in common phrases such as "Let's not waste time." Among Buddhists the adage "Something cannot become nothing" expresses belief that life continues in new forms after what Westerners call death. In the United States "The early bird gets the worm" implies that initiative is valuable, and "Nice guys finish last" suggests that winning is important and that it's more important to be aggressive than nice.

As Maria notes in her commentary, tension and misunderstanding can erupt when values and communication practices of different cultures clash.

Maria

I get hassled by a lot of girls on campus about being dependent on my family. They say I'm too close to my folks and my grandparents and aunts and uncles and cousins. But what they mean by "too close" is I'm closer with my family than most whites are. It's a white standard they're using, and it doesn't fit me. Strong ties with family and the community are important, good Mexican values.

Co-cultures are groups of people who live within a dominant culture yet also are members of another culture, or social group, that is part of the larger one. For many years social groups that lived in a dominant culture and belonged to a second culture were called *subcultures*. However, the prefix *sub* connotes inferiority, as if subcultures are somehow less than "regular cultures." The terms *co-culture* and *social group* are used now to describe groups of people who hold dual membership in the dominant culture and one or more particular groups within it (Samovar & Porter, 1994).

Cultures and Co-Cultures Develop Distinct Forms of Communication

One of the best indicators that a culture or co-culture exists is communication (Hecht, Collier, & Ribeau, 1993; Kochman, 1981). Because we learn to communicate in the process of interacting with others, people from different cultures use communication in different ways and attach different meanings to communicative acts. For example, many Asian cultures emphasize harmony and cooperation, whereas Western culture encourages conflict and competition. When Westerners and Easterners work together, their different ways of communicating may cause misunderstandings.

Yet it would be a mistake to think that all Westerners or all Easterners communicate exactly alike. Even within a culture or co-culture, there are individual differences. Furthermore, not everyone who technically belongs to a particular culture adopts the communication practices that are typical of that culture. For instance, many middle-class and upper-class blacks do not communicate in ways that research has shown are common in traditional black communities. Likewise, not all women communicate in ways consistent with the patterns typical of feminine social communities, and not all men communicate in ways that scholars have identified as common in masculine communities.

Gender as a Co-Culture

Of the many co-cultures, or specific social groups, that exist, gender has

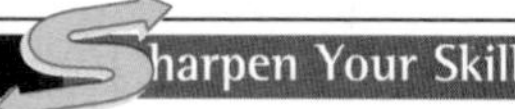

WHAT'S YOUR CULTURE SAYING?

What do common sayings and proverbs in the United States tell us about cultural values? What cultural values are expressed by sayings such as "You can't be too rich or too thin," "A stitch in time saves nine," "A watched pot never boils," "You can't take it with you," and "You've made your bed, now lie in it"? What other sayings can you think of that express key Western values?

received particularly intense study. Because we know more about it than other co-cultures, we'll explore gender as an example of a co-culture, yet the ideas that we'll discuss also apply to other co-cultures. Scholars have investigated how the sexes are socialized in separate co-cultures and how their communication differs in practice. One of the earliest studies reported that children's play is sex segregated, and boys and girls tend to play different kinds of games (Maltz & Borker, 1982).

Games that girls favor, such as house and school, involve few players, require talk to negotiate how to play because there aren't clear-cut guidelines, and depend on cooperation and sensitivity among players. Baseball, soccer, and war, which are typical boys' games, require more players and have clear goals and rules, so less talk is needed to play. Most boys' games are highly competitive, both between teams and for individual status within teams. Interaction in games teaches boys and girls distinct understandings of why, when, and how to use talk. Figure 7.1 summarizes the rules of communication that are typical of feminine and masculine social groups.

Research on women's and men's communication reveals that the rules we learn through play remain with many of us as we grow older. For instance, women's talk generally is more expressive and focused on feelings and relationships, whereas men's talk tends to be more instrumental and competitive (Aries, 1987; Beck, 1988; Becker, 1987; Johnson, 1989, 1996; Wood, 1998, 2001b, 2001c). In professional contexts women often engage in more personal communication with subordinates and peers than do men (Helgeson, 1990; Natalle, 1996). Many women favor management styles that are more collaborative than are typical of men. In personal relationships women tend to be more interested in talking about relationship issues than men.

Larry

Finally, I see what happens between my girlfriend and me. She always wants to talk about us, which I think is stupid unless we have a problem. I like to go to a concert or do something together, but then she says that I don't want to be with her. We speak totally different languages.

Another general difference is what each gender regards as the primary basis of relationships. For many men who were socialized in masculine communities, activities tend to be a primary foundation of close friendships and romantic relationships (Inman, 1996; Swain, 1989; Wood & Inman, 1993). Thus men typically cement friendships by doing things together (playing soccer, watching sports) and doing things for one another (trading favors, doing laundry). On the other hand, many women perceive communication as the crux of relationships. Communication is not only a means to instrumental ends but an end in itself (Aries, 1987; Riessman, 1990; Wood, 1997).

In general, men and women also have different styles of listening. Socialized to be responsive and expressive, many women tend to make listening

Figure 7.1 Rules of Gender Communication Co-Cultures

Feminine Communication Rules

- **Include others. Use talk to show interest in others and respond to their needs.**
- **Use talk cooperatively. Communication is a joint activity, so people have to work together. It's important to invite others into conversation, wait your turn to speak, and respond to what others say.**
- **Use talk expressively. Talk should deal with feelings, personal ideas, and problems and should build relationships with others.**

Masculine Communication Rules

- **Assert yourself. Use talk to establish your identity, expertise, knowledge, and so on.**
- **Use talk competitively. Communication is an arena for proving yourself. Use talk to gain and hold attention, to wrest the talk stage from others; interrupt and reroute topics to keep you and your ideas spotlighted.**
- **Use talk instrumentally. Talk should accomplish something, such as solving a problem, giving advice, or taking a stand on issues.**

fyi

TROUBLE WITH TALKING ABOUT TROUBLES

Differences in socialization often show up when men and women talk about their troubles. Perhaps a woman tells a man about something that is troubling her, and he responds with advice or a solution. His view of communication as instrumental leads him to want to do something. Because many women see communication as a way to build connections with others, however, women often want empathy and discussion of feelings before advice. Thus, women sometimes feel men's responses to their concerns are uncaring and insensitive. On the other hand, men may feel frustrated when women offer empathy and support instead of advice for solving problems.

Sources: Tannen, 1990; Wood, 1996, 1997.

noises such as "mm-hmm," "yeah," and "I know what you mean" when others are talking (Tannen, 1990; Wood, 1996). This is how they communicate that they are following and interested. Masculine socialization, however, places more emphasis on using communication instrumentally, so many men tend to offer verbal responses only if they have a point to make. Thus, on the job and in personal relationships women sometimes feel men aren't listening because men don't express attention in the ways women do. Also, men may misperceive women's listening noises as signaling agreement, not just attention.

Other Co-Cultures Gender isn't the only co-culture that affects communication. Research finds that communication patterns vary among social classes. For example, lower-income people tend to use shorter, simpler sentences, less elaborate explanations, and more conventional grammar than middle-income people (Bernstein, 1973).

Different racial and ethnic groups encourage distinct ways of interacting. Communication scholar Mark Orbe (1994) describes the United States as separate societies divided by race. A recent report finds that African Americans generally communicate more assertively than European Americans (Ribeau, Baldwin, & Hecht, 1994). What some African Americans consider authentic, powerful exchanges may be perceived as antagonistic by people from different social groups who have learned different rules for what counts as wit, play, and antagonism. Notice, however, that these are generalizations and they do not describe the communication of all blacks or all whites. Although membership in specific ethnic groups influences how we communicate, it is not the only influence and it is not one that affects all members of groups in the same way.

Another feature of traditional African American speech is extensive verbal artistry in which members play the dozens (a game of exchanging insults), speak indirectly (sometimes called *signifying*), and use highly dramatic language (Figure 7.2). These forms of communication allow historically oppressed social groups to express aggression and creativity indirectly when it might be unsafe to express them explicitly (Garner, 1994). As a group, African Americans reflect greater commitment to collective interests such as family or race in their communication, whereas European Americans tend to be more individualistic in their communication (Gaines, 1995). As a rule, African Americans also communicate more interactively than European Americans (Hecht et al., 1993; Weber, 1994). This explains why African Americans sometimes call out responses such as "Tell it," "All right," and "Keep talking" during speeches, church sermons, and classes. What Caucasians regard as interruptions of a speaker some African Americans perceive as complimentary participation in communication.

Michelle

I'm offended when I read that blacks communicate differently than whites. I don't, and neither do a lot of my black friends. Both of my parents were professionals, and I attended good schools, including a private one for two years. I speak the same way whites do. When the author of our

Figure 7.2 A Translation Guide

Term	*European American Meaning*	*Traditional African American Meaning*
Sister	**Female sibling**	**Black woman**
Brother	**Male sibling**	**Black man**
I'm going to buy you a watch.	**I am going to buy you a watch.**	**You're late (signifying).**
You call that dancing? My kid can dance better.	**You are a poor dancer (an insult).**	**Want to engage in "slammin'" or "jonin'"? (a game of reciprocal insults).**
I'm so good at my job they ought to make me president.	**Arrogant bragging**	**Verbal wit, not intended seriously (braggadocio)**

book says blacks signify and engage in call and response or talk differently than whites, it makes it sound like blacks are different from whites—like we don't know how to communicate like they do. If the author isn't black, how does she know how we communicate?

Michelle raises an important point. She wrote this comment to me after she read a previous edition of this book. In a conversation with Michelle, I explained that statements in this book about black communication patterns are based on research, including research conducted by black communication scholars. What you've read about traditional African American communication is not my opinion. Instead, the patterns we've discussed reflect the findings of careful scholarship. I include this research because many minority students have complained to me about textbooks that present only white communication patterns and present those as standard or correct. They have told me that this makes them feel erased, nonexistent. This point of view is reflected in Jason's comment, which he wrote after reading the same book Michelle criticized.

Jason

This is the first time since being at this school that I've seen blacks really included in a textbook or a class, other than my Af-Am classes. I think that's good, like it affirms my identity as a black. If I have to study how whites communicate, why shouldn't they learn how I communicate and why I communicate that way? I think we're all broadened if we know more about more kinds of people and how they think and act and talk.

My goal of weaving social diversity into the communication field leads me to include credible research on a variety of social groups so that we understand a range of ways in which people communicate. Yet it's critical to remember that statements about any group's communication are generalizations, not universal truths. Each of us communicates in some ways that are consistent with the patterns of particular social groups, and in other ways our communication departs from norms for each specific group. In part, that is because we belong to many groups. Michelle is not only black (a racial–ethnic group), but also upper middle class. Jason is also black, but he is from a working-class family. This may shed light on why Jason identifies with what African American scholars report as traditional black communication patterns and why Michelle does not.

Intan

Eye contact is the hardest part of learning American culture. In my home it would be very rude to do that. We look away or down when talking so as not to give insult. In America if I look down, it is thought I am hiding something or am dishonest. So I am learning to look at others when we talk, but it feels very disrespectful still to me.

BLACK TALK

Geneva Smitherman is a linguist who studies distinctive features of African American oral traditions. In her 1994 book, *Black Talk: Words and Phrases from the Hood to the Amen Corner,* Smitherman documents the richness and uniqueness of African American language. A sampling from *Black Talk:*

Chill: Relax.

Sweet: Outstanding.

All that: Excellent, great, all that something seems to be (example: "That woman is bad. She is definitely all that.").

Amen corner: Place in black churches where elders, especially women, traditionally sit.

Drop a dime: Tell on someone who is doing something wrong or illegal; report the person.

Git ovah: Make it over to a spiritually good life after struggling to overcome sin.

Jump salty: Become angry.

Mojo: Originally, mojo was a magical charm. In modern usage it is a source of personal magic that a person may draw upon to put others under a spell.

Scared of you: A compliment that acknowledges another person's achievements (example: "I'm scared of you now that you've been promoted.").

That how you living?: A criticism that asks why someone is acting a particular way.

Source: Smitherman, 1994.

Although members of a society may share a common language, we don't necessarily all use it the same way. Cultures and co-cultures, which exist both within and between countries, teach us rules for talking and interpreting others. Because communication rules vary among genders, races, and classes, we can't assume communication means the same things to all people or in all contexts.

Communication Expresses and Sustains Cultures

Communication simultaneously reflects and sustains cultural values. Each time we express cultural values, we also perpetuate them. When some Asian Americans veil their emotions, they fortify and express the value of self-restraint and the priority of reason over emotion. When some Westerners argue, push their ideas, and compete in conversations, they uphold the values of individuality and assertiveness. Communication, then, is a mirror of a culture's values and a primary means of keeping them woven into the fabric of everyday life.

Communication Is a Source of Cultural Change

In addition to reflecting culture, communication is a source of cultural change. Co-cultures in the United States have used communication to resist the

fyi

CODE TALKERS

During World War II a special group of soldiers serving in Iwo Jima developed a private code that enemy intelligence never broke. Because all the soldiers in this group were Navaho, the code they devised was based on the Navaho language, which is not written down and not understood by non-Navaho. Dubbed the "code talkers," this group of soldiers invented a 400-word code that was extremely secure. Drawing on the strong nature theme in Navaho life and language, the code included the Navaho words for *owl* (observer), *hawk* (dive bomber), and *egg* (bomb).

mainstream's efforts to define their identity. Whenever a group says, "No, the way you describe Americans doesn't fit me," that group initiates change in the cultural understandings.

A primary way in which communication propels change is by naming things in ways that shape how we understand them. For instance, the term *date rape* was coined in the late 1980s. Although historically many women had been forced to have sex by men they were dating, until recently the language had no term that named what happened as a violent invasion and a criminal act (Wood, 1992b, 2001b). Similarly, the term *sexual harassment* names a practice that certainly is not new but only lately has been labeled and given social reality. Mary's commentary explains how important the label is.

Mary

It was 15 years ago when I was just starting college that a professor sexually harassed me, only I didn't know to call it that then. I felt guilty, like maybe I'd done something to encourage him, or I felt maybe I was overreacting to his kissing me and touching me. But after the Clarence Thomas–Anita Hill hearings in 1991, I had a name for what happened—a name that said he was wrong, not me. It was only then that I could let go of that whole business.

As a primary tool of social movements, communication impels significant changes in cultural life. In the civil rights movement, powerful speakers such as Martin Luther King Jr. and Malcolm X raised black Americans' pride in their identity and heritage and inspired them to demand their rights in Western culture. Simultaneously, African American leaders used communication to persuade the nonblack public to rethink its attitudes and practices. Marches for gay pride and AIDS awareness are symbolic activities that challenge social attitudes that aim to devalue or ignore gay men and lesbians.

In addition to instigating change directly, communication accompanies other kinds of cultural change. Inventions such as antibiotics had to be explained to medical practitioners and a general public that believed infections were caused by fate and accident, not viruses and bacteria. Ideas and practices borrowed from one culture must be translated into other cultures. The Japanese system of management has been adapted to fit the culture of many U.S. companies. Calamities also must be defined and explained: Did the volcano erupt because of pressure in the earth or anger of the gods? Did we lose the war because we had a weak military or because our cause was wrong? Cultures use communication to define what change means and implies for social life.

Both an overall culture and our standpoint as members of particular social groups shape how we perceive and communicate. Yet we can learn to recognize and appreciate different cultural systems and the diverse forms of communication they foster. Doing so enables us to adapt our communication effectively in response to the diverse people with whom we interact.

GUIDELINES FOR ADAPTING COMMUNICATION

To communicate effectively, we need to adapt to different contexts and people. Effective adaptation allows us to tailor our verbal and nonverbal symbols and our ways of perceiving, creating climates, listening, and responding. We'll consider four guidelines for adapting communication skillfully.

Engage in Person-Centered Communication

The single most important guideline for adapting communication effectively is to engage in person-centered communication. From our discussion in Chapter 2 you'll recall that person-centeredness involves recognizing another person's perspective and taking that into account as you communicate. For instance, it's advisable to refrain from using a lot of idioms when talking with someone for whom English is a second language. Similarly, a man who has dual perspective might realize that a woman might appreciate empathy and supportive listening more than advice. The point is that competent communicators adapt to the perspectives of those with whom they interact.

We don't need to abandon our perspectives to accommodate those of others. In fact, it would be as unethical to stifle your views as to ignore those of others. Person-centeredness requires understanding both ours and another's point of view and respecting each when we communicate. Most of us can accept and grow from differences, but we feel disconfirmed if others don't recognize or acknowledge our perspectives.

Respect What Others Present as Their Feelings and Ideas

Has anyone ever said to you, "You shouldn't feel that way"? If so, you know how infuriating it can be to be told that your feelings aren't valid, appropriate, or acceptable. Equally destructive is being told our thoughts are wrong. When someone says, "How can you think something so stupid?" we feel disconfirmed. Effective communicators don't disparage others' thoughts and feelings. Even if you don't feel or think the same way, you can still respect another person as the expert on her or his perspective.

Susan

I hate it when people tell me they understand what it's like to have a learning disability. For one thing, there are a lot of learning disabilities, and I resent being lumped in a broad category. For another thing, if someone doesn't have dyslexia, which is my problem, they don't know what it means. They have no idea what it's like to see letters scrambled or wonder if you are seeing words right. People shouldn't say "I understand" what they haven't experienced.

One of the most disconfirming forms of communication is speaking for others when they are able to speak for themselves (Alcoff, 1991; Wood, 1998). Recently, I had a conversation with a couple at a party in which one person spoke for another. In response to my questions to the man, his wife said, "He's having trouble balancing career and family," "He's really proud of sticking with his exercise program," and "He's worried about how to take care of his parents now that their health is declining." She didn't allow her husband to assess whether he had trouble balancing career and family, felt pride about exercising, or was worried about his parents. Her rapid answers to questions I addressed to her husband left him voiceless. The same pattern occurs when parents speak for children who are capable of responding themselves. Generally, it's rude and disempowering to speak for others.

Just as we should not speak for others, we should not assume we understand how they feel or think. As we have seen, distinct experiences and cultural backgrounds make each of us unique. We seldom completely grasp what another person feels or thinks. Although it is supportive to engage in dual perspective, it isn't supportive to presume that we understand experiences we haven't had.

fyi

RESPECTING OTHERS' EXPERIENCES

Marsha Houston, an accomplished communication scholar, explains how claiming understanding can diminish a person. She writes that white women should never tell African American women that they understand their experiences as black women. Here's Houston's explanation:

> I have heard this sentence completed in numerous, sometimes bizarre, ways, from "because sexism is just as bad as racism," to "because I watch *The Cosby Show*," to "because I'm also a member of a minority group. I'm Jewish . . . Italian . . . overweight." . . . Similar experiences should not be confused with the same experience; my experience of prejudice is erased when you identify it as "the same" as yours.

Source: Houston, 1994, p. 138.

Recently, a Latina student in one of my classes commented on discrimination she faces, and a white male student said, "I know what you mean. Prejudice really hurts." Although he meant to be supportive, his response angered the woman, who retorted, "You don't know what I mean. You have no right to pretend you do until you've been female and nonwhite." When we claim to share what we haven't experienced, we take away from others' lives and identities.

Respecting what others say about their thoughts and feelings is a cornerstone of effective communication. We grow when we open ourselves to perspectives that differ from ours. If you don't understand what others say, ask them to explain. This shows that you are interested and respect their experience. It also paves the way for greater understanding between people with diverse backgrounds.

Resist Ethnocentric Bias

Most of us unreflectively use our home culture as the standard for judging other cultures. Some European Americans may regard rapping as noisy and theatrical because this form of communication is more dramatic than those whites conventionally use. On the other hand, some African Americans may perceive European Americans as stodgy and cold because their communication is more restrained (Houston, 1994). Asians may regard Westerners as rude for maintaining direct eye contact, whereas Westerners may perceive Asians as evasive for averting their eyes. European Americans' self-references may appear egocentric to Koreans, and Koreans may seem passive to Westerners. How we judge others depends more on the perspective we use to judge than on what others say and do (Wood, 1997, 1998).

Although it is natural to use our culture as the standard for judging other cultures, this can interfere with good communication. **Ethnocentrism** is the tendency to regard ourselves and our way of life as superior to other people and other ways of life. Literally, ethnocentrism means to put our ethnicity (*ethno-*) at the center (*centrism*) of the universe. Ethnocentrism encourages negative judgments of anything that differs from our ways. In extreme form, ethnocentrism can lead one group of people to feel it has the right to dominate other groups and suppress other cultures. The most abhorrent example of ethnocentrism was Nazi Germany's declaration that Aryans were the "master race," followed by the systematic genocide of Jewish people. Years later the Chinese forced Tibetans out of their homeland and into exile, where they remain today. Yet we need not look to dramatic examples like Nazi Germany to find ethnocentrism. It occurs whenever we judge someone from a different culture as less sensitive, honest, ambitious, good, or civilized than people from our culture.

To reduce ethnocentrism, we should remember that what is considered normal and right varies among cultures. **Cultural relativism** recognizes that cultures vary in how they think and behave, as well as in what they believe and value. Cultural relativism is not the same as moral relativism. We can acknowledge that a particular practice makes sense in its cultural context without approving of it. We may condemn clitoridectomies performed on young girls in some societies and also realize that genital surgery is rooted in ancient traditions that have meaning in those societies. Cultural relativism reminds us that something that appears odd or even wrong to us may seem natural and right from the point of view of a different culture. This facilitates respect, even when differences exist.

Recognize That Adapting to Diversity Is a Process

Developing skill in intercultural communication takes time. We don't move suddenly from being unaware of how people in other cultures interact to being totally comfortable and competent in talking with them. Dealing with diversity is a gradual process that requires time, experience with a variety of people, and a genuine desire to be part of a society that includes a range of people and communication styles. Five distinct responses to diversity range from total rejection to complete acceptance (Figure 7.3). At particular times in our lives we may find ourselves adopting different responses to diversity or to specific forms of diversity. That's natural in the overall process of recognizing and responding to diversity in life.

Resistance A common response to diversity is **resistance,** which occurs when we reject the beliefs of particular cultures. Resistance denies the value and validity of particular cultural styles (Berger, 1969). Without education or reflection, many people evaluate others based on the standards of their own culture. Some people think their judgments reflect universal truths. They aren't aware that they are imposing the arbitrary yardstick of their particular culture and ignoring the yardsticks of other cultures. Devaluing whatever differs from our ways limits human experience and diminishes cultural life.

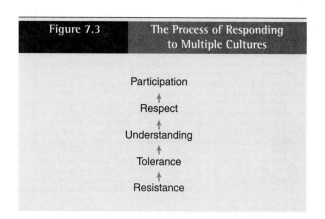

Figure 7.3 The Process of Responding to Multiple Cultures

Participation
↑
Respect
↑
Understanding
↑
Tolerance
↑
Resistance

Reid

I don't care what anyone says, I know that certain things are right or better than other things. I don't need to appreciate how women or blacks talk to be successful, and I sure don't need to learn how to talk their ways myself.

Resistance may be expressed in many ways. Hate crimes pollute campuses and the broader society. Denial of other cultures leads to racial slurs, anti-Semitic messages, and homophobic attacks. Resistance may also motivate members of a culture or co-culture to associate only with each other and to remain unaware of commonalities among people with diverse backgrounds. Insulation within a single culture occurs in both majority and minority groups.

Members of co-cultures may also resist and deny their group identities in order to fit into the mainstream. **Assimilation** occurs when people give up their ways and take on the ways of the dominant culture. Philosopher Peter Berger (1969) calls this *surrendering* because it involves giving up an original cultural identity for a new one. For many years assimilation was the dominant response of immigrants to the United States. The idea of America as a "melting pot" encouraged newcomers to melt into the mainstream by surrendering any ways that made them different from native-born citizens. More recently, the melting pot metaphor has been criticized as undesirable because it robs individuals of their unique heritages. Jesse Jackson proposed the alternative metaphor of the family quilt. This metaphor portrays the United States as a country in which diverse groups' values and customs are visible, as are the individual squares in a quilt, and at the same time each group contributes to a larger whole, just as each square contributes to a quilt's overall beauty.

Some people use another form of resistance to provoke change in cultural practices and viewpoints.

For example, heterosexuals who refuse to refer to their partners as "spouses" are resisting mainstream culture's refusal to grant legal status to gay and lesbian commitments. When culturally advantaged people resist and challenge the devaluation of disadvantaged groups, they can be powerful agents of change.

Chuck

My parents taught me homosexuality was immoral, and I'd never questioned that. In my freshman year I got to be good friends with Jim until he told me he was gay. I dropped him flat. Later I found out a guy on my floor was gay, and this year two of my brothers at the house came out. I still don't really approve, but it doesn't bother me so much now.

Tolerance A second response to diversity is **tolerance,** which means that people accept differences, although they may not approve of or even understand them. Tolerance involves respecting others' rights to their ways even though you may think their ways are wrong, bad, or offensive. Judgment still exists, but it's not actively imposed on others. Tolerance is open-mindedness in accepting the existence of differences, yet it is less open-minded in perceiving the value of alternative lifestyles and values. Although tolerance is not as divisive as resistance, neither does it actively foster a community in which people appreciate diversity and learn to grow from encountering differences.

Understanding A third response to diversity involves **understanding** that differences are rooted in cultural teachings and that no customs, traditions, or behaviors are intrinsically better than any others. This response builds on the idea of cultural relativism, which we discussed earlier. Rather than assuming that whatever differs from our ways is a deviation from a

universal standard (ours), a person who understands realizes that diverse values, beliefs, norms, and communication styles are rooted in distinct cultural perspectives. People who respond to diversity with understanding might notice that a Japanese person doesn't hold eye contact but would not assume that the Japanese person was devious. Instead, an understanding person would try to learn what eye contact means in Japanese society in order to understand the behavior in its native cultural context. Curiosity, rather than judgment, dominates in this stage as we make active efforts to understand others in terms of the values and traditions of their cultures.

Respect Once we move beyond judgment and begin to understand the cultural basis for ways that differ from ours, we may come to **respect** differences. We can appreciate the distinct validity and value of placing family above self, arranged marriage, and feminine and masculine communication styles. We don't have to adopt others' ways in order to respect them on their terms. Respect allows us to acknowledge genuine differences among groups yet remain anchored in the values and customs of our culture (Simons, Vázquez, & Harris, 1993). Learning about people who differ from us increases our understanding of them and thus our ability to communicate effectively with them. What is required to respect others is the ability to see them and what they do on their terms, not ours. In other words, respect avoids ethnocentrism.

Participation A final response to diversity is **participation,** in which we incorporate some practices and values of other groups in our lives. More than other responses, participation encourages us to develop skills for participating in a multicultural world in which all of us can take part in some of each other's customs. Harvard professor Henry Louis Gates (1992) believes that the ideal is a society in which we build a common civic culture that celebrates both differences and commonalities. Participation calls for us to be **multilingual,** which means we are able to speak and understand more than one language. Many people are already at least bilingual, which is also called being skilled at code switching. Many African Americans know how to operate in mainstream Caucasian society and in their distinct ethnic communities (Orbe, 1994). Many women know how to communicate in both feminine and masculine ways, and they adapt their style to the people with whom they interact (Henley, 1977). Bilingualism, or code switching, is also practiced by many Asian Americans, Mexican Americans, lesbians and

■ *How are this man and woman different? How might interacting enlarge the perspective of each person?*

gay men, and members of other groups that are simultaneously part of a dominant and a minority culture (Gaines, 1995).

My partner, Robbie, and I have learned how to communicate in both feminine and masculine styles. He was socialized to be assertive, competitive, instrumental, and analytical in conversation, whereas I learned to be more deferential, cooperative, relationship oriented, and creative. When we were first married, we were often frustrated by differences in our communication styles. I perceived him as domineering, sometimes insensitive to feelings, and overly analytical in his conversational style. He perceived me as being too focused on relationship issues and inefficient in moving from problems to solutions. Gradually, each of us learned to understand the other's ways of communicating and to respect our differences without judging them. Still later we came to participate in each other's style so that now both of us are fluent in both languages. Not only has this improved communication between us, but it has made us more competent communicators in general.

People reach different stages in their ability to respond to particular cultures. The different responses to cultural diversity that we've discussed represent parts of a process of learning to understand and adapt to diverse cultural groups. In the course of our lives many of us will move in and out of various responses as we interact with people from multiple cultures. At specific times we may find we are tolerant of one cultural group, respectful of another, and able to participate in yet others.

Summary

Because communication is systemic, it must be understood as existing within and being influenced by multiple contexts. We've focused on cultures and co-cultures as particularly important contexts that shape and are shaped by communication. Four principles summarize the relationships between culture and communication. First, we learn about our culture and its rules in the process of communicating with others. Second, distinct cultures and co-cultures may coexist within a single geographic location, and people may belong to multiple cultures. Third, we learned that cultures teach members distinct styles of communicating. Every culture's understandings about communication and its rules for interacting reflect and sustain the values shared by members of that group. The final principle is that communication and culture influence each other. On one hand, communication expresses and sustains cultural values and traditions. At the same time, communication is a potent force for changing cultural life.

In the final section of this chapter we considered four guidelines for adapting communication in a socially diverse world. The most fundamental is to engage in person-centered communication, which enables us to adapt to the perspectives and communication styles of others. Extending this, the second guideline is to respect what others present as their feelings and ideas. In most situations speaking for others is presumptuous, and disregarding what they express is rude. The third guideline for adapting communication is to resist ethnocentrism, which is the greatest threat to effective cross-cultural communication. Finally, we learned that adapting to diversity is a process in which we may find ourselves at different junctures at different times. Moving beyond narrow judgments based on our culture allows us to understand, respect, and sometimes participate in a diverse world and to enlarge ourselves in the process.

Although this chapter has focused on differences among people, it would be a mistake to be so aware of differences that we overlook our commonalities. No matter what culture we belong to, we all have feelings, dreams, ideas, hopes, fears, and values. Our common humanity transcends many of our differences, an idea beautifully expressed in a 1990 poem by Maya Angelou.

Human Family
I note the obvious differences
between each sort and type,
but we are more alike, my friends
than we are unalike.
We are more alike my friends
than we are unalike.

FOR FURTHER REFLECTION AND DISCUSSION

1. To understand how your standpoint influences perceptions, enter a culture different from the one you are used to. If you are Caucasian, you might attend services at a black church or a meeting of an African American community group. Do you notice your whiteness more in this context? If you are not Caucasian, reflect on the differences in how you perceive situations in which Caucasians are the majority and your race is the minority. With others in your class, discuss the effect of standpoint on perceptions and communication.
2. Some scholars claim that the United States has a multitude of co-cultures. Examples are people with disabilities and elderly people. Do you agree that these groups qualify as distinct co-cultures? What is required for a group to be considered a co-culture?
3. Continue the exercise started on page 153 by listing common sayings or adages in your culture. Decide what each saying reflects about the beliefs, values, and concerns of your culture.
4. Use *InfoTrac College Edition* to learn more about gendered patterns of nonverbal communication. Go to EasyTrac, type "gender and nonverbal," click *search,* then read the articles that appear.
5. Consider metaphors for U.S. society. For many years it was described as a melting pot, a metaphor that suggested that all the differences among people from various cultures would melt down and merge into a uniform culture. In recent years, however, the idea of a melting pot has been criticized for trying to obliterate differences rather than respect them. Jesse Jackson refers to the United States as a family quilt, whereas others say it's a collage in which differences exist and are noted as parts of the overall diverse whole society. Flora Davis (1991) calls the United States a salad bowl. What do you think she means by using the metaphor of salad bowl? What metaphor would you recommend?
6. As a class, discuss the tension between recognizing individuality and noting patterns common in specific social groups. Is it possible to recognize that people have standpoints in social groups and that members of any group vary? You might recall the concept of totalizing from Chapter 4 to assist your consideration of this issue.
7. To learn more about connections between culture and communication, check recent issues of these journals in the *InfoTrac College Edition* library: *International Journal of Comparative Sociology, Journal of American Ethnic History,* and *Sex Roles.*

KEY TERMS

Openness
Homeostasis
Culture
Standpoint
Standpoint theory
Co-culture
Ethnocentrism
Cultural relativism
Resistance
Assimilation
Tolerance
Understanding
Respect
Participation
Multilingual

Communication and Personal Identity

LEARNING OBJECTIVES

To understand

1. What the self is
2. How communication influences personal identity
3. How to resist destructive patterns in communication with yourself
4. How to create climates that foster your personal growth
5. Whether there are any vultures in your life

When my niece, Michelle, was three years old, she told me, "I am a girl." When her brother, Daniel, was born a year later, she told me, "I am Daniel's sister, and I have to take care of him." At her sixth birthday party she announced, "Now I'm a grown-up." I asked her what that meant, and she explained, "It means I have to clean my room, and I can go to school, and I can learn to be a lawyer and mommy like my mom."

Like Michelle, each of us has a sense of who we are. Like Michelle's, our sense of ourselves changes as we grow older and experience new relationships and contexts of life. Much of Michelle's sense of herself comes from how others have interacted with her during the early years of her life. Similarly, how you see yourself and what you imagine to be your future reflects how others have communicated to you since you were born.

In this chapter we will explore how the **self** is formed and changed in the process of communicating with others and with ourselves. First, we will define the self and explore the central role of communication in creating the self. In the second section of the chapter we'll consider special challenges and opportunities for communication with ourselves. Before we begin our discussion, complete the Sharpen Your Skill exercise that follows.

Sharpen Your Skill

DEFINING YOURSELF

Complete each of the ten statements with a noun or adjective that you consider descriptive of yourself:

1. I am ______________________.
2. I am ______________________.
3. I am ______________________.
4. I am ______________________.
5. I am ______________________.
6. I am ______________________.
7. I am ______________________.
8. I am ______________________.
9. I am ______________________.
10. I am ______________________.

COMMUNICATION AND PERSONAL IDENTITY

The self is an ever-changing system of perspectives that is formed and sustained in communication with others and ourselves. This definition emphasizes that the self is a process. Each of us continuously evolves and changes in response to experiences throughout our lives. The definition also calls attention to the idea that the self consists of perspectives: views about ourselves, others, and social life that change over time as we interact with others. Finally, the definition highlights communication as a critically important influence on who we are and how we see ourselves.

The Self Arises in Communication with Others

George Herbert Mead (1934) spent most of his career studying how humans develop selves. His conclusion was that the self is not innate but is acquired in the process of communicating with others. Infants aren't born with clear understandings of who they are and what their value is. Instead, we develop these understandings in the process of communicating with others who tell us who we are, how valuable we are, and what is expected of us. As we take others' perspectives into ourselves, we come to perceive ourselves through their eyes. Mead discussed two kinds of others who influence personal identity.

Eugenio

My father was not at home much when I was growing up. He worked in Merida where the tourists go and spend money. My grandfather lived with us and he raised me. He taught me to read and to count, and he showed me how to care for our livestock and repair the roof on our house after the rains each year. He is the one who talked to me about life and what matters. He is the one who taught me how to be a man.

Particular Others

The first perspectives that affect us are those of **particular others.** As the term implies, these are specific people who are significant to us. Mothers, fathers, siblings, peers, and often day-care providers are others who are significant to us in our early years. In addition, many families include aunts, uncles, grandparents, and friends who live together. Latinas and Latinos, Asians and Asian Americans, and African Americans generally have families more extensive than those of most

European Americans. Children in extended families have a number of significant others who affect how they come to see themselves, others, and the social world (Gaines, 1995).

As we grow older, peers increase in importance, as do teachers and co-workers. The friends and romantic partners we choose throughout life become primary anchors for our identity because we see ourselves in the looking glass of their eyes. As we interact with others, we internalize their views of us as ways that we see ourselves.

Generalized Other The second perspective that influences how we see ourselves is called the perspective of the **generalized other.** The generalized other is the collection of rules, roles, and attitudes endorsed by the whole social community in which we live (Mead, 1934). In other words, the generalized other represents the views of society and our social groups or co-cultures.

Broadly shared social perspectives are communicated both by other people who have internalized those views and by media and institutions that reflect cultural values. For example, when we read popular magazines and go to movies, we are inundated with messages about how we are supposed to look and act. We learn how the culture defines success, and we are likely to internalize this view. Communication from media infuses our lives, repeatedly telling us how we are supposed to be, think, act, and feel. Access to the Web and the Internet expands the perspectives we encounter, which may become part of how we view the world and experiences within it.

The institutions that organize our society uphold and express values that further convey social perspectives. For example, our judicial system asserts that as a society we value laws and punish those who break them. The Western institution of marriage communicates society's view that when people marry they become a single unit, which is why the law assumes that married couples have joint ownership of property. In other societies parents arrange marriages, and newlyweds become part of the husband's family. And many societies recognize, both legally and socially, marriages between members of the same sex. The number of schools and the levels of education inform us that Western society values learning. The number of prisons and ceaseless media attention to crime tell us that Western society values laws and lawful behavior.

At the same time, institutional processes reflect prevailing social prejudices. For instance, we may be a lawful society, but wealthy defendants can often buy better justice than poor ones. Similarly, although we claim to offer equal educational opportunities to all, students whose families have money and influence can often get into better schools than students whose families lack financial resources. These and other values are woven into the fabric of our culture, and we learn them with little effort or awareness. We have an ethical responsibility to reflect carefully on social values so that we can

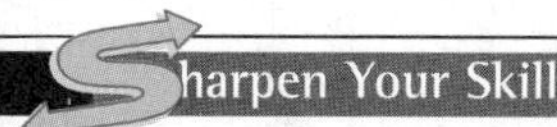

IDENTIFYING SOCIAL VALUES IN MEDIA

Select four popular magazines. Record the focus of articles and advertisements in the magazines. What do the articles and ads convey about what and who is valued in the United States? If you have a magazine aimed primarily at one sex, consider what cultural values it communicates about gender. What do articles convey about how women or men are regarded and what they are expected to be and do? Ask the same questions about advertisements. How many ads aimed at women focus on beauty, looking young, losing weight, taking care of others, and attracting men? How many ads aimed at men emphasize strength, virility, success, and independence?

To extend this exercise, note the cultural values conveyed by television, films, billboards, and news stories. Pay attention to who is highlighted and how different genders, races, and professions are represented.

make conscious choices about which ones we will accept for ourselves.

From the moment we enter the world, we interact with others. As we do, we learn how they see us and take their perspectives inside ourselves. Once we have internalized the views of significant others and the generalized other, we engage in internal dialogues in which we remind ourselves of social perspectives. Through the process of internal dialogues, or conversations with ourselves, we enforce the social values we have learned and the views of us that others communicate. How we perceive ourselves reflects the image of us that is reflected in the eyes of particular others and the generalized other.

Reflected Appraisals We see ourselves through the eyes of others, a process that is called **reflected appraisal,** or the looking glass self (Cooley, 1912). As infants interact with others, they learn how others see them. This is the beginning of a self-concept. Note that the self starts outside of us with others' views of who we are. Recognizing this, Mead said that we must first get outside ourselves to get into ourselves. By this he meant that the only way we can see ourselves is from the perspectives of others. If parents communicate to children that they are special and cherished, the children will come to see themselves as worthy of love. On the other hand, children whose parents communicate that they are not wanted or loved may come to think of themselves as unlovable. Reflected appraisals are not confined to childhood but continue throughout our lives. Sometimes a teacher first sees potential that students have not recognized in themselves. When the teacher communicates that a student is talented in a particular area, the student may come to see himself or herself that way. Later, in professional life we encounter co-workers and bosses who reflect their appraisals of us (we're on the fast track, average, or not suited to our positions). The appraisals of us that others communicate shape our sense of who we are.

Self-Fulfilling Prophesy One particularly powerful way in which communication shapes the self is **self-fulfilling prophesy,** which is acting in ways that bring about expectations or judgments of ourselves. If you have done poorly in classes where teachers didn't seem to respect you and done well with teachers who thought you were smart, you know what self-fulfilling prophesy is. Others usually first communicate the prophesies that we act to fulfill. However, because we import others' perspectives into ourselves, we may label ourselves as they do and then act to fulfill the labels we have internalized. We may try to live up or down to the ways we and others define

■ *Who are the people who form your looking glass self? For whom are you a looking glass?*

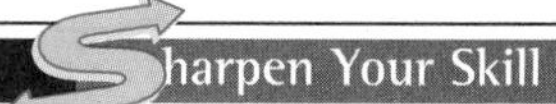

REFLECTING ON REFLECTED APPRAISALS

To understand how reflected appraisals have influenced your self-concept, try this exercise:

1. Refer to the Sharpen Your Skill exercise on page 168. Look at the ten words you used to describe yourself.
2. Next, identify five particular people who have been or are especially significant in your life.
3. Identify how the views these people communicated to you influenced you to develop the traits you listed in step 1. How did they express their appraisals of what you define as important parts of yourself?

Can you trace how you see yourself to the appraisals reflected by particular others in your life?

us. A friend of mine constantly worries about his weight. If he gains a few pounds, he criticizes himself as being fat. As a child he was overweight and his family constantly called him Fatty and Tubby. In elementary school some of his peers also teased him about being fat. Now this man is slender, but he can't see that. He still sees himself in terms of outdated labels. As a result, he worries excessively about weight and he thinks of himself as fat. He continues to accept the views others communicated when he was a child, and he continues to fulfill the prophesy by seeing himself as fat when he is not.

Like my friend, many of us believe things about ourselves that are inaccurate. In some cases the labels were once true but aren't any longer, yet we continue to apply them to ourselves (remember indexing, which we discussed in Chapter 4). In other cases the labels were never valid, but we are trapped by them anyway. Sometimes children are mislabeled as slow or stupid when the real problem is that they have physiological difficulties such as impaired vision or hearing or they are from other cultures and struggling with a second language. Even when the true source of difficulty is discovered, the children may have adopted a destructive self-fulfilling prophesy. If we accept others' judgments, we may fulfill their prophesies. To extend our discussion of the importance of communication from others in shaping how we see ourselves, we'll now elaborate the influence on self of family, friends, and society.

Communication with Family Members

For most of us, family members are the first and most important influence on how we see ourselves. Because family interaction dominates our early years, it usually sculpts the foundations of our self-concepts. Parents and other family members communicate who we are and what we are worth through direct definitions, scripts, and attachment styles.

Direct Definition

As the name implies, **direct definition** is communication that explicitly tells us who we are by labeling us and our behaviors. Parents and other family members define us by the symbols they use to describe us. For instance, parents might say, "You're my little girl" or "You're a big boy" and thus communicate to the child what sex it is. Having been labeled boy or girl, the child then pays attention to other communication about boys and girls to figure out what it means to be a certain sex. Family members guide our understandings of gender by directly defining what boys and girls do and don't do. Parents typically communicate their gender stereotypes to children, so they tell daughters, "Good girls don't play rough," "Be nice to your friends," and "Don't mess up your clothes." Sons, on the other hand, are more likely to hear, "Go get 'em," "Stick up for yourself," and "Don't cry." As we hear these definitions, we pick up our parents' gender expectations.

A POSITIVE PROPHESY

For years Georgia Tech ran a program called Challenge, which was a course designed to help disadvantaged students succeed academically. Yet when administrators reviewed the records, they found that students enrolled in Challenge did no better than disadvantaged students who did not attend.

Norman Johnson, a special assistant to the president of Georgia Tech, explained the reason for the dismal results of Challenge. He said, "We were starting off with the idea the kids were dumb. We didn't say that, of course, but the program was set up on a deficit model." Then Johnson suggested a new strategy: "Suppose we started with the idea that these youngsters were unusually bright, that we had very high expectations of them?"

Challenge teachers were then trained to expect success from their students and to communicate their expectations through how they treated students. The results were impressive: In 1992 10% of the first-year Challenge students had perfect 4.0 averages for the academic year. That 10% was more than all the minority students who had achieved 4.0 averages in the entire decade of 1980–1990. By comparison, only 5% of the students who didn't participate in Challenge had perfect averages. When teachers expected Challenge students to do well and communicated those expectations, the students in fact did do well—a case of a positive self-fulfilling prophesy.

Source: Raspberry, 1994, p. 9A.

Allena

My parents wanted a boy and had picked out Allen as his name. They got me instead. One of my strongest memories from childhood is hearing, "You were supposed to be a boy." I grew up believing that I was a mistake.

Family members provide direct communication about many aspects of who we are through statements they make. Positive labels enhance our self-esteem: "You're so smart," "You're sweet," "You're great at soccer." Negative labels can damage children's self-esteem: "You're a trouble maker," "You're stupid," and "You're impossible" are messages that can demolish a child's sense of self-worth. Direct definition also takes place as family members respond to children's behaviors. If children clown around and parents respond by saying, "What a cut-up; you really are funny," the children learn to see themselves as funny. If a child dusts furniture and receives praise ("You're great to help me clean the house"), being helpful to others is reinforced as part of the child's self-concept. From direct definition children learn what parents value, and this shapes what they come to value and how they regard themselves.

Identity Scripts Another way family members communicate who we are is through **identity scripts.** Psychologists define identity scripts as rules for living and identity (Berne, 1964; Harris, 1969). Like scripts for plays, identity scripts define our roles, how we are to play them, and basic elements in the plot of our lives. Think back to your childhood to identify some of the principal scripts that operated in your family. Were you told, "We are responsible people," "Save your money for a rainy day," "Always help others," "Look out for yourself," or

"Live by God's word"? These are examples of identity scripts people learn in families.

Most psychologists believe that the basic identity scripts for our lives are formed early, probably by age five. This means that fundamental understandings of who we are and how we are supposed to live are forged when we have virtually no control. We aren't allowed to coauthor or even edit our initial identity scripts because adults have power and children aren't even conscious of learning scripts. It is largely an unconscious process by which we internalize scripts that others write, and we absorb them with little, if any, awareness. As adults, however, we are no longer passive tablets on which others can write out who we are. We have the capacity to review the identity scripts that were given to us and to challenge and change those that do not fit the selves we now choose to be.

Attachment Styles Finally, parents communicate who we are through their **attachment styles**, which are patterns of parenting that teach us who we and others are and how to approach relationships (Figure 8.1). From his studies of interaction between parents and children, John Bowlby (1973, 1988) concluded that we learn attachment styles in our earliest relationships. In these formative relationships, others communicate how they see us, others, and relationships.

Most children form their first human bond with a parent, usually the mother because women do more of the caregiving in our society (Wood, 1994d). Many clinicians believe that the first bond is especially important because it forms expectations for later relationships (Ainsworth, Blehar, Waters, & Wall, 1978; Bartholomew & Horowitz, 1991; Miller, 1993). Four distinct attachment styles have been identified. **Secure attachment** is the most positive. This style develops when the caregiver responds in a consistently attentive and loving way to a child. In response, the child develops a positive sense of self-worth ("I am lovable") and a positive view of others ("People are loving and can be trusted"). People with secure attachment styles tend to be outgoing, affectionate, and able to handle the challenges and disappointments of close relationships without losing self-esteem.

Fearful attachment is cultivated when the caregiver in the first bond communicates in negative, rejecting, or even abusive ways to a child. Children who are treated this way often infer that they are unworthy of love and that others are not loving. Thus, they learn to see themselves as unlovable and others as rejecting. Not surprisingly, people with

Sharpen Your Skill

REFLECTING ON YOUR IDENTITY SCRIPTS

To take control of our lives we must first understand influences that shape it currently. Identify identity scripts your parents taught you.

1. First, recall explicit messages your parents gave you about "who we are" and "who you are." Can you hear their voices telling you codes you were expected to follow?
2. Next, write down the scripts. Try to capture the language your parents used in teaching the scripts.
3. Now review each script. Which ones make sense to you today? Are you still following any that have become irrelevant or nonfunctional for you? Do you disagree with any of them?
4. Commit to changing scripts that aren't productive for you or that conflict with values you now hold.

In some cases we can rewrite scripts. To do so, we must become aware of the scripts we were taught and take responsibility for scripting our lives.

Figure 8.1 Styles of Attachment

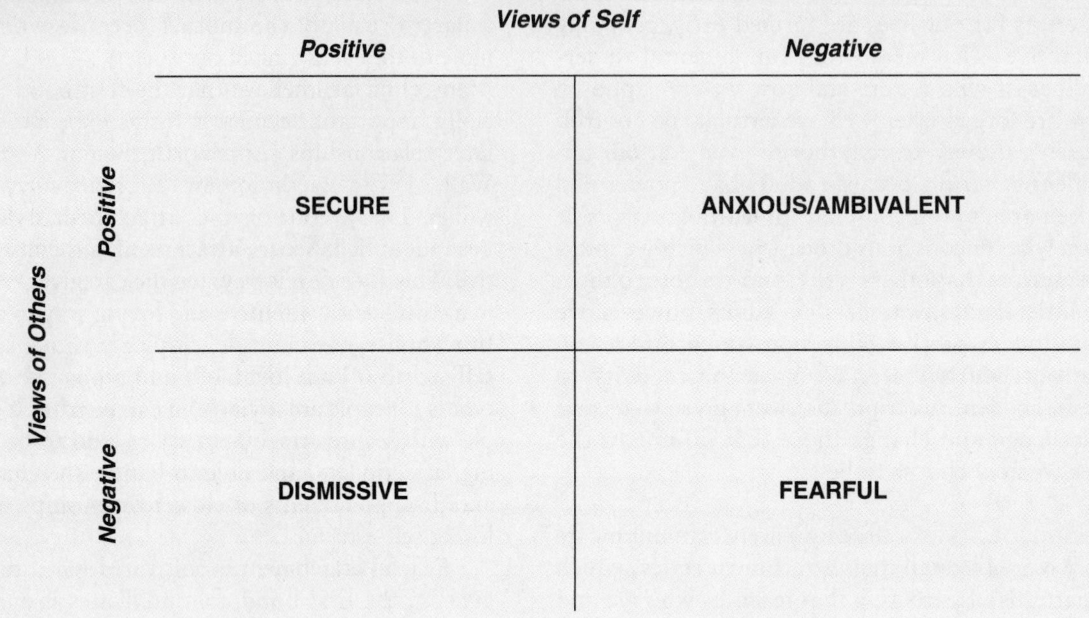

Views of Others \ Views of Self	Positive	Negative
Positive	SECURE	ANXIOUS/AMBIVALENT
Negative	DISMISSIVE	FEARFUL

fearful attachment styles are apprehensive about relationships. Although they often want close bonds with others, they fear others will not love them and that they are not lovable. Thus, as adults they may avoid others or feel insecure in relationships.

Zondi

In South Africa where I was born I learned that I was not important. Most daughters learn this. My name is Zondomini, which means between happiness and sadness. The happiness is because a child was born. The sadness is because I am a girl, not a boy. I am struggling now to see myself as worthy as a woman.

Dismissive attachment is also promoted by caregivers who are disinterested, rejecting, or abusive toward children. Yet people who develop this style do not accept the caregiver's view of them as unlovable. Instead, they dismiss others as unworthy. Consequently, children develop a positive view of themselves and a low regard for others and relationships. This leads them to a defensive view of relationships as unnecessary and undesirable. A final pattern is **anxious/ambivalent attachment,** which is the most complex of the four. Each of the other three styles results from some consistent pattern of treatment by a caregiver. The anxious/ambivalent style, however, is fostered by *inconsistent* treatment from the caregiver. Sometimes the adult is loving and attentive, yet at other times she or he is indifferent or rejecting. The caregiver's communication is not only inconsistent but also unpredictable. He or she may respond positively to something a child does on Monday and react negatively to the same behavior on Tuesday. An accident that results in severe punishment one day may be greeted with indulgent laughter on another day. Naturally, this unpredictability creates great anxiety in a child (Miller, 1993). Because children tend to assume others are right and they are wrong, they believe they are the source of any problem: They are unlovable or deserve others' abuse. In her commentary Noreen explains how inconsistent behaviors from her father confused and harmed her as a child.

Noreen

When I was little my father was an alcoholic, but I didn't know that then. All I knew was that sometimes he was nice to me, and sometimes he was really nasty. Once he told me I was his sunshine, but later that same day he said he wished I'd never been born. Even though now I know the alcohol made him mean, it's still hard to feel I'm okay.

In adult life people who have anxious/ambivalent attachment styles tend to be preoccupied with relationships. On one hand, they know others can be loving, so they're drawn to relationships. On the other hand, they realize that others can hurt them and be unloving, so they are uneasy with closeness. Reproducing what the caregiver did, people with anxious/ambivalent attachment styles may act inconsistently. One day they invite affection, the next day they rebuff it and deny needing closeness.

The attachment styles we learned in our first close relationship tend to persist (Bartholomew & Horowitz, 1991; Belsky & Pensky, 1988; Bowlby, 1988). However, this is not inevitable. We can modify our attachment styles by challenging the unconstructive views of us that were communicated in our early years and by forming relationships that foster secure connections today.

Communication with Peers

A second group of people whose communication influences our self-concept is peers. From childhood playmates to work associates, friends, and romantic partners, we interact with peers throughout our lives. As we do, we learn how others see us, and this affects how we see ourselves.

Reflected Appraisals Just as we reflect the appraisals of us that were communicated by family members, we also reflect the appraisals of us that peers communicate. If others communicate that they think we are smart, we are likely to reflect that appraisal in how we act and think about ourselves. If others communicate that they see us as dumb or unlikable, we may reflect their appraisals by thinking of ourselves in those ways. Reflected appraisals of peers join with those we saw in the eyes of family members and shape our self-images. Peers' appraisals of us have impact throughout our lives. We're affected by our co-workers' judgments of our professional competence, our neighbors' views of us, and the appraisals of friends.

Social Comparisons A second way in which communication with peers affects self-concept is through **social comparison,** which involves comparing ourselves with others to form judgments of our talents, abilities, qualities, and so forth. Whereas reflected

fyi

EMOTIONAL ABUSE

Andrew Vachss is an attorney who has devoted his life to helping children who have been abused. He has worked with children who have been sexually assaulted, physically maimed, abandoned, starved, and otherwise tortured. Yet Vachss regards emotional abuse as the most cruel. He says,

> Of all the many forms of child abuse, emotional abuse may be the cruelest and longest-lasting of all. Emotional abuse is the systematic diminishment of another. It may be intentional or subconscious (or both), but it is always . . . designed to reduce a child's self-concept to the point where the victim considers himself unworthy—unworthy of respect, unworthy of friendship, unworthy of the natural birthright of all children: love and protection. . . . There is no real difference between physical, sexual, and emotional abuse. All that distinguishes one from the other is the abuser's choice of weapons.

Source: Vachss, 1994, p. 4.

Sally Forth

Reprinted with special permission of King Features Syndicate.

appraisals are based on how others view us, social comparisons occur when we use others to evaluate ourselves. We gauge ourselves in relation to others in two ways. First, we compare ourselves to others to decide whether we are like them or different from them. Are we the same age, color, religion? Do we interact with the same people? Do we have similar backgrounds, political beliefs, and social commitments? Are we equally attractive? Assessing similarity and difference allows us to decide with whom we fit. Research has shown that people generally are most comfortable with others who are like them, so we tend to gravitate toward those we regard as similar (Pettigrew, 1967; Whitbeck & Hoyt, 1994). However, this can deprive us of diverse perspectives of people whose experiences and beliefs differ from ours. When we limit ourselves only to people like us, we impoverish the social perspectives that form our understandings of the world.

We also use social comparison to assess specific aspects of ourselves. Because there are no absolute standards of beauty, intelligence, musical talent, athletic ability, and so forth, we measure ourselves in relation to others. Am I as good a batter as Hendrick? Do I play the guitar as well as Sam? Am I as smart as Serena? Through comparing ourselves to others, we crystallize a self-image based on how we measure up on various criteria. This is normal and

harpen Your Skill

REVIEWING YOUR SOCIAL COMPARISONS

Find out whether your social comparisons are realistic.

1. Refer again to the Sharpen Your Skill exercise on page 168. Identify descriptions of yourself that you consider positive and descriptions that you consider negative. For example, you may have written, "I am kind," "I am smart," "I am responsible," "I am clumsy," "I am selfish," "I am impatient."
2. Next, beside each self-description, write the names of two people you use to judge yourself on each quality. For "I am kind," you would list people you use to measure kindness (remember the prototypes we discussed in Chapter 2).
3. Now review the names and qualities. Are any of the people unrealistic comparison points for you? If so, whom might you select to make more realistic social comparisons?

necessary if we are to develop realistic self-concepts. However, we should be wary of using inappropriate standards of comparison. It isn't realistic to judge our attractiveness in relation to stars and models or our athletic ability in relation to professional players.

Communication with Society

As we noted earlier, particular others are not the only influence on how we define ourselves and our value. We now consider in more detail how communication with the generalized other, or the social communities to which we belong, shapes the self. As we interact with the generalized other, we learn which aspects of identity society considers important, how society views various social groups, and, by extension, how it views us as members of specific groups. Modern Western culture emphasizes race, gender, sexual orientation, and socioeconomic level as central to personal identity (Andersen & Collins, 1992; Wood, 2000a, 2000b, 2001b).

Race In North America race is considered a primary aspect of personal identity. The race that has been historically favored in the United States is Caucasian. In the early years of this country's life, some people considered it normal and right for white men to own black women, men, and children and to require them to work for no wages and in poor conditions. Later, some people considered it natural that white men could vote but black men could not. White men had rights to be educated, pursue professional careers, own property, and other basic freedoms that were denied blacks. Even today Caucasian privilege continues: White children often

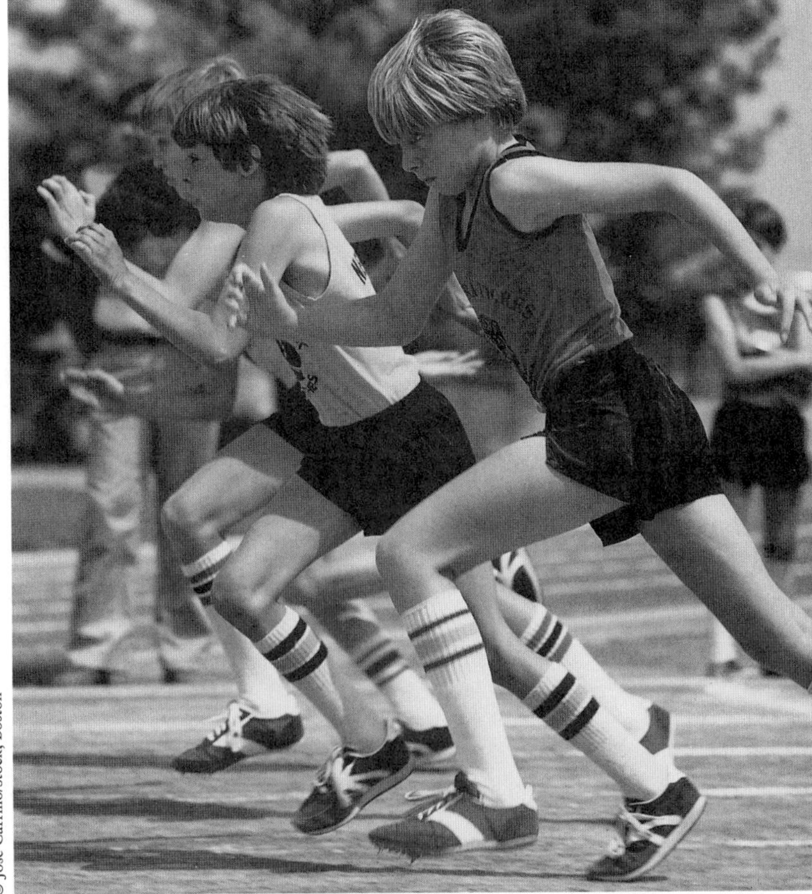

■ *Who are your sources for social comparisons today? How do you assess yourself relative to them?*

have access to better schools with more resources than do children of African American or Latin heritage. The upper levels of government, education, and businesses are dominated by European American men, whereas people of color continue to fight for equal rights in admission, hiring, and advancement. The color of one's skin makes a difference in how society treats us, our material lives, and who we are told we are.

Derrick

If my mama told me once, she told me a million times: "You got to work twice as hard to get half as far because you're black." I knew that my skin was a strike against me in this society since I can remember knowing anything. When I asked why blacks had to work harder, Mama said, "Because that's just how it is." I guess she was telling me that's how this society looks on African Americans.

Gender Gender is another category that is important in Western culture. Historically, Western society has valued men more than women and considered men more rational, competent, and entitled to various social advantages. In the 1800s women were not allowed to own property, gain professional training, or vote. Even today the United States and other cultures have strong gender prescriptions. Girls and women are expected to be caring, deferential, and cooperative, whereas boys and men are supposed to be independent, assertive, and competitive (Wood, 2001b). Consequently, women who assert themselves or compete are likely to receive social disapproval, be called bitches and otherwise reprimanded for violating prescriptions for their gender. Men who refuse to conform to social views of masculinity and who are gentle and caring risk being called wimps.

Inga

My parents treated me and my brother so different that you would think boys and girls were different species. I wasn't allowed to go out on my own because "someone could hurt you." But my brother was allowed to go anywhere he wanted because "he can take care of himself." I had a curfew because "girls have to be careful of their reputations," but my brother came home as late as he pleased. Even though I think a lot of the rules my parents enforced were sexist and unfair, I know that they were right in thinking girls are more vulnerable than boys.

Sexual Orientation A third aspect of identity that is salient in our culture's eyes is sexual orientation. Historically and today, heterosexuals are viewed as

fyi THE CONSTRUCTION OF RACE IN AMERICA

The term *white* wasn't used to describe people until Europeans colonized the United States. They invented the label *white* as a way to increase solidarity among European settlers who actually had diverse ethnic backgrounds. By calling themselves white these diverse groups could gloss over differences among them and use their light skin to distinguish themselves from dark-skinned people.

When slavery was an institution in the United States, Southern plantation owners invented a system of racial classification known as the One Drop Rule. According to this system, a person with as little as one drop of African blood was classified as black. Thus, racial divisions were established, though falsely.

Source: Bates, 1994.

normal, and lesbians, bisexuals, and gay men are regarded as abnormal. Society communicates this viewpoint not only directly but also through privileges given to heterosexuals but denied to gay men, lesbians, and bisexuals. For example, a woman and man who love each other can be married and have their commitment recognized religiously and legally. In the United States two men or two women who love each other and want to be life partners are denied social and legal recognition of their commitment. Many gay men and lesbians reject and resist negative social views of their identity, and they form communities that support positive self-images. These communities can serve as a generalized other that is different from that of the mainstream culture.

Socioeconomic Level A fourth facet of identity in our society is socioeconomic level. Because North America is an income-conscious society, the income level to which we belong affects everything from how much money we make to the kinds of schools, jobs, friends, and lifestyle choices we see as possibilities for ourselves. Socioeconomic level is difficult to pinpoint because, unlike sex and race, it is not visible. Socioeconomic level isn't just the amount of money a person has. It's a basic part of how we understand the world and how we think, feel, and act. Socioeconomics affect which stores we shop in, the restaurants we patronize, and the schools we attend. It influences how we dress, including our views of what it means to be well dressed. It also influences who our friends are, what forms of recreation we enjoy, where we live and work, even what kind of vehicle we drive (Langston, 1992).

Geneva

I don't fit in at this college. That hits me in the face every day. I walk across campus and see girls wearing shoes that cost more than all four pairs I own. I hear students talking about restaurants and trips that I can't afford. Last week I heard a guy complaining about being too broke to get a CD player for his car. I don't own a car. I don't know how to relate to these people who have so much money. Without my scholarship I could never have come here. I do know the people here see the world real differently than I do, and they see themselves as entitled to a lot more than I think I'm entitled to have.

Socioeconomic level influences our views of what we need. For example, people with economic security have the resources and leisure time to seek fulfillment of abstract needs such as self-actualization. They can afford therapy, yoga, retreats for spiritual development, and elite spas to condition their bodies. These are not feasible for people who are a step away from poverty. Members of the middle- and upper-income levels assume they will attend college and enter good professions, yet these often are not realistic options for lower-income people (Langston, 1992). Guidance counselors may

fyi A CROSS-CULTURAL LOOK AT SEXUAL IDENTITY

The Navajo and Mojave tribes once gave special respect to nadles, who were considered neither male nor female but a combination of the two sexes. The identity of nadle was sometimes conferred at birth on babies born with ambiguous genitals. People could also choose to be nadles later in life. When working on tasks assigned to women, nadles dressed and acted as women. When engaged in activities the society associated with men, nadles dressed and acted as men. Nadles could marry either women or men. Within their tribes nadles were regarded as wise and were given special privileges and deference.

Source: Olien, 1978.

encourage academically gifted lower-income students to go to work or pursue vocational education after high school, whereas they routinely steer middle-income students of average ability toward good colleges and high-status careers. In patterns such as this we see how the perspective of the generalized other shapes not just our sense of who we are but also the concrete realities of our lives.

Race, gender, sexual preference, and socioeconomic level are primary in our society's views of individuals and their worth. It's important to realize that these views of identity intersect with one another. Race interacts with gender, so that women of color experience double oppression and devaluation in our culture (Higginbotham, 1992; Lorde, 1992). Socioeconomic level and sexual preference also interact: Homophobia, or fear of homosexuals, is particularly pronounced among lower-income people, so a lesbian or gay person in a lower-income community may face unusually strong disapproval (Langston, 1992). Socioeconomic level and gender are also interlinked, with women far more likely to live at the poverty level than men (Stone, 1992). Gender and race intersect, so that black men face barriers not faced by white men (Gibbs, 1992).

In addition to race, gender, sexual preference, and socioeconomic level, society communicates other views that we may internalize. For instance, Western societies clearly value intelligence, competitiveness, individualism, and ambition. People, especially men, who conform to these social values receive more respect than those who don't. Mainstream Western society also values slimness, particularly in Caucasian women. Because society places such emphasis on slenderness in women, eating disorders are epidemic, and as many as 80 out of 100 fourth-grade girls diet, and most of them are well within normal weight limits (Wolf, 1991). Because preoccupation with self is a luxury of income level, the quest for thinness is more pronounced among Caucasian women than among women of color and in middle- and upper-income brackets more than in lower-income groups (Wood, 2001b). Today an estimated one in four college women has an eating disorder; without treatment, up to 20% of those with eating disorders die (Hicks, 1998). Society imposes physical requirements on men as well. Strength and sexual prowess are two expectations of "real men," which may explain why increasing numbers of men are having pectoral implants and penis enlargement surgery. People not born with bodies that society favors may feel compelled to construct them.

As we interact with particular others and participate in social life (the generalized other), we learn what and whom our society values. We also learn how our society sees us in terms of our race, gender,

fyi

RESOURCES ON EATING DISORDERS

If you or someone you know has an eating disorder, there are resources. Some of the best and most easy to access are on the Web. The following Web sites provide information on symptoms and consequences of eating disorders, personal accounts of living with and recovering from eating disorders, and treatment programs.

Ability's Bulimia Page: http://www.ability.org.uk/bulimia.html

Pale Reflections: http://members.aol.com/paleref/index.html

Bulimia Nervosa: http://www.ukhealthcare.uky.edu/disease/mentalhealth/edbulim

I'm Not Hungry: http://www.the-park.com/volunteer/safehaven/teenrescue/teens

Willough Treatment Center: http://www.thewillough.com/index.html

Sharpen Your Skill

INTERNALIZING THE GENERALIZED OTHER

Which views of the generalized other have you adopted?

1. How do you evaluate women? How important is physical appearance to your judgments?
2. How do you evaluate men? To what extent do strength and ambition affect your judgments?
3. What were you taught about African Americans, Latinos and Latinas, Native Americans, and people from Asian cultures? Which social views have you internalized?
4. How do you see heterosexuals, bisexuals, and gay men and lesbians? How did you develop these views?

Do you hold other social perspectives and attitudes that you don't really respect or like? If so, consider challenging them and reforming those parts of yourself.

sexual orientation, socioeconomic level, and other factors. However, social perspectives often do not remain outside us. If we do not reflect on the ethical and pragmatic implications of these values, we may import them into ourselves, and we thus come to share the views generally endorsed in our society.

Mike

I am a heterosexual white guy, but that doesn't mean that homophobia, racism, and sexism are irrelevant to me. Society isn't going to change if only people who are disadvantaged fight for equality. We're all involved.

We have seen that the self originates in communication. From interaction with family members, peers, and society as a whole we learn the prevailing values of our culture and of people who are significant to us. What we learn guides how we perceive and communicate with ourselves and others. We're now ready to discuss how what we've learned can help us meet two challenges related to personal growth.

CHALLENGES IN COMMUNICATING WITH OURSELVES

Throughout this chapter we've drawn on the basic communication processes covered in Part I of this book. For example, we've noted that others are an especially important influence on the process of perceiving ourselves. Our sense of identity evolves as we listen to others and observe their actions toward us. We've also learned that the symbols others use to define us shape how we perceive ourselves and that we can edit our self-talk to change our self-concepts. To demonstrate further how basic communication processes apply to interaction with ourselves, we will discuss two specific challenges to communicating in ways that foster personal growth and social well-being.

Reflecting Critically on Social Perspectives

We've seen that people tend to internalize the perspectives of the generalized other. In many ways this is useful, even essential, for collective life. If we all made up our own rules about when to stop and go at traffic intersections, wrecks would proliferate. If each of us operated by our own code for lawful conduct, we would have no shared standards regarding murder, tax payment, robbery, and so forth. Life would be chaotic.

Yet not all social views are as constructive as shared traffic rules and criminal law. The generalized other's unequal valuing of different social groups fuels discrimination against people whose only fault is not being what society defines as normal or good. Each of us has an ethical responsibility to exercise critical judgment about which social views we personally accept and use as guides for our behaviors, attitudes, and values. In addition, we have an ethical obligation to use our communication to promote positive social values and a fair social world.

The generalized other's perspective is not fixed, nor is it based on objective, absolute truths. Instead, the values endorsed by a society at any given time are arbitrary and subject to change. The fluidity of social values becomes especially obvious when we consider how widely values differ among cultures. For example, in Sweden, Denmark, and Norway marriages between members of the same sex are allowed and receive full legal recognition. In the early twentieth century people with disabilities were often kept in their homes or put in institutions. Today many schools place students who have physical or mental disabilities in regular classes. Prescriptions for femininity and masculinity also vary substantially across cultures. In some places men are emotional and dependent, and women are assertive and emotionally controlled. In many countries, race is less prominent than in North America, and mixed-race marriages are common. Some cultures even recognize more than two genders.

Social perspectives change in response to individual and collective efforts to revise social meanings. Each of us has an ethical responsibility to speak out against social perspectives that we perceive as wrong or harmful. By doing so we participate in the ongoing process of refining who we are as a society and the views of the generalized other that affect how we see ourselves and one another.

Seeking Personal Growth as a Communicator

Most of us perceive ways we could improve as communicators. Maybe we want to be more assertive, more mindful when listening, or more confident as

■ *Prescriptions for gender vary across cultures and over time. Within the dominant culture of the United States, what do you think gender will mean when these children are adults?*

public speakers. Three guidelines will help you grow as a communicator.

Set Realistic Goals Although willpower can do marvelous things, it has limits. We need to recognize that trying to change how we see ourselves works only if our goals are realistic. It's not realistic and usually not effective to expect radical growth immediately. If you are shy and want to be more extroverted, it's realistic to decide that you will speak up more and attend more social functions. On the other hand, setting the goal of being the life of the party may not be reasonable.

Realistic goals require realistic standards. Dissatisfaction with ourselves often stems from unrealistic expectations. In a culture that emphasizes perfectionism, it's easy to be trapped into expecting more than is humanly possible. If you set a goal of being a totally perfect communicator in all situations, you set yourself up for failure. More reasonable and more constructive is to establish a series of small goals that you can meet. You might focus on improving one communication skill. When you are satisfied with your ability at that skill, you can focus on a second one.

Assess Yourself Fairly Being realistic also involves making fair assessments of ourselves. This requires us to make reasonable social comparisons, place judgments of ourselves in context, realize that we are always in process, and assess ourselves in the perspective of time.

Remembering our discussion of social comparison, we know that selecting reasonable yardsticks for ourselves is important. Comparing your academic work with that of a certified genius is not appropriate. It is reasonable to measure your academic performance against others who have intellectual abilities and life situations similar to yours. Setting realistic goals and selecting appropriate standards of comparison are important guidelines when you want to bring about change in yourself.

Fenton

I thought I was prepared for college when I came here, but my first year was hard going. Most of the other guys in my dorm had a lot of experience with computers so they knew how to search online services to get information for papers in courses. My high school was in a poor rural county, so we didn't have many computers or instructors who could give us computer skills. I was really bummed out and thinking that I was inferior to the other freshmen here. Then I talked to my girlfriend back home, and she said something that gave me a new perspective on the situation. She said that I shouldn't be comparing my computer skills to those of people with a lot better training than I had. She reminded me that I knew more about using computers than most of my high school classmates. When I compared myself to them, I saw she was right. Then I could focus on upgrading my skills, but I didn't have to think I was stupid.

To assess ourselves effectively, we also should appreciate how our discrete qualities and abilities fit together to form the whole self. We treat ourselves unfairly if we judge specific aspects of our communication out of their overall context. Most often we do this by highlighting our shortcomings and overlooking what we do well. This leads to a distorted self-perception. Babe Ruth hit 714 home runs, and he also struck out 1,330 times. If he had defined himself only in terms of his strikeouts, he probably would never have become a world-renowned baseball player. One of my colleagues faults himself for being slow to grade and return students' papers. He compares himself to others in my department who return students' work more quickly. However, this man has twice as many office hours as any of his colleagues, which should temper his self-criticism about the length of time he takes to return papers. His judgment that he is negligent in returning papers is based on comparing himself to colleagues who spend less time talking with their students than he does. However, he doesn't compare himself to them when thinking about his office hours. In our efforts to improve self-concept, then, we should acknowledge our strengths and virtues as well as parts of ourselves we want to change.

To create and sustain a healthy self-concept, we also need to be attentive to unrealistic assessments of us that others may make. Bosses sometimes have unreasonable expectations. If we

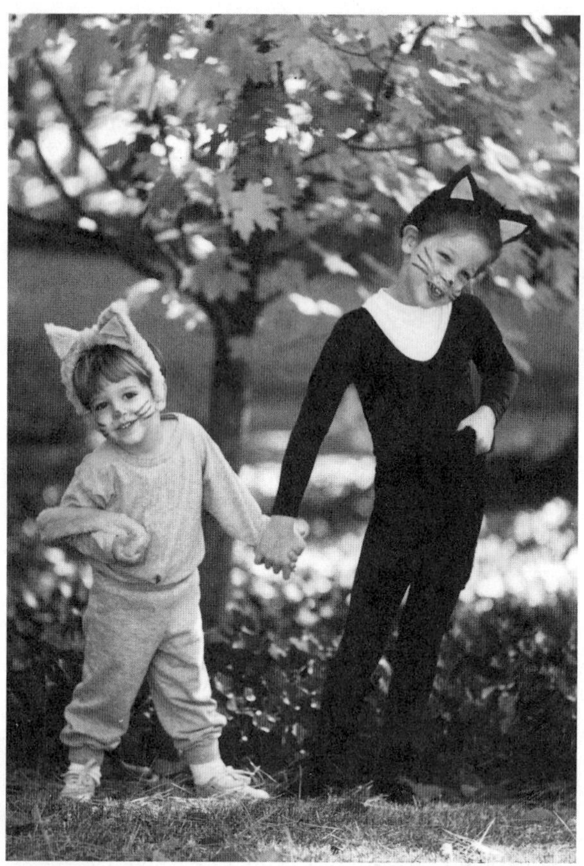
Carolyn C. Wood

■ *Halloween costumes allow children to experiment with different identities. What was your favorite costume when you were a child?*

measure our abilities by the unreasonable standards of our bosses, we may underestimate our effectiveness. Parents also can have expectations that are unrealistic or inconsistent with our goals and values. We should consider others' views of us, but we should not accept them uncritically.

A key foundation for improving self-concept is accepting yourself as in process. The human self is continuously in process, always becoming. This implies several things. First, it means that you need to accept who you are now as a starting point. You don't have to like or admire everything about yourself, but accepting who you are today as a basis for going forward is important. Your self has been shaped by all the interactions, reflected appraisals, and social comparisons made during your life. You cannot change your past, but neither do you have to be bound by it forever. Only by realizing and accepting who you are now can you move ahead.

Accepting yourself as in process also implies that you realize you can change. Who you are today is not who you will be in 5 or 10 years. Because you are in process, you are always changing and growing. Don't let yourself be hindered by negative self-fulfilling prophesies or the mindtrap that you cannot change (Rusk & Rusk, 1988). You can change if you set realistic goals, make a genuine commitment, and work for the changes you want. Just remember that you are not fixed as you are but are always in the process of becoming.

Create a Supportive Climate for Change Just as it is easier to swim with the tide than against it, it is easier to change our views of ourselves when we have some support for our efforts. You can do a lot to create a climate that supports your growth by choosing contexts and people who help you realize your goals.

First, think about settings. If you want to improve your physical condition, it makes more sense to participate in intramural sports than to hang out in bars. If you want to lose weight, it's better to go to restaurants that serve healthful foods and offer light choices than to go to cholesterol castles. If you want to become more outgoing, you need to put yourself in social situations rather than in libraries. But libraries are a better context than parties if your goal is to improve academic performance.

Bob

I never drank much until I got into this one group at school. All of them drank all the time. It was easy to join them. In fact, it was pretty hard not to drink and still be one of the guys. A while ago I decided I was drinking too much. It was hard enough not to drink because the guys were always doing it, but what really made it hard was the ways the guys got on me for abstaining. They let me know I was being uncool and made me feel like a jerk. Finally, I had to get a different apartment to stop drinking.

Who we are with has a great deal to do with how we see ourselves and how worthy we feel we are. This means you can create a supportive context by consciously choosing to be around people who believe in you and encourage your personal growth. It's equally important to steer clear of people who pull you down or say you can't change. In other words, people who reflect positive appraisals of us enhance our ability to improve who we are.

One way to think about how others' communication affects how we feel about ourselves is to recognize that people can be uppers, downers, and vultures (Simon, 1977). **Uppers** are people who communicate positively about us and who reflect positive appraisals of our self-worth. They notice our strengths, see our progress, and accept our weaknesses and problems without discounting us. When we're around uppers, we feel more upbeat and positive about ourselves. Uppers aren't necessarily unconditionally positive in their communication. A true friend can be an upper by recognizing our weaknesses and helping us work on them. Instead of putting us down, an upper believes in us and helps us believe in our capacity to change. Who are the uppers in your life? Are you an upper for yourself?

Downers are people who communicate negatively about us and our self-worth. They call attention to our flaws, emphasize our problems, and put down our dreams and goals. When we're around downers, we tend to feel down about ourselves. Reflecting their perspectives, we're more aware of our weaknesses and less confident of what we can accomplish. Downers, whether other people or ourselves, discourage belief in ourselves. Who are the downers in your life?

Vultures are an extreme form of downers. They not only communicate negatively about us but actually attack our self-concepts, just as actual vultures prey on their victims. Sometimes vultures initiate harsh criticism of us. They say, "That outfit looks dreadful on you," or "You really blew that one." In other cases vultures pick up on our doubts and magnify them. They discover our weak spots and exploit them, picking us apart by focusing on sensitive areas in our self-concept. For example, a friend of mine felt he was out of condition and decided to start a rigorous running program. One of his "friends" ridiculed him. The person said, "You're going to need to run a lot more if you want to see any change," "You look really out of shape when you put on your jogging shorts," and "Is 25 pounds all you can press? That's nothing." This harangue typifies a vulture's attack on self-worth. By telling us we are inadequate, vultures demolish our self-esteem. Reflect on how you feel about yourself when you're with uppers, downers, and vultures. Can you see how powerfully others' communication affects your self-concept? Have you internalized the perspectives of others so that you communicate with yourself as an upper, downer, or vulture?

As we've suggested in discussing uppers, downers, and vultures, others aren't the only ones whose communication affects our self-concepts. We also communicate with ourselves, and our messages influence our self-esteem. One of the most crippling kinds of self-talk in which we can engage is **self-sabotage.** This involves telling ourselves we are no good, we can't do something, there's no point in trying to change, and so forth. We may be repeating judgments others made of us or inventing negative self-fulfilling prophesies. Either way, self-sabotage defeats us because it undermines our belief in ourselves. Self-sabotage is poisonous; it destroys our motivation to grow. We can be downers or even vultures to ourselves, just as others can be. In fact, we can probably do more damage to our self-concept than others can because we are most aware of our vulnerabilities and fears. This may explain why vultures were originally described as people who put themselves down (Simon, 1977). We can also be uppers for ourselves. We can affirm our worth, encourage our growth, and fortify our sense of self-worth. Positive self-talk builds motivation and belief in yourself. It is also a useful strategy to interrupt and challenge negative messages from yourself and others. The next time you hear yourself saying, "I can't do this," or someone else says, "You'll never change," challenge the self-defeating message with self-talk. Say out loud to yourself, "I can do it. I will change." Use positive self-talk to resist counterproductive communication about yourself.

Before leaving this discussion, we should make it clear that improving your self-concept is not facilitated by uncritical positive communication. None of us grows and improves when we listen only to praise, particularly if it is less than honest. The true uppers in our lives offer constructive criticism as a way to encourage us to reach for better versions of ourselves.

Summary

In this chapter we explored the self as a process that evolves over the course of our lives. We saw that the self is not present at birth but develops as we interact with others. Through communication we learn perspectives of both particular others and the generalized other, or the broad social community. Reflected appraisals, direct definitions, and social comparisons further shape how we see ourselves and how we change over time. The perspective of the generalized other includes social views of aspects of identity, including race, gender, sexual preference, and income level. However, these are arbitrary social constructions that we can challenge. When we resist counterproductive social views, we promote change in society.

The final section of the chapter focused on concrete ways we can apply basic communication processes to foster a healthy society and personal growth. As members of a culture we have an ethical obligation to use our communication to speak out against social values that we consider wrong or harmful. In doing so we participate in the continuous evolution of our collective world.

In addition to advancing cultural life, communication can foster personal growth. Guidelines for doing this are to set realistic goals, assess yourself fairly, and create contexts that support the changes you seek. Transforming how we see ourselves is not easy, but it is possible. We can make amazing changes in who we are and who we will become when we embrace our human capacity to make choices.

FOR FURTHER REFLECTION AND DISCUSSION

1. Set one specific goal for personal growth as a communicator. Goals you could establish are to listen better, be more assertive, or learn about communication cultures that differ from yours. Apply what you learn during the semester to your personal goal.
2. Discuss society's views (the generalized other) of women and men. What are current social expectations for each sex? What behaviors, appearances, and attitudes violate social prescriptions for gender? Do you agree or disagree with these social expectations?
3. Use your *InfoTrac College Edition* to learn about areas of personal growth that are widely sought today. Select *Psychology Today,* skim the table of contents for the last four issues, and read two articles on personal growth topics.
4. To what extent do you feel you have an ethical responsibility to improve yourself and contribute to enhancing others? How does your standpoint as a member of specific social groups influence your views on this question?
5. On your *InfoTrac College Edition,* access the last year's issues of the *Journal of Family Practice.* What articles do you find that extend this chapter's discussion of the influence of families, especially parents, on children's self-concepts?

KEY TERMS

Self
Particular others
Generalized other
Reflected appraisal
Self-fulfilling prophesy
Direct definition
Identity scripts
Attachment styles
Secure attachment
Fearful attachment
Dismissive attachment
Anxious/ambivalent attachment
Social comparison
Uppers
Downers
Vultures
Self-sabotage

Communication in Personal Relationships

LEARNING OBJECTIVES

To understand

1. The difference between commitment and love
2. Whether it is normal not to always want to be with somebody you love
3. What kinds of communication sustain long-distance friendships and romances
4. Whether most romantic relationships are equitable for women and men
5. How couples can communicate effectively about safer sex

When my mother was no longer able to care for herself, my partner and I invited her to be part of our family. She lived in our home for the final 14 months of her life. As you might imagine, during this period I felt much sadness and grief. What you might not realize is that I also experienced a great deal of joy and personal growth, and important relationships in my life gained depth. Mother and I grew close in new ways, and my ties with Robbie, my sister, Carolyn, and close friends were deepened by sharing the fears and emotions that accompany losing a parent.

My experience is not unusual. All of us count on family, close friends, and romantic partners in good times as well as bad. Our intimates help us get through rough and unhappy moments, and they celebrate our joys and victories. Try to imagine that suddenly you have no close friends and no romantic partner. How would your life be different? What would be missing? If you're like most people, a great deal would be missing. Close relationships are important sources of growth, pleasure, comfort, and fulfillment. We need people who care about us and who let us care about them.

Healthy, effective communication is the heartbeat of healthy personal relationships. In previous chapters we've discussed self-disclosure, communication climate, and management of conflict as foundations of communication. In this chapter we focus on how those and other communication processes apply to the specific context of relationships with family, friends, and romantic partners. The first section of the chapter defines personal relationships and identifies their special features. In the second section of the chapter we'll examine four primary challenges for personal relationships in our era.

UNDERSTANDING PERSONAL RELATIONSHIPS

A **personal relationship** is a voluntary commitment between irreplaceable individuals who are influenced by rules, relationship dialectics, and surrounding contexts. This definition highlights important qualities that distinguish personal relationships from other kinds of human connections.

Features of Personal Relationships

Personal relationships are unique: Each has its distinctive qualities and style. In addition, commitment, rules, embeddedness in contexts, and relationship dialectics distinguish personal relationships from social connections. We'll discuss each of these features and then explore the evolutionary paths of friendships and romantic relationships.

Uniqueness The vast majority of our relationships are social, not personal. A **social relationship** is one in which participants interact within social roles rather than as individuals. For instance, you might exchange favors with a classmate, go roller-blading with people from your job, and talk about politics with a neighbor. In each case the person could be replaced by someone else who took the same role. You could find other people with whom to swap favors, go roller-blading, and have political conversations. In these relationships the specific people are less important than the roles they fulfill. The value of social relationships lies more in what participants do than in who they are because a variety of people could fulfill the same functions.

In personal relationships, however, the particular people and what they create between them define the connection. Many people are not so much committed to marriage in the abstract but to living their lives with a particular person. Friendships also involve unique bonds with specific people. Others cannot replace intimate partners (Blumstein & Kollock, 1988; Wood, 2000b). When a partner leaves or dies, that relationship ends, although it may remain strong in memory. We may later have other intimates, but a new spouse or best friend will not be a facsimile of the former one. Unlike social relationships, personal ones are unique and partners are irreplaceable.

■ *Over the years couples forge bonds that are unique and central to their happiness.*

Commitment The sparks and emotional high of being in love or discovering a new friend stem from **passion,** which is an intense feeling based on rewards from being involved with another person. Passion is why we feel butterflies in the stomach and fall head over heels. As exciting as passion is, it isn't the basis of enduring relationships.

Commitment is a decision to remain with a relationship. The hallmark of commitment is the intention to share the future (Beck, 1988). Committed friends and romantic partners assume they will stay together. Because commitment assumes a shared future, partners are unlikely to bail out if the going gets rough. Instead, they weather bad times (Lund, 1985). Unlike passion, commitment is a decision to stay together despite trouble, disappointments, sporadic restlessness, and lulls in emotional depth.

Commitment grows out of **investments,** which are what we put into relationships that we could not retrieve if the relationship were to end. When we care about another person, we invest time, energy, thought, and feelings into interaction. In doing this we invest *ourselves* in others. We also make material investments that can't be recovered if a relationship ends. Gifts, money spent going out, and joint property cannot be recovered fully if the relationship ends. Investments are powerful because they are personal choices to give things that can't be recovered. We can't get back the feelings and energy we invest in a relationship. We can't recover history shared with another. The only way to make good on investments is to stick with a relationship (Brehm, 1992). For good or ill, then, investments make it more difficult to end relationships.

Sarah

When Sean and I were first married, I was so happy I didn't care about anything else. My friends tried to talk me out of quitting school, but I wanted to work to put Sean through medical school. Then we had one baby and another and a third, and I was a stay-at-home mom who was totally involved in family. Then things started unraveling between Sean and me. After several years of feeling unhappy I thought about a divorce. But then I thought, "Where could I go? How could I support myself and the kids?" I hadn't finished college, so I couldn't earn a decent income. My job skills were rusty and out of date because I'd been out of the job market for 10 years. It was like I was trapped because I'd put too much in the marriage to leave.

Relationship Rules All relationships have **rules** that guide how partners communicate and interpret each other's communication. As in other communication contexts, rules in relationships define what is expected in certain kinds of relationships (friends should be loyal), the meaning of particular kinds of communication (hugs count as affection, silence as anger), and when, how, and in what circumstances various kinds of communication are appropriate. Typically, relationship rules are unspoken understandings between partners. Although friends and romantic partners may never explicitly discuss rules, they learn how important rules are if they violate one.

Miguel

Sherry and I had been dating for about six months when some of my friends from another school came to visit on their spring break. We decided to go out on Saturday night to hear a local band. It never occurred to me to check with Sherry because we hadn't made plans for that night. But she was so mad at me. She said, "We always go out on Fridays and Saturdays"—like it was written in stone or something.

As we noted in earlier chapters, two kinds of rules guide our communication. Constitutive rules define what various communications mean in personal relationships. For instance, some people count listening to problems as caring, whereas others count as caring engaging a friend or partner in activities to divert attention from problems (Tavris, 1992; Wood, 2001b, 2001c). Families often have constitutive rules that define what kinds of communication symbolize love and commitment (visiting at least three times a year, remembering birthdays). Romantic partners work out constitutive rules that define the kinds of communication that express loyalty, support, rudeness, love, joking, acceptance, and so forth.

Regulative rules govern interaction by specifying when and with whom to engage in various kinds of communication. For example, friends and family members often operate according to a regulative rule that says it's okay to criticize each other in private, but doing so in front of others is not acceptable. Many children learn it's impolite to interrupt others, particularly elders. Some romantic partners restrict physical displays of affection to private settings.

Friends, families, and romantic partners generate rules about what they want and expect of each other, such as support, time, and acceptance. Equally important are "shalt not" rules that define what each won't tolerate. For example, most Westerners

RULES OF FRIENDSHIP

Researchers asked Westerners what it takes to maintain a good friendship. Here are the common rules they identified:

1. Stand up for a friend who isn't around.
2. Share your successes and how you feel about them.
3. Give emotional support.
4. Trust and confide in each other.
5. Help a friend when she or he needs it.
6. Respect a friend's privacy.
7. Try to make friends feel good.
8. Tolerate your friend's friends.
9. Don't criticize a friend in front of others.
10. Don't tell a friend's confidences to other people.
11. Don't nag or focus on a friend's faults.

Source: Argyle & Henderson, 1984.

would consider it a betrayal if a friend became sexually involved with their romantic partner. Some families have strong "shalt not" rules that prohibit members from marrying outside their race, religion, or ethnic group. Rules regulate both trivial and important aspects of interaction. Not interrupting may be a rule, but breaking it probably won't wreck a good friendship. On the other hand, deceitful communication or verbal abuse sound the death knell for a friendship.

Embeddedness in Contexts Personal relationships are not isolated from the social world. Instead, the surroundings of relationships influence interaction between people (Allan, 1993; Baxter, 1993). Neighborhoods, social circles, family units, and society as a whole affect friendships and romances. For instance, Western culture values heterosexual marriage, which means that men and women who marry receive more social support than do singles, cohabiting heterosexuals, or gay and lesbian couples. Our families of origin shaped what we look for in intimates: the importance of social status, income, appearance, race, religion, intelligence, and so on. Our social circles establish norms for such activities as religious involvement, drinking, political activism, participation in community groups, studying, and partying. Circumstances in the overall society may also influence interaction among intimates. For instance, during deep recessions people who are laid off may experience a diminished sense of self-worth. Shifts in financial security and self-worth reverberate throughout close relationships, causing ripples of change throughout the systems. The many social contexts of our lives affect what we expect of relationships and how we communicate in them.

Barbara

I never realized how much your social group influences other relationships until I joined a sorority. All the girls there had the nicest clothes and the newest styles, and I felt pressured to buy expensive clothes myself. It was like the way I had dressed before (which wasn't bad) just wasn't good enough if I wanted to be part of the group.

Both particular others and the generalized other, which we discussed in Chapter 8, affect activities and expectations in personal relationships.

Families may voice approval or disapproval of our choices of intimates or the way we organize our private relationships. Our society's technological advances and mobility make long-distance relationships more possible, even inevitable, than in earlier times. The growing number of dual-career couples is revising traditional expectations about how much each partner participates in earning income, homemaking, and child care. As our society becomes more culturally diverse, interracial, interreligious, and interethnic relationships between people from diverse backgrounds become more common and socially accepted. Thus, both our social circles and the larger society are contexts that influence the relationships we form and the ways we communicate within them.

Relationship Dialectics A final quality of personal relationships is the presence of **relationship dialectics.** These are opposing and continuous tensions that are normal in all close relationships. Leslie Baxter, a scholar of interpersonal communication, has identified three relationship dialectics (Baxter, 1990, 1993).

Autonomy/connection is a tension between wanting to be separate and connected. Because we want to be deeply linked to others, we cherish spending time with our intimates, sharing experiences, and feeling connected. At the same time, each of us needs an independent identity. We don't want relationships to swallow our individuality, so we seek distance, even from our intimates.

Relationship counselors agree that a continuous friction in most close relationships arises from the contradictory desires for autonomy and connection (Beck, 1988; Scarf, 1987). Friends and romantic partners may vacation together and be with each other constantly for a week or more. They're often surprised when they return home and crave time apart. Intense immersion in togetherness prompts us to reestablish independent identity. When we get together with our families during holidays, we're often excited about catching up and talking intensely. Yet we often feel glad when the visit is over and we can part from families again for a time. Both autonomy and closeness are natural human needs. The challenge is to nurture both individuality and intimacy.

Novelty/predictability is a tension between wanting familiar routines and novelty. We like a certain amount of routine to provide security and predictability in our lives. Friends often have standard times to get together, families develop rituals for holidays and birthdays, and romantic couples settle on preferred times and places for going out. Yet too much routine is boring, so we seek novel experiences. Friends may take up a new sport together, families may plan unusual vacations, and romantic partners might explore a new restaurant or do something spontaneous and different to introduce variety into their customary routine.

The third dialectic, **openness/closedness,** involves tension between desires to be open and to maintain privacy. Although intimate relationships are sometimes idealized as totally open and honest, in reality complete openness would be intolerable (Baxter, 1988, 1993; Petronio, 1991). We want to share our inner selves with our intimates. Yet there may be times when we don't feel like sharing and there may be some topics that we don't care to talk about. All of us need some privacy, and intimates need to respect that in each other. Families often share deep feelings and thoughts but don't discuss sexual activities and attitudes. Friends and romantic partners, on the other hand, may talk about sex and other personal topics but not share intimacies that are part of family conversations. Wanting some privacy doesn't mean that people don't enjoy togetherness, nor does it signal that a relationship is in trouble.

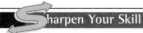

ANALYZING DIALECTICS IN YOUR RELATIONSHIPS

Trace the presence of the three dialectics in a close relationship of yours. How do you ensure enough autonomy and connection, openness and privacy, and novelty and routine? How do you feel when a relationship does not satisfy any of these six human needs?

It means only that we need both openness and closedness in our lives.

Researchers have identified four ways in which friends and romantic partners deal with dialectical tensions (Baxter, 1990; Baxter & Simon, 1993). One response, called **neutralization,** negotiates a balance between the opposing dialectical forces. This involves striking a compromise in which both needs are met to an extent, but neither is fully satisfied. A couple might agree to be generally open but not highly disclosive. **Separation** favors one need in a dialectic and ignores the other. For example, friends might agree to make novelty a priority and suppress their needs for routine. Separation also occurs when partners cycle between dialectical poles to favor each pole alternately. Couples involved in long-distance relationships often spend weekends in close contact and don't see each other during the week.

A third way to manage dialectics is **segmentation,** in which partners assign each pole to certain spheres, issues, activities, or times. For instance, friends might be open about many topics but respect each other's privacy and not pry in one or two areas. Family members are often connected about family matters but operate independently in other ways. Romantic partners might be autonomous in their professional activities yet connected in their interaction in the home and their involvement with children. Some couples symbolize autonomy in careers and connectedness in personal life by using a joint name in social circumstances (Smith-Jones) and individual names in professional circles (Ellen Smith, Frank Jones).

The final method of dealing with dialectics is **reframing.** This is a complex strategy that redefines apparently contradictory needs as not really in opposition. My colleagues and I found examples of reframing in a recent study of intimate partners (Wood et al., 1994). Some couples said that their autonomy enhances closeness because knowing they are separate in some ways allows them to feel safer when they are connected. Instead of viewing autonomy and closeness as opposing, these partners transcended the apparent tension between the two to define the needs as mutually enhancing.

Research suggests that separation by fulfilling one need and squelching the other in a dialectic is generally the least satisfying response (Baxter, 1990). Repressing any natural human impulse diminishes us. The challenge is to satisfy the variety of needs that we experience and that nurture our personal development. Understanding that dialectics are natural and constructive allows us to accept and grow from the tensions they generate.

Stanley

For a long time I've been stressed about my feelings. Sometimes I can't get enough of Annie, and then I feel crowded and don't want to see her at all. I never understood these switches, and I was afraid I was unstable or something. Now I see that I'm pretty normal after all.

The Evolutionary Course of Personal Relationships

Every personal relationship develops at its own pace and in unique ways. Yet the typical evolutionary courses of friendships and romances have some common occurrences.

Friendships Although friendships sometimes jump to life quickly, usually they unfold through a series of fairly predictable stages (Figure 9.1). Interpersonal communication researcher Bill Rawlins (1981, 1994) developed a six-stage model of how friendships develop.

Friendships begin with role-limited interactions. We might meet a new person at work, through membership on athletic teams or clubs, or by chance in an airport, store, or class. We might also meet a new person in a chat room or discussion forum and decide to move to private email conversations with him or her (Parks & Floyd, 1996). During initial encounters we tend to rely on standard social rules and roles. We are polite, stick with safe topics, and exercise care in making disclosures, although disclosures are sometimes made more quickly online than in person (Lea & Spears, 1995; Parks & Roberts, 1998; Turkle, 1997). Willingness to take some risks early in a relationship may be greater when people aren't interacting face to face.

The second stage of friendship is friendly relations, in which each person checks the other out to see whether they have common ground and interests.

Figure 9.1 The Developmental Course of Friendship

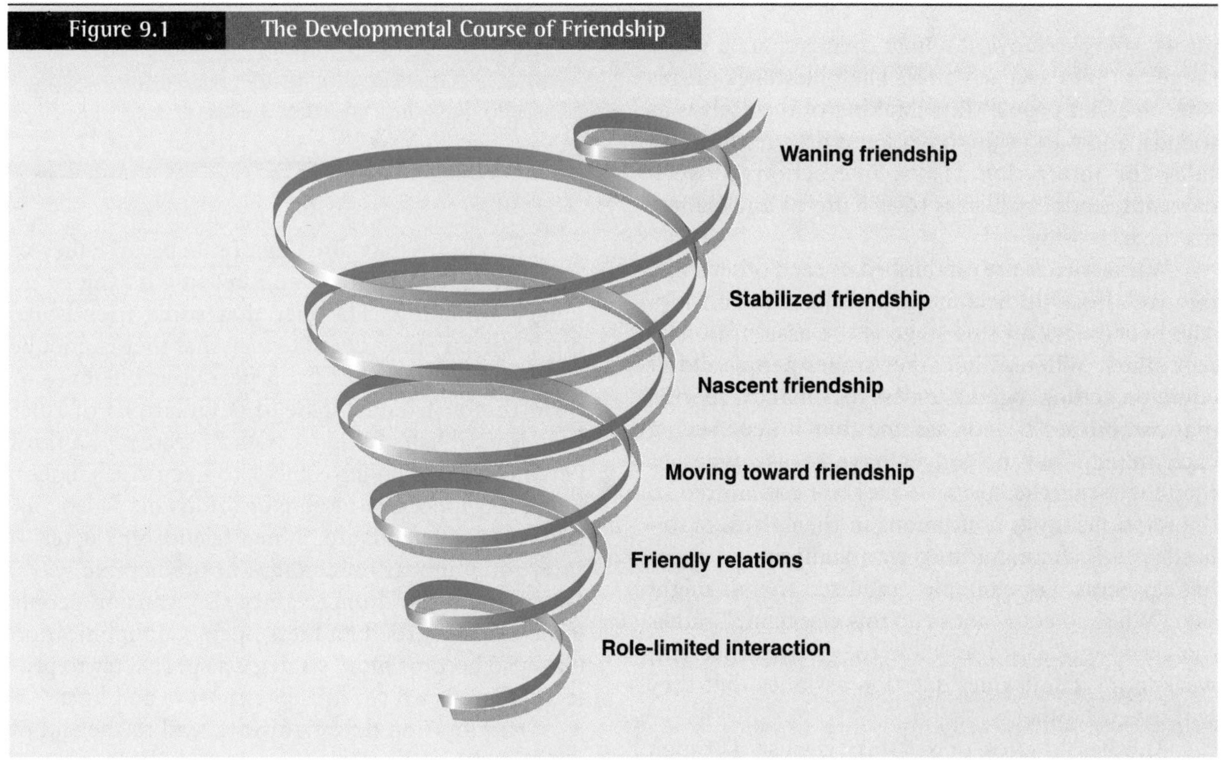

Riddick tells Jason that he really likes adventure movies. If Jason says he does too, they've found a shared interest. A businessperson engages in small talk to see whether an associate wants to get more personal. People who have formed friendly relations over the Internet often talk about experiences, books, films, and ideas. Although friendly exchanges are not dramatic, they allow us to explore the potential for a deeper relationship with another person.

The third stage, moving toward friendship, involves stepping beyond social roles. To signal that we'd like to personalize a relationship, we could introduce a more personal topic than those we have discussed so far in a relationship. We also move toward friendship when we arrange meetings or suggest shared activities. People who have gotten to know each other over the Internet or the World Wide Web sometimes develop enough interest to meet in person. As people interact more personally, they begin to talk about feelings, values, goals, and attitudes. This personal knowledge forms the initial foundation of friendship.

Sylvia

I think one of the greatest feelings in life is being on the brink of a new friendship. It's that moment when you realize this person is going to be important, really special, to you. It's like knowing something wonderful is going to happen and make your life richer. In a lot of ways it's like the infatuation you feel early in a romantic relationship—an anticipation and desire for more closeness.

Nascent friendship is a stage marked by increased involvement and caring. If initial interaction has been satisfying, people may begin to think of themselves as friends or as becoming friends. At this point social norms and roles become less important in regulating interaction, and friends begin to work out their private ways of relating. When my friend Sue and I were in graduate school, we developed a ritual of calling each day between 5 and 6 P.M. to catch up. Some friends settle into patterns of getting together for specific things (watching games, shopping, racquetball, meals, going to movies). Other friends share a wider range of times and activities. The milestones of this stage are that people start thinking of themselves as friends, and they begin to work out private roles and rules for interaction. Thus, interaction between nascent friends establishes basic patterns and climate for the friendship.

When friends are established in each other's life, their relationship becomes a stabilized friendship. The benchmark of this stage is the assumption of continuity. Whereas in earlier stages people didn't count on getting together unless they made a specific plan, stabilized friends assume they'll keep seeing each other. They no longer have to ask whether they'll get together because they are committed to the relationship as continuous in their lives. Stabilized friends communicate their assumption of ongoing closeness. For example, stabilized friends might say, "What do you want to do this weekend?" rather than asking, "Do you want to get together this weekend?" The former question assumes that they will see each other.

Another criterion of this stage is trust. Through disclosing private information and responding with acceptance, friends earn each other's trust. In turn, they feel safe sharing even more intimate information and revealing vulnerabilities that they usually conceal. Stabilized friendships may continue indefinitely, in some cases a lifetime.

Waning friendship exists when one or both people cease being committed to their relationship. Sometimes friends drift apart because each is pulled in different directions by career demands or personal circumstances. The common interests and experiences that once fueled the friendship are no longer a glue for closeness. Jean's commentary illustrates how changes can cause friendships to wither.

Jean

Clark and I had been friends with Ted and Cori ever since we were undergraduates, all the way through our graduate programs, and for several years after we were all working. Then Cori and Ted had a baby. At first I didn't think it would affect our friendship, but gradually it did. Cori and Ted were always talking about their baby, and they wanted to bring the baby with them if we went out to dinner or had them to our house. And they were interested in issues like cloth versus disposable diapers and things that were just irrelevant to Clark and me. After a while it seemed there was nothing we really shared anymore.

Friendships may also deteriorate because they've run their natural course and become boring or no longer enriching. The fact that some friendships don't last a lifetime doesn't mean that they cannot be special and important for a period in our lives. A third reason friendships end is violations of rules friends establish. Telling a friend's secrets to a third person violates an agreement to keep confidences. Being unsupportive in conversations may also violate rules of friendship. When friendships deteriorate, communication changes in predictable ways. Defensiveness and uncertainty rise, causing people to be more guarded and less open. Communication may also become more strategic as people try to protect themselves from further exposure and hurt.

Deterioration doesn't always lead to the end of the friendship. Even when serious violations occur between friends, relationships can sometimes be repaired. For this to happen, both friends must be committed to rebuilding trust and talking openly about their feelings and needs.

Romantic Relationships Like friendships, romances have a typical evolutionary path. We perceive romantic relationships as escalating, navigating, or deteriorating. Within these three broad phases of romance are more specific stages.

Escalating romantic involvements typically involve six stages of interaction. The first stage is people who aren't interacting. We are aware of ourselves as individuals with particular needs, goals, and qualities that affect what we look for in romantic relationships. Before forming romantic relationships, we also have learned a number of constitutive and regulative communication rules that affect how we interact with others and how we interpret their communication.

The second stage is invitational communication, in which people express interest in interacting. This stage involves both taking the initiative with others and responding to invitations they make to us. "Want to dance?" "Where are you from?" and "Did

FRIENDS OF THE HEART AND FRIENDS OF THE ROAD

Lillian Rubin has made a career of studying close relationships, particularly friendships. One of her more interesting findings is that there are two basic kinds of friends: friends of the heart and friends of the road. Friends of the heart are people we meet who become part of us in enduring ways. They are soulmates with whom we feel deeply and permanently connected. If friends of the heart move far away from each other, they often stay in touch and visit. Even if they don't maintain regular contact, they feel deeply woven into each other's lives.

Friends of the road are friends we make and from whom we part as we travel the road of life. We make friends wherever we are, and we provide support, companionship, fun, and so forth. When they or we move, we make no effort to stay in touch or maintain any continuing sense of connection. Friends of the road are people we enjoy for a time, then leave behind.

Source: Rubin, 1985.

you just start working here?" are examples of invitations to interact. Invitational communication usually follows a conventional script for social conversation. The meaning of invitational communication is found on the relationship level, not the content level. "I love this kind of music" literally means that a person likes the music. On the relationship level of meaning, however, the message is "I'm available and interested. Are you?" Of all the people we meet, we are romantically attracted to only a few. The two greatest influences on initial attraction are proximity and similarity.

Proximity influences initial attraction. We can interact only with people we meet, whether in person or in cyberspace. Consequently, where we live, work, and socialize and the electronic networks in which we participate constrain the possibilities for relationships. This reminds us that communication is systemic. From our discussion in Chapters 1 and 7 you may recall that the systemic character of communication means that context affects what happens when people transact. Some contexts, such as college campuses, promote meeting potential romantic partners, whereas other contexts are less conducive to meeting and dating. Specialized electronic networks and home pages are set up for people who want to talk about particular topics, develop friendships, or meet potential romantic partners.

FADED FRIENDSHIPS

Remember three friendships that were once close but have faded away. Describe the reasons they ended. How did boredom, differences, external circumstances, or violations contribute to decay of the friendships? How did communication patterns change as the friendships waned?

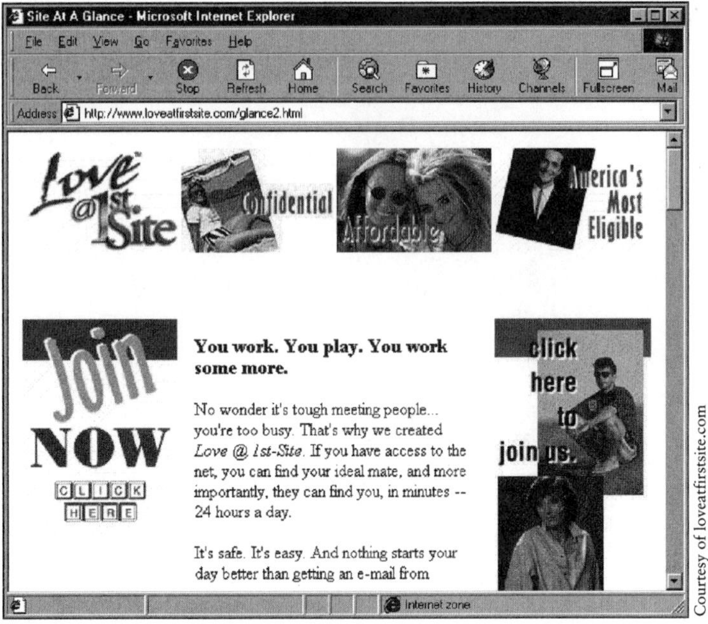

■ *A growing number of people visit web sites to meet potential dates and romantic partners.*

Courtesy of loveatfirstsite.com

Similarity is also important in romantic relationships. In the realm of romance, "birds of a feather" seems more true than "opposites attract." In general, we are attracted to people whose values, attitudes, and lifestyles are similar to ours. We tend to seek others who are similar to us in sexual orientation and values. Also important is similarity of social background because most people pair with others of their social background. In fact, social prestige influences dating patterns now more than it did in the 1950s (Whitbeck & Hoyt, 1994).

Similarity of personality is also linked to long-term marital happiness (Caspi & Harbener, 1990). In general, people tend to match themselves with people who are about as physically attractive as they are. We may fantasize about relationships with stunning people, but in reality we're likely to pass them by for someone at our level of attractiveness. In general, we seek romantic partners who are similar to us in many respects. In order for similarities between people to enhance attractiveness, the pair must recognize and communicate the similarities (Duck, 1994a, 1994b). In other words, attraction grows when people discuss common feelings, experiences, values, beliefs, and goals.

Exploratory communication is a stage in which people explore the possibilities for a relationship. We communicate to announce our identities and learn about others'. As in early stages of friendship, potential romantic partners fish for common interests. "Do you like jazz?" "What's your family like?" "Do you follow politics?" As we continue to interact with others, both breadth and depth of information increase. People may talk about difficulties in their lives, reasons for divorces, and so forth. Because most of us perceive self-disclosure as a sign of trust, it tends to escalate intimacy (Berger & Bell, 1988). At this early stage of interaction, both people expect reciprocity of disclosure so that neither is more vulnerable than the other (Duck, 1992; Miell & Duck, 1986).

Ginder

Last year I went out with a guy for a couple of months. After we'd been seeing each other a while, I told him some private stuff about me. The problem was that he didn't tell me anything personal about him. I felt really exposed with him knowing more about me than I did about him. Plus I felt like he must not trust me if he wouldn't reveal anything.

If early interaction increases attraction, the relationship may escalate. Intensifying communication is a stage in which a relationship gains depth as a result of the increasing amount and intimacy of

Zits

interaction. My students nicknamed this stage "euphoria" to emphasize the intensity and happiness it typically embodies. During this phase partners spend more and more time together, and they rely less on external structures such as movies or parties. Instead, they immerse themselves in the budding relationship and may feel they can't be together enough. They make further disclosures, fill in their biographies, and increasingly learn how the other feels and thinks. A recent study by Brenda Meeks, Susan Hendrick, and Clyde Hendrick (1998) showed that satisfaction with romantic relationships is linked to making and receiving disclosures and being able to understand the partner's perspective.

The intensifying stage often involves idealizing and personalized communication. Idealizing occurs when we see a relationship and partner as more wonderful, exciting, and perfect than they really are (Hendrick & Hendrick, 1988, 1996). During euphoria, partners often exaggerate each other's virtues, downplay or don't notice vices, and overlook problems in the relationship. It is also during euphoria that partners begin to develop relationship vocabularies that include nicknames and private codes. Sometimes Robbie and I greet each other by saying *namaste*. This is a Nepali greeting that expresses good will. Saying it reminds us of our trek in the mountains of Nepal. Private language heightens partners' sense of being a special couple. Partners invent words and nicknames for each other, and they develop ways to send private messages in public settings. Private language both reflects and enhances intimacy ("Public Pillow Talk," 1987).

Revising communication, although not part of escalation in all romantic relationships, occurs often enough to merit our consideration. During this stage partners come down out of the clouds to talk about their relationship's strengths, problems, and potential for the future. With the rush of euphoria over, partners consider whether they want the relationship to last. If so, they work through problems and obstacles to long-term viability. Some gay and lesbian partners have to resolve differences in openness about their sexual orientations. Couples may need to work out differences in religions and conflicts in location and career goals.

■ *Euphoria!*

WHAT DRIVES ESCALATION IN ROMANTIC RELATIONSHIPS?

According to researchers, events and circumstances sometimes push a couple toward commitment. Timing, approval from friends and family, good jobs, and so forth are events that can drive relationships forward. Relationship factors—feelings and fit between two particular people—seem to drive other relationships. Trust, compatibility, history, shared values, and self-disclosure are examples of relationship events that drive romance forward. Long-term satisfaction with marriage is more positively associated with relationship-driven commitments than event-driven ones. Here are examples:

Emeka and Fred started dating in their senior year. Both families supported the relationship, and it seemed that all of Emeka's and Fred's friends were getting married the summer after graduating. When they both got job offers in the same city, they decided it was time to marry. They did so a month after graduation but separated a year later.

Tyrone and Ella dated for three years. Although many of their friends remained single, Tyrone and Ella felt they were ready to start building a life together. By the time they walked down the aisle, they knew each other well and had learned how to be a compatible couple. Three years later, they are satisfied with the marriage.

Source: Surra, Arizzi, & Asmussen, 1988.

As you might expect, during this phase of romance communication often involves negotiation and even conflict. This is natural because revising communication requires partners to talk about negative features of a relationship and ways to improve them. These topics seldom arise in earlier stages of romance because difficulties are not a serious problem until the couple contemplates a long-term future. Many couples are able to revise their relationships in ways that make them stronger and more able to endure. Other couples cannot resolve problems. Thus people often fall in love and move through the intensifying stage, yet choose not to stay together. We can love a person with whom we don't want to share our life.

Commitment is a stage marked by the partners' decision to stay with a relationship permanently. This decision transforms a relationship from one based on past and present experiences and feelings into one with a future. Before they make a commitment, partners don't view the relationship as continuing forever. With commitment the relationship

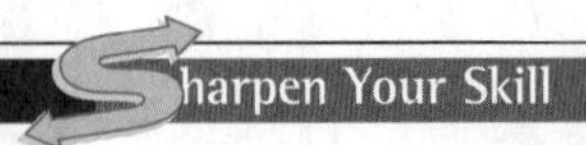

PRIVATE LANGUAGE

What are the special words and nonverbal codes in a close relationship of yours? Do you have a way to signal each other when you're bored at a party and ready to leave? Do you use nicknames and private words? What would be lost if you had no private language in your relationship?

fyi

STYLES OF LOVING

Just as people differ in their tastes in food and ways of dressing, so do we differ in how we love. Researchers have identified six different styles of loving, each of which is valid, although not all styles are compatible with one another. See whether you can identify your style of loving in the descriptions that follow:

Eros is a style of loving that is passionate, intense, and fast moving. Not confined to sexual passion, eros may be expressed in spiritual, intellectual, or emotional ways.

Storge (pronounced "store-gay") is a comfortable "best friends" kind of love that grows gradually to create a stable and even-keeled companionship.

Ludus is a playful, sometimes manipulative style of loving. For ludic lovers, love is a challenge, a puzzle, a game to be relished but not to lead to commitment.

Mania is an unsettling style of loving marked by emotional extremes. Manic lovers often are insecure about their value and their partners' commitment.

Agape is a selfless kind of love in which a beloved's happiness is more important than one's own. Agapic lovers are generous, unselfish, and devoted.

Pragma is a pragmatic and goal-oriented style of loving. Pragmas rely on reason and practical considerations to select people to love.

Sources: Hendrick & Hendrick, 1996; Hendrick, Hendrick, Foote, & Slapion-Foote, 1984; Lee, 1973, 1988.

becomes a given around which they arrange other aspects of their lives. This stage is analogous to stabilized friendship because the basis of both is assumed continuity.

Navigating is the ongoing process of communicating to sustain intimacy over time and in the face of changes in partners, the relationship, and surrounding contexts. Although navigating can be an extended stage in romantic intimacy, it is not stable. It is dynamic. Couples continuously work through new problems, revisit old ones, and accommodate changes in their individual and joint lives. To use an automotive analogy, navigating involves both preventive maintenance and periodic repairs (Canary & Stafford, 1994). Navigating communication aims to keep intimacy satisfying and healthy and to deal with problems and tensions that arise.

The nucleus of intimacy is **relationship culture,** which is a private world of rules, understandings, meanings, and patterns of interacting that partners create for their relationship (Wood, 1982). Relationship culture includes how a couple manages relationship dialectics. Mei-Ling and Gregory may do a great many things together, whereas Lana and Kaya emphasize autonomy. Brent and Carmella may be open and expressive, whereas Marion and Senona prefer more privacy in their marriage. There aren't right and wrong ways to manage dialectics because individuals and couples differ in what they need. The unique character of each relationship culture reflects how partners deal with tensions between autonomy and connection, openness and privacy, and novelty and routine (Fitzpatrick & Best, 1979; Wood, 2000b).

A relationship culture includes communication rules that partners work out. Couples develop agreements, usually unspoken, about how to signal anger, love, sexual interest, and so forth. They also develop routines for contact. Some couples catch up while they fix dinner each day, whereas other couples reserve weekends for staying in touch. Especially important in navigating is small talk, through which partners weave the fabric of their history and their current lives, experiences, and dreams.

Steve Duck (1992) proposed a five-phase model of relationship deterioration (Figure 9.2). **Dyadic breakdown** is the first stage, and it involves degeneration of established patterns, understandings, and routines that make up a relationship culture. Partners may stop talking after dinner, no longer bother to call when they are running late, and in other ways neglect the little things that tie them together. As the fabric of intimacy weakens, dissatisfaction mounts.

General gender differences are among the causes of dyadic breakdown (Wood, 1993c, 1993d, 2001b). For women, unhappiness with a relationship most often arises when communication declines in quality or quantity. Men are more likely to be dissatisfied by specific behaviors or the lack of valued behaviors. For instance, men report being dissatisfied when their partners don't greet them at the door and make special meals (Riessman, 1990). For many men, dissatisfaction also arises if they have domestic responsibilities that they feel aren't a man's job (Gottman & Carrère, 1994). It seems that women feel a relationship is breaking down if "we don't really communicate with each other anymore," whereas men tend to feel dissatisfied if "we don't do fun things together any more." Another gender difference is in who notices problems in a relationship. As a rule women are more likely than men to perceive declines in intimacy. Because many women are socialized to be sensitive to interpersonal nuances, they are likely to notice tensions and early symptoms of relationship distress (Cancian, 1989; Tavris, 1992).

The **intrapsychic phase** involves brooding about problems in the relationship and dissatisfactions with a partner (Duck, 1992). It's easy for the intrapsychic phase to become a self-fulfilling prophesy: As gloomy thoughts snowball and awareness of positive features of the relationship ebb, partners may actually bring about the failure of their relationship. During the intrapsychic phase partners may begin to think about alternatives to the relationship.

The **dyadic phase** of relationship decline doesn't always occur (Duck, 1992). When it does, the phase

Figure 9.2 Developmental Phases in Romantic Relationships

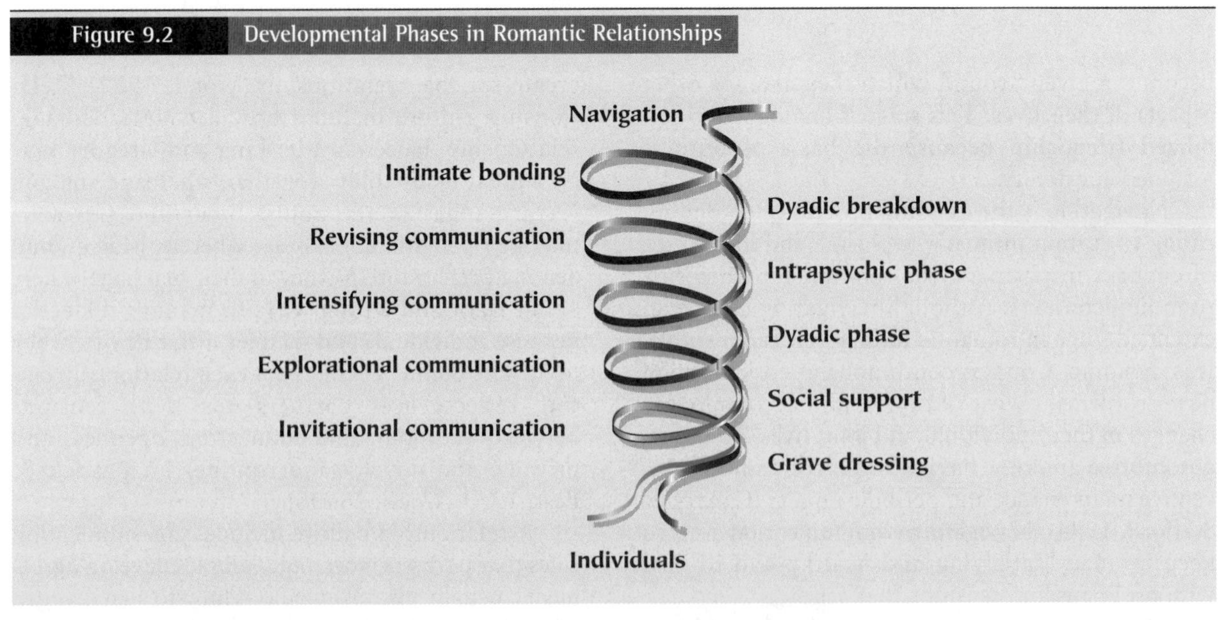

© Frank Siteman/Index Stock

■ *What do you think about when a romantic relationship seems to be ending?*

tends to involve conflict. Communication scholars report that many people avoid talking about problems, refuse to return calls from partners, and in other ways evade confronting difficulties (Baxter, 1984; Metts, Cupach, & Bejlovec, 1989). We have an ethical responsibility to ask whether we should avoid problems and conceal our thoughts and feelings from a partner. Although it is painful to talk about problems, avoiding discussion does nothing to resolve them and may make them worse. What happens in the dyadic phase depends on how committed partners are, whether they perceive attractive alternatives to the relationship, and whether they have the communication skills to work through problems constructively. A recent study (Battaglia, Richard, Datter, & Lord, 1998) found that many college undergraduates follow a cyclical pattern when breaking up. They pull apart and get back together several times before actually ending the relationship.

Jacob

I'll never forget the day I came home and Shelly was gone. She took all her personal things and just left me a note that said, "There's no point in trying to fix things." She never even gave us a chance to work out our difficulties, she didn't even let me be part of deciding what would happen. She just moved out. I think that hurt me as much as the actual end of the relationship.

If partners lack commitment or the communication skills they need to restore intimacy, they enter the **social phase** of disintegration, which involves figuring out how to explain their breakup. Either separately or in collaboration, partners decide how to explain their breakup to friends, coworkers, children, in-laws, and social acquaintances. When partners don't craft a joint explanation for breaking up, friends may take sides, gossip, and disparage one or the other partner as the bad guy (La Gaipa, 1982).

Social support is a phase in which partners look to friends and family for support during the breakup. Others can provide support by being available and by listening. Partners may give self-serving accounts of the breakup in order to save face and secure sympathy

Sharpen Your Skill

CHARTING YOUR RELATIONSHIP'S EVOLUTION

Recall a romantic relationship of yours that ended. Trace how it evolved from first meeting through final encounter. Do the stages we've discussed apply to the evolution of your romantic relationship? If not, how would you change or add to the stages we've described?

and support from others. Thus, Vera may tell her friends all the ways in which Frank was at fault and portray herself as the innocent party. During this phase former partners often criticize each other and expect friends to take sides (Duck, 1992). Although self-serving explanations of breakups are common, they aren't necessarily constructive. We have an ethical responsibility to monitor communication during this period so that we don't say things we'll later regret.

Grave dressing is the final phase in relationship decline, and it involves burying the relationship and accepting its end. During grave dressing we work to make sense of the relationship: what it meant, why it failed, and how it affected us. Typically, we mourn a relationship that has died. Even the person who initiates a breakup is often sad about the failure to realize what seemed possible at one time. Grave dressing completes the process of relationship dissolution by putting the relationship to rest so partners can get on with their individual lives.

The stages we've discussed describe how many people experience the evolution of friendship and romance. However, not everyone follows the pattern presented here. Some people skip one or more stages, and many of us cycle more than once through certain stages. For example, a couple might soar through euphoria, work out some tough issues in revising, then go through euphoria a second time. It's also normal for long-term partners to move out of navigation periodically as they experience both euphoric seasons and intervals of dyadic breakdown. Similarly, friends may drift into the stage of waning friendship and then revive their closeness. What remains constant as long as intimacy exists are partners' commitment to a future and investment in the relationship.

CHALLENGES IN PERSONAL RELATIONSHIPS

To sustain fulfilling personal relationships, partners rely on communication to deal with internal tensions and external pressures from other people and commitments. How skillfully we manage these challenges is a major influence on the endurance and quality of personal relationships. We'll consider four specific challenges that many friends and romantic partners face.

Dealing with Distance

Geographic separation can be difficult for friends and romantic couples. Many of us will be involved in long-distance romantic relationships because they are increasingly common. Fully 70% of college students are or have been in long-distance romances (Rohlfing, 1995), and even more have been or are involved in long-distance friendships. The number of long-distance relationships is likely to increase in the years ahead.

Perhaps the two greatest problems for long-distance commitments are the lack of daily communication about small events and issues and unrealistic expectations about interaction when partners are together. The first problem—not being able to share small talk and daily routines—is a major loss, especially for partners who can't communicate over the Internet. As we have seen, communication about ordinary topics weaves partners' lives together. Mundane conversations between friends and romantic partners are the foundation of relationships.

Greg

When Annie and I first moved to different cities, I don't know whether it was harder being apart or together. I missed her so much when we were apart for weeks at a time, and I really missed just being together in a laid-back kind of way. But whenever we were together, we both felt really pressured to be together every minute and not to have any disagreements or bad times. That's just not possible, and expecting it really caused us a lot of grief. Now we are careful to call and stay in touch with email so that we feel part of each other's regular lives. And we've learned that it's okay to have some private time even when we're together for only a few days.

A second common problem is unrealistic expectations for time together. Because partners have so little time when they are physically together, they often believe every moment must be perfect. They feel there should be no conflict and they should spend every minute together. Yet this is an unrealistic expectation. Conflict and needs for autonomy are natural in all romantic relationships. They may be even more likely in long-distance couples because partners are used to living alone and have established independent rhythms that may not mesh well.

The good news is that these problems don't necessarily sabotage long-distance romance. Most researchers report that partners can maintain satisfying commitments despite geographic separation (Rohlfing, 1995). To overcome the difficulties of long-distance love, many couples engage in creative communication to sustain intimacy. The FYI feature on page 206 summarizes some ways romantic intimates bridge distance. Since the early 1980s, when the research behind this material was conducted, developments in communication technologies have enlarged upon the ways couples and families who live apart can stay in touch. In addition to visiting each other several times each year, my sister and I send each other videocassettes. I tape segments of parties or trips that Robbie and I take and let Carolyn see us in those experiences. Her tapes most often feature her kids, Michelle, Daniel, and Harrison, engaged in mischief and the endless adventures of childhood. Exchanging videotapes allows us to stay aware of the rhythms of each other's lives.

Managing Dual-Career Relationships

Today most adults work outside the home. Thus, partners in a relationship must balance the demands and pressures of two careers with investment in the relationship itself. Research shows that the greatest problem dual-career couples face is not geographic distance or trade-offs in career opportunities. Instead, it is equity—or the lack of equity—of the two partners' contributions toward joint responsibilities.

Equality between partners affects satisfaction with relationships. Researchers report that the happiest dating and married couples feel that partners invest equally (Buunk & Mutsaers, 1999; Hecht, Marston, & Larkey, 1994). When we think we are investing more than a partner is, we tend to be resentful. When it seems our partner is investing more than we are, we may feel guilty. Imbalance of either sort erodes satisfaction.

Although few partners demand moment-to-moment equality, most of us want our relationships to be equitable over time. Equity has multiple dimensions. We may evaluate the fairness of financial, emotional, physical, and other contributions to a relationship. One area that strongly affects satisfaction of spouses and cohabiting partners is equity in housework and child care. Inequitable division of domestic obligations fuels dissatisfaction and resentment, both of which harm intimacy (Gottman & Carrère, 1994; Wood, 1998). Marital stability is more closely linked to equitable divisions of child care and housework than to income or sex life (Fowers, 1991; Suitor, 1991).

More than four in five marriages today include two wage earners (Wilkie, 1991). Unfortunately, divisions of family and home responsibilities have not changed much in response to changing employment patterns. Even when both partners in heterosexual relationships work outside the home, in 80% of dual-career families women do the vast majority

COPING WITH GEOGRAPHIC SEPARATION

Students report nine strategies for long-distance love:

1. Recognize that long-distance relationships are common; you're not alone.
2. Create more social support systems (friends) while separated from a romantic partner.
3. Communicate creatively; send video- and audiotapes.
4. Before separating, work out ground rules for going out with friends, phoning, visiting, and writing.
5. Use time together wisely: Be affectionate and have fun. Being serious all the time isn't smart.
6. Maintain honesty. Especially when partners live apart, they need to be straight with each other.
7. Build an open, supportive communication climate so you can talk about issues and feelings.
8. Maintain trust by abiding by ground rules that were agreed on, phoning when you say you will, and keeping lines of communication open.
9. Focus on the positive aspects of separation, such as career advancement or ability to focus on work.

Source: Westefield & Liddell, 1982.

of child care and homemaking (Nussbaum, 1992; Okin, 1989). In only 20% of dual-career families do men assume equal domestic responsibilities (Hochschild & Machung, 1989).

How do gay and lesbian partners manage domestic responsibilities? Lesbian couples create more egalitarian relationships than either heterosexuals or gay men. More than any other type of couple, lesbians are likely to communicate collaboratively to make decisions about domestic work and parenting (Huston & Schwartz, 1995). Consequently, lesbians are least likely to have negative feelings involving inequity (Kurdek, 1993). Gay men, like their heterosexual brothers, use the power derived from income to authorize inequitable contributions to domestic life. In gay couples the man who makes more money has and uses more power, both in making decisions that affect the relationship and in avoiding housework (Huston & Schwartz, 1995). This suggests that power is the basis of gendered divisions of labor and that men, more than women, seek the privileges of power, including evasion of domestic work.

As a rule, women assume a greater portion of **psychological responsibility,** which involves remembering, planning, and coordinating domestic activities. Parents may alternate who takes children to the doctor, but it is usually the mother who remembers when the kids need checkups, makes the appointments, and reminds the father to take the children. Both partners sign cards and gifts, but in many families it is women who assume responsibility for remembering birthdays and buying cards and gifts. Successful long-term relationships in our era require partners to communicate collaboratively to design equitable divisions of responsibility.

Molly

It really isn't fair when both spouses work outside the home but only one of them takes care of the home and kids. For years that was how Sean's and my marriage worked, no matter how much I tried to talk with him about a fairer arrangement. Finally, I had just had it, so I quit doing everything. Groceries didn't get bought, laundry piled up and he didn't have clean shirts, he didn't remember his mother's birthday (and for the first time ever I didn't remind him), bills didn't get paid. After a while he suggested we talk about a system we could both live with.

Resisting Violence and Abuse Between Intimates

Although we like to think of romantic relationships as loving, many are not. Violence and abuse are unfortunately common between romantic partners, and they cut across lines of socioeconomics, race, and ethnicity (French, 1992; West, 1995). Violence is high not only in heterosexual marriage but also in dating relationships (French, 1992; Muehlenhardt & Linton, 1987; Stets, 1990; Thompson, 1991). It also appears that cohabiting couples have the highest incidence of violence of all couples: Women who cohabit suffer 1.5 to 2 times more physical violence than married women (Stets & Straus, 1989). In addition to physical abuse, verbal and emotional brutality poison all too many relationships.

The majority of detected violence and abuse in intimacy seems to be committed by men against women. In the United States today a woman is beaten every 12 to 18 seconds by a husband or intimate, and four women are beaten to death each day (Brock-Utne, 1989; Wood, 2001b). Date rape is escalating, especially when people have been drinking ("What Teens Say," 1994). Too often people don't leave abusive relationships because they feel trapped by economic pressures or by relatives and clergy who counsel them to stay (West, 1995).

Violence seldom stops without intervention. Instead, it follows a predictable cycle: Tension mounts in the abuser, the abuser explodes by being violent, the abuser then is remorseful and loving, the victim feels loved and reassured that the relationship is working, and then tension mounts anew and the cycle begins again (Figure 9.3). Relationships that are abusive are unhealthy for everyone involved. They violate the trust that is a foundation of intimacy. In addition, they jeopardize the comfort, health, and sometimes the life of victims of violence. Less obvious is the damage abusers do to themselves. Using physical force against others is a sign of weakness—an admission that a person must resort to the most crude and unimaginative methods of influence. Abusers can lower their self-esteem and destroy relationships that they want.

LEARNING ABOUT GENDERED VIOLENCE

In 1995 President Clinton announced formation of the Violence Against Women Office, which aims to improve law enforcement and prosecution of those who enact violence against women, to increase services to women who are victims of violence, and to educate the public about violence against women. You can find out more about this organization by visiting the Web site of the U.S. Department of Justice's Violence Against Women Office: http://www.usdoj.gov/vawo. A related Web site that you might want to visit is the National Domestic Violence Hotline: http://www.ndvh.org.

Figure 9.3 Cycle of Abuse

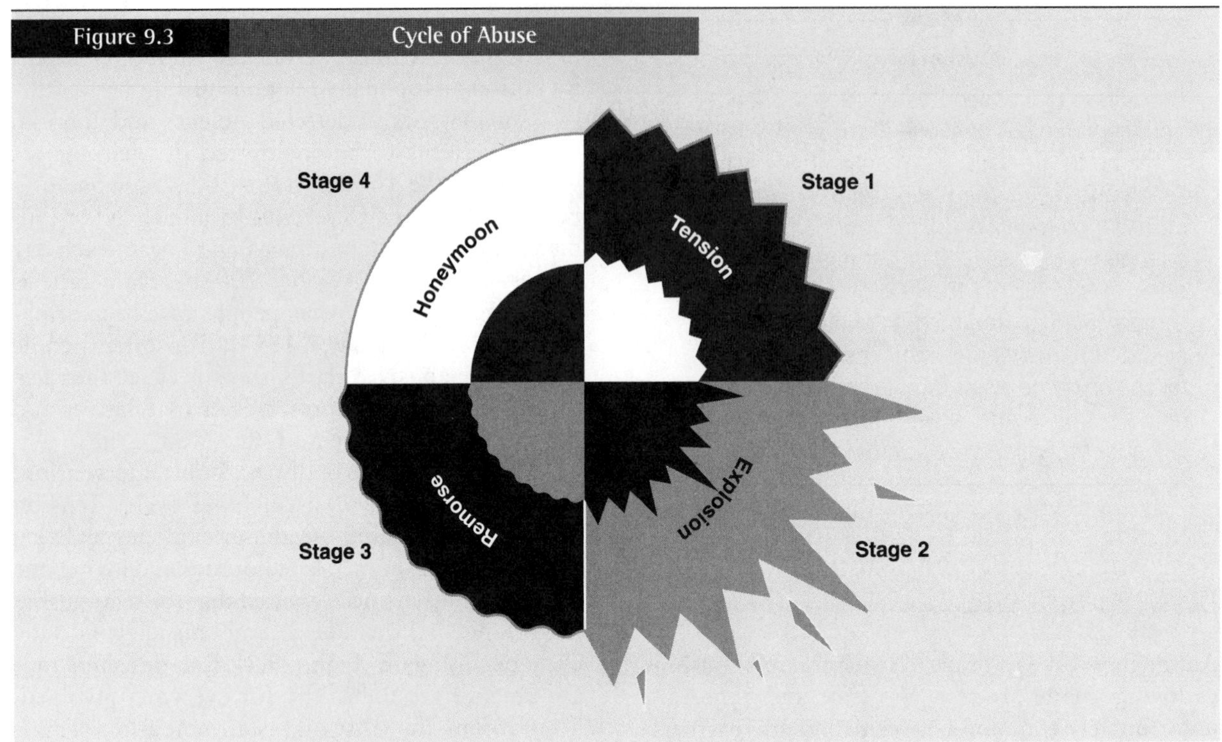

Communication and violence are related in two ways. Most obviously, patterns of communication between couples and abusers' patterns of intrapersonal communication can fuel tendencies toward violence. Some partners deliberately annoy and taunt each other, a pattern that can lead to serious abuse. Also, the language that abusers use to describe physical assaults on partners includes denial, trivializing the harm done, and blaming the partner or circumstances for "making me do it" (Stamp & Sabourin, 1995). These intrapersonal communication patterns allow abusers to deny their offenses, justify unjustifiable actions, and cast responsibility outside themselves.

Cultural communication practices that normalize violence also promote violence between intimates. Rape and other physical violations of women saturate the media. From magazines to films to television, violence is pervasive. News accounts camouflage the brutality of violence when they refer to "loving her too much" and "love that gets out of hand" (Meyers, 1994).

Violent relationships are *not* the fault of victims. Other than self-defense, there is no justification for physical violence against an intimate. A person cannot earn battering, nor do victims encourage it (Goodrich, Rampage, Ellman, & Halstead, 1988). If you know or suspect that someone you care about is a victim of abuse, don't ignore the situation and don't assume it's none of your business. It is an act of friendship to notice and offer to help. Victims of violence must make the ultimate decision about what to do, but the support and concern of friends can help them.

Negotiating Safer Sex

In the era of HIV/AIDS, sexual activities pose serious, even deadly threats. Despite vigorous public educa-

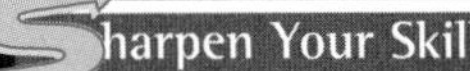

REASONS FOR NOT PRACTICING SAFER SEX

Students and members of singles organizations list these as the top five reasons for not practicing safer sex:

1. I knew my partner. We'd discussed our past sexual experiences.
2. I use another form of birth control.
3. A condom wasn't available at the time.
4. Things happened too fast.
5. I didn't feel I was at risk.

Source: Reel & Thompson, 1994.

tion campaigns, a great many people still don't practice safer sex, which includes abstinence, restricting sexual activity to a single partner who has been tested and found to be free of HIV, and using latex condoms (Reel & Thompson, 1994). In a recent nationwide survey, only 48% of men and 32% of women reported using condoms (Clements, 1994).

Sexual attraction and sexual activity are not necessarily restricted to romantic relationships. Friendships between heterosexual men and women, gay men, or lesbians sometimes include sexual tensions. Because Western culture so strongly emphasizes gender and sex, it's difficult not to perceive people in sexual terms (Johnson, Stockdale, & Saal, 1991; Nardi & Sherrod, 1994; O'Meara, 1989). Even if sexual activity doesn't occur, sexual undertones may ripple beneath the surface of friendships. Sexual attraction, tension, or invitations can be problems between friends when one party does not want to have a sexual relationship. Trust may be damaged if someone you consider a friend makes a pass at you. Once a friend transgresses the agreed-upon boundaries of a friendship, it's hard to know how to act with each other and what to expect. If friends decide sexual activity is appropriate for them, they should communicate about safer sex.

Although most college students know about HIV/AIDS, they don't consistently follow safer sex techniques. Communication scholars have found two primary reasons. First, ironically, many people find it more embarrassing to talk about sex than to engage in it. They find it awkward to ask direct questions of partners ("Have you been tested for HIV?"; "Are you having sex with anyone else?") or to make direct requests of partners ("I want you to wear a condom"; "I would like for you to be tested for HIV before we have sex"). Naturally, it's difficult to talk explicitly about sex and the dangers of HIV/AIDS. However, it is far more difficult to live with HIV or the knowledge that you infected another person.

A second reason people sometimes fail to negotiate safer sex is that alcohol or other drugs have diminished their rational thought and control. In a series of studies of college students' sexual activities, communication researchers Sheryl Bowen and Paula Michal-Johnson (1995, 1996) report that when people drink heavily they are especially likely to neglect safer sex precautions. The National Council on Alcoholism and Drug Dependence reports that sexually active teens are less likely to use condoms after drinking ("What Teens Say," 1994). Alcohol and other drugs loosen inhibitions, including appropriate concerns about personal safety.

Discussing and practicing safer sex may be awkward, but there is no sensible option. Good communication skills help ease the discomfort of negotiating safer sex. It is more constructive to say, "I feel unsafe having unprotected sex" than "Without a condom you could give me AIDS" (note that the first statement uses *I* language, whereas the second one relies on *you* language). Using relationship language fosters a positive communication climate; for example, it's more positive to talk about *our safety and our relationship* when negotiating sexual activity (Reel & Thompson, 1994). People who care about themselves and their partners are honest about their sexual histories and assertive about safer sex practices.

Summary

In this chapter we've explored communication in personal relationships, which are defined by commitment, uniqueness, relationship dialectics, relationship rules, and interaction with surrounding contexts. We traced the typical evolutionary paths of friendships and romances by noting how partners communicate during escalating, stabilizing, and declining stages of personal relationships. As we saw, communication is a primary dynamic in intimacy, influencing how we meet and get to know others, the patterns of interaction between friends and romantic partners, and the creation of relationship cultures that, ideally, are healthy and affirming.

In the final section of the chapter we considered four important challenges that friends and romantic partners face today. The communication principles and skills we have discussed in this and previous chapters can help us meet the challenges of sustaining intimacy across geographic distance, creating equitable relationships, resisting violence, and negotiating safer sex. Good communication skills are essential to managing these challenges so that we, our intimates, and the relationships we create survive and thrive over time.

FOR FURTHER REFLECTION AND DISCUSSION

1. Think about the distinction between love and commitment and the role each plays in personal relationships. Describe relationships in which commitment is present but love is not. Describe relationships in which love exists, but there's no commitment. What can you conclude about the impact of each?
2. Review the rules of friendship that researchers have identified (see the FYI box on page 192). Do these match with your experiences in friendships? Do you have additional rules that are unique to your close friendships?
3. Think about differences in the goals and rules for friendships and romantic relationships. Does comparing the two kinds of relationships give you any insight into the difficulties that commonly arise when two people who have been friends become romantically involved? What are the difficulties of trying to be friends with someone with whom you've been romantically involved?
4. Are you now or have you been involved in a long-distance personal relationship, either friendship or romance? How did you communicate to bridge the distance? Do your experiences parallel the chapter's discussion of challenges in long-distance relationships?
5. Visit an online dating service. Notice what qualities men and women claim they have and what qualities men and women are looking for in romantic partners. What similarities and differences can you identify?

KEY TERMS

Personal relationship
Social relationship
Passion
Commitment
Investment
Rules
Relationship dialectics
Autonomy/connection
Novelty/predictability
Openness/closedness
Neutralization
Separation
Segmentation
Reframing
Eros
Storge
Ludus
Mania
Agape
Pragma
Relationship culture
Dyadic breakdown
Intrapsychic phase
Dyadic phase
Social phase
Social support
Grave dressing
Psychological responsibility

Communication in Groups and Teams

LEARNING OBJECTIVES

To understand

1. Why groups and teams are increasingly popular
2. The differences between groups and teams
3. The strengths of group discussion
4. The potential limits of group discussion
5. Whether groups need single leaders
6. Why conflict can enhance work in groups and teams
7. How communication shapes group climate

Janet

I love groups! When people work together, creativity goes into high gear. I've never been in a group that didn't come up with better ideas than any of us had to start with.

Karl

There's a reason for the saying that a camel is a horse designed by a committee. They [committees] take forever to decide anything, and they dilute the ideas of the best members. I would much rather work on my own any day of the week.

Do you agree more with Karl or Janet? For every person who has Janet's enthusiasm for group work, someone has Karl's misgivings. Research shows sound reasons for both points of view. Groups generally do take more time to reach decisions than individuals, yet group decisions often are superior to those made by a single person. Although group interaction stimulates creativity, it may also suppress individuals and their ideas.

Whether your experiences in groups have been positive, negative, or a mix of the two, you have probably belonged to a number of groups during your life. Pick up any newspaper and you will see announcements for social groups, volunteer service committees, personal support groups, health teams, focus groups run by companies trying out new products, and political action coalitions. It is a rare person in the United States who doesn't participate in many groups.

In this chapter we'll build on what you've learned about communication to explore interaction in groups. The first part of the chapter defines groups and teams, traces their rising popularity, identifies features that affect communication in groups, and points out potential strengths and weaknesses of groups. The second part of the chapter describes challenges for effective participation in groups.

UNDERSTANDING COMMUNICATION IN GROUPS AND TEAMS

There are many kinds of groups, each with distinctive goals and communication patterns. Social groups provide us the stimulation of conversation and recreation with people we enjoy. Communication in social groups tends to be relaxed, informal, and more focused on the interpersonal climate than the tasks at hand. Personal growth groups enable people to deal with significant issues and problems in a supportive context. In personal growth groups, communication aims to help members clarify and address issues in their lives. Task groups exist to solve problems, develop policies, or achieve other substantive goals. The communication of task groups concentrates on evidence, reasoning, and ideas, as well as on organizing, discussion, and maintaining a healthy climate for interaction.

Although different types of groups have distinct primary purposes and focuses, most groups include attention to climate, personal topics, and tasks. For example, social groups often move into task discussion, as when one friend asks another for advice in solving a problem. Groups that exist to accomplish a task typically include some social communication, and therapy groups typically involve both task and social dimensions that contribute to the primary goal of personal growth.

For all types of groups, communication is a primary influence on productivity and the climate of interaction. Communication in groups and teams involves the basic processes we discussed in earlier chapters. For example, constructive group communication requires that members use effective verbal and nonverbal communication, check perceptions with one another, listen mindfully, build good climates, and adapt communication to each other and various group goals and situations.

Defining *Groups* and *Teams*

What is a group? Are six people standing in line for tickets a group? Are five individuals studying their individual materials in a library a group? Are four businesspeople in an airport lounge a group?

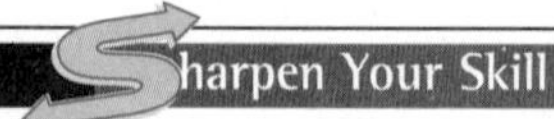

GROUPS IN YOUR LIFE

How many groups do you belong to? List the groups in which you currently participate.

- Social groups
- Personal support groups
- Work groups
- Volunteer service committees

■ *What can you tell about this group from the photo? Look for nonverbal clues regarding leadership, formality, and climate.*

Unless people are interacting and involved in collective endeavors, a group does not exist. The foregoing examples describe collections of individuals but not groups.

For a group to exist, the people must interact and be interdependent, have a common goal, and share some rules of conduct. Thus we can define a **group** as three or more people who interact over time, depend on one another, and follow shared rules of conduct to reach a common goal. Individual members of a group may have goals that differ from or are in tension with the collective goal, but a common goal still exists (Keyton, 1999b). Group members perceive themselves as interdependent—as needing one another to achieve something, such as developing a policy for the workplace, fostering social ties among people, or promoting personal growth.

A **team** is a special kind of group characterized by different and complementary resources of members and by a strong sense of collective identity (Hirokawa & Keyton, 1995). Like all groups, teams involve interaction, interdependence, shared rules, and common goals. Yet teams are distinct in two respects. First, teams consist of people who bring specialized and different resources to a common project. Second, teams develop greater interdependence and a stronger sense of identity than is standard for most groups. Team members perceive themselves as a unit much more than do members of most groups (Lumsden & Lumsden, 1997). In other words, all teams are groups, but not all groups are teams.

Groups and teams develop rules that members understand and follow. You will recall from earlier chapters that constitutive rules state what counts as what. For example, in some groups disagreement counts as a positive sign of involvement and critical thinking, whereas other groups regard disagreement as negative. Regulative rules regulate how, when, and with whom we interact. For instance, a group might have regulative rules that hold that members do not interrupt each other and that any tensions among members are not discussed with outsiders. Groups generate rules in the process of interacting and figuring out what works for them (Figure 10.1).

Shared goals is another characteristic of groups. Citizens form groups to accomplish political goals, establish community programs, protest zoning decisions, and protect the security of neighborhoods. Workers form groups to safeguard benefits and job security, and they work in teams to develop and market products, evaluate and refine company programs, and improve productivity. Other groups form to promote personal growth (therapy groups), share a life (families), socialize (recreational clubs), and participate

TEAM EXCELLENCE AND EXCELLENCE IN TEAMS

The Xerox Corporation discovered the value of team work more than a decade ago. Paul Allaire, CEO of Xerox in 1990, described himself as a firm believer in teams, in which more than 75% of Xerox employees at all levels are actively involved. They are responsible for everything from reducing costs of delivery and improving customer satisfaction to designing new products.

Xerox's annual Team Excellence Award, presented at a formal ceremony, is a monetary reward shared by members of the winning team. One winner was the "Fly-by-Nites," a team that reduced the cost of overnight air shipments by a dramatic $1.9 million and improved speed of deliveries, which increased customer satisfaction.

Source: Bowles, 1990.

in sports (intramural teams). Many online groups are defined by members' shared interest in some activity, issue, or hobby. If a common goal dissolves, the group disbands or redefines its purpose.

Mieko

When I first came here to go to school, I felt very alone. I met some other students from Japan, and we formed a group to help us feel at home in America. For the first year that group was most important to us because we felt uprooted. The second year it was not so important because we'd all started finding ways to fit in here, and we felt more at home. The third year we decided not to be a group anymore. The reason we wanted a group no longer existed.

The Rise of Groups and Teams

The tendency toward teamwork is especially pronounced in the workplace (Hirokawa & Keyton, 1995). Whether you are an attorney working with a litigation team, a health care professional on a medical team, or a factory worker on a team assigned to

Figure 10.1 Stages of Group Development

Bruce Tuckman (1965) reviewed research on therapy, learning, and task groups. Regardless of purpose, the groups followed a four-phase sequence of development:

Forming	**is the initial stage of group life in which members define a purpose and get acquainted.**
Storming	**is typically marked by conflict about goals, personalities, information, and so forth. Members may also struggle for power.**
Norming	**is a phase in which members work out guidelines, rules, and roles to regulate how they interact.**
Performing	**exists when members settle down to business after resolving conflicts and establishing norms.**

Source: Tuckman, 1965.

reduce production time, working with others probably will be part of your career. Your raises and advancement are likely to depend significantly on how effectively you communicate in groups. Reliance on groups is increasing because groups often produce better results than individuals. As group members communicate, creativity is stoked, solid ideas emerge, and members enjoy participating. Task groups aim to accomplish some defined objective, such as creating a policy, making a decision, solving a problem, evaluating a product, advising others, or generating ideas. Because task groups pervade professional and civic life, we'll concentrate on this type of group here. Of course, much of the information we'll discuss pertains to other types of groups as well.

The task group, which is often a team, has emerged as a major feature of modern life. Earlier in this century the majority of people worked fairly independently. Each person had her or his individual job responsibilities and coordinated with others only when necessary. In recent years, however, six kinds of groups have become prevalent in business and civic life (Sher & Gottlieb, 1989).

Project Teams Many businesses and professions rely on project teams, which consist of people who have expertise related to different facets of a project and who combine their knowledge and skills to accomplish a common goal. The objective might be to establish a quality control system, create a public relations campaign for a new product, or promote a corporation's image in a community.

Communication in project teams allows each member to develop a holistic vision that infuses collective work. To launch a new product, pharmaceutical companies often put together product teams that include scientists and doctors who understand the technical character of the new drug and other personnel who have knowledge of marketing, product design, advertising, and customer relations. Working together, team members develop a coherent plan for testing, packaging, advertising, and marketing the new product to the public. If the individuals worked separately in their specific areas, they would generate a less effective plan.

Focus Groups Focus groups are used to find out what people think about a specific idea, product, issue, or person. Focus groups are a mainstay of advertisers who want to understand attitudes, preferences, and responses of people whom they want to buy their product, vote for their candidate, and so forth. What do 21- to 25-year-olds think of a new light beer? How do retirees respond to a planned advertising campaign for cruises? Focus groups are also popular in political life: What do middle-income women and men think of a mayoral candidate's environmental record? How do young voters feel about economic issues? Do African Americans regard the candidate as trustworthy?

Focus groups are guided by a leader or facilitator who encourages members to communicate their ideas, beliefs, feelings, and perceptions relevant to the topic. The contributions of group members serve as the foundation for later decisions, such as how to refine the recipe for the light beer, increase perceptions of a political candidate's trustworthiness, and tailor advertising for cruises. The facilitator seldom offers substantive comments but encourages group members to express themselves, respond to each other, and elaborate on their thoughts and feelings. Usually, facilitators develop a list of questions in advance and use these to encourage participants to talk (Lederman, 1990).

Brainstorming Groups Group discussion is especially effective in stimulating creative thinking. Interaction seems to spark imagination, so groups are often superior to individuals in generating ideas. When idea generation is the goal, brainstorming groups are appropriate. The goal of **brainstorming** is to come up with as many ideas as possible. Because criticism tends to stifle creativity, brainstorming groups bar criticism. They encourage creativity and even wild thinking in order to come up with the most imaginative ideas possible. If a group starts to run out of ideas, members can suggest new dimensions of a topic or ways to extend ideas already generated. (Rules for brainstorming appear in Figure 10.2.)

Perhaps you are concerned that brainstorming might produce unrealistic ideas. That's not really a problem because evaluative discussion follows brainstorming. During evaluation members work together to appraise the ideas generated through brainstorming. Criticism now is appropriate and constructive because the group must decide which idea or ideas merit more focused attention. During this stage the group discards impractical ideas, refines weak or undeveloped contributions, consolidates related suggestions, and further discusses promising ones.

Leaders or facilitators of brainstorming groups should set a tone for creative communication. To do this, they should demonstrate energy, stoke members' imaginations, and respond enthusiastically to

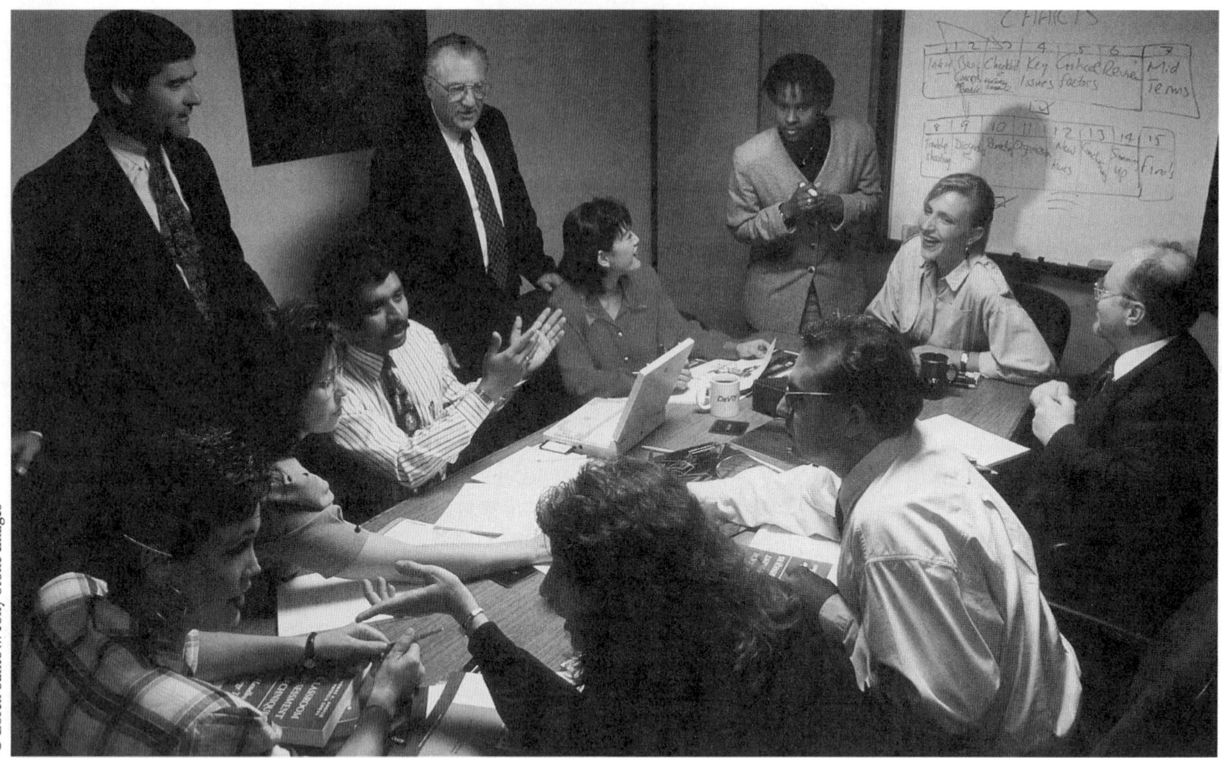

■ *How involved is this group in brainstorming? What is the facilitator doing to encourage creativity?*

members' ideas. If the group runs out of ideas, leaders may prompt members by saying, "Let's try to combine some of the ideas we already have," or "We're being too restrained—how about some wild proposals?"

Advisory Groups Advisory groups do not actually make policies or decisions. Instead, they submit recommendations to others who make the final decisions. Advisory groups are constituted to provide expert briefing to an individual or another group that is empowered make a decision. For example, in my department I chair the teaching committee, an advisory group that makes recommendations to the faculty as a whole. Our committee has recommended policies for peer evaluation of faculty teaching and for greater emphasis on teaching in tenure and promotion decisions. In 1995 Vice President Al

Figure 10.2 Rules for Brainstorming

- **Do not evaluate ideas in any way. Both verbal and nonverbal criticism are inappropriate.**
- **Record all ideas on a board or easel so that all members of the group can see them.**
- **Go for quantity: The more ideas, the better.**
- **Build on ideas. An idea presented by one member of the group may stimulate an extension by another member. This is desirable.**
- **Encourage creativity. Welcome wild and even preposterous ideas. An idea that seems wacky may lead to other ideas that are more workable.**

Gore worked with an advisory group consisting of leaders of major environmental organizations in the United States. Bringing together a handful of key players to discuss national environmental policy accomplished two objectives. First, it quelled the infighting to which these groups are prone. Second, discussion among group members generated perspectives richer than those presented by any individual member before the group formed.

Advisory groups may also consist of peers who advise each other. In a 1995 *Wall Street Journal* column addressed to small business owners, management consultant Howard Upton described a system of peer advisory groups developed by chief executives of the Petroleum Equipment Institute. The executives created groups of ten to twelve presidents of the 700 distributorships in the United States and Canada. By conferring regularly, these presidents were able to advise each other on common problems, practices, and goals. The members found that by pooling experience and reports on methods of problem solving, they were able to enhance everyone's effectiveness.

High-ranking authorities in government and business are seldom experts on the range of issues relevant to decisions they must make. Those who track business trends say that "it is impossible for the head of any company, large or small, to succeed without benefit of outside advice" (Upton, 1995, p. A14). The solitary manager, president, or CEO who relies only on his or her ideas is not functional in modern life. Advisory groups allow decision makers to benefit from other experts' information and advice pertinent to developing effective policies and making informed decisions.

Quality Circles A **quality circle** includes three or more people who are employed in different areas of an organization and who work together to improve quality in the organization (Lumsden & Lumsden, 1997). Originally, quality circles were part of total quality management, a system that calls for intensive teamwork and highly participative work structures to maximize the quality of an organization's output (Deming, 1982). A variety of organizations, not all of which endorse total quality management, now use quality circles. Quality circles mix not just people with differing areas of expertise but also people at different levels in an organization's hierarchy. Thus, a secretary may contribute as much as a mid-level manager to a discussion of ways to improve office productivity.

The first few meetings of a quality circle typically focus on complaining about problems (Scorpion, 1991). This doesn't necessarily foster a negative climate because complaining about shared frustrations allows members to become comfortable with one another and to establish some common ground. In addition, this opening talk generally alerts the group to special concerns and areas of knowledge that each member can contribute. After the initial venting of frustrations, quality circles focus on identifying needs

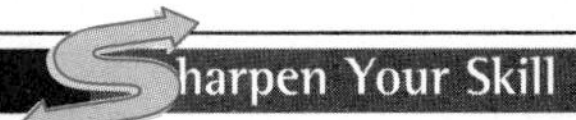

BRAINSTORMING

To learn the value of brainstorming, try this. First, write down as many ideas as you alone can think of in response to one of the items listed here. Then spend 10 minutes generating ideas in discussion with four to six other members of your class. Be sure to follow the rules for brainstorming that appear in Figure 10.2.

1. List ways to incorporate technology into teaching on your campus.
2. How could the number of people who vote in local elections be increased?
3. Develop ideas for your class's graduation gift to your school.

What do you conclude about the value of brainstorming as a method of promoting creative communication in groups?

or problems, ways in which organizational functioning could be improved, and areas of stress or discontent for employees.

For quality circles to be effective, management must guarantee its support for their work and recommendations. Nothing is more frustrating than to be asked to work on a problem but be denied authority to implement changes or assurance that others will implement them. When given support, quality circles often generate impressive and creative solutions to organizational problems such as high costs, on-the-job accidents, and low worker morale. Quality groups usually make reports on a regular basis (weekly or monthly) to keep management informed of their ideas and suggestions.

Decision-Making Groups A sixth kind of task group exists to make decisions. In some cases decision-making groups form to make a specific decision: What should the company's policy on medical leave be? What benefits and personnel should we cut to achieve a 15% decrease in annual expenses? Other standing groups or committees make decisions about training and development, public relations, budgets, and other matters. Members of decision-making groups are responsible for creating a supportive communication climate, organizing discussions productively, and ensuring critical analysis and sound reasoning (Figure 10.3).

Task groups and teams are prominent in professional and civic life. When members and leaders are effective communicators, task groups often allow people with different backgrounds, abilities, expertise, and talents to generate results that are more creative and better informed than those they could devise individually.

Features of Small Groups

What happens in groups and teams depends largely on members' abilities to communicate verbally and nonverbally, listen mindfully, coordinate perceptions, build a climate that fosters high-quality work, and adapt to one another and their situation. If members are not skilled in basic communication processes, groups are unlikely to achieve their potential for productivity and creativity (Keyton, 1999a). Thus, we need to understand influences on participation in groups as well as the influence of communication itself on group process and productivity. We'll consider five features of small groups that affect and are affected by participation.

Cohesion **Cohesion** is the degree of closeness among members and sense of group spirit. In highly cohesive groups, members see themselves as tightly linked and committed to shared goals. This results in greater sat-

Figure 10.3 The Standard Agenda for Problem Solving

Task groups generally aim to solve problems, ranging from how to improve morale to what policy to implement. A time-tested method for effective problem solving is the agenda, based on philosopher John Dewey's (1910) model of reflective thinking:

Phase 1: **Define the problem.**

Phase 2: **Analyze information relevant to the problem.**

Phase 3: **Generate criteria to assess solutions.**

Phase 4: **Identify potential solutions.**

Phase 5: **Select the best solution.**

Phase 6: **Implement the solution (or recommend it).**

Phase 7: **Develop an action plan to monitor the effectiveness of the solution.**

Sources: Dewey, 1910; Wood, 2001a.

isfaction than members of noncohesive units feel. High cohesion and the satisfaction it generates tend to increase members' commitment to a group and its goals. Consequently, cohesiveness is important to effective and satisfying group communication.

Cohesion grows out of communication that builds group identity and creates a climate of inclusion for all members. One way to promote cohesion is to emphasize the group or team and the goals members share. Comments that stress pulling together and collective interests build cohesion by reinforcing group identity. Cohesion is also fostered by communication that highlights similarities among members: interests, experiences, and ways of thinking that are common to members of the group. A third way to enhance cohesion is to be responsive so that all members feel valued by and committed to the group (Gibb, 1961, 1964; Schutz, 1966).

Cohesion and participation are reciprocal in their influence. Cohesion is promoted when all members are involved and communicating in the group. At the same time, because cohesiveness generates a feeling of identity and involvement, once established it fosters participation. Thus, high levels of participation tend to build cohesion, and strong cohesion generally fosters vigorous participation. Encouraging all members to be involved in discussion and responding to each person's contributions fuel cohesion and continued participation. Although cohesion is important for effective group communication, excessive cohesion can actually undermine sound group work. When members are too close, they may be less critical of each other's ideas and less willing to engage in analysis and arguments that are necessary to develop the best outcomes.

Extreme cohesion sometimes leads to **groupthink,** in which members cease to think critically and independently. Groupthink has occurred in high-level groups such as presidential advisory boards and national decision-making bodies (Janis, 1977; Wood, Phillips, & Pedersen, 1986). Members tend to perceive their group so positively that they assume it cannot make bad decisions. Consequently, members do not critically screen ideas generated in deliberations. The predictable result is group outcomes that are inferior and that often fail.

Group Size The number of people in a group affects the amount and quality of communication. Conversation between two people involves only two people who create, perceive, and listen to messages. In a group of five people, each idea must be received and interpreted by four others, each of whom may respond with comments that four others must receive and interpret. As group size increases, the contributions of each member tend to decrease. You may have experienced frustration when participating in large online chat rooms and discussion forums: It can be hard to get your ideas in, and the

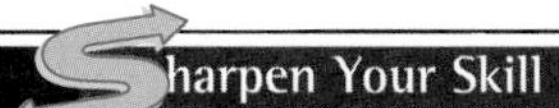

COMMUNICATION AND COHESION

Select a group to which you belong and rate its level of cohesion as high, moderate, or low. Next, pay attention to the communication among members of the group during one meeting. Based on the discussion, answer these questions:

1. To what extent does communication emphasize the group or team?
2. To what extent does talk among members emphasize collective goals?
3. To what degree do members talk about pulling together and collaborating?
4. To what extent do members comment on similarities among their goals, interests, experiences, and the like?
5. To what degree do members communicate affection and respect to one another?

sheer number of people contributing ideas can mean that no idea receives much feedback. Because participation is linked to commitment, larger groups may generate less commitment to group outcomes than smaller groups. Because participation also affects cohesion, larger groups may also be less cohesive than smaller ones.

Yolanda

The worst group I was ever on had three members. We were supposed to have five, but two dropped out after the first meeting, so there were three of us to come up with proposals for artistic programs for the campus. Nobody would say anything against anybody else's ideas, even if we thought they were bad. For myself, I know I held back from criticizing a lot of times because I didn't want to offend either of the other two. We came up with some really bad ideas because we were so small we couldn't risk arguing.

The disadvantages of large groups might lead you to assume that small groups would be ideal. However, groups can be too small as well as too large. With too few members a group has limited resources, which diminishes a primary value of group decision making. Also, in small groups members may be unwilling to criticize each other's ideas because alienating one member would dramatically weaken the group. Most researchers agree that five to seven members is the optimal size for a group (Wood, 1992a).

Power Structure Power structure is a third feature that influences participation in small groups. **Power** is the ability to influence others (Wood et al., 1986). There are two distinct ways of influencing others. **Power over** is the ability to help or harm others. This form of power usually is expressed in ways that emphasize and build the status of the person wielding influence. A team leader might exert positive power over a member by providing mentoring, giving strong performance reviews, and assigning the member high-status roles on the team. A leader could also exert negative power over a member by withholding these benefits, assigning unpleasant tasks, and responding negatively to the member's communication during meetings.

Power to is the ability to empower others to reach their goals (Boulding, 1990; Staley, 1988). People who empower others do not emphasize their status. Instead, they act behind the scenes to enlarge others' influence and visibility and to help others succeed. This brand of power aims to create opportunities for others, recognize achievements, and help others to accomplish their goals. It builds team spirit so that group members are productive and satisfied (Boulding, 1990). This style of influence fosters a

fyi

GENDERED POWER PATTERNS

Research (Helgesen, 1990) reveals general differences in how women and men define and use power. Men tend to see power as finite and as something to guard closely. Women are more likely to regard power as unlimited and to share it freely. Another difference is how the sexes see the ends of power. In general, men see power as something an individual has and uses to enhance individual status. The tendency among women is to perceive power as a resource for empowering others and building strong collaborative teams. Differences in orientations toward power are consistent with gender communication cultures and the divergent rules of communication they teach women and men.

win—win group climate in which each member's success is perceived to advance the collective work. Members view themselves as a unit that benefits from the successes of individual members.

Within groups power may be earned and distributed in distinct ways. Power may result from position (CEO, president, professor, best friend of the boss), or it may be earned (demonstrated competence or expertise). If all members of a group have roughly equal power, the group has a distributed power structure. On the other hand, if one or more members have greater power than others, the group has a hierarchical power structure. Hierarchy may take the form of one person who is more powerful than all others, who are equal in power to one another. Alternatively, hierarchy may mean multiple levels of power. A leader might have the greatest power, three others might have power equal to each other's but less than the leader's, and four other members might have little power.

How are individual power and group power structure related to participation? First, members with high power tend to be the centers of group communication; they talk more and others talk more to them. **Social climbing** is the process of trying to increase personal status in a group by winning the approval of high-status members. If social climbing doesn't increase the status of those doing it, they often become marginal participants in groups. In addition, members with a great deal of power often have greater influence on group decisions. High-power members tend to find discussion more satisfying than members with less power (Wood et al., 1986). This makes sense because those with power get to participate more and get their way more often.

Power both influences communication and is influenced by it (Barge & Keyton, 1994). In other words, how members communicate can affect the power they acquire. People who make good substantive comments, cultivate a healthy climate, and organize deliberations tend to earn power quickly. These are examples of earned power that is conferred because a member provides skills valued by the group. Members who demonstrate that they have done their homework and respond thoughtfully likewise gain power.

Interaction Patterns Another important influence on communication in groups is interaction patterns (Figure 10.4). Centralized patterns allow one or two people to have key positions, and most or all communication either goes to them or is funneled through them to other group members. Decentralized patterns promote more balanced communication. As you might suspect, the power of individual members often affects interaction patterns. If one or two members have greater power, a centralized pattern of interaction is likely to emerge. Decentralized patterns are more typical when members have roughly equal power.

One strategy for controlling communication in groups is to manage proxemics, the nonverbal communication relevant to space. If you want a centralized communication structure (and hierarchical power), you might arrange chairs so that one person has the central position. On the other hand, if you want a decentralized structure, you should arrange chairs so that no person is more central than any other. Equalized participation directly enhances satisfaction with belonging to a group and commitment to a group's decisions.

Group Norms A final feature of small groups that affects communication is **norms.** Like rules, which we have discussed, norms are guidelines that regulate how members act, as well as how they interact with each other. Group norms control everything from trivial to critical aspects of a group's life. More inconsequential norms may regulate meeting time and whether eating is allowed during meetings. More substantive norms govern how members express and analyze ideas, listen to one another, and manage conflict.

Norms grow directly out of interaction. For example, at an initial meeting one person might disparage another's idea, and members might not pay attention when others are speaking. If this continues, a norm for disrespect will develop and members will form a habit of not being good listeners. On the other hand, one member might disparage an idea and another person might say, "I don't agree. Let's consider the point." If the group does consider the idea, a norm for respectful communication may develop.

Figure 10.4 Patterns of Interaction in Groups

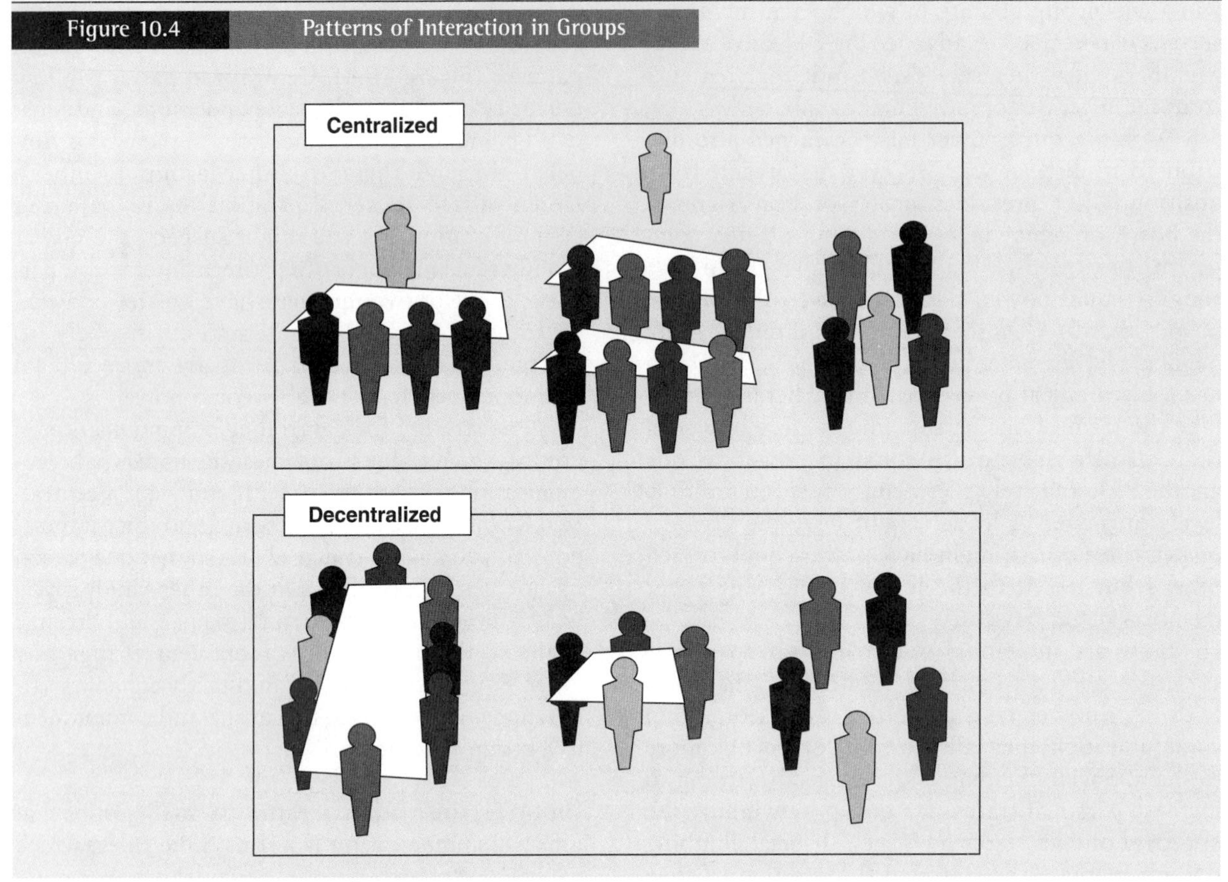

Baxter

When our team first formed, everyone was pretty casual. There was a lot of kidding around before we got down to work at each meeting, and members often drifted in late. I didn't want to crack down at the beginning because I thought that might dampen group spirit. With 20–20 hindsight, I now see I should have imposed some rules at the outset. I've tried to get members to get to meetings on time and buckle down to work, but I'm fighting against a history of being laid-back.

As Baxter's commentary reflects, norms become entrenched early in a group's life, so it's important to pay attention to them from the outset. By noticing patterns and tendencies, you can exert influence over the norms that govern conduct in a group. Cohesion, size, power structure, interaction patterns, and norms are features of groups that affect participation, productivity, and satisfaction.

Potential Limitations and Strengths of Groups

A great deal of research has compared individual and group decision making. As you might expect, the research identifies both potential weaknesses and strengths of groups.

Limitations of Groups

The two most significant disadvantages of group discussion are the time required for group process and the potential of conformity pressures to interfere with high-quality work from groups.

Non Sequitur
THE EFFICIENCY OF COMMITTEE MANAGEMENT
OK, THE BOARD HAS FINALLY COME TO A CONSENSUS HERE... TWO LARGE PEPPERONIS ON THIN CRUST, WITH LIGHT CHEESE AND EXTRA SAUCE...
WILEY 10-14

Operating solo, an individual can think through ideas efficiently and choose the best one. In group discussion, however, all members have an opportunity to voice their ideas and to respond to the ideas others put forward. It takes substantial time for each person to describe ideas, clarify misunderstandings, and respond to questions or criticisms. In addition, groups require time to deliberate about alternative courses of action. Thus, group discussion probably is not a wise choice for routine policy making and emergency tasks. When creativity and thoroughness are important, however, the values of groups may be more important than the time they require.

Groups also have the potential to suppress individuals and encourage conformity. This can happen in two ways. First, conformity pressures may exist when a majority has an opinion different from that of a minority or a single member. Holding out for your point of view is difficult when most or all of your peers have a different one. In effective groups, however, all members understand and resist conformity pressures. They realize that the majority is sometimes wrong and the minority, even a single person, is sometimes right. Members have an ethical responsibility to communicate in ways that encourage expression of diverse ideas and open debate about different viewpoints.

Conformity pressures may also arise when one member is extremely charismatic or has more power or prestige than other members. Even if that person is all alone in a point of view, other members may conform. Sometimes a high-status member doesn't intend to influence others and may not overtly exert pressure. However, the other members still perceive the status, and it may affect their judgments. President Kennedy's advisers, for example, regarded him so highly that in some cases they suspended their individual critical thinking and agreed with whatever he said (Janis, 1977). As this example illustrates, often neither the high-status person nor others are consciously aware of pressures to conform. This implies that members should be on guard against the potential to conform uncritically.

Lance

I used to belong to a creative writing group where all of us helped each other improve our writing. At first all of us were equally vocal, and we had a lot of good discussions and even disagreements that helped us grow as writers. But then one member of the group got a story accepted by a big magazine, and all of a sudden we thought of her as a better writer than any of us. She didn't act any different, but we saw her as more accomplished, so when she said something everybody listened and nobody disagreed. It was like a wet blanket on our creativity because her opinion just carried too much weight once she got published.

Strengths of Groups The primary potential strengths of groups in comparison to individuals are greater resources, more thorough thought, heightened creativity, and enhanced commitment to decisions (Wood, 1992a). A group obviously exceeds any individual in the ideas, perspectives, experiences, and expertise it can bring to bear on solving a problem. Especially in teams, the different resources of individual members are a key to effectiveness. One member knows technical aspects of a product, another understands market psychology, a third is talented in advertising, and so forth. Health care teams consist of specialists who combine their knowledge to care for a patient.

Groups also tend to be more thorough than individuals, probably because members check and balance each other. The parts of an issue one member doesn't understand another person does; the details of a plan that bore one person interest another; the holes in a proposal that some members overlook are perceived by others. Greater thoroughness by groups isn't simply the result of more people. It reflects interaction among members. When conformity pressures are controlled, discussion can promote critical and careful analysis because members propel each other's thinking (Wood, 1992a). **Synergy** is a special kind of energy that enlarges the efforts, talents, and strengths of individual members (Lumsden & Lumsden, 1997). A third value of groups is that they are generally more creative than individuals. Again, the reason seems to lie in the synergy of groups. When members know how to communicate effectively, they spark good ideas, integrate thinking, and increase creativity. Any individual eventually runs out of new ideas, but groups seem to have almost infinite generative ability. As members talk, they build on each other's ideas, refine proposals, and see new possibilities in each other's comments. The result is often a greater number of overall ideas and more creative solutions.

Laura

When the supervisor said all of us in my department were to meet and brainstorm ways to cut costs for the company, I thought it was silly and each person should just submit suggestions individually. But I was wrong. When my group started, each of us had one or two ideas. But the six of us came up with more than 25 ideas after we'd talked awhile.

Finally, an important strength of groups is their ability to generate commitment to outcomes. The greater commitment fostered by group discussion arises from two sources. First, participation enhances commitment to decisions. Thus, groups with balanced participation build commitment among members, which is especially important if members will be involved in implementing the decision. Second, because groups have greater resources than an individual decision maker, their decisions are more likely to take into account the points of view of the various people needed to implement a decision. This is critical because a decision can be sabotaged if the people it affects dislike it or feel that their perspectives weren't considered.

Greater resources, thoroughness, creativity, and commitment to group goals are powerful values of group process. To incorporate these values, members must be willing to invest the time that discussion requires and must resist pressures to conform or induce others to conform.

CHALLENGES OF COMMUNICATING IN GROUPS AND TEAMS

For groups to realize their potential strengths, members must meet a number of communication challenges. Three that we will consider are participating constructively, providing leadership, and managing conflict so that it benefits the group and its outcomes.

Participating Constructively

There are four kinds of communication in groups (Figure 10.5). The first three—task, procedural, and climate communication—are constructive because they foster good group climate and outcomes. The fourth kind of communication is egocentric, or dysfunctional, communication. It tends to detract from a healthy group climate and effective decision making.

Figure 10.5 Types of Communication in Groups

Task Communication	**Initiates ideas** **Seeks information** **Gives information** **Elaborates on ideas** **Evaluates, offers critical analysis**
Procedural Communication	**Establishes agenda** **Provides orientation** **Curbs digressions** **Guides participation** **Coordinates ideas** **Summarizes others' contributions** **Records group progress**
Climate Communication	**Establishes and maintains healthy climate** **Energizes group process** **Harmonizes ideas** **Recognizes others** **Reconciles conflicts** **Builds enthusiasm for group**
Egocentric Communication	**Is aggressive toward others** **Blocks ideas** **Seeks personal recognition (brags)** **Dominates interaction** **Pleads for special interests** **Confesses, self-discloses, seeks personal help** **Disrupts task** **Devalues others** **Trivializes group and its work**

Task Communication **Task communication** focuses on the problem, issues, or information before a group. It provides ideas and information, clarifies members' understanding, and critically evaluates ideas. Task contributions may initiate ideas, respond to others' ideas, or provide critical evaluation of information. Task comments also include asking for ideas and criticism from others.

Procedural Communication If you've ever participated in a disorganized group, you understand the importance of **procedural communication.** It helps a group get organized and stay on track in its decision making. Procedural contributions establish an agenda, coordinate comments of different members, and record group progress. In addition, procedural contributions may curb digressions and tangents, summarize progress, and regulate participation so that everyone has opportunities to speak and nobody dominates.

Climate Communication A group is more than a task unit. It is also people who are involved in a relationship that can be more or less pleasant and open. **Climate communication** focuses on creating and maintaining a constructive climate that encourages members to contribute freely and to evaluate ideas critically. Climate comments emphasize a group's strengths and progress, recognize others' contributions, reconcile conflicts, and build enthusiasm for the group and its work.

Egocentric Communication The final kind of group communication is not recommended, but it sometimes surfaces in groups. **Egocentric communication**, or dysfunctional communication, is used to block others or to call attention to oneself. It detracts from group progress because it is self-centered rather than group centered. Examples of egocentric talk are devaluing another member's ideas, trivializing group efforts, being aggressive toward other members, bragging about personal accomplishments, dominating, disrupting group work, and pleading for special causes that aren't in a group's interest.

Task, procedural, and climate communication work together to foster productive, organized, and comfortable group discussion. Most of us are already skilled in one or two kinds of communication. For instance, some people have a gift for reconciling conflicts and using humor to break tension. Other people have keen organizational talents that allow them to offer procedural leadership. Still others are especially skillful in analyzing information. The kinds of communication that you associate with yourself reflect your self-concept, which we discussed in Chapter 8.

Egocentric communication, on the other hand, does not contribute to enjoyable group interaction or high-quality outcomes. Egocentric comments can sabotage a group's climate and hinder its progress in achieving its goals. If it occurs, others in the group should intervene to discourage it. Communicating clearly that egocentric behavior will not be tolerated in your group fosters norms for effective interaction. Figure 10.6 breaks an excerpt from a student discussion into the types of communication we have identified.

Figure 10.6 includes all four kinds of communication that we have discussed. Note how skillfully Ann communicates to defuse tension between Bob and Jan before it disrupts the group. You might also notice that Ed provides the primary procedural leadership for the group, and Bob is effective in interjecting humor to build a good climate. Several members recognize contributions to the discussion.

Understanding how varied types of communication affect collective work allows you to make informed choices about when to use each type of communication in your participation in groups. Although you may not be proficient in all three positive kinds of group communication now, you can enlarge your repertoire of group communication skills.

Providing Leadership

All groups need leadership in order to be effective. For decades society assumed that leaders are born, not made. Researchers studied personal qualities, ranging from intelligence to emotional balance and physical energy, in an effort to understand the traits of born leaders. This line of study failed to reveal any consistent traits of leaders. The lack of identifiable

Sharpen Your Skill

YOUR COMMUNICATION IN GROUPS

1. How do you contribute to small group discussions?
2. Do you specialize in task, procedural, or climate communication?
3. Observe yourself in a small group setting and record the focus of your comments. Which kinds of group communication do you do well? In which areas do you want to develop greater skill?

Figure 10.6 Coding Group Communication

Ed: Let's start by talking about our goals. [procedural]
Jan: That's a good idea. [climate]
Bob: I think our goal is to come up with a better meal plan for students on campus. [task]
Ed: What do you mean by "better"? Do you mean cheaper or more variety or more tasteful? [task]
Ann: I think it's all three. [task]
Ed: Well, we probably do care about all three, but maybe we should talk about one at a time so we can keep our discussion focused. [procedural]
Bob: Okay, I vote we focus first on taste—like it would be good if there were some taste to the food on campus! [task and climate (humor)]
Jan: Do you mean taste itself or quality of food, which might also consider nutrition? [task]
Bob: Pure taste! When I'm hungry, I don't think about what's good for me, just what tastes good. [task and possibly climate (humor)]
Jan: Well, maybe we want the food service to think about nutrition because we don't. [task]
Bob: If you're a health food nut, that's your problem. I don't think nutrition is something that's important in the food service on campus. [task; may also be egocentric if his tone toward Jan is snide]
Ed: Let's do this: Let's talk first about what we would like in terms of taste itself. [procedural] Before we meet next time, it might be a good idea for one of us to talk with the manager of the cafeteria to see whether they have to meet any nutritional guidelines in what they serve. [task]
Ann: I'll volunteer to do that. [task]
Ed: Great. Thanks, Ann. [climate]
Bob: I'll volunteer to do taste testing! [climate (humor)]
Jan: With your weight you'd better not. [egocentric]
Bob: Yeah, like you have a right to criticize me. [egocentric]
Ann: Look, none of us is here to criticize anyone else. We're here because we want to improve the food service on campus. [climate]. We've decided we want to focus first on taste [procedural] so who has an idea of how do we go about studying that? [task]

leader traits led researchers to realize that leadership is not an individual quality or a constant set of qualities. Instead, leadership is a set of functions that assist groups in accomplishing tasks and maintaining a good climate.

Leadership, Not Leader Leadership may be provided either by one member or by several members who contribute to guiding group process and ensuring effective outcomes. Leadership exists when one or more members communicate in order to establish a good working climate, organize group processes, and ensure that discussion is substantive. You may have noticed that leadership communication parallels types of constructive communication that group members make. A fourth function of leadership is to control disruptive members, who engage in egocentric communication. Leadership, then, is effective participation.

When a single person provides leadership, that person performs the functions necessary for effective group discussion. When leadership is not vested in one person, several members share responsibilities. Whether there is one leader or shared leadership, the primary responsibilities are to organize discussion, ensure sound research and reasoning, promote norms for mindful listening and clear verbal and nonverbal communication, create a productive climate, build group morale, and discourage egocentric communication that detracts from group efforts.

Krystal

The most effective group I've ever been in had three leaders. I was the person who understood our task best, so I contributed the most to critical thinking about the issues. But Belinda was the one who kept us organized. She could get us off tangents, and she knew when it was time to move on from one stage of work to the next. She also pulled ideas together to coordinate our thinking. Kevin was the climate leader. He could always tell a joke if things got tense, and he was the best person I ever saw for recognizing others' contributions. I couldn't point to any one leader in that group, but we sure did have good leadership.

When we realize that leadership is a series of functions that move groups along, we understand that more than one person may engage in leadership in a specific group or team. Sometimes one member communicates to provide guidance on task and procedures, and another member communicates to build a healthy group climate. A group needs both climate and task leadership to be maximally effective. Also, different people may provide leadership at different times in a group's life. The person who guides the group at the outset may not be the one who advances the group's work in later phases. Depending on what a group needs at a specific time, different leadership functions are appropriate and may come from different members. Even when an official leader exists, other members may contribute much of the communication that provides leadership to a group. Although the official leader has the responsibility for a group's decision (and gets the credit or blame), others may provide a substantial amount of leadership.

In sum, leadership is a dynamic process of meeting the various needs for effective communication in small groups. Whether provided by one or several members, effective leadership involves communication that advances a group's task, organizes deliberations, builds group morale, controls disruptions, and fosters a constructive climate.

Managing Conflict Constructively

In Chapter 3 we learned that conflict is natural and can be productive. In groups and teams, conflict stimulates thinking, helps members consider diverse perspectives, and enlarges members' understanding of issues involved in making decisions and generating ideas. To achieve these goals, however, conflict must be managed carefully. The goal is to manage conflict so that it enriches group processes and helps groups achieve their collective goals. Trey's commentary is instructive. Although many of us may not enjoy conflict, we can nonetheless recognize its value—even its necessity—to effective group work. Just as conflict in relationships can enlarge perspectives and increase understanding, conflict in groups can foster critical, thorough, and insightful deliberations.

Trey

I used to think conflict was terrible and hurt groups, but last year I was a member of a group that had no—I mean, zero—conflict. A couple of times I tried to bring up an idea different than what had been suggested, but my idea wouldn't even get a hearing. The whole goal was not to disagree. As a result, we didn't do a very thorough job of analyzing the issues, and we didn't subject the solution we developed to critical scrutiny. When our recommendation was put into practice, it bombed. We could have foreseen and avoided the failure if we had been willing to argue and disagree in order to test our idea before we put it forward.

Types of Conflict Effective members promote conflict that is constructive for task and climate and discourage conflict that disrupts healthy discussion. Figure 10.7 highlights features of these two forms of group conflict. Disruptive conflict exists when disagreements interfere with effective work and healthy communication climate. Typically, disruptive conflict is marked by communication that is competitive as members vie with each other to wield influence and get their way. Accompanying the competitive tone of communication is a self-interested focus in which members talk about only their ideas, their solutions, their points of view. The competitive and self-centered communication in disruptive conflict fosters a win–lose orientation to conflict and diminished cohesion.

Group climate deteriorates during disruptive conflict. Members may feel unsafe volunteering ideas because others might harshly evaluate or scorn them. Personal attacks may occur as members criticize one another's motives or attack one another personally. Recall the discussion in Chapter 3 of communication that fosters defensiveness; we saw that defensive climates are promoted by communication that expresses evaluation, superiority, control orientation, neutrality, certainty, and closed-mindedness. Just as these forms of communication undermine healthy climates in personal relationships, they also interfere with group climate and productivity.

Constructive conflict occurs when members understand that disagreements are natural and can help them achieve their shared goals. Communication that expresses respect for diverse opinions reflects this attitude. Members also emphasize shared interests and goals. The cooperative focus of communication encourages a win–win orientation. Discussion is open and supportive of differences, and disagreements focus on issues, not personalities.

To encourage constructive conflict, communication should demonstrate openness to different ideas, willingness to alter opinions when good reasons exist, and respect for the integrity of other members and the views they express.

Constructive conflict allows members to broaden their understandings and subject all ideas to careful cooperative analysis. Constructive conflict is most likely to occur when the appropriate groundwork has been established by creating a supportive open climate of communication. Group climate is built throughout the life of a group, beginning with the first meeting among members. Thus, it is important to communicate in ways that build a strong climate from the start so that it is established when conflict arises.

Figure 10.7 Characteristics of Group Conflict

Disruptive Conflict	Constructive Conflict
Competitive	Cooperative
Self-interested focus	Collective focus
Win-lose approach	Win-win approach
Closed climate	Open climate
Defensive communication	Supportive communication
Personal attacks	Focus on issues

Summary

In this chapter we've considered what small groups are and how they operate. We defined groups as three or more people who meet over time, share understandings of how to interact, and have a common goal. Group members must recognize and manage the potential weaknesses of group discussion, notably conformity pressures and time, to realize the important advantages of group decision making.

Task teams are increasingly popular in modern professional life because they are often more effective than individuals in producing creative, high-quality decisions and securing members' commitment. Many factors, including cohesion, size, power, norms, and interaction patterns, influence communication in task groups and teams. Each of these features shapes the small group system within which communication transpires. Understanding and managing these influences should enable you to enhance the climate of groups, the quality of outcomes, and the efficiency of group processes.

In the latter part of this chapter we discussed three challenges for effective communication in groups and teams. The first one, participating effectively, requires task, climate, and procedural contributions that foster good group climate and outcomes. Developing skill in constructive types of communication and avoiding egocentric comments will make you a valuable member of any group. The second challenge for effective communication in groups and teams is to ensure leadership, which may be provided by a single person or several members. Good leadership exists when one or more members communicate to organize discussion, ensure careful work on the task, and build cohesion, morale, and an effective climate for collective work.

A third challenge is to manage conflict so that it enhances, rather than detracts from, group processes. In our discussion we identified communication that fosters constructive conflict, which improves the quality of group decision making. Constructive conflict in groups, as we have seen, grows out of a supportive communication climate that is built over the course of a group's life.

FOR FURTHER REFLECTION AND DISCUSSION

1. Interview a professional in the field you hope to enter after college. Ask her or him to identify how various groups and teams discussed in this chapter are used on the job. If you are already employed in a career, reflect on your experiences with groups on the job.
2. Recall the last group in which you participated. Did you find it effective in achieving its task goals? Was the climate comfortable? Now describe your group according to key features discussed in this chapter: cohesion, size, interaction patterns, power, norms, leadership, and conflict. Do these features explain the climate and task effectiveness of your group?
3. Use your *InfoTrac College Edition* to review research on the use of focus groups to discover public opinions on issues and products. Go to PowerTrac and access recent issues of *Public Relations Journal, Public Relations Quarterly,* and *Public Relations Review.*
4. Ask several people who have lived in non-Western cultures whether the cultural values that affect group communication in the United States are present in the countries where they lived. In your conversation explore how differences in cultural values affect group interaction.
5. Agree on a topic to discuss in groups of five to seven students. Half of the groups should meet

outside of class and discuss the topic. The other half should discuss the topic online. When the class meets again, compare the two kinds of discussions in terms of task productivity, climate, and members' satisfaction. Identify distinct characteristics of in-person and online discussion.

6. Observe a group discussion on your campus or in your town. Record the contributions made by members by classifying them as task, climate, procedural, or egocentric. Do the communication patterns you observe explain the effectiveness or ineffectiveness of the group?

KEY TERMS

Group
Team
Brainstorming
Quality circle
Cohesion
Groupthink
Power
Power over
Power to
Social climbing
Norms
Synergy
Task communication
Procedural communication
Climate communication
Egocentric communication

Communication in Organizations

LEARNING OBJECTIVES

To understand

1. What organizational culture is
2. Whether being involved in the informal networks of organizations is important
3. How rituals and routines affect life in organizations
4. Challenges for personal relationships on the job
5. The challenges for organizations in the years ahead

Josh is a senior system analyst at MicroLife, an innovative technology firm in Silicon Valley. Although he typically works more than 40 hours a week, his schedule varies according to his moods and his responsibilities for caring for his daughter, Marie. Some days Josh is at his desk by 8 A.M., and on other days he gets to the office around noon. Life on the job is casual, as is dress. Sneakers, t-shirts, and jeans are standard attire for all employees at MicroLife. People drop in at each other's offices without appointments and sometimes even without specific business to conduct.

When Josh first joined MicroLife, drop-by chats with longer-term employees gave him insight into the company. He can still remember hearing stories about Wayne Murray—Wild Man Wayne—who launched the company from a makeshift workstation in his basement. He also heard tale after tale of oddball ideas the company backed that became highly profitable. Josh really enjoys the creative freedom at MicroLife: Everyone is encouraged to think innovatively, to try new ways of doing things. Weekly softball games provide friendly competition between the Nerds (the team of system analysts) and the Words (the team of software writers).

Jacqueline slips her shoes off under her desk, hoping nobody will see because Bankers United has a strict dress code requiring suits, heels (for women), and clean-shaven faces (for men). On her first day at work a manager took her out to lunch and mentioned two recent hires who "just didn't work out" because they didn't dress professionally. Jacqueline got the message. From other employees she heard about people who had been given bad performance reviews for being late more than once in a 6-month period. When Jacqueline suggested a way to streamline mortgage applications, she was told, "That isn't how we do things here." It didn't take a genius to figure out that at Bankers United the operating mode was rigid rules and rigid enforcement of them. Although she sometimes feels constrained by the authoritarian atmosphere of Bankers United, Jacqueline also likes having clear-cut rules to follow.

Would you rather work for MicroLife or Bankers United? Why? If you're a relaxed person who enjoys informality and does well in unstructured environments, MicroLife may appeal to you. On the other hand, if you like clear rules and a traditional working environment, Bankers United may be more attractive to you. Neither company is better in an absolute sense. Some businesses and professions can be flexible about dress and hours, especially if employees are not meeting with the public. As long as the work gets done—programs debugged, phone calls answered—it doesn't matter how people dress and when they work. Other organizations must accommodate a time clock and must follow inflexible procedures to meet their objectives. Hospitals must schedule operating rooms, and doctors, nurses, and anesthesiologists must be on time for surgery. Perhaps a good goal for each of us is to join an organization whose work philosophy is compatible with our individual talents, needs, and lifestyle.

Communication in organizations is the topic of this chapter. In the first section of the chapter we'll focus on the overall culture of an organization, which is what creates the interpersonal and task climate for its members. As we will see, organizational culture is created and expressed in communication. Every organization has a distinct culture that consists of traditions, structures, and practices that reflect and reproduce a particular form of work life and on-the-job relationships. In the second section of the chapter we'll consider three challenges of communicating in organizations in our era: adapting to the needs, values, and situations of diverse workers; moving in and out of work teams; and managing personal relationships with co-workers.

UNDERSTANDING COMMUNICATION AND ORGANIZATIONAL CULTURES

If you're like most people, you've had different experiences in various jobs. Perhaps you have worked in a casual organization like MicroLife, as well as in an organization that operated by strict, unbending rules, similar to those at Bankers United. Perhaps you've had jobs in which employees routinely engaged in friendly socializing and other jobs in which business and personal life were kept separate. Every organization has a distinct way of doing things that reflects its particular identity and traditions.

Traditionally, organizations have been viewed in terms of lines of authority, channels of communication, productivity, and other formal aspects of structure. To complement that emphasis, many communication scholars today focus on **organizational culture,** which consists of ways of thinking, acting, and viewing work that are shared by members of an organization and reflect an organization's distinct identity. Just as ethnic cultures consist of meanings shared by members of the ethnic groups, organizational cultures consist of meanings shared by members of organizations. Just as new members of ethnic cultures are socialized into preexisting meanings and traditions, new members of organizations are socialized into preexisting meanings and traditions. Just as a culture's way of life continues even though specific people leave or die, an organization's culture persists despite the comings and goings of specific workers.

Scholars have gained insight into the ways in which communication creates, sustains, and expresses the culture of organizations (Pacanowsky & O'Donnell-Trujillo, 1982, 1983; Pacanowski, 1989; Riley, 1983; Smircich, 1983). The relationship between communication and organizational culture is reciprocal: communication among members of organizations creates, sustains, and sometimes alters the culture. At the same time, organizational culture influences patterns of communication among members.

When employees interact in any way, they produce and reproduce their organization's culture (Pacanowsky, 1989; Van Maanen & Barley, 1985). Among the communication practices that express and uphold organizational cultures are four that we will explore: vocabularies, stories, rites and rituals, and structures. These symbolic activities continuously vitalize and reinforce shared meanings that keep an organization coherent and give it a character that endures beyond the presence of particular members.

Vocabulary

The most obvious communication dimension of organizational culture is vocabulary. Just as the language of an ethnic culture reflects and expresses its history, norms, values, and identity, the language of an organization reflects and expresses its history, norms, values, and identity.

Hierarchical Language Many organizations and professions have vocabularies that distinguish levels of status among members. The military, for example, relies on language that continuously acknowledges rank ("Yes, sir," "chain of command"), which reflects the close ties of status, respect, and privilege to official rank. Salutes, as well as stripes and medals on uniforms, are part of the nonverbal vocabulary that emphasizes rank and status. In a study of police, researchers noted the pervasiveness of derogatory descriptions of suspects and informants. Officers routinely referred to *creeps, dirtbags,* and *maggots* to emphasize the undesirable element with which police often deal (Pacanowsky & O'Donnell-Trujillo, 1983).

Unequal terms of address also communicate rank. For instance, the CEO may use first names ("Good morning, Jan") when speaking to employees. Unless given permission to use the CEO's first name, however, lower-status members of an organization typically refer to the CEO as Mr. Smith, Ms. Smith, Sir, or Ma'am. Professors generally use students' first names, whereas students tend to use titles to address their teachers: Dr. Armstrong, Ms. Armstrong, Mr. Armstrong, or Professor Armstrong. Bosses may call secretaries by their first name, but secretaries do not have the same freedom unless the boss grants it.

Masculine Language Some organizations rely on language that emphasizes interests and experiences more typical of men than women. Consider the number of phrases in the working world that are taken from sports (home run, ballpark estimate,

NOTICE INSTITUTIONAL CULTURE

What is the culture of your school? Does it portray itself as an institution of higher learning, a place for personal and intellectual growth, or a school devoted to the liberal arts? Can you locate specific documents, school rituals, and so forth that express the proclaimed identity of your school?

Now identify specific practices in which you and other students engage that reflect and sustain the identity your school claims. Going to classes, making notes, studying, taking exams, and so forth are all activities that support a campus's identity as a place in which learning is the preeminent goal and value.

Locate archives that hold historical records of your school (usually in the library or central administration). Trace the persistence of basic threads in your school's identity throughout the decades since its founding.

■ *Symbols of hierarchy are more obvious in the military than in many other organizations. How might the strong focus on rank affect communication?*

© Andrew Lichtenstein/Impact Visuals

touchdown, develop a game plan, be a team player, the starting lineup), military life (battle plan, mount a campaign, plan of attack, under fire, get the big guns, defensive move, offensive strike), and male sexual parts and activities (a troublesome person is a prick, you can hit on a person, screw someone, or stick it to them, and bold professionals have balls). Whether intentional or not, such language reflects men's bodies and experiences more than those of women and serves to bind men together in a community in which many women may feel unwelcome or uncomfortable (Wood, 2001b).

Language in the workplace may also normalize sexist practices, including sexual harassment. From practices such as calling women "hon" and "sweetheart" to blatantly sexualized comments about women's appearances, this kind of language spotlights women's sexuality and obscures their professional abilities and status. In 1992, Mary Strine analyzed the ways in which academic institutions define and describe sexual harassment so as to make it seem normal and acceptable. Shereen Bingham (1994, 1996) and others (Taylor & Conrad, 1992; Wood, 1992b, 1994a) have documented additional ways in which sexual harassment is normalized or resisted in the workplace. In related work, Carol Blair, Julie Brown, and Leslie Baxter (1994) examined the power of masculine norms of thought and speech in some academic institutions to marginalize women faculty and teachings about gender.

Stories

Scholars of organizational culture recognize that humans are, by nature, storytellers. We tell stories to weave coherent narratives out of experience and to create meaning in our lives. Furthermore, the stories we tell do some real work in establishing and sustaining organizational cultures. Michael Pacanowsky and Nick O'Donnell-Trujillo (1983) identified three kinds of stories within the organizational context.

Corporate Stories

Corporate stories convey the values, style, and history of an organization. Stories are a way of passing on legends, traditions, and key experiences in the life of a culture. Just as families have favorite stories about their history and identity that they retell often, organizations have favorite stories that reflect their collective vision of themselves.

One important function of stories is to socialize new members into the culture of an organization. Newcomers learn about the history and identity of an organization by listening to stories of its leaders, as well as its trials and triumphs. For example, both Levi Strauss and Microsoft are known for their informal style of operation. New employees are regaled with tales about the laid-back character of the companies: casual dress, relaxed meetings, and nonbureaucratic ways of getting things done. These stories socialize new employees into the cultures of the companies.

When retold among veteran members of an organization, stories foster feelings of connection and vitalize organizational ideology. You've heard the term *war stories,* which refers to frequently retold stories about key moments such as crises, successes, and takeovers. When long-term members of organizations rehash pivotal events in their shared history, they cement the bonds between them and their involvement with the organization.

Personal Stories Members of organizations also tell stories about themselves. Personal stories are accounts that announce how people see themselves and how they want to be seen by others. For example, if Sabra perceives herself as a supportive team player, she could simply tell new employees this by saying, "I am a supportive person who believes in teamwork." On the other hand, she could define her image by telling a story: "When I first came here most folks were operating in isolation, and I thought a lot more could be accomplished if we learned to collaborate. Let me tell you something I did to make that happen. After I'd been on staff for three months, I was assigned to work up a plan for downsizing our manufacturing department. Instead of just developing a plan on my own, I talked with several other managers, and then I met with people who worked in manufacturing to get their ideas. The plan we came up with reflected all of our input." This narrative gives a concrete, coherent example of how Sabra sees herself and wants others to see her.

Jed

I sing with the Gospel Choir, and we have a good following in the southeast. When I first joined the group, the other members talked to me. In our conversations what I heard again and again was the idea that we exist to make music for God and about God, not to glorify ourselves. One of the choir members told me about a singer who had gotten on a personal ego trip because of all the bookings we were getting, and he started thinking he was more important than the music. That guy didn't last long with the group.

Collegial Stories The third type of organizational story offers one person's account of other members of the organization. "If you need help getting around the CEO, Jane's the one to see. A year ago I couldn't finish a report by deadline, so Jane rearranged his calendar so that he thought the report wasn't due for another week." "Roberts is a real stickler for rules. Once when I took an extra 20 minutes on my lunch break, he reamed me out." "Pat trades on politics, not performance. Pat took several of the higher-ups out for lunch and golfed with them for the month before bonuses were decided." Whether positive or negative, collegial stories assert identities for others in an organization. They are part of the informal network, or rumor mill, that teaches new members of an organization how to get along with various other members of the culture.

Rites and Rituals

Rites and rituals are verbal and nonverbal practices that express and reproduce organizational cultures. They do so by providing standardized ways of expressing organizational values and identity.

Rites Rites are dramatic, planned sets of activities that bring together aspects of cultural ideology in a single event. Harrison Trice and Janice Beyer (1984) identified six kinds of organizational rites. Rites of passage are used to mark entry into different levels in organizations. For example, larger offices with nicer artwork may symbolize promotions. Special handshakes are nonverbal rites that symbolize communality among members of clubs and other groups. A desk plaque with a new employee's name and title is a rite that acknowledges a change in identity. Rites of integration affirm and enhance the sense of community in an organization. Examples are holiday parties, annual picnics, and graduation ceremonies at campuses.

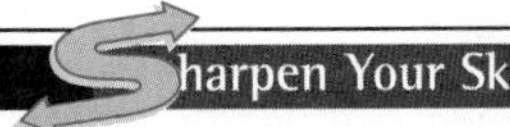

NOTICING STORIES AND THE WORK THEY DO

Think about an organization to which you belong, perhaps one in which you worked or one that you have had many opportunities to observe. Identify corporate, personal, and collegial stories you were told when you first entered the organization. How did these stories shape your understandings of the organization? Try extending the idea of organizational stories to your family's culture. What family stories taught you your family's history and values? What personal stories did your parents tell you to define who they are and what they stand for? Did family members talk about others? If so, what collegial stories did you hear about other relatives? Do the stories told in your family form a coherent account of its identity?

Organizational cultures also include rites that blame or praise people. Firings and demotions are common blaming rites. In the military, being put on k.p. duty is a ritual meant to punish trainees and lower their status. The counterpart to blaming rites is enhancement rites that shower praise and glory on individuals or teams that represent the organization's self-image. Campuses that value teaching, for instance, bestow awards on faculty who are especially committed and gifted teachers. Many sales companies give awards for productivity (most sales of the month, quarter, or year, for example). Many organizations use their local networks to post congratulations to employees. In my department, faculty meetings always open with announcements about honors and achievements of individual faculty members. This recognition rite gives each of us moments in the limelight.

Audrey

In my sorority we recognize sisters who make the dean's list each semester by putting a rose on their dinner plates. That way everyone realizes who has done well academically, and we can also remind ourselves that scholarship is one of the qualities we all aspire to.

Organizations also develop rites for managing change. Renewal rites aim to revitalize and update organizations. Training workshops serve this purpose, as do periodic retreats in which organizational members discuss their goals and the institution's health. A nonverbal symbol of change may be moving an employee's office from the second to the fourth floor after a promotion. Organizations also develop rituals for managing conflicts between members of the organization. Conflict resolution rites are standard methods of dealing with differences and discord. Examples are arbitration, collective bargaining, mediation, executive fiat, voting, and ignoring or denying problems. The conflict resolution rite that typifies an organization reflects the values of its overall culture.

Rituals Rituals are forms of communication that occur regularly and that members of an organization perceive as familiar and routine parts of organizational life. Rites differ from rituals in that the latter don't necessarily bring together a number of aspects of organizational ideology into a single event. Rather, rituals are repeated communication performances that communicate a particular value or role definition.

Organizations have personal, task, and social rituals. Personal rituals are performances in which individuals routinely engage to define themselves. In their study of organizational cultures, Pacanowsky and O'Donnell-Trujillo (1983) noted that Lou Polito, the owner of a car company, opened all the company's mail every day. Whenever possible, Polito hand-delivered mail to the divisions of his company to communicate his openness and his involvement with the day-to-day business.

Social rituals are standardized performances that affirm relationships among members of organizations. Some organizations have a company dining room to encourage socializing among employees. Others have break rooms and break times that permit informal interaction. Smiles are nonverbal indicators of friendliness and camaraderie. Email chatting and forwarding of jokes are methods of socializing on the job. Tamar Katriel (1990) identified a social ritual of griping among Israelis. *Kiturim,* the name Israelis give to their griping, most often occurs during Friday night social events called *mesibot kiturim,* which translates as "gripe sessions." Unlike much griping by Westerners, *kiturim* focuses on national issues, concerns, and problems rather than personal complaints. Some Jewish families engage in ritualized *kvetching,* which is personal griping that aims to air frustrations but not necessarily to resolve them. The point of the ritual is to complain, not to solve a problem.

Task rituals are repeated activities that help members of an organization perform their jobs. Perhaps a special conference room is used for particular tasks such as giving sales presentations, holding performance reviews, or making sales proposals. Task rituals are also evident in forms and procedures that members of organizations are expected to use to do various things. These forms and procedures standardize task performance in a manner consistent with the organization's view of itself and how it operates. In their study of a police unit, Pacanowsky and O'Donnell-Trujillo (1983) identified the routine that officers are trained to follow when they stop drivers for violations. The set of questions officers are taught to ask ("May I see your license, please? Do you know why I stopped you? Do you know how fast you were going?") allows them to size up traffic violators and decide whether to give them a break or a closer look.

Sharon

Where I work we have this ritual of spending the first half-hour or so at work every Monday complaining about what we have to get done that week. Even if we don't have a rough week ahead, we go through the motions of moaning and groaning. It's kind of like a bonding ceremony for us.

Structures

Organizational cultures are also represented through structural aspects of organizational life. As the name implies, **structures** organize relationships and interaction among members of an organization. We'll consider four structures that express and uphold organizational culture: roles, rules, policies, and communication networks.

Roles

Roles are responsibilities and behaviors expected of people because of their specific positions in an organization. Most organizations formally define roles in job descriptions:

> *Training coordinator:* Responsible for assessing needs and providing training to northwest branches of the firm, supervises staff of 25 professional trainers, coordinates with director of human relations.
>
> *Instructor:* Duties include teaching three classes per term, supervising graduate student theses, serving on departmental and university committees, and conducting research. Ph.D. and experience required.

The critical quality of a role is that it is not tied to any particular person. Rather, a role is a set of functions and responsibilities that could be performed by any number of people who have particular talents, experiences, and other relevant qualifications. If one person quits or is fired, another can be found as a replacement. Regardless of who is in the role, the organization will continue with its structure intact. The different roles in an organization are a system, which means they are interrelated and interacting. Each role is connected to other roles within the system. Organizational charts, such as the one featured in Figure 11.1, portray the relationships among different roles in an organization. The chart shows who is responsible to whom and clarifies the hierarchy of power among roles in the organization.

Rules Rules, which we discussed in Chapter 1, are patterned ways of interacting. Rules are present in organizational contexts, just as they are in other settings of interaction. As in other contexts, organizational rules may be formal (in the contract or organizational chart) or informal (norms for interaction). Within organizations, constitutive rules specify what various kinds of communication symbolize. Some firms count working late as evidence of commitment. Socializing with colleagues after work may count as showing team spirit. Sending copies of email to all team members may count as showing team spirit. Taking on extra assignments, attending training sessions, and dressing like upper management may communicate ambition.

Lyle

I found out the hard way that a company I worked for was dead serious about the organizational chart. I had a problem with a co-worker so I talked with a guy in another department I was friends with. Somehow my supervisor found out and he blew a gasket. He was furious that I had "gone outside of the chain of command" instead of coming straight to him.

Regulative rules specify when, where, and with whom communication should occur. Organizational charts formalize regulative rules by showing who reports to whom. Other regulative rules may determine that problems should not be discussed with people outside the organization and that social conversations are (or are not) permitted during working hours. Some organizations have found that employees spend so much time online that productivity suffers, so rules regulating online time are instituted.

Policies **Policies** are formal statements of practices that reflect and uphold the overall culture of an organization. For example, my university's mission statement emphasizes the importance of teaching. Consistent with the organizational identity reflected in that mission statement, we have policies that require teaching evaluations and policies that tie good teaching performance to tenure, promotion, and raises. Most organizations codify policies governing such aspects of work life as hiring, promotion, benefits, grievances, and medical leave. The content

Figure 11.1 An Organizational Chart for the Editorial Staff of a Newspaper

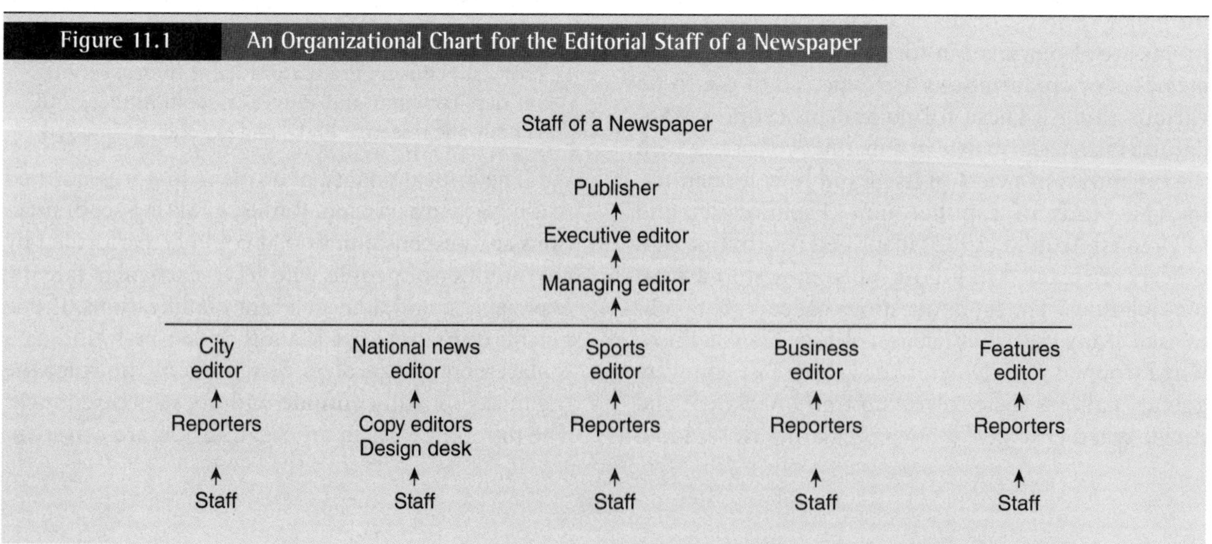

"I've never actually seen a corporate ladder before."

From *The Wall Street Journal*; permission, Cartoon Features Syndicate.

of policies in these areas differs among organizations in ways that reflect the distinct cultures of diverse work environments.

Organizational policies also reflect the larger society within which organizations are embedded. For example, as public awareness of sexual harassment has increased, most organizations have developed formal policies that define sexual harassment, state the organization's attitude toward it, and detail the procedure for making complaints. Because of the prevalence of dual-career couples, many organizations have created departments to help place spouses of people they want to hire.

Communication Networks **Communication networks** link members of an organization together through formal and informal forms of interaction. Job descriptions and organizational charts, which specify who is supposed to communicate with whom, are formal networks. Formal networks provide the order necessary for organizations to operate. They define lines of upward communication (subordinates to superiors; providing feedback, reporting results), downward communication (superiors to subordinates; giving orders, establishing policies), and horizontal communication (peer to peer; coordinating among departments).

The informal communication network is more difficult to describe because it is not formally defined and not based on fixed organizational roles. Friendships, alliances, enmities, and casual conversations may be part of the informal network through which information flows. Most professionals have others within their organization with whom they regularly check perceptions and past whom they run certain ideas.

Communication outside the formal channels of an organization is sometimes called the *grapevine*, a

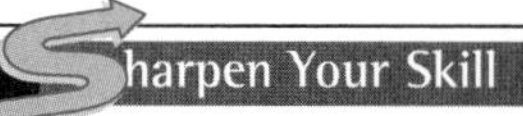

DETECTING VALUES IN POLICIES

To understand how policies reflect organizational cultures, consider the values suggested in these policies:

- Some organizations allow employees to work flexible hours in order to meet responsibilities to their families.
- Some organizations provide full or partial salary to employees on family leave.
- Some organizations allow gay and lesbian employees to insure their partners and name their partners as beneficiaries for pensions.
- Some organizations support employee education by allowing time off for classes with no salary penalty or by paying the employee's tuition.
- Some organizations provide incentives such as raises, bonuses, or extra time off to employees who quit smoking, participate in an exercise program, and otherwise take care of their health.

term that suggests their free-flowing style. Grapevine communication, although continuous in organizational life, is especially active during periods of change (Davis, 1977, 1980). This makes sense because we engage in communication to reduce our uncertainty and discomfort with change. New information (a fresh rumor) activates the grapevine. Although details often are lost or distorted as messages travel along a grapevine, the information conveyed informally has a surprisingly high rate of accuracy: 75% to 90% (Hellweg, 1992). If details are important, however, the grapevine may be a poor source of information.

To view organizations as cultures is to see that they are systems of meaning that are produced, reproduced, and modified in the process of communicating. As members of organizations use language, tell stories, and engage in rites and rituals, they continuously create and refine the identity of their workplace. Roles, rules, networks, and policies are structures that further reflect and shape the identity of organizations and the people who belong to them.

VIRTUALLY NETWORKING

In addition to informal and formal communication networks in physical places of work, an increasing number of workers are part of electronic networks. Made possible by new technologies, telecommuting allows millions of people to work from their homes or mobile offices. Using computers, email, and faxes, these telecommuters do their work and maintain contact with colleagues without going to the physical job site. Research to date finds that telecommuting raises the productivity and morale of employees. Many employers like it because it cuts the costs of providing office space.

Source: Shellenbarger, 1995.

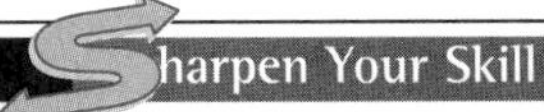

I HEARD IT THROUGH THE GRAPEVINE

This exercise requires six students outside your class. Communicate the message provided here to the first person and ask her or him to pass it along and to keep the message moving until it gets to the last person. Then ask that person to communicate the message to you.

> There's going to be a change in how the school schedules classes starting next fall. All students will take only two courses at a time and will attend those classes for 3 hours, 5 days a week for a total of 4 weeks. Then there will be a 1-week break, and students will start another term in which they take two more courses. The purposes of the new system are to encourage more intensive study in each area and to reduce competing demands among courses. The short-term system has been tried successfully at other schools, and not only have students liked it, but their grades have gone up.

What details did students eliminate as they passed the message along the grapevine? What aspects of the message were distorted or changed? Did the basic message get through accurately?

CHALLENGES FOR COMMUNICATING IN ORGANIZATIONS

Participating effectively in organizational life poses continuous challenges for all of us. Of the many challenges you may encounter, we'll discuss three that are particularly relevant to organizational communication in our era.

Adapting to Diverse Needs, Situations, and People

Consider the following descriptions of people who work in one company in my community:

> *Eileen is 28,* single, Jewish, bilingual, and the primary caregiver for her disabled mother.
>
> *Frank is 37,* a father of two, and a European American married to a full-time homemaker. He is especially skilled in collaborative team building.
>
> *Denise is 30,* single, European American, an expert public speaker, and mother of a 4-year-old girl.
>
> *Sam is 59,* African American, father of two grown children, and married to an accountant. He is widely regarded as supportive and empathic.
>
> *Ned is 42,* divorced, European American, and recovering from a heart bypass operation.
>
> *Javier is 23* and married to a woman who works full time. They are expecting their first child in a few months.

These six people have different life situations, abilities, and goals. The differences between them affect what they need and want in order to be effective on the job. Eileen and Denise need flexible working hours so that they can take care of a mother and young child. Eileen may also expect her employer to respect Rosh Hashanah, Yom Kippur, Hanukkah, and other holidays of her religion. Ned may need extended disability leave and a period of part-time work while he recuperates from his heart surgery. Javier may want to take family leave when his child is born, a benefit that wouldn't be valued by Frank or Sam.

Eileen, Frank, Denise, Ned, Sam, and Javier are typical of the workforce today. They illustrate the

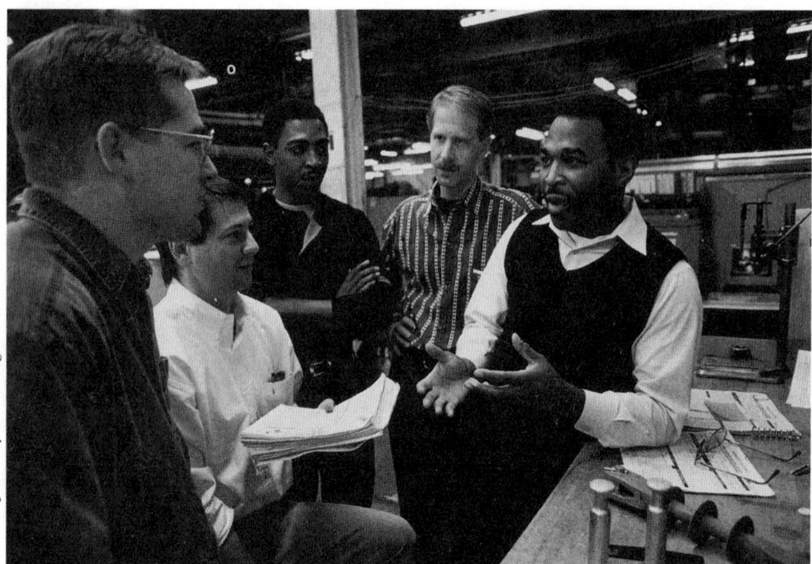

© David Joel/Tony Stone Images

■ *How would this photograph of professionals be different if it had been taken 20 years ago?*

diversity of people, life situations, and needs that characterizes the modern workplace. The variety of workers is a major change, one that requires organizations to adapt.

The industrial revolution, which occurred in the mid-1800s, transformed what had been a largely agrarian economy into one dominated by factories and centralized workplaces. The assembly line is not just how factories produced products; it is also a metaphor for how factories treated workers. All employees were expected to fit into the same mold: identical work hours and benefits and identical dedication to their jobs, without complications from personal or family life. Many workers were men who, like Frank, had a wife who took care of home and family life. Other workers—men with wives who worked outside the home, single parents—had to devise child care arrangements through kinship networks, babysitters, or a combination of the two. The workplace was not expected to accommodate employees' personal situations and needs.

In our era, a quite different picture of organizational life is emerging. Workers are demanding conditions and benefits tailored to their individual circumstances. Many organizations have a cafeteria-style benefits package that allows employees to select benefits from a range of options (Figure 11.2).

Someone with primary caregiving responsibilities might sacrifice vacation time for additional family

fy*i* TOMORROW'S ORGANIZATIONS

One of the best ways to learn about social and organizational trends that are reshaping the world of work is to read online magazines. *Entrepreneurial Edge Online* discusses emerging trends and resources for entrepreneurs: http://www.edgeonline.com. Another savvy site is *Idea CafÈ,* which says it offers "a fun approach to serious business." It provides advice on running a business, using technologies, and networking: http://www.ideacafe.com.

leave. A person nearing retirement might want maximum insurance and medical coverage but little family leave time. Flextime, which allows people to adjust working hours to their lifestyles, would be a valuable benefit for many workers. Employer-sponsored classes would be sought by workers who want to learn new skills that might accelerate their advancement. Still another increasingly cherished option is telecommuting, which allows workers to work in their homes or other locations removed from a central office. More than 9 million people work in virtual offices, and more will in the future (Pescovitz, 1995, p. 8).

The organizations that survive and thrive in an era of diversity will be those that adapt effectively to meet the expectations and needs of different workers. Flexible rules and policies, rather than a one-size-fits-all formula, will mark the successful workplaces of the future. By extension, the most competent and effective professionals will be those who are comfortable with a stream of changes in people and ways of working. You might work closely with a colleague for several years and then see little of that person if he or she modifies working hours to accommodate changes in family life. If you choose to telecommute, you will need to develop new ways of staying involved in the informal network (which may operate largely on the Internet) and having the amount of social contact you enjoy. Managers will need to find ways to lead employees who work in different locations and who work different hours. Project teams may interact through email bulletin boards as often as or more often than they interact face to face.

The workplace of today is different from that of yesterday, and it is not what we will see in days ahead. Because rapid change is typical in modern work life, an adaptive orientation is one of the most important qualifications for success. Being open to change and willing to experiment are challenges for effective participation in organizations.

Figure 11.2 A Menu of Job Benefits

Flexible working hours
Family leave
Vacation time
Personal or sick days
On-site day care
Life insurance
Medical insurance
Dental insurance
Disability insurance
Employer-subsidized continuing education
Part-time work
Telecommuting
Self-selected holidays (usually a fixed number)

Moving In and Out of Teams

Another challenge for communication in the organizations of today and tomorrow is participating in a variety of teams. Effective communication on the job requires interacting intensely with members of teams that may form and dissolve quickly. Whereas autonomous workers—single leaders, mavericks, and independent professionals—were prized in the 1940s, the team player is most highly sought today.

The skills we've discussed will help you perceive carefully, listen well, use verbal and nonverbal communication effectively, promote constructive climates, and adapt your style of interacting to the diverse people on your teams. The challenge is to be able to adjust your style of communicating to the expectations and interaction styles of a variety of people and to the constraints of a range of situations. The greater your repertoire of communication skills, the more effectively you will be able to move in and out of teams on the job.

John

My job is entirely different today than when I started it 13 years ago. When I came aboard, each of us had his own responsibilities, and management pretty much left us alone to do our work. I found authors and helped them develop their ideas, Andy took care of all art for the books, someone else was in charge of marketing, and so forth. Each of us did our job on a book and passed the book on to the next person. Now

fyi

FAMILY LEAVE: NOT FOR EVERYONE

Many people assume that the Family and Medical Leave Act, which became law in 1993, guarantees family leave for all workers. Not exactly. There are some hitches.

First, only workers who have worked in a company for at least 1 year and have worked a minimum of 1,250 hours a year are covered, so millions of part-time and new employees cannot count on family leave. Second, companies are not required to provide family leave to employees at the top 10% of the pay scale. Third, the act applies only to organizations with at least fifty employees, so many small businesses don't offer family leaves. Finally—and this is the greatest limitation—the law does not require companies to pay full or partial salary to workers on family leave. Thus family leave is a realistic option only for employees who can live for a period of time without a paycheck. Legislative proposals to extend the Family and Medical Leave Act are currently under consideration. Contrast U.S. policies on family leave with those of other countries. In Sweden workers receive 51 weeks of family leave with 90% of their salary. Italian workers can count on a minimum of 20 weeks of family leave with 80% salary. Germany provides no less than 14 weeks of family leave at full salary. And in the Netherlands workers are entitled to at least 7 weeks of family leave at 100% salary.

the big buzzword is team. *Everything is done in teams. From the start of a new book project the author and I are part of a team that includes the art editor, marketing director, manuscript designer, and so forth. Each of us has to coordinate with the others continuously; nobody works as a lone operator. Although I had reservations about teams at first, by now I'm convinced that they are superior to individuals working independently. The books we're producing are more internally coherent, and they are developed far more efficiently when we collaborate.*

Managing Personal Relationships on the Job

A third challenge of organizational life involves participating in relationships that are simultaneously personal and professional. You probably will be involved in a number of such relationships during your work life. In a 1995 study titled "Bosses and Buddies," Ted Zorn described his long friendship with a colleague who became his supervisor. Zorn went on to note that close relationships between people who work together are common. Although management has traditionally discouraged personal relationships among employees, the relationships have developed anyway. Because the vast majority of U.S. residents work at least 40 hours a week, it's not surprising that we form personal relationships with people on the job.

Anna

It's hard for me now that my best friend has been promoted over me. Part of it is envy, because I wanted the promotion too. But the hardest part is that I resent her power over me. When Billie gives me an assignment, I feel like as my friend she shouldn't dump extra work on me. But I also know that as the boss she has to give extra work to all of us sometimes. It just doesn't

HUMAN RELATIONS IN ORGANIZATIONS

The Web site of the International Society for the Psychoanalytic Study of Organizations is a forum for researchers, teachers, and clinicians who are interested in how human relationships and communication affect organizations and those who work in them. To read current research, go to http://www.sba.oakland.edu/ispso/index.html.

feel right for my best friend to tell me what to do and evaluate my work.

Friendships between co-workers or supervisors and subordinates involve tension between the role expectations for friends and colleagues (Figure 11.3). A supervisor may have difficulty rendering a fair evaluation of a subordinate who is also a friend. The supervisor might err by overrating the subordinate–friend's strengths or might try to compensate for personal affection by being especially harsh in judging the friend–subordinate. Friendship may also constrain negative feedback, which is essential to effective performance on the job (Larson, 1984). On the positive side, personal relationships may enhance commitment to a job and communication between co-workers (Zorn, 1995).

Romantic relationships between people who work together also pose challenges (Dillard & Witteman, 1985). They are likely to involve many of the same dialectical tensions that operate in friendships between supervisors and subordinates. In addition, romantic relationships are especially likely to arouse co-workers' resentment and discomfort. Romantic breakups also tend to be more dramatic than friendships that end. Thus, when a romance dies, workplace relationships and climate may feel repercussions.

Figure 11.3 Dialectical Tensions in Friendships Between Supervisors and Subordinates

Autonomy/connection **Distance is often characteristic of relationships between people at different levels of an organizational hierarchy. Closeness is typical of friends.**

Novelty/predictability **On the job, friends tend to regard novelty as inherent in their hierarchical relationships and as a source of stress. They seek predictability, perhaps to compensate for the uncertainty arising from different levels of power.**

Openness/closedness **Friends usually value and expect openness with one another. Yet supervisors may need to keep certain information from subordinates, and subordinates may not feel free to speak openly to people who have power over them.**

Equality/superiority **Friends generally seek equality and downplay differences in status, power, and so forth. Supervisors, however, have inarguably greater status, access to information, and salaries than subordinates, thus creating inequality. It is difficult to report to your friend-boss and difficult to reprimand your friend-subordinate.**

Privilege/uniformity **Friends typically have privileges with each other, access to secrets, private feelings and thoughts, and special treatment. Yet on-the-job relationships are supposed to be free of favoritism, and bosses are expected to treat all subordinates fairly and equally.**

Source: Zorn, 1995.

It's probably unrealistic to assume we can avoid personal relationships with people on the job. The challenge is to manage those relationships so that the workplace doesn't interfere with the personal bond and the intimacy doesn't jeopardize professionalism. Friends and romantic partners may need to adjust their expectations and styles of interacting so that personal and work roles are separated. It's also advisable to make sure that on-the-job communication doesn't reflect favoritism and privileges that could cause resentment in co-workers. This suggests that it's important to invest extra effort to maintain an open communication climate with other co-workers.

Eugene

Once I got involved with a woman where I was working. We were assigned to the same team and really hit it off, and one thing led to another and we were dating. I guess it affected our work some since we spent a lot of time talking and stuff in the office. But the real problem came when we broke up. It's impossible to avoid seeing your "ex" when you work together in a small office, and everyone else acted like they were walking on eggshells around us. She finally quit, and you could just feel tension drain out of everyone else in our office.

Summary

In this chapter we've seen the importance of daily performances, such as rituals and storytelling, in upholding an organization's identity and a shared set of meanings for members of the organization. The culture of an organization is created, sustained, and altered in the process of communication among members of an organization. As they talk, interact, and develop policies and participate in the formal and informal networks, they continuously weave the fabric of their individual roles and collective life.

Organizations, like other contexts of communication, involve a number of challenges, three of which we discussed in this chapter. One challenge is to develop a large repertoire of communication skills so that you can adapt effectively to diverse people, situations, and needs in the workplace. A second challenge is to become effective in teamwork because teams pervade modern organizations. Finally, managing personal relationships in the workplace is a challenge that is increasingly common. It's likely that you and others will form friendships and perhaps romantic relationships with people in the workplace. Communication skills that we've discussed throughout this book will help you navigate the tensions and challenges of close relationships on the job.

FOR FURTHER REFLECTION AND DISCUSSION

1. Use your *InfoTrac College Edition* to read the newest research on trends affecting organizational life. Two good sources are the *Journal of Occupational and Organizational Psychology* and *The Futurist.*
2. Locate a copy of your college's policies governing students. What can you infer about the culture the college wants to promote from its policies concerning class attendance, consumption of drugs, and dishonorable conduct? (Note how dishonorable conduct is defined; this differs among schools.)
3. Reflect on the corporate, personal, and collegial stories you heard during your first few weeks on a new job. What did these stories say about the organizational culture?
4. Have you ever had a close friendship or romantic involvement with a co-worker? What were the advantages and disadvantages of the dual roles in the relationship?
5. Think about a group to which you belong. It may be a work group or social group, such as a fraternity or interest club. Describe some common rites and rituals in your group. What do

these rites and rituals communicate about the group's culture?

6. Take two blank sheets of paper. On one, sketch the formal communication network for an organization for which you work or have worked in the past. On the second sheet of paper, draw the informal communication network for the same organization. Describe the kinds of information you get from each network.
7. Interview a person older than 45 who has a career that interests you. Ask the person to describe changes she or he has seen in her or his profession, such as the prominence of teams and changes in benefit packages, work schedules, and other features of professional life.
8. Visit the Web site of an organization you think you might like to join. Explore different links on the site to learn about the organization's policies and the image of itself it presents. What can you infer about the organization's culture from material on its site?

KEY TERMS

Organizational culture
Structures
Roles
Policies
Communication network

Communication in Interviews

LEARNING OBJECTIVES

To understand

1. The purposes of interviewing
2. The basic pattern most interviews follow
3. What a stress interview is
4. What topics employment interviewers cannot legally raise
5. How you can prepare to communicate effectively in hiring interviews
6. The value of interviewing as means of gathering information

You've probably participated in a number of interviews during your life. It's likely that you have been an interviewee many times. Perhaps you were interviewed by committees that appoint students to leadership positions at your school. You may have had interviews with members of groups you sought to join. Few of us have escaped telephone interviews regarding our opinions of political candidates, products, and social policies. It's likely that you've interviewed more than once for part-time or full-time jobs. You've probably also been on the other side of the interviewing process; you may have interviewed people who were applying to join organizations to which you belong. Perhaps you've had jobs that required you to conduct telephone or in-person interviews. You may have interviewed experts to gain information about a topic on which you were writing a paper or preparing a speech.

Many college students think immediately of hiring or employment interviews when the topic of interviewing comes up. Yet hiring is only one of many functions interviews serve. As we shall see, interviews are part of professional, civic, and social life. Because interviews are common, learning to communicate effectively in interviews is important to your personal effectiveness.

In this chapter we will discuss interviewing and identify ways you can enhance your effectiveness as an interviewer and interviewee. The opening section of the chapter describes communication during interviews. First, we will identify a range of purposes or types of interviews in which you may participate during your life. Second, we will discuss the structure and style of interviews.

Third, we will describe different kinds of questions interviewers use. The second section of this chapter identifies challenges that are part of interviewing. We will focus on hiring interviews because those are particularly important to many college students. Our discussion will provide tips for preparing to interview and dealing with inappropriate or illegal questions.

UNDERSTANDING COMMUNICATION IN INTERVIEWS

An **interview** is a communication transaction that emphasizes questions and answers (Lumsden & Lumsden, 1997, p. 266). Rob Anderson and George Killenberg (1999, p. 2) elaborate this definition by noting that the word *interview* suggests "a sharing of views" in which the interviewer and interviewee are involved in a "partnership." In interviewing, listening and speaking are equally important (Purdy & Borisoff, 1997), so think about the implications for listening as well as talking as your read about various kinds of interviews.

Types and Purposes of Interviews

Communication scholars (Anderson & Killenberg, 1999; Goyer, Redding, & Rickey, 1964; Stewart & Cash, 1991) have identified distinct types of interviews. Each interview is defined by its primary purpose, although interviews often have multiple and sometimes conflicting purposes. For example, a job

YOUR INTERVIEWING EXPERIENCE

Each question asks about one of eleven distinct types of interviews. Reflect on your experiences to determine how many of these you have experienced.

1. Have you ever provided information to someone who asked to talk with you about your attitudes, purchasing or voting patterns, or behaviors?
2. Have you ever talked with someone to find out about their attitudes, purchasing or voting patterns, or behaviors?
3. Has anyone ever tried to persuade you to buy a product or service, endorse a candidate or policy, or accept an idea?
4. Have you ever talked with someone in an effort to resolve a mutual problem?
5. Have you ever met with an expert to get counseling on personal problems or financial or legal matters?
6. Have you ever been interviewed for a job or membership in an organization or interviewed another person for a job or membership?
7. Have you ever spoken with someone to make a complaint about a product, service, or person?
8. Have you ever had a conference in which your performance was appraised or in which you appraised another person's performance?
9. Have you ever met with someone about problems in your work, activities, or attitudes, or have you ever talked with someone else about problems of theirs?
10. Have you ever talked with someone who seemed to want to make you feel stressed and uneasy?
11. Have you ever been interviewed about your experiences in a school or job after you announced you would be leaving?

candidate may want to be honest and get a job offer, and the two goals may be at odds. The next Sharpen Your Skill exercise invites you to think about types of interviews in which you've participated.

Information-Giving Interviews The first type of interview provides information to another person. Doctors engage in **information-giving interviews** when they explain to patients how to take medicines and observe symptoms. Academic advisers give students information about curricular requirements, specific courses, and administrative processes. Team leaders often inform new members of a work unit about expectations and operating procedures.

Information-Getting Interviews In this type of interview the interviewer asks questions to learn about the interviewee's opinions, knowledge, attitudes, behaviors, and so forth. Public opinion polls, census taking, and research surveys are common examples of **information-getting interviews.** Physicians also use these to gain insight into patients' medical histories and current conditions. Journalists devote a great deal of time to information-getting interviews to obtain background material for stories they are writing, as well as to learn about experts' opinions on newsworthy topics. Information-getting interviews are useful whenever we are trying to learn about something—perhaps to write a paper, prepare a speech, or enlarge our personal understanding of some issue.

Persuasive Interviews Interviews designed to influence attitudes or actions are **persuasive interviews** (Anderson, 1995). The best-known example of these is the sales interview, in which a salesperson attempts to persuade a customer to buy a product or service. Persuasive interviews can sell more than products. They may also promote people (a door-to-door campaign to persuade residents to support a particular political candidate) and ideas (persuading an administrator to act on your team's report, convincing a company to implement regulations needed to protect the environment).

Problem-Solving Interviews When people need to solve some problem, they may engage in **problem-solving interviews.** Perhaps you have met with a professor to discuss difficulties in a course. The two of you may have collaborated to identify ways to improve your note taking, study habits, and writing. Supervisors sometimes hold problem-solving interviews with employees to discover and resolve impediments to maximally effective work. Colleagues often talk to each other to resolve problems in morale, productivity, or other work-related issues. By seeking each

■ *Interviewing allows us to learn about first-hand experiences of other people.*

CONDUCTING AN EFFECTIVE INFORMATION-GATHERING INTERVIEW

Twelve guidelines will help you communicate effectively when you are conducting an information-gathering interview.

Before the interview

1. Learn about the person you will interview. What is her or his job title, and what experiences relevant to your topic has she or he had?
2. Learn about the topic of the interview. What do you know now, and what do you need to know to be informed about the topic so that you can frame good questions and have a perspective for understanding the interviewee's responses?
3. Prepare a list of key questions. You should have at least one question for each 2 minutes of the interview. Put your questions in order of priority so that you ask the most important ones first in case time runs out.
4. Call the interviewee to schedule the interview. You should explain who you are, why you would like to interview him or her, how long you estimate the interview will take, and what will be done with the interview (Will the person be quoted? Where?). Ask the interviewee where he or she would prefer to meet (his or her office, a nearby coffee shop, etc.).
5. If you plan to record the interview, check your recording equipment. Make sure you have a clean tape and fresh batteries.

During the interview

6. Begin by thanking the person for granting the interview. Then reintroduce yourself, restate the purpose of the interview, and state how long the interview will take. You may want to state a range, such as 20 to 30 minutes.
7. If you want to record the interview, ask the interviewee's permission.
8. If you are using an informed consent form, ask the interviewee to read and sign it.
9. Ask your first question and listen mindfully to the response. Follow up on it with mirror, probing, and hypothetical questions. Respect what the interviewee says and attend to his or her ideas, as well as to your goals for the interview.
10. Continue with questions and follow-up comments and queries until you have the information that you need.
11. Summarize the interview: Review what you have learned, invite the interviewee to add to or correct your summary, and thank him or her for the time and information.

After the interview

12. Send a brief note or email to thank the person for granting the interview and to let her or him know that it was helpful to you.

other's perspective we can broaden our understanding of problems and our insight into potential solutions.

Leroy

Mark and I have worked together for 10 years in the same department. Whenever there is a problem at the factory, one of us finds the other and we sit down and talk it through until we come up with a solution. Sometimes I lead with the questions and sometimes Mark does; sometimes the hang-up is in his area, sometimes it's in mine. He understands the production end of the business better than I do, and I have more knowledge of personnel. Between the two of us we can fix almost any problem.

Counseling Interviews Like problem-solving interviews, **counseling interviews** focus on understanding and resolving a problem. In counseling interviews, however, the problem is not mutual. A client has a problem, such as stress, depression, or compulsiveness, that she or he wants to overcome. The counselor attempts to help the client understand the problem more fully and collaborates with the client to develop strategies for coping with or overcoming the difficulty (Anderson, 1997; Smith, 1996). Counseling interviews also occur outside the therapeutic setting: We may seek counseling from attorneys to address (or avoid) legal problems, accountants to get help with financial matters, religious leaders to deal with spiritual issues, and architects to gain assistance in designing a home.

Employment Interviews The purpose of **employment interviews** is to allow employers and job candidates to assess each other and determine whether there is a good fit between them. Typically, employment interviews include periods of information giving and information getting, as well as persuasive efforts on the part of both participants. The prospective employer wants to convince the job candidate of the quality of the company, and the candidate wants to convince the prospective employer of the quality of his or her qualifications. Ideally, both participants gain enough information to make a sound judgment of the fit between the candidate and the job. Later in this chapter, we'll look at the employment interview in greater detail.

Complaint Interviews **Complaint interviews** allow people to register complaints about a product, service, or person. Many firms have departments whose sole purpose is to accept and respond to complaints. Of primary importance is letting the people who complain know their feelings matter (see Lenny's commentary). The interviewer (company representative)

fyi ELECTRONIC JOB APPLICATIONS AND INTERVIEWS

An increasingly popular method of interviewing relies on video technology that allows recruiters to stay in their offices and "meet" job candidates on their computer screens ("Desktop Video," 1995; Sixel, 1995). Schools are responding by investing in video equipment and software. Although both recruiters and campus placement offices are enthusiastic about video interviews, the format has drawbacks. Todd Landis, who manages college recruiting for a major department store, says, "I never got to shake the person's hand."

Getting an interview is also becoming a virtual process. More and more companies are accepting online job applications. In 1997 only 17% of companies accepted applications on their Web sites; by 1999, 38% were accepting online applications ("USA Snapshots," 1999).

attempts to gain information about the customer's dissatisfaction: What was defective or disappointing about the product? Was service inadequate? What would it take to satisfy the customer now? The person conducting complaint interviews should call recurring complaints to the attention of others who can diagnose and solve the underlying problems.

Lenny

I worked in the complaint department of a department store. The person who trained me for that position told me the number one way to satisfy customers was to let them complain without trying to argue, correct them, or tell them they misused the product. He told me that mainly people just need to be heard and have what they say accepted. I found that was true. When I let them talk and didn't defend the company or correct them, they were usually satisfied even if I didn't authorize reimbursement or replacement. It's amazing how much it matters to people to feel somebody really listens to them.

Performance Reviews Most organizations require **performance reviews,** or performance appraisals, at regular intervals. By building performance appraisals into work life, organizations continuously monitor employees' performance and foster their professional growth. The performance review is an occasion on which a supervisor comments on a subordinate's achievements and professional development, identifies any weaknesses or problems, and collaborates to develop goals for future performance. During the interview subordinates should offer their perceptions of their strengths and weaknesses and participate actively in developing goals for professional development. Supervisors should comment on strengths, as well as areas for improvement, and may act as coaches to encourage professional development (Waldroop & Butler, 1996).

Reprimand Interviews When a person's work is unsatisfactory or the person is creating tensions with co-workers, a supervisor may conduct a **reprimand interview.** The goals are to identify lapses in professional conduct, determine sources of problems, and establish a plan for improving future performance. Because reprimands tend to evoke defensiveness, developing a constructive, supportive communication climate for these interviews is especially important. Supervisors may foster a good climate by opening the interview with assurances that the goal is to solve a problem together, not punish the subordinate. Supervisors should also invite subordinates to express their perceptions and feelings fully.

Gloria

My supervisor at my summer job called me in one day. I knew I had made mistakes in keeping records, so I figured I was in hot water. But she was really nice. The first thing she said when I got to her office was that we had a problem and she wanted to work it out so that I could continue working there. That took a lot of the tension out of the conference for me because the worst thing that could happen (getting fired) wasn't going to happen. We talked for about 20 minutes and fig-

ured out how I could keep my records in order. It was a totally helpful experience.

Stress Interviews **Stress interviews** are designed to create anxiety in respondents or interviewees. Although they may involve gaining or giving information, persuading, or other interview purposes, stress interviews are unique in their deliberate intent to apply pressure. Typical communication techniques for inducing stress are rapid-fire questions, intentional misinterpretations and distortions of the interviewee's responses, and hostile or skeptical nonverbal expressions. Why, you might ask, would anyone deliberately pressure another person? Actually, stress interviews may be useful in several situations. Attorneys may intentionally intimidate reluctant or hostile witnesses or people whose honesty is suspect. Similarly, prison administrators and police officers may communicate aggressively with people they think are withholding important information. This kind of interview also may be used in hiring interviews for jobs that involve high stress. By deliberately trying to rattle the job candidate, the interviewer can assess how well he or she manages stress.

Exit Interviews In academic and professional life, **exit interviews** are an increasingly popular form of communication. The goal of this type of interview is to gain information, insights, and perceptions about a place of work or education from a person who is leaving. While people are in a job or learning environment, they may be reluctant to mention dissatisfactions or to speak against those who have power over them. When people leave an organization, however, they can offer honest insights and perceptions with little fear of reprisal. Thus exit interviews can be especially valuable in providing information about policies, personnel, and organizational culture. The chair of my department routinely has exit interviews with graduate students when they complete their degrees. From these conferences he gains important information that allows us to refine our curriculum, program requirements, and opportunities for graduate students.

Clarence

When my company told all managers to conduct exit interviews, I admit I wasn't convinced they would achieve much. But I was wrong. When I talk to people who are leaving my division, I learn about all kinds of problems—people problems, policy glitches, role confusion—that I had no idea existed. When people are working for a company, they have to be careful not to alienate co-workers and not to be critical of people who control their salaries and placement. But when they leave, they have nothing to lose by being honest. They'll tell you the straight scoop.

Our discussion of eleven common types of interviews makes it clear that interviewing is not an unusual form of communication. Most of us have participated and will participate in many of the interviews we've identified.

The Basic Structure of Interviews

To be effective, interviews should follow a structure that builds a good communication climate, allows both the interviewer and interviewee to deal with substantive matters, and involves listening by all parties. Experienced interviewers, even ones without professional training, tend to organize interview communication into a three-stage sequence. Interviewees who understand the purpose of each stage in the sequence increase their ability to participate effectively.

The Opening Stage The initial stage of an interview tends to be brief and aims to create an effective climate for interaction, clarify the purpose, and preview issues to be discussed (Wilson & Goodall, 1991). Typically, opening small talk encourages a friendly climate: "I see you're from Buffalo. Are the winters there still as harsh as they used to be?"; "It's been 6 months since our last performance review. Any new developments in your life?"; "I noticed you got your B.A. from State University. I graduated from there too. Did you ever take any courses with Doctor Mayberry in anthropology?"

After opening small talk, effective interviewers state the purpose of the interview and how they plan to accomplish that purpose: "As you know, I'm on campus today to talk with liberal arts majors who are interested in joining Hodgeson Marketing. I'd like to ask some questions about you and your background, and then I want to give you an opportunity to ask me anything you want about Hodgeson." "Pat, the reason I asked you to meet with me today is that there have been some complaints about your attitude from others on your work team. I know you are good at your job and have a fine history with the firm, so I want us to put our heads together to resolve this matter. Let's begin with me telling you what I've heard, and then I'd like to hear your perceptions of what's happening." These examples show how the opening stage of an interview establishes a comfortable climate for communication and defines the purpose of the interview.

The Substantive Stage The second stage of an interview, which generally consumes the bulk of time, deals with substance, or content, relevant to the purpose of the interview. For example, in reprimand interviews the substantive stage would zero in on identifying problem behaviors and devising solutions. In a hiring interview the substantive stage might concentrate on the job candidate's background, experience, and qualifications.

Because the goal of the substantive stage is to exchange information, it requires careful planning and thought. Most interviewers prepare lists of topics or questions and use their notes to make sure they cover all important topics during an interview. They may also take notes of responses during the interview. Communication during this phase tends to progress from broad topic areas to increasingly narrow, detailed, and demanding questions within each topic. After introducing a topic, the interviewer may ask some initial general questions and then follow up with more detailed probes. Because the pattern of communication moves from broad to narrow, it is called the **funnel sequence** (Figure 12.1; Cannell & Kahn, 1968; Moffatt, 1979). The interviewer may repeat the funnel sequence for each new topic area in an interview.

During the substantive stage an interviewer may invite the interviewee to take the lead in communication by posing questions or volunteering perceptions and ideas in response to what has been covered thus far. To be an effective interviewee, you should be prepared with questions and topics you want to introduce. This portrays you as someone who is self-initiating and responsible.

The Closing Stage Like the opening stage, the closing stage tends to be brief (Figure 12.2). Its purposes are to summarize what has been discussed, state what follow-up, if any, will occur, and create good will in parting. Summarizing the content of the interview increases the likelihood that an accurate and complete record (written or in memory) of the interview will survive. If the interviewer overlooks any topics, the interviewee may appropriately offer a reminder. Interviewees also may ask about follow-up if interviewers fail to mention this.

Most interviews follow the three-step sequence we've discussed. Occasionally, they do not. Some interviewers are ineffective because they are disorganized, unprepared, and inadequately trained in effective interviewing. They may ramble for 15 minutes or more and fail to provide any closing other than "Gee, our time is up." In other instances interviewers may deliberately violate the standard pattern to achieve their goals. For example, in stress interviews designed to test how well a person responds to pressure, the interviewer may skip any opening comments and jump immediately into tough, substantive questions. This allows the interviewer to assess how well the respondent copes with unexpected stress. Understanding the communication characteristic of each stage allows you to determine which stage you are in at any point in an interview. Based on your assessment of which stage you are in, you can adapt your communication appropriately.

Figure 12.1 The Funnel Sequence

Tell me a little bit about yourself and your interests.

So you especially enjoy working with others, right?

Have you ever supervised others?

Are you comfortable dealing with conflict?

Tell me about a situation in which you had a conflict with a co-worker.

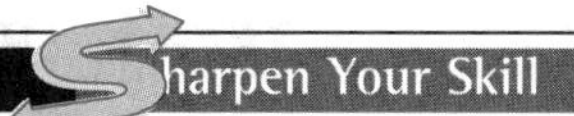

RESEARCH FOR EMPLOYMENT INTERVIEWS

1. Identify a particular job (a position) that you are interested in obtaining: ___________________.
2. Identify one firm that has such positions and with which you would like to interview: ___________________
3. Research the firm and position by going to your library, an online service, or the campus placement office. Based on what you learn about the company, develop one question designed to achieve each of the following objectives:
   a. To show that you understand the company's long-term vision for itself: ___________________.
   b. To demonstrate that you fit with the organizational culture of the company: ___________________.
   c. To show that you understand the company's history and patterns of growth: ___________________.
   d. To demonstrate your interest in growth within the company through training, special assignments, or other routes this company favors: ___________________.

Styles of Interviewing

Like other forms of communication, interviews have climates that shape what happens in interaction. The climate between participants in interviews is influenced by the degree of confirmation provided and the openness, equality, problem orientation, empathy, spontaneity, and descriptiveness embodied in communication, as discussed in Chapter 3. Formality and balance of power also affect the climate of an interview.

Formality Interviews may be more or less formal. In highly formal interviews, participants tend to stay

Figure 12.2 Effective and Ineffective Closings

Effective
I've learned a good deal about your background and interests in our conversation today. Your academic training in teamwork and leadership certainly prepares you for a management trainee position with our firm, and your work experience further qualifies you. When I get back to the main office, I'm going to suggest that the company fly you out for an on-site interview. You should hear from me or someone else with the company within a week to ten days. Meanwhile, good luck with those exams—I remember how stressful exam week can be.

Ineffective
I really enjoyed talking with you. Thanks for your time. I'll be in touch.

closely within social and professional roles. They do little to acknowledge each other as unique individuals. Instead, the interviewer acts as the potential employer, the corrective supervisor, or whatever role is pertinent to the type of interview being conducted. The interviewee also acts from a defined role: prospective employee, repentant subordinate, and so forth. The content of highly formal interviews tends to follow a standard format, often a format stipulated by the organizations that all interviewers follow to ensure consistency. Nonverbal communication provides further clues to formality: business dress, formal meeting room, stilted postures, and stiff handshakes are signs of formality.

In contrast, informal interviews are more relaxed, personal, and flexible. The interviewer attempts to engage the interviewee as an individual, not just a person in a general role. In turn, the interviewee tends to communicate with the interviewer in more individualistic ways. Typically, informal interviews aren't as rigidly structured as formal interviews. The interviewer may have a list of standard topics (either mental or written down), but those are only guidelines, not a straitjacket for communication. Either participant may introduce unusual topics, and they may devote more time than planned to issues that arise. Informal interviews often include nonverbal cues such as smiling, relaxed postures, casual surroundings, and informal dress.

Most interviews fall between the extremes of formality and informality. Also, interviews may become more or less formal as a result of communication between participants. A person who communicates in a stilted manner is likely to encourage formality in the other person. Conversely, a person who communicates casually promotes a relaxed style of response. Although both participants affect the formality of an interview, the interviewer usually has primary control, and the interviewee adapts accordingly.

Balance of Power Another influence on the communication climate in interviews is the balance of power between interviewer and interviewee (Figure 12.3). Power may be evenly balanced between participants or may be skewed toward either the interviewer or the interviewee.

Interviewees have the greatest power to direct the content of communication with a mirror style of interview. A **mirror interview,** or reflective interview, is one in which the interviewer consistently reflects the interviewee's comments to the interviewee. This may be done by restating verbatim what an interviewee says, paraphrasing an interviewee's comments, or making limited inferences about an interviewee's thoughts and feelings based on the communication. Skillful listening is essential for effectively using the mirror style (Banville, 1978). Consider this sample excerpt from a mirror interview:

INTERVIEWER: Tell me about your studies.

INTERVIEWEE: I'm a communication major.

INTERVIEWER: So you've studied communication?

INTERVIEWEE: Yes, especially organizational communication and leadership.

INTERVIEWER: Then you're particularly interested in leadership in organizations?

INTERVIEWEE: Yes. I think communication is the heart of effective leadership, so studying it has taught me a lot about how to lead well.

INTERVIEWER: Tell me what you mean when you say that communication is the "heart of effective leadership."

INTERVIEWEE: Well, I see leadership as motivating others and empowering them to achieve their goals. A person who knows how to communicate clearly, listen well, and establish rapport with others is most able to motivate them.

Figure 12.3 Power Balances in Interviews

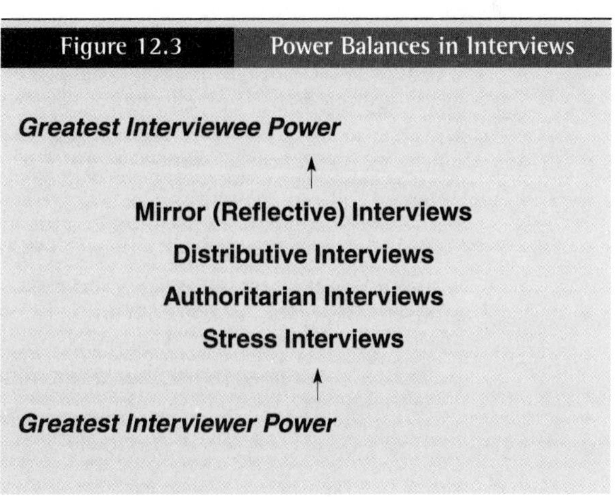

In this exchange the interviewer lets the interviewee lead. What the interviewee says is the basis for the interviewer's subsequent questions and probes. Astute interviewees realize that mirror interviews give them significant opportunity to highlight their strengths and introduce topics they want to discuss.

Distributive interviews are those in which power is equally divided (or distributed) between participants. Both ask and answer questions, listen and speak, and contribute to shaping the direction and content of communication. The distributive style of interviewing generally is used when participants are equal in professional or social standing. Distributive interviews may also be used between people with unequal power if the interviewer wants to create a relaxed exchange. Recruiters often use distributive styles to put job candidates at ease.

Authoritarian interviews are those in which the interviewer exercises primary control over interaction. The interviewer may avoid or quickly cut off discussion of any topics not on the list and may give the interviewee little or no opportunity to ask questions or initiate topics. Efficiency is the primary strength of the authoritarian style of interviewing: Many topics can be covered in a down-to-business manner. Balanced against the advantage of efficiency are significant drawbacks. The authoritarian style of interviewing can be frustrating to interviewees, and the interviewer may miss relevant information by failing to specifically seek it and not giving the interviewee an opportunity to initiate topics.

Stress interviews, which we discussed earlier in this chapter, are those in which the interviewer has primary control, as in authoritarian interviews. Unlike authoritarian interviews, however, stress interviews are a deliberate attempt to create anxiety in the interviewee. Thus, the interviewer has control not only of the pace and content of interaction but also of the psychological agenda. Interviewees have even less control than in authoritarian interviews because stress interviews often rely on trick questions, surprise turns in topic, and unsettling responses to interviewees. If you find yourself in a stress interview, recognize that it is probably a deliberate attempt to test your ability to cope with pressure. Stay alert and flexible to deal with unpredictable communication from the interviewer.

■ *How do you read the degree of formality and balance of power in this interview? What nonverbal behaviors influence your perceptions?*

Forms of Questions in Interviews

Most interviews follow a question–answer pattern in which each person speaks only briefly before the other person speaks. Consequently, skill in asking and responding to questions is central to effectiveness. Skillful interviewers understand that different kinds of questions shape responses, and effective interviewees recognize the opportunities and constraints of distinct forms of questions (Dillon, 1990; Foddy, 1993). We'll consider seven of the most common types of questions and discuss the responses invited by each.

Open Questions Open questions are general queries that initiate new topics: "What can you tell me about yourself?" "What is your work experience?" Because open questions are broad, they allow interviewees a wide latitude of appropriate responses. Thus interviewees have an opportunity to steer communication toward specific topics that interest or reflect well on them.

Closed Questions Questions that call for specific and brief responses are called closed questions. Unlike open questions, they do not invite broad answers. Instead, they ask for a concrete narrow reply, often in the form of yes or no. Closed questions often are used to follow up on general replies to open questions: "How many business courses have you taken?" "What was your position at the summer camp?" "How did you handle that situation?" Closed questions call for short direct answers, and an interviewer may interpret more general responses negatively.

Mirror Questions Mirror questions paraphrase, or reflect off, the previous communication. If an interviewee says, "I have worked in a lot of stressful jobs," the interviewer might respond reflectively by saying, "So you can handle pressure, right?" At the content level of meaning a mirror question seems pointless because it merely repeats what preceded it. At the relationship level of meaning, however, mirror questions say, "Elaborate; tell me more." Thus, they represent opportunities to expand ideas.

Ranier

My counselor uses mirror questions all the time. Whatever I say, she paraphrases it back to me. At first that frustrated me because I expected her to provide me with some answers, or at least some direction in dealing with my problems. But now I realize that what she's doing is teaching me to solve my own problems. By nudging me to reflect on my feelings she helps me identify what I do feel.

Hypothetical Questions Hypothetical questions ask a person to respond to a speculative situation. The questioner may describe a hypothetical scenario and then ask the respondent to react. Recruiters often pose hypothetical questions to see how well job candidates think on their feet. A student of mine provided the following example of a hypothetical question she received in a job interview: "Assume you are supervising an employee who is consistently late to work and sometimes leaves early. What would you do?" My student responded that her first course of action would be to talk with the employee to determine the reason for her tardiness and early departures. Next, she said, she would work with the employee to eliminate the source or, if company policies allowed it, to rearrange the schedule to accommodate the employee's circumstances. This response revealed that the job candidate was collaborative and supportive with subordinates—precisely the qualities the recruiter wanted to assess. Hypothetical questions are designed to find out how you grasp and respond to complex situations. The content of your answer may be less important than the process through which you approach the situation.

Probing Questions When we probe something, we go beneath its surface to find out more about it. During interviews, probing questions go beneath the surface of a response to gather additional information and insight. Consider this example of several probing questions that follow an open question and a broad response:

INTERVIEWER: Tell me about your work history.

INTERVIEWEE: I've held ten jobs while I've been attending college.

INTERVIEWER: Why have you held so many different jobs instead of sticking with one of them?

INTERVIEWEE: I kept switching in the hope of finding one that would be really interesting.

INTERVIEWER: What makes a job interesting to you?

INTERVIEWEE: It would have to be challenging and have enough variety not to bore me.

INTERVIEWER: Are you easily bored?

Note how the interviewer probes to learn more about responses that the interviewee makes. Each probe seeks more details about the interviewee's attitudes toward work.

Leading Questions Leading questions—also called loaded questions—predispose a certain response. For example, "You believe in teamwork, don't you?" encourages "yes" as a response, whereas "You don't

Sharpen Your Skill

RESPONDING TO HYPOTHETICAL QUESTIONS

Here are two questions based on hypothetical scenarios. Read each and then respond quickly and out loud, as you would in an actual interview:

A. You find out that two co-workers under your supervision are romantically involved. They are of equal rank, so the relationship cannot lead to promotions or demotions. Would you be concerned about the relationship? Would you do anything about it?

B. You learn that one person in your department is pilfering company supplies. The person is taking only small things (stationery, tape, and so forth). Would you be concerned? What, if anything, would you do?

In scenario A, an effective initial response would be to ask whether the company has specific policies regarding consensual relationships between employees. If the answer is yes, your follow-up comment might demonstrate your intention to enforce existing policies. If the answer is no, your follow-up comment might suggest you would talk with both people to make sure that they understand the problems that can accompany collegial romances. This would communicate that you are concerned about the people who work for you as well as about the company.

Scenario B poses a moral dilemma and calls upon you to make a moral judgment. An effective response would begin by stating your position on the ethical issue of stealing. Next, the response should reflect whether you would try to resolve the problem by speaking privately with the person (which shows a concern for protecting subordinates and a willingness to avoid excessive punishment) or reporting the person to others in the firm (which shows respect for chain of command and the letter of the law).

Are you satisfied with your ability to respond quickly and effectively to a hypothetical question? If not, practice answering additional hypothetical questions posed by a friend or classmate.

drink on a regular basis, do you?" encourages "no" as a response. Leading questions generally are not a good way to get candid responses because they suggest how you want a person to respond (Stewart & Cash, 1991). Leading questions can be useful, however, if an interviewer wants to test an interviewee's commitment to an idea. An acquaintance of mine who recruits employees for sales positions that require a lot of travel often poses this leading question: "After a year or two of travel the novelty wears off. I assume you expect a permanent location after a year or so with us, right?" Applicants who answer "yes" do not get job offers because travel is an ongoing part of the sales positions.

Summary Questions A final kind of question is a summary question that covers what has been discussed. Although summary questions often are phrased as statements, they function as questions. For example, "I believe we've covered everything," should be perceived as "Do we need to discuss anything else?" "It seems we've agreed on expectations for your performance during the next quarter," should be perceived as, "Do you feel we have a common understanding of what's expected of you?" Communication that summarizes an interview provides an opportunity for participants to check whether they agree about what they've discussed and what will follow.

OBSERVING INTERVIEWS

Watch one television program that features interviews of newsmakers. *Face the Nation, 20/20, Meet the Press,* and *Sixty Minutes* are examples of programs that feature news interviews. Also watch one television program that features interviews with celebrities or people in the limelight. The talk shows of Sally Jesse Raphael and Oprah Winfrey are examples of this genre.

Identify the form of each question posed (open, closed, leading, etc.) and the response it generates. Do the different kinds of interviews rely on distinct types of questions? Why? What do you conclude about the importance of question style to the content and pace of interviews?

What you've learned about the types, purposes, and structures of interviews and the communication dynamics within them provides a foundation for thinking about two important challenges for communicating in interviews.

CHALLENGES WHEN COMMUNICATING IN INTERVIEWS

Like all kinds of interaction, interviewing presents challenges that require basic communication skills. We will discuss two specific challenges: preparing to be interviewed and dealing with illegal questions. We will use the hiring interview to illustrate these challenges, but the ideas we'll discuss pertain to other kinds of interviews.

Preparing to Interview Effectively

My students often have told me that they can't prepare for interviews because they don't know what the interviewer will ask. Even without knowing exactly what questions will arise, you can do a great deal to prepare yourself for a successful interview.

Conduct Research Every type of interview benefits from advance research, although the appropriate research varies according to the interview's purpose. Before performance appraisals, both the supervisor and the subordinate should review any previous performance appraisals. In addition, both participants should think about what has happened since the last appraisal. Have goals that were set been met? Have there been notable achievements such as development of new skills, awards, and so forth? It's also appropriate to talk with others to learn what is expected of employees at various stages in their careers.

Wall Street Journal reporter Rochelle Sharpe (1995) notes that only about 5% of job applicants do any research on a company before interviewing for a job with it. You can put yourself ahead of 95% of job applicants by doing advance research. To learn about a hiring organization, you'll want information about its self-image, history, benefits, organizational culture, and so forth. If you know someone who works for the company, ask that person to share perceptions and information with you. If you aren't personally acquainted with employees at the company, check for materials in your library or placement office or an online service. Standard references such as *Moody's Manuals* and *Standard & Poor's Index* provide information about organizations' size, locations, salary levels, structure, employee benefits, and financial condition. If you prefer to research companies online, most have Web sites that provide substantial information on their history and policies, as well as profiles of their workforce.

Research enhances your effectiveness in two ways. First, the information you gather provides a basis for questions that show that you've done your homework and understand the company. Second, when you know something about a company's or program's priorities, image, and goals, you can adapt your communication to meet the expectations and norms of the company. For example, if you learn that

© CORBIS

Many companies have Web sites that provide up-to-date information that interviewees can use to prepare for meeting company officials.

a particular employer is highly committed to a team approach, during an interview you might emphasize your experience in working on teams. If you learn that the organization expects employees to operate independently, you might highlight your experience working solo during the interview. It is not ethical to misrepresent yourself; however, it is appropriate to spotlight aspects of your experience and interests that match the culture of the organization.

Engage in Person-Centered Communication In Chapter 2 we discussed person-centered communication, in which one person recognizes and respects the perspective of another person. To prepare for an interview, ask yourself, "What would I want to know if I were interviewing me for this position?" Don't ask what you want to tell the interviewer about yourself or what you think is most important about your record. Instead, take the position of the interviewer as you anticipate the interaction.

Glenn

I'm on the selection committee for study abroad, so I interview a lot of students. You'd be amazed at how few of them have bothered to learn about the history and goals of the program. When I ask applicants why they want to study abroad, most of them talk about their personal interests and totally ignore the program's purpose of serving as an ambassador of good will to people in other countries. Students who have bothered to research the program and who can link their goals to those of the program have a real edge in getting accepted.

fyi THE VIRTUAL INTERVIEWING ASSISTANT

The Virtual Interviewing Assistant provides links to help you learn to participate in many types of interviews, including appraisal, counseling, selection, and reprimand. This site also provides information on how to prepare for and follow up on interviews. Visit it at http://www.ukans.edu/cwis/ units/coms2.via/index.html.

CULTURAL DIVERSITY IN INTERVIEWS

The U.S. Department of Labor (1992) cautions interviewers to be sensitive to cultural diversity, which affects how interviewees represent themselves. For example, Western culture encourages people to be assertive and to highlight their strengths. In contrast, some Eastern cultures teach members to be modest about personal achievements and abilities. This can result in misunderstandings and poor decisions about job candidates.

One case study highlighted in an educational pamphlet from the Labor Department features Tran, who is Vietnamese by birth. When Tran applies for a supervisory job, he is interviewed by a woman named Marie. She is impressed by his résumé, which is professionally written and shows that Tran has a great deal of experience and qualifications for the position. When Marie asks Tran to expand on the résumé by telling her about his skills, he says only that the résumé completely states his experience and qualifications. After several efforts to get Tran to elaborate on his abilities, Marie decides he lacks the self-confidence necessary for a supervisory position, and she decides not to hire him. What Marie doesn't understand is that Tran's culture emphasizes the importance of modesty and humility. He was taught that it is unbecoming to call attention to his talents and qualifications. His reluctance to elaborate on his experience and abilities reflects his cultural learnings, not a lack of self-confidence.

You are not likely to know the interviewer personally, so you can't realistically expect to understand him or her as a unique individual. What matters is to recognize that in the interview situation the recruiter is a representative of a particular company with distinct goals, history, expectations, and culture. If you have researched the company, you will be able to adapt your communication to the interviewer's frame of reference.

Practice Responding One of the most common complaints of employment recruiters is that candidates are unprepared for interviews (DeVito, 1994). Examples of appearing unprepared include not bringing a résumé to the interview, not knowing about the company, and not commanding specific information, such as names of former supervisors and dates of employment. The ability to recall specific information is particularly important because it

DELIVERY MATTERS IN INTERVIEWS

Communication scholar Mary Mino (1996) wanted to know how much nonverbal delivery skills and substantive content influenced perceptions of interviewees. To find out, she studied mock hiring interviews. Mino discovered that interviewers were impressed by candidates who articulated clearly and whose nonverbal communication conveyed enthusiasm, assertiveness, and an outgoing personality. However, cautions Mino, dynamic nonverbal communication alone doesn't impress interviewers. When slick speaking is combined with poor content, interviewees are perceived as insincere.

Figure 12.4 Common Questions in Employment Interviews

1. Why did you decide to attend this school?
2. What did you choose as your major?
3. What do you consider the best course you've taken? Why?
4. Why are you interested in our company (firm)?
5. How does your academic background pertain to this job?
6. What do you consider your most serious weakness?
7. What are your long-term professional goals?
8. Which of the jobs you've held has been most satisfying to you? Why?
9. What is the most difficult situation you have ever been in? How did you handle it?
10. Who has been the biggest influence in your life?
11. What are your hobbies? How do you spend spare time?
12. How do you define success in sales (marketing, management, training, etc.)?
13. Why should we hire you instead of another person?
14. What kind of people do you prefer to work with? Why?
15. Are you willing to travel?
16. Do you plan to pursue further education in the future?
17. What do you think of the president's budget proposal (or another current national issue)?
18. Describe your closest friend.
19. How long would you expect to remain with our company?
20. Do you think recent developments in technology are particularly relevant to our company? Why? How?
21. What can you do for this company?
22. What do you see as disadvantages of this job?
23. Define teamwork. Give me an example of a team on which you worked.
24. What do you expect your employer to do for you?
25. Tell me about yourself.

suggests that you are prepared and knowledgeable. Yet many people fumble when asked about specifics. Why? Because they assume they know about themselves, so they don't bother to review details and to practice responses.

You can avoid appearing unprepared by taking time before an interview to review your experiences and accomplishments and to remind yourself of key names, places, and dates. It's also a good idea to rehearse actual answers by responding aloud to questions that are likely to be posed. Figure 12.4 provides twenty-five questions commonly asked in employment interviews. Practice answering these and you will be ahead of most interviewees. You

MAKING THE EXTRA EFFORT

One way to distinguish yourself from other interviewees is to write a follow-up letter to your interviewer. Within a week of the interview, send a short letter thanking the interviewer for his or her time, restating your interest in the job, and saying that you are looking forward to hearing from the company. It's also appropriate to mention a specific topic that came up in the interview—perhaps a play-off game that has now been played or a restaurant the interviewer mentioned intending to visit.

may find it useful to ask a friend to ask the questions and let you respond because this simulates the interaction during interviews. Responding while looking in a mirror is another way to practice. Conducting research, engaging in person-centered communication, and practicing responses will not prepare you for everything that can happen in an interview. However, they will make you better prepared and more impressive than people who don't follow the guidelines we've discussed.

Managing Illegal Questions in Interviews

Just a couple of years ago a student who was completing a professional degree was asked this question by a job recruiter: "What methods of birth control do you use?" Fortunately, this student knew the question was discriminatory, so she refused to answer and reported the interviewer to our campus placement service.

Know the Law

The Equal Employment Opportunity Commission (EEOC) is a federally created entity that monitors various kinds of discrimination in hiring decisions. In 1970 the EEOC issued initial guidelines pertinent to employment interviews, and these have been updated periodically. EEOC guidelines also apply to tests, application forms, and other devices used to screen job applicants.

EEOC regulations prohibit discrimination on the basis of criteria that are legally irrelevant to job qualifications. Because the EEOC is an arm of the federal government, it protects interviewees in all states from intrusive questions about race, ethnicity, marital status, age, sex, disability, and arrests. Individual states and institutions may impose additional limits on information about candidates that may be

BONAFIDE JOB QUALIFICATION

EEOC guidelines specify categories of questions that are *generally* discriminatory in job interviews. Yet the EEOC recognizes one important exception to its guidelines: the BFJQ, or bonafide job qualification. This means that if a question that is generally illegal is relevant to a qualification required to do a particular job, an interviewer may ask about it. For example, being female might be considered a qualification for a rape crisis counselor. When a topic pertains directly to requirements for performing a job, it is legal to ask about it. However, the burden of proving the relevance of any question lies with the interviewer and the organization.

used in hiring decisions. My school, for instance, has a policy against discrimination based on military service and sexual orientation.

Illegal questions may reflect either an interviewer's ignorance of laws or willful disregard of an interviewee's rights. People who conduct interviews should review restrictions on questions in a good source such as Arthur Bell's 1989 book. Whether interviewers intend to ask illegal questions or not, it's important for interviewees to know what questions are not legally permissible in employment interviews. Interviewees who do not understand the legal boundaries on questions cannot protect their rights. Figure 12.5 provides examples of some of the most commonly asked illegal questions.

Responding to Illegal Questions Knowing which questions are out of bounds doesn't tell us what to do if we are asked an inappropriate question. You may choose to respond if it doesn't bother you. You also have the right to object and point out to an interviewer that a question is inappropriate. If you don't care about the job, this is a reasonable way to respond. Even if you exercise your rights diplomatically, doing so may lessen an interviewer's willingness to recommend you for employment.

Often interviewers who ask inappropriate questions don't intend to violate EEOC guidelines, so it's unwise to assume they have bad motives (Wilson & Goodall, 1991). One effective way to respond to unlawful questions is to provide only information

Figure 12.5 Legal and Illegal Questions in Interviews

The Equal Employment Opportunity Commission (EEOC) and legal statutes and case law have defined questions that may and may not be asked of job candidates. In general, it is unlawful to ask about race; national origin; religion; family status and plans for marriage, children, child care, or birth control; physical characteristics; disabilities; or religion. Here are examples of legal and illegal questions.

It's legal to ask	*But illegal to ask:*
1. Are you a law-abiding person?	1. Have you ever been convicted of a felony?
2. Do you have the physical strength to do this job?	2. Are you physically disabled?
3. Are you fluent in any languages other than English?	3. Are you a native speaker of English?
4. Could you provide proof that you are old enough to meet the age requirements for this job?	4. How old are you?
5. Your transcript shows you took a course in socialism. Did you find it interesting?	5. Are you a socialist?
	6. Would you be willing to live in a town without a church, synagog, or temple?
	7. Does your religion allow you to work on Saturdays?
	8. May I have a picture of you to put with your file?
	9. Are you married/Do you intend to marry?
	10. Do you have children/ Do you have reliable child care?
	11. Do you own a car? A house?
	12. What is your political affiliation?

that may be sought legally. This strategy preserves a supportive climate in the interview by not directly reprimanding the interviewer with "You can't ask that question." For instance, if an employer asks whether you are a native Chinese speaker, you might respond, "I am fluent in both English and Chinese." If you are asked whether you belong to any political organizations, be wary because this is often an effort to determine your religion or political affiliation. You might answer, "The only organizations to which I belong that are relevant to this job are the Training and Development Association and the National Communication Association."

If a diplomatic response, such as a partial answer, doesn't satisfy the interviewer, it is appropriate for you to be more assertive. You might ask, "How does your question pertain to qualifications for this job?" This more direct response can be effective in protecting your rights without harming the climate if your nonverbal communication is open and friendly (a questioning tone, a pleasant facial expression) rather than challenging (an accusatory tone, a glare). It is possible to be both assertive and cordial, and this is generally advisable.

Summary

Interviews are common in everyday life. They occur when we respond to pollsters' questions, apply for a job or promotion, conduct research, engage in counseling, and so forth. In this chapter we have gained insight into the structure and processes involved in interviewing. We have learned that most interviews follow a three-part sequence and that different styles and forms of question are used to achieve different objectives in interview situations.

In the second section of the chapter we focused on three guidelines for effective communication when interviewing, especially in the context of job seeking. The first guideline is to prepare by researching the company and the interviewer, reviewing your qualifications and experience, and practicing dealing with questions, including difficult ones. A second guideline for effectiveness in interviews is to be person-centered in your communication. Adapting the content and style of your communication to the person with whom you are interacting is important. A final suggestion is to become familiar with legal issues relevant to interviewing. Whether you are an interviewer or an interviewee, you should know and abide by laws concerning what can and cannot be asked in interviews.

FOR FURTHER REFLECTION AND DISCUSSION

1. Arrange an information-seeking interview with a person in the field you hope to enter. Ask the person to tell you about the job—its advantages and disadvantages and the skills it requires.
2. Visit the Web site of a company you might like to join. Record the information provided on the Web site. Based on what you find on the site, make a list of five questions you could ask in an interview to show that you have researched the company.
3. Schedule an interview with a peer on a topic of mutual interest. During the interview, experiment with different forms of questions: open ended, closed, mirror, stress, leading, and hypothetical. How do the different types of questions affect the interviewee's comfort and responses?
4. The chapter said that interviewees may choose to respond to illegal questions if the questions are not personally offensive or bothersome. For instance, Christians might think they have nothing to lose

by responding honestly to the question, "Can you work on Saturdays?" What do you regard as the pragmatic and ethical implications of responding to questions that don't harm you? If only members of minority religions refuse to answer questions about religion, how effective are the legal protections provided by EEOC guidelines? If all Protestants answer honestly questions about religion, are members of other religions jeopardized?

5. Use the Virtual Interviewing Assistant to practice your interviewing skills. The Web site was identified in an FYI box in this chapter.

KEY TERMS

Interview
Information-giving interview
Information-getting interview
Persuasive interview
Problem-solving interview
Counseling interview
Employment interview
Complaint interview
Performance review
Reprimand interview
Stress interview
Exit interview
Funnel sequence
Mirror interview
Distributive interview
Authoritarian interview

Public Communication

LEARNING OBJECTIVES

To understand

1. What public speaking is
2. Whether ordinary people do much public speaking
3. How speakers earn credibility
4. How speakers organize and support their ideas
5. Whether speaking anxiety is common or normal
6. How to listen critically to the public communication of others

Many people think that public speaking is something done by a few high-visibility people. Yet most of us have occasions to speak in public during our lives. Think about public situations in which you might want to speak:

- A developer wants to build a shopping center in your neighborhood, and you oppose the idea. The town council has announced that it will hear public statements on the developer's proposal at its next meeting.
- You strongly believe that we need greater controls on industrial pollution. You want to get your ideas across to legislators and members of your community.
- Your supervisor asks you to speak to a group of high school students about the company.
- You are responsible for reporting your project team's findings to the CEO of your firm.
- You are taking a course in which all students are required to make an oral presentation.
- You attend a public presentation in which the speaker misuses statistics to support the claim that children's television programs are not violent. You want to challenge the speaker and give accurate information to other listeners.

Speaking in public allows you to be an informed and active citizen, an effective professional, a responsible member of your community, and someone who influences what others believe, think, and do. Thus skill in public speaking is important for both individuals and society. Equally important is skill in listening critically to the public communication of others. People who can present their ideas effectively and listen critically to the ideas of others are able to be active vigorous participants in all spheres of life.

This chapter focuses on public speaking. In the first part of the chapter we will discuss the many uses of public speaking, and we will describe different kinds of speeches and distinctive features of public speaking. The second section of the chapter provides an overview of what is involved in planning and presenting public speeches. In the third section we identify three particular challenges for effective public communication: reducing speaking anxiety, adapting to audiences, and listening critically to public discourse. The complex process of public speaking cannot be taught in a single chapter. The *Student Companion* that accompanies this book provides detailed guidelines for crafting speeches. This chapter's goal is to give you a conceptual understanding of what is involved in public communication. The information we will cover will be especially useful in helping you become a more critical listener when you attend to others' public communication.

PUBLIC SPEAKING AS ENLARGED CONVERSATION

In 1938 James Winans, a distinguished professor of communication, remarked that effective public speaking is enlarged conversation. What Winans meant was that in many ways public speaking is quite similar to everyday talk. As John Motley and Jennifer Molloy more recently stated, "Except for preparation time and turn-taking delay, public speaking has fundamental parallels to everyday conversation" (1994, p. 52). Whether we are talking with a couple of friends or speaking to an audience of 100 people, we need to adapt to others' perspectives, create a good climate for interaction, use effective verbal and nonverbal communication, organize what we say so others can follow our ideas, support our claims, present our ideas in an engaging and convincing manner, and listen and respond to those with whom we interact. In public speaking, as in everyday conversation, these are skills of effective communication.

Thinking of public speaking as enlarged conversation reminds us that most public speaking usually is not stiff or exceedingly formal. In fact, some of the most effective public speakers use an informal personal style that invites listeners to feel that they are interacting with someone, not being lectured to. This means that public speaking doesn't require an entirely different set of communication skills. Instead,

■ *This Native American man is speaking at a protest rally. His goal is to raise awareness of Native Americans' heritage and current status.*

© Bob Daemmrich/Stock, Boston

THE FIRST AMENDMENT: FREEDOM OF RELIGION, SPEECH, AND THE PRESS

Congress shall make no law respecting an establishment of religion, or prohibiting the free exercise thereof; or abridging the freedom of speech, or of the press, or the right of people peaceably to assemble, and to petition the Government for a redress of grievances.

good public communication requires and builds on skills and principles that apply to communication in all contexts, as discussed in Part I of this book.

I learned that effective public speaking is much like conversation when I first taught a large lecture course. I lectured in a fairly formal style because I thought that was appropriate in a class of 150 students. One day a student asked a question and I responded with another question. He replied, then another student added her ideas, and an open discussion was launched. Both the students and I were more engaged with one another and the course material than we had been when I lectured formally. That's when I realized that even in large classes effective teaching is enlarged conversation.

Public Speaking in Everyday Life

In *Successful Public Speaking,* Cheryl Hamilton (1996) observes that public speaking is part of everyday life for most people. According to Hamilton, public speaking is a means to three important goals. First, we gain personal satisfaction when we're able to give voice to values and ideas that matter to us. Second, being able to speak in public allows us to be effective citizens who affect what happens in our communities, state, and nation. Third, the ability to make public presentations is linked to professional success and advancement. According to research conducted at Stanford University, the single best predictor of a person's earning power is whether that person enjoys giving public speeches (Sandholtz, 1987).

Cedric

When I studied to be a computer programmer, I never thought I would have to do any public speaking. After starting my job, I found out that addressing groups is a big part of what I do. Nearly every week I meet with personnel in other departments. I explain new computer programs to them and teach them to use them. I

Sharpen Your Skill

NOTICING CONVERSATIONAL SPEAKING STYLE

Think about professors you found most and least effective in communicating course content to you. For each group of professors, answer these questions:

1. Did they use a formal or informal speaking style?
2. Did the professors state clearly what was important?
3. Did the professors give reasons for ideas and opinions they expressed?
4. Could you follow the professors' train of thought?
5. Did they adapt their ideas to your knowledge and interests?
6. Did you feel involved in the classroom communication?

make speeches to groups as small as seven and as large as forty. If I couldn't make effective public presentations, I couldn't do my job, even though I am a technical specialist.

Public speaking is not restricted to professionals in high-status positions. Most members of organizations, from CEOs to entry-level and midlevel employees, are expected to speak both within organizations and to the public. Skill in public speaking is important for parents who are concerned about a high school's reading list, law enforcement officers who need to calm crowds or educate groups on laws and self-defense, doctors, politicians and experts who give press conferences, and professionals who want to persuade their companies to adopt or modify policies.

Types and Goals of Public Speeches

Tradition recognizes three speaking purposes: entertaining, informing, and persuading. You probably realize that these purposes often overlap. For example, informative speeches routinely include humor or interesting comments to entertain listeners. Some of your favorite professors probably include stories and interesting examples to enliven informational lectures. Persuasive speeches often contain information about issues, as well as content that is entertaining. Speeches intended to entertain may also inform and persuade, perhaps through the use of humor or dramatic narratives. Although purposes for speaking overlap, most speeches have one primary purpose.

Speaking to Entertain In **speeches to entertain** the primary objective is to engage, interest, amuse, or please listeners. You might think that only accomplished comics and performers present speeches to entertain. Actually, many of us will be involved in speaking to entertain during our lives. You might be asked to give an after-dinner speech, present a toast at a friend's wedding, or make remarks at a retirement party for a colleague. In each case the primary goal is to entertain, although in the process of entertaining others a speaker might include information about the occasion, the couple being married, or the achievements of the colleague who is retiring. Even when your primary purpose in speaking is not to entertain, you'll want to interest listeners whom you intend to inform or persuade. If you intend to entertain listeners, it's a good idea to test your jokes or amusing comments in advance. It's unwise to assume that others will find humor in something you think is funny or that audiences will respond to jokes as

MOVED TO SPEAK

Candace Lightner had never thought of herself as a public speaker. She had never sought the limelight and had seldom been required to speak out to others. Then in 1980 her 13-year-old daughter was killed by a teenage drunk driver. Once she recovered from the immediate grief of her daughter's untimely death, Lightner began a crusade to pass strict laws against drunk driving.

She founded Mothers Against Drunk Driving (MADD), which now has thousands of members. In addition, Lightner persuaded state and federal legislators to approve stiffer laws and penalties for drunk driving and to raise the age for drinking to 21. Although not an outstanding speaker when she began her crusade, Lightner became a skillful speaker in order to get her message across.

Sources: Lightner, 1990; Sellinger, 1994.

Courtesy Candace Lightner

■ *Here Candace Lightner holds up a photo of her daughter, who was killed by a drunk driver. Lightner's speeches led to laws that crack down on drunk drivers.*

your friends do; after all, friends often think alike and have similar senses of humor. It is also a good idea to avoid jokes and remarks that might offend some people. Even if you find them funny, they could alienate listeners, as Joanna's commentary illustrates.

Joanna

I am so angry about a lecture I went to last week. The speaker was trying to sound like he was with it or something, so right at the start of his talk he tried to tell a joke. He asked, "How many State coeds does it take to change a tire?" You should have heard the groan from all the women in the audience. He lost us right there.

Humor doesn't dominate in all speeches that have the goal of entertaining. We also entertain when we tell stories. **Narrative speaking** involves rendering a story to share experiences, build community, pass on history, or teach a lesson. Narrative speaking often occurs in families as parents share stories of their courtship with children, discuss friends and relatives, and keep family memories alive. You probably heard a great many family stories as you were growing up. Narrative speaking is also important in cultures that emphasize oral communication. In some other countries and many co-cultures in the United States, individual and collective histories are kept alive through storytelling. African Americans, southerners, and members of Italian and Vietnamese communities in the United States have particularly strong traditions of weaving families and communities together by telling stories that create common knowledge and understandings.

Speaking to Inform **Speeches to inform** have the primary goal of increasing listeners' understanding, awareness, or knowledge of some topic. For example, a speaker might want listeners to understand what behaviors do and do not spread HIV. Another example of informative speaking is a speech to make listeners aware of recycling programs. In both cases the primary purpose is to enrich listeners' knowledge, although clearly the two topics have persuasive implications. Speeches to inform may also take the form of demonstrations, in which the speaker shows how to do something while giving a verbal explanation. For instance, a demonstration speech might show listeners how to use a new computer program or how to distinguish between poisonous and nonpoisonous species of mushrooms.

■ *Narrative speaking is a vital part of many cultures. In these communities, storytelling weaves the past into the present.*

©Lawrence Migdale/Photo Researchers

Gladys

I've taught second grade for eight years, and there's one thing I've learned: If you don't get the students' interest, you can't teach them anything. My education classes taught us to focus on content when planning lessons. But working in real classrooms with real children taught me that before a teacher can get content or information across to students, she has to first capture their interest.

Speeches to inform may also teach listeners something entirely new. Sasha, a student in one of my classes, gave a speech on arranged marriages, which are still common in her native country. Her goal was for students to understand the history of arranged marriages and why they work for many people. Although her primary goal was to inform, her speech had a persuasive aspect because she encouraged listeners not to impose their values on practices in other cultures. This reinforces our earlier discussion of overlapping purposes in public speaking.

Speaking to Persuade

Speeches to persuade aim to change listeners' attitudes, beliefs, or behaviors or to motivate them to some action. Persuasive goals are to influence attitudes, change practices, and alter beliefs. Rather than being primarily an entertainer or teacher, the persuasive speaker is an advocate who argues for a cause, issue, policy, attitude, or action. In one of my classes a student named Chris gave a speech designed to persuade other students to contribute to the Red Cross blood drive. He began by telling us that he was a hemophiliac whose life depended on blood donations. He then explained the procedures for donating blood (a subordinate informational purpose) so that listeners would not be deterred by fear of the unknown. Next, he described several cases of people who had died or become critically ill because adequate supplies of blood weren't available. In the two weeks after his speech, more than a third of the students donated blood.

Distinctive Features of Public Communication

Although public speaking is enlarged conversation, it differs in some ways from casual interaction. Two

fyi LISTENING TO FAMOUS SPEECHES

Webcorp Inc. has created Historic Audio Archives that allow you to listen to significant speeches by famous people, including Martin Luther King, John Fitzgerald Kennedy, Malcolm X, Richard Nixon, Adolf Hitler, and Winston Churchill. Visit the site at http://www.webcorp.com/sounds/index.html.

features generally distinguish public speaking from other kinds of communication. First, public speeches tend to involve more planning and preparation than casual conversations. Second, in public speaking situations the audiences' contributions are less obvious and immediate than those of speakers. We will discuss both features and identify the responsibilities they imply for speakers.

Greater Responsibility to Plan and Prepare When a friend asks your opinion on gun control, you respond without conducting research, carefully organizing your ideas, and practicing your delivery. Before speaking to a group of fifty people about gun control, however, you would be likely to do some research, organize your ideas, and practice delivering your speech. In public speaking situations you have a responsibility to provide evidence and reasoning to support your beliefs, structure your ideas clearly, and practice your presentation so that your delivery is engaging.

Listeners' expectations affect the planning and preparation that go into public speaking. We expect more evidence, clearer organization, and more polished delivery in public speeches than in casual conversations. Thus, public speakers who do not take advantage of the opportunity to prepare their communication are likely to disappoint listeners and be judged inadequate. This implies that when you are giving a public speech, you have a responsibility to analyze listeners, do research, organize ideas, and practice and polish delivery.

Less Interaction Public speaking also tends to be less interactive than many forms of communication, such as personal conversations, interviews, and team deliberations. In many contexts communicators take turns talking, but speakers tend to dominate the

fyi WISDOM FROM ANCIENT TEACHERS

Ancient teachers of rhetoric taught students to master five specific canons, or arts, of public speaking that remain relevant today.

- Invention: the art of discovering ideas for speaking, arguments, or proofs to support claims and increase a speaker's credibility.
- Organization: the art of arranging ideas so that they are understandable and effective and so that a speaker's credibility is enhanced.
- Style: the art of speaking well, with grace, clarity, and vitality.
- Memory: the art of familiarizing oneself with the content of a speech so that the speaker's energies can be devoted to delivery and interaction with listeners.
- Delivery: the art of presenting a speech effectively and in ways that enhance credibility.

airwaves in public presentations. It would be a mistake, however, to think that listeners don't participate actively in public presentations. They are sending messages even as they listen: head nods, frowns, perplexed expressions, applause, smiles. Listeners communicate throughout a speech, primarily in nonverbal ways. As Cheryl Hamilton notes, effective public speakers "realize that successful communication is a two-way street" (1996, p. 29). In other words, good public speakers pay attention to what listeners are "saying" throughout a speech.

Even though listeners participate actively, public speaking places special responsibility on speakers. To be effective they must anticipate listeners' attitudes and knowledge and must adapt their presentation to the views of listeners. One of the first steps in planning a good public speech is to ask what audience members are likely to know about a topic and how they are likely to feel about it. Based on what you know or learn about listeners, you can make informed choices about what information to include and how to support and organize your ideas.

While actually giving the speech, you can also meet your responsibility to adapt to listeners by being attentive to their feedback. If some listeners look confused, you might add an example or elaborate an idea. If listeners' nonverbal behaviors suggest that they are bored, you might alter your volume, incorporate gestures, change your speaking position, or offer a personal example to enliven your talk. Later in this chapter we'll return to the topic of adapting to listeners. For now you should realize that because public speaking gives the speaker primary control, the speaker has a special responsibility to be sensitive to listeners' ideas, values, interests, and experiences. With this background, we're ready to summarize guidelines for planning and presenting public communication.

PLANNING AND PRESENTING PUBLIC SPEECHES

Effective public speaking is a process, not an isolated event. The process begins with understanding credibility and ways to earn it. The next steps are to plan a speech and conduct research. Speakers then organize their ideas so that they are logical and easy to follow. Finally, speakers select delivery styles and practice presentation. We will discuss each step. For more detailed guidance, refer to the *Student Companion* to this book.

Earning Credibility

Effective public speaking (and, indeed, communication in all contexts) requires credibility. **Credibility** exists when listeners believe in a speaker and trust what the speaker says and does. Credibility is based on listeners' perceptions of a speaker's position, authority, knowledge (also called expertise), dynamism, and trustworthiness (also called character). Thus, to earn credibility speakers should demonstrate that they are informed about their topics, are dynamic communicators, and are ethical in using evidence and reasoning.

A speaker's credibility is not necessarily static. Some speakers have high **initial credibility,** which is the expertise, dynamism, and character that listeners attribute to them before they begin to speak. Initial credibility is based on titles, experiences, and achievements that are known to listeners before they hear a speech. For example, Ralph Nader has high initial credibility in the area of consumer protection.

Ricardo

Last month I went to a lecture about getting started in financial planning. I figured the speaker was someone who just wanted to sell me something, so I didn't have too high a regard for him. But during his talk he quoted lots of information from unbiased sources, so I saw that he really knew his stuff. He also didn't try to sell us anything, so I began to trust what he said. And he made the ideas really easy to follow with charts and handouts. By the time he was through, I thought he was excellent.

Speakers may gain **derived credibility,** which listeners grant as a result of how speakers communicate during presentations. Speakers may earn derived credibility when they provide clear and well-organized information and convincing evidence and when they have an engaging delivery style. Speakers may also increase credibility during a presentation if listeners regard them as likeable and as having good will toward the listeners (McCroskey & Teven, 1999). **Terminal credibility** is a cumulative combination of initial and derived credibility. Terminal credibility may be greater or less than initial credibility, depending on how effectively a speaker communicates.

Soyana

The greatest teacher I ever had taught a class in government policies and practices. Before coming to campus he had been an adviser to three presidents, and he had held a lot of different offices in government, so he really knew what he was teaching us about from the inside. Everything he said had so much more weight than what I hear from professors who've never had any practical experience.

As we discuss specific aspects of planning and presenting public speeches, keep the issue of credibility central in your thinking. It should influence each decision you make as you prepare for and engage in public speaking.

Planning Public Speeches

A well-crafted speech begins with careful planning. Speakers should select a limited topic, define a clear purpose, and develop a concise thesis statement.

Selecting a Topic Speakers should select topics about which they are informed and that matter to them. When you choose a topic that you care about, you have a head start in both knowledge and enthusiasm. Thus listeners are more likely to perceive you as knowledgeable and dynamic.

Speakers should also choose topics that are appropriate to listeners. It's important to consider listeners' values, backgrounds, attitudes, knowledge, and interests so that you can select topics and adapt how you address them in ways that respect the perspectives and interests of listeners.

Topics for speeches should be appropriate to the situation. If you are asked to speak at a professional meeting, your speech should address the concerns and issues of that profession. If you are speaking about someone who has won an award or is retiring, the situation calls for a speech that praises the person.

Finally, effective topics are limited in scope. You may be concerned about education, but that topic is too broad for a single speech. You might narrow it to a speech on funding for education or training of teachers or some other specific aspect of your general area of interest.

Defining the Purpose The second step in planning a speech is to define your general and specific

Garfield

Reprinted by permission of Universal Press Syndicate.

purposes. The general purpose is to entertain, inform, or persuade—a traditional goal of public speeches. The **specific purpose** is exactly what you hope to accomplish. For example, specific purposes are getting 25% of the audience to sign up to donate blood, enabling listeners to give correct answers to a quiz on how HIV is spread, getting 50% of the audience to sign a petition against gun control that you will send to Congress, or getting listeners to laugh at your jokes and enjoy the talk.

Developing the Thesis A clear **thesis statement,** which is the main idea of the entire speech, guides an effective speech: "Everyone should wear seat belts," "we should vote for stronger regulations on industrial waste," or "the electoral college should be abolished in the United States". Each of these thesis statements succinctly summarizes the key idea of a speech. The specific purpose of a speech, which we discussed earlier, should be consistent with the thesis: "I want listeners to buckle up," "I want listeners to call their representatives to voice support for legislation on industrial waste," "I want listeners to support a constitutional amendment abolishing the electoral college."

Researching and Supporting Public Speeches

A second way to earn credibility is to provide listeners with reasons to believe what you say. **Evidence** is material used to support claims a speaker makes. Supporting your ideas may involve clarification or proof. In addition, support may enhance interest and emotional response to ideas. Evidence serves a number of important functions in speeches. First, it can be used to make ideas clearer, more compelling, and more dramatic. Second, evidence fortifies a speaker's opinions, which are seldom sufficient to persuade intelligent listeners. Finally, evidence heightens a speaker's credibility. A speaker who supports ideas well comes across as informed and prepared. Thus, including strong evidence allows speakers to gain derived credibility during a presentation.

The effectiveness of evidence depends directly on whether listeners understand and accept it. This reinforces the importance of adapting to listeners, which we have emphasized throughout this book and which we will discuss again later in this chapter. Even if you quote the world's leading authority, the evidence won't be effective if your listeners don't find the

CONDUCTING RESEARCH FOR PUBLIC SPEECHES

Libraries and online services hold a wealth of information. A good way to begin library research is by conducting a computer search with programs that quickly identify books and articles related to your topic.

Specialized references can direct you to materials directly pertinent to your topic. *The Reader's Guide to Periodical Literature* summarizes articles published in 125 popular magazines. *The Public Affairs Information Service Bulletin* indexes books, pamphlets, and other materials relevant to public affairs. *American Demographics* provides a splendid summary of information on Americans' patterns, behaviors, possessions, and so forth. *Psychological Abstracts* surveys articles published on psychological topics, and other disciplines have similar references.

Computerized databases allow you to search library holdings from a terminal. The *InfoTrac College Edition* that accompanies your textbook provides a fully searchable virtual library. There you can find information on any topic. Among the more popular sources of general information included in *InfoTrac College Edition* is *Information Please Almanac* (with subdirectories for sports, environment, and other topics).

authority credible (Olson & Cal, 1984). No matter how valid evidence is, it is effective only if listeners believe it. Consequently, your choices of evidence for your speech should take listeners' perspectives into account. You want to include support that they find credible while also making sure your evidence is valid.

The next issue is what type of evidence to use. Five forms of support are widely respected, and each tends to be effective in specific situations and for particular goals.

The kinds of evidence are **statistics, examples, comparisons, quotations,** and **visual aids.** Figure 13.1 summarizes the types of evidence and their uses.

Harihar

Last week at the meeting of Nepalese Americans we had a speaker talk to us about principles of ethical conduct. He quoted Jesus for principles such as to love your neighbors and to be kind to others. But all of us in the group are Buddhist, and there are Buddhist precepts that say the same thing. For us Buddha would have been a better person than Jesus to illustrate moral principles.

Before including any form of evidence in a speech, speakers have an ethical responsibility to check the accuracy of material and the credibility of sources. It is advisable to ask questions such as these:

- Are the statistics still valid? Population demographics, social trends, and other matters are quickly dated, so it's important to have current statistics.
- Does the person being quoted have any personal interest in endorsing a certain point of view? For example, tobacco companies' statements about the harmlessness of tobacco may reflect personal and financial interests.
- Is a person being quoted an expert on the topic? It is inappropriate to rely on the **halo effect,** in which people who are well known in one area (sports stars, for instance) are quoted in an area outside their expertise (nutritional value of a cereal, for instance).
- Is an example representative of the point it is used to support? Is it typical of the general case?
- Are any comparisons fair? For instance, it might be appropriate to compare Christianity and Buddhism as spiritual paths, but it would not be appropriate to compare them as religions that believe in a single god.
- Are visual aids clear, visible by all listeners, and accurate in their images?

When presenting evidence to listeners, speakers have an ethical obligation to identify the source and tell listeners its date. You can cite sources verbally by saying, "Doctor Montelbond, who won the 1988 Nobel Prize in physics, published a study in 1996 in which she reported that . . ." or "As Senator Bollinger remarked in 1997. . . ." Oral footnotes enable listeners to evaluate the speaker's evidence. They also give appropriate acknowledgment to the person or group that initially generated the evidence.

Organizing Speeches

Organization increases speaking effectiveness in several ways (Spicer & Bassett, 1976). First, people like structure, and they expect ideas to come to them in some ordered way rather than in a jumble. Organization also affects comprehension of ideas. Listeners can understand, follow, and remember a speech that is well planned and ordered. Listeners are less likely to retain the key ideas in a poorly organized speech. Furthermore, experimental evidence shows that listeners are more persuaded by an organized than a disorganized speech (McCroskey & Mehrley, 1969). Finally, organization enhances speakers' credibility, probably because a carefully structured speech reflects well on a speaker's preparation and respect for listeners (Baker, 1965). When someone gives a disorganized speech, listeners may regard the person as incompetent or unprepared. This lessens derived and terminal credibility.

Organizing an effective speech does not rely on the same principles used to organize written work. Oral communication requires more explicit organization, greater redundancy, and simpler sentence structure. Unlike readers, listeners cannot refer to an earlier passage if they become confused or forget a point already made. Providing signposts to highlight organization and repeating key ideas increase listeners' retention of a message (Woolfolk, 1987).

Figure 13.1 Types of Evidence and Their Uses

Examples **provide concrete descriptions of situations, individuals, problems, or other phenomena.**

Types:	Short (instance) Detailed Hypothetical Anecdotal
Uses:	To personalize information and ideas To add interest to a presentation To enhance dramatic effect

Comparisons (analogies) **compare two ideas, processes, people, situations, or other phenomena.**

Types:	Literal analogy (A heart is a pump.) Figurative analogy (Life is a journey.) Metaphor Simile
Uses:	To show connections between phenomena To relate a new idea to one that is familiar to listeners To provide interest to a presentation

Statistics **provide numerical summaries of information.**

Types:	Percentages and ratios Demographic data Frequency counts Correlations Trends
Uses:	To summarize many instances of some phenomena To show relationships between two or more phenomena (cause or correlation) To demonstrate trends or patterns

Quotations (testimony) **restate or paraphrase the words of others, with appropriate credit to the sources of the words.**

Types:	Short quotation Extended quotation Paraphrase
Uses:	To add variety and interest to a presentation To support a speaker's claims To draw on the credibility of people whom listeners know To include particularly arresting phrasings of ideas

Visual aids **reinforce verbal communication and provide visual information and appeals.**

Types:	Hand-made charts and graphs Overheads/transparencies Computer-created charts and graphs Powerpoint slides Objects, pictures, handouts, film clips
Uses:	To strengthen and underscore verbal messages To translate statistics into pictures that are understandable To add variety and interest to a presentation To give listeners a vivid appreciation of a topic, issue, or point

Consistent with the need for redundancy in oral communication, good speeches tell listeners what the speaker is going to tell them, present the message, and then remind listeners of the main points. This translates into preparing an introduction, a body, and a conclusion. In addition, speakers should include transitions to move listeners from point to point in the speech.

The Introduction The introduction is the first thing an audience hears. It should gain their attention, state the thesis, and preview how the speaker will develop the topic (Miller, 1974).

The first objective of an introduction is to gain listeners' attention. You might open with a dramatic piece of evidence: a startling statistic (in the United States four women are battered to death by intimates every day), striking visual aid (photo of victim of battering), or dramatic example (detailed story of one woman who was battered). You could also pose a question that invites listeners to think actively about the topic: "Have you ever feared for your life and had no way to escape?" Speakers may also gain listeners' attention by referring to personal experience with the topic: "For the past year I have worked as a volunteer in the local battered women's shelter." Your method of capturing listeners' attention should make clear why your speech is relevant to listeners.

A good introduction includes the thesis statement that we discussed earlier. Your thesis should be a clear, short sentence that captures the main theme of your talk.

The final purpose of an introduction is to preview major points so that listeners understand how you plan to develop your thesis. Typically, a preview lists the main points in a concise manner: "In my talk I will show you that vegetarianism is a healthful diet, and I will demonstrate that it is also delicious" or "To inform you about your legal rights in an interview, I will first discuss laws that prohibit discrimination and protect privacy. Next, I will tell you what questions are illegal. Finally, I will tell you what you can do if an interviewer violates your rights."

In summary, a good introduction

- Captures listeners' attention
- Informs listeners of the main idea (thesis) of the speech
- Explains how the thesis will be developed by previewing claims or key points in the speech

The Body of the Speech The body of a speech develops the thesis by organizing content into points that are distinct yet related. In short speeches of 5 to 10 minutes, two or three points are usually all that a speaker can develop well. Longer speeches may include more points. You can organize speeches

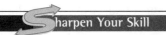

DEVELOPING EFFECTIVE THESIS STATEMENTS

Here are ineffective thesis statements. Rephrase them so that they are concise and clear theses for speeches.

Ineffective	Effective
1. We all need to think about HIV.	1. Accurate information about HIV can protect you from infection.
2. Vegetarianism is a healthful way of life.	______________
3. It's hard to tell how computers will affect individuals' lives.	______________
4. Cyberhate is all around us.	______________

in many ways, and each organizational pattern has distinct effects on the overall meaning that is created. Temporal, or time, patterns organize ideas chronologically. They emphasize progression, sequences, or development. Spatial patterns organize ideas according to physical relationships. They are useful in explaining layouts, geographic relationships, or connections among parts of a system. Topical patterns (also called classification patterns) order speech content into categories or areas. This pattern is useful for speeches in which topics break down into two or three areas that aren't related temporally, spatially, or otherwise. Comparative patterns compare two or more phenomena (people, machines, planets, situations). This pattern may be used to demonstrate either similarities between phenomena ("In many ways public speaking is like everyday conversation") or differences between phenomena ("Public speaking requires more planning than everyday conversation").

Persuasive speeches typically rely on organizational patterns that encourage listeners to change attitudes or behaviors. Problem–solution patterns allow speakers to describe a problem and propose a solution. Cause–effect and effect–cause patterns order speech content into two main points: cause and effect. This structure is useful for persuasive speeches that aim to convince listeners that certain consequences will follow from particular actions.

A final way to organize a speech is the motivated sequence pattern (Gronbeck, McKerro, Ehninger, & Monroe, 1994; Monroe, 1935). This pattern is effective in diverse communication situations, probably because it follows a natural order of human thought. The motivated sequence pattern includes five sequential steps. The attention step focuses listeners' attention on the topic with a strong opening ("Imagine this campus with no trees whatsoever"). The need step shows that a real and serious problem exists ("Acid rain is slowly but surely destroying the trees on our planet"). Next is the satisfaction step, in which a speaker recommends a solution to the problem described ("Stronger environmental regulations and individual efforts to use environmentally safe products can protect trees and thus the oxygen we need to live"). The visualization step intensifies listeners' commitment to the solution by helping them imagine the results that the recommended solution would achieve ("You will have air to breathe and so will your children and grandchildren. Moreover, we'll have trees to add beauty to our lives"). Finally, in the action step the speaker appeals to listeners to take concrete action to realize the recommended solution ("Refuse to buy or use any aerosol products. Sign this petition that I am sending to our representatives on Capitol Hill").

The organization chosen for a speech affects the content. Figure 13.2 illustrates how a single topic could be organized in three distinct ways. Note how the organizational pattern influences overall meaning.

Conclusion A good speech ends on a strong note (Baird, 1974). The conclusion is a speaker's last chance to emphasize ideas and gain listeners' support. A good conclusion should accomplish two goals. First, it should summarize the main ideas of the speech. Second, it should leave listeners with a memorable final idea (a dramatic quote or example, a challenge, a memorable computer graphic, and so forth). These two functions of the conclusion echo the attention and preview steps in the introduction to a speech.

Transitions The final aspect of organizing a speech is developing **transitions,** which are words, phrases, and sentences that connect the ideas. Transitions signal listeners that you have finished talking about one idea and are ready to move to the next one. Within the development of a single point, speakers usually rely on such transitional words and phrases as "therefore," "and so," "for this reason," and "as the evidence suggests." To make transitions from one point to another, the speaker may use phrases: "My second point is . . ."; "Now that we have seen how many people immigrate to the United States, let's ask what they bring to our country." Speakers typically use one or more sentences to create transitions between the major parts of a speech (introduction, body, conclusion). A student in one of my classes moved from the body to the conclusion of his speech with this transition: "I have discussed in some detail why we need protection for wetlands. Before I leave you, let me summarize the key ideas."

Developing Effective Delivery

As we have seen, dynamism is one dimension of a speaker's credibility. Thus, an engaging delivery is important. **Oral style** should be more personal than

Figure 13.2 The Influence of Organization on Messages

Topic: The Arctic National Wildlife Refuge

Speech 1: Temporal Organization

Thesis: The history of the Arctic National Wildlife Refuge should guide our vision of its future.

Claim 1: The Arctic National Wildlife Refuge has provided sanctuary to many endangered species of animals.

Claim 2: Today mining and tourism industries are seeking to open the Arctic National Wildlife Refuge up to development.

Claim 3: A better future is one in which the sanctuary is preserved for wildlife.

Speech 2: Spatial Organization

Thesis: We must preserve the Arctic National Wildlife Refuge as one of the few remaining wild spaces in our nation.

Claim 1: Most of the land in the United States has been developed for human use and profit.

Claim 2: All that remains of truly wild lands are a few national parks, a few acres in Utah, and the Arctic National Wildlife Refuge.

Claim 3: If we allow the Arctic National Wildlife Refuge to be opened to development, we will lose one of the last wild spaces we have.

Speech 3: Cause–Effects

Thesis: Opening the Arctic National Wildlife Refuge to development would result in losses for fragile animals, biodiversity, and humans.

Claim 1: If the refuge is opened to mining and industrial development, ten species of endangered animals will perish forever.

Claim 2: Allowing development of the refuge would make unique biological forms extinct.

Claim 3: If the refuge is opened to mining and industrial development, humans will lose a rare and precious national treasure.

written style (Wilson & Arnold, 1974). Speakers may include personal stories and personal pronouns, referring to themselves as *I* rather than *the speaker*. Also, speakers may use phrases instead of complete sentences, and contractions (*can't*) are appropriate. Speakers should also sustain eye contact with listeners and show that they are approachable. If you reflect on speakers you have found effective, you will probably realize that they seemed engaging, personal, and open to you.

Effective oral style is also more immediate and active than written style tends to be (Wilson & Arnold, 1974). This is important because listeners must understand ideas immediately, as they are spoken, whereas readers can take time to comprehend ideas. Speakers foster immediacy by using short sentences instead of complex sentences. Immediacy also involves following general ideas with clear, specific evidence or elaboration. Rhetorical questions ("Would you like to know that a good job is waiting for you when you graduate?"), interjections ("Good grief!"; "Look!"), and redundancy also enhance the immediacy of a speech.

Throughout this book we've seen that we should adapt our communication to its context. This basic

fyi PERSONAL STYLE AND EFFECTIVE TEACHING

Teachers, like others who speak to large groups, are more effective when they come across as individuals. A substantial amount of research shows that teachers who seem warm and approachable, show interest in talking with students, maintain eye contact when lecturing, and use humor in class are better liked than teachers who are more impersonal. Personal style not only affects how much students like teachers but also increases students' motivation to study and learn. These effects have been found with students in courses in high schools, colleges, and even in off-campus televised programs.

Sources: Christophel, 1990; Gorham & Zakahi, 1990; Hackman & Walker, 1990; Mongeau & Blalock, 1994.

communication principle guides a speaker's choice of a presentation style. The style of speaking that is effective at a political rally is different from the style appropriate for an attorney's closing speech in a trial; delivering a toast at a wedding requires a different style than testifying before Congress. Each speaking situation suggests guidelines for presentation, so speakers must consider the context when selecting a speaking style.

Four styles of delivery are generally recognized and each is appropriate in certain contexts. **Impromptu delivery** involves little or no preparation. It can be effective for speakers who know their material thoroughly. Many politicians speak impromptu when talking about their experience in public service and policies they advocate. Impromptu speaking generally is not advisable for novice speakers or for anyone who is not thoroughly familiar with a topic.

Probably the most commonly used presentational style is **extemporaneous delivery.** Extemporaneous speaking involves substantial preparation and practice, but it stops short of memorizing the exact words of a speech and relies on notes. Speakers conduct research, organize materials, and practice delivering their speeches, but they do not rehearse so much that speeches sound canned. Attorneys, teachers, politicians, and others who engage in public speaking most often use an extemporaneous style of presentation.

Manuscript delivery, as the name implies, involves presenting a speech from a complete written manuscript. In addition to the preparation typical of extemporaneous delivery, manuscript style requires speakers to write out the entire content of a speech and to rely on the written document or a teleprompter projection when making presentations. Few people can present manuscript speeches in an engaging, dynamic manner. However, manuscript delivery is appropriate, even advisable, in situations that call for precision. For instance, presidents generally use manuscripts for official presentations. In these circumstances, speakers cannot run the risk of using imprecise language.

An extension of the manuscript style of speaking is **memorized delivery,** in which a speaker commits an entire speech to memory and presents it without relying on a written text or notes. This style shares the primary disadvantage of manuscript speaking: the risk of a canned delivery that lacks dynamism and immediacy. In addition, the memorized style of delivery entails a second serious danger: forgetting. If speakers are nervous or if something happens to disrupt a presentation, they may become rattled and forget all or part of the speech. Without the written text, they may be unable to get back on track. When choosing a style of delivery, speakers should consider the advantages and disadvantages of each speaking style and the constraints of particular communication situations. No single style suits all occasions. Instead, the most effective style is one that suits the particular speaker and the situation.

Regardless of which delivery style speakers use, effective ones devote thought and practice to their verbal and nonverbal communication. Selecting words that convey your intended meanings and that create strong images for listeners is important. Equally important is using effective gestures, paralanguage, and movement. Because public speaking is enlarged conversation, nonverbal behaviors generally should be more vigorous and commanding than those we use in personal communication.

CHALLENGES IN PUBLIC SPEAKING

Like other forms of communication, public speaking includes challenges. We'll discuss three challenges that are particularly important in public presentations.

Understanding and Controlling Speaking Anxiety

One of the most common challenges for public speakers is anxiety. Contrary to what many people think, however, communication apprehension (sometimes called stage fright) is common and can actually enhance speaking effectiveness. The communication situations that prompt apprehension vary among people, as the commentaries by Tomoko and Trish illustrate.

Tomoko

Talking to a big group of people is no problem for me. I like being able to prepare what I want to say in advance and to control what happens. But I get very nervous about one-on-one talking. It's too personal and spontaneous for me to feel secure about what will happen.

Trish

I can talk all day with one friend or a few of them and be totally at ease, but put me in front of a group of people and I just freeze. I feel I'm on display or something and everything I say has to be perfect and it all depends on me. It's just a huge pressure.

Both Trish and Tomoko are normal in feeling some anxiety about specific communication situations. Few people don't sometimes feel apprehensive about talking with others (Richmond & McCroskey, 1992). What many people don't realize is that a degree of anxiety is natural and may actually improve communication. When we are anxious, we become more alert and energetic, largely because our bodies produce adrenaline and extra blood sugar, which enhance our vigilance (Bostrom, 1988). The burst of adrenaline increases vitality, which can make speakers more dynamic and compelling (Bradley, 1978). You can channel the extra energy that accompanies public speaking into gestures and movement that enhance your presentation.

You should also realize that anxiety is common for seasoned speakers. Many politicians feel nervous before and during a speech, even though they have made hundreds or even thousands of speeches. Likewise, teachers who have taught for years usually feel tension before meeting a class, and seasoned journalists such as Mike Wallace claim they get butterflies when conducting interviews. The energy that communication anxiety fosters allows politicians, teachers, and journalists to be more dynamic and interesting.

Although a degree of anxiety about speaking is natural, too much can interfere with effectiveness. When anxiety is great enough to hinder our ability to interact with others, communication apprehension exists. **Communication apprehension** is a

COMMUNICATION ANXIETY AMONG DEAF COMMUNICATORS

Is communication anxiety experienced only by people who communicate orally? To find out, communication researchers Melanie and Steve Booth-Butterfield (1994) studied eighty-nine students in three publicly funded residential schools for the deaf. They discovered that deaf people, like those who use oral communication, are affected by communication apprehension. Their signing is less clear, less effective, weaker, smaller, and less intense as their communication anxiety increases. They also found that deaf students have lower overall communication apprehension levels than students who hear and speak.

detrimental level of anxiety associated with real or anticipated communication encounters (McCroskey, 1977; Richmond & McCroskey, 1992). Communication apprehension exists in degrees and may occur at times other than when we're actually speaking. Many people feel anxious primarily in advance of communication situations; they worry, imagine difficulties, and dread the occasion long before the communication occurs.

Tim

The CEO at my company wants us to be like a family, so he drops into our offices to be friendly and has parties at his home. We all know he means well, but, to tell the truth, it makes us uncomfortable. We're not equals, he decides our salaries, so we can't relax and communicate naturally when he's around. I can feel the knots in my stomach when he comes into my office and initiates small talk.

Causes of Communication Apprehension Communication apprehension may be situational or chronic. Research has identified five situational factors that may generate apprehension. First, we tend to be anxious when interacting with people who are unfamiliar to us or whom we perceive as different from us. This is why intercultural communication can evoke anxiety. Second, we may feel apprehensive about communicating in uncertain situations. The first few job interviews are novel experiences that produce anxiety in many people. Third, we may feel apprehensive when we are in the spotlight. We tend to feel self-conscious and anxious that we might embarrass ourselves by acting inappropriately. Evaluation is another cause of apprehension. We are often uneasy when we're being evaluated or interacting with someone who has more status or power than we do (Motley & Molloy, 1994). For example, people sometimes feel apprehensive about talking with professors, socializing with supervisors, or meeting the parents of the person they are dating. In such cases we may feel we're inadequate and fear we won't be accepted, and that stimulates anxiety.

A final situational reason for apprehension is a past failure or failures in speaking situations. If you have had bad experiences leading groups on five occasions, chances are you will have anxiety about leading a sixth group. We may also be apprehensive if we have had one particularly dramatic failure. For example, my doctor called me one day to ask whether I would coach her for a speech she had to give to a medical society. When I asked why she thought she needed coaching, Eleanor told me that the last speech she had given was eight years earlier in medical school. She was an intern, and it was her turn to present a case to the other interns and in front of the resident who supervised her. Just before the speech she had lost her first patient to a heart attack and she was badly shaken. All her work preparing the case and rehearsing her presentation was eclipsed by the shock of losing a patient. As a result, she was disorganized, flustered, and generally ineffective. That single incident, which followed a history of successful speaking, was so traumatic that Eleanor developed acute speaking anxiety.

Some people experience communication apprehension that is not confined to specific situations. Chronic anxiety appears to be learned. In other words, we can learn to fear communication, just as some of us learn to fear dogs, heights, or lightning (DeFleur & Ball-Rokeach, 1989).

One source of learned communication apprehension is observation of other people who are anxious about communicating. A child whose parents are afraid of speaking in public and who talk about the risks and failures that accompany speaking may learn to fear communicating. If we see friends perspiring heavily and being stressed about making presentations, we may internalize their anxiety as an appropriate response to speaking situations.

Why don't all people who have anxious models develop communication apprehension? Reinforcement may be the answer (Beatty, Plax, & Kearney, 1985). Children might become chronically apprehensive if they are reprimanded for speaking in class, repeatedly told to be quiet during dinner, and punished for talking when adults are conversing. Because these children get consistently negative responses to efforts to communicate, they may learn to avoid communicating and to fear situations that require it.

Michael

To this day I have vivid memories of my father's being sick—I mean, throwing up sick—any time

Sharpen Your Skill

PERSONAL REPORT OF COMMUNICATION APPREHENSION

Instructions: Here are twenty-four statements that ask how you feel about communicating. Don't worry if some statements seem similar to other statements. In the space to the left of each item, rate the extent to which the statement describes you. Record your first impressions without analyzing the statements closely. Use the following scale:

1 = Strongly agree that the statement describes me

2 = Agree that the statement describes me

3 = Undecided how well the statement describes me

4 = Disagree that the statement describes me

5 = Strongly disagree that the statement describes me

1. I dislike participating in group discussions.
2. Generally, I am comfortable while participating in group discussions.
3. I am tense and nervous while participating in group discussions.
4. I like to get involved in group discussions.
5. Engaging in group discussion with new people makes me tense and nervous.
6. I am calm and relaxed while participating in group discussions.
7. Generally, I am nervous when I have to participate in a meeting.
8. Usually, I am calm and relaxed while participating in meetings.
9. I am calm and relaxed when I am called on to express an opinion at a meeting.
10. I am afraid to express myself at meetings.
11. Communicating at meetings usually makes me uncomfortable.
12. I am relaxed when answering questions at a meeting.
13. While participating in a conversation with a new acquaintance, I feel nervous.
14. I have no fear of speaking up in conversation.
15. Ordinarily, I am tense and nervous in conversations.
16. Ordinarily, I am calm and relaxed in conversations.
17. While conversing with a new acquaintance, I feel relaxed.
18. I'm afraid to speak up in conversations.
19. I have no fear of giving a speech.
20. Certain parts of my body feel tense and rigid while I'm giving a speech.
21. I feel relaxed while giving a speech.
22. My thoughts become confused and jumbled when I am giving a speech.
23. I face the prospect of giving a speech with confidence.
24. While giving a speech, I get so nervous I forget facts I really know.

(continued)

(continued)

Computing Your Score

This test allows you to calculate your overall communication apprehension score and your communication apprehension scores for particular speaking situations.

Group Score

Add scores for items 2, 4, and 6.

Subtract scores for items 1, 3, and 5.

Add 18 points = _________

Meeting Score

Add scores for items 8, 9, and 12.

Subtract scores for items 7, 10, and 11.

Add 18 points = _________

Dyad Score

Add scores for items 14, 16, and 17.

Subtract scores for items 13, 15, and 18.

Add 18 points = _________

Public Speaking Score

Add scores for items 19, 21, and 23.

Subtract scores for items 20, 22, and 24.

Add 18 points = _________

Total

Add the four subscores together.

Total communication apprehension score = _________

The overall scores may range from 24 to 120. (If your score is higher than 120 or less than 24, you calculated incorrectly.)

Scores of 83 or more indicate high communication apprehension. People who score in this range tend to talk little, are shy, and are somewhat withdrawn and nervous in speaking situations.

Scores of 55 or less indicate low communication apprehension. People who score in this range tend to enjoy being with others, like to talk, and feel confident in their communication ability.

Source: McCroskey, 1982.

he had to make a presentation to his work team. He would start getting edgy weeks before the presentation, then he'd get nervous, then he'd be unable to hold food down. By the day of a presentation he was a basket case. That's probably why I was so fearful of speaking until I got help.

Reducing Communication Apprehension

Michael's last sentence is important. If communication apprehension is learned, it can also be unlearned or reduced. Communication scholars have developed several methods of reducing speaking apprehension. Although we cannot discuss every method, we will examine four well-tested programs. If you have more communication apprehension than you would like, reading this section will inform you of ways to deal with it.

Systematic desensitization is a method of treating many fears, from fear of flying to fear of speaking. It focuses on reducing the tension that surrounds the feared event. When we are apprehensive, our heart rate quickens, muscles tighten, and breathing becomes more shallow (Beatty & Behnke, 1991). Systematic desensitization teaches people how to relax and thereby reduce the physiological features of anxiety. Once people learn to control their breathing and muscle tension, counselors ask them to think systematically about speaking situations of progressive difficulty. The goal is to learn to associate feeling relaxed with images of themselves in communication situations.

A second method of reducing communication apprehension is **cognitive restructuring,** which is a process of revising how people think about speaking situations. According to this method, speaking is not the problem; rather, the problem is irrational beliefs about speaking. For example, if you think you must be perfect, totally engaging, and liked by everyone who hears you, you have set yourself up for anxiety. A key part of cognitive restructuring is learning to identify and challenge negative self-statements. Users of this method would criticize the statement "My topic won't interest everyone" for assuming that others will not be interested and that any speaker can hold the attention of everyone. Michael Motley and Jennifer Molloy (1994) report that apprehension decreases when people read a short booklet that encourages them to develop new and rational views of communication. The heart of this method is to change people's perspective on public speaking so that they view it not as a unique kind of communication but as similar to conversations that they have every day.

A third technique for reducing communication apprehension is **positive visualization,** which aims to reduce speaking anxiety by guiding apprehensive speakers through imagined positive speaking experiences. This technique allows people to form mental pictures of themselves as effective speakers and to then enact those mental pictures in actual speaking situations (Hamilton, 1996). Researchers report that positive visualization is especially effective in reducing chronic communication apprehension (Ayres & Hopf, 1990; Bourhis & Allen, 1992).

The goal of positive visualization is to create detailed positive images of yourself in progressively challenging speaking situations. Instead of thinking about all the things you might do wrong and

fyi

IN YOUR MIND'S EYE

Positive visualization can enhance success in a variety of situations. In professional life, managers are coached to visualize successful negotiations and meetings. Athletes are taught to imagine playing well, and those who engage in positive visualization improve as much as athletes who physically practice their sport.

Research (Lau, 1989; Porter & Foster, 1986) shows that during positive visualization, we act like the person we see ourselves as being. Applying this to athletics, business, or speaking, successful people seem to be those who see themselves as successful.

POSITIVE VISUALIZATION

Imagine thinking about an issue that really matters to you. A friend drops by, and you talk with him about the topic. As you talk, you notice that he seems really attentive and interested in what you have to say.

Now imagine that your friend asks you to talk to his class about the topic. You can see that he thinks you could present your ideas well and that other students would be interested in hearing what you have to say.

Next, imagine that you agree to speak to his class. You go to the classroom. Notice how it looks. Visualize the sun shining in and the informal arrangement of chairs. Look at the twenty-two students in the class. Notice how they look like friends of yours: open, willing to learn something new.

Hear your friend introducing you as someone who has something important to say. You walk to the front of the class and look at the students. Several are smiling at you.

Visualize yourself starting your talk. You begin by saying that you're not used to speaking in public. Several students nod as they identify with you. Notice how you are relaxing and gaining self-confidence as they accept you. Then you state your thesis. Hear how your words flow smoothly and confidently. See the students nodding with interest. Visualize yourself moving through the short talk. Note how the students remain engaged during your speech. When you finish, the students break into applause.

negative responses listeners might have, create a vivid and detailed mental image of yourself speaking successfully. It's important to avoid self-sabotaging communication, which we discussed in Chapter 8. In positive visualization the goal is to create a positive self-fulfilling prophecy by allowing only positive thoughts about your communication.

Skills training is a fourth method of reducing communication apprehension. Whereas other approaches assume that anxiety causes communication problems, skills training assumes that lack of speaking skills causes us to be apprehensive. This method focuses on teaching people such skills as how to start conversations, organize ideas, and respond effectively to others (Phillips, 1991).

After reading about these methods of reducing communication apprehension, you may be thinking that each seems useful. If so, your thinking coincides with research that finds that a combination of all three methods is more likely to relieve speaking anxiety than any single method (Allen, Hunter, & Donahue, 1989). The major conclusion is that communication apprehension is not necessarily permanent. Ways to reduce it exist. Eliminating all communication anxiety is not desirable, however, because some vigilance can enhance a speaker's dynamism and alertness. If you experience communication apprehension that interferes with your ability to express your ideas, ask your instructor to direct you to professionals who can work with you.

Adapting to Audiences

A second challenge for public speakers is adapting to audiences, a topic we discussed earlier in this chapter and in Chapter 7. Listeners are the whole reason for speaking; without them, communication does not occur. Thus, speakers should be sensitive to listeners and adapt to their perspectives and expectations.

You should take into account the perspectives of listeners if you want them to consider your views. We consider the views of our friends when we talk with them. We think about others' perspectives when we engage in business negotiations. We use dual perspective when communicating with children, dates, and neighbors. Thus, audience analysis is important to effectiveness in all communication encounters. This implies that we should adapt our communication to the ideas, concerns, knowledge, and communication styles of those to whom we speak. To do this we must understand who our listeners are and what is most likely to inform, entertain, or persuade them.

Learning About Listeners In one of my classes, a student named Odell gave a persuasive speech designed to convince listeners to support affirmative action. He was personally compelling and dynamic in his delivery, and his ideas were well organized. The only problems were that his audience had little knowledge about affirmative action and he didn't explain exactly what the policy involves. He assumed listeners understood how affirmative action works and he focused on its positive effects. His listeners were not persuaded because Odell failed to give them information necessary to their support. Odell's speech also illustrates our earlier point that speeches often combine more than one speaking purpose; in this case, giving information was essential to Odell's larger goal of persuading listeners.

In another class, a student named Christie spoke passionately about the morality of vegetarianism. She provided dramatic evidence of the cruelty animals suffer as they are raised and slaughtered. When we polled students after her speech, only two had been persuaded to consider vegetarianism. Why was Christie ineffective? She did not recognize and address listeners' beliefs that vegetarianism is not healthful and that vegetarian foods are unappetizing. Christie mistakenly assumed that listeners would know that it is easy to eat nutritiously without consuming meat, and she assumed they would understand that vegetarian foods can taste good. However, her listeners didn't know these things, and they weren't about to consider a diet that they thought wasn't nutritious or palatable.

The mistake that Christie and Odell made was not adapting to their audiences. It is impossible to entertain, inform, or persuade people if we do not consider their perspectives on our topics. Speakers need to understand what listeners already know and believe and what reservations they might have about what we say (McGuire, 1989). To paraphrase the advice of an ancient Greek rhetorician, "The fool persuades me with his or her reasons, the wise person with my own." The advice that effective speakers understand and work with listeners' reasons, values, knowledge, and concerns is as wise today as it was more than two thousand years ago.

Tailoring Speeches to Listeners To adapt communication to listeners, effective speakers ask themselves what their listeners already know about the topic. What attitudes and beliefs do they have about the topic? Answers to key questions such as these provide a speaker with important information for crafting an effective speech.

Although politicians and corporations can afford to conduct sophisticated polls to find out what people know, want, think, and believe, most of us don't have the resources to do that. So how do ordinary people engage in goal-focused analysis? One answer is to be observant. Usually, a speaker has some experience in interacting with listeners or people similar to listeners. Drawing on past interactions, a speaker may be able to discern a great deal about the knowledge, attitudes, and beliefs of listeners.

Gathering information about listeners through conversations or surveys is also appropriate. For example, once I was asked to speak on women leaders at a governor's leadership conference. To prepare my presentation, I asked the conference planners to send me information about the occupations and ages of people attending the conference. In addition, I asked the planners to survey conferees about their experience as leaders and working with women leaders. The material I received informed me about the level of experience and the attitudes and biases in my listeners. Then I could adapt my speech to what they knew and believed.

By taking listeners into consideration, you build a presentation that is interactive and respectful. As we learned earlier in this chapter, listeners tend to confer credibility on speakers who show that they understand listeners and who adapt presentations to listeners' perspectives, knowledge, and expectations.

Listening Critically to Speakers

A final challenge is to listen critically to public discourse that others present. Because we often find ourselves in the role of listener, we should know how to listen well and critically to ideas that others present. As you will recall from Chapter 6, critical listening involves attending mindfully to communication in order to evaluate its merit. Critical listeners assess whether a speaker is informed and ethical and whether a speech is soundly reasoned and supported.

The first step in critical listening is to take in and understand what a speaker says. You cannot evaluate an argument or idea until you have grasped it and the information that supports it. Thus, effective listening requires you to concentrate on what a speaker says. You can focus your listening by asking questions such as

- What does the speaker announce as the purpose of the talk?
- What evidence does the speaker provide to support claims?
- Does the speaker have experience that qualifies him or her to speak on this topic?
- Does the speaker have any vested interest in what she or he advocates?

You probably noticed that these questions parallel those we identified in our earlier discussion of ways to improve your credibility when you are making speeches. The questions help you zero in on what others say so that you can make informed judgments of their credibility and the credibility of their ideas.

To listen critically, you should suspend your preconceptions about topics and speakers. You need not abandon your ideas, but you should set them aside long enough to listen openly to a speech, especially if you are predisposed to disagree with it. By granting a full and fair hearing to others and ideas that differ from yours, you increase the likelihood that your perspective and ideas will be well informed and carefully reasoned.

Summary

In this chapter we have discussed the role of public speaking in everyday life. We began by dispelling the widely held misperception that only a few highly visible people engage in public speaking. As we saw, most of us will engage in public presentations in the normal course of professional, civic, and personal life.

In the first part of the chapter we noted that although public speaking is similar in many ways to other kinds of communication, it is distinct in the greater planning and practice it involves and the less obvious contributions of listeners. We also identified entertaining, informing, and persuading as general purposes of public speaking, and we noted that these goals often overlap.

In the second section of this chapter we described what's involved in planning, researching, organizing, and delivering public speeches. Throughout our discussion we highlighted how each aspect of developing a speech influences the credibility that listeners confer on speakers. To earn credibility, speakers should demonstrate that they are knowledgeable (mentioning personal experience with the topic and including good evidence), trustworthy (making ethical choices that show respect for listeners and the integrity of evidence), and dynamic (engaging delivery).

The third section of the chapter focused on three challenges for communicating in public situations. Perhaps the most common challenge is communication apprehension, which is normal and can be helpful in energizing speakers. If speaking anxiety is sufficient to hinder effective communication, ways to reduce it exist, and we reviewed four of these. A second challenge, adapting to listeners, is critical to effective public speaking. In our discussion, we emphasized that speakers have an ethical responsibility to consider listeners' perspectives, knowledge, and expectations as they plan, prepare, and present speeches. A final challenge is listening critically to public speeches by others. Good listeners suspend their views long enough to give a full and fair hearing to what others say. As they listen, they identify and evaluate the quality of speakers' experience, evidence, and reasoning, which allows them to make informed critical assessments of the ideas presented.

Public communication is vital to personal and professional success and to the health of our society. Not reserved for people who have high status or are in the public limelight, public speaking is a basic skill for us all. In this chapter we have seen what is involved in presenting and listening to public presentations, and we have identified ways to enhance our effectiveness in this vital realm of social life.

FOR FURTHER REFLECTION AND DISCUSSION

1. What was your overall score on the Personal Report of Communication Apprehension? Which of your subscores was the highest? Are the results of your test congruent with your perceptions of your comfort in talking with others? Are you concerned about your anxiety in any communication situations? If so, what might you do to reduce it?
2. Think about presentations that you hear (lectures by professors, talks on campus). How much do these speakers seem to take the audience into consideration in what they say? Does this affect the speakers' effectiveness?
3. Note examples of narrative speaking in everyday life. Preachers, rabbis, and priests use stories, or parables, to make points in their sermons. Teachers rely on stories to bring conceptual material to life. How much is storytelling part of communication in your community?
4. Use your *InfoTrac College Edition* to find examples of public speeches. Using *PowerTrac,* select *Vital Speeches*. You may then instruct the program to search for speeches by a particular speaker, such as Martin Luther King, Jr., or by a topic, such as health care. Read two speeches and identify how they conform to or depart from principles discussed in this chapter.
5. During the next week, pay attention to evidence cited by others in public presentations. You might note what evidence is used on news programs, by professors in classes, and by special speakers on your campus. Evaluate the effectiveness of evidence that others use. Are visuals clear and uncluttered? Do speakers explain the qualifications of sources they cite, and are those sources adequately unbiased? What examples and analogies are presented, and how effective are they?
6. Note the use of stories to add interest and effect to public presentations. Describe a speaker who uses a story effectively and one who uses a story ineffectively. What are the differences between them? What conclusions can you draw about the effective use of stories in public presentations?
7. To appreciate the difference between written and oral styles, select *Vital Speeches* on your *InfoTrac College Edition.* Print out one speech and identify examples of oral style in the speech.
8. In class, give short one- to two-minute impromptu speeches about your favorite activity or some other topic with which you are already familiar. Next, spend two days preparing an extemporaneous speech on the same topic. How do the two speeches differ in quality and effectiveness?

KEY TERMS

Speech to entertain
Narrative speaking
Speech to inform
Speech to persuade
Credibility
Initial credibility
Derived credibility
Terminal credibility
Specific purpose
Thesis statement
Evidence
Statistics
Examples
Comparisons (analogies)
Quotations
Visual aids
Halo effect
Transitions
Oral style
Impromptu delivery
Extemporaneous delivery
Manuscript delivery
Memorized delivery
Communication apprehension
Systematic desensitization
Cognitive restructuring
Positive visualization
Skills training

Mass Communication

LEARNING OBJECTIVES

To understand

1. How the media shape our thinking
2. How mass communication affects our perceptions of events and people
3. Whether mass communication fosters a global village
4. What the mean world syndrome is
5. How to think critically about mass communication

To launch our discussion of mass communication, answer these four questions:

1. In an average week, what do you think is the chance that you will be involved in some form of violence?
   A. One in 100.
   B. Ten in 100.
   C. Twenty-five in 100.
   D. One in 200.
2. During the feminist movement of the 1960s how many bras were burned in public protest?
   A. One hundred bras were burned.
   B. Ten bras were burned.
   C. One bra was burned as a symbolic protest.
   D. No bras were burned in public protest.
3. On an annual basis, what percentage of crimes in the United States are violent crimes such as murder, rape, robbery, and assault?
   A. 75%.
   B. 50%.
   C. 25%.
   D. 10%.
4. Who left the first-year class at the Citadel during the first week of school in 1995?
   A. Shannon Faulkner.
   B. Shannon Faulkner and five male cadets.
   C. Shannon Faulkner and ten male cadets.
   D. Shannon Faulkner and more than twenty male cadets.

The correct answer for each item is *D*. The more time you spend watching television, the more likely you are to have answered one or more questions incorrectly. Mass media, especially television, exaggerate the extent of violence in the world. The more television you watch, the more likely you are to overestimate the amount of violent crime in the United States (question 3) and the probability that you personally will be a victim of violent crime (question 1). Heavy television viewers also tend to underestimate the number of people arrested and convicted in trials.

Mass media also shape (or misshape) our perceptions of events. Many of my students believe that radical feminists staged a public bra burning to protest the Miss America Pageant's focus on women as sex objects. In reality, no public bra burning occurred in the 1960s. Feminists considered burning a bra in protest but rejected the idea. However, a reporter heard of the plan and reported it as factual. The story was picked up by newspapers, radio, and television (Faludi, 1991; Hanisch, 1970). Millions of Americans accepted the report as true, which may explain why even today some people refer to "bra-burning feminists." In 1995 media spotlighted Shannon Faulkner's decision to leave the Citadel during Hell Week, the initial training period for all entering students at the formerly all-male military school. What media did *not* emphasize was that more than 20 of the 600 male cadets also quit that week. The media's decision to focus on Faulkner's withdrawal and not on all the men who also left created in many people the false idea that only the lone woman had departed.

Mass communication powerfully affects our attitudes and beliefs, as well as our perspective on social life. Today **mass communication** is a major source of information, companionship, and entertainment. Yet mass communication does more than report information and entertain us. It also presents us with views of human beings, events, issues, and cultural life. Mass communication also grants a hearing and visibility to some people and points of views, whereas it mutes other voices and viewpoints. Thus mass communication affects our perceptions of issues, events, and people.

The first section of this chapter describes the evolution of mass communication and some of its effects and functions. We'll explore relationships between media, our views of the world, and how we think, feel, and act. In the second section of this chapter we'll consider challenges for us as we interact with mass communication.

UNDERSTANDING MASS COMMUNICATION

Mass communication includes all media that address mass audiences. Included in mass communication are books, film, television, radio, newspapers, magazines, and other forms of visual and print communication that reach masses of people. Mass communication also includes computer technologies such as the Web and WebTV that reach a great number of people, but it does not include one-on-one electronic communication such as email messages exchanged by friends.

Media History of Human Civilization

More than 30 years ago Marshall McLuhan emerged as a prophet of the media. He claimed that the dominant media at any given time in a society strongly shape both individual and collective life. To explain his ideas, McLuhan traced changes in Western society by identifying media that emerged and dominated in four distinct eras (Figure 14.1; McLuhan, 1962, 1964; McLuhan & Fiore, 1967).

The Tribal Epoch During the **tribal epoch** the oral tradition reigned. People communicated face to face and gave and got immediate feedback. Oral cultures were knitted together by stories and rituals that passed along the history and traditions of a culture, as well as by oral transmission of information and forms of entertainment. Reliance on the spoken word for information and recreation fostered cohesive communities and made hearing a dominant sense (McLuhan, 1969). Tribal communities and the oral tradition they foster have not

Figure 14.1 Media Epochs in Human History

Tribal Epoch	Literate Epoch	Print Epoch	Electronic Epoch
	2000 B.C.	1450	1850
talking (hearing)	alphabet (sight)	book (sight)	telegraph (hearing)

disappeared altogether. Although they no longer prevail in the United States, oral cultures continue among insulated communities in regions such as Appalachia, as well as groups that deliberately isolate themselves from mainstream culture (such as the Amish). Oral cultures also prevail in many undeveloped countries.

The Literate Epoch Invention of the phonetic alphabet ushered in the **literate epoch** in many societies. Writing was based on a symbol system that allowed people to communicate without face-to-face interaction. With written communication came changes in human life. The emergence of written communication allowed people to gain information privately, away from others in their communities. Because we can reread printed materials, they require less memory than oral communication. The alphabet also fostered ascendance of sight as a primary sense. For those who could read and write, sight supplanted hearing as a dominant sense. Writing also established a linear form for communication. In writing, letter follows letter, word follows word, sentence follows sentence. According to

fyi

THE MEDIUM IS THE MESSAGE/MASSAGE

Marshall McLuhan is probably best known for his statement, "The medium is the message." For him, it had multiple meanings (McLuhan & Fiore, 1967). It implied, first, that the medium of communication determines the substance of communication. In other words, although the content of communication is not irrelevant, it is less important than the form or medium of communication. For example, McLuhan argued that the act of watching television shapes how we think, regardless of what we watch on television. He wrote that the dominant media of an age are more influential in our lives than any specific content conveyed by those media.

"The medium is the message" had other meanings for McLuhan. By changing only one letter, the statement becomes "The medium is the massage." This implies that media massage our consciousness and transform our perceptions. Finally, McLuhan sometimes made a play on words by saying "The medium is the mass-age," by which he meant that the dominant medium had become mass communication.

■ *Here a Pueblo Indian man holds a homemade drum while telling his niece about her Pueblo heritage.*

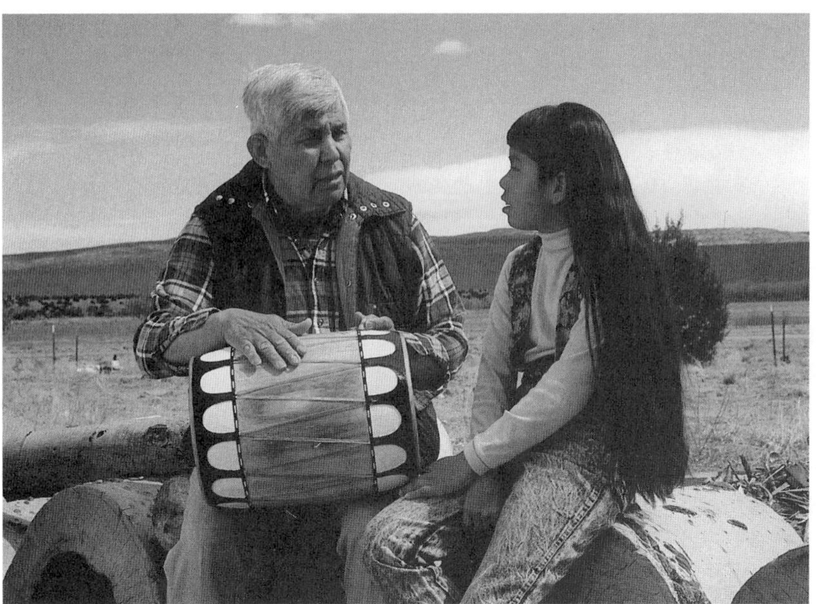

© Lawrence Migdale/Tony Stone Images

McLuhan, the continuous sequential order of print cultivated linear thinking and, with that, the development of disciplines such as mathematics that are based on linear logic. Diminished in prominence was the more fluid, weblike communication form typical of storytelling.

Derek

I spent two years as a Peace Corps volunteer in some of the smaller and poorer countries in Africa. It was an incredible experience to live in societies that had no mass communication. Information was passed along by visitors who traveled into villages or by villagers who traveled to one of the larger cities and returned with news. What I noticed most about these societies is that people interact with each other more and more intensely than in the United States. Talking is living, talking is information, talking is entertainment, talking is history in oral cultures.

The Print Epoch Although invention of the alphabet made written communication possible, print did not immediately gain prominence as the preferred medium of communication. When the alphabet was first developed, monks and scribes laboriously copied individual books and other written materials. There was no way to mass-produce the written word. Thus reading and access to print media were restricted to the more elite classes of society. They were not immediately available to the majority of people.

The **print epoch** began when Gutenberg invented the printing press in the fifteenth century, and literacy ascended in human history. The printing press made possible the printing of thousands of copies of a single book at moderate cost. Thus the printed word was no longer restricted to people with status and money; instead, it was increasingly accessible to members of all socioeconomic groups, making print a mainstream medium. McLuhan asserted that the printing press was the first mechanism for mass production, which is why he credited it with inaugurating the industrial revolution (McLuhan, 1962). Like other evolutions in media, the printing press changed human life. Reliance on the visual sense was no longer restricted to the elite who had access to individually copied books and print matter. The capability to mass-produce printed material made visual perception dominant and pervasive. In addition, mass-produced writing cultivated homogeneity because the same message could be delivered to many people. At the same time, widely available printed material further fragmented communities because people no longer needed to be together to share information and tell stories. Each woman and man could read a book, newspaper, or magazine in isolation from others. No longer was face-to-face contact necessary for communication to occur (McLuhan & Fiore, 1967).

The Electronic Epoch The dominance of print as a medium and the eye as a primary sense organ diminished with the invention of the telegraph, which was the forerunner of the **electronic epoch** in human history. Reliance on print and the distance between people who mass-produced written material declined, and electronic communication once again brought people together. According to McLuhan (1969), electronic media revived the oral tradition and made hearing and touch preeminent.

The telegraph was only the first of a long line of electronic media with the potential to revitalize a sense of community among people. We listen to the radio and understand what is happening in Rwanda or Zambia, we see a newscast and know what our president said and how he looked when he spoke, and we read a magazine and learn about everything from economic conditions to fashion trends. No longer do we know only about people and events in our immediate physical locations. The increased contact made possible by electronic communication led McLuhan to claim that we are becoming "a global village" (McLuhan & Fiore, 1967). Other people worry that electronic communication isolates people from one another because each of us interacts with a television, radio, or personal computer instead of interacting with other human beings.

To understand McLuhan's ideas, reflect on the changes brought about with the emergence of new media in each of the epochs we have just discussed. Humans adapt to their environments by developing

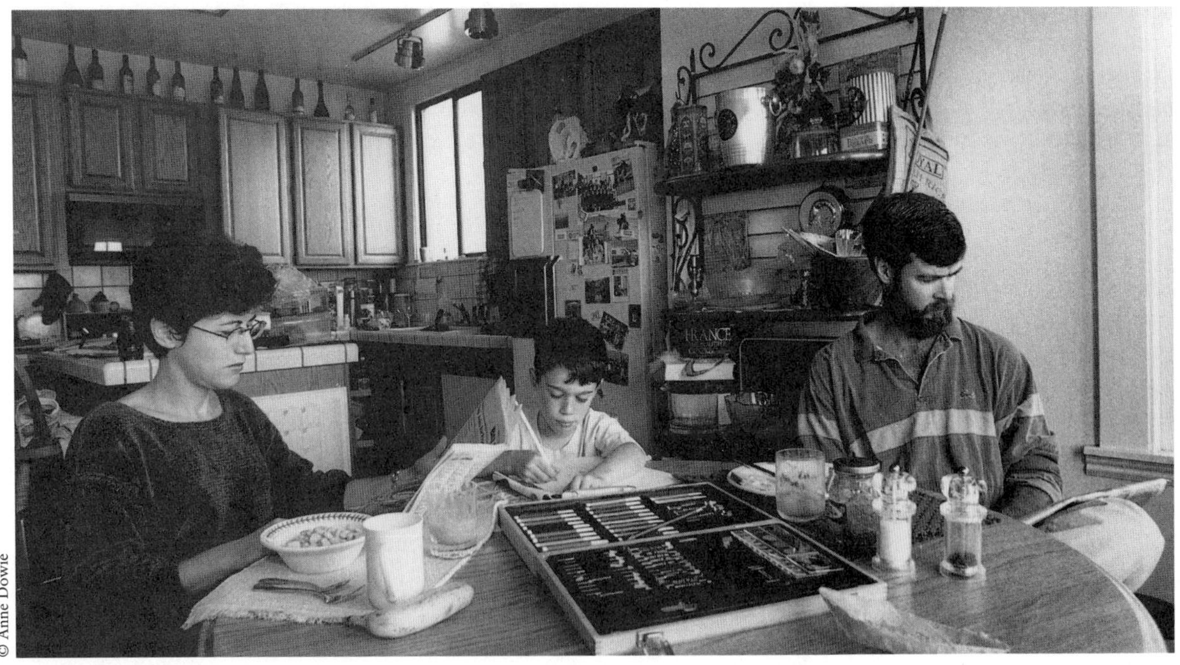

■ *Does mass communication discourage face-to-face interaction? How many families share a table without talking?*

Sharpen Your Skill

MASSAGING THE MESSAGE

Call to mind a recent experience in your life. Describe that experience using a pen and sheet of paper. Next, share the experience with someone by talking in person. Third, recount the experience in an email message to an acquaintance.

How does the message change as you change the medium of conveying it? How does your sense of the message vary with the different media for transmitting it?

sensory abilities that enhance their ability to survive and function. When listening and speaking were the only ways to convey information, we developed keen oral and aural senses and prodigious memories. Once people could rely on printed forms of communication, sight supplanted hearing and speaking as the dominant sense, and memory became less important.

McLuhan died in 1980. He left a partial manuscript that described the computer as a new medium that would change human beings again. Media scholar Paul Levinson (1999) maintains that much of McLuhan's thinking correctly anticipated the impact of digital communication. Were McLuhan alive today, he probably would be calling attention to ways in which communication technologies are shaping how we think and how our senses are adapting in response to the media of this era.

Meggan

I think the Web has done more to expand individuals than anything ever invented. You can browse and learn all kinds of things and get involved with an amazing range of people that you would never meet in person. Computers have opened so many new doors for communication among people.

Shelton

My 6-year-old spends more time with his computer than he does with family or friends. He's on the Internet each morning before he goes to school. He refuses to be in extracurricular activities because after-school meetings would reduce time on the Web. I worry he won't develop social skills and learn to adjust to different people when 90% of the time he's using the computer to talk with groups that share his interests. That's not very broadening.

Functions and Effects of Mass Communication

In this section we'll focus on four views of the functions and effects of mass communication.

Gratification Think about the last time you went to a movie. Did you attend because the story mattered to you? Did you go to escape from problems and worries? Did you attend because it featured stars you like? According to a perspective called **uses and gratification theory,** we choose to attend to mass communication in order to gratify ourselves (Communication Research, 1979; Katz, Blumler, & Gurevitch, 1974). In our quest for both immediate and deferred gratification, we select media that we think will reward us. For example, if you are bored and want excitement, you might watch an action film. If you are interested in national affairs, you might listen to National Public Radio. If you are concerned about rain for the game, you might watch the Weather Channel.

A GRATIFYING FORMULA

Uses and gratification theorists (Schramm & Porter, 1982) advance the following formula to explain why people select specific media:

Promise of reward ÷ Effort required = Probability of selection

Rewards may be immediate or delayed. Effort includes the difficulty of obtaining media and the time and expense required. The probability that you will choose a specific medium is the promise of reward divided by the effort required to obtain it. Consider an example. Perhaps you want some entertainment to take your mind off a problem. You consider watching television, going out to a movie, reading a novel, and renting a film. If all media offer equally gratifying choices, you are likely to watch TV because that requires the least effort. If the TV offers nothing exciting, however, the reward of that medium is lower, so you might select the novel, film, or video.

Uses and gratification theory assumes that people are active agents who make deliberate choices among media in order to gratify themselves. We use media to gain information, alleviate loneliness, divert us from problems, and so forth. In other words, uses and gratification theory assumes that people exercise control over media, a view that not all media scholars share. The exploding number of satellite and cable channels expands our options for choosing media that gratify us.

Agenda Setting A second view of media effects asserts that media establish an agenda for us by spotlighting some issues, events, and people and downplaying others. Agenda setting is the media's ability to select and call to the public's attention ideas, events, and people (Agee, Ault, & Emery, 1996). In the example of cadets who withdrew from the Citadel in 1995, the media selected Shannon Faulkner and called her to the public's attention. Thus, we were aware of her departure from the

A NOVEL KIND OF NOVEL

Imagine reading a novel that has no definite beginning, plot line, or ending. If a particular character or plot line interests you, you can follow it and ignore the rest of the novel. If you don't like the way a plot is evolving, you can change it. It's rather like reading a book that was meant to have its pages shuffled. Hypertext fiction is here. Unlike conventional novels, hypertext tales have no fixed progression. Instead, readers can structure the story as they move through it. On each page, there are words, phrases, and images that readers can click with a mouse to link them to other pages. Users can download some links to hear recorded dialogue and sound effects. As the links in a story multiply, so do the ways different readers can structure it. Different readers of hypertext fiction are not likely to experience the same story.

Source: Blanton, 1996.

fyi

WHO'S SETTING YOUR AGENDA?

Ralph Nader criticizes media not just for what they do, but also for what they do *not* do and what they do *not* cover. And he criticizes us as consumers of mass media for not noticing absences in coverage. In a 1996 article, Nader wrote, "It does not occur to 14 million college students that there is no thirty-minute weekly national television program focusing on significant campus activities outside of the athletic arena. Few workers critical of the powers-that-be seem to think there should be television and radio programs devoted to labor as there are to business" (p. 10). Nader urges us to think critically about what media do and do not offer us and how both what's offered and what's missing affect how we think about ourselves and society.

military school but may not have realized that a number of male cadets also left. Shortly after the Clintons moved to the White House, the media focused on Hillary Rodham Clinton's hairstyle and gave far less attention to her activities.

Alex Edelstein (1993) observes that media don't actually tell us what to think but rather tell us what to think about. In other words, media set the agenda for topics in public consciousness. Consider the amount of current interest in the sexual activities (real or rumored) of public figures, especially politicians. Historical accounts document extramarital sexual activities of many past presidents, but media at the time didn't put these on the public agenda. In our era, media do call the sexual lives of public figures to our attention, making us more aware of this issue than the public was in previous times.

Kurt Lewin coined the term **gatekeeper** in 1947 to describe the people and groups that decide which messages pass through the gates that control information flow to reach consumers. Since Lewin introduced the term, communication researchers have studied the ways in which individuals and groups control what stories and ideas are included in mass communication (Altheide, 1974; Gitlin, 1980; Shaw, 1999; Shoemaker, 1991). Gatekeepers screen messages, stories, and perspectives to create messages (programs, interviews, news clips) that shape our perceptions of events and people.

Mass communication has many gatekeepers. Editors of newspapers, books, and magazines screen the information that gets to readers; owners, executives, and producers filter information for radio and television programs; advertisers and political groups may also intervene to influence which messages get through to end users of mass communication. For example, radio stations that are owned and financed by conservatives air Rush Limbaugh's comments but not those of progressives and liberals. Radio stations owned and funded by more liberal groups are likely to shut the gate on Rush Limbaugh but include Molly Ivins and Mark Shields. As a result, listeners of the two stations are likely to be aware of different issues and to have different perspectives on social life. America Online (AOL), a major Internet service provider, chooses which companies, groups, and issues to highlight on the pop-up menus that greet users each time they sign on. This gives visibility to the groups, people, and issues that AOL, not users, decides to emphasize.

Gatekeepers screen not only information content but also sources of information. Writers, producers, and others who control programming decide which experts to feature, which people in the news to cover, and which perspectives on events to include. An example of bias in mass communication is the tendency to use members of minority groups almost exclusively as authorities on issues involving

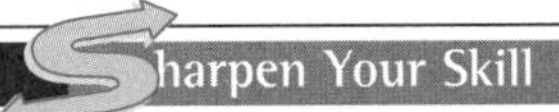

GATEKEEPING THE GATEKEEPERS

Watch several episodes of a popular talk show hosted by such people as Oprah Winfrey, Geraldo, or Sally Jesse Raphael. List the topics of the shows and describe the people who were featured on them. What conclusions can you draw about the biases and perspectives that shape the gatekeeping of each host?

race. This can foster the misperception that members of minorities have expertise only about ethnicity.

There is also evidence of racial bias in media accounts of crime stories. Oscar Gandy (1994), a professor at the Annenberg School for Communication, is concerned that newspapers present minority citizens as violent criminals more often than they present European Americans as violent criminals and more often than they present minorities in positive stories. Gandy claims that this pattern distorts our perceptions of the extent to which members of different races perpetrate violent crimes. This is important because, as Gandy notes, "The framing of stories influences what we understand about the world in which we live" (p. 47).

Racial bias has also been found in programming on the three major commercial television networks. According to communication professor Ralph Entman (1994), black defendants are more likely than white ones to be unnamed and to be shown in mug shots, which places them in a context associated with criminality. White defendants, reports Entman, are more likely to be named as individuals and to be portrayed in a series of videos and still photos that provide less criminal and more individual visions of them.

Cultivating Worldviews A third view of the effects of mass communication is based on **cultivation theory,** which claims that television cultivates, or promotes, a worldview that is inaccurate but that viewers nonetheless assume reflects real life. This theory is concerned exclusively with the medium of television, which it claims creates a synthetic reality that shapes heavy viewers' perspectives and beliefs about the world (Gerbner, 1990; Gerbner, Gross, Morgan, & Signorielli, 1986; Signorielli & Morgan, 1990).

Cultivation is the cumulative process by which television fosters beliefs about social reality. According to the theory, television fosters particular and often unrealistic understandings of the world as being more violent and dangerous than statistics on actual violence show it is. Thus, goes the reasoning, watching television promotes distorted views of life. The word *cumulative* is important to understanding cultivation. Researchers don't argue that a particular program has significant effects on what viewers believe. However, they claim that watching television over a long period of time affects viewers' basic views of the world. By extension, the more television people watch, the more distorted their ideas about life are likely to be. Simply put, the theory claims that television cumulatively cultivates a synthetic worldview that heavy viewers are likely to assume represents reality.

To open this chapter I asked you to answer questions based on surveys conducted in research on cultivation theory. Heavy television viewers are more likely to have beliefs that reflect the worldview portrayed by television, which is not equivalent to a worldview based on empirical data. In television entertainment programming, 77% of major characters who commit crimes perpetrate acts of violence. Compare this to the fact that roughly 10% of reported real crimes are violent. In prime-time entertainment programming on commercial networks, 86% of the depictions of the criminal justice system in the United States portray criminals as never being brought to trial or as getting off at trial (Choi, Massey, & Baran, 1988). Yet

fyi THE ROOTS OF CULTIVATION THEORY

Cultivation theory emerged in 1967 when George Gerbner lent his scientific expertise to two national efforts to understand media's effects: the National Commission on the Causes and Prevention of Violence, which met in 1967 and 1968, and the Surgeon General's Scientific Advisory Committee on Television and Social Behavior, which conferred during 1972. Both councils were concerned with violence and potential connections between televised violence and increases in both violence and tolerance of violence. The genesis of cultivation theory in national studies of violence explains why it concentrates on how television cultivates attitudes and beliefs about violence and views of the world as a dangerous place.

of the nearly 11,000 felony arrests in California in 1 year, 80% went to trial, and 88% of the trials resulted in convictions. Prime-time entertainment programs portray 64% of characters as involved in violence, so heavy viewing of television is likely to cultivate the belief that being a victim of violence is common. In the real world, however, the average person has a 1 in 200 chance of being involved in a violent crime in any week.

The world of television teems with violence. As I was writing this chapter in the summer of 1999, The Annenberg Public Policy center reported that 28% of children's shows include four or more acts of violence and fully 75% of these programs do not carry the FV (fantasy violence) rating ("Value of Children's Shows," 1999). By age 6 the average child in the United States has watched 5,000 hours of television; by age 18 the average person has watched

THE MEAN WORLD SYNDROME

The basic worldview studied by cultivation theorists is exemplified in research on the **mean world syndrome** (Gerbner et al., 1986). The mean world syndrome is the belief that the world is a dangerous place, full of mean people who cannot be trusted and who are likely to harm us. Although less than 1% of the U.S. population is victimized by violent crime in any year, television presents the world as a dangerous place in which everyone is at risk.

fully 19,000 hours of television. What happens during all the hours in front of the television set? According to one researcher, the average 18-year-old in the United States has viewed 200,000 separate acts of violence on television, including 40,000 murders (Zuckerman, 1993). Given the incidence of violence on television, it's no wonder that many heavy viewers think the world is more violent than crime reports show it is.

Kelly

I didn't think much about sex and violence on TV until my daughter was old enough to watch. When she was four, I found her watching an MTV program that was absolutely pornographic. What does seeing that do to the mind of a four-year-old girl? We don't let her watch TV now unless we can monitor what she sees. I think we're going to get one of those V-chips to block out programs she shouldn't see.

Why is violence so much greater on television than in real life? The answer varies with different kinds of programs. Violence in best-selling action novels, prime-time entertainment shows, and cartoons may be used to interest and stimulate consumers. Although most people in real life aren't shooting and mugging each other, many people might find it dull to watch shows with little action. The high incidence of violence in news programming reflects in part the fact that the abnormal is more newsworthy than the normal (Mander, 1999). It isn't news that 99.9% of couples are either getting along or working out their problems in nonviolent ways; it is news when Lorena Bobbitt amputates her husband's penis or O. J. Simpson's wife is murdered (D. Hunt, 1999). It isn't news that most of us grumble about big government but refrain from violent protest; it is news when someone blows up the Federal Building in Oklahoma City and cites dissatisfaction with big government as a motive. Simply put, violence is news.

In a study of more than 2,000 children's programs aired between 1967 and 1985, Nancy Signorielli (1990) found that 71% of prime-time and 94% of weekend programs included acts of violence. Each hour of prime-time programming averaged more than five acts of violence and weekend programming averaged more than six. Signorielli then surveyed people at five different times to learn their views of the world. Her findings show that heavy viewers are more likely to see the world as a mean place and people as untrustworthy than are lighter viewers. This study is consistent with cultivation theory's claim that television viewing has a cumulative effect on basic views of the world.

Another reason for the inordinate violence shown on news programs is the breadth of coverage that most news broadcasts attempt. A 30-minute news program presents approximately fifteen news items. When we subtract the time for the twenty-five to thirty commercials in a half-hour news program, the total time for presenting news is closer to 23 minutes (Ferrante, 1995). Because so much information is presented so quickly, there is little analysis, depth, or reflection. Instead, the stories are capsuled in

Sharpen Your Skill

WHY NEWS DOESN'T STICK WITH US

Make a list of all the news events (not sports reports or weather information) you recall from last night's news program (or the most recent news program you watched). How many specific news events do you recall? If you're like most people, you don't remember many events presented on television news because they are presented so quickly and superficially that viewers seldom absorb or reflect on them. What does this experience suggest to you about the newsworthiness of news programming?

dramatic film clips. In his 1985 book *Amusing Ourselves to Death,* cultural critic Neil Postman argues that the fast and furious format of news programming creates the overall impression that the world is unmanageable, beyond our control, and filled with danger and violence. Consequently, reports on crime and violence may do less to enhance understanding and informed response than to agitate, scare, and intimidate us.

Perhaps you are thinking that few people confuse what they see on television with real life. Research shows that this may not be the case. Children's sex-role stereotypes seem directly related to the amount of commercial television (but not educational television) they watch. In a comparison of communities that did not have television with ones that did, one researcher (Kimball, 1986) found that children who watched commercial television had more sex-stereotypical views of women and men than children who didn't view television. When television was introduced into the communities that had not had it, children's sex-stereotypical attitudes increased.

The effects of television on our views of reality are also evident in the finding that nonstereotypical portrayals of the sexes on television actually decrease viewers' sex stereotypes (Rosenwasser, Lingenfelter, & Harrington, 1989). Research also finds that media views of relationships cultivate unrealistic views of what a normal relationship is. MTV programming strongly emphasizes eroticism and sublime sex, and people who watch a lot of MTV have been shown to have expectations for sexual perfectionism in their relationships (Shapiro & Kroeger, 1991). Relatedly, people who read a lot of self-help books tend to have less realistic views of relationships than people who read few or no self-help guides. Investigations have also shown that people who watch sexually violent MTV are more likely to regard sexual violence as normal in relationships, and this is true of both female and male viewers (Dieter, 1989).

If we believe that all relationship problems can be fixed, sex can always be sublime, and couples live happily ever after, we're likely to be dissatisfied with real relationships that can't consistently live up to these synthesized images. If we believe violence is normal in intimate relationships, we may accept it—and its sometimes lethal consequences—in our relationships. Furthermore, if we believe that the images broadcast by media are accurate, we're likely to reject normal relationships in which people work out problems in a futile quest for the unrealistically perfect relationships depicted on television.

Kasheta

To earn money I babysit two little boys four days a week. One day they got into a fight and I broke it up. When I told them that physical violence isn't a good way to solve problems, they reeled off a list of TV characters that beat up on each other. Another day one of them referred to the little girl next door as a "ho." When I asked why he called her that, he started singing the lyrics from an MTV video he'd been watching. In that video women were called "hos." It's scary what kids absorb.

fy*i*

MEDIA-CREATED BODY IMAGES

In 1999 anthropologist and psychiatrist Anne Becker reported research that suggests that media are very powerful in shaping—or distorting—body images. For centuries the people of Fiji had been a food-loving society. People enjoyed eating and considered fleshy bodies attractive in both women and men. In fact, when someone seemed to be losing weight, acquaintances chided her or him for "going thin." All of that changed in 1995 when television stations in Fiji began broadcasting American programs such *Melrose Place, Seinfeld,* and *Beverly Hills 90210.* Within three years, an astonishing number of Fijian women began dieting and developing eating disorders. When asked why they were trying to lose weight, young Fijian woman cited characters such as Amanda (Heather Locklear) on *Melrose Place* as their model (Becker, 1999; "Fat-Phobia," 1999; Goodman, 1999).

Accounting for Cultivation What accounts for television's ability to induce belief in false worldviews? Cultivation theorists identify two mechanisms to explain the cultivation process: **mainstreaming** and **resonance.**

Mainstreaming is the effect of stabilizing and homogenizing views within a society. If television programs, from Saturday morning cartoons to prime-time dramas, feature extensive violence, viewers may come to believe that violence is common. As they interact with others, heavy viewers communicate their attitudes and thus affect the attitudes of others who watch little or no television. Thus, televised versions of life permeate the mainstream.

Describing the power of television to create mainstream views of cultural life, Gerbner and his colleagues assert that "television cultivates from infancy the very predispositions and preferences that used to be acquired from other primary sources. . . . Television has become the primary common source of socialization and everyday information (mostly in the form of entertainment) of an otherwise heterogeneous population" (1986, p. 18). Gerbner (1997a, 1997b) is highly critical of the media's impact on the public. He worries that the prevalence of media, especially television, undermines democratic principles and democratic control over national life. When media executives and advertisers control programming, media have too much power to cultivate the values, desires, and worldviews consumers hold.

The second explanation for television's capacity to cultivate worldviews is resonance, which is the extent to which media representations are congruent with personal experience. For instance, a person who has been robbed, assaulted, or raped is likely to identify with televised violence. In so doing, viewers heighten the influence of the televised message by fortifying it with their experience. In other words, when media correspond with our experiences, we are more likely to assume that they accurately represent the world in general.

Supporting Dominant Social Systems Critical scholars of communication identify a fourth function of mass communication: supporting the prevailing power relations and perspectives of society. Because individuals and groups that have benefited from the existing social structure control mass communication, they tend to approve of and support the system that has privileged them. Support of the status quo is evident in the content of mass communication, which is more likely to portray white men as good, powerful, and successful than it is to describe women or minority men in those ways. Capitalism generally is presented positively, whereas welfare typically is portrayed negatively.

Sharpen Your Skill

TESTING THE MEAN WORLD HYPOTHESIS

The following are statements adapted from the mean world index used in research. Ask ten people whether they basically agree or disagree with each statement. After respondents have answered, ask them how much television they watch on an average day. Do your results support the claim that television cultivates a mean world syndrome?

1. Most public officials are not interested in the plight of the average person.
2. Despite what some people say, the lot of the average person is getting worse, not better.
3. Most people mostly look out for themselves rather than trying to help others.
4. Most people would try to take advantage of you if they had a chance.
5. You can't be too careful in dealing with people.

Robert McChesney is a media scholar who believes that media have become a significant antidemocratic force in our society. In his recent book, *Rich Media, Poor Democracy* (1999), McChesney argues that the information revolution that was supposed to equalize citizens' access to information has benefited primarily wealthy investors, corporations, advertisers, and media itself. He says the media do not serve the people well.

Mass media are particularly powerful in representing the ideology of privileged groups as normal, right, and natural (Hall, 1986a, 1986b, 1988, 1989a, 1989b; Wood, 2001a). Television programs, from children's shows to prime-time news, represent white, heterosexual, able-bodied males as the norm in the United States, although they are actually not the majority. Magazine covers and ads, as well as billboards, portray young, able-bodied, attractive white people as the norm. Despite critiques of bias in media, minorities continue to be portrayed most often as criminals, victims, subordinates, or otherwise less than respectable people (Entman, 1994; Gandy, 1994; Wong, 1994). As I was writing this chapter, programs were announced for the fall 1999 prime-time television season. Of the 26 new comedies and dramas scheduled on major broadcast networks, not a single one features a black person in a leading role, and even in supporting roles blacks are scarce (Braxton, 1999). Even more scarce in the world of television are Latinos and Latinas, the fastest growing ethnic–racial group in the United States. Not a single one of these shows features a Latino or Latina in a leading role (Haubegger, 1999).

In books and television women continue to be depicted as dependent and in the primary identities of homemaker and mother, although most women in the United States work outside the home and have for many years (Wood, 2001b). In these and other respects, media present a worldview that is out of sync with the facts but squarely supports the dominant ideology of the culture.

We've considered four views of the functions and effects of mass communication. Uses and gratification theory asserts that people actively use media to gratify themselves. In contrast, agenda-setting and cultivation theories emphasize the ways in which media shape our perceptions through various means, including gatekeeping and the cultivation of synthetic reality. Probably each view of mass communication has some validity. Surely, we make some fairly conscious choices about how to use media. At the same time, mass communication probably influences us in ways that we don't notice. Media may foster distorted perceptions as a result of selectivity in

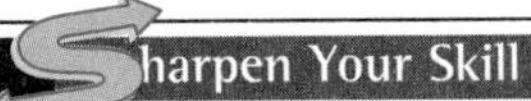

DETECTING DOMINANT VALUES IN MEDIA

Watch two hours of prime-time commercial television. Pay attention to the dominant ideology that is represented and normalized in the programming. Who are the good and bad characters? Which personal qualities are represented as admirable and which are represented as objectionable? Who are the victims and victors, the heroes and villains? What goals and values are endorsed?

issues covered and voices heard, as well as misrepresentations of social life. A fourth view, developed by critical scholars, highlights the role of mass communication as a conservative force that supports prevailing social systems and perspectives. Our discussion gives us insight into how mass communication shapes individual and cultural consciousness.

CHALLENGES FOR INTERACTING WITH MASS COMMUNICATION

Because mass communication surrounds and influences us, we have an ethical obligation to be responsible and thoughtful consumers. Two critical challenges for interacting with mass communication are to exercise critical thought and respond actively.

Exercising Critical Thought

The first challenge is to think critically about mass communication. To do this, we should first adopt a critical attitude in judging the extent to which mass communication affects people. In addition, we should exercise skills of critical listening and interpretation when we use sources of mass communication.

Develop a Balanced View of the Power of Mass Communication Because this chapter focuses on mass communication, we've concentrated on its operation and influence. Yet mass communication does not operate in isolation. It interacts with all the other elements in our world. To develop an appropriately balanced view of the influence of mass communication, we need to place this form of communication within larger social contexts that affect meaning.

Melvin DeFleur and Sandra Ball-Rokeach (1989) assert that assuming television is the only cause of viewers' attitudes is naive. They argue that television, individual viewers, and society interact in complex ways. The same argument would hold true for the influence of other mass media, such as radio, film, billboards, magazines, and newspapers. If this is so, it's inaccurate to presume that a linear relationship exists between media and individuals' attitudes.

Our view of how media affect people should also be informed by standpoint theory. As you will recall, this theory highlights the ways in which the social, symbolic, and material circumstances of different groups affect members' perceptions and knowledge. To assume that everyone responds similarly to the synthetic worldview depicted on the tube reflects the belief that all viewers have common experiences that have shaped their perceptions and interpretations. Gender, ethnicity, socioeconomic group, sexual orientation, spiritual commitments, and age are some of the many factors that create differences in human experience and thus the perspectives we bring to bear on our interaction with mass communication.

A critical attitude acknowledges the important distinction between two views of mass communication: Mass communication determines individual attitudes and social perspectives, and mass communication is one of many influences on individual attitudes and social perspectives. The former claim's untempered assertion that mass communication determines human consciousness and social life is both naive and overstated. It obscures the complex multiple influences on how we think as individuals and how we organize social life (Boulding, 1967). The latter claim represents a thoughtful critical awareness of the qualified influence of mass communication and our ability to exercise control over its effects.

Listen and Interpret Critically A second ethical principle for interacting with mass communication is to be critical in how we listen to and interpret what is presented to us. Rather than accepting news accounts unquestioningly, we should be thoughtful and skeptical. It's important to ask questions such as these:

- Why is this story getting so much attention? Whose interests are served and whose are muted?
- What is the source of statistics and other forms of evidence? Are the sources current? Do the sources have any interest in taking a specific position? (For example, tobacco companies have vested interest in denying or minimizing the harms of smoking.)
- Whose views aren't being heard?
- Are stories balanced so that a range of viewpoints is given voice (for example, in a report on environmental bills pending in Congress, do news reports include statements from the Sierra Club, industry leaders, environmental scientists, and so forth)?
- How are different people and viewpoints framed by gatekeepers (reporters, photographers, experts, etc.)?

It's equally important to be critical in interpreting other kinds of mass communication, such as music, magazines, billboards, and computer-mediated messages. When listening to popular music, ask what view of society it portrays, who and what it represents as normal, and what views of women and men it fosters. Raise the same questions about the images in magazines and on billboards. Asking questions such as these allows you to be critical and careful in assessing what mass communication presents to you.

Responding Actively

Our discussion of the influence of mass communication on individuals may have led you to think we are passive victims of media. That would be an inap-

A RIOT IN THE WORLD OF MUSIC

In Olympia, Washington, in 1990 two new bands began to attract a following. Bikini Kill and Bratmobile, the two bands, are unusual in that the band members and fans were mostly female. Rather than following the conventional route of successful bands, Bikini Kill, Bratmobile, and other women's bands created a support network for female musicians and their fans. The collective movement that resulted was named Riot Grrrls, in which fans and members of the bands are equally considered to be riot grrrls. This radically egalitarian structure opposes the idea of hierarchy that is a central thread in the dominant worldview in Western culture.

Specializing in hard-core punk music, these bands challenge prevailing practices. According to Bikini Kill, "Riot Grrrl is . . . because us girls crave records and books and fanzines that speak to us, that we feel included in . . . because we are angry at a society that tells us girl = dumb, girl = bad, girl = weak, because we see fostering and supporting girl scenes and girl artists of all kinds as integral." Shunning conventional views of femininity, Riot Grrrls bands embody anger, resistance, and assertion. They speak openly about sexual experience, and they refuse to devalue feminine experiences and qualities.

Sources: Hall, 1995; Bikini Kill, 1991, p. 1.

propriate conclusion, and it would undermine your ability to meet the ethical challenge to respond actively to mass communication.

People may respond to mass communication and the worldviews that it portrays in three ways (Fiske, 1987; S. Hall, 1982, 1989b). First, we may uncritically consume messages and their ideological underpinnings. This response is one in which we accept the view of reality that is expressed by tools of the culture, especially media. A second response is to qualify our acceptance of dominant ideology as reflected in media. For example, you might agree that in general people should be judged on merit (acceptance of a dominant cultural premise) but decide that a history of discrimination justifies some extra consideration to members of some social groups (refusal to give unconditioned assent to the dominant worldview).

A third response is to oppose prevailing perspectives. Engaging in this response requires us first to recognize that the worldviews presented in mass communication are not unvarnished truth but instead are partial, subjective perspectives that serve the interests of some individuals and groups while oppressing the interests of others in society. Second, we must find or create an alternative worldview to substitute for the one we are resisting. Individuals have strongly criticized advertising that encourages women to be passive, deferential, and obsessed with weight and appearance (Rakow, 1992). Both women and men have opposed sexual harassment, which cultural institutions historically tolerated. The Riot Grrrls invented a novel kind of music and bands that privilege women and their experiences and that reject the conventional hierarchy between performers (stars) and fans (followers).

REMAKING LANGUAGE, REMAKING THE SOCIAL WORLD

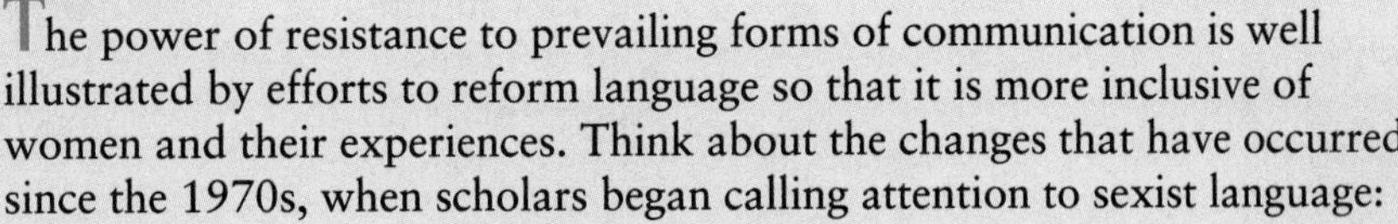

The power of resistance to prevailing forms of communication is well illustrated by efforts to reform language so that it is more inclusive of women and their experiences. Think about the changes that have occurred since the 1970s, when scholars began calling attention to sexist language:

- *Ms.* is now widely accepted as a title for women.
- Male generic terms (*he, chairman*) have been replaced by nonsexist alternatives (*he or she, chair*).
- Many women who marry choose to keep their birth names or to hyphenate their birth names and their husbands' birth names.
- Most book and journal publishers have an explicit policy prohibiting sexist language.
- The newest conventional dictionaries—*Webster's*, for instance—reflect a conscious effort to reduce the sexism and male bias in language.
- Terms such as *sexual harassment, date rape,* and *marital rape* that describe experiences nearly exclusive to women have entered general vocabulary in society.

The Web offers abundant resources to let you learn to identify and avoid sexist language, including male generic terms. Among the Web sites worth visiting is this one: http://uwc.server.fac.utexas.edu/handouts/nonsex/html. You can also use your *InfoTrac College Edition* to read research on sexist language. On EasyTrac, type "sexism and language," select *key words,* select *search,* and view recent articles on the topic.

HOW TO GET INVOLVED

If you want to learn more about gender and media or if you want to become active in working against media that devalue women and celebrate violence, visit these Web sites:

MediaWatch: http://www.mediawatch.com/
National Coalition on Television Violence: http://www.nctvv.org

Assume Agency To become an active responder, you must recognize that you are an agent who can affect what happens around you. Believing that we are powerless to control how mass communication affects us can become a self-fulfilling prophesy. Thus, not recognizing your agency could induce you to yield the degree of control you could have.

Manuel

I was really angry about a story in the local paper. It was about Mexicans who come to the U.S. The story only mentioned Mexican Americans who get in trouble with the law, are on welfare, or are illegal residents. So I wrote a letter to the editor and said the story was biased and inaccurate. The editor invited me to write an article for the opinion page and I did. In my article I described many Mexican Americans who are hard-working honest citizens who are making this country better. There were a lot of responses to my article, so I know I made a difference.

Manuel's experience demonstrates that assuming agency is not just personally empowering; it also enriches cultural life. People have an ethical responsibility to resist and redefine the messages of mass communication that they consider inaccurate or harmful (Newcomb, 1978).

Summary

In this chapter we have examined mass communication. We began our discussion by considering McLuhan's ideas about how epochs dominated by different media affected individual lives and social organization. We also considered four views of the functions and effects of mass communication. One view is that people use mass communication to gratify their interests. Two other views, agenda setting and cultivation theory, give greater emphasis to the ways in which mass communication influences what we think about (the agenda for public discussion) and how we perceive social life (the worldview that is cultivated by media). A final view is that mass communication functions to support dominant social relations, roles, and perspectives and to make them seem normal and right. Mass communication, along with other institutions and practices, creates, legitimizes, and sustains particular and partial views of social life that define the roles of specific groups within an overall culture. If you think about mass communication in your life, you'll probably realize that each of these views has some merit.

The second section of the chapter focused on two ethical challenges for our participation in mass communication. One is to adopt a critical orientation toward mass communication. This requires first that we develop a realistic, balanced perspective on the power of mass communication. Media do not exist in isolation, nor do we as consumers of mass communication. Each of us participates in multiple and diverse social systems that shape our responses to mass communication and the worldviews it presents. To be responsible participants in social life, we need to question what is included—and what is made invisible—in mass communication.

A second challenge is to assume an active voice by responding to mass communication. We have an ethical responsibility to speak out against communication that we think is inaccurate, hurtful, or wrong. And speaking out can make a difference. In 1995 Calvin Klein discontinued an ad campaign because so many individuals and groups objected to the ads. Other companies have withdrawn ads and even products in response to voices of resistance.

Power relationships and social perspectives are never fixed in cultural life. They are always open to change and negotiation among voices that offer rival views of reality. One means of negotiating social meanings is our response to mass communication. Without our consent and support, mass communication cannot exist.

FOR FURTHER REFLECTION AND DISCUSSION

1. As a class, discuss competing views of the functions and effects of mass communication. Class members should review their experiences to find support for findings of research presented in this chapter.
2. Should there be some control over the violence presented in media? Do you think viewers, especially children, are harmed by the prevalence of violence in media? Are you concerned about the lack of correspondence between the synthetic world of television violence and the actual incidence of violence in social life? If you think there should be some controls, what groups or individuals would you trust to exercise them?
3. Use your *InfoTrac College Edition* to review the last year's issues of *Broadcasting & Cable*. Identify new trends in mass communication and discuss how they fit with theories and research covered in this chapter.
4. If you know people from cultures that are still primarily oral, talk with them about communication and social life in their cultures. How do their experiences differ from those of native-born citizens of the United States? It would be worthwhile to organize a guest panel of people from other cultures to speak with your class about patterns of interaction and thought in cultures that have different dominant media.
5. Make a list of the forms of mass communication you use most often. Include newspapers, magazines, television programs, types of films, radio stations, and so forth. Describe your media environment. How do your choices of mass communication reflect and shape your identity and your social perspectives?
6. Embrace the challenge advanced in this chapter by taking an active role in responding to mass communication. Write a letter to the editor of a local paper, or write to a manufacturer to support or criticize its product or the way it advertises its product. As a class, discuss your means of assuming a voice in the life of our culture. Visit the Web sites mentioned in the FYI box on page 318 to learn about your opportunities for becoming a more involved consumer and controller of mass media.

KEY TERMS

Mass communication
Tribal epoch
Literate epoch
Print epoch
Electronic epoch
Uses and gratification theory
Gatekeeper
Cultivation theory
Cultivation
Mean world syndrome
Mainstreaming
Resonance

Technologies of Communication

LEARNING OBJECTIVES

To understand

1. What communication technologies are
2. Guidelines for online communication
3. The difficulty of managing the ever-increasing flow of information in our society
4. The democratic and nondemocratic potentials of communication technologies
5. How online communities differ from face-to-face communities
6. Issues involved in regulating communication technologies

Consider this riddle: What is the size of a matchbook and provides the power to access people and organizations all over the world?

If you answered a hard drive that should be available within 2 years, you're correct. In 1999 Steven Levy reported that researchers at IBM are shrinking computer hard drives to the size of a matchbook. At the same time, other tech-savvy companies are developing sprinkler systems that will check weather reports and activate only if rain is not forecast and allow you to turn on the lights in your home while you are driving so that you don't come home to a dark house. Want to have the inventory in your refrigerator checked and restocked continuously? That too is in the works: It's called the Internet refrigerator, which checks food supplies and orders more from the supermarket. How about a coffee pot that is wired to your daily schedule so it knows when to start your morning brew and adjusts to changes in your wake-up time? Would you like your dishwasher to contact the manufacturer if something goes wrong? These and other inventions will soon be available.

Both the nature of changes and the rapidity of them define the era in which we live. Every sphere of life, from friendship to business negotiations to government operations, increasingly involves communication technologies that have emerged only in recent years. The years ahead will see communication technologies integrated even more fully into our lives. Thus, your ability to participate effectively in social and professional life will depend on your competence in understanding and using communication technologies.

In this chapter we will learn about communication technologies that shape how we live and work. The first section of the chapter explores a range of communication technologies that are part of our lives. In this section, we will also look ahead to technological forms of communication that are on the horizon, and we'll contemplate their implications for how we live, work, and interact. The second section of the chapter identifies four challenges that accompany life in the information age.

UNDERSTANDING COMMUNICATION TECHNOLOGIES

Communication technologies include well-established systems such as the telephone and television and newer systems such as the Internet, World Wide Web, and videoconferencing. Yet these are no longer isolated technologies. Instead, individual technologies are transformed as they converge and interact with one another (Levy, 1999; Straubhaar & LaRose, 1995). Already in use is WebTV, which transforms the television into an interactive technology that allows the user to set viewing menus and surf channels while watching a program (Parkes & Larsen, 1999). Former Disney executive Michael Ovitz has an even more ambitious plan. Teamed up with Ron Burkle, Ovitz wants to develop CheckOut, which would be the "be-all and end-all dispenser of pop culture on the Net" (Rafter, 1999, p. 86). Using CheckOut, you could click to get news on Madonna and then be transported to listings of her videos and CDs and taken into her chat room.

Some communication technologies are familiar to almost everyone; others are newer and fewer people are comfortable with them. In our discussion we'll move from established to newer technologies of communication. If you are a seasoned user of newer technologies, you might share your knowledge with classmates who are less experienced.

Written Communication

Although you might not think of writing as a technology, it is a way to record and transfer information. Historically, written communication was the way that people who were separated by distance exchanged messages. People wrote letters for both personal and business reasons. Another form of conventional written communication is the memorandum, a word that comes from the Latin word *memorare,* which means "to bring remembrance." Written memoranda, or memos, were once ubiquitous in business settings, especially when companies needed permanent records. People still write letters and memoranda because both modes of communication remain useful, even ideal, in some situations. The primary advantage of written communication is its paper trail, which we can review at any time to refresh our memory and isn't lost if a hard disk crashes. Written records can protect people from misrepresentation. For example, a file might contain written documentation of an employee's negative performance reviews and infractions of rules. If the employee protests when fired by the supervisor, written records will justify the dismissal. Without permanent records, the employee might successfully claim that the dismissal was based on malice or bias.

Letters and memos also have drawbacks. Both require time and effort to prepare thoughtfully. Writing a personal letter that conveys warmth and closeness is difficult. Equally difficult can be composing a business letter that is precise and thorough in anticipating the reader's questions and potential misunderstandings. Furthermore, some people have difficulty finding appropriate words, constructing sentences that are logical and graceful, and using correct grammar, syntax, punctuation, and spelling. Finally, letters take time to reach their destinations (three to five days by regular mail) or money to move quickly ($7 or more for express service).

Memoranda also have disadvantages. The primary one is that they may be ignored. A colleague of mine refers to his trash can as his memo file. Like him, many people feel that memos are unimportant and may skim them or not read them at all. Many professionals today assume that any urgent news will be sent by email or fax, so hard-copy memos aren't considered high priority. Another disadvantage of memos is that they cannot be transmitted quickly to people outside a limited physical site.

Telephone Communication

When Alexander Graham Bell invented the telephone in 1875, he revolutionized communication. Phones allowed people to hear each other across many miles, even across oceans. This made it possible to feel personally connected or, as the marketing slogan touts, to "reach out and touch someone" in a manner more immediate than letters.

Rhoda

Telephones are a lifeline for me. I keep up with my friends with long telephone calls. Most evenings I have 1- or 2-hour-long conversations with members of my family or friends. I am wheelchair bound, so I don't get out as much as some people. I go to work everyday and do my shopping and go to temple each week. If I want to go out to socialize, I have to make a detailed plan. I have to get my chair ready and plan a route that is accessible. I can't just jump in my car and go like able-bodied people do. The telephone lets me stay involved with people I love without the physical stress of getting myself from here to there.

We are a nation of telephone callers, with the average U.S. resident making more than three calls a day and spending more than 30 minutes a day on the phone (Straubhaar & LaRose, 1995, p. 4). We use phones to stay in touch with friends and family, order merchandise, conduct business, and gain information (Katz, 1999). Answering machines and voice mail systems increase the number of calls we receive and make every day. In addition, voice mail has the important advantage of allowing people to retrieve messages when they are away from the home or office.

William

It drives me crazy when I call someone and get one of those obnoxious voice mail greetings. When I called a classmate last week, the answering machine blared some kind of music. I couldn't even understand the words and I had to wait through about a minute of noise before I could leave a message. It's really rude to force anyone who calls to listen to that.

Another communication technology based on the telephone is the facsimile system, or fax. In

© CORBIS

■ *Which facets of communication does the telephone accent and obscure?*

TELEPHONE ETIQUETTE

Telephone conversations can be useful and enjoyable or offensive and counterproductive. What makes the difference is whether callers observe basic rules of etiquette.

- Identify yourself. Unless you are calling an intimate, always identify yourself when you place a call or return a call, and identify yourself fully on the cover sheet of fax transmissions. It's also advisable to repeat your name at the end of a call with someone who doesn't know you well.
- Put people before phones. If you are talking with someone face to face, it's inconsiderate to engage in phone conversations or read faxes that come in. Have your calls held, turn on your answering machine, or answer the phone, explain to the caller that you have company, and say you will call back later.
- Respect private time. Make business calls during business hours (those in the time zone of the person you are calling) and to and from business locations. Most people labor hard at their jobs and look forward to getting away from work pressures in their time off.
- Return calls promptly. You communicate a loud message of disrespect when you don't return a call or wait a long time before returning it.
- Schedule extended phone conversations. Don't assume someone you call is willing to engage in an extended conversation. If you need to talk at length with another person, ask when the person would have time for extended communication.
- Be discreet. Phone calls and fax transmissions aren't necessarily private. Cellular phones are especially vulnerable to monitoring because they do not have private bands. It's unwise to communicate personal information by phone or fax.
- Avoid calling during meal times. A few years ago a number of marketers began calling people in their homes between 5 and 8 P.M. They reasoned that people would be home for dinner and so would answer the phone. What they learned is that many people fiercely resent intrusions in their dinner hour. Don't repeat the marketers' mistake. If a friend or business associate calls at meal time, it's acceptable not to answer or to answer, explain your schedule, and offer to return the call later. If a salesperson or pollster interrupts a meal with a phone call, it's appropriate to inform them, firmly but politely, that you are eating (or preparing to eat) and say goodbye.
- Exclude sensitive communication from messages. Other people, such as assistants at work and family members at home, sometimes screen messages left on voice mail or transmitted via fax. When leaving a message on voice mail, say only what you are willing to have heard by someone other than the person you called. When sending a fax, refrain from including highly personal or confidential content.

(continued)

(continued)

- Avoid sensational greetings. Greetings on voice mail communicate a good deal about the caller. Some greetings jeopardize personal security. "I'm not home right now, but please leave your name and number" tells any thief that your home is an easy target. Less dangerous, but no less irritating to many people, are frivolous greetings. Riddles, jokes, music (sung by the greeter or another person), and imitations of the voices of famous personalities annoy some callers. The best greeting is straightforward: "I can't answer the phone right now, but I'll return your call if you leave your name and number."
- Share the conversation. Typically, the person placing a call has a purpose, such as sharing news, getting advice, or passing on information. Before ending the call, however, the caller should ask whether the other person has issues or topics to discuss.

addition to being fast, fax transmissions are inexpensive. A two-page document can be transmitted across the country for less than the cost of a 33-cent stamp. Fax systems are standard equipment in most businesses and many homes.

Computer-Mediated Communication

In the 1970s I was working on my master's degree. To analyze data for my thesis I had to go to a building that housed a mainframe computer that was huge, noisy, and slow. In the decade that followed, chunky personal computers, or PCs, replaced the cumbersome mainframe computers. By the 1990s streamlined PCs replaced their husky predecessors. Before the new millennium arrived, palm-sized PCs were on the market and in users' hands. As the size and cost of computers decrease, they will be integrated into more and more appliances, such as the coffee pot and refrigerator mentioned earlier in this chapter.

The Internet is an especially popular feature of computer technology. Linking people and databases around the world, the Internet allows unprecedented access and interaction (Abbate, 1999). In 1995 more than 24 million people in the United States and Canada used the Internet an average of five hours each day (Sandberg, 1995). Only four years later, in 1999, 1 million PCs were sold per year, with access to the Internet wired into nearly all of them (Gates, 1999).

Computer technologies that allow people to send and receive information quickly are central to the information era in which we live. More than three-quarters of the economic activity in the United States today involves producing, processing, or distributing information (Straubhaar & LaRose, 1995). The ability to exchange information rapidly across long distances changes what and where the workplace is. The traditional pattern of housing all employees in one location competes with new patterns of work made possible by technologies. More than nine million Americans telecommute (Pescovitz, 1995). Dubbed virtual offices, separated private work spaces linked by computers are likely to become increasingly popular in the years ahead.

Kara

When my little sister was born, Mom continued working from home. She is an account executive at a bank so most of her work involves supervising transactions and advising clients. Her computer at home is linked to the main one at the bank in town, so she has access to all the information she needs. She uses the phone or email to talk with clients. She says she is at least as productive working at home as when she worked in the main office.

CYBERSPEAK: THE LANGUAGE OF THE NET

Every social system has a language, and the virtual world is no exception. Many people already know cyberspeak, but here are some basic terms (Krol, 1994; Spellerberg, 1999):

Domain: A group of interconnected computers. The group may be as small as a network in a particular office or as large as the Internet.

Emoticons: This is a new word made up of two familiar ones: *emotions* and *icons*. Emoticons are pictures, often best viewed sideways, used to express feelings in electronic communication. :) is a smile and :(is a frown. Online communication also uses abbreviations, such as *LOL* for "laughing out loud" and *BTW* for "by the way."

Flame: An argumentative or insulting online message. As a verb, it means "to insult" ("I flamed him").

Hyperlink: An icon, graphic, or word in a file that can be clicked to open another file.

Hypertext: A method of presenting information in which a user can "expand" certain words in on-screen text. Pointing to a specific word links the user to related documents that provide a definition, background information, biographical sketches, and so forth.

Internet service provider (ISP): The link between a computer and the Internet. The ISP allows a person to dial into its computers, which connect the user to the Internet.

Java: A programming language that allows people to write programs that can be downloaded from the Internet.

Local area network (LAN): A group of computers, usually desktops, within a specified area such as an office or company. LANs link people by allowing them to send and receive messages. A related system is an intranet, which works like the Internet but is used in a single office or company.

Online service: A commercial service that provides access to features such as email, news reports, financial services, and the Web.

Spam: Unsolicited email, usually bulk email for advertising purposes.

Universal resource locator (URL): A standardized system of addressing documents and media available on the Internet.

World Wide Web (Web, WWW): A graphical interface for the Internet that consists of Internet servers that give users access to documents, including ones with hyperlinks to other documents.

fyi

CYBERCOMMUNICATION

What do people communicate in cyberspace? We all know that people use the net to exchange information related to work, shop, pay bills, keep in touch with friends, and chat with people who share their interests and hobbies. But that's not all that's being communicated in cyberspace. Here are two of the more unusual kinds of communication on the net:

Cybermemorials are one or more pages dedicated to a person who has died. Cybermemorials began appearing on the Internet in 1990 (Hower, 1999). They range from simple, single-page tributes to elaborate multimedia scrapbooks with the deceased's favorite music, photos of the deceased, and chronologies of the dead person's life. Web sites dedicated to cybermemorials, some of which provide links to support groups include Virtual Memorials (virtual-memorials.com/), After-Death Communication (www.afterdeath.com/memorials/index.htm), and In the Memory Of (www.inthe-memoryof.com/).

Cybersex is sexual talk, often intense, that takes place on the Internet, usually between people who have never met in person. Before you dismiss cybersex as something only a few people would consider, take note of a few facts: In every month of 1998 at least 9 million people visited a sexually oriented adult Web site. There are several hundred sex-related bulletin boards on which users can post illicit messages. Many of the hundreds of sex chat rooms are full by midday (Bass, 1999; Schnarch, 1997).

Electronic mail is one of the most popular uses of the Internet. It allows us to have conversations with friends and professional associates without tiresome iterations of telephone tag ("I am returning the message you left on my machine by leaving this one on your machine") and the inconvenience of coordinating different time zones. Using email, I advise students, conduct business, serve as a consultant for attorneys, debate campus issues with colleagues in my department, and collaborate with academics in other states and countries. In addition, I stay in daily touch with friends who live far away from me. Because email is an extension of conventional written communication, it has the advantage of allowing writers the time to compose thoughtful messages and to communicate when it's convenient for them. However, email does not necessarily have the advantage of automatically producing hard copy, and it lacks the advantage of privacy that accompanies conventional written messages.

Bryan

One of the best things about computer technology is that I can talk to my father on a regular basis without the cost of long-distance phone calls. He has email at his office, and I have a free account at school, so we talk nearly every day. Before I used email I called home only when there was something important to discuss; there had to be some issue to justify a call. Now we chat about everyday stuff, and I feel we're a lot more connected.

© Sarah Putnam/Index Stock

■ *In the 1970s futurist Alvin Toffler predicted that the United States would become a nation of "electronic cottages"—what we know today as home offices.*

Cindy

I don't like communicating on email. It feels awkward to me to send a message to someone, not knowing when they'll see it and not being able to tell how they respond. It doesn't seem like real communication.

Although the net and the Web allow us to get information more quickly and through different channels than other modes of communication, it would be a mistake to think that computer-mediated communication is only a matter of form. Cyberspace is a unique environment that affects not just *how* we communicate, but also *what* we communicate (Fraser, 1999). On the net, many people communicate differently than they do in face-to-face settings or when they exchange written communication. According to psychology professor John Suler (1999), many people feel they have more freedom to express themselves on the Internet. Screen names and aliases, for example, allow people to say what they want without being easily identifiable. Avatars, colorful icons that people use to represent their identities in cyberspace, release identity from any conventional name. In a recent interview (Bookmark, 1999, p. A29), Suler said, "On line, people are free to express aspects of themselves that they wouldn't in other kinds of encounters. There are people who have whole collections of avatars to represent different aspects of their personalities."

The Internet also allows people to take control of parts of their lives and activities that historically have been controlled by government agencies and corporations (Shapiro, 1999). For example, people who invest in the stock market traditionally have had to work through a broker and rely on the broker to execute trades and inform them. Today, many people buy and sell stocks online directly without having to depend on a broker. We can also access government reports immediately on the Web instead of having to write or call the government agency to request a written report. One notable downside of this easy access is that users may unknowingly leave cyberprints that allow others to monitor their interests, habits, and so forth.

Ty

I think email is the greatest thing since soccer. I can send a message when it suits me and read my mail when I feel like it, unlike telephone conversations when you have to answer when the phone rings. I also like knowing that I'm not disturbing friends when I send them messages, because they can read them when they feel like it. I think email makes communication a lot easier and more relaxed.

NETIQUETTE (EMAIL ETIQUETTE)

Just as there is an etiquette for using the phone or any other medium of communication, there is a protocol for prudent use of email. Here are ten good general guidelines for email (Hollis, 1989; *Guide to the Web,* 1999):

- Identify the topic. In the subject field of a message header, type a key word or words that provide a quick description of your subject. This allows your recipient to recognize the topic immediately and to recall it from a message that has been stored, perhaps for some time.
- Be brief. In the world of electronic communication, short really is sweet, especially in business exchanges. Messages that run longer than a full screen might be better managed through oral discussion. Remember, many users have to pay for time on the Internet, so longer messages cost them more.
- Assume that any message you send will survive indefinitely and in multiple places. Recipients, including those you may not intend, may save messages forever. Gossip, personal aspersion, and secrets may come back to haunt you. When an institution owns the equipment on which you send messages, they may be stored indefinitely.
- Use the pyramid form to compose messages. This means you should put the most important information or topic first and discuss less significant details or other messages later in your message.
- Reflect before responding. It's advisable not to respond to personal criticism or messages that upset you when you are emotional. If a message you read angers or upsets you, wait a few hours and reread it before sending any response, especially if your message may be stored.
- Think and write literally. Emotions and nuances are difficult to express in existing modes of written communication, whether electronic or not. Thus, some emotions and subtleties of meaning may be misinterpreted by readers. Humor may be taken literally because you can't use vocal inflection and winks to signal that you are joking. Irony may also not be evident in written messages. Emoticons won't always clarify feelings.
- Double-check the names of recipients. Much email is sent to multiple recipients or members of a list. When you reply to messages sent to multiple recipients, everyone who received the first message will receive your reply unless you instruct your server to send your reply only to a specified individual or individuals.
- Consider timing. Refrain from sending messages that are likely to prompt immediate and strong responses if you will not be available to continue the conversation. For example, don't send upsetting news or make a statement that requires response just before leaving on a trip.

(continued)

ntinued)

Avoid flaming. Flaming is the sending of emotional and derogatory messages to or about another person or group. Flaming is more likely to incite anger than thought, and it may silence people and thus lessen the potential of critical democratic participation in conversation.

- Verify transmission. Don't assume your message gets through just because you send it. Often servers are down, so a message may not be transmitted, and your server may not inform you that the message didn't get through. Also, email addresses change as people switch from one system to another. If you don't receive a reply to a message you sent, follow up with a phone call, letter, or fax to see whether your email got through.
- Don't open email from strangers. Viruses are rampant and they can be very destructive. If you don't know the person sending you an email, the safest plan is not to open the message. Instead, reply (without opening the note) saying that you don't open email from strangers and ask the sender to call or fax a message.

Find out about the newest netiquette by visiting Netiquette's home page: http://www.albion.com/netiquette.

Teleconferencing

Not long ago the word *conference* referred to a meeting in which people discussed one or more topics. Today the meaning of *conference* has been modified to include meetings that don't involve in-person interaction. ***Teleconferencing*** is a term based on the Greek word *tele,* which means "at a distance." Teleconferencing is conducting meetings among people who are geographically separated. Teleconferencing can take several forms, and they differ in the extent to which they emulate face-to-face meetings.

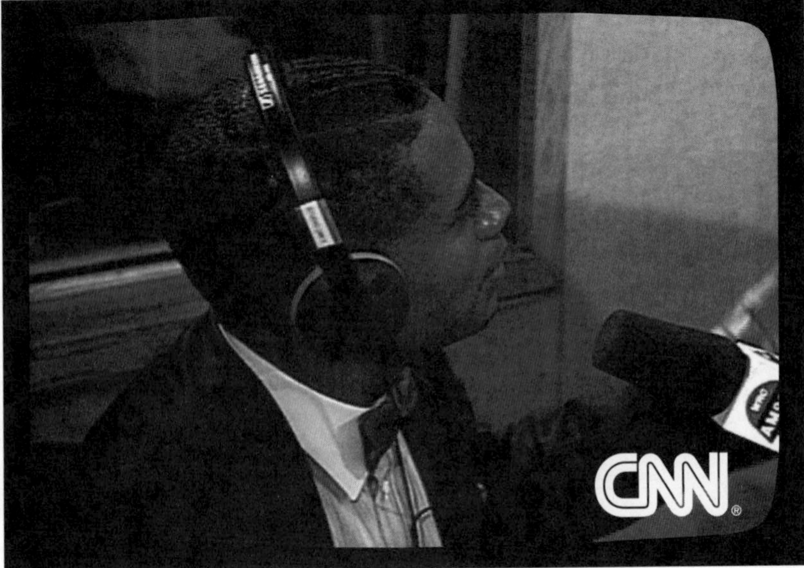

■ *Communication technologies allow people to see and hear each other across distance.*

Courtesy of CNN

Audioconferencing allows people at different locations to participate in a discussion over the telephone. If you have ever been involved in a conference call, you are familiar with this form of teleconferencing. Rooms equipped with high-quality speakers and microphones provide more sophisticated audioconferencing. One of the most important advantages of audioconferencing over in-person meetings is the lower expense. The cost of a telephone conference is far less than that required for travel, accommodations, meals, and incidentals for several people. Audioconferencing has the additional advantage of only slightly disrupting schedules. The time required to participate in a conference call is much less than the time required to travel to a face-to-face meeting. Probably the most serious disadvantage of audioconferencing is its inability to convey visual dimensions of nonverbal communication. From our discussion in Chapter 5 you'll recall that face and body motion, artifacts, and personal appearance are meaningful forms of nonverbal communication. In audioconferences we are unable to see what others look like or to detect facial responses, gestures, and posture that might provide clues about how they feel about their messages and ours.

Computer conferencing allows multiple participants to send and receive email in sequential exchanges. Most Internet service providers today offer chat mode and instant messaging so that people can engage in communication simultaneously. Discussion forums with threaded discussion allow team members to discuss a project and students and teachers to participate in distance learning. Notable benefits of computer conferencing are low cost, minimum advance notice required to s ence, and ability of participants to stay ular work environments. Because most conferencing relies on typed messages, howev linear and requires each participant to wait for o ers to type and transmit their messages. In addition, computer conferencing without video means that communicators cannot see and hear one another or give and receive immediate nonverbal feedback (Rogers, 1986).

Videoconferencing is rapidly expanding in popularity, largely because it combines the advantages of other kinds of teleconferencing while avoiding many of their disadvantages. You probably have witnessed examples of videoconferencing, which is common on news programs. Using satellites to transmit visual images, people in distant locations appear on screen with newscasters in a studio (Widner, 1986). The outstanding advantage of videoconferencing is that it most closely emulates in-person communication. Because participants can see and hear one another, they can communicate verbally and nonverbally. This allows greater perspective: more complete and immediate feedback and instantaneous interaction. In addition, videoconferencing has the advantage of allowing participants to share visual materials such as charts, film clips, models, and pictures. The disadvantage of expense tempers these benefits. Videoconferencing is considerably more costly than other forms of teleconferencing, although its cost is likely to decrease as technology improves and the market becomes more competitive. Even now it is less expensive than face-to-face meetings that require travel, accommodations, and so forth. The advantages of

fyi

A VIRTUAL PH.D.?

Walden University in Minneapolis, Minnesota, advertises itself as a pioneer in "dispersed residency doctoral programs." Translated, this means that Walden allows students to earn their doctoral degrees without ever setting foot on the campus. That's a good thing, because Walden University does not have a physical campus.

Calling itself "a university without walls," Walden relies on the Walden Information Network (WIN) to provide students with many conventional features of campus life: courses, conferences with instructors, online access to a graduate library, small student group discussions, and even advertising to sell cars, books, and so forth.

ICTION AND FACTS ABOUT THE INTERNET

ommon misperceptions about the Internet and corrections o the Web, 1999; Krol, 1994).

are connected to the Internet if you send and receive email.

ot necessarily. If your computer allows you to dial into a remote system, you can read and write email, but you aren't directly connected to the Internet.

Fiction: The Internet is free.

Fact: Somebody pays for every connection to the Internet. Often companies and colleges don't pass the fees on to the actual users, which is why many people think access is free.

Fiction: The Internet is a network.

Fact: Actually, the Internet is a network of networks that are connected to one another. Each network may have its own policies and rules, which are coordinated among connected networks.

Fiction: The Internet was developed in the 1990s.

Fact: Although widespread use of the Internet is a phenomenon of the 1990s, the Internet actually was developed in the mid-1970s. In original form the Internet connected an experimental U.S. Defense Department network known as the ARPAnet with other radio and satellite networks.

videoconferencing have led such companies as Hewlett-Packard and Texas Instruments, as well as government agencies such as the Environmental Protection Agency and the military, to use it.

Interconnected Communication Technologies

What many people call new technologies of communication are actually extensions and convergences of traditional forms of communication (Figure 15.1). They store and send communication in ways that differ from traditional media, using digital technologies instead of conventional analog ones. As communication professor Fred Williams has noted, "New media forms seldom fully replace old ones" (1992, p. 142). In other words, radio did not replace newspapers, and television did not replace radio. However, convergence of technologies radically alters how we conduct business, engage in research, share information and ideas, and sustain personal relationships.

Interconnectivity is the key word for the future of communication technologies. And interconnectivity promises to be good news for people who are not tech-savvy. The idea of interconnectivity is to connect various devices to each other and the net so that users don't have the hassles of configuring each new system. One of the key people firing the interconnectivity revolution is Bill Joy, Sun Microsystems' chief scientist. Joy is a tireless crusader for simplicity in the technological revolution. He believes that people shouldn't have to deal with the current complexities of making technology work. Instead, Joy thinks computers should and will work more like simple appliances such as the toaster, dishwasher, alarm clock, or electric drill (Sandberg, 1999). Soon,

Figure 15.1 Traditional and Convergent Forms of Communication

Level	*Traditional Form*	*Technological Form*
Interpersonal	Face to face, letter, phone call	Mail, audio conference, computer conference
Group	Face to face	Teleconference, Internet
Organizational	Face to face, memo, intercom, telephone, meetings	Mail, LAN, fax, audio conference, video conference
Public	Newspapers, radio, television, magazines, books, films	Videotape, video disk, cable TV, satellite TV, videotext, teletext, digital information systems
International	Mass media, including global broadcast links, telex, films	Global satellite coverage, direct broadcast satellite, videotape video disk

Source: Adapted from Williams, 1992, p. 142.

he says, we will buy computerized products, plug them in, and have them work automatically.

Central to making interconnectivity a reality is getting away from the idea of a single PC in your home or office. Instead, each appliance or device would have its own computer that could be easily connected to other devices, and all of the devices would be wired to the net. Another leader of the technological revolution agrees this is the future. In a 1998 speech, Bill Gates said that the next decade will bring more change than we've seen in the past 25 years, and one of the greatest changes will be the move from single do-it-all PCs to multiple computer-driven devices, most or all of which will be linked to the net (McCollum, 1998). Gates also predicts that "PCs gave the world a whole new way to work, play and communicate. The PC-plus era will be just as revolutionary. It will take the PC's power and make it available almost anywhere, on devices that haven't yet been dreamed up" (Gates, 1999, p. 64).

CHALLENGES OF CONVERGING COMMUNICATION TECHNOLOGIES

Changes inevitably entail challenges. Nowhere is this more true than in relation to communication technologies. Of the many challenges that accompany the information age, we will focus on four that are particularly compelling.

Managing Information Flow and Overload

When I became a faculty member in 1975, I received several phone calls and a handful of letters and memos each day. If I wasn't in my office when people called, they had to try later or give up. Today, less than 25 years later, I am deluged by communication from others. In addition to the phone calls and letters, each day I receive at least a dozen voice mail messages, thirty or more email notes from friends and colleagues, and often as many as forty email messages from my students. My daily faxes and FedEx correspondence dwarf what arrives through regular mail. I feel inundated by the sheer volume of communication I receive and to which I must respond.

My situation is common. Many people in our era are swamped with communication and information, all of which demands our attention. A 1999 survey of email use found that, on average, workers send and receive 36 email messages every day (Jones, 1999). How will we manage the unremitting deluge? Are we capable of understanding, processing,

fy*i*

THE PC-PLUS ERA

What does interconnectivity mean for you? It means your home, office, car, and other locations will be filled with devices that talk to each other and the net, and you shouldn't have to even think about how they work, much less deal with the hassles of configuring new systems. Here are a few of the things that those leading the technological revolution say we can expect in the next 10 to 15 years (Gates, 1999; Hempel, 1999; Levy, 1999):

Smart homes: The coffee maker will talk to your calendar and decide when to start your morning coffee. Your refrigerator will notice when a product has reached its expiration date and email the supermarket to send more. Your dishwasher will notice if you buy a new dishwashing detergent, email the manufacturer, and remotely upgrade your machine to adjust to the new detergent. Lamps will turn on automatically. Your TV will be connected to the Web and will know your viewing preferences. The mirror over the bathroom sink will show you the news headlines while you wash and shave in the morning. Your security system will recognize Fido and Tigger as your dog and cat, so the alarm won't go off as they enter rooms or leap about.

Smart cars: If you're lost and there is nobody from whom to get directions, your car will be able to connect to the Net and call out directions. It will also notice if your battery is getting weak or your alternator is about to die, and it will give you directions to the closest service station that has the expertise and parts to repair your car. Your car will also be able to forewarn you about traffic jams and suggest alternative routes.

Smart offices: You'll use smart staples that link files in your PC to those in your digital tablet. When you change an appointment in your palmtop, that change will be noted automatically by a minicomputer woven into your jacket. Voice recognition will be readily available, so you won't even have to type to get information into your systems.

and responding to this amount of communication on a continuous basis? If not, do we inevitably fall behind in our careers while those who manage information better advance?

Amy

Sometimes I wish I hadn't bought an answering machine. When I get back to my apartment after a day on campus and at work, the red message light is always blinking. I feel like I have to listen to the messages and return calls. Instead of my apartment's being a place where I can get away from the pressure, it's a source of more pressure.

Mark

I love having voice mail and email. Before I had them, I used to worry when I wasn't home that I might miss important calls from friends. Now I can stay out as long as I want, and I don't miss anything. If someone calls, they leave a message and I call back. If someone sends me an email note, it's there when I open my mailbox. New technologies definitely increase my personal freedom.

Like Amy, many people feel overwhelmed by the sheer volume of information and its seemingly relentless pursuit of us. Yet perhaps the change has been less in amount than in form. Williams (1992) suggests that communication often takes the place of transportation. For example, instead of traveling to a conference, many professionals today converse by computer, teleconferencing, or videoconferencing. Instead of traveling to shopping malls, many consumers today let their keyboards and televisions do the walking as they shop online. Instead of physically traveling to libraries, many people today rely on virtual libraries that can be accessed on the Web. Another trend is online magazines and newspapers. Whereas conventional newspapers and magazines are mass printed and mailed or delivered, an increasing number of users now download these documents in their homes or offices, and they can tailor the downloading to their interests.

It isn't clear whether the amount of information means we are destined to feel overloaded. Perhaps the effects of expanded information will depend on our ability to control information rather than being controlled by it. Some people limit their online communication to a set amount of time each day or week, some refuse to have voice mail, and some tell people (clients, students, co-workers) they prefer to discuss business in person and will not reply to email messages. These options show that there are ways that we can control the amount of information that communication technologies deliver to us.

Another option for managing information overload was developed by Dr. Email, the 36-year-old president and CEO of General Interactive, Inc. Working with colleagues, Dr. Email (also known as V. Shiva) created EchoMail, a software program that uses sophisticated pattern recognition technology to read, store, and classify incoming email messages. Clients such as Nike, Allstate, Calvin Klein, and Unilever have spent up to $1 million to install EchoMail into their networks so that they can recognize patterns in customers' messages and can be more responsive to customers' needs and requests (Imperato, 1999).

Ensuring Democratic Access

Some scholars (Buck, 1988; Chesebro, 1995; Gergen, 1991) believe communication technologies are ushering in a global community in which everyone can participate without the barriers of geography. Almost instant communication with people who are miles, even continents, away is possible. Furthermore, information and education can now be made available to people who were previously excluded because of distance.

Other scholars and social critics (Hyde, 1995; Markhoff, 1989) have less optimistic views of what new technologies may mean. One significant concern is that they may magnify existing social divisions as

fyi — INFORMATION VERSUS KNOWLEDGE

Few people doubt that we live in an information era, but does this mean we have more knowledge? Philosopher David Rothenberg (1999), who teaches at the New Jersey Institute of Technology, worries that we are confusing information with knowledge. The Web allows us to get more information and get it faster than ever before, but do we know what to do with all the information we can gather so easily? Rothenberg (1999, p. B8) points out that "Information is the details, all those data that are not so easy to locate. Knowledge is being able to put the details together and draw a clear conclusion." Knowledge requires more than gathering information. It requires evaluating the credibility of sources of information, thinking about how bits of information fit together, and connecting information. Rothenberg encourages his students not to use the Web just to get information, but rather to use it to connect with other people and to explore ideas, both of which can lead to knowledge.

THE DIGITAL DIVIDE

Not everyone in the United States has equal access to communication technologies. On July 8, 1999, the National Telecommunications and Information Administration, which is part of the U.S. Commerce Department, released a report titled "Falling Through the Net" (http://www.ntia.doc.gov/ntiahome/digitaldivide). The report details disturbing trends in use of the Internet. Age, rural versus urban setting, and education are all factors that affect who has access to telecommunication. Among the many factors, two stand out: income and race. Only 12.1% of people with annual incomes under $10,000 use the Internet, whereas 58.9% of people with incomes of $75,000 or more use the Internet.

There is also a marked racial divide in use of the Internet. In the United States the Internet is used by 37% of whites, 35.9% of Asian and Pacific Islanders, 19% of blacks, and 16.6% of Hispanics.

Go to the Web site listed in this box to read the full report.

some people have better access to new technologies. An information elite could easily develop because use of new technologies requires both knowledge and resources that not everyone has. For example, fiberoptic networks are so costly that they might be laid between two prosperous urban areas but not be routed into poorer rural communities (Markhoff, 1989). This would mean that people living in the already advantaged urban areas would have increased access to video, audio, and computer technologies, whereas members of rural communities would be relegated to the margins of the information revolution and the personal and professional enrichment it allows.

As ordinary citizens, workers, and voters, we have an ethical responsibility to identify and work to realize the potential of technologies of communication to enrich us as individuals and as members of a common world. To promote equal opportunity in the information age, we cannot restrict access to new and converging technologies to individuals and groups who are already privileged by their social, professional, and economic status. As a society we have a responsibility to provide access and training to people who cannot afford it. In the short run, this would be expensive. In the long run, however, it would be far less costly than the problems of a society in which a small technology elite is privileged and the majority of citizens are excluded from full participation. The Public Electronic Network (PEN) project illustrates the potential of new technologies to enlarge participation in civic life (see the FYI box).

Rethinking What Community Means

What does the term *community* mean to you? Conventionally, it has connoted a physical world made up of people who live together in a continuing manner. Yet today we hear much about virtual communities in which people are linked in cyberspace but share no concrete physical location. Are these new kinds of communities or merely new ways of building familiar communities?

In traditional communities people lived together and had to make compromises and accommodations to get along. Electronic communities don't require such accommodations. As Steven Jones points out, "Community membership is in no small way a simple matter of subscribing or desubscribing to a bulletin board or electronic news group" (1995, p. 11). We are free to join communities when we

DIFFERENT PEOPLE, DIFFERENT VISIONS

Here is a sample of opinions of what communication technologies do or will mean for individuals and society. Which views do you find most and least plausible?

"CMC [computer-mediated communication] is not just a tool; it is at once technology, medium, and engine of social relations" (Jones, 1995, p. 16).

Virtual communities formed by CMC are "incontrovertibly social spaces in which people still meet face-to-face, but under new definitions of both 'meet' and 'face'" (Stone, 1991, p. 85).

"The computer creates anonymity, which leads to a decrease in social inhibition and an increase in flaming" (Baym, 1995, p. 153).

The anonymity of computer communication means that "users are able to express and experiment with aspects of their personality that social inhibition would generally encourage them to suppress" (Reid, 1991, p. 22).

CMC has the potential to "promote efficiency at the expense of social contact" (Chesebro & Bonsall, 1989, p. 221).

"When the VR [virtual reality] revolution really gets rolling, we are likely to be too busy tuning into whatever we are tuning into to analyze or debate the consequences" (Rheingold, 1991, p. 350).

"In no way has the computer had even 10 percent of the impact that I expect in the years ahead" (Gates, 1998 as quoted by McCollum, 1998, p. A25).

■ *Public access to technologies allows people with few resources to participate in the information revolution.*

THE PEN SYSTEM AND CIVIC PARTICIPATION

In Santa Monica, California, the local government has committed to an experiment in radical democracy (Schmitz, Rogers, Phillips, & Pascal, 1995). First, local officials such as the mayor and council members invited constituents to correspond with them by email. Second, to ensure that contact is not limited to those who can afford computers and modems, the government set up terminals in public locations, such as libraries and malls. The project was dubbed Public Electronic Network (PEN).

The designers of PEN assumed that the public terminals would increase participation by workers and taxpayers who didn't have personal computers. What they didn't assume was that the public terminals would also be used by people who didn't work or pay taxes: homeless citizens. But that is precisely what happened. Santa Monica's substantial homeless population began using the system to talk about the homeless problem. Within a few months proposals for assisting homeless citizens were developed. One provided email addresses to the homeless so that they could apply for jobs and have an address to give to potential employers; another set up a nonprofit organization called SHWASHLOCK, which furnished showers, laundry rooms, and storage lockers for homeless citizens so that they could clean themselves and their clothes and safely store clothes in order to make a good appearance when applying for jobs.

PEN dramatically illustrates the potential of new technologies of communication to democratize access to information and public officials. As several homeless people in Santa Monica have noted, their shabby appearance does not constrain their ability to "talk" with officials about their problems and to apply for jobs. Email makes appearance irrelevant, so others respond to them on the basis of their ideas.

want and to leave when they no longer interest us. We need not accommodate people and topics that don't engage us. For this reason, some scholars worry that electronic communities promote narcissism, in which we talk only about ourselves and only with people like ourselves (Caldwell & Taha, 1993; Kelly, 1997; Walther, 1996). Using cellular phones, portable modems, satellite dishes, and personal digital assistants, we can tap into our communities no matter where we travel (Baym, 1995; Carey, 1989; Pescovitz, 1995). Does the ease of joining and leaving electronic communities lessen ties between members? Does it diminish the sense of collectivity and continuity that traditionally has been associated with community?

Another quality of traditional communities that is not necessarily part of electronic communities is face-to-face contact and all that it implies. When people interact in person, they know certain things about one another, such as sex, race, approximate age, and physical appearance. In online communication such basic aspects of personal identity may not be clear. They may even be fabricated. People sometimes represent themselves falsely. Men define themselves as women and vice versa; people claim appearances and physical conditions that they don't have (Lea & Spears, 1995; Papin & Bharadway, 1998). Does electronic communication allow, or even promote, deception? Or, as some claim, does it enhance communication by reducing attention to

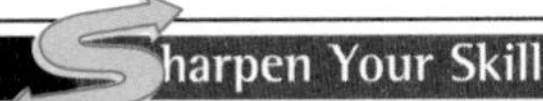

KEEPING UP WITH THE PACE OF CHANGE

The information revolution moves rapidly. Many technologies that are avant-garde today will be outmoded within a year or two. Many ideas that people are now talking about as possibilities will be realities in no time.

Writing this chapter was frustrating because communication technologies change so rapidly. Between the time I wrote the manuscript (summer 1999) and the time the book was published (summer 2000), some of what I wrote has become outdated. To grasp the speed of change, review this chapter and identify information that is already out of date. Which ideas that I describe as on the frontier are now established? Which possibilities have become realities?

such aspects of identity as physical appearance and gender? Some people invent different identities for themselves to fit different moods and goals. Is this honest, good, and liberating, or troublesome? These ethical questions are unresolved, and they will become increasingly prominent as more and more people engage others in cyberspace.

Regulating Cyberspace

A fourth challenge of new technologies is how, if at all, we should regulate them. What guidelines are reasonable? What guidelines infringe on freedom of speech and the press? We have regulations for written and oral communication. Yet technologies of communication have outpaced our ability to develop rules to safeguard people's comfort, health, privacy, and dignity. We need to think carefully about what kinds of regulations we want and how to implement them.

One form of communication on the net that irritates many people is advertising that they don't want and can't escape. The Web is saturated with ads, and many of them have to download before the content of a Web page appears, forcing the user to confront the ad. In the future the Web and net are likely to include even more advertising than today. If you go to a site to read a review of a movie, you may also get—without asking for them—offers to buy the soundtrack, video version, and other items connected with the movie (Rafter, 1999). Should ads be regulated on individuals' private computers? Should users be able to opt not to have ads precede or accompany Web pages they access? If so, should users have to accept the expense of buying programs to avoid the ads (Tanaka, 1999)? Does the pervasiveness of advertising on the net blur the boundary between content and advertising?

Privacy is a key issue that regulations must address (Tung, 1999; Shapiro, 1999). Many online advertisers collect **cookies,** which are bits of data that Web sites collect and store in users' personal browsers. This gives advertisers information about you that you might not choose to release. Currently Congress is debating bills that would limit the extent to which online companies could gather and share information about users, and the Federal Trade Commission (FTC) is considering prohibiting online companies from gathering information from children without parental consent (Hunt & Murray, 1999). In 1999 the FTC reprimanded two companies for online privacy invasions, but neither company was actually penalized (Lash, 1999). Software manufacturers are developing programs to disable cookies, but this will help only people who buy and install the programs (Tanaka, 1999).

Many people mistakenly assume that their online communication is private and cannot be released without their permission. One threat to privacy is hackers, who break into computers and

fyi

CYBERHATE

Many people are concerned about cyberhate. The Web has many sites where people can engage in hate speech, and there is little regulation of these sites or their implications for actions such as killings, bombings, and persecutions. Should anyone be allowed to create a site that proclaims hate of particular groups and that exhorts others to hate the groups and act against them? Should anyone be allowed to visit sites that exist to promote hate? Is this kind of communication protected by the constitutional right to freedom of speech?

To learn more about hate speech, codes regulating it in specific contexts, and opinions on whether it should be regulated, go to this site: http://www.stedwards.edu/hum/durmmond/haters.html.

collect whatever they want. Another restriction on privacy is employers. A recent survey revealed that 60.9% of workers were not aware of an email tracking system in their places of work (*E-mail Abuse Survey,* 1999). Yet companies are increasingly instituting systems to monitor employees' online communication. During a random check of employees' online activities, a chapter of the American Heart Association discovered that an employee had repeatedly visited a pornographic Web site. He was dismissed (Jones, 1999). Increasingly, employers are screening employees' email to filter out profanity, pornography, and sexist and racist jokes and language (Jones, 1999). Employees who protest that this is an invasion of privacy are learning that the courts regard email and Web access as company resources that employees are allowed to use. Court rulings do not support any expectation of privacy in email and Web communication on the job.

Hackers and employers aren't the only ones who can gain access to your personal electronic communication. FBI agents and other law enforcement personnel routinely get search warrants that require Internet service providers to turn over information about users who are being investigated for illegal activity. AOL alone handles about twenty warrants each month (Weise, 1999). Whether a person is sending an intimate message to a loved one, posting child pornography, or discussing murder, there is a long and enduring electronic trail. After the shootings at Columbine High School in Colorado, FBI agents went to AOL for information that showed suspect Eric Harris had been engaged in online communication about making bombs. David Smith, who created and unleashed the Melissa virus in 1998, was caught through tracking his online communication. And don't assume you're safe if you post material anonymously on Web sites. The person who posts a message can be traced. Hitting the delete key doesn't erase a message from storage in the computer on which it was composed, the computer on which it was received, and often other computers between the source and destination.

Privacy is not the only issue at stake in questions of how, if at all, to regulate electronic communication. Your physical health may also be at stake if some kinds of online communication are not regulated. A drug company set up a shop on the Internet and arranged for pharmacies in two states to ship prescription drugs to patients. The only problem was that the drug company needed doctors to write prescriptions, which are required for dispensing drugs that are not sold over-the-counter. The company hired doctors to review questionnaires submitted electronically by people who wanted prescriptions. One doctor who agreed to issue prescriptions online was cited by his state's medical quality assurance commission for unprofessional conduct; he was an orthopedic

ANNOY.COM

Apollo Media Corporation thought it had a sure way to make lots of money. The idea was that people would tell off public officials if they could do so anonymously. So Apollo offered a new Web site, www.annoy.com. For a fee, annoy.com would send an insulting message to a public official without including the client's name. The messages it sent on behalf of anonymous disgruntled citizens often were laced with profanities and obscenities.

Not so fast, said the Supreme Court. On April 19, 1999, the high court affirmed a lower court's ruling that annoy.com's activities violated the 1996 Communications Decency Act, which prohibits the transmission of "communication which is obscene, lewd, lascivious, filthy or indecent with the intent to annoy, abuse, threaten or harass another person" ("Ban on Annoying," 1999, p. 4A). Obscenity, said the Supreme Court, is not protected by the First Amendment's guarantee of free speech.

surgeon who was writing prescriptions for Viagra (used to treat male impotence) for patients he never examined ("Cybermedicine," 1999). Prescribing medications online entails special dangers, including the possibility that patients will have undetected conditions or be taking other medications that make particular drugs dangerous for them. From the annoyance of unwelcome advertising to the dangers of indiscriminate prescriptions, content on the Internet and Web remains unregulated and the idea of regulation remains highly controversial.

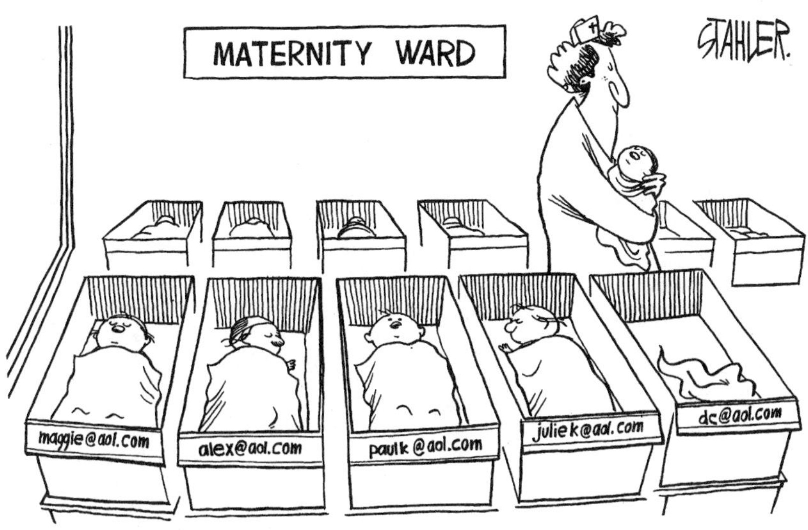

Jeff Stahler reprinted by permission of Newspaper Enterprise Association, Inc.

Summary

Called the information age, ours is a time of rapid changes in the means of communication. Media affect not only the form but also the content and meaning of communication. The same words spoken face to face and transmitted via email may be interpreted quite differently. Furthermore, we communicate differently when we use different media. Online communication tends to be more impulsive and less reflective than face-to-face communication. We should try to choose media that fit our messages, the situation, and those with whom we communicate.

The information revolution is less an outgrowth of dramatically new technologies than the convergence of multiple technologies. As telephones, computers, and televisions are increasingly able to work together, the ways we can communicate and the kinds of information available to us proliferate geometrically.

Communication technologies pose a number of challenges for us. One of the most remarked-upon challenges of our era is the deluge of information that sometimes threatens to overwhelm us. Learning to control and manage the steady stream of information that flows in daily is a priority for people today. Another challenge of the information age is avoiding the possibility of a society divided into the technologically elite and the people without resources and knowledge to use new communication technologies. If we are to realize the potential of new technologies to expand and enrich national life, we must find ways to include all segments of society in them. A third challenge of our era is creating communities in new ways. Unlike traditional communities, those formed in cyberspace require less commitment and less adjustment and accommodation among members. Finally, we face the challenge of regulating communication in cyberspace: How do we provide reasonable safeguards for individual and collective well being while preserving our constitutional right to freedom of speech and the press? In the years ahead each of us will play a role in responding to these and other challenges of the information age.

FOR FURTHER REFLECTION AND DISCUSSION

1. Can you suggest ways we might avail ourselves of the advantages for personal and professional growth that new technologies offer without experiencing some of the real and potential disadvantages discussed in this chapter?
2. How do relationships between people who never meet face to face differ from relationships between people who can see each other? What are the advantages and limitations of forming and sustaining relationships electronically?
3. This chapter follows Marshall McLuhan's idea that the form, or medium, of communication affects the substance of communication. Identify differences and similarities in how you communicate with people in person and electronically.
4. Interview two people who telecommute. Ask them to describe the advantages and disadvantages of working in a location physically removed from a central office and contact with co-workers.
5. Do you think we need regulations for communication on the Web and the Internet? If so, who should be responsible for developing and enforcing rules of conduct? If you do favor regulations to govern conduct, what are the implications for free speech of regulating communication that flames, harasses, or discriminates against individuals and groups? Should the First Amendment to the U.S. Constitution apply to communication in which the sender's identity is or can be concealed?
6. Some people think that new technologies foster wide democratic participation in social life, whereas others claim that the cost and expertise required by new technologies will foster a society of haves and have-nots in which only the elite participate fully. What is your position? What social programs, policies, and laws might influence the extent to which converging technologies of communication invigorate democratic life?
7. Write out your scenario for the presence and use of communication technologies 5 years from now in the profession you intend to join. Describe how you think existing technologies will figure in that environment and what new kinds of communication systems may be invented that will affect that context.

KEY TERMS

Teleconferencing

Cookies

Closing

We have traveled a long way since the introductory chapter. Our journey has introduced us to many different forms and contexts of communication. At the same time, we've seen that common elements make up the mosaics of human communication. To close this book I'd like to highlight the central theme that unifies all that we've discussed.

Communication Mosaics: Common Elements, Different Forms

The central idea of this book is that basic processes and skills take on different emphases and forms as they are incorporated in various kinds of communication. Six skills are foundations of effectiveness in talking with yourself, interacting in personal relationships, deliberating in groups, participating in organizational life, interviewing, giving public speeches, interacting with mass communication, and using communication technologies. Let's review the six basic skills discussed in *Communication Mosaics* and recall how these common elements vary as they are placed in diverse kinds of communication.

Perceiving and Understanding

Perceiving and understanding people are basic skills that surface in diverse communication situations. We have learned that perception is an active personal process through which we interpret people, situations, and interactions. To interpret phenomena, we notice, organize, and attach meaning to only some of the many stimuli around us at any moment. What we notice and how we interpret it depends on many factors, including our needs and goals, the relationship we are in, and the context of interaction. For example, we might notice relationship-level meanings more than content-level meanings in a conversation with a romantic partner or when listening to support a friend. On the other hand, we might focus more on content-level meanings in a performance review interview or when listening to a public presentation on social policies. We become more effective communicators when we realize how keenly our own ways of perceiving shape what people and things mean to us.

Creating Communication Climates

Creating climates for interaction is the second skill we discussed. Like the other basic skills, creating climate is relevant to all contexts and forms of communication.

The climate, or psychological tone of interaction, influences what people communicate and how they feel about each other. The nature of an effective climate varies according to communication contexts and goals. A warm, intimate feeling may be ideal in romantic relationships, whereas a tone of respect and cooperation may be more appropriate in work teams and organizational life. Once you realize that communication is a primary influence on climate, you can make informed choices about what kinds of climates you want to create and which forms of communication will foster them.

Engaging in Verbal Communication

Creating meaning with verbal communication is the third skill we discussed. We use language to express our thoughts and feelings, inform and persuade others, reflect on our experiences, create a sense of community with friends and co-workers, and gain information from others. We also respond to the language others use when intimates share private feelings with us, co-workers explain new projects, public officials try to win our support, interviewers ask us questions, and media present news and entertainment.

Engaging in Nonverbal Communication

A fourth basic skill is using nonverbal communication effectively. As we interact with others, we move our hands, alter our positions, vary our facial expressions, inflect our voices, change our speaking volume, and use silence. We also express ourselves with the clothes we wear and the artifacts we have. In contexts ranging from private to public, the many dimensions of nonverbal communication affect the meanings we attach to others and their messages and the meanings they attach to us and what we communicate.

Listening and Responding to Others

A fifth basic skill is listening, which is important in all communication situations. Communication is not just talking; it is also listening and responding. As we learned, we listen for different reasons: to gain information, to make critical judgments about what others say, and to understand and support people who matter to us. Different listening goals are best served by specific skills. For instance, evaluating a message is appropriate when listening critically, but it may be inadvisable when listening to a friend who is disclosing a personal problem. Showing concern and support is desirable when our listening goal is to help an intimate but may be irrelevant when the purpose in listening is to assess a politician's credibility. Although goals and behaviors of listening vary across situations, listening is present and important in all communication encounters.

Adapting to Other People and Situations

The final basic communication skill is adapting to other people and situations. This skill integrates and extends the other five skills by highlighting the importance of adapting these skills to particular contexts and people with whom we communicate. As we have seen, each of us learns how to communicate by participating in our social groups. Naturally, diverse social groups develop different patterns of interaction, and these are reflected in the communication of members of those groups. We should recognize and respect diverse styles of interacting and learn how to be effective in them by adapting our verbal and nonverbal communication, ways of perceiving, styles of listening, and expectations of climate.

These six skills are foundations of communication in its many forms and contexts. If you master these skills, you should be effective in personal relationships, professional interactions, and civic and social life.

The Road Ahead

Although this book is ending, what you have learned in it and the class it accompanies will continue to be of value throughout your life. Because communication is central to all facets of life, the understandings and skills you have gained will serve you for all the years ahead.

You will find that what we've discussed helps you understand and interact effectively with diverse others in a range of situations you will encounter. Whether you are watching television, counseling a friend, interacting with a colleague, or corresponding on the Internet, what you have learned in this book will enrich your life. The skills we have discussed and the contexts we have explored provide you with understandings that should allow you to communicate in ways that enhance your personal credibility and the effectiveness of your communication.

I hope that you have found this book worthy of the time you've invested in reading and studying it. And I hope the concepts, processes, and skills we have discussed will be valuable to you in the years ahead as you encounter a rich array of communication challenges and opportunities.

Glossary

Abstract Removed from concrete reality. Symbols are abstract because they are inferences and generalizations abstracted from reality.

Acknowledgment Second of three levels of interpersonal confirmation. Acknowledgment communicates that you hear and understand another's feelings and thoughts.

Agape One of six styles of loving. Agapic love is selfless and focused on the other's happiness.

Ambiguous Subject to multiple meanings. Symbols are ambiguous because their meanings vary from person to person, context to context, and so forth.

Ambushing Listening carefully for the purpose of attacking a speaker.

Analogies Type of comparison that asserts likeness between two things.

Anxious/ambivalent attachment One of four styles of attachment. The anxious/ambivalent style is fostered by inconsistent treatment by a caregiver and results in a preoccupation with relationships, both wanting and fearing intimacy.

Arbitrary Random or nonnecessary. Symbols are arbitrary because there is no necessary reason for any particular symbol to stand for a particular referent.

Artifacts Personal objects we use to announce our identities and personalize our environments.

Assimilation Occurs when people give up their ways and take on the ways of the dominant culture.

Attachment styles Patterns of interaction between a child and primary caregiver that teach children who they are, who others are, and how to approach relationships. Four attachment styles have been identified.

Attribution Account that explains why things happen and why people act as they do. Attributions are not necessarily correct interpretations of others and their motives.

Authoritarian interview Interviewing style in which interviewer has and exerts greater power than interviewee.

Autonomy/connection One of three relationship dialectics. This one involves tension between the need for personal autonomy, or independence, and connection, or intimacy.

Bracketing Identifying issues that are peripheral to a current conflict and setting those issues aside for discussion at a later time.

Brainstorming Group technique for generating potential solutions to a problem. Brainstorming encourages ideas to flow freely, without immediate criticism.

Chronemics A type of nonverbal communication concerned with how we perceive and use time to define identities and interaction.

Climate communication One of three constructive forms of participation in group decision making. Climate communication refers to creating and sustaining an open, engaged atmosphere for discussion.

Co-cultures Groups of people who live within a dominant culture yet also are members of another culture that is not dominant in a particular society.

Cognitive complexity Determined by the number of constructs used, how abstract they are, and how elaborately they interact to create perceptions.

Cognitive restructuring A method of reducing communication apprehension that involves teaching people to revise how they think about speaking situations.

Cognitive schemata Mental structures people use to organize and interpret experience. Four schemata have been identified: prototypes, personal constructs, stereotypes, and scripts.

Cohesion The degree of closeness, or feeling of esprit de corps, among members of a group.

Commitment A decision to remain with a relationship. Commitment is one of three dimensions of enduring romantic relationships, and it has more influence on relationship continuity than does love alone. It is also an advanced stage in the process of escalation in romantic relationships.

Communication A systemic process in which people interact with and through symbols to create and interpret meanings.

Communication apprehension Anxiety associated with real or anticipated communication encounters.

Communication apprehension is common and can be constructive.

Communication climate The overall feeling, or emotional mood, between people.

Communication network Links members of an organization. Communication networks may be formal (e.g., as specified in an organizational chart) or informal (friendship circles).

Communication rules Shared understandings of what communication means and what behaviors are appropriate in various situations.

Comparison Form of evidence that uses associations between two things that are similar (or strikingly different) in some important way or ways.

Complaint interview An interview that allows people to register complaints about a product, service, person, or company.

Conflict Exists when people who depend on each other express different views, interests, or goals and perceive their differences as incompatible or as in opposition.

Cookies Bits of data that Web sites collect and store in users' personal browsers.

Constitutive rules Communication rules that define what communication means by specifying how certain communicative acts are to be counted.

Constructivism Theory that states that we organize and interpret experience by applying cognitive structures called schemata.

Content level of meaning One of two levels of meaning in communication. The content level of meaning is the literal information in a message.

Counseling interview An interview in which one person with expertise helps another to understand a problem and develop strategies to overcome or cope more effectively with the difficulty.

Covert conflict Conflict that is expressed indirectly. Covert conflict generally is more difficult to manage constructively than overt conflict.

Credibility Willingness to believe in a person or to trust what a person says and does. Credibility exists in the minds of listeners and they confer it, or refuse to confer it, on speakers.

Critical listening Listening to analyze and evaluate the content of communication or the person speaking.

Critical research methods Data analysis that aims to identify, critique, or change communication practices that oppress, marginalize, or otherwise harm people.

Cultivation Cumulative process by which television fosters beliefs about social reality, including the belief that the world is more dangerous and violent than it actually is.

Cultivation theory Claims that television promotes a worldview that is inaccurate but that viewers assume reflects real life.

Cultural relativism Recognition that cultures vary in how they think, act, and behave, as well as in what they believe and value. Cultural relativism is not the same as moral relativism.

Culture Beliefs, understandings, practices, and ways of interpreting experience that are shared by a number of people.

Defensive listening Perceiving personal attacks, criticisms, or hostile undertones in communication when none is intended.

Derived credibility The expertise and trustworthiness that listeners recognize in a speaker as a result of how the speaker communicates during a presentation.

Direct definition Communication that explicitly tells us who we are by specifically labeling us and reacting to our behaviors. Direct definition usually occurs first in families and also in interaction with peers and others.

Dismissive attachment One of four attachment styles. This one is fostered by a caregiver's disinterested, rejecting, or abusive treatment of a child. It results in a view of others as unworthy of love and the self as adequate yet removed from intimate relationships.

Distributive interview Style of interviewing in which power is roughly equal between interviewer and interviewee.

Downer Person who communicates negatively about us and our worth.

Dyadic breakdown The first stage of relationship decay. Dyadic breakdown involves degeneration of established patterns, understandings, and routines that make up a relationship culture and sustain intimacy on a day-to-day basis.

Dyadic phase Stage in relationship deterioration in which partners discuss problems and alternative futures for the relationship. Not all partners engage in this phase.

Egocentric communication An unconstructive form of group contribution that is used to block others or to call attention to oneself.

Electronic epoch Fourth era in media history of civilization. The electronic epoch was ushered in by the invention of the telegraph, which made it possible for people to communicate personally across distance.

Empathy Ability to feel with another person—to feel what he or she feels in a situation.

Employment interview An interview in which employers and job candidates assess each other and determine whether there is a good fit between them.

Endorsement Third of three levels of interpersonal confirmation. Endorsement communicates acceptance of another's thoughts and feelings. Endorsement is not the same as agreement.

Environmental distractions Occurrences in communication situations that interfere with listening.

Environmental factors Nonverbal elements of settings that affect how we think, feel, act, and communicate.

Eros One of six styles of loving. Eros is passionate, intense, and erotic.

Ethics Branch of philosophy that deals with the goodness or rightness of particular actions. Ethical issues infuse all areas of the communication field.

Ethnocentrism The tendency to assume that one way of life is normal and superior to other ways of life.

Evidence Material used to interest, move, or persuade people. Types of evidence are statistics, examples, comparisons, quotations, and visual aids.

Examples Form of evidence that uses single instances to make a point, dramatize an idea, or personalize information. The four types of examples are undetailed, detailed, hypothetical, and anecdotal, or stories.

Exit interview An interview designed to gain information, insights, and perceptions about a place of work or education from a person who is leaving.

Extemporaneous delivery Presentational style that includes preparation and practice but not memorization of actual words and nonverbal behaviors.

Fantasy themes Ideas that spin out in a group and capture its social or task themes.

Fearful attachment One of four styles of attachment. Fostered by a caregiver's dismissive, rejecting, or abusive treatment, the fearful style may lead people to perceive themselves as unworthy of love.

Feedback Response to a message that may be verbal or nonverbal. Feedback appeared first in interactive models of communication.

Funnel sequence A pattern of communication in interviews that moves from broad, general questions to progressively more narrow and probing questions.

Gatekeeper Person, group, or institution that controls what topics are presented by media and how those topics are presented to viewers, listeners, or readers.

Generalized other Perspective that represents a person's perception of the collection of rules, roles, and attitudes endorsed by social groups or the whole social community to which the person belongs.

Grace Granting forgiveness or putting aside our needs or helping another save face when no standard says we should or must do so.

Grave dressing Final stage in the deterioration of romantic relationships in which partners put the relationship to rest.

Group More than two people who interact over time, are interdependent, and follow shared rules of conduct in order to reach a common goal. One type of group is a team.

Groupthink Exists when members cease to think critically and independently about ideas generated by a group.

Halo effect Occurs when an expert in one area is assumed to also be an expert in other areas that may be unrelated to the person's expertise.

Haptics Form of nonverbal communication that involves physical touch.

Hearing A physiological activity that occurs when sound waves hit our eardrums. Unlike listening, hearing is a passive process.

Homeostasis State of equilibrium that systems strive for but cannot sustain.

Hypertext Method of presenting information within new technologies. Hypertext allows users to get extensive information about specific words and concepts that appear on a computer screen.

Hypothetical thought Thinking about experiences and ideas that do not exist in the everyday reality.

I Creative, spontaneous, impulsive aspect of self. The *I* is complemented by the *me.*

Identity script Guide to action based on rules for living and identity. Initially communicated in families, scripts define our roles, how we are to play them, and basic elements in the plot of our lives.

Impromptu delivery Involves little preparation. Speakers think on their feet as they talk about ideas and positions with which they are familiar.

Indexing Technique of noting that statements reflect a specific time and circumstances and may not apply to other times or circumstances.

Individualism Pronounced Western value that holds that each person is unique and important and should be recognized for her or his individual activities.

Inference An interpretation that goes beyond the facts known.

Informational listening Listening to understand information and ideas.

Information-getting interview An interview in which one person asks questions to learn about a person's qualifications, background, experience, opinions, knowledge, attitudes, behaviors, and so forth.

Information-giving interview An interview that provides information to another person.

Initial credibility The expertise and trustworthiness listeners grant a speaker before a presentation begins. Initial credibility is based on titles, positions, experiences, or achievements known to listeners before they hear a speech.

Internet International network of networks that are connected to one another.

Interpersonal communication Deals with communication between people, usually in close relationships such as friendship and romance.

Interpretation The subjective process of organizing and making sense of perceptions.

Interview A communication transaction that emphasizes questions and answers.

Intrapersonal communication Communication with ourselves, or self-talk.

Intrapsychic phase The second phase in disintegration of romantic relationships, which involves brooding about problems in the relationship and dissatisfactions with a partner.

Investment Something put into a relationship that cannot be recovered should the relationship end. Investments, more than rewards and love, increase commitment.

Kinesics Body position and body motions, including those of the face.

Listening A complex process that consists of being mindful, hearing, selecting and organizing information, interpreting communication, responding, and remembering.

Literal listening Listening only to the content level of meaning and ignoring the relationship level of meaning.

Literate epoch Second era in media history of civilization. Invention of the phonetic alphabet inaugurated the literate epoch in which common symbols allowed people to communicate with writing.

Loaded language An extreme form of evaluative language that relies on words that strongly slant perceptions and thus meanings.

Local area network (LAN) LANs are interconnected groups of computers in a specified area such as an office or campus.

Lose–lose One of three orientations to conflict. Lose–lose assumes that everyone loses when conflict occurs.

Ludus One of six styles of love. Ludic love is playful and sometimes manipulative.

Mainstreaming The effect of television in stabilizing and homogenizing views within a society. Mainstreaming is one of two processes used to explain television's cultivation of synthetic worldviews.

Mania One of six styles of loving. Mania is an obsessive style of loving that often reflects personal insecurity.

Manuscript delivery Presentational style that involves speaking from a complete manuscript of a speech.

Mass communication All media that address mass audiences.

Me Reflective, analytical, socially conscious aspect of self. *Me* complements the *I* aspect of self.

Meaning The significance we bestow on a phenomenon—what it signifies to us.

Mean world syndrome Belief that the world is dangerous and full of mean people.

Memorized delivery Presentational style in which a speech is memorized word for word in advance.

Message complexity Exists when a message is highly complex, is full of detailed information, or involves intricate reasoning. Message complexity can interfere with effective listening.

Message overload Occurs when we receive more messages than we can interpret, evaluate, and remember. Message overload can interfere with effective listening.

Mindfulness A concept from Zen Buddhism that refers to being fully present in the moment. Being mindful is the first step of listening and the foundation for all others.

Mind reading Assuming that we understand what another person thinks or how another person perceives something.

Minimal encouragers Communication that gently invites another person to elaborate by expressing interest in hearing more.

Mirror interview Style of interviewing in which an interviewer's questions reflect previous responses and comments of the interviewee. Mirror interviews give substantial power to interviewees.

Monitoring The capacity to observe and regulate your communication.

Monopolizing Hogging the stage by continuously focusing communication on ourselves instead of the person who is talking.

Multilingual Having the ability to speak and understand more than one language.

Narrative speaking Rendering a story to share experiences, build community, pass on history, or teach a lesson.

Neutralization One of four responses to relationship dialectics. Neutralization involves balancing or finding a compromise between two dialectical poles.

Noise Anything that interferes with the intended meaning of communication. Noise includes sounds (e.g., traffic) as well as psychological interferences (e.g., preoccupation).

Nonverbal communication All forms of communication other than words themselves. Nonverbal communication includes inflection and other vocal qualities as well as several other behaviors.

Norms Informal rules that guide how members of a culture or group think, feel, and act. Norms define what is normal, or appropriate, in various situations.

Novelty/predictability One of three relationship dialectics. This one involves tension between wanting spontaneous, new experiences and wanting routines and familiar experiences.

Openness Extent to which a system interacts with its surrounding environment.

Openness/closedness One of three relationship dialectics. This one involves tension between wanting to share private thoughts, feelings, and experiences with intimates and wanting to preserve personal privacy.

Oral style Visual, vocal, and verbal aspects of the delivery of a public speech or other communication.

Organizational culture Understandings about identity and codes of thought and action that members of an organization share.

Overt conflict Conflict that is expressed directly and in a straightforward manner.

Paralanguage Communication that is vocal but not verbal. Paralanguage includes accent, inflection, volume, pitch, and sounds such as murmurs and gasps.

Paraphrasing A method of clarifying another's meaning by reflecting our interpretations of their communication to them.

Participation Response to cultural diversity in which people incorporate some practices, customs, and traditions of other groups into their lives.

Particular others Specific people who are significant to the self and who influence the self's values, perspectives, and esteem.

Passion Intensely positive feelings and desires for another person. Passion is based on rewards from involvement and is not equivalent to commitment.

Perception An active process of selecting, organizing, and interpreting people, objects, events, situations, and activities.

Performance review An occasion for a supervisor to comment on a subordinate's achievements and professional development, identify any weaknesses or problems, and collaborate to develop goals for future performance. Subordinates should offer perceptions of their strengths and weaknesses and participate actively in developing goals for professional development. Also known as a performance appraisal.

Personal constructs Bipolar mental yardsticks that allow us to measure people and situations along specific dimensions of judgment.

Personal relationship Defined by uniqueness, rules, relationship dialectics, commitment, and embeddedness in contexts. Personal relationships, unlike social ones, are irreplaceable.

Person-centeredness The ability to perceive another as a unique and distinct individual apart from social roles and generalizations.

Persuasive interview An interview designed to influence attitudes, beliefs, values, or actions.

Physical appearance Type of nonverbal communication that is concerned with how people look, as well as cultural meanings, values, and expectations associated with aspects of physical appearance.

Policy Formal statement of practice that reflects and upholds organizational culture.

Positive visualization A technique for reducing speaking anxiety in which people visualize themselves communicating effectively in progressively challenging speaking situations.

Power The ability to influence others. This feature of small groups affects participation.

Power over The ability to help or harm others. Power over others usually is communicated in ways that highlight the status and influence of the person using power over others.

Power to The ability to empower others to reach their goals. People who use power to help others generally do not highlight their own status and influence.

Pragma One of six styles of loving. Pragmatic love is based on practical considerations and criteria for attachment.

Print epoch Third era in media history of civilization. Invention of the printing press made it possible to mass-produce written materials so that reading was no longer restricted to elite members of society.

Problem-solving interview An interview in which people collaborate to identify sources of a mutual problem and to develop means of addressing or resolving it.

Procedural communication One of three constructive ways of participating in group decision making. Procedural communication orders ideas and coordinates contributions of members.

Process Something that is ongoing and continuously in motion for which it is difficult to identify beginnings and endings. Communication is a process.

Prototypes Knowledge structures that define the clearest or most representative examples of some category.

Proxemics A type of nonverbal communication that includes space and how we use it.

Pseudolistening Pretending to listen.

Psychological responsibility Obligation to remember, plan, and coordinate domestic work and child care. In general, women assume psychological responsibility for child care and housework, even if both partners share in the actual doing of tasks.

Punctuation Defining the beginning and ending of interaction or interaction episodes. Punctuation is subjective and not always agreed upon by people involved in interaction.

Qualitative research methods Interpretive techniques used to understand the character of experience, particularly how people perceive and make sense of communication. Qualitative methods include textual analysis and ethnography.

Quality circle Group in which people from different departments or areas in an organization collaborate to solve problems, meet needs, or increase quality of work life.

Quantitative research methods Techniques used to gather data that are quantifiable. Quantitative methods include descriptive statistics, surveys, and experiments.

Quotations Form of evidence that uses exact citations of statements made by others. Also called testimony.

Recognition Most basic level of interpersonal confirmation. Recognition communicates awareness that another person exists and is present.

Reflected appraisal Process of seeing and thinking about ourselves in terms of the appraisals of us that others reflect.

Reframing One of four responses to relationship dialectics. The reframing response transcends the apparent contradiction between two dialectical poles and reinterprets them as not in tension.

Regulative rules Communication rules that regulate interaction by specifying when, how, where, and with whom to talk about certain things.

Relationship culture A private world of rules, understandings, and patterns of acting and interpreting that partners create to give meaning to their relationship. Relationship culture is the nucleus of intimacy.

Relationship dialectics Opposing forces, or tensions, that are normal parts of all relationships. Three relationship dialectics are autonomy/connection, novelty/predictability, and openness/closedness.

Relationship level of meaning One of two levels of meaning in communication. The relationship level of meaning expresses the relationship between communicators.

Relationship listening Listening to support another person or understand how another person thinks, feels, or perceives some situation, event, or other phenomenon.

Remembering The process of recalling what you have heard. This is the sixth part of listening.

Reprimand interview An interview conducted by a supervisor to identify lapses in a subordinate's professional conduct, determine sources of problems, and establish a plan for improving future performance.

Resistance Response to cultural diversity that occurs when we attack the cultural practices of others or proclaim that our cultural traditions are superior.

Resonance The extent to which something (specifically phenomena on television) is congruent with personal experience. Resonance is one of two mechanisms used to explain television's ability to cultivate synthetic worldviews.

Respect Response to cultural diversity in which we value others' customs, traditions, values, and so forth even if we do not actively incorporate them into our lives.

Responding Symbolizing your interest in what is being said with observable feedback to speakers during interaction. This is the fifth of six elements in listening.

Role Responsibilities and behaviors expected of a person by virtue of his or her position.

Rules Patterned ways of behaving and interpreting behavior. All relationships develop rules.

Schemata Cognitive structures we use to organize and interpret experiences. Four types of schemata are prototypes, personal constructs, stereotypes, and scripts.

Scripts One of four cognitive schemata. Scripts define expected or appropriate sequences of action in particular settings.

Secure attachment One of four styles of attachment. The secure style is fostered by a caregiver who communicates with an infant in consistently loving and attentive ways. This pattern of early interaction inclines people to view themselves and others as worthy and to be comfortable both alone and in intimate relationships.

Segmentation One of four responses to relationship dialectics. Segmentation responses meet one dialectical need while ignoring or not satisfying the contradictory dialectical need.

Selective listening Focusing on only selected parts of communication. We listen selectively when we screen out parts of a message that don't interest us or that we disagree with and when we rivet attention on parts of communication that interest us or with which we agree.

Self A multidimensional process that involves forming and acting from social perspectives that arise and evolve in communication with others and ourselves.

Self-disclosure Revealing personal information about ourselves that others are unlikely to discover in other ways.

Self-fulfilling prophesy Acting in ways that bring about others' or our expectations or judgments of ourselves.

Self-sabotage Self-talk that communicates we are no good, we can't do something, we can't change, and so forth. Self-sabotaging communication undermines belief in ourselves and motivation to change and grow.

Self-serving bias Tendency to attribute our positive actions and successes to stable, global, internal influences that we control and to attribute negative actions and failures to unstable, specific, external influences beyond our control.

Separation One of four responses to relationship dialectics. The separation response occurs when friends or romantic partners assign one pole of a dialectic to certain spheres of activities or topics and assign the contradictory dialectical pole to distinct spheres of activities or topics.

Silence Lack of sound. Silence can be a powerful form of nonverbal communication.

Skills training A method of reducing communication apprehension that assumes that anxiety results from lack of speaking skills and thus can be reduced by learning skills.

Social climbing The process of trying to increase personal status in a group by winning the approval of high-status members.

Social comparison Comparing ourselves with others to form judgments of our talents, abilities, qualities, and so forth.

Social phase Part of relationship disintegration in which partners figure out how to inform outsiders that the relationship is ending.

Social relationship Unlike personal relationships, social ones tend to follow broad social scripts and rules, and participants in them tend to assume conventional social roles in relation to one another. Social relationships, unlike personal ones, can be replaced.

Social support Phase of relationship decline in which partners look to friends and family for support during the trauma of breaking up.

Specific purpose Objective that a speaker aims to accomplish as a result of presenting a speech. Specific purposes often are stated as behavioral objectives.

Speech to entertain Speech in which the primary goal is to amuse, interest, and engage listeners.

Speech to inform Speech in which the primary goal is to increase listeners' understanding, awareness, or knowledge about some topic.

Speech to persuade Speech in which the primary goal is to change listeners' attitudes, beliefs, or behaviors or to motivate listeners to action.

Standpoint The social, symbolic, and material conditions common to a group of people that influence how they understand themselves, others, and society.

Standpoint theory Claims that a culture includes a number of social groups that differently shape the perceptions, identities, and opportunities of members of those groups.

Static evaluation Assessments that suggest that something is unchanging or static. "Bob is impatient" is a static evaluation.

Statistics Form of evidence that uses numbers to summarize a great many individual cases or that demonstrates relationships among phenomena.

Stereotypes Predictive generalizations about people and situations.

Storge One of six styles of loving. Storgic love is based on friendship and is even-keeled.

Stress interview Style of interviewing in which an interviewer deliberately attempts to create anxiety in an interviewee.

Structures Organized relationships and interactions between members of an organization. Structures include roles, rules, policies, and communication networks.

Symbols Arbitrary, ambiguous, and abstract representations of other phenomena. Symbols are the basis of language, much nonverbal behavior, and human thought.

Synergy A special kind of energy that combines and goes beyond the energies, talents, and strengths of individual members.

System A group of interrelated elements that affect one another. Communication is systemic.

Systematic desensitization Method of reducing communication apprehension that first teaches people how to relax physiologically and then helps them practice feeling relaxed as they imagine themselves in progressively more difficult communication situations.

Task communication One of three constructive forms of participation in group decision making. Task communication focuses on giving and analyzing information and ideas.

Team A special kind of group that is characterized by different and complementary resources of members and by a strong sense of collective identity. All teams are groups, but not all groups are teams.

Teleconferencing Refers to meetings, formal or informal, conducted among people who are geographically separated. Teleconferencing can take several forms, and they differ in the extent to which they emulate face-to-face meetings.

Terminal credibility The cumulative expertise and trustworthiness listeners recognize in a speaker as a result of initial and derived credibility. Terminal credibility may be greater or less than initial credibility, depending on how effectively a speaker communicates.

Thesis statement The main idea of an entire speech. It should capture the key message in a concise sentence that listeners can remember easily.

Tolerance Response to diversity in which we accept differences, although we may not approve of or even understand them.

Totalizing Responding to a person as if one aspect of that person is the total of who the person is.

Transitions Words and sentences that connect ideas and main points in a speech so that listeners can follow a speaker.

Tribal epoch First era in a media history of civilization. During the tribal epoch the oral tradition reigned, and face-to-face talking and listening were primary forms of communication.

Understanding Response to cultural diversity that assumes that differences are rooted in cultural teachings and that no traditions, customs, or behaviors are intrinsically better than others.

Uppers People who communicate positive messages about us and our worth.

Uses and gratification theory Theory that claims people use media to gratify their needs, interests, and desires.

Verbal communication Words and only words. Verbal communication does not include inflection, accent, volume, pitch, or other paralinguistic features of speech.

Visual aids Form of evidence that uses visual objects such as charts, graphs, photographs, and physical objects to reinforce ideas presented verbally or to provide information.

Vultures People who attack a person's self-esteem. Vultures may be others or people who attack themselves.

Win–lose One of three orientations toward conflict. The win–lose orientation assumes that one person wins and the other(s) lose in any conflict.

Win–win One of three orientations to conflict. The win–win orientation assumes that everyone involved in a conflict can win and attempts to bring about a mutually satisfying solution.

World Wide Web (WWW) Newest information service on the Internet. The WWW is based on hypertext.

References

Abbate, J. (1999). *Inventing the Internet.* Reading, MA: Addison-Wesley-Longman.

Acitelli, L. (1988). When spouses talk to each other about their relationship. *Journal of Social and Personal Relationships, 5,* 185–199.

Acitelli, L. (1993). You, me, and us: Perspectives on relationship awareness. In S. W. Duck (Ed.), *Understanding relationship processes, 1: Individuals in relationships* (pp. 144–174). Thousand Oaks, CA: Sage.

Agee, W., Ault, P., & Emery, E. (1996). *Introduction to mass communications* (12th ed.). Reading, MA: Addison-Wesley.

Ainsworth, M. D., Blehar, M. C., Waters, E., & Wall, S. (1978). *Patterns of attachment: A psychological study of the strange situation.* Mahwah, NJ: Erlbaum.

Alcoff, L. (1991, Winter). The problem of speaking for others. *Cultural Critique,* 5–32.

Alexander, E. R., III. (1979). The reduction of cognitive conflict: Effects of various types of communication. *Journal of Conflict Resolution, 23,* 120–138.

Allan, G. (1993). Social structure and relationships. In S. Duck (Ed.), *Understanding relationship processes, 3: Social context and relationships* (pp. 1–25). Thousand Oaks, CA: Sage.

Allen, M., Hunter, J., & Donahue, W. (1989). Meta-analysis of self-report data on the effectiveness of public speaking anxiety treatment techniques. *Communication Education, 38,* 54–76.

Altheide, D. (1974). *Creating reality.* Thousand Oaks, CA: Sage.

Andersen, M. L., & Collins, P. H. (Eds.). (1992). *Race, class, and gender: An anthology.* Belmont, CA: Wadsworth.

Andersen, P. (1993). Cognitive schemata in personal relationships. In S. Duck (Ed.), *Understanding relationship processes, 1: Individuals in relationships* (pp. 1–29). Thousand Oaks, CA: Sage.

Anderson, H. (1997). *Conversation, language, and possibilities: A postmodern approach to therapy.* New York: Basic Books.

Anderson, R. (1995). *Essentials of personal selling: The new professionalism.* Englewood Cliffs, NJ: Prentice Hall.

Anderson, R., & Killenberg, G. (1999). *Interviewing: Speaking, listening, and learning for professional life.* Mountain View, CA: Mayfield.

Angelou, M. (1991). *I shall not be moved.* New York: Random House.

Angier, N. (1999, March 27). Not your average Joe. *Fairbanks Daily News Miner,* p. C1.

Argyle, M., & Henderson, M. (1984). The rules of friendship. *Journal of Social and Personal Relationships, 1,* 211–237.

Argyle, M., & Henderson, M. (1985). The rules of relationships. In S. W. Duck & D. Perlman (Eds.), *Understanding personal relationships: An interdisciplinary approach* (pp. 63–84). Thousand Oaks, CA: Sage.

Aries, E. (1987). Gender and communication. In P. Shaver (Ed.), *Sex and gender* (pp. 149–176). Thousand Oaks, CA: Sage.

AXIS Center for Public Awareness of People with Disabilities. Guidelines for Communicating with People with Disabilities. [Pamphlet] Columbus, OH: Author.

Axtell, R. (1990a). *Dos and taboos around the world* (2nd ed.). New York: Wiley.

Axtell, R. (1990b). *Dos and taboos of hosting international visitors.* New York: Wiley.

Ayres, J., & Hopf, T. S. (1990). The long-term effect of visualization in the classroom: A brief research report. *Communication Education, 39,* 75–78.

Bach, G. R., & Wyden, P. (1973). *The intimate enemy: How to fight fair in love and marriage.* New York: Avon.

Bailey, A. (1998, February 29). Daily bread. *The Durham Herald–Sun,* p. C5.

Baird, J. E., Jr. (1974). The effects of speech summaries upon audience comprehension of expository speeches of varying quality and complexity. *Central States Speech Journal, 25,* 124–135.

Baker, E. E. (1965). The immediate effects of perceived speaker disorganization on speaker credibility and audience attitude change in persuasive speaking. *Western Journal of Speech Communication, 29,* 148–161.

Ban on annoying, obscene e-mail upheld. (1999, April 20). *Raleigh News & Observer,* p. 4A.

Banville, T. (1978). *How to listen—how to be heard.* Chicago: Nelson-Hall.

Barge, K., & Keyton, J. (1994). Contextualizing power and social influence in groups. In L. Frey (Ed.), *Group communication in context: Studies of natural groups* (pp. 85–105). Mahwah, NJ: Erlbaum.

Bargh, J. (1997). *The automaticity of everyday life.* Mahwah, NJ: Erlbaum.

Bargh, J. (1999, January 29). The most powerful manipulative messages are hiding in plain sight. *Chronicle of Higher Education,* p. B6.

Barker, L., Edwards, R., Gaines, C., Gladney, K., & Holley, F. (1981). An investigation of proportional time spent in various communication activities by college students. *Journal of Applied Communication Research, 8,* 101–109.

Barnes, M. K., & Duck, S. (1994). Everyday communicative contexts for social support. In B. Burleson, T. Albrecht, & I. Sarason (Eds.), *The communication of social support* (pp. 175–194). Thousand Oaks, CA: Sage.

Bartholomew, K., & Horowitz, L. M. (1991). Attachment styles among young adults: A test of a four-category model. *Journal of Personality and Social Psychology, 61,* 226–244.

Bass, A. (1999, June 30). Web of isolation: When cybersex subs for a social life. *Raleigh News & Observer,* p. 4E.

Bates, E. (1994, Fall). Beyond black and white. *Southern Exposure,* 11–15.

Bateson, M. C. (1990). *Composing a life.* New York: Penguin/Plume.

Battaglia, D., Richard, F., Datter, D., & Lord, C. (1998). Breaking up is (relatively) easy to do: A script for the dissolution of close relationships. *Journal of Social and Personal Relationships, 15,* 829–845.

Baxter, L. A. (1984). Trajectories of relationship disengagement. *Journal of Social and Personal Relationships, 7,* 141–178.

Baxter, L. A. (1985). Accomplishing relational disengagement. In S. Duck & D. Perlman (Eds.), *Understanding personal relationships: An interdisciplinary approach* (pp. 243–265). Thousand Oaks, CA: Sage.

Baxter, L. A. (1987). Symbols of relationship identity in relationship cultures. *Journal of Social and Personal Relationships, 4,* 261–279.

Baxter, L. A. (1988). A dialectical perspective on communication strategies in relationship development. In S. W. Duck, D. F. Hay, S. E. Hobfoll, W. Iches, & B. Montgomery (Eds.), *Handbook of personal relationships* (pp. 257–273). London: Wiley.

Baxter, L. A. (1990). Dialectical contradictions in relational development. *Journal of Social and Personal Relationships, 7,* 69–88.

Baxter, L. A. (1993). The social side of personal relationships: A dialectical perspective. In S. Duck (Ed.), *Understanding relationship processes, 3: Social context and relationships* (pp. 139–165). Thousand Oaks, CA: Sage.

Baxter, L. A., & Simon, E. P. (1993). Relationship maintenance strategies and dialectical contradictions in personal relationships. *Journal of Social and Personal Relationships, 10,* 225–242.

Baym, N. K. (1995). The emergence of community in computer-mediated communication. In S. G. Jones (Ed.), *Cybersociety: Computer-mediated communication and community* (pp. 138–163). Thousand Oaks, CA: Sage.

Beatty, M. J., & Behnke, R. R. (1991). Effects of public speaking trait anxiety and intensity of speaking task on heart rate during performance. *Human Communication Research, 18,* 147–176.

Beatty, M. J., Plax, T., & Kearney, P. (1985). Reinforcement vs. modeling theory in the development of communication apprehension: A retrospective analysis. *Communication Research Reports, 12,* 80–95.

Be civil. (1994, July 5). *Wall Street Journal,* p. A1.

Beck, A. (1988). *Love is never enough.* New York: Harper & Row.

Becker, A. (1999, June 2). Personal email communication.

Becker, C. S. (1987). Friendship between women: A phenomenological study of best friends. *Journal of Phenomenological Psychology, 18,* 59–72.

Bell, A. (1989). *The complete manager's guide to interviewing.* Homewood, IL: Dow Jones–Irwin.

Bellah, R., Madsen, R., Sullivan, W., Swindler, A., & Tipton, S. (1985). *Habits of the heart: Individualism and commitment in American life.* Berkeley: University of California Press.

Belsky, J., & Pensky, E. (1988). Developmental history, personality, and family relationships: Toward an emergent family system. In R. A. Hinde & J. Stevenson-Hinde (Eds.), *Relationships within families: Mutual influences* (pp. 193–217). Oxford, UK: Clarendon.

Benjamin, D., & Horwitz, T. (1994, July 14). German view: "You Americans work too hard—and for what?" *Wall Street Journal,* pp. B1, B6.

Berg, J. H. (1987). Responsiveness and self-disclosure. In V. J. Derlega & J. H. Berg (Eds.), *Self-disclosure: Theory, research, and therapy.* New York: Plenum.

Berger, C. K., & Bell, R. A. (1988). Plans and the initiation of social relationships. *Human Communication Research, 15,* 217–235.

Berger, P. (1969). *A rumor of angels: Modern society and the rediscovery of the supernatural.* Garden City, NY: Doubleday.

Berger, P., & Kellner, H. (1964). Marriage and the construction of reality: An exercise in the microsociology of knowledge. *Diogenes, 46,* 1–24.

Bergner, R. M., & Bergner, L. L. (1990). Sexual misunderstanding: A descriptive and pragmatic formulation. *Psychotherapy, 27,* 464–467.

Berko, R., Wolvin, A., & Wolvin, D. (1992). *Communicating: A social and career focus* (5th ed.). Boston: Houghton Mifflin.

Berne, E. (1964). *Games people play.* New York: Grove.

Bernstein, B. (Ed.). (1973). *Class, codes, and control* (Vol. 2). London: Routledge & Kegan Paul.

Bikini Kill. (1991). *Bikini Kill, 1,* n.p.

Bingham, S. (Ed.). (1994). *Conceptualizing sexual harassment as discursive practice.* Westport, CT: Praeger.

Bingham, S. (1996). Sexual harassment: On the job, on the campus. In J. T. Wood (Ed.), *Gendered relationships* (pp. 233–252). Mountain View, CA: Mayfield.

Birdwhistell, R. (1970). *Kinesics and context.* Philadelphia: University of Pennsylvania Press.

Blair, C., Brown, J., & Baxter, L. (1994). Disciplining the feminine. *Quarterly Journal of Speech, 80,* 383–409.

Blanton, J. (1996, March 28). A novel medium. *Wall Street Journal,* p. R10.

Blumstein, P., & Kollock, P. (1988). Personal relationships. *Annual Review of Sociology, 14,* 467–490.

Bolton, R. (1986). Listening is more than merely hearing. In J. Stewart (Ed.), *Bridges, not walls* (4th ed., pp. 159–179). New York: Random House.

Bookmark. (1999, July 9). *Chronicle of Higher Education,* p. A29.

Booth-Butterfield, M., & Booth-Butterfield, S. (1994). Communication anxiety and signing effectiveness: Testing an interference model among deaf communicators. *Journal of Applied Communication Research, 22,* 273–286.

Bordo, S. (1999). *The male body: A new look at men in public and in private.* New York: Farrar, Straus & Giroux.

Bormann, E. G. (1975). *Discussion and group methods: Theory and practice.* New York: Harper & Row.

Bormann, E. G., Putnam L. L., & Pratt, J. M. (1978). Power, authority, and sex: Male response to female dominance. *Communication Monographs, 45,* 119–155.

Bostrom, R. N. (1988). *Communicating in public: Speaking and listening.* Santa Rosa, CA: Burgess.

Boulding, K. (1967). The medium is the massage. In G. E. Stearn (Ed.), *Hot and cool* (pp. 56–64). New York: Dial.

Boulding, K. (1990). *Three faces of power.* Thousand Oaks, CA: Sage.

Bourhis, J., & Allen, M. (1992). Meta-analysis of the relationship between communication apprehension and cognitive performance. *Communication Education, 41,* 68–76.

Bowen, S. P., & Michal-Johnson, P. (1995). HIV/AIDS: A crucible for understanding the dark side of sexual interactions. In S. Duck & J. T. Wood (Eds.), *Understanding relationship processes, 5: Confronting relationship challenges* (pp. 150–180). Thousand Oaks, CA: Sage.

Bowen, S. P., & Michal-Johnson, P. (1996). Being sexual in the shadow of AIDS. In J. T. Wood (Ed.), *Gendered relationships* (pp. 177–196). Mountain View, CA: Mayfield.

Bowlby, J. (1973). *Separation: Attachment and loss* (Vol. 2). New York: Basic Books.

Bowlby, J. (1988). *A secure base: Parent–child attachment and healthy human development.* New York: Basic Books.

Bowles, J. G. (1990, September 24). The human side of quality. *Fortune.*

Bozzi, V. (1986, February). Eat to the beat. *Psychology Today,* p. 16.

Bradbury, T. N., & Fincham, F. D. (1990). Attributions in marriage: Review and critique. *Psychological Bulletin, 107,* 3–33.

Bradley, B. (1978). *Fundamentals of speech communication: The credibility of ideas* (2nd ed.). Dubuque, IA: Wm. C. Brown.

Braxton, G. (1999, June 5). Minorities glaringly absent from fall television lineup. *Richmond Times–Dispatch,* pp. F8–F9.

Brehm, S. (1992). *Intimate relations* (2nd ed.). New York: McGraw-Hill.

Brock-Utne, B. (1989). *Feminist perspectives on peace and peace education.* New York: Pergamon.

Buber, M. (1957). Distance and relation. *Psychiatry, 20,* 97–104.

Buber, M. (1970). I and thou (Walter Kaufmann, Trans.). New York: Scribner's.

Buck, R. (1988). Nonverbal communication: Spontaneous and symbolic aspects. *American Behavioral Scientist, 31,* 341–354.

Buckley, M. F. (1992). Focus on research: We listen a book a day; we speak a book a week: Learning from Walter Loban. *Language Arts, 69,* 622–626.

Burgoon, J. K., Buller, D. B., Hale, J. L., & deTurck, M. A. (1984). Relational messages associated with nonverbal behaviors. *Human Communication Research, 10,* 351–378.

Burgoon, J. K., Buller, D. B., & Woodhall, G. W. (1989). *Nonverbal communication: The unspoken dialogue.* New York: Harper & Row.

Buunk, B., & Mutsaers, W. (1999). Equity perceptions and marital satisfaction in former and current marriage: A study among the remarried. *Journal of Social and Personal Relationships, 16,* 123–132.

Caldera, Y. M., Huston, A. C., & O'Brien, M. (1989). Social interactions and play patterns of parents and toddlers with feminine, masculine, and neutral toys. *Child Development, 60,* 70–76.

Caldwell, B., & Taha, L. (1993). Starving at the banquet: Social isolation in electronic communication media. Online, accessed June 8, 1999: http://jan.ucc.nau.edu/ipct-j/1993/caldwell.txt.

Campbell, K. (1989). *Man cannot speak for her: II. Key texts of the early feminists.* New York: Greenwood.

Canary, D., & Stafford, L. (Eds.). (1994). *Communication and relational maintenance.* New York: Academic Press.

Cancian, F. (1989). Love and the rise of capitalism. In B. Risman & P. Schwartz (Eds.), *Gender in intimate relationships* (pp. 12–25). Belmont, CA: Wadsworth.

Cannell, C., & Kahn, R. (1968). Interviewing. In G. Lindzey & E. Aronson (Eds.), *The handbook of social psychology* (Vol. 2, 2nd ed., pp. 569–584). Reading, MA: Addison-Wesley.

Capella, J. N. (1991). The biological origins of automated patterns of human interaction. *Communication Theory, 1,* 4–35.

Carey, J. (1989). *Communication as culture.* Boston, MA: Unwin-Hyman.

Carnes, J. (1994, Spring). An uncommon language. *Teaching Tolerance,* pp. 56–63.

Caspi, A., & Harbener, E. S. (1990). Continuity and change: Assortive marriage and the consistency of personality in adulthood. *Journal of Personality and Social Psychology, 58,* 250–258.

Cassirer, E. (1944). *An essay on man.* New Haven, CT: Yale University Press.

Chesebro, J. W. (1995). Communication technologies as cognitive systems. In J. T. Wood & R. B. Gregg (Eds.), *The future of the field* (pp. 15–46). Cresskill, NJ: Hampton.

Chesebro, J. W., & Bonsall, D. G. (1989). *Computer-mediated communication.* Tuscaloosa: University of Alabama Press.

Choi, Y. S., Massey, K. K., & Baran, S. J. (1988, May). *The beginnings of political communication research in the United States: Origins of the "limited effects" model.* Paper presented to the annual convention of the International Communication Association, San Francisco.

Christensen, A., & Heavey, C. (1990). Gender and social structure in the demand/withdraw pattern in marital conflict. *Journal of Personality and Social Psychology, 59,* 73–81.

Christophel, D. M. (1990). The relationships among teacher immediacy behaviors, student motivation, and learning. *Communication Education, 39,* 323–340.

Cissna, K. N. L, & Sieburg, E. (1986). Patterns of interactional confirmation and disconfirmation. In J. Stewart (Ed.), *Bridges, not walls* (4th ed., pp. 230–239). New York: Random House.

Civickly, J. M., Pace, R. W., & Krause, R. M. (1977). Interviewer and client behaviors in supportive and defensive interviews. In B. D. Ruben (Ed.), *Communication yearbook, I* (pp. 347–362). New Brunswick, NJ: Transaction Books.

Clair, R. P. (1993). The use of framing devices to sequester organizational narratives: Hegemony and harassment. *Communication Monographs, 60,* 113–136.

Clements, M. (1994, August 7). Sex in America today. *Parade,* pp. 4–6.

Cloven, D. H., & Roloff, M. E. (1991). Sense-making activities and interpersonal conflict: Communicative cures for the mulling blues. *Western Journal of Speech Communication, 55,* 134–158.

Communication Research, 6. (1979, January). Special issue devoted to uses and gratification theory.

Condry, S. M., Condry, J. C., & Pogatshnik, L. W. (1983). Sex differences: A study of the ear of the beholder. *Sex Roles, 9,* 697–704.

Conley, T. (1990). *Rhetoric in the European tradition.* New York: Longman.

Connecting with the Future. (1999). New York: National Association of State Universities and Land-Grant Colleges. (Also available online at http://www.nasulgc.org/finalit.pdf.)

Conquergood, D. (1986). Is it real? Watching television with Laotian refugees. *Directions, 2,* 71–74.

Conquergood, D., Friesema, P., Hunter, A., & Mansbridge, J. (1990). *Dispersed ethnicity and community integration: Newcomers and established residents in the Albany Park area of Chicago.* Evanston, IL: Center for Urban Affairs and Policy Research, Northwestern University.

Conrad, C. (1995). Was Pogo right? In J. T. Wood & R. B. Gregg (Eds.), *The future of the field* (pp. 183–208). Cresskill, NJ: Hampton.

Cooley, C. H. (1912). *Human nature and the social order.* New York: Scribner's.

Cox, J. R. (1989). The fulfillment of time: King's "I have a dream" speech (August 28, 1963). In M. C. Leff & F. J. Kaufeld (Eds.), *Texts in context: Critical dialogues on significant episodes in American rhetoric* (pp. 181–204). Davis, CA: Hermagoras.

Crockett, W. H. (1965). Cognitive complexity and impression formation. In B. A. Maher (Ed.), *Progress in experimental personality research* (Vol. 2, pp. 47–90). New York: Academic Press.

Cronen, V., Pearce, W. B., & Snavely, L. (1979). A theory of rule-structure and types of episodes and a study of perceived enmeshment in undesired repetitive patterns ("URPs"). In D. Nimmo (Ed.), *Communication yearbook* (Vol. 3). New Brunswick, NJ: Transaction Books.

Crowley, G. (1995, March 6). Dialing the stress-meter down. *Newsweek,* p. 62.

Cunningham, J. A., Strassberg, D. S., & Haan, B. (1986). Effects of intimacy and sex-role congruency on self-disclosure. *Journal of Social and Clinical Psychology, 4,* 393–401.

"Cybermedicine" raises ethical questions. (1999, June 28). *Raleigh News & Observer,* p. 7A.

Dance, F. E. X. (1970). The concept of communication. *Journal of Communication, 20,* 201–210.

Davis, F. (1991). *Moving the mountain: The women's movement in America since 1960.* New York: Simon & Schuster.

Davis, K. (1977). The care and cultivation of the corporate grapevine. In R. Huseman, C. Logue, & D. Freshley (Eds.), *Readings in interpersonal and organizational communication* (3rd ed., pp. 131–136). Boston: Holbrook.

Davis, K. (1980). Management communication and the grapevine. In S. Ferguson & S. Ferguson (Eds.), *Intercom: Readings in organizational communication* (pp. 55–66). Rochelle Park, NJ: Hayden.

DeFleur, M. L., & Ball-Rokeach, S. (1989). *Theories of mass communication* (5th ed.). White Plains, NY: Longman.

DeFrancisco, V. (1991). The sounds of silence: How men silence women in marital relations. *Discourse & Society, 2,* 413–423.

Delia, J., Clark, R. A., & Switzer, D. (1974). Cognitive complexity and impression formation in informal social interaction. *Speech Monographs, 41,* 299–308.

Deming, W. E. (1982). *Out of the crisis.* Cambridge, MA: Cambridge University Press.

Derlega, V. J., & Berg, J. H. (1987). *Self-disclosure: Research, theory, and therapy.* New York: Plenum.

Derlega, V. J., Metts, S., Petronio, S., & Margulis, S. (1993). *Self-disclosure.* Thousand Oaks, CA: Sage.

Desktop video interviews catch recruiters' eyes. (1995, November 21). *Wall Street Journal,* p. 1A.

DeVito, J. (1994). *Human communication: The basic course* (6th ed.). New York: HarperCollins.

Dewey, J. (1910). *How we think.* Boston: Heath.

Did you know? (1998, September 30). *Raleigh News & Observer,* p. F1.

Dieter, P. (1989, March). *Shooting her with video, drugs, bullets, and promises.* Paper presented at the meeting of the Association of Women in Psychology, Newport, RI.

Dillard, J. P., & Witteman, H. (1985). Romantic relationships at work: Organizational and personal influences. *Human Communication Research, 12,* 99–116.

Dillon, J. (1990). *The practice of questioning.* New York: Routledge.

Dindia, K. (1994). A multiphasic view of relationship maintenance strategies. In D. Canary & L. Stafford (Eds.), *Communication and relational maintenance* (pp. 91–112). New York: Academic Press.

Dixson, M., & Duck, S. W. (1993). Understanding relationship processes: Uncovering the human search for meaning. In S. W. Duck (Ed.), *Understanding relationship processes, 1: Individuals in relationships* (pp. 175–206). Thousand Oaks, CA: Sage.

Duck, S. W. (1990). Relationships as unfinished business: Out of the frying pan and into the 1990s. *Journal of Social and Personal Relationships, 7,* 5–24.

Duck, S. W. (1992). *Human relationships* (2nd ed.). Thousand Oaks, CA: Sage.

Duck, S. W. (1994a). *Meaningful relationships.* Thousand Oaks, CA: Sage.

Duck, S. W. (1994b). Steady as (s)he goes: Relational maintenance as a shared meaning system. In D. Canary & L. Stafford (Eds.), *Communication and relational maintenance* (pp. 45–60). New York: Academic Press.

Duck, S. W., & Wood, J. T. (Eds.). (1995). *Understanding relationship processes, 5: Confronting relationship challenges.* Thousand Oaks, CA: Sage.

Eadie, W. F. (1982). Defensive communication revisited: A critical examination of Gibb's theory. *Southern Speech Communication Journal, 47,* 163–177.

Eckman, P., Friesen, W., & Ellsworth, P. (1971). *Emotion in the human face: Guidelines for research and an integration of findings.* Elmsford, NY: Pergamon.

Edelstein, A. (1993). Thinking about the criterion variable in agenda-setting research. *Journal of Communication, 48,* 85–99.

Egan, G. (1973). Listening as empathic support. In J. Stewart (Ed.), *Bridges, not walls.* Reading, MA: Addison-Wesley.

Ellis, A., & Harper, R. (1977). *A new guide to rational living.* North Hollywood, CA: Wilshire.

E-mail abuse survey. (1999). Cambridge, MA: Elron Software, Inc.

Entman, R. (1994). African Americans according to TV news. Special issue: Race: America's rawest nerve. *Media Studies Journal, 8,* 29–38.

Ernst, F. Jr. (1973). *Who's listening? A handbook of the transactional analysis of the listening function.* Vallejo, CA: Addresso'set.

Estes, W. K. (1989). Learning theory. In A. Lessold & R. Glaser (Eds.), *Foundations for a psychology of education.* Mahwah, NJ: Erlbaum.

Evans, D. (1993, March 1). The wrong examples. *Newsweek,* p. 10.

Falling through the net. (1999, July 8). Report of the National Telecommunications and Information Administration. Washington, DC: U.S. Department of Commerce (http://www.ntia.doc.gov/ntiahome/digitaldivide/).

Faludi, S. (1991). *Backlash: The undeclared war against American women.* New York: Crown.

Fat-phobia in the Fijis: TV-thin is in. (1999, May 31). *Newsweek,* p. 70.

Fehr, B. (1993). How do I love thee? Let me consult my prototype. In S. W. Duck (Ed.), *Understanding relationship processes, 1: Individuals in relationships* (pp. 87–122). Thousand Oaks, CA: Sage.

Ferrante, J. (1995). *Sociology: A global perspective* (2nd ed.). Belmont, CA: Wadsworth.

Fincham, F. D., & Bradbury, T. N. (1987). The impact of attributions in marriage: A longitudinal analysis. *Journal of Personality and Social Psychology, 53,* 510–517.

Fisher, B. A. (1987). *Interpersonal communication: The pragmatics of human relationships.* New York: Random House.

Fisher, J. D., & Byrne, D. (1975). Too close for comfort: Sex differences in response to invasions of personal space. *Journal of Personal and Social Psychology, 32,* 15–21.

Fiske, J. (1987). *Television culture.* London: Methuen.

Fitzpatrick, M. A. (1988). *Between husbands and wives: Communication in marriage.* Thousand Oaks, CA: Sage.

Fitzpatrick, M. A., & Best, P. (1979). Dyadic adjustment in relational types: Consensus, cohesion, affectional expression, and satisfaction in enduring relationships. *Communication Monographs, 46,* 167–178.

Fletcher, G. J., & Fincham, F. D. (1991). Attribution in close relationships. In G. J. Fletcher & F. D. Fincham (Eds.), *Cognition in close relationships* (pp. 7–35). Mahwah, NJ: Erlbaum.

Foddy, W. (1993). *Constructing questions for interviews and questionnaires.* Cambridge, UK: Cambridge University Press.

Foss, S., Foss, K., & Trapp, R. (1991). *Contemporary perspectives on rhetoric* (2nd ed.). Prospect Heights, IL: Waveland.

Fowers, B. J. (1991). His and her marriage: A multivariate study of gender and marital satisfaction. *Sex Roles, 24,* 209–221.

Fraser, A. (1999, August 6). Colleges should tap the pedagogical potential of the World-Wide Web. *Chronicle of Higher Education,* p. B8.

French, M. (1992). *The war against women.* New York: Summit.

Gabriel, S. L., & Smithson, I. (Eds.). (1990). *Gender in the classroom: Power and pedagogy.* Urbana: University of Illinois Press.

Gaines, S., Jr. (1995). Relationships between members of cultural minorities. In J. T. Wood & S. W. Duck (Eds.), *Understanding relationship processes, 6: Understudied relationships: Off the beaten track* (pp. 51–88). Thousand Oaks, CA: Sage.

Gandy, O. H., Jr. (1994). From bad to worse: the media's framing of race and risk. Special issue: Race: America's rawest nerve. *Media Studies Journal, 8,* 39–48.

Garner, T. (1994). Oral rhetorical practice in African American culture. In A. Gonzaléz, M. Houston, & V. Chen (Eds.), *Our voices: Essays in culture, ethnicity, and communication* (pp. 81–91). Los Angeles: Roxbury.

Gates, B. (1999, May 31). Why the PC will not die. *Newsweek,* p. 64.

Gates, H. L. (1992). *Loose canons: Notes on the culture wars.* New York: Oxford University Press.

Gerbner, G. (1990). Epilogue: Advancing on the path of righteousness (maybe). In N. Signorielli & M. Morgan (Eds.), *Cultivation analysis: New directions in media effects research* (pp. 250–261). Thousand Oaks, CA: Sage.

Gerbner, G. (1997a). *The crisis of the cultural environment: Media and democracy in the 21st century.* Northampton, MA: Media Education Foundation (http://www.mediaed.org).

Gerbner, G. (1997b). *The electronic storyteller: Television and the cultivation of values.* Northampton, MA: Media Education Foundation (http://www.mediaed.org).

Gerbner, G., Gross, L., Morgan, M., & Signorielli, N. (1986). Living with television: The dynamics of the cultivation process. In J. Bryant & D. Zillmann (Eds.), *Perspectives on media effects* (pp. 17–40). Mahwah, NJ: Erlbaum.

Gergen, K. (1991). *The saturated self: Dilemmas of identity in contemporary life.* New York: Basic Books.

Gerstel, N., & Gross, H. (1985). *Commuter marriage.* New York: Guilford.

Gibb, J. R. (1961). Defensive communication. *Journal of Communication, 11,* 141–148.

Gibb, J. R. (1964). Climate for trust formation. In L. Bradford, J. Gibb, & K. Benne (Eds.), *T-group theory and laboratory method* (pp. 279–309). New York: Wiley.

Gibb, J. R. (1970). Sensitivity training as a medium for personal growth and improved interpersonal relationships. *Interpersonal Development, 1,* 6–31.

Gibbs, J. T. (1992). Young black males in America: Endangered, embittered, and embattled. In M. L.

Andersen & P. H. Collins, (Eds.), *Race, class, and gender: An anthology* (pp. 267–276). Belmont, CA: Wadsworth.

Gilman, S. (1999a). *Creating beauty to cure the soul: Race and psychology in the shaping of aesthetic surgery.* Durham, NC: Duke University Press.

Gilman, S. (1999b). *Making the body beautiful: A cultural history of aesthetic surgery*. Princeton, NJ: Princeton University Press.

Gitlin, T. (1980). *The whole world is watching: Mass media in the making and unmaking of the new left.* Berkeley: University of California Press.

Goodman, E. (1999, May 29). Western culture pounds away at paradise. *Raleigh News & Observer,* p. 24A.

Goodrich, T. J., Rampage, C., Ellman, B., & Halstead, K. (1988). *Feminist family therapy: A casebook.* New York: Norton.

Gorham, J., & Zakahi, W. R. (1990). A comparison of teacher and student perceptions of immediacy and learning. *Communication Education, 39,* 46–62.

Gottman, J. M. (1993). The roles of conflict engagement, escalation or avoidance in marital interaction: A longitudinal view of five types of couples. *Journal of Consulting and Clinical Psychology, 61,* 6–15.

Gottman, J. M., & Carrère, S. (1994). Why can't men and women get along? Developmental roots and marital inequities. In D. Canary & L. Stafford (Eds.), *Communication and relational maintenance* (pp. 203–229). New York: Academic Press.

Gottman, J. M., Markman, H. J., & Notarius, C. (1977). The topography of marital conflict: A sequential analysis of verbal and nonverbal behavior. *Journal of Marriage and the Family, 39,* 461–477.

Gouran, D. S. (1982). *Making decisions in groups: Choices and consequences.* Glenview, IL: Scott, Foresman.

Goyer, S., Redding, W. C., & Rickey, J. (1964). *Interviewing principles and techniques.* Dubuque, IA: Wm. C. Brown.

Gronbeck, B. (1999). *Paradigms of speech communication studies: Looking back toward the future.* Needham Heights, MA: Allyn & Bacon.

Gronbeck, B. E., McKerro, R., Ehninger, D., & Monroe, A. H. (1994). *Principles and types of speech communication* (12th ed.). Glenview, IL: Scott, Foresman.

Grossberg, L. (1997). *Bringing it all back home: Essays in cultural studies.* Durham, NC: Duke University Press.

Guide to the Web, vol. 7. (1999). Lincoln, NE: Sandhills.

Hackman, M. Z., & Walker, K. B. (1990). Instructional communication in the televised classroom: The effects of system design and teacher immediacy on student learning and satisfaction. *Communication Education, 39,* 196–206.

Haiken, E. (1997). *Venus envy: A history of cosmetic surgery*. Baltimore: Johns Hopkins University Press.

Hall, A. D., & Fagen, R. (1956). Definition of a system. *General Systems, 1,* 18–28.

Hall, D. (1995). *Revolution grrrl style now!: The rhetoric and subcultural practices of Riot Grrrls.* Unpublished master's thesis in the Department of Communication Studies at the University of North Carolina, Chapel Hill.

Hall, E. T. (1968). Proxemics. *Current Anthropology, 9,* 83–108.

Hall, E. T. (1969). *The hidden dimension.* New York: Anchor.

Hall, E. T. (1977). *Beyond culture.* New York: Doubleday.

Hall, J. A. (1987). On explaining gender differences: The case of nonverbal communication. In P. Shaver & C. Hendricks (Eds.), *Sex and gender* (pp. 177–200). Thousand Oaks, CA: Sage.

Hall, S. (1982). The rediscovery of "ideology": Return of the repressed in media studies. In M. Gurevitch, T. Bennett, J. Curran, & J. Woollacott (Eds.), *Culture, society, and the media* (pp. 56–90). London: Methuen.

Hall, S. (1986a). Cultural studies: Two paradigms. In R. Collins (Ed.), *Media, culture, and society: A critical reader.* London: Sage.

Hall, S. (1986b). The problem of ideology: Marxism without guarantees. *Journal of Communication Inquiry, 10,* 28–44.

Hall, S. (1988). *The hard road to renewal: Thatcherism and the crisis on the left.* London: Verso.

Hall, S. (1989a). Ideology. In E. Barnouw et al. (Eds.), *International encyclopedia of communication* (Vol. 2, pp. 307–311). New York: Oxford University Press.

Hall, S. (1989b). Ideology and communication theory. In B. Dervin, L. Grossberg, B. O'Keefe, & E. Wartella (Eds.), *Rethinking communication theory* (Vol. 1, pp. 40–52). Thousand Oaks, CA: Sage.

Hamachek, D. (1992). *Encounters with the self* (3rd ed.). New York: Harcourt, Brace, Jovanovich.

Hamilton, C. (1996). *Successful public speaking.* Belmont, CA: Wadsworth.

Hampden-Turner, C. (1982). *Maps of the mind: Charts and concepts of the mind and its labyrinths.* New York: Macmillan/Collier.

Hanisch, C. (1970). What can be learned? A critique of the Miss America protest. In L. Tanner (Ed.), *Voices from women's liberation* (pp. 123–136). New York: Signet.

Hansen, J. E., & Schuldt, W. J. (1984). Marital self-disclosure and marital satisfaction. *Journal of Marriage and the Family, 46,* 923–926.

Haraway, D. (1988). Situated knowledges: The science question in feminism and the privilege of partial perspective. *Signs, 14,* 575–599.

Harding, S. (1991). *Whose science? Whose knowledge? Thinking from women's lives.* Ithaca, NY: Cornell University Press.

Harris, T. J. (1969). *I'm OK, you're OK.* New York: Harper & Row.

Haubegger, C. (1999, July 12). The legacy of generation —. *Newsweek,* p. 61.

Hayakawa, S. I. (1962). *The use and misuse of language.* New York: Fawcett.

Hayakawa, S. I. (1964). *Language in thought and action* (2nd ed.). New York: Harcourt, Brace & World.

Hecht, M. L., Collier, M. J., & Ribeau, S. A. (1993). *African American communication: Ethnic identity and cultural interpretation.* Thousand Oaks, CA: Sage.

Hecht, M. L., Marston, P. J., & Larkey, L. K. (1994). Love ways and relationship quality in heterosexual relationships. *Journal of Social and Personal Relationships, 11,* 25–44.

Hegel, G. W. F. (1807). *Phenomenology of mind* (J. B. Baillie, Trans.). Germany: Wurzburg & Bamburg.

Heider, F. (1958). *The psychology of interpersonal relations.* New York: Wiley.

Helgeson, S. (1990). *The female advantage: Women's ways of leadership.* New York: Doubleday/Currency.

Hellweg, S. (1992). Organizational grapevines. In K. L. Hutchinson (Ed.), *Readings in organizational communication* (pp. 159–172). Dubuque, IA: Wm. C. Brown.

Hempel, C. (1999, July 9). The brains in the family may be your wired home. *Raleigh News & Observer,* pp. 1D, 6D.

Hendrick, C., & Hendrick, S. (1988). Lovers wear rose colored glasses. *Journal of Social and Personal Relationships, 5,* 161–184.

Hendrick, C., & Hendrick, S. (1996). Gender and the experience of heterosexual love. In J. T. Wood (Ed.), *Gendered relationships* (pp. 131–148). Mountain View, CA: Mayfield.

Hendrick, C., Hendrick, S., Foote, F. H., & Slapion-Foote, M. J. (1984). Do men and women love differently? *Journal of Social and Personal Relationships, 2,* 177–196.

Henley, N. M. (1977). *Body politics: Power, sex and nonverbal communication.* Englewood Cliffs, NJ: Prentice Hall.

Hicks, J. (1998, November 5). A thin line. *Raleigh News & Observer,* pp. 1E, 3E.

Higginbotham, E. (1992). We were never on a pedestal: Women of color continue to struggle with poverty, racism, and sexism. In M. L. Andersen & P. H. Collins (Eds.), *Race, class, and gender: An anthology* (pp. 183–190). Belmont, CA: Wadsworth.

Hirokawa, R., & Keyton, J. (1995). Perceived facilitators and inhibitors of effectiveness in organizational work teams. *Management Communication Quarterly, 8,* 424–446.

Hochschild, A., & Machung, A. (1989). *The second shift.* New York: Viking.

Hojat, M. (1982). Loneliness as a function of selected personality variables. *Journal of Clinical Psychology, 38,* 136–141.

Hollis, R. (1989, June 10). E-mail etiquette. *MacWeek, 24,* p. 26.

Honeycutt, J. M., Woods, B., & Fontenot, K. (1993). The endorsement of communication conflict rules as a function of engagement, marriage, and marital ideology. *Journal of Social and Personal Relationships, 10,* 285–304.

Houston, M. (1994). When black women talk with white women: Why dialogues are difficult. In A. Gonzaléz, M. Houston, & V. Chen (Eds.), *Our voices: Essays in culture, ethnicity, and communication* (pp. 133–139). Los Angeles: Roxbury.

Houston, M., & Wood, J. T. (1996). Difficult dialogues, expanded horizons: Communicating across race and class. In J. T. Wood (Ed.), *Gendered relationships* (pp. 39–56). Mountain View, CA: Mayfield.

How Americans communicate: http://www.natcom.org/research/Roper/how_americans_communicate.htm

Hower, W. (1999, June 29). Cybermemorials. *Raleigh News & Observer,* p. 1E.

Hunt, A., & Murray, A. (1999, August). Privacy, please: How the "second generation of e-business" plans to invade your space. *Smart Money,* 73–74.

Hunt, D. (1999). *O. J. Simpson facts and fictions: News rituals in the construction of reality.* Cambridge University Press.

Huston, M., & Schwartz, P. (1995). Relationships of lesbians and gay men. In J. T. Wood & S. W. Duck (Eds.), *Understanding relationship processes, 6: Understudied relationships: Off the beaten track* (pp. 89–121). Thousand Oaks, CA: Sage.

Hyde, M. J. (1995). Human being and the call of technology. In J. T. Wood & R. B. Gregg (Eds.), *The future of the field* (pp. 47–79). Cresskill, NJ: Hampton.

Imperato, G. (1999, May). The email prescription. *Fast Company,* pp. 90–99.

Inman, C. C. (1996). Men's friendships: Closeness in the doing. In J. T. Wood (Ed.), *Gendered relationships* (pp. 95–110). Mountain View, CA: Mayfield.

James, K. (1989). When twos are really threes: The triangular dance in couple conflict. *Australian and New Zealand Journal of Family Therapy, 10,* 179–186.

Janis, I. L. (1977). *Victims of groupthink*. Boston: Houghton Mifflin.

Johnson, C. B., Stockdale, M. S., & Saal, F. E. (1991). Persistence of men's misperceptions of friendly cues across a variety of interpersonal encounters. *Psychology of Women Quarterly, 15,* 463–465.

Johnson, F. L. (1989). Women's culture and communication: An analytic perspective. In C. M. Lont & S. A. Friedley (Eds.), *Beyond the boundaries: Sex and gender diversity in communication.* Fairfax, VA: George Mason University Press.

Johnson, F. L. (1996). Women's friendships: Closeness in dialogue. In J. T. Wood (Ed.), *Gendered relationships* (pp. 79–94). Mountain View, CA: Mayfield.

Jones, E., & Gallois, C. (1989). Spouses' impressions of rules for communication in public and private marital conflicts. *Journal of Marriage and the Family, 51,* 957–967.

Jones, S. G. (Ed.). (1995). *Cybersociety: Computer-mediated communication and community.* Thousand Oaks, CA: Sage.

Jones, S. (1999, July 24). Some don't get the message. *Raleigh News & Observer,* pp. 1D, 6D.

Jones, W. H., & Moore, T. L. (1989). Loneliness and social support. In M. Hojat & R. Crandall (Eds.), *Loneliness: Theory, research, and applications* (pp. 145–156). Thousand Oaks, CA: Sage.

Katriel, T. (1990). "Griping" as a verbal ritual in some Israeli discourse. In D. Carbaugh (Ed.), *Cultural communication and intercultural contact* (pp. 99–114). Mahwah, NJ: Erlbaum.

Katz, E., Blumler, J., & Gurevitch, M. (1974). Uses of mass communication by the individual. In W. P. Davidson & F. Yu (Eds.), *Major issues and future directions* (pp. 11–35). New York: Praeger.

Katz, J. (1999). *Connections: Social and cultural studies of the telephone in American life.* New Brunswick, NJ: Transaction Press.

Kaufman, J. (1996, January 18). Feng shui puts your furniture and your life in order. *Wall Street Journal,* p. A12.

Keeley, M. P., & Hart, A. J. (1994). Nonverbal behavior in dyadic interaction. In S. W. Duck (Ed.), *Understanding relationship processes, 4: Dynamics of relationships* (pp. 135–162). Thousand Oaks, CA: Sage.

Kelley, H. H. (1967). Attribution theory in social psychology. In D. Levine (Ed.), *Nebraska symposium on motivation* (Vol. 15, pp. 192–238). Lincoln: University of Nebraska Press.

Kelly, G. A. (1955). *The psychology of personal constructs.* New York: Norton.

Kelly, T. (1997). *Conversational narcissism in hyperpersonal interaction.* (Online, accessed April 19, 1999: http://odin.cc.pdx.edu/~psu17799/sp511.htm.)

Keyes, R. (1992, February 22). Do you have the time? *Parade,* pp. 22–25.

Keyton, J. (1999a). Relational communication in groups. In L. Frey, D. Gouran, & S. Poole (Eds.), *Handbook of group communication theory and research* (pp. 192–222). Thousand Oaks, CA: Sage.

Keyton, J. (1999b). *Group communication: Process and analysis.* Mountain View, CA: Mayfield.

Kimball, M. (1986). Television and sex-role attitudes. In T. M. Williams (Ed.), *The impact of television: A natural experiment in three communities* (pp. 265–301). Orlando, FL: Academic Press.

Klopf, D. W. (1991). *Intercultural encounters: The fundamentals of intercultural communication* (2nd ed.). Englewood, CO: Morton.

Knapp, M. L. (1972). *Nonverbal communication in human interaction.* New York: Holt, Rinehart, & Winston.

Kochman, T. (1981). *Black and white styles in conflict.* Chicago: University of Chicago Press.

Korzybski, A. (1933). *Science and sanity.* Lakeville, CT: Institute of General Semantics.

Korzybski, A. (1948). *Science and sanity* (3rd ed.). Lakeville, CT: International Non-Aristotelian Library.

Krol, E. (1994). *The whole Internet: User's guide and catalog.* Seabastopol, CA: O'Reilly & Associates.

Kruger, P. (1999, June). A leader's journey. *Fast Company,* pp. 116–138.

Kurdek, L. A. (1993). The allocation of household labor in gay, lesbian, and heterosexual married couples. *Journal of Social Issues, 49,* 127–139.

La Gaipa, J. J. (1982). Rituals of disengagement. In S. W. Duck (Ed.), *Personal relationships, 4: Dissolving personal relationships.* London: Academic Press.

Lakoff, G., & Johnson, M. (1980). *Metaphors we live by.* Chicago: University of Chicago Press.

Langer, S. (1953). *Feeling and form: A theory of art.* New York: Scribner's.

Langer, S. (1979). *Philosophy in a new key: A study in the symbolism of reason, rite, and art* (3rd ed.). Cambridge, MA: Harvard University Press.

Langston, D. (1992). Tired of playing monopoly? In M. L. Andersen & P. H. Collins, (Eds.), *Race, class, and gender: An anthology* (pp. 110–119). Belmont, CA: Wadsworth.

Larmer, B. (1999, July 12). Latino America. *Newsweek,* 48–51.

Larson, J. R. (1984). The performance feedback process: A preliminary model. *Organizational Behavior and Human Performance, 33,* 42–76.

Lash, A. (1999, August 2–9). Privacy, practically speaking. *Industry Standard,* pp. 121–124.

Laswell, H. D. (1948). The structure and function of communication in society. In L. Bryson (Ed.),

The communication of ideas. New York: Harper & Row.

Lau, B. (1989). Imagining your path to success. *Management Quarterly, 30*, 30–41.

Lea, M., & Spears, R. (1995). Relationships conducted over electronic systems. In J. T. Wood & S. W. Duck (Eds.), *Understanding relationship processes, 6: Understudied relationships: Off the beaten track* (pp. 197–233). Thousand Oaks, CA: Sage.

Leathers, D. G. (1986). *Successful nonverbal communication: Principles and applications*. New York: Macmillan.

Lederman, L. (1990). Assessing educational effectiveness: The focus group interview as a technique for data collection. *Communication Education, 39*, 117–127.

Lee, J. A. (1973). *The colors of love: An exploration of the ways of loving*. Don Mills, Ontario: New Press.

Lee, J. A. (1988). Love-styles. In R. J. Sternberg & M. L. Barnes (Eds.), *The psychology of love* (pp. 38–67). New Haven, CT: Yale University Press.

Lee, W. (1994). On not missing the boat: A processual method for intercultural understandings of idioms and lifeworld. *Journal of Applied Communication Research, 22*, 141–161.

Le Poire, B. A., Burgoon, J. K., & Parrott, R. (1992). Status and privacy restoring communication in the workplace. *Journal of Applied Communication Research, 4*, 419–436.

Levinson, P. (1999). *Digital McLuhan: A guide to the information millennium*. New York: Routledge.

Levy, S. (1999, May 31). The new digital galaxy. *Newsweek*, pp. 57–62.

Lewin, K. (1947). *Human relations*. New York: Harper & Row.

Lichter, S. R., Lichter, L. S., Rothman, S., & Amundson, D. (1987, July–August). Prime-time prejudice: TV's images of blacks and Hispanics. *Public Opinion*, 13–16.

Lightner, C. (1990). *Giving sorrow words: How to cope with grief and get on with your life*. New York: Warner.

Lorde, A. (1992). Age, race, class, and sex: Women redefining difference. In M. L. Andersen & P. H. Collins (Eds.), *Race, class, and gender: An anthology* (pp. 495–502). Belmont, CA: Wadsworth.

Luft, J. (1969). *Of human interaction*. Palo Alto, CA: Natural Press.

Lumsden, G., & Lumsden, D. (1997). *Communicating in groups and teams*. Belmont, CA: Wadsworth.

Lund, M. (1985). The development of investment and commitment scales for predicting continuity of personal relationships. *Journal of Social and Personal Relationships, 2*, 3–23.

Lytton, H., & Romney, D. M. (1991). Parents' differential socialization of boys and girls: A meta-analysis. *Psychological Bulletin, 109*, 267–296.

Major, B., Schmidlin, A. M., & Williams, L. (1990). Gender patterns in social touch: The impact of setting and age. In C. Mayo & N. M. Henley (Eds.), *Gender and nonverbal behavior* (pp. 3–37). New York: Springer-Verlag.

Malandro, L. A., & Barker, L. L. (1983). *Nonverbal communication*. Reading, MA: Addison-Wesley.

Maltz, D. N., & Borker, R. (1982). A cultural approach to male–female miscommunication. In J. J. Gumpertz (Ed.), *Language and social identity* (pp. 196–216). Cambridge, UK: Cambridge University Press.

Mander, M. (Ed.). (1999). *Framing friction: Media and social conflict*. Urbana: University of Illinois Press.

Markhoff, J. (1989, November 5). Here comes the fiber-optic home. *New York Times*, sec. 3, pp. 1, 15.

McChesney, R. (1999). *Rich media, poor democracy: Communication politics in dubious times*. Urbana: University of Illinois Press.

McClure, M. (1997). Mind/body medicine: Evidence of efficacy. *Health and Healing, 1*, 3.

McCollum, K. (1998, October 23). In a speech to Indiana U. students, Bill Gates paints a glowing future for computing. *Chronicle of Higher Education*, p. A25.

McCollum, K. (1999, May 14). Students find sex, drugs, and more than a little education on line, survey finds. *Chronicle of Higher Education*, p. A31.

McCroskey, J. C. (1977). Oral communication apprehension: A summary of recent theory and research. *Human Communication Research, 4*, 78–96.

McCroskey, J. C. (1982). *Introduction to rhetorical communication* (4th ed.). Englewood Cliffs, NJ: Prentice Hall.

McCroskey, J. C., & Mehrley, R. S. (1969). The effects of disorganization and nonfluency on attitude change and source credibility. *Speech Monographs, 36*, 13–21.

McCroskey, J., & Teven, J. (1999). Goodwill: A reexamination of the construct and its measurement. *Communication Monographs, 66*, 90–103.

McGee-Cooper, A., Trammel, D., & Lau, B. (1992). *You don't have to go home from work exhausted*. New York: Bantam.

McGuire, W. J. (1989). Theoretical foundations of campaigns. In R. E. Rice & C. K. Atkin (Eds.), *Public communication campaigns* (2nd ed., pp. 43–65). Thousand Oaks, CA: Sage.

McLuhan, M. (1962). *The Gutenberg galaxy*. Toronto: University of Toronto Press.

McLuhan, M. (1964). *Understanding media*. New York: McGraw-Hill.

McLuhan, M. (1969, March). Interview. *Playboy,* pp. 53–54, 56, 59–62, 64–66, 68, 70.

McLuhan, M., & Fiore, Q. (1967). *The medium is the message.* New York: Random House.

Mead, G. H. (1934). *Mind, self, and society.* Chicago: University of Chicago Press.

Meeks, B., Hendrick, S., & Hendrick, C. (1998). Communication, love, and satisfaction. *Journal of Social and Personal Relationships, 15,* 755–773.

Mehrabian, A. (1981). *Silent messages: Implicit communication of emotion and attitudes* (2nd ed.). Belmont, CA: Wadsworth.

Metts, S., Cupach, W. R., & Bejlovec, R. A. (1989). "I love you too much to ever start liking you": Redefining romantic relationships. *Journal of Social and Personal Relationships, 6,* 259–274.

Meyers, M. (1994). News of battering. *Journal of Communication, 44,* 47–62.

Miell, D. E., & Duck, S. W. (1986). Strategies in developing friendship. In V. J. Derlega & B. A. Winstead (Eds.), *Friendship and social interaction.* New York: Springer-Verlag.

Miller, E. (1974). Speech introductions and conclusions. *Quarterly Journal of Speech, 32,* 118–127.

Miller, G. R., & Parks, M. R. (1982). Communication in dissolving relationships. In S. W. Duck (Ed.), *Personal relationships 4: Dissolving personal relationships* (pp. 127–154). London: Academic Press.

Miller, J. B. (1993). Learning from early relationship experience. In S. W. Duck (Ed.), *Understanding relationship processes, 2: Learning about relationships* (pp. 1–29). Thousand Oaks, CA: Sage.

Mino, M. (1996). The relative effects of content and vocal delivery during a stimulated employment interview. *Communication Research Reports, 13,* 225–238.

Mirzoeff, N. (Ed.). (1998). *The visual culture reader.* New York: Routledge.

Moffatt, T. (1979). *Selection interviewing for managers.* New York: Harper & Row.

Mongeau, P. A., & Blalock, J. (1994). Student evaluations of instructor immediacy and sexually harassing behaviors: An experimental investigation. *Journal of Applied Communication Research, 22,* 256–272.

Monroe, A. H. (1935). *Principles and types of speech.* Glenview, IL: Scott, Foresman.

Montgomery, B. M. (1988). Quality communication in personal relationships. In S. W. Duck (Ed.), *Handbook of personal relationships* (pp. 343–366). New York: Wiley.

Morreal, S. P., & Vogl, M. (Eds.). (1998). *Pathways to careers in communication* (5th ed.). Annandale, VA: National Communication Association.

Motley, M., & Molloy, J. (1994). An efficacy test of a new therapy ("communication-orientation motivation") for public speaking anxiety. *Journal of Applied Communication Research, 22,* 48–58.

Muehlenhardt, C. L., & Linton, M. A. (1987). Date rape and sexual aggression in dating situations: Incidence and risk factors. *Journal of Counseling Psychology, 34,* 186–196.

Munter, M. (1993). Cross cultural communication for managers. *Business Horizons, 36,* 68–77.

Murphy, B. O., & Zorn, T. (1996). Gendered interaction in professional relationships. In J. T. Wood (Ed.), *Gendered relationships* (pp. 213–231). Mountain View, CA: Mayfield.

Nader, R. (1996, January 1). Imagine that! *The Nation,* p. 10.

Nardi, P. M., & Sherrod, D. (1994). Friendship in the lives of gay men and lesbians. *Journal of Social and Personal Relationships, 11,* 185–199.

Natalle, E. (1996). Gendered issues in the workplace. In J. T. Wood (Ed.), *Gendered relationships* (pp. 253–274). Mountain View, CA: Mayfield.

Newcomb, H. (1978). Assessing the violence profile studies of Gerbner and Gross. *Communication Research, 5,* 264–282.

Nichols, M. (1996). *The lost art of listening.* New York: Guilford.

Nichols, R., & Stevens, L. M. (1957). Listening to people. *Harvard Business Review, 35,* 85–92.

Noller, P. (1986). Sex differences in nonverbal communication: Advantage lost or supremacy regained? *Australian Journal of Psychology, 38,* 23–32.

Noller, P. (1987). Nonverbal communication in marriage. In D. Perlman & S. Duck (Eds.), *Intimate relationships: Development, dynamics, and deterioration* (pp. 149–176). Thousand Oaks, CA: Sage.

Nussbaum, J. E. (1992, October 18). Justice for women! *New York Review of Books,* pp. 43–48.

Okin, S. M. (1989). *Gender, justice, and the family.* New York: Basic Books.

Olien, M. (1978). *The human myth.* New York: Harper & Row.

Olson, J. M., & Cal, A. V. (1984). Source credibility, attitudes, and the recall of past behaviors. *European Journal of Social Psychology, 14,* 203–210.

O'Meara, J. D. (1989). Cross-sex friendship: Four basic challenges of an ignored relationship. *Sex Roles, 21,* 525–543.

Orbe, M. P. (1994). "Remember, it's always the white's ball": Descriptions of African American male communication. *Communication Quarterly, 42,* 287–300.

Pacanowsky, M. (1989). Creating and narrating organizational realities. In B. Dervin, L. Grossberg, B.

O'Keefe, & E. Wartella (Eds.), *Rethinking communication: Paradigm exemplars* (pp. 250–257). Thousand Oaks, CA: Sage.

Pacanowsky, M., & O'Donnell-Trujillo, N. (1982). Communication and organizational cultures. *Western Journal of Speech Communication, 46,* 115–130.

Pacanowsky, M., & O'Donnell-Trujillo, N. (1983). Organizational communication as cultural performance. *Communication Monographs, 30,* 126–147.

Papin, G., & Bharadway, L. (1998). Pick a gender and get back to us: How cyberspace affects who we are. (Online, accessed March, 1999: http://www.uwm.edu/~gianna/soc/pic_a_gender.html.)

Parkes, C., & Larsen, P. (1999, May 8–9). The box in the living room comes to life. *Financial Times,* p. 7.

Parks, M., & Floyd, K. (1996). Making friends in cyberspace. *Journal of Communication, 46,* 80–97.

Parks, M., & Roberts, L. (1998). "Making MOOsic": The development of personal relationships on line and a comparison to their off-line counterparts. *Journal of Social and Personal Relationships, 15,* 517–537.

Patterson, M. L. (1992). A functional approach to nonverbal exchange. In R. S. Feldman & B. Rime (Eds.), *Fundamentals of nonverbal behavior* (pp. 458–495). New York: Cambridge University Press.

Patton, B. R., & Ritter, B. (1976). *Living together: Female/male communication.* Columbus, OH: Charles E. Merrill.

Pearce, W. B., Cronen, V. E., & Conklin, F. (1979). On what to look at when analyzing communication: A hierarchical model of actors' meanings. *Communication, 4,* 195–220.

Peiss, K. (1998). *Hope in a jar: The making of America's beauty culture.* Highland Park, IL: Metropolitan Books.

Pescovitz, D. (1995, October). The future of telecommuting. *Wired,* p. 8.

Petronio, S. (1991). Communication boundary management: A theoretical model of managing disclosure of private information between married couples. *Communication Theory, 1,* 311–335.

Pettigrew, T. E. (1967). Social evaluation theory: Consequences and applications. In D. Levine (Ed.), *Nebraska symposium on motivation* (pp. 241–311). Lincoln: University of Nebraska Press.

Phillips, G. M. (1991). *Communication incompetencies.* Carbondale: Southern Illinois University Press.

Phillips, G. M., & Wood, J. T. (1983). *Communication and human relationships.* New York: Macmillan.

Porter, K., & Foster, J. (1986). *The mental athlete: Inner training for peak performance.* New York: Ballantine.

Postman, N. (1985). *Amusing ourselves to death.* New York: Penguin.

Public Broadcasting Service. American games, Japanese rules. (1988). Frontline documentary. Cited in J. Ferrante (1992), *Sociology: A global perspective* (p. 102). Belmont, CA: Wadsworth.

Public pillow talk. (1987, October). *Psychology Today,* p. 18.

Purdy, M., & Borisoff, D. (Eds). (1997). *Listening in everyday life: A personal and professional approach* (2nd ed.). Lanham, MD: University of America Press.

Quindlen, A. (1994, September 13). The image of a modern girl. *Raleigh News & Observer,* p. 9A.

Rafter, M. (1999, August 2–9). Check it out. *The Industry Standard,* pp. 87–90.

Rakow, L. (1992). "Don't hate me because I'm beautiful": Feminist resistance to advertising's irresistible meanings. *Southern Journal of Speech Communication, 36,* 11–26.

Raspberry, W. (1994, July 5). Major gains in minorities' grades at Tech. *Raleigh News & Observer,* p. 9A.

Rawlins, W. K. (1981). *Friendship as a communicative achievement: A theory and an interpretive analysis of verbal reports.* Doctoral dissertation, Temple University, Philadelphia.

Rawlins, W. K. (1994). Being there and growing apart: Sustaining friendships during adulthood. In D. Canary & Laura Stafford (Eds.), *Communication and relational maintenance* (pp. 275–294). New York: Academic Press.

Reel, B. W., & Thompson, T. L. (1994). A test of the effectiveness of strategies for talking about AIDS and condom use. *Journal of Applied Communication Research, 22,* 127–141.

Reid, E. M. (1991). *Electropolis: Communication and community on Internet relay chat.* Electronic document cited in N. Baym (1995).

Reis, H. T., Senchak, M., & Soloman, B. (1985). Sex differences in the intimacy of social interaction: Further examination of potential explanations. *Journal of Personality and Social Psychology, 48,* 1204–1217.

Rheingold, H. (1991). *Virtual reality.* New York: Summit.

Ribeau, S. A., Baldwin, J. R., & Hecht, M. L. (1994). An African-American communication perspective. In L. Samovar and R. Porter (Eds.), *International communication: A reader* (7th ed., pp. 140–147). Belmont, CA: Wadsworth.

Richmond, V. P., & McCroskey, J. C. (1992). *Communication: Apprehension, avoidance, and effectiveness* (3rd ed.). Scottsdale, AZ: Gorsuch Scarisbrick.

Riessman, C. (1990). *Divorce talk: Women and men make sense of personal relationships.* New Brunswick, NJ: Rutgers University Press.

Riley, P. (1983). A structurationist account of political culture. *Administrative Science Quarterly, 28,* 414–437.

Rogers, E. M. (1986). *Communication technology: The new media in society.* New York: Free Press.

Rohlfing, M. (1995). "Doesn't anybody stay in one place anymore?": An exploration of the understudied phenomenon of long-distance relationships. In J. T. Wood & S. W. Duck (Eds.), *Understanding relationship processes, 6: Understudied relationships: Off the beaten track* (pp. 173–196). Thousand Oaks, CA: Sage.

Root, M. P. (1990). Disordered eating habits in women of color. *Sex Roles, 22,* 525–536.

Rosenwasser, S. M., Lingenfelter, M., & Harrington, A. F. (1989). Nontraditional gender role portrayals on television and children's gender role perceptions. *Journal of Applied Developmental Psychology, 10,* 97–105.

Rothenberg, D. (1999, July 16). Use the Web to connect with "ideas in motion." *Chronicle of Higher Education,* p. B8.

Ruberman, T. R. (1992, January). Psychosocial influences on mortality of patients with coronary heart disease. *Journal of the American Medical Association, 267,* 559–560.

Rubin, L. (1985). *Just friends: The role of friendship in our lives.* New York: Harper & Row.

Rusbult, C. E. (1987). Responses to dissatisfaction in close relationships: The exit–voice–loyalty–neglect model. In D. Perlman & S. W. Duck (Eds.), *Intimate relationships: Development, dynamics, and deterioration* (pp. 109–238). London: Sage.

Rusbult, C. E., Johnson, D. J., & Morrow, G. D. (1986). Impact of couple patterns of problem solving on distress and nondistress in dating relationships. *Journal of Personality and Social Psychology, 50,* 744–753.

Rusbult, C. E., & Zembrodt, I. M. (1983). Responses to dissatisfaction in romantic involvement: A multidimensional scaling analysis. *Journal of Experimental Social Psychology, 19,* 274–293.

Rusbult, E. E., Zembrodt, I. M., & Iwaniszek, J. (1986). The impact of gender and sex-role orientation on responses to dissatisfaction in close relationships. *Sex Roles, 15,* 1–20.

Rusk, T., & Rusk, N. (1988). *Mind traps: Change your mind, change your life.* Los Angeles: Price Stern Sloan.

Sadker, M., & Sadker, D. (1986, March). Sexism in the classroom: From grade school to graduate school. *Phi Delta Kappan,* pp. 512–515.

Sallinen-Kuparinen, A. (1992). Teacher communicator style. *Communication Education, 41,* 153–166.

Samovar, L., & Porter, R. (1991). *Communication between cultures.* Belmont, CA: Wadsworth.

Samovar, L., & Porter, R. (Eds.). (1994). *Intercultural communication: A reader* (7th ed.). Belmont, CA: Wadsworth.

Sandberg, J. (1995, October 30). On-line population reaches 24 million in North America. *Wall Street Journal,* p. B3.

Sandberg, J. (1999, May 31). The quiet genius who brings it all together. *Newsweek,* p. 63.

Sandholtz, K. (1987, Fall). *Managing your career.* Special supplement to the *Wall Street Journal.*

Scarf, M. (1987). *Intimate partners: Patterns in love and marriage.* New York: Random House.

Schmitz, J., Rogers, E. M., Phillips, K., & Pascal, D. (1995). The public electronic network (PEN) and the homeless in Santa Monica. *Journal of Applied Communication Research, 23,* 26–43.

Schnarch, D. (1997). Sex, intimacy, and the Internet. *Journal of Sex Education and Therapy, 22,* 15–20.

Schneider, A. (1999, March 26). Taking aim at student incoherence. *Chronicle of Higher Education,* pp. A16–A18.

Schramm, W. (1955). *The process and effects of mass communication.* Urbana: University of Illinois Press.

Schramm, W., & Porter, W. (1982). *Men, women, messages, and media.* New York: Harper & Row.

Schutz, A. (1999). It was your fault! Self-serving bias in autobiographical accounts of conflicts in married couples. *Journal of Social and Personal Relationships, 16,* 193–208.

Schutz, W. (1966). *The interpersonal underworld.* Palo Alto, CA: Science and Behavior Books.

Schwartz, T. (1989, January–February). Acceleration syndrome: Does everyone live in the fast lane nowadays? *Utne Reader,* pp. 36–43.

Scorpion. (1991, Winter). Quality circles help sharpen competitive edge. *The Scorpion: The Official All-State Legal Supply Employee Publication,* p. 12.

Sebeok, T. A., & Rosenthal, R. (Eds.). (1981). *The Clever Hans phenomenon: Communication with horses, whales, apes, and people.* New York: New York Academy of Sciences.

Secord, P. F., Bevan, W., & Katz, B. (1956). The Negro stereotype and perceptual accentuation. *Journal of Abnormal and Social Psychology, 54,* 78–83.

Seligman, M. E. P. (1990). *Learned optimism.* New York: Simon & Schuster/Pocket Books.

Sellinger, M. B. (1994, July 9). Candy Lightner prods Congress. *People,* pp. 102, 105.

Shannon, C., & Weaver, W. (1949). *The mathematical theory of communication.* Urbana: University of Illinois Press.

Shapiro, A. (1999). *The control revolution.* New York: HarperCollins.

Shapiro, J., & Kroeger, L. (1991). Is life just a romantic novel? The relationship between attitudes about intimate relationships and the popular media. *American Journal of Family Therapy, 19,* 226–236.

Sharlet, J. (1999, July 2). Beholding beauty: Scholars nip and tuck at our quest for perfection. *Chronicle of Higher Education,* pp. A15–A16.

Sharpe, R. (1995, October 31, 1995). The checkoff. *Wall Street Journal,* p. A1.

Shattuck, T. R. (1980). *The forbidden experiment: The story of the wild boy of Aveyron.* New York: Farrar, Straus, & Giroux.

Shaw, C. (1999). *Deciding what we watch: Taste, decency, and media ethics in the UK and the USA.* UK: Oxford University Press.

Shellenbarger, S. (1995, August 23). Telecommuter profile: Productive, efficient, and a little weird. *Wall Street Journal,* p. B1.

Sher, B., & Gottlieb, A. (1989). *Teamworks!* New York: Warner.

Shimanoff, S. B. (1980). *Communication rules: Theory and research.* Thousand Oaks, CA: Sage.

Shoemaker, P. (1991). *Gatekeeping.* Thousand Oaks, CA: Sage.

Shotter, J. (1993). *Conversational realities: The construction of life through language.* Thousand Oaks, CA: Sage.

Sights, sounds and stereotypes. (1992, October 11). *Raleigh News & Observer,* pp. G1, G10.

Signorielli, N. (1990). Television's mean and dangerous world: A continuation of the cultural indicators perspective. In N. Signorielli & M. Morgan (Eds.), *Cultivation analysis: New directions in media effects research* (pp. 85–106). Thousand Oaks, CA: Sage.

Signorielli, N., & Morgan, M. (Eds.). (1990). *Cultivation analysis: New directions in media effects research.* Thousand Oaks, CA: Sage.

Silverstone, D., Greenbaum, M., & MacGregor, S., III. (1987). *The preferred college graduate as seen by the N.Y. business community.* Unpublished manuscript.

Simon, S. B. (1977). *Vulture: A modern allegory on the art of putting oneself down.* Niles, IL: Argus Communications.

Simons, G. F., Vázquez, C., & Harris, P. R. (1993). *Transcultural leadership: Empowering the diverse workforce.* Houston: Gulf.

Sixel, L. M. (1995, August 6). Companies do college interviews by video. *Raleigh News & Observer,* p. 10F.

Smircich, L. (1983). Concepts of culture and organizational analysis. *Administrative Quarterly, 28,* 339–358.

Smith, R. (1996). *The patient's story: Integrated patient–doctor interviewing.* Boston: Little, Brown.

Smitherman, G. (1994). *Black talk: Words and phrases from the hood to the amen corner.* Boston: Houghton Mifflin.

Spain, D. (1992). *Gendered spaces.* Chapel Hill: University of North Carolina Press.

Spear, W. (1996). *Feng shui made easy: Designing your life with the ancient art of placement.* New York: HarperCollins.

Spellerberg, D. (1999). The pocket guide to the Internet. In *Guide to the Web* (pp. 139–144). Lincoln, NE: Sandhills.

Spencer, M. (1982). *Foundations of modern sociology.* Englewood Cliffs, NJ: Prentice Hall.

Spencer, T. (1994). Transforming personal relationships through ordinary talk. In S. W. Duck (Ed.), *Understanding relationship processes, 4: Dynamics of relationships* (pp. 58–85). Thousand Oaks, CA: Sage.

Spender, D. (1989). *Invisible women: The schooling scandal.* London: Women's Press.

Spicer, C., & Bassett, R. E. (1976). The effect of organization on learning from an informative message. *Southern Speech Communication Journal, 41,* 290–299.

Spitz, R. (1965). *The first year of life.* New York: International Universities Press.

Staley, C. C. (1988). The communicative power of women managers: Doubts, dilemmas, and management development programs. In K. Valentine & N. Hoar (Eds.), *Women and communicative power* (pp. 36–48). Annandale, VA: Speech Communication Association.

Stamp, G., & Sabourin, T. (1995). Accounting for violence: An analysis of male spousal abuse narratives. *Journal of Applied Communication Research, 23,* 284–307.

Stephenson, S. J., & D'Angelo, G. (1973, May). *The effects of evaluative/empathic listening and self-esteem on defensive reactions in dyads.* Paper presented to the International Communication Association, Montreal.

Sterling, C. (1995). Commentary. In F. Williams, *The new communications* (4th ed.). Belmont, CA: Wadsworth.

Stets, J. E. (1990). Verbal and physical aggression in marriage. *Journal of Marriage and the Family, 52,* 501–514.

Stets, J. E., & Straus, M. A. (1989). The marriage license as a hitting license: A comparison of assaults in dating, cohabiting, and married couples. *Journal of Family Violence, 41,* 33–52.

Stewart, C., & Cash, W. (1991). *Interviewing: Principles and practices* (6th ed.). Dubuque, IA: Wm. C. Brown.

Stone, A. R. (1991). Will the real body please stand up? Boundary stories about virtual cultures. In M. Benedikt (Ed.), *Cyberspace* (pp. 81–118). Cambridge, MA: MIT Press.

Stone, R. (1992). The feminization of poverty among the elderly. In M. L. Andersen & P. H. Collins (Eds.), *Race, class, and gender: An anthology* (pp. 201–214). Belmont, CA: Wadsworth.

Straubhaar, J., & LaRose, R. (1995). *Communications media in the information society*. Belmont, CA: Wadsworth.

Strine, M. S. (1992). Understanding "how things work": Sexual harassment and academic culture. *Journal of Applied Communication Research, 20,* 391–400.

Suitor, J. J. (1991). Marital quality and satisfaction with the division of household labor across the family life cycle. *Journal of Marriage and the Family, 53,* 221–230.

Suler, J. (1999). *The psychology of cyberspace* (http://www.rider.edu/users/suler/psycyber/psycyber.html).

Surra, C., Arizzi, P., & Asmussen, L. (1988). The association between reasons for commitment and the development and outcome of marital relationships. *Journal of Social and Personal Relationships, 5,* 47–64.

Swain, S. (1989). Covert intimacy: Closeness in men's friendships. In B. Risman & P. Schwartz (Ed.), *Gender and intimate relationships* (pp. 71–86). Belmont, CA: Wadsworth.

Sypher, B. (1984). Seeing ourselves as others see us. *Communication Research, 11,* 97–115.

Tanaka, J. (1999, July 5). Mad about online ads. *Newsweek,* p. 66.

Tannen, D. (1990). *You just don't understand: Women and men in conversation.* New York: Morrow.

Tavris, C. (1992). *The mismeasure of woman.* New York: Simon & Schuster.

Taylor, B., & Conrad, C. (1992). Narratives of sexual harassment: Organizational dimensions. *Journal of Applied Communication Research, 20,* 401–418.

Templin, N. (1995, October 5). The PC wars: Who gets to use the family computer? *Wall Street Journal,* pp. B1, B2.

Thomas, V. G. (1989). Body-image satisfaction among black women. *Journal of Social Psychology, 129,* 107–112.

Thompson, E. H., Jr. (1991). The maleness of violence in dating relationships: An appraisal of stereotypes. *Sex Roles, 24,* 261–278.

Toffler, A. (1970). *Future shock.* New York: Morrow.

Toffler, A. (1980). *The third wave.* New York: Morrow.

Tolhuizen, J. H. (1989). Communication strategies for intensifying dating relationships: Identification, use, and structure. *Journal of Social and Personal Relationships, 6,* 413–434.

Triandis, H. C. (1990). Cross-cultural studies of individualism and collectivism. In J. J. Berman (Ed.), *Cross-cultural perspectives* (pp. 41–133). Lincoln: University of Nebraska Press.

Trice, H., & Beyer, J. (1984). Studying organizational cultures through rites and ceremonials. *Academy of Management Review, 9,* 653–669.

Trotter, R. J. (1975, October 25). "The truth, the whole truth, and nothing but. . . ." *Science News, 108,* 269.

Tuckman, B. W. (1965). Developmental sequences in small groups. *Psychological Bulletin, 63,* 384–399.

Tung, B. (1999). *Kerberas: A network authentication system.* Reading, MA: Addison-Wesley.

Turkle, S. (1997). *Life on the screen.* New York: Touchstone.

Ueland, B. (1992, November–December). Tell me more: On the fine art of listening. *Utne Reader,* pp. 104–109.

Upton, H. (1995, May 8). Peerless advice from small-business peers. *Wall Street Journal,* p. A14.

USA Snapshots. (1999, May 10). *USA Today,* p. 1B.

U.S. Census Bureau. (1998). *How we are changing.* Washington, DC: Author.

U.S. Department of Labor. (1992). *Cultural diversity in the workplace.* Washington, DC: Government Printing Office.

Vachss, A. (1994, August 28). You carry the cure in your own heart. *Parade,* pp. 4–6.

Value of children's shows is questionable, study finds. (1999, June 28). *Raleigh News & Observer,* p. 5A.

Van Maanen, J., & Barley, S. (1985). Cultural organization: Fragments of a theory. In P. J. Frost et al. (Eds.), *Organizational culture* (pp. 31–54). Thousand Oaks, CA: Sage.

Villarosa, L. (1994, January). Dangerous eating. *Essence,* pp. 19–21, 87.

Vocate, D. (Ed.). (1994). *Intrapersonal communication: Different voices, different minds.* Mahwah, NJ: Erlbaum.

von Bertalanffy, L. (1951). *Problems of life.* New York: Harper & Row.

von Bertalanffy, L. (1967). *Robots, men, and minds.* New York: Braziller.

Waldroop, J., & Butler, T. (1996, November/December). The executive as coach. *Harvard Business Review,* pp. 111–117.

Walker, M. B., & Trimboli, A. (1989). Communicating affect: The role of verbal and nonverbal content. *Journal of Language and Social Psychology, 8,* 229–248.

Walther, J. (1996). Computer-mediated communication: Impersonal, interpersonal, and hyperpersonal interaction. Special issue of *Communication Research, 23,* 3–43.

Watzlawick, P., Beavin, J., & Jackson, D. D. (1967). *Pragmatics of human communication.* New York: Norton.

Weaver, C. (1972). *Human listening: Processes and behavior.* Indianapolis: Bobbs-Merrill.

Weber, S. N. (1994). The need to be: The sociocultural significance of black language. In L. Samovar & R.

Porter (Eds.), *Intercultural communication: A reader* (7th ed., pp. 221–226). Belmont, CA: Wadsworth.

Weise, E. (1999, May 10). Electronic evidence hot new tactic. *USA Today,* pp. 1A, 2A.

Weiss, K. (1999, January 25). http://www.latimes.com/home/news/asection/t000007602.html.

Weiss, S. E. (1987). The changing logic of a former minor power. In H. Binnendijk (Ed.), *National negotiating styles* (pp. 44–74). Washington, DC: Department of State.

Wells, W., & Siegel, B. (1961). Stereotyped somatotypes. *Psychological Reports, 8,* 77–78.

Werner, C., Altman, I., & Oxley, D. (1985). Temporal aspects of homes: A transactional perspective. In I. Altman & C. M. Werner (Eds.), *Home environments: vol. 8: Human behavior and environment: Advances in theory and research* (pp. 1–32). Thousand Oaks, CA: Sage.

West, C., & Zimmerman, D. H. (1987). Doing gender. *Gender and Society, 1,* 125–151.

West, J. (1995). Understanding how the dynamics of ideology influence violence between intimates. In S. W. Duck & J. T. Wood (Eds.), *Understanding relationship processes, 5: Confronting relationship challenges* (pp. 129–149). Thousand Oaks, CA: Sage.

Westefield, J. S., & Liddell, D. (1982). Coping with long-distance relationships. *Journal of College Student Personnel, 23,* 550–551.

What teens say about drinking. (1994, August 7). *Parade,* p. 9.

Whitbeck, L. B., & Hoyt, D. R. (1994). Social prestige and assortive mating: A comparison of students from 1956 and 1988. *Journal of Social and Personal Relationships, 11,* 137–145.

Whorf, B. (1956). *Language, thought, and reality.* New York: MIT Press/Wiley.

Widner, D. (1986). *Teleguide.* Washington, DC: Public Service Satellite Consortium.

Wiemann, J. M., & Harrison, R. P. (Eds). (1983). *Nonverbal interaction.* Thousand Oaks, CA: Sage.

Wilkie, J. R. (1991). The decline in men's labor force participation and income and the changing structure of family economic support. *Journal of Marriage and the Family, 53,* 111–122.

Williams, F. (1992). *The new communications* (3rd ed.). Belmont, CA: Wadsworth.

Wilson, G., & Goodall, H., Jr. (1991). *Interviewing in context.* New York: McGraw-Hill.

Wilson, J. F., & Arnold, C. C. (1974). *Public speaking as a liberal art* (4th ed.). Boston: Allyn & Bacon.

Winans, J. A. (1938). *Speechmaking.* New York: Appleton-Century-Crofts.

Wolf, N. (1991). *The beauty myth.* New York: Morrow.

Wong, W. (1994). Covering the invisible "model minority." Special issue: Race: America's rawest nerve. *Media Studies Journal, 8,* 49–60.

Wood, J. T. (1982). Communication and relational culture: Bases for the study of human relationships. *Communication Quarterly, 30,* 75–84.

Wood, J. T. (1992a). *Spinning the symbolic web: Human communication as symbolic interaction.* Norwood, NJ: Ablex.

Wood, J. T. (1992b). Telling our stories: Narratives as a basis for theorizing sexual harassment. *Journal of Applied Communication Research, 4,* 349–363.

Wood, J. T. (1993a). Diversity and commonality: Sustaining their tension in communication courses. *Western Journal of Communication, 57,* 367–380.

Wood, J. T. (1993b). Engendered relations: Interaction, caring, power, and responsibility in intimacy. In S. W. Duck (Ed.), *Understanding relationship processes, 3: Social context and relationships* (pp. 26–54). Thousand Oaks, CA: Sage.

Wood, J. T. (1993c). Enlarging conceptual boundaries: A critique of research on interpersonal communication. In S. P. Bowen & N. J. Wyatt (Eds.), *Transforming visions: Feminist critiques in communication studies* (pp. 19–49). Cresskill, NJ: Hampton.

Wood, J. T. (1993d). Gender and moral voice: From woman's nature to standpoint theory. *Women's Studies in Communication, 15,* 1–24.

Wood, J. T. (1994a). Saying it makes it so: The discursive construction of sexual harassment. In S. Bingham (Ed.), *Conceptualizing sexual harassment as discursive practice* (pp. 17–30). Westport, CT: Praeger.

Wood, J. T. (1994b). Engendered identities: Shaping voice and mind through gender. In D. Vocate (Ed.), *Intrapersonal communication: Different voices, different minds* (pp. 145–167). Mahwah, NJ: Erlbaum.

Wood, J. T. (1994c). Gender and relationship crises: Contrasting reasons, responses, and relational orientations. In J. Ringer (Ed.), *Queer words, queer images: The construction of homosexuality* (pp. 238–264). New York: New York University Press.

Wood, J. T. (1994d). *Who cares? Women, care, and culture.* Carbondale: Southern Illinois University Press.

Wood, J. T. (1995). Feminist scholarship and research on personal relationships. *Journal of Social and Personal Relationships, 12,* 103–120.

Wood, J. T. (Ed.). (1996). *Gendered relationships.* Mountain View, CA: Mayfield.

Wood, J. T. (1997). Diversity in dialogue: Communication between friends. In J. Makau and R. Arnett (Eds.),

Ethics of communication in an age of diversity (pp. 5–26). Urbana: University of Illinois Press.

Wood, J. T. (1998). *But I thought you meant . . . : Misunderstandings in human communication.* Mountain View, CA: Mayfield.

Wood, J. T. (1999). *Interpersonal communication: Everyday encounters* (2nd ed.). Belmont, CA: Wadsworth.

Wood, J. T. (2000a). *Communication in our lives* (2nd ed.). Belmont, CA: Wadsworth.

Wood, J. T. (2000b). *Relational communication: Continuity and change in personal relationships* (2nd ed.). Belmont, CA: Wadsworth.

Wood, J. T. (2001a). *Communication theories in action* (2nd ed.). Belmont, CA: Wadsworth.

Wood, J. T. (2001b). *Gendered lives: Communication, gender and culture* (4th ed.). Belmont, CA: Wadsworth.

Wood, J. T. (2001c). He says/she says: Misunderstandings between men and women. In D. Braithwaite & J. Wood (Eds.), *Case studies in interpersonal communication: Processes and problems* (pp. 93–100). Belmont, CA: Wadsworth.

Wood, J. T., Dendy, L., Dordek, E., Germany, M., & Varallo, S. (1994). Dialectic of difference: A thematic analysis of intimates' meanings for differences. In K. Carter & M. Presnell (Eds.), *Interpretive approaches to interpersonal communication* (pp. 115–136). New York: State University of New York Press.

Wood, J. T., & Duck, S. W. (1995a). Off the beaten track: New shores for relationship research. In Wood, J. T., & Duck, S. W. (Eds.), *Understanding relationship processes, 6: Understudied relationships: Off the beaten track* (pp. 1–21). Thousand Oaks, CA: Sage.

Wood, J. T., & Duck, S. W. (Eds.). (1995b). *Understanding relationship processes, 6: Understudied relationships: Off the beaten track.* Thousand Oaks, CA: Sage.

Wood, J. T., & Inman, C. C. (1993). In a different mode: Masculine styles of communicating closeness. *Journal of Applied Communication Research, 21,* 279–295.

Wood, J. T., Phillips, G. M., & Pedersen, D. J. (1986). *Group discussion: A practical guide to participation and leadership* (2nd ed.). New York: Harper & Row.

Woolfolk, A. E. (1987). *Educational psychology.* Englewood Cliffs, NJ: Prentice Hall.

Wydra, N. (1998). *Look before you love: Feng Shui techniques for revealing anyone's true nature.* Lincolnwood, IL: Contemporary Books.

Yerby, J., Buerkel-Rothfuss, N., & Bochner, A. (1990). *Understanding family communication.* Scottsdale, AZ: Gorsuch Scarisbrick.

Zorn, T. (1995). Bosses and buddies: Constructing and performing simultaneously hierarchical and close friendship relationships. In J. T. Wood & S. W. Duck (Eds.), *Understanding relationship processes, 6: Understudied relationships: Off the beaten track* (pp. 122–147). Thousand Oaks, CA: Sage.

Zuckerman, M. B. (1993, August 2). The victims of TV violence. *U.S. News & World Report,* p. 64.

Index

Boldface page numbers refer to definitions of terms and page numbers followed by the italicized letter *f* indicate figures

Q